FIFTY YEARS OF
AMERICAN EDUCATION

1900 - 1950

*A Historical Review and
Critical Appraisal*

By

EDGAR W. KNIGHT

KENAN PROFESSOR OF EDUCATIONAL HISTORY
UNIVERSITY OF NORTH CAROLINA

THE RONALD PRESS COMPANY · NEW YORK

2

To
ANNE KNIGHT FLEMING
AND
JANE KNIGHT LUDLOW

PREFACE

This book was prepared in order to tell the story of the growth of education in the United States during the first half of the twentieth century, a growth that was then more conspicuous than in any other period of the nation's history. Moreover, the history of American education during those decades was a significant part of the progress in economic and industrial, political, and other social developments with which it was closely interwoven.

Changes in the scene between 1900 and 1950 were striking in elementary, secondary, higher, and professional schools, and also in the extension of educational effort which was not commonly accepted when the century began. Elementary education was expanding and becoming more favorably accepted than in any other period since the inception of the universal school, public secondary education was becoming more widespread than in any earlier period, and new opportunities in higher education were little if any less prominent. At the same time, other developments were appearing in directions that were little thought of in 1900. These, which are here set out as faithfully as the records permit, form an extraordinary story of educational growth in a half century that is perhaps unmatched in history.

The chapters that follow undertake to report on and discuss these developments in the United States, which, during the half-century, was a participant in two frightful world wars and underwent a devastating economic depression. In those emergencies, education in this country was confronted with trials and tests of merit to which it had never before been subjected. The story of its fortunes in those crises is a fascinating part of the entire democratic epic of America.

During the half century, education in the United States reached its most lofty quantitative triumphs. In the less easily measurable aspects of American life during that time, there appeared changes which, although perhaps less striking than those in economic, industrial, and educational growth, were nevertheless observable. And unless human experience is strangely misleading, the big task ahead of education during the second half of the twentieth century is to do qualitatively what has been quantitatively done so well ever since 1900.

One of the happy and wholesome parts of the vast educational development during this period was the fact that the American people were apparently becoming more vitally aware of the persistent issues that faced them. As never before, those issues came to be clearly outlined against a pattern of world events, and education seemed to promise to become one of the most potent instruments of peace. Probably at no other time in history was there such wide discussion of acute educational issues as in the second quarter of the twentieth century. Nor in any other period had there been such severe criticism of the work of the schools.

Most of the materials in this book have been experimented with for several years in a course on "Contemporary Trends and Issues in American Education" at the University of North Carolina, for two summers at the University of Michigan, and for a semester and a summer at Duke University, in courses that in all instances dealt with much of the subject matter contained in this book. Students whose major interests were in elementary, secondary, or higher education, or in educational administration, found that many of the materials here presented threw fresh light on current but persistent problems in those and other fields.

Experience at these institutions also showed that, in addition to the materials presented, students seemed more eager than is commonly believed for an opportunity to make as wide use as possible of original sources in the study of educational and social history. One purpose of this book, therefore, is to call the attention of students and teachers to the vital importance of original sources and to provide such persons with the opportunity to work with them. Among these sources are the proceedings of national and local educational associations and societies, acts of legislatures, decisions of courts, and discussions in the daily press and in periodicals that are not altogether professionally educational in character. Encouraging students to make use of such materials stimulates their interest in the important role that education has come to play, and shows them that the roots of many of the educational issues which confront them today reach back into the past. In this book an effort has been made to direct the attention of students and teachers to the important historical antecedents of contemporary educational issues and problems.

To facilitate the use of this book, a preview of each chapter is presented, and at the end of each chapter is a carefully annotated list of readings and questions which it is hoped will be found useful to both students and teachers.

I am grateful to Mrs. Mabel T. Hill for help in the preparation of the material; to Clifton L. Hall for reading some of the proof; and to Isaac Copeland for assistance in making the index.

EDGAR W. KNIGHT

Chapel Hill, February, 1952

CONTENTS

TABLES

Fifty Years of
American Education

Chapter 1

THEN AND NOW

PREVIEW OF THE CHAPTER

Who could have predicted in 1900, the editor of the *NEA Journal* asked in early 1950, what could have happened in these fifty years? The first half of the twentieth century saw phenomenal changes in most aspects of American life. . . . Changes in the educational scene—elementary, secondary, and higher—were very striking. . . . Conditions in 1900, as shown by the *New York Times,* contrasted most sharply with those in 1950. . . . The forming of educational associations and the expansion of educational journalism were also conspicuous developments in the first half of the century. . . . The economic interests of the American people were strong in 1900, but they were far more vigorous in 1950 when there was wide public concern over economic conditions. The national debt stood at more than $260 billion, and the gross debts of the states were at an all-time high. . . . Significant educational events marked the closing decade of the first half of the century, which also witnessed an increase in the relations of the national government to education and a new emphasis on education and internationalism. . . . Events and discoveries "moved with lightning speed" in a period that has been called "the age of conflict." . . . Around 1900, religion seemed to be gaining strength after a critical period in conflict with Darwinism, and in 1950 it was enjoying its greatest boom, with a revivalistic movement sweeping the country. But there was much evidence of confusion among the American people even before the crisis in Korea. . . . Prominent persons commented on the scene in 1900 and also in 1950, but some of the predictions of the earlier date turned out to be far from accurate. . . . Serious books had no wider sale at the beginning of the century than they had had in the 1870's when readers were fewer and less wealthy. Best sellers in 1900 were in marked contrast with those of 1950. While the American people were spending $100 million a year on their libraries, this sum was reported to be only two thirds of what they spent on bowling alleys and billiards, and one third of the people were without library facilities in 1950. . . . Developments in science between 1900 and 1950 were almost incredible, but there was evidence of a growing dissatisfaction with the laboratory. . . . The first half of the century witnessed many efforts to purge teachers by loyalty oaths, and the issue of academic freedom in 1950 was more acute than ever.

Predictions of 1900.—In March of 1950, the editor of the *NEA Journal* asked: "Who can tell what lies ahead?" He went on to inquire who could have predicted or guessed in 1900 that by 1950 the population of the United States would have doubled; that enrollments in the high schools would have increased from 630 thousand to about 7 million, and collegiate enrollments from fewer than a quarter of a million to nearly two and a half million; that the average life expectancy of the American people would increase from fifty years to more than sixty-five through advances in medical science, sanitation, and improved educational facilities; that telephones would increase from 1.35 million to more than 40 million, and automobiles from about 4 thousand to more than 40 million; that in 1949 there would be 83 million radios and more than 3 million television sets in the United States; that within forty-seven years, from the first successful mechanical airplane flight in December of 1903, by the Wright brothers from Kill Devil Hill on the coast of North Carolina, aviation would so greatly develop that Americans would in 1950 be flying annually more than 9 billion passenger miles, and that there would be airplanes that would exceed the speed of sound? Who in 1900 could have predicted that within four decades the United States would ride out the most severe economic dislocation in its history and also play the decisive role in two world wars; that the Communist International or Comintern, which was causing so much trouble in the world in 1950, would have been organized in Russia (1919); that in 1920 the League of Nations would automatically come into existence under the Versailles Peace Treaty, and that a quarter of a century later the League would vote itself out of existence and turn over its physical assets to the United Nations, whose charter became effective in 1945? Who could have predicted, even in 1935 when President Roosevelt signed the social security law, that by 1950 more than $24 billion would have been paid under its provisions to individual American beneficiaries, and that in 1950 amendments to the original statute would bring thousands of other Americans into the sheltering arms of the national government? In 1950 the American people were "in the middle of the most amazing century in the long upward struggle of the race," and with their record and resources they should have no fear of the future. The world, Joy Elmer Morgan hopefully declared, had "no problems which high ideals and intelligent persistence will not solve . . ."

In the same publication for May of 1950, David H. Russell wrote under the caption "What's Right with Our Public Schools?" and noted that it was occasionally healthy to point to the good features of public education and other democratic institutions, "not with smugness but with justifiable pride in achievement." He pointed out that the public school was the greatest agency for citizenship which the American people had developed; that it contributed to the moral and spiritual growth of youth; that it had given the people of this country a very high literacy rate; that it had tended to raise the standard of living and to improve the physical well-being and health and safety habits of the people; and that it was teaching more efficiently than ever before. He also noted that public education was healthy when the people were willing to consider what was wrong with it. But in the same issue of that publication appeared an article on "Who Teaches Our Children?" by Edgar Dale, who asked whether it was the teachers, the movies, the comics, the radio, or advertising. It came out that in homes having television, reading had declined 18 per cent, evening radio listening 68 per cent, attendance at movies 20 per cent, and other outside entertainment 24 per cent. In the fifty fabulous years that followed 1900, the face of the earth and almost all that was in it, including education, changed very rapidly and also very surprisingly.

Changes in the Educational Scene.—Of the hundred half centuries that have passed since the recorded story of mankind began five thousand years ago, not one of them revealed such extraordinary material progress as the first half of the twentieth century. Changes in the American educational scene between 1900 and 1950 were also conspicuous. In 1900 there were about 15 million pupils in the free public elementary and secondary schools, about 500 thousand of them in secondary schools. At mid-century there were about 25 million, and enrollments in secondary schools were twelve times greater than in 1900, with private secondary schools increasing in number and enrollments between 1890 and 1900. It was predicted in 1950 that a decade later there would be 34 million children in elementary and more than 8 million in secondary schools. Expenditures per pupil in average daily attendance in 1900 were about $16.88; in 1950 the figure was about $185. Expenditures for school construction in 1900 were about $35 million. In 1910 these were about $70 million; in 1920, about $154 million; in 1930, about $371 million; in 1940, about $258 million; in 1949, about a half billion; and at current costs of construction, by 1960 it would require at least 10 billion to provide adequate housing for the rapidly increasing school population. New York City alone was reported to need by 1956 at least 165 new elementary and junior high schools, 31 senior high schools, and 103 additions to existing buildings, the total cost of which would be $511 million.

Conditions in 1900.—In 1900 the average annual public school term was about 144 days; in 1948 it was about 177 days. In 1948 it was reported that among Americans twenty-five years of age or over, 4 per cent had not gone to school at all; 13 per cent had not finished the fourth grade; 56 per cent had had an eighth-grade education or less; and 75 per cent had not finished high school, but more than one third of all the grown people in the United States hoped to get more schooling after the Second World War, and 50 per cent of them desired cultural and professional studies. In 1900 the total receipts from all sources for public school purposes were about $220 million; in 1949 the figure was $4.3 billion. Salaries of teachers were very low in 1900. In cities of over 8,000 people, the average annual salary of teachers and supervising officers was only about $670. In 1950 the average annual salary of teachers was about $2,886, California leading with $3,940, followed by New York with $3,875. Mississippi remained at the bottom of the list with $1,393, "or $27.78 a week, compared with a national average of $55.37 a week." In 1950 a serious shortage of teachers continued to plague American education. In that year, one in every ten teachers in the United States, a total of more than 86 thousand, was employed on an emergency or substandard certificate.

Changes in higher education were no less conspicuous than in elementary and secondary education. Enrollments in higher educational institutions in 1900 were less than 250 thousand. Two decades later these had reached 597 thousand. By 1930 the enrollments were about 1.1 million, and by 1940 they had reached 1.5 million. In 1950 the number was about 2.5 million, and in 1947 President Truman's Commission on Higher Education had made recommendations that would send the enrollments up even higher. The value of the total property of institutions for higher education in 1900 was about $360 million, a trifling sum compared with its value in 1950. The total income of institutions for higher education in 1900 was about $29 million. In 1950 it was close to a billion. The cost of a college education had so greatly increased by mid-century that further increases in tuition and fees were viewed as unsound public policy. One of the considerations that led the President's Commission on Higher Education to recommend huge federal funds for scholarships and fellowships was the great increase in the cost of higher education.

By 1900 the American people had already become very degree-conscious, and thirty-nine different kinds of academic degrees were that year conferred on 11,177 men and 4,795 women. In 1950 the number was 496,900: bachelor's 428,000; master's 62,000; doctorates 6,900. The almost blind faith of the American people in the economic value of a college education had by 1950 produced a condition which could not have been anticipated in 1900: what effect would the mass production of holders of academic degrees have on the American economy? "What would be the result of a rapidly expanding proletariat of the A.B. and the Ph.D.?" One economist wrote on the dismal prospect of "Millions of B.A.'s, But No Jobs," and he predicted that within a few years there would be three college graduates for every job for which they had been trained.

In 1900 several states had not yet enacted compulsory school attendance legislation, the movement being very slow in the southern states. Beginning with Massachusetts in 1852, twenty-six states and the District of Columbia had enacted legislation on the subject by 1890. By 1918, when Mississippi enacted such legislation, all the other states had already done so. Practically every state, however, had to overcome much stubborn opposition by those who argued that such laws were un-American in principle in that they interfered with the personal liberty of the parent and arrogated new powers to the state.

On Monday, January 1, 1900, one year before the end of the nineteenth century, the *New York Times* published 82,106 copies of a fourteen-page issue, plus a thirty-two page supplement that reviewed the business and economic developments of the previous year. At that time that paper cost one cent on weekdays and three cents on Sunday. Fifty years later, the same paper had an average daily circulation of 544,974 copies which sold for five cents on weekdays and fifteen cents on Sundays.

The financial situation in 1900 was reviewed by the financial editor of the newspaper. "The United States the Envy of the World" was written by the president of the New York Clearing House; the subject of national finances was reviewed by Secretary of the Treasury Lyman J. Gage; trade conditions throughout the world were discussed by the London correspondent of the *New York Times;* the range of prices in iron, cotton, wheat, and corn was exhibited by charts; the probable increase in imports was discussed by Worthington C. Ford, to mention a few of the subjects of business and commerce that were treated in the special supplement. The nation of 76 million was pronounced prosperous. The leading editorial of the *Times* said that 1899 had been "a year of wonders, a veritable *annus mirabilis* in business and production," and an editorial writer said: "Unquestionably, to the great body of business men, the outlook on the threshold is extremely bright."

That day the leading news in that paper had to do with the seizure of a German ship, the "Bundesrath," by the British, who suspected it of taking volunteers to join the Boers in South Africa. Kaiser Wilhelm was angry about it and ordered two German cruisers to Delagoa Bay in Portuguese East Africa to protect German shipping and other interests. The international situation was nervous then, as it was again to be in 1950. On January 1 of 1900, the German press was demanding a larger German navy to match Britain's. In middle 1950 the United States was diplomatically sending out a Macedonian call to the other members of the United Nations for help in the Korean crisis, and President Truman was asking the Congress for $10 billion for military purposes, in excess of the $13 billion he had already requested. The same issue of the *Times* carried a story of "the American campaign against the Aguinaldo rebels in the Philippines." The Pullman Company had just absorbed the Wagner Company, a rival manufacturer of railway cars. President William McKinley was entertaining in the White House, Governor Theodore Roosevelt in Albany, and Queen Victoria, ailing at eighty, who was resting at her country place in Osborne, Isle of Wight, died January 22 of that year. There was a severe snowstorm in the Southeast and a man in Georgia had frozen to death.

New York City, with its 3.6 million people (in 1950 its population was officially set at 7.8 million), had had a gay time the night before with the celebration centering on lower Broadway and the crowds so dense in front of Trinity Church that pedestrians had difficulty in moving. At St. Patrick's Cathedral, Archbishop Corrigan "began a solemn high mass" at midnight. The newspaper described the gayeties of New Year's Eve in part as follows: "High carnival, with the tin horn at its greatest altitude of evolution, ushered in the year which ends the nineteenth century." There was wide discussion of the question of the end of the old and the start of the new century, which, however, did not start until January 1, 1901.

Exports in 1899 had been more than a billion and a quarter dollars. The production of wheat was 547 million bushels, and of bituminous coal 190 million tons. Roast beef could be had at eight cents a pound, eggs at twenty-two cents a dozen, sugar at four cents a pound, butter at twenty-five cents a pound, women's muslin "corset covers" at fourteen cents each, a "cambric undershirt, trimmed with tucks, lace insertion, and ruffle of lace" at forty-nine cents, gingham at five cents a yard, and men's box-calf shoes at $2.50 a pair. A New Year's dinner could be had at the Broadway Central Hotel for six bits. A business house was looking for a stenographer at seven dollars a week. The average wage for a week of fifty-nine hours was thirteen dollars. A letter to the editor of the *New York Times* complained that "the leakage and waste at the Croton Reservoir prove that what we need is not water, but greater care and economy of what we have." Fifty years later, when prices of all commodities were out of sight, the shortage of water in the big city made big headline news. In 1900 the big issue in Congress, which was to reconvene January 3, was a bill to appropriate $50 million for the Army of the United States, most of it on account of the Philippines. Fifty years later the activities of the armed forces, including the Atomic Energy Commission, were costing $20.5 billion without the unestimated cost of Korea and Formosa. The cost of the political and social insanity of war was dipping deep into the pockets of posterity.

In 1900 the United States was sovereign over 3.7 million square miles, a tremendous expansion since 1790 when the figure was 900 thousand square miles, and complete expansion had not yet been achieved. In 1900 there were only forty-five states: Oklahoma was admitted to the Union in 1907, and Arizona and New Mexico were admitted in 1912. In addition to the 76 million people in the continental United States in 1900, nearly 9 million others were under its jurisdiction as a result of the war with Spain. The population figures were constantly increasing through immense numbers of immigrants who came in steady streams from many parts of the world. In addition to the 67 millions of white European stock, there were about 9 millions of African Negro descent, about 237 thousand American Indians, and about 114 thousand of Oriental descent. The trend toward the centralization of the population in the rapidly growing cities was striking and was commented upon by observers of the American scene, among them James Bryce, who was greatly impressed with the phenomenon in 1905. In 1900, one third of the total population could be found in 547 cities of at least 8 thousand people, an extraordinary change from the 5 million who in 1860 had lived in 141 such cities. In 1950 the American people were becoming predominantly urban.

Educational Associations and Journalism.—The principle in social history that education reflects life about it finds illustration in the genius of American educational workers for organization, propaganda, and publicity. The forming of educational organizations and the expansion of educational journalism in the latter part of the nineteenth and the first half of the twentieth century were conspicuous features of the American educational scene. Educational journalism, which had modestly begun in 1818 with the publication of *The Academician* in New York by Albert and John W. Pickett, had by 1950 become big business. In that year more than seven hundred and fifty separate educational periodicals were listed under forty-three different classifications, according to a report of the Educational Press Association. At mid-twentieth century, the number of the many educational associations and organizations, most of which had their specialized "house organs," reads like the catalogue of a mail-order house. (See Chapter 10.)

American Economic Interests.—If the economic interests of the American people appeared strong in 1900, these were far more vigorous fifty years later. In early January of 1949, President Truman presented his economic report to the Congress and said that the American people had "just enjoyed another year of bountiful prosperity," a condition which enabled them not only to strengthen their domestic economy but also to aid in the recovery of "freedom-loving peoples elsewhere who seek lasting peace." The strength of the economy of the United States was being tested. The ability and willingness of the American people to protect their prosperity were being challenged. But in 1948 employment was up and unemployment was down. Production, the agricultural output, and wages were encouraging. Business investment continued at a high level, the supply of housing was increasing, and President Truman said that the goal the American people sought was "the greatest prosperity for the whole country and not the special gain of any particular group." In April of 1950 President Truman reported the nation still in a prosperous condition, international relations on the upgrade, and he anticipated continued domestic prosperity and more healthy foreign relations. It was then known that on top of a deficit of $5.5 billion for the fiscal year ending June 30 of 1950, an additional deficit was expected for the fiscal year 1951, but these estimates were made before the assault on the Republic of Korea which called for more spending by the United States. In 1950 it was pointed out that from the days of President George Washington through the second term of President Franklin D. Roosevelt, total governmental expenditures were $179 billion, and that during five years of President Truman's administration the total was $191 billion. The Second World War and its aftermath, and American help to friendly nations through the Marshall Plan and the North Atlantic Pact, had greatly increased the costs of the government of the United States. The national debt was $1.263 billion in 1900. In 1950 it was reported at $260 billion. The gross debts of the forty-eight states had reached an all-time high of $4.1 billion by 1950 and would probably go higher before they went down. Heavy state and federal spending had significant implications for American education.

Despite President Truman's optimism, there was wide public concern at mid-century over economic conditions and over the failure of the national government to reduce "its extravagant spending." Fifty-three million Americans were paying an average income tax of one dollar a day to the government, whose debt at the end of 1950 was ten times larger than it had been at the end of the First World War, and the total cost of federal governmental expenditures was nearly thirteen times greater than in 1930. Equally cheerless were other facts: in 1950 Americans were paying fifteen times as much in income taxes as they had paid in 1930. But the government in 1930 was composed of only thirty-eight major departments. In 1950 there were sixty-one such departments. In 1930 the government employed 600 thousand workers, and in 1950 more than 2 million. In 1930 the American people were supporting the government of only one nation. In 1950 they were helping to support a score or more in addition to their own. In 1930 the population of the United States was about 123 million as against 150 million whom the government was serving in 1950. As the first half of the twentieth century was coming to a close, governmental pay rolls were approaching the $22 billion a year mark, federal, state, and local governments accounting for nearly one out of every six dollars paid out for salaries and wages, including the members of the armed forces and school employees.

And there was evidence of considerable confusion in education at mid-century. Although in the main the American people were better fed and clothed and in better health than at other periods, apparently they were confused and uncertain. While pessimists could take refuge in the thought that a common shipwreck is a consolation to everybody, some of the stouthearted seriously inquired whether some of the fair promises of American democracy and American education were unfulfilled. A century or more earlier, idealists and energetic educational advocates had rather consistently pointed to universal education, which had been substantially achieved by 1950, as the sovereign solvent of all economic, political, social, and moral ills of the American people. Most Americans in 1900 probably saw progress as inevitable; most of them in 1950, although uncertain of the future, probably tended to cling to the same view. In that year they had access to more educational opportunities than they had ever before enjoyed. But the high rate of failures of high school and college students, and its accompanying waste, caused educational workers to search their hearts and also examine their handiwork. Only about half of the 1.7 million students who entered upon secondary education in 1949 would remain to be graduated; and the story of college students was also dismal. Truancy, failures, and the dropping of students out of school and college were giving concern to the National League to Promote School Attendance which deplored this "waste of human resources." Some thoughtful observers were beginning to ask whether the effort to provide American education "from the gutter to the university" was turning out to be too much of a dream.

The National Government and Education.—Several significant educational events and developments marked the closing years of the first half of the twentieth century. As already noticed, enrollments in the colleges and universities were increasing, even in the face of a declining number of veterans under the G.I. Bill of Rights. But of the 2.5 million students in higher educational institutions in 1950, more than one tenth (288 thousand) were in ten institutions: New York University, 47.9 thousand; University of California, 43.4 thousand; College of the City of New York, 30.1 thousand; Columbia University, 29.2 thousand; University of Minnesota, 25.1 thousand; University of Illinois, 25 thousand; Northwestern University, 22.8 thousand; Ohio State University, 22.4 thousand; Indiana University, 21.8 thousand; University of Wisconsin, 20.7 thousand. Nevertheless the rapid growth of the junior and community college across the nation was a very impressive fact. The United States Office of Education announced in March of 1950 that during the past two years about 150 colleges had been added to the list of recognized institutions, and seventy-five more were expected to be added before the end of the year. The directory of that agency listed 500 two-year colleges, with enrollments of a half million students. This remarkable growth in community colleges meant that many communities were undertaking to extend higher educational opportunities to as many of their citizens as possible.

The decade of the 1940's had witnessed an increase in the relations of the national government to education and a new emphasis on education and internationalism. The issue of Church and State was sharper in the United States than ever before, and the exchange of opinions between Francis Cardinal Spellman and Mrs. Eleanor Roosevelt in the summer of 1949 was considered a very significant event. The shelving of the proposal for federal educational aid after long discussion; decisions of the Supreme Court on religious and racial issues and increased pressure to end educational discrimination against minorities; fresh attempts to purge teachers by means of loyalty oaths; recommendations of President Truman's Commission on Higher Education; the organization of the National Citizens' Commission for the Public Schools; the launching in the southern states of a regional plan for specialized collegiate and professional education; the sending of "education missions" to Japan and Germany; the novel form of federal educational aid through the G.I. Bill of Rights; the passage of the Fulbright Act; the establishment of Japan's International University in whose activities the United States would cooperate; the establishment by the State of New York of a mammoth university; the activities of UNESCO; the wide discussion of and publications on liberal education and the humanities; the nation-wide observance of John Dewey's birthday; and Harvard's going "coed, but incognito" were some of the events that attracted wide notice and discussion in the 1940's.

At the age of ninety in October of 1949, John Dewey, America's great philosopher, was regarded by his disciples and his critics "as the nation's most characteristic intellectual expression, notably in its emphasis on practical reasons for ordered change," as Irwin Edman wrote in the *New York Times Magazine* on October 16 of that year. More than half a century earlier Dewey had become famous "as a fresh voice and a liberating energy in American philosophy and education," and his intellectual influence was showing no signs of waning at mid-century.[1]

The year 1948 marked the centennial of the public health movement which had been set in motion in England when the first public health act and the organization of the first general board of health in London were achieved. From those modest beginnings had developed extraordinary improvements in sanitary and hygienic services which during the first half of the twentieth century had made human life more comfortable and happier throughout the entire civilized world. But accidents affected the national economy more than any disease, and insurance companies and the National Safety Council were try-

[1] See also William W. Brickman, "John Dewey's Foreign Reputation as an Educator," *School and Society*, LXXX (October 22, 1949), pp. 257-65.

ing to drive that fact home. More than 32 thousand people had been killed and 1.47 million had been injured by motor vehicles alone in 1948. Conditions had become so critical that many schools were giving courses in safety, which led some critics to inquire whether the curriculum was not already too much inflated.

The "Age of Conflict."—Events and discoveries "moved with lightning speed" in the first half of the twentieth century, which has also been called the "age of conflict." It witnessed two world-wide wars, the most depressing economic dislocation the world had ever seen, the disintegration of a half dozen empires out of which new nations were born, and revolutionary discoveries that startled mankind and promised to promote both the arts of war and the arts of peace. The first five decades of the century moved with gigantic strides.

When, on August 6, 1945, President Truman announced that a Japanese city had been subjected to the devastation of the atomic bomb, a dramatic intimation that the Second World War was approaching its end, one commentator noted "the fulfillment of the strangest, most dreadful dream that has ever entered the mind of man." Most people who read the frightful news probably heard of Hiroshima and uranium for the first time. The "basic energy of the universe" had been harnessed, whether for good or ill the future would reveal. Although the scientific discovery presumably promised peace on earth and good will to man, it was at the same time a threat to human existence everywhere; and those who sat in the seats of the mighty in 1945 laid heavy emphasis on the "tragic significance" and the "awful responsibility" which the atomic age would inevitably bring. The event "changed not only the outlook of the world but the entire future prospect of human life," and it seemed clear that most human beings understood less and not more than ever before the facts of life of the real world in which they lived. Certainly a new era of warfare had opened to speed the surrender of Japan. American educational organizations were soon selecting as the theme of their conventions, "Education in the Atomic Age."

In early 1901, less than a year after the death of Alexandrina Victoria, who had been queen of Great Britain and Ireland since 1837 and empress of India since 1876, Guglielmo Marconi, an Italian inventor who acquired fame for developing wireless telegraphy on a commercial basis, transmitted the first radio signal across the Atlantic, and two years later the Wright brothers made their successful aircraft flight. In September of 1905 the war between

Japan and Russia ended, with Japan emerging as a great world power, to be cut down four decades later. England, France, and Russia in 1907 formed the Triple Entente to counteract the Triple Alliance of Germany, Austria-Hungary, and Italy, and five years later the Manchu Empire collapsed in revolution and China became a republic. Two years later, Archduke Francis Ferdinand, heir to the Austro-Hungarian throne, was assassinated while visiting in Sarajevo in the province of Bosnia, and that event became the immediate cause of the First World War. Less than two months later the Panama Canal was opened to strengthen the power of the United States in the affairs of the world, and in the same month Germany defeated Russia at Tannenburg, the first military reverses that led to the downfall of the czar. Within two weeks the first Battle of the Marne paved the way for Germany's ultimate defeat in the First World War, and on April 6, 1917, the United States declared war on Germany. Seven months later Lenin seized power in Russia and set off the Communist Revolution. And on November 11, 1918, Germany surrendered and the First World War was brought to a close. The Treaty of Versailles was signed June 28, 1919, but it imposed unenforceable terms of peace. Five months later, the Senate of the United States rejected the League of Nations, a fact that had much to do with the ultimate failure of that organization. In 1922, the United States, Britain, Japan, France, and Italy agreed at the Washington Naval Conference to scrap their battleships and accept ratios of naval armaments. But the same year Benito Mussolini made a successful march on Rome and seized power in Italy. The promise that the Locarno Conference in October of 1925 would bring stability to Europe was to be unfulfilled.

Two years later, on May 20-21, Charles Lindbergh stimulated interest in aviation by flying nonstop from New York to Paris. On October 29 of 1929 the New York Stock Exchange collapsed, a terrifying event which helped to bring on a world-wide depression. In 1931 Japan blew up a part of the South Manchurian Railroad as an excuse for military aggression in China. In 1933 Marshal Hindenburg summoned Adolph Hitler to power and a reign of terror of a dozen years began under the Nazis. In March of that year Franklin Delano Roosevelt became president of the United States and promptly introduced what came to be known as the "New Deal Program." Three years later, on March 7, 1936, Germany violated the treaties of Versailles and Locarno by reoccupying the Rhineland, and two months later Italy ignored the sanctions of the League of Nations and completed the conquest of Ethiopia.

The same year General Francisco Franco, with help from Hitler and Mussolini, began a civil war and a totalitarian regime in Spain. Hitler launched a new period of German aggression by annexing Austria in March, 1938, and in September of that year the Munich Pact was signed, marking the climax of British-French efforts to appease the dictator of Germany. In 1939 the German-Russian Pact was signed. This prepared the way for the Second World War, which began September 1, when Hitler invaded Poland, and within less than a year he continued his conquest of Western Europe by attacking the Netherlands. In August of 1940 the United States definitely took sides with England by exchanging destroyers for British bases, and in September of that year successful air defenses saved England from invasion. In 1941 the United States became the "arsenal of democracy" by adopting the Lend-Lease Program. On June 22 of that year Germany attacked Russia. In less than two months the Atlantic Charter was signed to give an idealistic purpose to the Second World War. Then came the "day of infamy," December 7, 1941, when the Japanese attacked Pearl Harbor and forced the United States to become an active and complete participant in the war. In early June of 1942 the United States won a naval victory at Midway to halt the advance of Japan, within five months American forces launched a vigorous campaign in North Africa, and in June of 1944 the complete defeat of Germany was presaged by successful landings in Normandy. The statement at the Yalta Conference in February of 1945 by Winston Churchill, Franklin D. Roosevelt, and Joseph Stalin made concessions to Russia in efforts to secure the cooperation of that country. The death of Adolph Hitler came that year and the early surrender of the Nazis. Shortly afterward, fifty nations met in San Francisco to elaborate and implement the Moscow Pact, the Declaration of the Dumbarton Oaks Conference, and the Yalta Conference into the charter of the United Nations, the objectives of which were "to save succeeding generations from the scourge of war"; "to reaffirm faith in fundamental rights, in the dignity and worth of the human person, in the equal rights of men and women and of nations large and small"; and "to promote social progress and better standards of life in larger freedom" by the practice of tolerance, by cooperation to guarantee international peace and security; by preventing the use of armed force "save in the common interest"; and by the use of international efforts to encourage the economic, social, and educational welfare of all the peoples of the earth. It was hoped that a new era in international understanding was dawning at the end of a half-century in which men had fought the most destructive wars in all human history. Specialized agencies under the supervision of the United Nations included the International Bank, the International Stabilization Fund, the International Labor Organization, the Food and Agriculture Organization, and the United Nations Educational, Scientific, and Cultural Organization (UNESCO).

Other events that were characterized by surprise and speed included the defeat of the Conservatives by the Labor Party in England and the beginning of a socialistic regime in that country; the end of the appeasement era, when President Truman's plan for military aid to Greece and Turkey in order to fight communism was approved in 1947; and the adoption by the United States in 1948 of the Marshall Plan to help finance the recovery of Europe and its fight against communism. In early November of 1948, President Truman was re-elected, to the surprise of many people, and the era of the "fair deal" was continued. In 1949 the Atlantic Pact promised to unite Western Europe against aggression, and a few weeks later Russia ended the blockade of Berlin which marked a major victory of the airlift in the "cold war." In June of 1950 the Republic of Korea was invaded by the Communists, and the anxieties, doubts, and misgiving of scores of millions of human beings throughout the world were greatly increased. If hope for peace in the world remained in the human heart, it may have been because two world-wide conflicts had demonstrated the vanity and futility of war. International conditions at mid-twentieth century did not lighten the task of education in the United States but made it more heavy and confusing. The crisis in Korea did not make for educational quietude. The schools already had more children than could be taken care of, and the numbers were rapidly increasing. Congested conditions and part-day sessions were more disturbing than ever before in the entire history of American education, in which in 1950 there was deep confusion. The National Education Association pointed out that a real crisis in American education lay immediately ahead unless plans were made for the inevitable.

Religion and Education.—At the turn of the century religion seemed to be gaining strength after passing through a critical period during which it was beset by many threats. These had come especially from wide discussion of the Darwinian hypothesis, from what came to be known as the "higher criticism," and from the questioning of the validity of the Bible. Many violent conflicts raged between fundamentalism and modernism from the 1870's to the 1890's, only to break out again in the 1920's. In 1950 it was reported that religion was enjoying its greatest boom, with an evangelistic and revivalistic spirit spreading throughout the country. Membership in the churches was at an all-time high. But the cause or causes of the extraordinary religious interest did not readily appear, although many explanations were offered for it. A rather common belief was that, faced by the fears of atomic warfare and economic insecurity, many people were searching for refuge from fear and confusion. By mid-twentieth century, considerable dissatisfaction with the arrogance of science also appeared to be growing. Earlier there was even evidence of disillusion with the laboratory, as Joseph Wood Krutch had written in 1928.[2]

Comments of Some Prominent Persons.—The mystery of the "flying saucers" was given fresh attention in 1950 and did not increase confidence and quietude. Experts of the Air Force had spent two years investigating and measuring reports and rumors that the weird things had been seen in the sky, and their conclusion, made public at the end of 1949 after "sifting almost 400 cases," was that all of them could be accounted for by misinterpretation of balloons, meteors, birds, or other conventional objects because of a "mild form of mass hysteria" or "pure hoaxes." President Truman was reported as saying in April of 1950 that he was as much puzzled by the things as anybody else. The report of the air experts did not calm the curiosity and imagination of the public as theories about "the celestial crockery" increased. One theory was that the disks were "aircraft of a revolutionary design—a combination of heliocopter and fast jet plane"—being developed by the Navy itself, but the story was officially and emphatically denied. Another speculation was of Russian experimentation; another of meteors flashing across the sky or to the planet Venus, then close to the earth; and another was that of optical illusions, the experts pointing out that the sun, the stars, and the senses had "the habit of playing tricks on us." Whatever the explanation, and despite the frequency with which the "saucers" were reportedly turning up, most persons seemed to "have difficulty discussing them with a straight face." Whether a mild form of mass hysteria or hoax, discussion of the saucers may have reflected the wave of uncertainty that seemed to be sweeping over many Americans in the age of materialistic philosophy that had

2 *Atlantic Monthly*, March, 1928.

gained powerful strength by the middle of the twentieth century and had made for confusion in education as well as in other phases of American life.

But Americans were not alone in their fears and misgivings. On Easter Sunday of 1950 the *New York Times* said editorially [3] that one phase of the materialistic philosophy "has even imposed itself by force on a third or more of the earth's population. This philosophy allows man certain virtues, such as courage and intelligence, but it treats him as an animal, guided in the last analysis by the primitive motives." The world, it said, had had its wars, "sordid struggles for material gain," its evils by man to man, but Western civilization had had "its ethical code, too..." The great heresy throughout the ages had been "the doctrine that men must be ruled by terror, cruelty, and greed." While nineteen hundred Easters had passed and bells had rung, "hopes have grown green and expectations have blossomed—and then, too often, there has been tragedy. We cannot, perhaps dare not, look far into the future. We do not know what ordeals humanity has yet to endure. There are dreadful doctrines abroad, dreadful weapons have been invented, in some ways the earth is not so safe or happy as it was a century or several centuries ago. But we know there can be no final defeat for the hopes that rise today. Neither weapons nor marching men, neither lies nor treachery, can win that ancient battle. The immortal aspiration, the yearning for peace and justice, goodness and freedom, cannot be killed. When this spring has withered, there will come other springs —in nature and in the affairs of men." What a task for education— not schooling merely—in the years ahead if spring were to come in the affairs of men! For in the first fifty years of the twentieth century, education in the United States obviously had not escaped the materialistic philosophy that seemed to be engulfed in its environment.

In the same issue of the *Times* in which that editorial appeared, A. J. Carlson, professor emeritus of physiology of the University of Chicago, was reported as saying that civilization could not long survive "unless educational standards are changed to give priority to the maxim that the proper study of mankind is man." The schools must teach children and youth "about man, his nature, and the manner in which he is fashioned. The study of man would teach people to think ahead as far as man's past, which is at least a billion years." In Rome twenty centuries ago, he said, the "slogan was 'bread and circuses.' In our own country today some fellow citizens insist on

[3] Quoted by permission of the *New York Times*.

the slogan, 'security from the cradle to the grave.' Both slogans are bad biology. Both are off the beam, as I understand man, past and present." On the same Sunday, Pope Pius XII was pleading in a tremendous Holy Year Easter celebration "for a return to the spirit of the gospel and social justice." He said that by bitter experiences human beings had come to know that "crimes, massacres, and wars" had been caused by neglect of that spirit and that justice. Another speaker that day said that the "four horsemen of the new Apocalypse —inflation, unemployment, hunger, and the atomic bomb—are ready to ride with a ruthlessness never before seen."

A few weeks later came the crisis in Korea. The national head-quarters of the Selective Service in an advisory, not mandatory, ruling, jolted those students in college who expected to be deferred from military service: only those should be deferred who had completed at least one full academic year of a full-time course, whose scholastic rank was in the upper half of their class, and who had shown intentions, prior to August first, of entering upon a full-time college course in the fall. While energetic preparations for defense were being made in the summer of 1950, the Atomic Energy Commission published its long-awaited book, *The Effects of Atomic Weapons,* which sketched the gory details of destruction and death which had become so familiar to the people of the United States who had been hearing for five years that there was no defense against atomic bombing. The AEC did give some rules, whether comforting or not, for protection against surprise attack by the infernal contraption.

Comments on the current scene by important people around the turn of the century were generally optimistic and "even self-laudatory," but there were also comments on the menaces and afflictions that could face the twentieth century.[4] The *Indianapolis Journal* said that the most remarkable and significant feature of the nineteenth century had been "the improvement in the condition of the working classes." The Reverend Newell Dwight Hillis saw the century as "one of the most fascinating chapters in the story of man's upward progress." A newspaper in Providence, Rhode Island, predicted that the day was coming when nearly every household would have a telephone. Dr. S. P. Langley, the Smithsonian scientist, said that his experiments had convinced him that a "great universal highway overhead" was soon to be opened and that airplanes could be built "to travel at speeds higher than any with which we are familiar." But the *Popular Science Monthly* commented that Langley seemed

4 For predictions for the future in 1900, see Mark Sullivan, *Our Times* (New York: Chas. Scribner's Sons, 1926), Vol. I, pp. 362-72.

to be claiming too much and that he "should be extremely careful not to do anything that may lend itself to an interpretation that will bring injury on the scientific work of the government or of the country."

Langley should have placed his knowledge of aviation at the disposal of the army and "expert mechanicians, and this would have been better than to attempt to become an inventor in a field where success is doubtful and where failure is likely to bring discredit, however undeserved, on scientific work." But in 1903 Thomas A. Edison would bet that he could take a car of his own design and make a return trip to Chicago more quickly and with more pleasure "than any other machine in existence," and the trip could be made at twenty-five miles an hour. Englishman H. G. Wells predicted that the motor car would soon be capable of three hundred or more miles in a day, but he did not believe that the airplane would ever develop "as a serious modification of transport and communication," and he refused to see the submarine do anything except "suffocate its crew and founder at sea." The *Literary Digest* said October 14, 1899, that the "horseless carriage would never come into as common use as the bicycle."

Albert Shaw predicted in the *Review of Reviews* that the twentieth century would become famous "for the expanded and altered nature of international relations." William Jennings Bryan said that the greatest menace to the new century would be the increasing influence of wealth that would lead "to increasing disregard of the inalienable rights of men." Samuel Gompers saw danger in the competition of Oriental labor with American labor. President Jacob Gould Schurman of Cornell University saw the greatest menace to be the "exaltation, worship, and pursuit of money as the foremost good of life." President Arthur T. Hadley of Yale University believed that "legislation based on the self-interest of individuals, or classes, instead of on public sentiment and public spirit" would be the greatest affliction of the new century. Andrew Carnegie was hopeful that before the twentieth century closed "the earth will be purged of its foulest shame, the killing of men in battle under the name of war." John Jacob Astor, one of the richest men in the United States, predicted that "war will become so destructive that it will probably bring its own end." He also said that "keeping horses in large cities would doubtless be prohibited by the Board of Health, as stabling cows, pigs, or sheep is now. Second-story sidewalks, composed largely of translucent glass, leaving all the present street level to vehicles, are already badly needed, . . . and will doubtless have made their appearance in less than twenty years." But when the Archbishop of Canterbury was asked his opinion of the greatest menace to the twentieth century he is reported to have replied, "I have not the slightest idea."

In 1950 the mood of the times was reflected in what people were quoted as saying about American and world conditions. As the year began to advance, some important persons commented on the current scene, as important persons had done at the opening of the century. William Benton, senator from Connecticut, on the need for positive measures to combat Communism, was quoted as saying that the American people were burying their heads "in the sands of our own frustration"; Herbert Hoover, as saying that about the time they thought they could "make ends meet, somebody moves the ends"; D. H. Wilkinson, of Cambridge University, as saying, "Our brightest hope is that the hydrogen bomb will very nearly, but not quite, work"; the Reverend Paul C. Potter, of Colorado, testifying before the Joint Congressional Atomic Energy Commission, as saying, "Any modern system of national defense which does not give specific attention to the panic-proofing of personnel, civilian as well as military, is as useless as a gun with a cardboard barrel"; Robert Frost, who admitted embarrassment at being described as poet, as saying, "I call myself a teacher on my income-tax report. But next year I'm going to put down 'resigned.' When they ask me, 'Resigned from what?' I'll say, 'Resigned to everything.'" Seventy-eight-year-old American artist John Sloan, philosophizing about late recognition of his lifetime work of painting, was quoted as saying, "I'm lucky, because I've never been hindered by financial success or by approval." Wayne Coy, chairman of the Federal Communications Commission, "on off-color video programs," was quoted as saying, "The boy who used to express himself with chalk on a wall is now provided with a television screen."

John Foster Dulles was quoted as saying, "The peace agreement the Soviet leaders seem to want would, at best, be no more than an arrangement whereby they would promise not to wage a war they do not plan with weapons they do not have." Gloria Swanson, star of stage and screen, was quoted as saying, "There's no justification in spending all the money we do for defense when heart trouble has killed more people than the most bloody war in history." Archibald MacLeish, American poet, former Librarian of Congress and former Assistant Secretary of State, was quoted as saying, "Confidence in peace, confidence in the future, the natural, normal, decent confidence of men of courage and character in their country and themselves, has all but vanished from the Congress of the United States." The Reverend Edward N. West, Canon of the Cathedral of St. John the Divine, on how to get more people to church, was quoted as saying, "Comfortable, movable chairs is the only answer." Arthur Motley, head of a group of sales executives, was quoted as saying, "In the United States, durable goods are goods that will last until time payments are completed." Monsignor John S. Middleton, education secretary of the Catholic Archdiocese of New York, urging the re-examination by teachers of their motives and aims, was quoted as saying, "So many teachers are tempted to look with flirtatious longing on administrative posts—the moment of liberation arriving when someone gets out of the classroom and into the office." Educational administration had rapidly become the tail that wagged the educational dog. In his report for 1915, Nicholas Murray Butler, president of Columbia University, had written: "There is some measure of truth in the cynical suggestion that administration may best be defined as the doing extremely well of something that had better not be done at all. The tendency not only in universities but in all forms of public business to multiply and to complicate the details of routine administration is as strong as it is mischievous."

Thomas H. Briggs, formerly of Columbia University, commenting on the heavy criticism of American education, was quoted as saying, "Hunters have to buy licenses, and if lay critics of schools had to buy licenses, we might have enough money to run the public schools."[5] "It's a wonderful country we live in," commented the *Kalends* of the Waverly Press in the early part of 1950, "but just the same, we Americans have seven and a half billion headaches a year, an average of fifty a year for each one of us. The expert on medicines who made that estimate also says that we buy eleven million pounds of aspirin a year. It may be a headache to you, but it means jobs to people who make the aspirin." A poll taken by Dr. George Gallup's Institute of Public Opinion toward the end of mid-century showed that of eight North American nations, the American people suffered most from insomnia, and annually took 3.36 million sleeping pills, twenty-four for each person.

Bookselling and Education.—A comparison of "best sellers" around 1900 and in 1950 shows that 1899 had left the impression of being an unusually busy year for the publishers who reported, according to the *Publishers' Weekly*,[6] 5,321 new publications during that

[5] *New York Times Magazine*, March 5 and 26 and April 2, 1950.
[6] January 27, 1900.

year, more than in 1897 or in 1898, but fewer than in 1895 and 1896. The war with Spain had seriously interrupted publication in 1898. In 1899 fiction led in new publications, and Paul Leicester Ford's *Janice Meredith,* and Winston Churchill's *Richard Carvel* and *The Crisis,* took the lead and achieved remarkable popularity. The publication of *Resurrection,* by the "Great Master of the North," Count Lev Nickolaevich Tolstoi, was announced in 1900, and this great novel that touched upon so many issues and tragedies in the Russia of that time was published simultaneously in that country, Germany, France, Austria, Denmark, Great Britain, and the United States. Another popular book of the period was Edward N. Westcott's *David Harum,* which reached a sale of 400 thousand in a year. James Bryce, British statesman, jurist, and author, wrote in 1905 that serious books had no wider sale in the United States at that time than these had had in the 1870's when readers were fewer and less wealthy.

The best selling books of fiction in the United States in 1949 were reported to be *The Egyptian* by the Finnish writer, Mika Waltari; *The Big Fisherman* by Lloyd Douglas; *Mary,* a Biblical novel by Sholem Asch; John O'Hara's *A Rage to Live;* John P. Marquand's *Point of No Return;* Thomas B. Costain's *High Towers;* Van Wyck Mason's *Cutlass Empire;* Frank Yerby's *Pride's Castle;* and Edward Streeter's *Father of the Bride.* An interesting feature of nonfiction at mid-twentieth century was what could be called picture books: *White Collar Zoo* and *Home Sweet Zoo* by Clare Barnes, Jr.; *The Frenchman* by Phillipe Halsman; *The Baby;* and Francis L. Golden's *Fellow Citizens* had wide sales. Books on canasta swept the country. So also did religious books. As already noted, in 1950 there was an upsurge of religious interest in the United States, as there had been in the latter part of the nineteenth century. But according to the Public Library Inquiry,[7] the average adult in the United States in 1950 was spending one fourth of his waking hours reading newspapers, magazines, and books, and listening to the radio or looking at movies or television. The Inquiry reported 7,408 public libraries whose condition, however, was only fair, due, it was believed, to public apathy. The American people were spending $100 million a year on their libraries, but that sum was only two thirds of what they spent on bowling alleys and billiards. At mid-century one third of the people of the United States were reported without library facilities.

[7] *The Public Library in the United States* (New York: Columbia University Press), 1950.

Dissatisfaction with Scientific Progress.—Differences in science in 1900 and in 1950 were very glaring. In 1900 science was relatively young as compared with scientific developments and interest in 1950, when billions of dollars were being spent on experimentation with and the production of the terrifying energy of the atom, which was throwing the fear of God into millions of human beings. True, advances in medical science since 1900 had become one of the great marvels of the world. Remarkable developments in the ability of men to control their physical environment distinguished 1950 from 1900. But as noted above, there was noticeable a growing dissatisfaction with science, due, perhaps, to what the great scientist, Michael Pupin, had called "the spiritual unpreparedness" of men to enjoy the gifts of science.

The Questioning of Academic Freedom.—At mid-twentieth century, the issue of academic freedom was probably more acute than it had ever been in this country. In the Revolutionary War and in the Civil War, tests of loyalty had been required, but during and after the First World War, in the years of depression and during and after the Second World War, as in other crises, there were feverish efforts, agitation, discussion, and considerable recrimination and occasional suits at law on loyalty oaths and attempts to purge teachers by legislation or regulations. In the 1920's, efforts had been made in many states to pass "monkey" and "pure" history bills. The movement to prohibit by law the teaching of the Darwinian hypothesis of evolution, reminiscent of the fights over that subject in the 1870's and 1880's in what has been called the "critical" period in religion in the United States, culminated in the widely publicized Scopes trial in Tennessee. As these efforts are more fully discussed in a later Chapter, it is sufficient here only to note that the specter of communism during and after the Second World War led to action by state legislatures and governing boards of higher educational institutions.

The first trial in the history of the school system in New York City to determine whether being a member of the Communist party was sufficient grounds for dismissing a teacher began September 18, 1950, in the office of the Board of Education. The teacher who was being tried was one of eight who had been suspended the previous May by Superintendent William Jansen. Seven were to be tried on charges of insubordination only, for refusing to say whether they were or ever had been members of the Communist party; but David L. Friedman, with twenty-three years' experience, was being tried on the charge of membership in the party. Superintendent Jansen was seeking to prove, and make the proof stand up in the courts, that membership in the Communist party unfitted a person to be a teacher in an American school. The teachers involved raised the question of their constitutional rights and of academic freedom. Since their suspension they had been without remuneration and they claimed that they had suffered other embarrassments.

Perhaps the case that attracted most notice and was most widely discussed in 1950 was that of the University of California, which by that time had become a year-long battle, and such a bitter one, that the American Psychological Association in September urged its 7.3 thousand members to stay away from positions in that institution. Six professors had refused to say whether or not they were members of the Communist party. In their meeting in July, the regents had voted to dismiss the professors for failure to sign a statement on the matter. At the same time, but by a narrow margin, they had voted to retain thirty-nine other professors, but they reversed themselves some weeks later and dismissed thirty-one. Of these, six professors gave in and signed the required statement, while the others sought relief in the courts. In the fall of 1951, however, the Board of Regents voted to rescind the oath requirement and "finis" was written to the hot dispute.

This chapter shows extraordinary changes in many directions in the United States during the first half of the twentieth century, which had its ups and downs. Educational developments were very remarkable, but these have been only briefly sketched. The extension of some educational efforts already begun by 1900, and the beginning of some educational practices not very common at that time, will be more fully treated in the chapters that follow. Among these are the reorganization and expansion in elementary and secondary education; the growth of the junior high school and the junior college; the rapid expansion of higher education and the launching of new college plans; the education of teachers, and national studies of that subject; the rapid growth of the summer session, university extension, and adult education; the strengthening of compulsory attendance and child labor legislation, and increased attention to the health and welfare of children; increased interest in vocational education, vocational guidance, and mental hygiene; feverish activities in the construction and the reconstruction of the curriculum; the growth of the so-called scientific study of education, and the development and use of tests, measurements, and educational surveys; reorganization in educational administration and finance, and the consolidation of rural schools; graduate and professional education; the growth of university presses; the educational views of school men, as these were given in educational associations, especially the National Education Association, and in educational journals; increased activities in federal-state educational relations; new and varied educational interests in international relations and the activities of the United Nations Educational, Scientific, and Cultural Organizations (UNESCO); the establishment of a mammoth university in the state of New York; a regional plan for higher education in the Southern states; significant court decisions, especially on religious and racial issues; the education of women; the education of the Negro; activities of regional standardizing educational associations; the impact of wars and of depression on education; the educational effects of the great increase in economic wealth and of the findings of the psychological laboratories; the rise of philanthropic foundations; academic freedom; efforts to make science and history pure by legislation and to purge teachers by oaths of loyalty; and other subjects. The next chapter deals with the evolving and expanding common school.

Some Suggested Questions and Exercises for Students

1. Study and report on the major economic, political, psychological, and social and religious forces and influences in American life that produced the phenomenal changes in the educational scene between 1900 and 1950.

2. Compare or contrast an elementary school, a secondary school, and a college in 1900 and in 1950 in as many ways as you can. For example, in organization and administration; in the courses offered; in the training and salaries of teachers; in extracurricular activities— athletics; dramatic, debating, literary, and other organizations in which students took part; in counseling and vocational guidance.

3. What effects were the mounting costs of government—federal and state—at mid-twentieth century likely to have on American education? On federal educational aid?

4. Account as best you can for what was described as the great "boom" in religion in 1950. Fear of economic insecurity? Of atomic warfare? Disillusion with science?

5. Study and report on the major discoveries in medical science since 1900 and their impact on the work of the schools.

6. Between 1920 and 1950 there was feverish activity in the study, construction, and reconstruction of the curriculum at all levels of education. What was the significance of such activity?

7. Explain the rapid rise of educational organizations and associations and the great expansion in educational journalism between 1900 and 1950.

8. Account for the great increase in attendance at secondary schools and higher educational institutions between 1900 and 1950.

9. There was much discussion in 1899 and early 1900 about the exact time that the nineteenth century ended and the twentieth century began. Exactly when did the first half of the twentieth century come to a close?

10. Examine the *Publishers' Weekly* at the close of each decade of this first half-century for any noticeable trends in the reading habits of the American people.

11. Trends in education during these fifty years appear in newspapers and nonprofessional periodicals which gave increasing attention to the subject during that time. The *New York Times* has for many years published a special educational page on Sundays. So also do such magazines as *Time* and *Newsweek*. Students find an examination of such materials a really exciting experience in the study of the educational history of this country during these years and of current trends. A lively interest in the subject may be awakened in students by having them select a publication for study and report in class. Besides those mentioned above, The *Atlantic Monthly, Harper's Magazine*, the *New Republic*, the *Nation*, the *Saturday Evening Post*, and others frequently carry interesting and illuminating discussions that are not always to be found in professional educational journals.

12. Another exercise that students find very useful is a study of educational trends as these appear in the discussions and proceedings of educational associations. Especially recommended are the *Proceedings*, and particularly the resolutions, of the National Education Association (see Chapter 9) and its *Journal*, for national educational trends and issues. For local trends and issues, the student should examine the proceedings of his state educational association and its journal.

SOME SUGGESTED REFERENCES AND READING

BARCK, OSCAR T., JR., and BLAKE, NELSON M. *Since 1900: A History of the United States in Our Times.* New York: The Macmillan Co., 1947.

Chaps. i ("The Good Old Days") and xxx ("Social Trends During Peace and War") give good descriptions of economic, social, and religious, of literary and other conditions in the United States in 1900. Examine pages 825-47 for suggestions for further reading which will throw light on topics discussed in this Chapter.

BEARD, CHARLES A. (ed.). *A Century of Progress.* New York: Harper & Bros., 1932.

Contains chapters that helpfully supplement the material on most of the topics discussed in this Chapter. It is recommended that students read Beard's brilliant chapter on the idea of social progress, and as much as they can in the chapters on invention, industry, transportation, agriculture, banking and finance, natural science, medicine, education, the changing position of women, and literature and the arts.

CRAVEN, AVERY, and JOHNSON, WALTER. *The United States: Experiment in Democracy.* Boston: Ginn & Co., 1947.

Chap. xxxi on "The Roaring Twenties" makes lively reading on some of the things that happened in this country in that decade: the revival of nativism, the ballyhoo years, the revolt of the younger generation, prohibition, technology, education, literature and the arts.

DULLES, F. R. *Twentieth Century America.* Boston: Houghton Mifflin Co., 1945.

Chap. iv, "American Life in 1900," shows that housekeeping had become "ready-made," that wide interest had developed in sports, melodrama, and hot dogs, and throws light on popular reading and popular music and on "fads and fancies" at that time. See also chap. x on American life on the eve of the First World War; chap. xxiii on American life in the 1920's; and chap. xxiv on American life in the 1930's.

FAULKNER, HAROLD U. *American Political and Social History.* New York: Appleton-Century-Crofts, Inc., 1943.

Chaps. xxviii ("The Gilded Age"), xxxiii ("The Age of Big Business"), and xxxiv ("The Era of Reform") are suggested as useful supplementary readings for this Chapter.

KNIGHT, EDGAR W., and HALL, CLIFTON L. *Readings in American Educational History.* New York: Appleton-Century-Crofts, Inc., 1951.

Contains considerable source materials that bear on some of the topics briefly discussed in this Chapter.

MONROE, WALTER S. *Encyclopedia of Educational Research* (rev. ed.). New York: The Macmillan Co., 1950.

This is a most useful book of reference for students of education who can find in it accounts of the findings of research on innumerable educational topics. Shows that between the middle 1890's and 1940 more than a hundred thousand pieces of "research" in education were reported. Between 1940 and 1950 the increase was phenomenal.

SULLIVAN, MARK. *Our Times.* New York: Chas. Scribner's Sons, 1926.

This work of six volumes is written in a breezy, gossipy, and occasionally somewhat jazzy but effective style, plentifully documented from newspapers and periodical literature. Chaps. i-iii; xiii, x, xiv, xvi, xviii, xix, xxii of Volume I, and chaps. i-vii, xi, and xxvii of Volume II afford interesting supplementary reading for this Chapter.

Chapter 2

THE EXPANDING COMMON SCHOOL

PREVIEW OF THE CHAPTER

The American elementary school has always been considered "the school of the people." There have been three clearly marked stages in its growth, but the greatest changes in its development came during the first half of the twentieth century. . . . European influences on elementary education after 1860 were very striking, but the principles of Pestalozzianism, Herbartianism, Froebelianism, and the educational philosophy of John Dewey were often misunderstood and misapplied and tended to "go to seed." . . . Efforts by Charles W. Eliot, William T. Harris, and others, and the work of national committees, especially the Committee of Fifteen on Elementary Education, were among the first to draw attention to the needs of the elementary schools. . . . Increase in attendance at elementary schools, in length of school term, in expenditures for schools, in the reduction of illiteracy, and in other advances were greatly marked between 1900 and 1950. . . . Studies by Leonard P. Ayres and others after 1900 stimulated interest in the problems of retardation and elimination in the elementary school. A growing concern for the individual pupil developed, but even at mid-century some of the old issues still persisted. . . . Interest in means by which the school would hold more of the older pupils was stimulated and led to the organization of the junior high schools; and the report of the Commission on the Length of Elementary Education (1927) provoked wide discussion. . . . Compulsory attendance and child labor laws tended to improve in the twentieth century and had a direct bearing on elementary education. But sociologist Franklin H. Giddings and psychologist Edward L. Thorndike raised some pointed questions about both forms of legislation. In 1950 the proposed federal child labor amendment to the Constitution of the United States had not been ratified. . . . Interest of specialists in the construction and reconstruction of the curriculum of the elementary school was very vigorous, especially after 1920, but considerable legislative control of the curriculum continued. . . . Publication in 1938 of findings by the Regents' Inquiry into the Character and Cost of Public Education in the State of New York, and in 1948 by the Educational Policies Commission of *Education for All American Youth,* stimulated wide discussion of educational issues and problems. . . . The percentage of the national income that went into education seems not to have kept pace with the phenomenal increase in national wealth between 1900 and 1950. The birth rate greatly increased between 1929 and 1949. The schools in 1950, very different from those in 1900, were becoming more and more secular.

The School of the People.—The elementary school in the United States has always been considered "the school of the people" and the fundamental unit of the common school system of this country. All the way from its origins in the seventeenth century to the middle of the twentieth, it has been a constituent part of American culture; and its history is one of the most fascinating and hopeful chapters in the whole story of the growth of American democracy. The history of the common elementary school is almost an epic account of idealism and resolution in a struggle with selfishness and vested interests, sometimes with mediocrity in management, and with other obstacles, including an indifferent public conscience that long stood stubbornly in its way. Born in poverty and obscurity, nurtured in its infancy by crumbs from the tables of charity and philanthropy, at times exploited by designing politicians and narrow ecclesiastics, the American common elementary school gradually gained sufficient strength to demand and get better care, which it began to receive in the second quarter of the nineteenth century, nearly two centuries after it first saw the light of day in Massachusetts in 1647 when the first common school law was enacted in this country. From that date to the present, the common elementary school has been an increasing concern of the people and of governing authorities; and at mid-twentieth century it was the largest single public enterprise of the American people.

Three rather clearly marked stages in the development of the common elementary school may be seen in its historical development. Prior to the educational awakening in the second quarter of the past century, the typical common elementary school was a "frontier" institution. It was generally an ungraded, meagerly equipped, district, one-teacher school with a very narrow curriculum. But it possessed the shining virtue of being democratic in its spirit, organization and management, and although it did not provide much schooling or education, that which it did provide was open to all the children of the local community. The teacher in the early days was often a law unto himself and essentially only the keeper of the school. The first treatise on teaching published in this country in English, by Samuel R. Hall in 1829, bore the title "Lectures on School-Keeping." The teacher's methods were individualistic and often wore the color of a cruel pedagogical Calvinism. Formal mental discipline and the "knowledge-aim" were powerful. The first great care of the teacher was to assign lessons and hear recitations. The pupils were on their own in trying to master the meager knowledge available through the elementary school, and the teacher rarely gave much help in improving their methods of study. There was much drill in the "tool subjects," a practice which was later to come to be frowned upon when so-called progressive education got going after 1920. The local educational officials orally examined the children on their knowledge of reading, spelling, the rudiments of arithmetic and of grammar, and they inspected the pupils' copybooks. Written examinations in the schools, and even in the colleges, were late in appearing. The first written examinations in the elementary schools seem to have been given in Boston in 1845; trustees continued until much later to examine students orally in some of the colleges.

The second stage in the growth of the common elementary school seems to have begun after 1860, when changes in practices came to be made by influences from Europe between that date and 1900. More emphasis than formerly came to be placed on materials and methods of teaching, on "psychological procedures," although psychology was hardly yet dry behind the ears, and on the education of teachers. During those decades, the normal school and other agencies for the training of teachers had rapid growth, and there was wider discussion than ever before of the purpose and the program of the elementary school and of the training of teachers. Among the earliest national committees to give attention to education was the Committee of Fifteen on Elementary Education, whose report in 1895 is discussed later in this Chapter.

Since 1900 elementary education in the United States has witnessed its greatest changes. The great increase in the economic wealth of the American people, the extension of democratic ideas, the findings of the psychologists, the overthrow of the doctrine of formal mental discipline, the discussion of individual differences—which have also had an effect on secondary and higher education—experimentation with the construction and reconstruction of the curriculum, and what has come to be called "the Dewey philosophy" have all had a more or less heavy impact on the theories and practices in elementary as in other levels of education. During this century improvements have also come in child labor and compulsory attendance legislation, and there has been an increasing humaneness toward children.

European Influences on Elementary Education.—Chief among the European influences on education after 1860 were Pestalozzianism, Herbartianism, and Froebelianism, all of which showed the influence of the writings of Jean Jacques Rousseau, eminent French philosopher and author. His educational writings, which were less original than revolutionary, were often misunderstood and led to some strange pedagogical behavior, including some of the theories of the so-called "progressives" in education in the United States after 1920.

Pestalozzianism, which had an influence on Herbart and Froebel, had its widest effect in the United States after 1860. Herbartianism found its way into this country, especially after 1890, through the influence of several Americans, among whom were Charles De Garmo and Charles and Frank McMurry, who had studied at the University of Jena, a center of the new pedagogical theory. Their writings on educational methods and on the curriculum "propagated" the Herbartian theories; and the organization of training and of practice-teaching in many American normal schools closely followed the practices at Jena. In the early 1890's, the National Herbart Society for the Scientific Study of Education was organized, and this further stimulated Herbartianism, which flooded many parts of the country. Interest in many of the Herbartian principles may be seen in addresses and papers before other educational organizations, especially the National Educational Association.

Froebel, founder of the modern kindergarten, was also an enthusiastic follower of Pestalozzi, but his theories reflected his own introspective and mystical temperament and his fondness for symbolism. The institutional result of his theories was the kindergarten, which between 1850 and 1875 was established in many American cities and towns. Apparently the first public kindergarten was established in the schools of St. Louis in the early 1870's under the superintendency of William T. Harris, who later became United States Commissioner of Education. The kindergarten had become a rather common practice in nearly two hundred of the larger cities of the United States by 1900, when it was reported that there were 1,400 public kindergartens with more than 95 thousand pupils. More than twice that number, however, were in private kindergartens. In recent decades this type of school has greatly increased under both private and public direction, with progress in the study of children and in child psychology bringing about reforms in some of the crude practices of the earlier kindergartens. Enrollments were about 773 thousand in public kindergartens and about 57 thousand in private ones in 1940. Numerous schools for exceptional or atypical children of kindergarten age were reported at that time, and kindergartens of both types were reported to be increasing in number at mid-twentieth century.

Froebel's influence was also extensive in the development of manual training or construction work in the schools in the United States, through the work of Colonel Francis W. Parker, a vigorous champion of improved practices in elementary education; of John Dewey, perhaps the greatest interpreter of education in an industrial society; and of others who were very influential in advocating the application to elementary education of principles not unlike those propounded by Froebel. In striking contrast to the work of the elementary school of earlier days, they emphasized the importance of artistic and industrial activities, of "training in thought through expression, and training in expression through thought," and Dewey, in particular, urged the study of industry as a central part of the curriculum "by having the children actively engaged to a certain extent in miniature industrial processes which are reproduced in the school."

Even if this theory of his had been sound, the distinguished philosopher must have assumed for the direction of such a "core curriculum" persons who were more broadly educated and who were also possessed of a higher historical, psychological, and sociological perspective than teachers of the time had. Some curious practices were bound to follow in the work of disciples who misunderstood the master. Later, Dewey had to rebuke, if not in fact cut the ground from under, some of the misguided zealots who obviously misunderstood his theories.[1] He found it difficult "to take stock of the achievements of progressive schools" in the decade of 1920 to 1930 because these were too diverse both in aims and in mode of conduct. But progressive schools testified to the "fact that the underlying motivation is so largely a reaction against the traditional school that the watchwords of the progressive movements are capable of being translated into inconsistent practices." While all progressive schools could not, in his view, be described by "sweeping generalizations," Dewey noted that "some of these schools indulge pupils in unrestrained freedom of action and speech, of manners and lack of manners. Schools farthest to the left (and there are many parents who share the fallacy) carry the thing they call freedom nearly to the point of anarchy."

[1] "How Much Freedom in New Schools?" *New Republic,* July 9, 1930, pp. 204-6.

About a month earlier, Boyd H. Bode had written in the same magazine that American education was "a confusing and not altogether edifying spectacle" to the casual observer. "It is productive of endless fads and panaceas; it is pretentiously scientific, and at the same time pathetically conventional; it is scornful of the past, yet painfully inarticulate when it speaks of the future. The tremendous activity now going on in education is evidence of far-reaching social changes, but we do not seem to know what these changes signify or how they are to be directed." The newer attitudes or movements in education—one emphasizing the need for making education, as Herbert Spencer had put it, a direct preparation for life, and the other the importance of full and free development—found fault with educational traditionalism but for very different reasons. There was reason, Bode thought, for believing that

...this assault on "scientific organization" has gone too far... The outstanding weakness of the newer educational movements . . . is that they have no program to offer as a substitute for the one they seek to displace . . . The doctrine of freedom, which is so much in evidence at present in our American schools, seems to be animated by the idea that programs are an obstacle to education—unless they are originated by the pupils themselves. Initiative on the part of the teacher is suppressed on the ground that purposes must not be "imposed" on pupils from without, and one is left to wonder why a teacher is needed at all. There is little ground for surprise that the more conservative members of the teaching profession view these innovations with scorn . . . The ideal of discipline through rigorous, systematic thinking and through allegiance to standards of taste and conduct is surrendered because the mob will have none of these things. Education is betrayed in its own household... The freedom theory, though always facile in quoting Dewey to its purpose, seems never to have acquired an understanding of Dewey's conception of freedom.

Dewey had insisted that freedom is achieved through the exercise of intelligence,

...whereas the less discriminating of his disciples understand him to mean that intelligence is achieved through the exercise of freedom . . . In terms of Dewey's conception of freedom, it is not at all evident that there is no place for compulsion or prescription. Any device is justified if it actually promotes thinking. Moreover, if adult psychology is any clue, it is conceivable that if children have a sense of responsibility and accountability, they feel themselves sustained thereby. The pupil who inquired, "Do we have to do what we want to do today?" seems to have had a sense that something was lacking.[2]

2 *New Republic,* June 4, 1930, pp. 61-64.

The conception of the kindergarten as a "miniature society" for young children, in which the young citizen could learn to move freely "but with consideration for his little fellows," and the large place of symbolism in Froebelianism, drew criticisms. John Dewey commented on the difficulty, if not the impossibility, for the small child to experience the symbolic meaning of a thing, as Froebel apparently expected him to do, and wrote that practically all the child got out of it was his

. . . own physical and sensational meaning, plus, very often, a glib facility in phrases and attitudes that he learns are expected of him by his teacher—without, however, any mental counterpart. We often teach insincerity and instill sentimentalism when we think we are teaching truths by means of symbols. The realities reproduced, therefore, by the child should be as familiar, direct, and real in character as possible. It is largely for this reason that in the kindergarten of our school, the work centers about the reproduction of home and neighborhood life.[3]

By 1950 "community education," "resource-use education," "outdoor education," and education promised under other strange titles seemed to the pedagogically uninitiated to have some of the symbols which Dewey tended to criticize. In many schools, children of tender age at mid-twentieth century were being plunged into make-believe studies of "community resources," and they and their parents were perhaps led to believe that these little folks could solve the economic, political, social, and racial problems which the wisest men of the past had failed to solve and which too few of their teachers were able to solve or instruct the children in solving. And the techniques of "panel discussions" and "workshops" and other devices of classroom escapism, which were very fashionable, encouraged "glib facility in phrases and attitudes" not unlike those that Dewey had criticized in 1900.

A very severe criticism of Froebelian symbolism came from the pen of the eminent psychologist, Edward L. Thorndike:

And what shall I say of those who by a most extraordinary intellectual perversity attribute to children the habit of using common things as symbols of abstractions which have never in any way entered their heads; who tell us that the girl likes to play with her doll because the play symbolizes to her motherhood; that the boy likes to be cut of doors because the sunlight symbolizes to him cheerfulness? . . .
If we live in houses because they symbolize protection, if we like to see Sherlock Holmes on the stage because he symbolizes to us craft, or Uncle Tom because he symbolizes to us slavery, or a clown from the circus because

[3] *Elementary School Record* (Chicago: University of Chicago Press, 1900).

he symbolizes to us folly; if we eat apples because they symbolize to us the fall of man, or strawberries because they symbolize to us the scarlet woman, then perhaps the children play with the ball because it symbolizes "infinite development and absolute limitation."

No one has ever given a particle of valid evidence to show any such preposterous associations in children's minds between plain things and these far-away abstractions.[4]

The formalized methods of Pestalozzianism were also severely criticized, and many of the criticisms, especially of "object" teaching, indicated the tendency of teachers to have children memorize facts about objects. But it is said that a valuable feature of the work and influence of Pestalozzi was reform in discipline through what he called a "thinking love" which tended to increase interest in gentleness and humaneness toward children in the schools.

Charles Dickens satirized the formalism of Pestalozzianism in the schools of England in *Hard Times,* when he described "Mr. Gradgrind, the town magnate and the school patron" who appeared in the model school of his own creation, where Mr. Choakumchild surcharges the youthful Coketowners with grim facts.   After a preliminary address to the teachers in this vein—

Now what I want is facts. Teach these boys and girls nothing but facts. Facts alone are wanted in life. Plant nothing else, and root out everything else. You can only form the mind of reasoning animals upon facts; nothing else ever will be of any service to them. This is the principle upon which I bring up my own children, and this is the principle upon which I bring up these children. Stick to facts, Sir!

And after this modest statement, which gratified Mr. Gradgrind's self-love in "witnessing the triumphs of his own educational scheming," he called out "by an appropriate management and catechizing," its distinctive features.

Sissy Jupe, Girl No. 20, the daughter of a strolling circus actor, whose life, no small share of it, has been passed under the canvas; whose knowledge of horse, generic and specific, extends back as far as memory reaches; familiar with the form and food, the powers and habits and everything relating to the horse; knowing it through several senses; Sissy Jupe has been asked to define horse. Astonished at hearing her father stigmatized as a veterinary surgeon, a farrier, and horse-breaker; bewildered by the striking want of resemblance between the horse of her own conceptions and the prescribed formula that represented the animal in the books of the Home and Colonial

[4] *Notes on Child Study* (New York: The Macmillan Co., 1903), pp. 77-80.

Society, she dares not trust herself with the confusing description, and shrinks from it in silence and alarm.

"Girl No. 20 unable to define a horse," said Mr. Gradgrind.

Girl No. 20 is declared possessed of no facts in reference to one of the commonest of animals, and appeal is made to one red-eyed Bitzer, who knows horse practically only as he has seen a picture of a horse or as he has, perhaps, sometimes safely weathered the perils of a crowded street crossing.

"Bitzer," (said Thomas Gradgrind,) "your definition of a horse!"

"Quadruped. Graminivorous. Forty teeth, namely: twenty-four grinders, four eyeteeth, and twelve incisive. Sheds coat in the spring; in marshy countries sheds hoofs too. Hoofs hard, but requiring to be shod with iron. Age known by marks in mouth." Thus (and much more) Bitzer.

"Now Girl No. 20," said Mr. Gradgrind, "you know what a horse is."

The importation of the Pestalozzian principles and practices into the United States had its impetus through the enthusiasm of Superintendent Edward A. Sheldon of the Oswego, New York, schools. In Toronto, Canada, Sheldon had seen an exhibition of materials in Pestalozzian methods, and he got the notion of copying them in his city and in the Oswego teacher-training school, which became a state normal school in 1866. The Board of Education of Oswego, upon examination of their work, reported favorably on the teachers in that city and published some examples of lessons taught on the Pestalozzian principle of "object" teaching. Among them was the following, a lesson on "shells," which illustrates how formal the "object" method became.

Given to a C class, primary; ages of children 5 to 6 years.

Object of the lesson was to lead the children to observe the parts of the shell, also to perceive the appropriateness of the names given to the parts.

The teacher, holding up a shell before the class, told them that an animal once lived in that shell, and then asked, "what do you live in?"

Children. Houses.

T. This was the house of an animal. Now I want you to look at it, and see if you can find different parts of this shell. James may point to some part of it.

The boy touched the small point at one end. The teacher said this part is called the *apex* of the shell. Now point to the apex of this cone; of the pyramid. The word *apex* was now printed on the blackboard.

Mary may touch some other part of the shell. She put her finger upon the largest part, or body of it; and the teacher said, this is called the *body* of the shell, and printed the word on the board.

Pointing to the whorl on the shell, the teacher said, "Look at this; see how it winds around the shell; this part looks as if it whirled around, so we call it the *whorl.*" This word was also printed on the board.

The opening of the shell was pointed at, and the children were asked to give it a name. No one replied, and the teacher requested a boy to open his mouth, and the other children to look at it, upon which several of them suggested the word *mouth* as a good name for the opening of the shell. This was printed on the board, and the children told that it is the name for that part of the shell.

Next the edges of the shell were pointed at, and the children referred to parts of their own mouths for a name. *Lips* were readily given, and printed on the board.

The groove leading to the mouth was pointed at, and the children were told to call it a *canal*. The word was then printed.

The attention of the children was directed to the lower part of the shell, containing the canal, and the children asked if they had ever seen any part of a bird that resembled it in shape. "The bird's beak?" was the reply. "That is right; and we will call this the *beak* of the shell," said the teacher. This word was also printed on the board.

A child was now called to take the shell and point out the parts as the children named them. The teacher pointed out the parts, and the children named them.[5]

In spite of some good principles which it represented, Herbartianism, just like Pestalozzianism, tended "to go to seed." Its disciples were often overzealous in advocating its adoption and in making promises for its magical powers. John Dewey knocked the Herbartian doctrine of interest into a cocked hat in an address before the National Herbart Society for the Scientific Study of Education in 1896 and drove the word "Herbart" out of the title of that organization. This doctrine, which could easily become misunderstood and be easily perverted, tended to make the teacher a sort of jumping jack, as one critic observed, and the same critic defined the doctrine of apperception as the "pedagogical holy ghost." The formal steps in instruction became very artificial, and the theory of recapitulation and of culture-epochs seemed farfetched when applied to education. Among the most energetic advocates of recapitulation were G. Stanley Hall and his students, one of whom published "Hydro-Psychoses," which dealt with mental states in relation to water and undertook to show that human beings, because their ancestors were fishes, tended to show certain attitudes toward water; and another, under the title "Dendro-Psychoses," dealt with the mental states in connection with trees. It sought to explain the attitudes of human beings toward climbing trees or toward falling trees because their ancestors had

[5] Henry Barnard, *Pestalozzi and His Educational System* (Syracuse, N. Y.: C. W. Bardeen, 1874), p. 419.

been monkeys.[6] The culture-epoch theory was very popular in academic discussions, and many uncritical educators seemed to accept it without much question of its validity, but it is now known that a rational curriculum could be had almost as well from a mail-order house as by fabrication on the culture-epoch theory. A satirist described the theory as the timing of the teaching of events or topics to corresponding stages in the pupil's life. According to this theory, he noted, internal disturbances such as civil wars could best be taught to children when they had spells of colic. The Herbartian principle of correlation also became a sort of fetish, but it was as vague and as difficult to understand as the fashionable "integration" and "fusion" were later to become. Examination of the history of the changing styles in pedagogy in the elementary schools of the United States during the past seven or eight decades shows that teaching has not been allowed to remain the simple process that it in fact is, but has been made complicated by theories that have their day and then cease to be. Of the many crimes committed by modern pedagogy, not the least flagrant and odious is its apparent tendency to make teaching very mysterious and ritualistic, something to be understood only by the craft.

Examining the Elementary School Curriculum.—As early as 1890, Charles W. Eliot, president of Harvard, had pointed out what he believed to be waste in time in certain phases of the work in elementary schools, and he reported an investigation he had made that showed the limited acquaintance which children were getting with literature in the grammar schools of Massachusetts, believed to be as good as any in this country.

I turned next to an examination of the quantity of work done in the grammar school under consideration—and, first, of the amount of reading. The amount of time given to reading and the study of the English language through the spelling book and the little grammar which are used in that school, and through a variety of other aids to the learning of English, is 37 per cent of all school time during six years. But what is the amount of reading in this time? I procured two careful estimates of the time it would take a graduate of a high school to read aloud consecutively all the books which are read in this school during six years, including the history, the reading lessons in geography, and the book on manners. The estimates were made by two persons reading aloud at a moderate rate, and reading everything that the children in most of the rooms of that school have been supposed to read

6 *American Journal of Psychology,* IX (July, 1898), pp. 449-506; X (January, 1899), pp. 171-229.

during their entire course of six years. The time occupied in doing this reading was forty-six hours . . . How small an acquaintance adults would make with English literature if their reading were [so] limited in amount . . . This test . . . is, of course, a very rough and inadequate one, . . . but it gives some clue to the very limited acquaintance with literature which the children get in the entire course of six years.[7]

In 1891 Eliot had written:

It would be for the advancement of the whole public school system if every reader were hereafter to be absolutely excluded from the school. I object to them because they are not real literature; they are but mere scraps of literature, even when the single lessons or materials of which they are composed are taken from literature. But there are a great many readers that seem to have been composed especially for the use of children. They are not made up of selections from recognized literature, and as a rule this class is simply ineffable trash. They are entirely unfit material to use in the training of our children. The object of reading with children is to convey to them the ideals of the human race; our readers do not do that and are thoroughly unfitted to do it. I believe that we should substitute in all our schools real literature for readers.[8]

Here it should be noted that Herbartianism, which flooded the United States in the latter part of the past century and the early part of the present one, emphasized literature and history in the elementary schools as effective means of moral education, and the use of "literary classics" was recommended in place of selected pieces in the reading books. More recently the tendency has apparently been away from literary "masterpieces" to reading materials more nearly adapted to the interests of children, with the result that more attention has been given to children's interests in reading and a large body of literature for children has been developed.

One of the earliest national efforts of American educators to examine the curriculum of the elementary schools was begun in 1893 when the Department of Superintendence of the National Educational Association appointed a committee of ten, later increased to fifteen, which became known as the Committee of Fifteen on Elementary Education. Its purpose was to investigate the organization of public-school systems, the correlation of studies in the primary and grammar schools, and the training of teachers.[9]

[7] "An Average Massachusetts Grammar School," in *Educational Reform*. New York: The Century Co., 1898.
[8] *Educational Review*, II (July, 1891), p. 145.
[9] The chairman of the committee was Superintendent William H. Maxwell of Brooklyn, New York. Other members were United States Commissioner of

Three subcommittees were formed from the larger committee, and their reports were made to and accepted by the Department of Superintendence in 1895. One of these was on the training of teachers; another on the correlation of studies in the elementary schools; and the third on the organization of city school systems. In discharging the committee by resolution, the Department expressed appreciation of "the great value of the report of the Committee of Fifteen in setting forth standards, defining educational values, and furnishing broad grounds for intelligent deliberation and discussion in the future . . ."

The subcommittee on the correlation of studies in the elementary schools undertook to find adequate answers to such questions as the following:

Should the course in the elementary school be eight years, and the course in the secondary school be four years, as was the case at that time? Or should the course in the elementary school be six years, and that in the secondary school six years?

Has each of the grammar-school studies—language (including reading, spelling, grammar, composition), mathematics (arithmetic, algebra, plane geometry), geography, history, natural science (botany, zoology, mineralogy), penmanship, drawing, etc., a distinct pedagogical value? If so, what is it?

Should other subjects . . . such as manual training (including sloyd, sewing, and cooking), physical culture, physics, music, physiology (including the effects of stimulants and narcotics), Latin, or a modern language be taught in the elementary-school course? If so, why?

Should the sequence of topics be determined by the logical development of the subject or by the child's power to apperceive new ideas? Or, to any extent, by the evolutionary steps manifested by the race? If so, by the evolution of the race to which the child belongs or that of the human race?

Other questions considered by this subcommittee concerned the purpose "of attempting a close correlation of studies"; the elimination of "nonessentials" in order to prevent duplication and save time and effort, although "nonessentials" were not clearly defined; the development of the apperceiving power of the minds of children; the possi-

---

Education, William T. Harris; Superintendent T. M. Balliet of Springfield, Massachusetts; Superintendent H. S. Tarbell of Providence, Rhode Island; Superintendent N. C. Dougherty of Peoria, Illinois; Superintendent W. B. Powell of Washington, D. C.; Superintendent L. H. Jones of Indianapolis, Indiana; Superintendent J. M. Greenwood of Kansas City, Missouri; State Superintendent A. B. Poland of New Jersey; and Superintendent Edward Brooks of Philadelphia. Added later to the committee were President Andrew S. Draper of the University of Illinois; Superintendent E. P. Seaver of Boston; Superintendent A. G. Lane of Chicago; Superintendent Charles B. Gilbert of St. Paul; and Superintendent Oscar H. Cooper of Galveston, Texas.

bility of correlating all the subjects in the elementary school; the possibility of "correlating the results of the work in all the groups" of subjects correlated; the length of recitation periods in each year; the proper time for introducing the new subjects mentioned in the third question above; how many hours a week for how many years should be given to each subject or group of subjects; the topics that should be covered in each subject or group of subjects; whether each subject or group of subjects should be treated differently for pupils who were to leave school at the end of the elementary period and for those who were going to high school; the possibility of describing the best method of teaching each subject or group of subjects; the point at which the specialization of teachers should begin; principles for promoting pupils from grade to grade, and who should determine those principles.

Some of these questions were to give American educators something to talk about in faculty meetings and conventions for many years. Conclusive and definitive answers were not readily found. And some of these questions or variations of them were still being given at least academic consideration at mid-twentieth century.

But there was agreement in the Committee on the following "propositions" in regard to the correlation of studies:

The civilization of the age—the environment into which the child is born—should determine the selection of the objects of study, to the end that the child may gain an insight into the world in which he lives and a command over its resources such as is obtained by a helpful cooperation with his fellows.

Psychology should determine the selection and arrangement of the topics within each branch so as to afford the best exercise of the faculty of the mind and to secure the unfolding of those faculties in their natural order.

Language, as a subject of study, has a distinct and definite relation to the introduction of the child into the civilization of his time, and has, therefore, a distinct pedagogical value, forming the true basis of correlating the elementary studies.

In correlating geography and history, the former should be subordinate to the latter.

Instruction in the elements of physics and chemistry, in so far as they are to be taught at all in the elementary school, should not be limited to the higher grades but should be given in all grades in connection with topics in physiology and physical geography.

Elementary geography should not be taught as a special study, but the topics usually included under this caption in the course of study should be incorporated into the course of form and nature study.

The use of good English, including the correct use of technical terms, should be required in all studies; all use of bad English, caused by, or significant of, confusion of thought, should be corrected by securing the elucidation of the thought; the child's best efforts in speech should be required in all recitations, oral or written; but solecisms [errors, barbarisms, improprieties in speech] should for the most part be corrected in the regular language lessons.

The study of English grammar should be made subordinate and auxiliary to the study of English literature.

Writing, as a special branch, should be taught only through the sixth year of the course.

Manual training in wood and metals should be made a part of the course for boys during the seventh and eighth years; and sewing and cooking should be taught to girls—the former in the fourth, fifth, and sixth years, the latter in the seventh and eighth years.

Music should be taught throughout the elementary courses, and the sight reading of music should have a prominent place in the study.

The following "propositions" were rejected by the Committee:

Algebra should take the place of arithmetic in the eighth year of the elementary school.

In the eighth year, an option should be given between Latin and a modern language.

United States history should be taken up during the eighth year, and should be studied only up to the date of the adoption of the Constitution.

The course of study for elementary schools should admit optional studies on educational grounds for the good of the pupil.

Concrete geometry should be taught under the head of drawing, and also under the head of mensuration in arithmetic.

During an eight-year course (beginning with the sixth year of age), the following subjects should be required from all pupils: English, mathematics, United States history and Constitution, drawing, and music Not more than one of the following subjects should be pursued in addition to those enumerated above: Latin, a modern language, natural science, manual training, or concrete geometry.

The following "propositions" were adopted by a majority of the members of the Committee:

Algebra (not to the exclusion of arithmetic) should be taught during one half of the last year of the course.

Latin should be studied during the eighth year instead of English grammar; and English grammar should be studied during the sixth and seventh years.

United States history should be studied for one and a half years.

The Constitution of the United States should be studied for ten weeks during the last year of the course.

If the community is at one on the course of study, all pupils should take the same branches of study, without any omission.

Reading should be both silent and oral. There should be at least four lines of connected reading, embracing literature, history, geography, and nature studies. Furthermore, prose and poetry, of an appropriate character, should be read to the classes throughout the grades in which pupils are too young to read such literature themselves.

Not more than sixty minutes of outside study should be required of any elementary school pupil.[10]

The report of the subcommittee on the correlation of studies in the elementary schools was the only one which dealt with the function of elementary education and its relation to secondary education. The subcommittee's interpretation of the meaning of correlation indicated that it meant a logical order of topics and branches of learning, a proper sequence of courses, and what was later to become known as "experiences." It also believed that the studies should form a symmetrical whole, a proper balance of the great divisions of human learning, and one branch or division should not be emphasized out of proportion to its importance. All subjects should be so presented as to prevent the abnormal development of the child; there should be psychological symmetry; and the entire course of the pupil should be correlated with the world in which he lived. The influence of Herbartianism on the report of this subcommittee seems evident.[11]

Increased Attendance in Elementary Schools.—About 21.4 million of the 76 million people in 1900 were between the ages of five and eighteen, about 17 million were enrolled in public and private schools, colleges, and universities, and about 525 thousand in special and evening schools, business schools, and private kindergartens. Of the 146 million people in the United States in 1948, about 30 million were between the ages of five and seventeen, and about 24 million were enrolled in elementary and secondary schools. About 31 per cent of the fourteen- or fifteen-year-olds in 1900 dropped out to go to work, as compared with 5 per cent in 1950. The proportion of grade school pupils who went to high school so greatly increased after 1900 that a major recommendation of the National Education Association in 1950 was for the immediate building of more schools.

[10] The chairman of the subcommittee on the correlation of studies was U. S. Commissioner of Education William T. Harris. Other members were superintendents J. M. Greenwood of Kansas City, Charles B. Gilbert of St. Paul, L. H. Jones of Indianapolis, and William H. Maxwell of Brooklyn.

[11] For the report of the Committee of Fifteen, see *Journal of Proceedings and Addresses* of the National Educational Association for 1895, pp. 232 ff. See also *Educational Review* (March, 1895).

The average annual public school term in 1880 was 130.3 days as compared with 144.3 days in 1900 and 177.6 in 1948. But the figures for the earlier years were made lower by including data for states with very short terms. The average pupil around 1900 probably attended school less than four months a year. Terms were very short in the southern states where the Conference for Education in the South, which was to promote an educational awakening during the next decade or more, had only a few years before starting its effective work. The average number of years of public schooling for Americans in 1900 was 4.44. Forty-four years later the National Education Association reported that among Americans twenty-five years of age or over, 4 per cent had never gone to school at all; 13 per cent had never completed the fourth grade; 56 per cent had had only an eighth-grade education or less; and 75 per cent had not finished high school. As against this dismal reminder, a survey by George Gallup's American Institute of Public Opinion about the same time showed that more than one third of all the grown people of this country hoped to get more schooling after the Second World War, and 50 per cent of them desired professional and cultural studies. Only 34 per cent desired "bread-and-butter vocational training."

The number of illiterates in the United States in 1900 was smaller by 145 thousand than in 1890, and was divided about equally between whites and Negroes. Illiterate males of both races represented about 10 per cent of the population over ten years of age, while illiterate females of both races represented about 11 per cent. About 1.4 million people in this country in 1900 could not speak English; of these about 670 thousand were men and 733 thousand were women.

In 1870 the percentage of illiteracy was reported as 20.0; in 1880 as 17.0; in 1890 as 13.3; in 1900 as 10.7; in 1910 as 7.7; in 1920 as 6.0; and in 1930 as 4.3. Illiteracy was defined as inability to read and write in any language. In 1930 the rate among Negroes was reported as 16.3; among whites as 1.5. Among Negroes in urban centers it was given as 5.0.

Data on illiteracy were last collected by the Bureau of the Census in 1930, and in 1940 these were supplemented by data on the number of years of formal schooling the American people had had. In 1947 the figures reported on persons between twenty and twenty-four years of age who had had from one to four years of grade schooling was 3.2; five to six years, 4.7; seven to eight years, 14.1. The percentage of those who had had from one to three years of high school was 24.7; four years of high school, 40.2. The percentage of those who had had one to three years of college was 9.9; four years or more,

2.5. The percentage of those not reporting their formal schooling was 0.7.

Total receipts from all sources for the public schools in 1900 were about $220 million, as compared with $4.3 billion in 1949. Nearly 70 per cent of receipts in 1900 came from local taxes, with state taxes representing only about 17 per cent. Forty-eight years later, according to a report of the Council of State Governments,[12] the percentage of receipts for public schools from local sources was 53.2; from state sources, about 39.8. County (5.7) and federal (1.3) provided the remainder. Practically all the federal funds provided directly for schools were for vocational education and vocational rehabilitation (other than funds for school lunches and educational funds for veterans). Instructional salaries in 1900 absorbed about $215 million of the $220 million total receipts. In 1948 these absorbed about $2.3 billion of the total expenditures of $4.3 billion. In 1900 the expenditure per pupil for current expenses was $20.21; in 1948 the figure was about $179.

Retardation in the Schools.—A little more than four decades ago a careful study [13] of the subject showed that about 33 per cent of all the pupils in the public schools of the United States were in the "retarded" class, and this condition was costing the taxpayers much money. "This gives an idea of the magnitude of the problem with which we are dealing. It is not at all a problem concerning a few undeveloped or feeble-minded children. It is one affecting most intimately perhaps 6 million children in the United States." Ayres pointed out that wherever the retarded children constituted a large part of the enrollment in the schools, many of them did not complete the elementary course. Children who were backward in their studies rarely remained to finish elementary school. Conditions varied widely, but the general tendency in the cities at that time was for the schools "to carry all of their children through the fifth grade, to take one half of them to the eighth grade, and one in ten through the high school." Five years earlier William H. Maxwell, superintendent of the New York City schools, reported that 39 per cent of the children in the elementary grades in that city were retarded— "above the normal age for the grades they were in."

In the discussions of retardation forty years ago, it was generally claimed by those who did not view the matter as very serious that average children in the schools had entered "at comparatively ad-

[12] *The Forty-eight State School Systems* (Chicago, 1949).
[13] Leonard P. Ayres, *Laggards in Our Schools* (New York: Charities Publication Committee), 1909.

vanced ages," and that even if some children did make a slow progress, these were offset to some extent "by an equal or greater
number" who progressed rapidly. The studies by Ayres found that
these two contentions had little basis in fact. As for the second claim,
it was found that for every child who was proceeding at more than
the normal rate, eight to ten children were "making abnormally slow
progress." The course of study, he concluded, was adapted neither
to the slow nor to the average child, "but to the unusually bright
one." In the country at large, one sixth of the children were "repeaters," and in the cities alone the "wasteful process" was costing
$27 million a year.

There was no one cause nor even a preponderant cause for retardation. Among the many causes were late entrance, irregular attendance, illness, certain physical defects, ignorance of the English
language (among foreigners), faulty practices of promotion, and the
number of times a child failed in his course. Inquiry into this last
condition "demonstrated that we are training our children well in
failure." But the most important set of facts brought to light by the
study had to do with the relative standing of boys and girls. The
schools were better adapted "to the needs of the girls than to those
of the boys." There were 13 per cent more retardation and 13 per
cent more repeaters among the boys than among the girls, and the
percentage of girls who finished the elementary schools was 17 per
cent greater than that of the boys.

These conditions and the remedies proposed for improvement
were not complimentary commentaries on the administration of public elementary education in the United States forty years ago.

If children are to progress regularly through the grades, they must be
present in the schools. This means that we must have better compulsory
attendance laws and better provision for their enforcement. If we are to
enforce the attendance laws, we must know where the children of school age
are. Therefore we must have better laws for taking the school census, and
better methods for utilizing the returns. If we are to have all of our children
complete the common school course, we must have an agreement which is
now commonly lacking between the length of the school course and the length
of the compulsory attendance period. It is a curious anomaly that we commonly have school courses eight or nine years in length and compel attendance
for six years only.

The administrative reforms which must be brought about consist mainly
of more thorough and better medical inspection, courses of study which will
more nearly fit the abilities of the average pupil, more flexible grading, and,
most important of all, a better knowledge of the facts. We must have better

school records and we must learn to interpret them more intelligently. It is far from creditable that in hardly a city in the country can the school authorities tell how many pupils begin each year, or how fast they advance, or what proportion finish, or why they fall out, or where and why they lose time.[14]

These statements were made concerning conditions in city school systems on which the study was based and in which educational administration was presumably more advanced than in rural communities. If conditions were so bad in urban places forty years ago, what must they have been in the rural schools?

The study by Ayres inquired into the truth of the assumption that the evils of retardation were of recent growth in the elementary schools of the United States. This assumption had grown out of the awakened interest in the subject of retardation and the agitation for vocational instruction in the elementary grades. Economic and social trends in the latter part of the nineteenth century and the early part of the twentieth seemed to strengthen arguments for vocational training. Students of the subject of retardation tried to find out whether the condition was improving and decreasing in seriousness; and whether, if retardation showed improvement, the decrease was "rapid enough to warrant us in feeling that the matter will take care of itself if no further attention be paid to it."

In the case of six cities, the data upon which inquiry on this question was made were not very abundant. But it appeared that the tendency was "one of general progress toward better conditions with no advance in the last five years." For example, Columbus, Ohio, seemed to show no decided change between 1895 and 1907. Kansas City, Missouri, showed decided improvement. The result in Los Angeles was negative. Portland, Oregon, showed steady improvement, and Springfield, Massachusetts, showed "continued and decided improvement." In the main, there appeared to be a slow but general tendency, which was by no means universal, "for our cities to increase the relative size of the enrollment in the upper grades as compared with that in the lower ones." But this hopeful tendency was "far from being either universal or decided." Although encouraging, the tendency was "so inconsiderable in degree as to indicate very plainly that retardation is not an evil which will be self-eradicating if neglected." In 1950 retardation was still an educational evil in the United States, chiefly because it had not been self-eradicating.

[14] *Ibid.,* p .7.

A prominent trend in elementary education in the United States during the past four or five decades appeared in the growing concern for the individual pupil. Many practices have developed that have definitely aimed to meet the individual needs of pupils. These practices include coaching and giving extra time to "laggards"; studying so-called "problem" cases; grouping the pupils according to their abilities; making individual assignments; providing "adjustment" rooms and guidance services; directing the study of the pupils more closely; socializing the recitations; making use of the so-called "problem-project" devices; arranging "ungraded" classes; planning and using the "activities" program, "units" of instruction, and other procedures in order to call out and develop the interests and activities of the pupils "within a socialized environment," as the pedagogical specialists promised. During recent decades the growing interest in the individual pupil in the work of the elementary school was clearly revealed by the various methods that had been introduced and experimented with, even though not all these were always clear and easily defined or described. The vagueness of some of the new procedures tended to confuse some of the teachers in elementary schools and to draw from critics the charge of relaxed discipline and the lack of thoroughness and system. Whatever the criticisms, however, one purpose of the new plans was to look upon the child more "as an active agent in learning and adaptation to situations" and less as a "passive recipient of teaching and training." The latter view was the one so long held in elementary schools, as in other levels of education in the United States. The tendency was from "teaching to learning," a phrase so often found in "progressive" educational writings and speeches.

The elementary school in the United States has remained a "graded" school, with subjects of instruction assigned to the various grade levels, although the graded system is not of very ancient origin. Where the system came from and how it became the common practice in this country led to a somewhat heated debate toward the end of the First World War, between Charles H. Judd of the University of Chicago and Paul Monroe of Columbia University, the former holding that "the elementary schools of the United States borrowed their plan of organization and the general definition of their course of study from Prussia," and Monroe arguing that they were indigenous to the American soil and not an importation from Prussia.[15] It seems clear, however, that educational influences from Prussia did

---

[15] See *School and Society*, VII (June 15 and 29, 1918), and VIII (September 7, 1918); also *New Republic*, XIV (April 20, 1918), and *Educational Review*, LVI (November, 1918).

find their way to the United States, particularly in the second quarter of the nineteenth century, when many reports on the Prussian system of education were made available and were apparently widely read in this country. Whatever its weaknesses, the graded system has remained a prominent feature of elementary education in this country. The pupils are placed in one grade or another chiefly according to their achievement in or "mastery" of the subjects of the various grades, although in the early schools instruction had been largely individual, each pupil proceeding as rapidly as his ability, interest, and effort would permit. But in a society so passionately devoted, as theoretically the United States is, to the promising principle of universal education, mass educational production will likely continue to be a conspicuous feature of the American scene. In spite of the increased and intelligent effort by school administrators, supervisors, and teachers during recent decades to solve the old problems of re-tardation and elimination, however, these evils have persisted in the elementary schools.

As the quality of the schools improved, their "holding power" became stronger, although failures in both secondary schools and colleges were still distressingly large in 1950. Of 1,000 children in the fifth grade in 1906, only 139 were graduated from high school in 1914, but of that number in that grade in 1934, about 467 were graduated from high school in 1942. The reduction of child labor and improvements in compulsory attendance legislation had also helped to keep children in school. In 1900 about 31 per cent of American children fourteen and fifteen years old were employed in gainful occupations. This figure dropped to 18 per cent by 1920, to 9 per cent by 1930, to 5 per cent by 1940, and at mid-century showed promise of further reduction through more intelligent legisla-tion on child labor and compulsory school attendance. Another con-dition that was having an effect on keeping more children in school was of an economic nature. In 1900 the average American income per capita, adjusted to the value of money in 1939, was about $400 a year. In 1947 it was about $900, when adjusted to the same value. As the American people have improved their economic status, their children have enjoyed the advantages of more years of schooling. This economic condition has particularly affected increases in en-rollments in the secondary schools, where many of the "dropouts" had been caused by the low economic status of families.

The Inception of the Junior High School.—The decade between 1910 and 1920 witnessed a new form of educational organization, known as the "junior high school," which seems to have had its beginnings in Berkeley and Los Angeles, California, and Columbus, Ohio. The new type of organization had followed the discussion for several years of some important questions: How can education be reorganized so that schooling will attract and retain a larger percentage of the older pupils who were dropping out, and more nearly meet the varying needs of the heterogeneous population then swarming into the schools? How can instruction be better adapted to the needs of the different social classes and thereby better adjust the work of the schools to the social and industrial conditions of the times? How can the work of the schools be better adjusted to the natural growth and mental development of children? Interest in these questions had been stimulated by John Dewey and by William Rainey Harper, president of the University of Chicago, by Charles W. Eliot, president of Harvard University, and by others. As early as 1888 Eliot had read a paper before the Department of Superintendence of the National Educational Association on "Can School Programs be Shortened and Enriched?" and four years later he gave a paper on "Shortening and Enriching the Grammar School Course" before the same organization. The same year he gave an address before the National Educational Association on "Undesirable and Desirable Uniformity in Schools." In this he said in part:

Let us first consider in some detail the undesirable uniformity in schools. The graded school of large towns and cities will supply our first illustration. In any room of a perfectly graded grammar school we find, in the fall, a single class of from forty to sixty children who are supposed to have had the same preparation for the coming year's work; who have had the same lessons, in the same books, at the same times, under the same teacher, throughout the year; who are to make as nearly as possible the same progress every day in each subject, and to submit to the same tests at the same intervals. They are all kept together, day by day, so far as is possible. The bright ones never work to their utmost and are frequently marking time; the slow ones are urged forward at a rate which drives some of them to despair; and the ideal of the class is that of equal preparation, equal capacity, equal progress, and equal attainments. If, at the beginning of the year, the children are obtrusively unequal in capacity or attainments, it is an inconvenience to be regretted. The teacher will not be able to "handle her class" so easily as she could if they were all of the same mental size and strength. If, at the end of the year, they have not been pretty well evened up, the teacher has been less successful than she could have wished. This is an extreme statement of the most undesirable uniformity in schools. This is the sense in which close grading is an educational curse. In my opinion, the right aims, in any room of a primary or grammar school, are to recognize at the beginning of the year, as promptly as possible, the different capacities and powers of the children; to carry them forward, throughout the year, each at his own gait and speed; and to turn them out at the end very much more different in capacity and attainments than they were at the beginning. It has always seemed to me that a teacher who did not discharge his pupils at the end of each year much more unlike in powers and acquisitions than they were at the beginning, was a proved failure. We all know that children, like adults, are not alike, but infinitely different; that the object of education, as of life, is to bring out the innate powers and to develop to the highest possible degree the natural and acquired capacities of each individual. An education or training, therefore, which at the end of four years, ten years, or twenty years leaves the subjects of it alike in skill, capacity, or power of service, must have been ill-directed. . . .

Let us take another illustration, at a higher grade—the secondary school, represented in the United States by the high school, the academy, and the private preparatory school. These schools hold the children until the seventeenth, eighteenth, or nineteenth year. By that time of life almost every peculiar mental or physcial gift which by training can be made of value to the individual or to society is already revealed to its possessor and to any observant friend, provided that the youth has had access to those various fields of human knowledge and research in which the various mental capacities and activities find play. If a youth has never had access to any studies except Latin, Greek, and mathematics, he will perhaps remain ignorant of his powers in scientific or historical study. If he has never had access to any language but his own, his linguistic gifts may be concealed from himself and his friends. This revelation to himself of a youth's natural predispositions and faculties is one of the principal objects of secondary education. Now if the only school that the youth has attended has had a narrow, uniform program, containing a limited number of subjects, without options among them, this important object in secondary education may not have been attained for the individual. A good secondary school must have a program of studies larger and wider than any single pupil can follow, else its range of subjects will be too small to permit the sure fulfillment of this all-important function of a good secondary school—the thorough exploration of all its pupils' capacities . . .

Anyone who has had much experience in schools or colleges must have learned that as the course of education goes on, and new subjects are set before a class or group of pupils, the bright and the dull children not infrequently change places—those that were accounted bright become apparently dull, and those that were accounted dull become, perhaps, leaders. The reason is that the dull children have finally been brought to a subject in which they excel; while the bright ones, who have been exercising a faculty which they possess in large measure, have been brought to a new field to which their powers are not adapted. Flexible and diversified school programs will give all the children their most favorable chance; stiff and uniform programs will not. No machine, like an army, a ship, or a factory, can be a democratic institution; for it demands from the many implicit obedience, and the subordination of the individual energy to the movements of the mass. So far as a school is a machine of uniform product, it must fail, on that account, to serve as it might the real interests of democratic society.[16]

A Significant Study.—Wide discussion of and increased interest in the reorganization of education in the 1920's were somewhat reminiscent of discussions that were going on when the Committee of Fifteen was preparing and presenting its report on elementary education in the early 1890's. In 1920 "The Educational Research Committee" was formed under the auspices of the Commonwealth Fund to promote research in the field of education, and one of its earliest activities was a study of the elementary schools of this country and Canada. The movement for the reorganization of education by means of the junior high schools, and the fact that there were in the various states clearly distinguishable examples of elementary schools with seven, eight, and nine grades, led pointedly to the question: "What is essential to a complete definition of elementary education?" In order to answer this question, the Commission on Length of Elementary Education was formed and undertook two types of investigation. One was to discover, if possible, the views held in representative school systems in the various states on the proper scope of elementary education; the other was to measure the achievements of pupils in certain selected centers of general comparability, and to examine contrasting practices in regard to the length of elementary education.[17]

Although in the decade of 1920 to 1930 enrollments in high schools had increased nearly 100 per cent—one of the significant facts about education in the United States during the first half of the twentieth century—the increase in enrollments in the elementary school was only about 10 per cent. The increase in the first grade was only about 4 per cent. And the decrease in the birth rate led to the prediction that by 1940 enrollments in the elementary school would become stationary or actually decrease. It was also predicted that the need for new elementary school buildings would probably grow less, and only the need to replace old buildings would remain. The story was very different before 1950 when the need for school buildings was greater than at any time in the history of the United States.

In general, the public schools were holding in daily average attendance a larger percentage of children than formerly. In 1920

[16] *Proceedings of the National Educational Association,* 1892, pp. 617-25.
[17] *Report of the Commission on Length of Elementary Education* (Chicago: The University of Chicago, 1927). The first chapter gives a summary of the report.

only 75 of the 100 children enrolled were attending daily; in 1930, 83 out of every 100 were doing so. The percentage of children five to seventeen years of age in the public schools increased from about 78 per cent in 1920 to nearly 82 per cent in 1930; and the average child was receiving nearly eleven days more schooling in 1930 than the average child had received ten years earlier.

But elementary education showed wide divergencies in practice throughout the country, as the report of the Commission on Length of Elementary Education revealed. Diversity in practice was due in part to the great mobility of the people, which served to spread ideas and customs in public affairs from one part of the country to another; the tendency of the managers and teachers of the schools to change their positions frequently; and the services of professional organizations and professional literature which informed the people in all parts of the country about what was going on elsewhere in education. Diversity appeared in the age of admission of pupils, policies of promotion, subjects in the curriculum, size of classes, preparation of teachers, length of the school day and school year, and the attitudes of the community towards compulsory education.

The commission had the cooperation of more than 600 typical school systems from which information was had. Its report showed that in some states, chiefly southern, the elementary schools in the middle 1920's had seven grades, some had eight grades, and in some states, especially Maryland, some systems had seven grades and some eight grades. In a few systems in New England, especially in the state of Maine, there were nine-grade elementary schools. The systems examined were organized in different ways, some having junior high schools, and some, other types of organization or mixed organization.

The school year varied from 111 days to 195 days, a difference which seemed to be somewhat closely related to the financial ability of the states. The school day varied from a minimum of less than 300 minutes to a maximum of more than 360 minutes. In general it appeared that the school day in junior and senior high schools was longer than in the elementary schools, a difference perhaps not due to economic conditions in the various states but more likely to the views of the communities with regard to the desirable organization of schools. Laws on compulsory attendance also varied in provisions, as could have been expected, the lowest age of compulsory attendance being six years and the highest eighteen years, with sixteen years being the upper limit in most of the states. The states in which the pupils were the youngest were Massachusetts, Maine, Indiana,

Wisconsin, Iowa, South Dakota, Minnesota, Montana, Connecticut, and Nebraska. Those states in which the pupils were the oldest were Virginia, North Carolina, South Carolina, Kentucky, North Dakota, Texas, New Mexico, Louisiana, Arizona, and Tennessee. There were marked differences in policies of promotion and in the retention of pupils. These differences appeared in the percentage of repeaters who ranged for the first grade from nearly 31 per cent in one state to a little more than 6 per cent in another. For the sixth grade, the maximum percentage of repeaters was about 15 per cent and the minimum was about $2\frac{1}{2}$ per cent.

Variations in the preparation of teachers were also striking. Many of them had only two years of professional training. These variations did not, it was believed, parallel the financial ability of the states. Apparently the judgments of communities with regard to the professional training of teachers were strong influences, as were also tradition and the ability of the communities to provide good salaries. Variations appeared in the content of curriculum. In general there was a tendency to retain up to the sixth grade the rudimentary and conventional elementary subjects. Reading and arithmetic, for example, were found almost everywhere for all the elementary grades. Geography was found in the first grade in more than 6 per cent of the school systems; in nearly 10 per cent in the second grade; in 63 per cent in the third grade; in 92 per cent in the fourth grade; in 96 per cent in the fifth grade; in 95 per cent in the sixth grade; in about 89 per cent in the seventh grade; in 37 per cent in the eighth grade; and in more than 12 per cent in the ninth grade. From these figures it was evident that there was a nucleus of subjects in the elementary schools composed of reading, penmanship, arithmetic, and English, including spelling and phonetics. Outside these subjects were others that were taught throughout the grades in about three fourths of the school systems—drawing, hygiene, physical training, and music. History was taught extensively in the fifth grade and beyond. Other subjects that appeared in about one fourth of the school systems were handwork, manual training, physiology, home economics, natural sciences, and social sciences. The commission's study of the curriculum seemed to show that the elementary school was generally recognized as the agency of society for training children in the mastery of the vernacular, the rudiments of mathematics, and the arts of reading and writing. There appeared to be agreement that certain bodies of information, such as that about the world, should be taught in the elementary school, but the exact limits of such instruction were hazy and the work in the upper classes of the

elementary curriculum seemed to pass easily over into the work of
the secondary school without any clear line of the proper jurisdiction
—where elementary education should end and where secondary education should begin.

The report concluded that the influences of tradition in states,
and of state departments of education, were very strong in causing
diversity in practice in elementary education. Some states concen-
trated on a limited range of subjects, while others undertook "to
enrich the curriculum" by the use of as many subjects as possible.
By 1950 there was increasing evidence that the curriculum had been
inflated or proliferated. One critic pointed out that the schools were
undertaking to teach everything "except how to get in out of the
rain." In spite of efforts at some enrichment in the middle 1920's,
courses in foreign languages, higher mathematics, and science were
rare in the elementary schools, and before they reached fourteen
years of age pupils were prevented from studying subjects which were
open to pupils in the secondary schools

. . . of every other civilized country at a much earlier age. If pupils in the
elementary schools of the United States are mature enough in the seventh
and eighth grades to study a number of the informational subjects which were
formerly regarded as advanced, this fact would seem to justify the statement
that they should be admitted to the study of foreign languages and advanced
mathematics if they need these in their preparation for later life. . . . In
America alone the progress of all pupils is blocked by the limited program
of elementary education.

A powerful influence which prevented the merging of the upper
grades of the elementary school with the high school was the high
school itself. Teachers in high schools were reluctant to accept any
proposals which tended to transform the work of the first high school
year or to readjust their subjects or the organization of their schools
so as to adapt the work to younger pupils. The result was that

. . . many American school systems continue to administer elementary education and secondary education on the schedule of grades that has existed
since the days of Horace Mann. This they do in spite of the introduction
of the junior high school, in spite of the expansion of the curriculum, in
spite of the example of successful seven-grade elementary schools, in spite
of the obvious maturity of many pupils, and in spite of the accumulating
evidence that the eight-grade elementary school is undergoing and should
undergo a fundamental transformation.

The study showed, for example, that in Maryland, where three
counties had eight-grade and the others seven-grade elementary

schools, "on the average, the pupils from the seven-grade elementary school were adequately prepared for high school." When the pupils from the two types of systems were followed into the colleges and normal schools of the state, any "distinction in scholastic standing disappeared." The quality of standing in higher education of pupils from the two systems paralleled information that had been reported for a number of years by the regional association of colleges and secondary schools. There appeared to be evidence to show from experience that elementary education of a satisfactory degree of richness of content could be provided in seven grades.

Some of the forces that influenced elementary education during the first half of the twentieth century were not unlike those that influenced secondary and higher education during that period. Among these were the great increase in economic wealth, the extension of democratic ideas, industrialism and the idea of industrial efficiency, the finding of psychological laboratories, a growing humaneness in the public attitude toward children, and the weakening of the old theological despotism. There had been a tendency under theology to make children imps of the devil and to beat him out of them. And although, as the twentieth century advanced, there appeared to be a tendency in some schools of psychology to make children chemical episodes, nevertheless the personality of children was being respected as perhaps never before in elementary education in this country.

Compulsory Attendance and Child Labor Legislation.—The enactment and enforcement of intelligent compulsory attendance and child labor legislation have been very closely related to the development of elementary education in this country. In 1852 Massachusetts had been the first of the American states to enact legislation on compulsory school attendance, and by 1890 the following states and territories had enacted laws on the subject:

State or Territory	Year	State or Territory	Year
Massachusetts	1852	Wyoming	1876
District of Columbia	1864	Ohio	1877
Vermont	1867	Wisconsin	1879
New Hampshire	1871	Rhode Island	1883
Michigan	1871	Illinois	1883
Washington	1871	Dakota	1883
Connecticut	1872	Montana	1883
Nevada	1873	Minnesota	1885
New York	1874	Nebraska	1887
Kansas	1874	Idaho	1887
California	1874	Colorado	1889
Maine	1875	Oregon	1889
New Jersey	1875	Utah	1890

Between 1890 and 1900, legislation on the subject was enacted as follows: New Mexico, 1891; Pennsylvania, 1895; Kentucky, 1896; Indiana and West Virginia, 1897; Arizona, 1899; Iowa and Maryland, 1902; Missouri and Tennessee, 1905; Delaware, North Carolina, and Oklahoma, 1907; Virginia, 1908; Arkansas, 1909; Louisiana, 1910; Alabama, Florida, South Carolina, and Texas, 1915; Georgia, 1916; and Mississippi, 1918. It will be noticed that the movement for compulsory school attendance legislation was slow in the southern states, the first legislation on the subject being enacted in Tennessee in 1905. Revisions, extensions, and improvements in this legislation have been made from time to time in most of the American states.[18]

The arguments for and against compulsory attendance laws, which reached back to the days of Martin Luther, were very vigorous in the United States far into the twentieth century. The arguments had been set out many times, but perhaps never more effectively than in 1872 by B. G. Northorp, secretary of the Connecticut State Board of Education, in his annual report for that year. Among other statements on the subject Northorp said:

Such a law would create a new crime. I reply, it ought to. To bring up children in ignorance *is* a crime and should be treated as such. As the most prolific source of criminality, it should be under the ban of legal condemnation and the restraint of legal punishment. All modern civilization and legislation has made new crimes. Barbarism recognizes but few. To employ children in factories who are under ten years of age or who have not attended school, or to employ minors under eighteen years of age more than twelve hours a day, is each a new crime.

It interferes with the liberty of parents. I reply again, it ought to when they are incapacitated by vice or other causes for the performance of essential duties as parents. Many other laws limit personal liberty. The requisition to serve on juries, or to aid the sheriff in arresting criminals, or the exactions of military service in the hour of the country's need—these and many other laws do this. If the law may prohibit the owner from practicing cruelty upon his horse or ox, it may restrain the parent from dwarfing the mind and debasing the character of his child. If the State may imprison and punish juvenile criminals, it may remove the causes of their crime and its consequences of loss, injury, and shame. The child has rights which not even a parent may violate. He may not rob his child of the sacred right of a good education. The law would justly punish a parent for starving his child, and more mischief is done by starving the mind than by famishing the body. The right of a parent to his children is founded on his ability and

[18] See *Report*, the U. S. Commissioner of Education, 1888-89, I, 471. U. S. Office of Education, Bulletin No. 4, 1935.

disposition to supply their wants of body and mind. When a parent is disqualified by intemperance, cruelty, or insanity, society justly assumes the control of the children. In ancient Greece the law gave almost unlimited authority to the father over his offspring. The same is true in some semi-barbarous nations now. In all Christian lands the rights of the parents are held to imply certain correlative duties, and the duty to education is as positive as to feed and clothe. Neglected children, when not orphans in fact, are virtually such, their parents ignoring their duties and thus forfeiting their rights as parents. The State should protect the helpless, and especially these, its defenseless wards, who otherwise will be vicious as well as weak.

It arrogates new power by the Government. So do all quarantine and hygienic regulations and laws for the abatement of nuisances. Now, ignorance is as noxious as the most offensive nuisance, and more destructive than bodily contagions. Self-protection is a fundamental law of society.

It is un-American and unadapted to our free institutions. To put the question in the most offensive form, it may be asked, "Would you have policemen drag your children to school?" I answer, "Yes, if it will prevent their dragging them to jail a few years hence." But this law in our land would invoke no "dragging" and no police espionage or inquisitorial searches. With the annual enumeration and the school registers in hand, and the aid of the teachers and others most conversant with each district, school officers could easily learn who are the absentees.

Compulsory education is monarchical in its origin and history. Common as is this impression, it is erroneous. Connecticut may justly claim to be one of the first states in the world to establish the principle of compulsory education. On this point our earliest laws were most rigid. They need but slight modification to adapt them to the changed circumstances of the present. Before the Peace of Westphalia, before Prussia existed as a kingdom, and while Frederick William was only "elector of Brandenburg," Connecticut adopted coercive education . . .

Attendance would be just as large without the law as it is now. It may be so. But so far from being an objection, this fact is strong proof of the efficiency of that law which has itself helped create so healthful a public sentiment. Were the law to be abrogated tomorrow, the individual and general interest in public education would remain. The same might have been said of Connecticut for more than 170 years after the adoption of compulsory education. During all that period, a native of this state, of mature age, unable to read the English language, would have been looked upon as a prodigy. Still, in Connecticut as well as in Germany, it was the law itself which greatly aided in awakening public interest and in fixing the habits, associations, and traditions of the people.[19]

[19] *Annual Report Connecticut Board of Education,* 1872, p. 32. In *Bulletin* No. 2, 1914, U. S. Bureau of Education, pp. 10, 11.

"The American people cannot shuffle with the question of compulsory education much longer," declared an editorial in the *Educational Review*[20] several years before the end of the nineteenth century, in pointing to the platform of a political party in an unnamed Western state in opposition to a law on the subject. The plank in the platform said: "We are opposed to state interference with parental rights and rights of conscience in the education of children, as an infringement of the fundamental democratic doctrine that the largest individual liberty consistent with the rights of others insures the highest type of American citizens and the best government." Then the editorial went on to say:

This rather sphinx-like utterance is found in the platform of one of the great political parties in a western state, distinguished for its excellent educational institutions and the high and law-abiding character of its citizenship. When interpreted, the passage quoted means that its framers are opposed to a compulsory education law. Its terms are sufficiently vague and general to prove hiding places for wary politicians, but its intent is clear.

The American people cannot shuffle with the question of compulsory education much longer. They must settle it one way or another, and that soon. The empty bombast of "pointing with pride to our unsurpassed system of public schools" has played its part. Our provisions for public instruction are admirable, to be sure; but ignorance and vice and low moral standards in public and private life are playing havoc with some of our much extolled "free institutions." European critics have pierced our armor of pride and self-assertion and are asking searching questions as to why certain things occur here in spite of all our advantages.

Character, not intelligence, it may be said, is the remedy. This is indisputable; but unless history and human experience are strangely misleading, character flourishes on a soil of knowledge, not on one of ignorance. The State's own safety is bound up with the character, and so in a measure with the intelligence, of its citizenship. To secure a minimum of both, so far as a system of public schools can do so, is the plain and accepted duty of the State. There is no natural right to be ignorant or vicious that limits the exercise of the State's power in securing this minimum. Compulsory education is, therefore, the logical consequent of universal suffrage. If the American people propose to allow religious feeling, or any other force, to set aside this principle, they should do so understandingly, with their eyes open to the consequences. Compulsory education should not, and need not, trench in the least on any parental right or any religious conviction. Antireligious public education is no more a necessity than sectarian proselyting at State expense. These facts should be preached incessantly from the platform and

[20] Vol. IV (June, 1892), pp. 95-96.

by the press. No cowardly attempt to avoid a direct argument on the school question should be permitted. Meet it fairly and squarely, not with passion or partisanship but with argument.

On the same day that the compulsory education law of Ohio was pronounced constitutional by the State Supreme Court, the decision of the Roman authorities concerning Archbishop Ireland's plan of fusing the parochial and the public schools was received by cable. It proves to be a most important document, not only for the Roman Catholic Church but for the American public school system. For twist and turn its guarded phrases and technical terms as we may, Archbishop Ireland is sustained, and his liberal, patriotic, and thoroughly religious policy is to be permitted to continue. It is true that it is an experiment, but it is a most hopeful and courageous one for the American common school, and all good citizens will support it by every means in their power.

The above comment on the educational plan of Archbishop John Ireland, of St. Paul, referred to the heated controversy in the Roman Catholic Church in this country over "the school question," which turned not only on state control over Catholic schools in return for some public aid to those schools, but even touched on the right of the state to educate. Archbishop Ireland had given an address before the National Educational Association in St. Paul in 1890 in which he praised the existing state school in giving secular instruction. "It is our pride and glory," he said. "The Republic of the United States has solemnly affirmed its resolve that within its borders no clouds of ignorance shall settle upon the minds of the children of its people. In furnishing the means to accomplish this, generosity knows no limit. The Free School of America! Withered be the hand raised in sign of its destruction! Can I be suspected of enmity to the state school because I would fain widen the expanse of its wings until all the children of the people find shelter beneath their cover; because I tell of defects which for very love of the state school I seek to remedy?"

But he found the parish school necessary because the public school tended "to eliminate religion from the minds and hearts of the youth of the country." He saw two solutions for the problem: (1) permeate the state school with the religion of the majority of the children; (2) "The Poughkeepsie Plan." In this plan the local board of education rented the building formerly used for a parish school and from nine o'clock in the morning until three in the afternoon the school was in every respect a state school. But there was the tacit understanding that so long as the teachers who were Catholic in faith passed their examination and did their work efficiently and as loyally as other teachers under the direction of the board of education, they should not be replaced by teachers of another faith. In the plan, which had the approval of John Cardinal McCloskey, Archbishop of New York, religious instruction was not given during school hours.

Pope Leo the XIII's *"Tolerari potest"* brought the controversy to a conclusion. On January 31, 1893, James Cardinal Gibbons, Archbishop of Baltimore, wrote to the pope suggesting an encyclical letter on the school question and "was gratified to hear from Monsignor O'Connell at Rome that Cardinal Rampolla, Papal Secretary of State, had remarked that 'the school question in America was decided.' " [21] In the encyclical, dated May 31, 1893, it was stated that "although the public schools are not to be entirely condemned (since cases may occur, as the Council itself had forseen, in which it is lawful to attend them), still every endeavor should be made to multiply Catholic schools and to bring them to perfect equipment." In connection with this controversy in the early 1890's, it is of interest to note here that the shelving of the proposal for federal educational aid in 1950 had its roots in part at least in the religious controversy that developed over the question of aid to private and parochial schools.

Franklin H. Giddings, eminent sociologist, raised before the National Education Association in 1905 some realistic and searching questions on the subject, and said that compulsory attendance legislation and child labor laws "are undoubtedly socialistic in character." For example, should the state pay the parents for the time their children are in school? Commenting on the social and legal aspects of current practices he said:

> The educational problem and the industrial problem of child labor cannot be separated. This is true, whether every parent is permitted to deal as he will with his child or whether he is compelled, as in most American commonwealths, to withhold his child from gainful employment and to keep him in a school, or otherwise to provide systematic instruction for him during certain weeks of each year. Child labor itself is a kind of education which, according to its nature and extent, may be consistent or altogether inconsistent with other kinds. The labor that American boys and girls had to perform on the farm a generation and more ago was often an invaluable discipline of mind

[21] For a detailed account of this subject see Daniel F. Reilly, *The School Controversy, 1891-1893* (Washington: The Catholic University of America Press, 1943). Because of the bitterness of the dispute in the Catholic Church "and the resultant wounded feelings," no extended study of it had been made before Reilly's doctoral dissertation. "Now that the acrimony of the controversy has disappeared with the demise of the participants, perhaps a new generation can begin to understand dispassionately, judge the questions at issue, and profit by them."

and character, fitting them for self-reliant and useful careers quite as effectively as their meager school training did. Such labor did not necessarily unfit the child for the enjoyment of the highest educational advantages. Exhausting confinement in stores, sweatshops, and factories is child labor of an altogether different sort. It is antagonistic to the child's mental and physical development and it cannot be combined with any sound educational policy.

Compulsory education by the state and the prohibition of child labor are policies undoubtedly socialistic in character. They assert the supremacy of the state's interest in the child as against any opposing interest of the parent. The American people have never been afraid of socialism to this extent, and within the last ten years it has greatly extended both compulsory education and the prohibition of the labor of children between ten and fourteen years of age. It would not be inaccurate to say that public sentiment at the present time in New England, in the Northwest, and in most of the North Central states demands an increasingly strict enforcement of child-labor legislation, and that a similar sentiment is rapidly growing in the South.

This policy encounters, however, important obstacles which call for intelligent examination. Not much difficulty has been encountered in the courts. The constitutionality of both compulsory school attendance and of the restriction of child employment in the interest of health, intelligence, morals, and citizenship is everywhere upheld. The real difficulties are of quite another character.

It is not easy to maintain the administrative machinery to enforce child-labor restriction and the truancy laws. Experience has shown that compulsory school attendance is itself the best enforcement of the laws against child labor; but this is difficult where school accommodations are inadequate, and where population is either dense and heterogeneous, as in the tenement-house quarters of our great cities, or sparse and indifferent to educational interests, as in the mountain regions of the South.

A very special difficulty, and one that puts all our theories and our devices to the severest test, is that which is presented by destitute families. The practical question, which has to be answered over and over, is: Is it right to take a strong, overgrown boy thirteen years of age from money-earning employment and force him to attend school, when by so doing we compel a widowed mother to apply to private or public agencies for help, thereby making her, and perhaps the boy also, a pauper?

The only answer to this question, consistent with the policy of compulsory education itself, is the proposition that in such cases adequate public assistance should be given, not as charity but as a right. To shrink from this course because it is socialistic is thoroughly illogical and inconsistent. Compulsory education itself, as I have said, is socialism pure and simple. State interference with the parent's disposition of the child's energy and time is a further extension of socialism. These policies have never been anything but socialistic. They never by any possibility can be anything less than socialistic. Let us, therefore, not balk at a further provision by the state which happens to be necessary to make them effective. Let us make our socialistic scheme complete and consistent or confess that it is altogether wrong and abandon it.

A final and deeper difficulty exists which has received curiously little attention. We hear a great deal lately about "race suicide." Large families are no longer seen, especially in the so-called middle classes. It is strange that no one has pointed out the connection between the increased demand upon parents to maintain their children in school, foregoing the earnings that children might add to the family income, and the diminishing size of the average family. The connection, however, is undoubtedly a real one, and the practical inference is obvious. If the restriction of child labor is desirable, if compulsory education is desirable, and if at the same time larger families are also desirable, the state must make up to the family at least some part of the income that children could earn if they were permitted freely to enter upon industrial employments. The question, therefore, that we shall have to face and to answer is this: Shall the state pay parents for keeping their children in school between the ages of ten and fourteen? This would be a policy of socialism, undoubtedly. I do not pretend to say whether the American people will or will not adopt it. I only say that, as a matter of social causation, they will be compelled to adopt it if they try to maintain both large families and compulsory education while prohibiting child labor in department stores and factories. It is not my intention to advocate the measure or to argue against it. My purpose is served in calling your attention to the logic of facts.[22]

As late as 1914, four years before the last American state enacted a compulsory attendance law, W. S. Deffenbaugh summarized the current arguments against such legislation which were similar to those pointed out by Northorp in 1872:

Though nearly all the States in the Union have enacted compulsory attendance laws, each State has had to overcome much opposition on the part of those who argued that such laws are un-American in principle, in that they interfere with the personal liberty of the parent. In 1891 and 1893 Governor Pattison, of Pennsylvania, vetoed compulsory education bills on that ground. In 1895, when Governor Hastings signed a similar bill, he did so only because he did not wish to obtrude his judgment in the matter, which was against the bill.

The plea that such laws interfere with personal liberty has, however, never been recognized by the courts, and all such laws now on the statutes of the several States are considered constitutional.

Among the arguments offered by those opposed to the enactment of compulsory attendance laws are these: (1) a new crime is created; (2) it interferes with the liberty of parents; (3) new powers are arrogated by the

[22] *Proceedings,* National Educational Association, 1905, pp. 111-13.

government; (4) it is un-American and not adapted to our free institutions; (5) compulsory education is monarchical in its origin and history; (6) attendance is just as great without the law.[23]

Edward L. Thorndike, distinguished psychologist, in 1932 raised some questions about the theories and practices of compulsory attendance legislation and on the distribution of education, just as an eminent sociologist had done in 1905. But Thorndike's questions differed from those by Giddings. He said:

The general spirit of our country for the past hundred years has been to make great efforts to increase the amount of education but to pay relatively little attention to its distribution. The plea of reformers has been for more education, regardless of who received it. There has been an indiscriminate urge toward more schools, longer school years, and later compulsory-attendance ages. Education of any sort for any person has been recommended as a national investment, without much consideration of the differences in safety and income which may attach to the investment in certain boys and girls rather than in others. The mere volume of education has been taken as a measure of idealism, somewhat as the mere volume of gifts to beggars of all sorts used to be taken as a measure of philanthropy and charity.

In so far as any attention has been paid to the question of who were receiving much and who were receiving little education, the general tendency has been to try to equalize the distribution by aiding backward communities, increasing the number of days schools were in session, delaying the permissible age for leaving school, enforcing attendance laws, and other lines of effort designed to raise the amount for those who were receiving less than others. The doctrine that equalization of education is beneficent, partly by remedying certain definite accidents and injustices and partly by a mysterious power to advance democracy and social justice, has been very popular. Its influence has been potent not only in the distribution of education so as to give most to those who have least, but also in the efforts of teachers to bring backward pupils up to grade, and in the establishment of special classes for the deficient and dull.

It may be doubted whether either the policy of striving for indiscriminate increase in the volume of education or the policy of favoring especially those who would otherwise have very little schooling was ever the best for the general welfare. A very strong argument could have been made at any time in the last half century for exercising careful discrimination in the distribution of education, the most being given to those who would use it best for the common good. A fairly strong argument could also have been made that those who would use more education best for the common good would be those who already had a great deal of it—for example, promising young

23 "Compulsory Attendance Laws in the United States," *Bulletin* No. 2, 1915, U. S. Bureau of Education, p. 10.

students of science, who, with more education, might make discoveries of great benefit to the world, or promising young physicians, clergymen, engineers, and the like, who, with more education, might serve their communities much better. However, so long as there were many children who had only a few years of schooling, each of less than a hundred days, the benevolent doctrine of changing distribution in such a way as to favor the least educated was rarely questioned. The prevention of illiteracy and the extension of education so that every child would have at least a thousand days of schooling seemed a wise as well as a humane policy, even if not in the end the wisest.

When the school year was lengthened, the age of compulsory attendance raised to fourteen or sixteen, and provision made for special classes for the very dull, some thinkers began to consider the interests of the intellectually able pupils and the public's interest in making the most out of its human resources. These thinkers asked, "Who are receiving the most education? Are they the ones who will use it best for the common good?" But they asked these questions usually in such forms as: "Who are going to college?" "Who should go?" "Who are proceeding on to high school?" "Who should?"

When the questions are asked in these forms, the answer to the first is that the high schools do get a selection that is superior in intellect, and the colleges and professional schools a selection that is still more so. The facts concerning the relation of intelligence to grade reached among the American soldiers of the World War, the facts revealed by surveys of high-school populations, and the facts shown by the tests of intellect or "scholastic aptitude" which have been more and more widely adopted by colleges since 1920, were, in spite of numerous individual misfits and dubious educational investments, accepted as comforting. Those who were found at the higher levels of schooling were much abler than those who had been eliminated by the way.

The question, "Who are receiving the most education?" is not, however, answered adequately by answering the questions: "Who go to college?" "Who go to high school?" "Who attend medical schools?" or any other questions that ask who receive certain higher levels of education. "Most education" may mean two things: most education in actual amount of educational effort spent on the person or most education in amount of change made in the person. The former is roughly measured by the money spent on the pupil or by the days or years of schooling he receives. The latter is roughly measured by the amount he learns, or the grade he reaches, or the abilities which promotions, degrees, and diplomas are intended to represent. Both meanings are important, but they must not be confused. The facts just mentioned about the superior quality of students in higher institutions do not prove that the ablest children are receiving the most education in years. They may conceivably prove that the ablest children learn the most and advance the farthest, though having little more, or no more education in the first meaning than the average or the dull . . .

Present distributions are surely bad. It certainly is not reasonable that the intellectually ablest 5 per cent of boys should be kept in school to an age only four months beyond that to which the least able are kept. Suppose that we had eighty years of schooling to distribute among these eighty boys. Surely it would be wasteful and essentially unjust to give each boy one year more. More schooling of the sort they have had will make the low twentieth very little happier or more useful, but it can be guaranteed that two years more for some of the top twentieth would enrich their individual lives and produce substantial benefits to the community. Indiscriminate advances in the compulsory-school age beyond sixteen seem, in view of the actual facts, a weak and wasteful procedure.

What shall we say of laws or customs which systematically and emphatically distribute the most schooling to those least able to get profit from it for themselves or for the community? Are they not intolerably unwise and unjust? Yet they have been very common. Thus a child of a certain age (say fourteen) is allowed to go to work if he has reached a certain advanced stage (say graduation from Grade VIII); but, if he has only reached Grade V, for example, he must be given more schooling. Of our forty especially able boys, five left school before they were fifteen; not one of the dull forty left at such an early age. We need laws to prevent greedy or perverse parents from depriving gifted children of schooling, not laws to force them to keep in school children who have neither the ability nor the interest to profit thereby.

The problem of providing schooling in some reasonable relation to the intellectual ability of the recipients is only one part of the general problem of the quantitative distribution of education. It would be a very inadequate treatment of the matter to use intellectual superiority alone as the measure of fitness for more education. Moreover, the problems of the qualitative distribution of education are at least as important as those of quantity. We have to ask not only, "How much schooling shall each sort of individual receive?" but also, "What kind of schooling shall it be?"

There is no time to do more than mention these questions and recommend them as worthy subjects for thought and research. I must use the time that remains to reinforce your memories of the message I have tried to deliver.

Zeal to produce more schooling, that is, to increase the amount of schooling given in our country, has been one of America's fine idealisms. Such zeal should be maintained, but with it there should be equal zeal to distribute this education so that those will have most who can use it best. What evidence we now have indicates that the ablest receive very little more than the least able. For every boy in the top forty of our 785 who stayed in school beyond the age of eighteen, there were nearly ten boys below average ability who did so. The passion for equalization which had a certain nobility when a large percentage of children barely learned to read and write becomes unwise, almost ridiculous, when the question is of spending our resources to keep in school boys of sixteen, or seventeen, or eighteen who would be happier and more useful at work or at play. Our increased resources should be used to aid young men and women whom nature and nurture have chosen to profit from schooling.

Doubtless, great ability will often manage to get education outside of schools or to get along without it, but those who can do so much for the world with so little are the very ones who should be given more. In the wars we are incessantly waging against disease, misery, depravity, injustice, and ugliness, we should not provide our best marksmen with the poorest weapons nor ask our bravest to fight with their naked hands.[24]

Compulsory school attendance legislation is very closely related to child labor legislation, and in development the two humanitarian movements have gone somewhat hand in hand. Early and even late proposals in the states for child labor laws encountered selfishness and the cupidity of manufacturers and often also of parents, a Federal Constitution that was drawn up for an agricultural age, conservative courts, and hostility to the alleged invasion of the rights of parents to the labor of their children. But acting under the police power, many states passed child labor laws which fixed a minimum age limit for work, limitation on the hours of labor, prohibitions against certain employments that were considered dangerous to health, and the requirement of certain educational attainments before children would be permitted to go to work. In 1907 the Congress appropriated $150 thousand to investigate the labor of children, and in 1912 it created the Children's Bureau. In 1924 the National Child Labor Committee, which had been established in 1904, estimated that two million boys and girls under fifteen years of age were gainfully employed, most of them as laborers on farms. By 1932 all states had provided some form of legislation regulating the labor of children, and most of the states had some provision for mothers' pensions.

In general, the term "child labor law" seems to have to do with the employment of persons under the age of twenty-one years, but its meaning varies according to the specific definition given in the law of each state. So also with the term "minor," which generally means one under the age of twenty-one, but again a lower age may be specified in the statute. Most improvements in such legislation came

---

[24] "The Distribution of Education," *The School Review*, XL (May, 1932), pp. 337-45. His conclusions in this article were based on a careful study of "the educational careers of 785 boys constituting a representative sample of eighth grade pupils in New York City. . . . The years of schooling (of approximately 180 days) varied from 6.5 to 16.5 . . . The age at leaving school permanently varied from thirteen to twenty-five. If the sampling had been taken for an age or for a much lower grade, the variation would have been even greater. Even in our sample, some boys have 2.5 times as many years of schooling as have others." P. 336. In December, 1951, President Colgate W. Darden, Jr., of the University of Virginia, startled some educational people by severe criticisms of compulsory educational practices.

in the twentieth century; but a glance at the initial laws serves to indicate the low social conscience of the American people in their concern for the welfare of children, and it also reflects occupational interests and opportunities. Legislation on child labor and on compulsory school attendance is an important part of social history.[25]

Every state at mid-twentieth century had a child labor law which usually applied to the employment of minors up to sixteen or eighteen years of age. In some cases the legislation applied to the employment of young people up to the age of twenty-one. Improvements in child labor legislation had been worked out in part through a wide exchange of experiences among the states, and in the main such laws generally followed a rather definite pattern. Nevertheless the laws varied widely in the conditions and standards set up for the employment of minors, and were very uneven in some occupations. Some provisions applied to all gainful occupations, and some exempted certain types of occupation such as agriculture, domestic service, and the sale and distribution of magazines and newspapers. The result was that even within a state, the law did not always apply equally to all children.[26] In many of the states the minimum age for work in factories was still fourteen years, and children of fourteen or fifteen or even under fourteen could be employed while schools were in session. The United States Department of Labor was recommending the following minimum-age standard: "No minor under sixteen years of age shall be employed, permitted, or suffered to work in any gainful occupation during school hours, and no minor under sixteen years of age shall be employed, permitted, or suffered to work in, or in connection with, any manufacturing or mechanical establishment." The minimum age of this proposed standard would approximate that fixed under the standards of the Federal Fair Labor Standards Act of 1938.

All attempts to secure action by the national government on the labor of children in occupational activities had failed by 1950, although the need for protecting children from exploitation had long been recognized. Attempts to secure Congressional acts that prohibited the labor of children, or an amendment to the Constitution of the United States on that subject, had frequently been made. In 1906 Senator Alfred J. Beveridge, of Indiana, proposed an amendment by which the shipment through interstate commerce of goods

[25] See Miriam E. Loughran, *The Historical Development of Child-Labor Legislation in the United States* (Washington: The Catholic University of America, 1921).
[26] See U. S. Department of Labor, *State Child-Labor Standards*. Bulletin No. 114, 1949.

produced in factories or mines that employed children would be prevented, but nothing came of the proposal. A decade later the Congress passed legislation which contained provisions similar to those proposed by Senator Beveridge, but the Supreme Court of the United States in 1918 held the law unconstitutional. The following year Congress undertook by different means to solve the problem by enacting a law which imposed heavy taxation on the products of factories that employ children in their work. Three years later the Supreme Court of the United States declared this legislation unconstitutional on the ground that it was an illegal use of the power to tax. In 1924 further effort in the solution of the problem was made by Congress when it approved the proposed amendment to the Constitution which would give the national government the power "to limit, regulate, and prohibit the labor of persons under eighteen years of age," but in 1950 not enough states had ratified the proposal to make it a part of the Constitution.

There were many arguments against ratification of the proposed federal amendment, some of which were not unlike the arguments offered earlier against compulsory attendance and child labor legislation by the states. The fear of invasion by the national government into the rights of the states and into the rights of parents was strong. Opponents of such an amendment to the Constitution also argued the educational value of child labor, as the following statements, which were made in 1925, indicate:

I am one of those who oppose this amendment...

Below are a few of the evils which some claim our present educational and child-labor laws are producing. It is claimed that the schools are now turning out young men with ideals of luxury and idleness, without the ability to do mental work and unwilling to do physical. That many of these resort to crime so that at the present time, when less people are driven to crime through need, education is supplying the lack. That the schools are turning American boys away from the factory work that offers them the best opportunity in life, leaving the best of the factory jobs to those of foreign birth and education. That the schools are destroying ideals of craftsmanship so that ordinary jobs are becoming more a matter of money only. They are thereby one of the greatest causes of labor unrest, strikes, etc.

Personally, I think that each of these claims has a certain amount of truth, but that the observed evils would largely disappear if the boys were given a proper working experience before and during their high-school and college course. But I do not mean that modern, makeshift, vocational work in the school which can never be made of educational value comparable with work in the factory. We should recognize that the person or the law that keeps a twelve-year-old boy away from his job is depriving him of his education and "an opportunity for a fair start in life" to as great an extent as the one who keeps him away from school.

We must recognize that there are evils in connection with child labor, that they are serious evils which give the child-labor agitators an excuse for their work. But why is it that the national government has spent large sums of money for propaganda against child labor and for the schools, but is not willing to make the comparatively small appropriation that would be necessary to get some real information as to the two? They have often published the results of comparisons of the earnings of men of high intelligence and school training, but they have never made any attempt to compare those equal in intelligence and other respects, but differing in school training.

There are evils connected with athletics, but we would not want to abolish athletics for that reason. There are evils of hypocrisy and others in the church, but we would not think of abolishing churches. Child labor has an educational value quite comparable with either of these, and we should be just as reluctant to abolish it.[27]

Construction and Reconstruction of the Curriculum.—Interest and activity in the construction and reconstruction of the curriculum of the elementary school during the first half of the twentieth century, and especially after 1920, were conspicuous educational phenomena and represented most popular pedagogical efforts. Stimulated by Pestalozzianism, Herbartianism, Froebelianism, developments in psychology, and the child study movement, and later by progressive education and other influences, efforts to bring about changes in the curriculum had been promoted by the work of national committees, beginning with the Committee of Ten, under the chairmanship of Charles W. Eliot, president of Harvard, and composed of five college presidents, one college professor, two headmasters of private secondary schools, one principal of a public school, and the United States Commissioner of Education. The report of the Committee was made in 1893. While this Committee was primarily concerned with the curriculum of secondary education, it at least had to take notice of the curriculum of elementary education. It was the view of the Committee that a satisfactory program for the secondary school could not be made if

. . . limited to a period of four years and founded on the present elementary school subjects and methods. In the opinion of the Committee, several subjects now reserved for the high schools—such as algebra, geometry, natural science, and foreign languages—should be begun earlier than now, and therefore within the schools classified as elementary; or, as an alternative, the secondary-school period should be made to begin two years earlier than

[27] B. C. Forbes, *School and Society,* XXI (February 21, 1925), p. 232.

at present, leaving six years instead of eight for the elementary subjects and elementary school period. Under the present organization, elementary subjects and elementary methods are, in the judgment of the Committee, kept in use too long.

Although the report of this Committee, which is discussed more fully in the next chapter, was politely and fairly well received, its immediate effect was not impressive. In the 1880's and 1890's there was much confusion in secondary education, and that condition led to the formation of the regional standardizing associations of colleges and secondary schools, which are also discussed in the next chapter.

From the report and discussion of the work of the Committee of Ten until 1950, the curriculum of the elementary school increasingly claimed the wide attention of the profession and of experts on the construction of the curriculum, and at mid-century it continued to claim attention. In the 1930's and 1940's many state departments of education and many city school systems feverishly engaged in making new curricular programs, some of which were widely publicized and highly touted as panaceas for the conditions revealed especially by war and depression and by growing interest in national and international affairs, in contrast with local and state affairs. Publication on curricular issues became voluminous, but some of it was somewhat vague. Courses in the curriculum came to be widely offered by teachers' colleges and by schools and departments of education in the colleges and universities. State agencies for the certification of teachers encouraged the movement. Books on the subject poured from the presses, and it became fashionable for educational institutions to establish "curriculum laboratories." [28] One result of all these efforts was the proliferation of the curriculum in elementary education (which was also taking place in secondary schools) almost to the point of inflation. At mid-twentieth century the question was whether the schools were trying to do too much.[29]

[28] At the University of Osceola, a candidate for an advanced degree in education was asked by an avid advocate of curriculum-making the difference between a library and a "curriculum laboratory." He replied, with disrespect if not with scorn, that in a library a student could generally find what he was looking for. For a breezy satire on the subject, see Leon Eubanks, "I Attend A Curriculum 'Laboratory,'" *School and Society,* October 5, 1940.

[29] See Mortimer Smith, *And Madly Teach* (Chicago: Henry Regnery Co., 1949); Albert Lynd, "Quackery in the Public Schools," *Atlantic Monthly,* March, 1950, pp. 33-38. See also Bernard Iddings Bell, "The School Can't Take the Place of the Home," *New York Times Magazine,* May 9, 1948. For what may be considered an answer to these and other critics of the schools, see Walter Biddle Saul, "I'll Stick Up for the Schools," *Saturday Evening Post,* April 15, 1950, pp. 22-23, 65-66, 70, 73-74.

It would be reckless for one uninitiated in the mysterious ritual of making, remaking, coring, and perhaps also "yo-yoing" the curriculum to attempt appraisal of these efforts, although it is apparent that they reflected confusion in and about the purposes of the schools. But to list some of the names under which some of the curricular proposals have circulated during the past two or three decades may not be dangerous. These may be found in the writings on the subject and could be documented. Reported, they should be given in alphabetical rather than in chronological order, because old educational ideas, whether sound or diseased, have a habit of reappearing under new but often unrecognizable names.

The student of curricular activity in the United States during recent decades will run on numerous names of plans whose slogans and watchwords teachers and students learned to make glib phrases about, after the manner of the catchwords that had flourished under the spells of Pestalozzianism, Herbartianism, Froebelianism, and later "progressism." Even the casual student of proposals for changes in the curriculum in recent decades will find the following without undue effort: the activity curriculum; areas-of-living curriculum; Batavia curriculum; challenging curriculum; broad-fields curriculum; child-centered curriculum; contract curriculum; cooperative curriculum; core-curriculum; developmental curriculum; cycle curriculum; Dalton curriculum; dynamic curriculum; dynamics-of-behavior curriculum; emerging curriculum; energizing curriculum; experiencing curriculum; formal curriculum; functional curriculum; fusion-curriculum; Gary curriculum; guidance-curriculum; individual-differences curriculum; multiple-track curriculum; opportunistic curriculum; orientation-curriculum; personal-problems-of-living curriculum; planless curriculum; project-curriculum; problem-curriculum; shared-experiences curriculum; subject-centered curriculum; teacher-curriculum; unit curriculum; Winnetka curriculum; world-wide curriculum.

The education of teachers in service has often been given as one of the important purposes of programs to revise the curriculum. Committees of teachers are formed, usually by the "coordinator" of instruction, the principal, superintendent, or other official, and the work of revision is undertaken cooperatively. But it has been pointed out that enthusiasm for constructing or reconstructing the curriculum may tend to cause the teachers to spend so much time in that endeavor that they will have little time left to do anything with it after it has been constructed or reconstructed.

It has also been noted that while continuous cooperative efforts to improve the curriculum by committees of teachers and others were marked in the first half of the twentieth century and were continuing vigorously at mid-century, state legislatures also continued to exercise control over what was taught in the schools, as they had always done. Such control the profession and experts on curriculum-making considered undesirable, but legislatures jealously guarded their prerogative in the matter, as they had always done, chiefly because they were aware of the close relation between the people and their common schools. Legislatures can and do very largely say what can and what cannot be taught in the schools. For a long time statutory legislation on this subject was very general, but within the present century it tended to become more specific. Jesse K. Flanders reported in *Legislative Control of the Elementary Curriculum* [30] more than 2,200 legislative acts prescribing for the elementary curriculum in 1903, 1913, and 1923. A study of legislative action since 1923 would doubtless also be very revealing. The tendency, especially in economic and military crises, to prohibit the teaching of certain subjects and to require the teaching of others, forms an important chapter in the history of American education and represents the influence of pressure groups on legislative action. Witness the attempts in the 1920's to enact "pure history" and "monkey" bills; to make children salute the American flag; and the numerous statutes enacted from time to time on "loyalty oaths" for teachers. In recent years there has also been a tendency for the courts to become school boards, especially for the Supreme Court of the United States to become the national school board. That tribunal held in 1948, in the widely publicized McCollum case from Illinois, that religious instruction could not be given in public school buildings. And its decisions on racial issues and education in recent years have also been of the highest significance.

The Famous New York "Regents' Inquiry."—A "charter" for elementary education was presented in 1938 by the extensive *Regents' Inquiry into the Character and Cost of Public Education in the State of New York.*[31] The inquiry observed that the educational needs of children of elementary school ages required "a more definite and appropriate elementary school program." This was to be achieved by beginning with children of about the age of five years and making

[30] (New York: Teachers College, Columbia University), 1925.

[31] *Education for American Life* (New York: McGraw-Hill Book Co., 1938), pp. 49-51. For its plan for secondary education in that state, see Chapter 3, below.

preprimary or kindergarten work a part of the regular program of the elementary school, and complete the work of the elementary school at the end of the sixth grade. Continuing, the report said:

Every elementary school should be part of a system maintaining a complete secondary school program, and promotion within the elementary school and from the elementary to the secondary school should be determined locally in terms of the good of the child and in general accord with standards to be approved by the State, but without the use of uniform Regents' Examinations.

Make every elementary school large enough, but not too large (desirable limits are 180 to 600 pupils), so that classes may be of economical size, the educational facilities may be more adequate, some specialized teaching may be introduced, and the pupils may engage in group activities.

Make character development a central aim of the school program by providing inspiring teachers, introducing meaningful experiences into the curriculum, bringing parents actively into school affairs, introducing the pupil to outstanding ethical literature and standards, and coordinating the school program and that of the other community agencies concerned with the child.

Emphasize the importance of the basic mental tools—reading, writing, speech, and arithmetic—and expect every normal pupil to have a mastery of them by the end of the sixth grade. See to it that these skills are learned through their use of carefully selected experiences in which the learner can see how they function in daily life. See to it that the contents of the course of study are better geared to the psychological development of the child, especially in the fields of arithmetic, language, and the social studies. Greatly enrich the work in literature and reading.

Revise the elementary school curriculum. Try to reduce the number of isolated, piecemeal elements of the curriculum, discontinue the present practice of adding new bodies of content by specific legal enactment, and repeal such existing legal requirements. Integrate the curriculum more fully by bringing out the relationships among the major fields of human experience which should form the basis of its structure.

Organize instruction so as to provide more adequately for differences in the abilities of children. Provide more fully for the education of the gifted and talented children of the community. Take steps to reduce the high percentage of nonpromotion found in many of the schools of the State. Study more fully the factors both in and out of school that may be conditioning the educational product unfavorably. Establish local or regional educational guidance clinics to provide the expert assistance needed to make such a program a success.

Strengthen the educational provisions for mentally and physically handicapped children, and, subject to state regulations, require adjoining districts to cooperate in the maintenance of such services.

Take steps to make available for teachers more adequate and up-to-date instructional supplies, materials, and equipment. Make more extensive use of modern means of instruction, such as the radio, motion pictures, and other visual aids. Make certain that all schools have good library facilities and that the curriculum makes use of them. Introduce the wider use of field trips, excursions, visits to museums and to art galleries, and other trips, with the aid of school buses. Amend the law to require the provision of free textbooks and essential supplies to all children in public schools.

Organize a planned cooperative state and local program of research and experimentation dealing with all aspects of the educational process, including organization, curriculum, teaching procedures, appraisal, materials of instruction, and personnel.

In 1948 the Educational Policies Commission published a volume under the title *Education for All American Children* [32] because the Commission believed "that elementary education is now entering a period of significant change. Such a time of transition is the best occasion for the development of long-range plans in the light of coherent policies." Part I of this volume described "a series of hypothetical schools and school systems as we hope and believe they may be developed in the next ten years." That part of the book was prepared so as to describe those schools *as they might appear to an observer in 1958.* The study stated that the curriculum of an elementary school consisted of

. . . those experiences which the child has at the school or under its jurisdiction. Through those experiences, plus those outside the school's program, the child grows and learns . . . The curriculum in a good elementary school reveals a combination of thoughtful planning, intelligent guidance of children's experiences, and meaningful appraisal. It is never supposed that the curriculum is made when a book is published; rather it is made as children live.

It goes on to state that the making of a curriculum "should be a continuous process to which a great number of persons make a variety of contributions," and that it should be planned "to insure both to pupils and society the benefits of valuable learnings whose effects are cumulative toward desired goals." At every stage in the development of the curriculum, "the teacher should be a strategic factor." The closing paragraph of the section dealing with the curriculum got a bit exhortative and was perhaps not too clear to many of those who went about the Middletowns teaching in elementary schools. It admonished: "Let the elementary-school curriculum derive its goals from the demands and values of the social scene. Let its methods conform to the demands and values of human growth and develop-

[32] Washington, D. C.: National Education Association, 1948.

ment. The good elementary school is not concerned exclusively either with the nature of society or with the nature of childhood. The good elementary school is developmental, with a social criterion, conserving democratic values."

National Income and the Increasing Birth Rate.—At about the close of the first half of the twentieth century, the birth rate continued to be so high that estimates of educational needs ("Today's babies are tomorrow's school children") had to be revised. Some careful observers seemed to believe that the birth rate would "flatten out," as it had done after World War I; but the figures that were coming in did not show this to be an accurate prophecy. The increases in births in the continental United States in the period from 1929 to 1949 were approximately those shown below.

Year	Births	Year	Births
1929	2,169,000	1940	2,360,000
1930	2,203,000	1941	2,513,000
1931	2,112,000	1942	2,808,000
1932	2,074,000	1943	2,934,000
1933	2,081,000	1944	2,794,000
1934	2,167,000	1945	2,735,000
1935	2,155,000	1946	3,288,000
1936	2,144,000	1947	3,699,000
1937	2,203,000	1948	3,599,000
1938	2,286,000	1949	3,592,000
1939	2,265,000		

The elementary school of the mid-twentieth century was a very different institution from what it had been in 1900, radical changes in both its philosophy and practices having been made. The concept of the purposes of elementary education had greatly widened. Few persons in 1900 had much respect for the personality of the child, which in 1950 most persons had or professed to have or were generally encouraged to have. In 1900 the emphasis in the elementary school was on the "knowledge aim," the memorizing of "facts," after the manner of Mr. Gradgrind and Mr. Choakumchild in Charles Dickens's *Hard Times*. The acquisition of facts was the thing. What is nowadays known as the "all-round" development of the child was practically unheard of in 1900. What is now called "social understanding" on the part of children was undreamed of by most parents and teachers. But there were some theorists in 1950 who may have been a bit too enthusiastic in suggesting that young children must get "social understanding" if they were to be spared the disillusion and cynicism that this harsh world engenders; they must early learn to solve perplexing social and economic, political, and racial problems, and thus build for their generation a better, fairer, and a brighter world.[33]

The aims of elementary education in 1900 were fewer and simpler and therefore apparently more easily attained than in 1950 when life had become more complex and the aims of education had greatly increased in number and were less clear and therefore more difficult to attain than a half century earlier. Little was known in 1900 about the nature of children as compared with what was believed to be known in 1950. The term "child growth and development," which in 1950 was on the lips of nearly everybody engaged in educational work in this country, and which almost any professor of education could give courses in or on, would have had no meaning to the pedagogues of 1900 and may have been even as unpronounceable by them as Shibboleth was by the fleeing Ephraimites centuries before. No one in his right mind in 1900 would have considered the experiences of children as a sound basis for a curriculum, but these experiences in 1950 were considered very modish as its basis. Opportunities for children to engage in socially valuable enterprises, so strongly urged in 1950 in books and articles on elementary education, were, however, abundantly provided in 1900 in natural rather than artificial ways. The necessities of the times had seen to that.

Many issues faced the schools of the United States at mid-twentieth century, but one of the most acute faced the elementary schools. The problem had come to those schools as a result of the unprecedented increase of children of elementary school age, the serious shortage of teachers, and the menacing lack of adequate school buildings. The United States Office of Education was reported in September of 1950 as estimating a jump of at least a million children in the public elementary schools over 1949, an estimate that turned out to be very accurate. Never before had American communities been called on during one year to take care of such an increase of elementary school children, although they had been warned about what was likely to happen; many communities had not made sufficient preparation for the great increase. As the schools opened in the fall of 1951, there was still a lack of available space for teaching, classes were congested, many of the teachers were inadequately qualified for their work, and instruction was not so effective as it should have been.

Congestion in the parochial schools was also reported. Enrollments in about 11 thousand Catholic schools with about 110 thousand

---

[33] Here Carl L. Becker's *How New Will the Better World Be?* is suggested for examination by the student. (New York: Alfred A. Knopf, 1944.)

teachers were at an all-time high, about 3.5 million pupils. The largest increases were in the elementary and high schools, about 2.5 million, with about 500 thousand of these in secondary schools. About 70 thousand were in Catholic colleges for women, about 240 thousand in colleges and universities for men, about 24 thousand in seminaries, and about 7 thousand in colleges and training schools for teachers.

The crisis in Korea in 1950 made the educational situation in the United States less tolerable. There was danger that teaching staffs would be depleted by military demands, and there was much anxiety over the possible shortage of materials and labor for the construction of school buildings. Added to these difficulties was the uncertainty of adequate financial support for educational purposes and the threat of increasing taxes for military and other governmental activities.

The shortage of teachers for the elementary schools was perhaps the most gloomy part of the entire educational picture in 1950. About 90 thousand more teachers than had been employed in 1949 were needed, and only about 20 thousand were being prepared or had been technically prepared and certificated in 1949-1950. About 90 thousand teachers were on substandard certificates. Teaching in the elementary school was still looked upon as a less manly undertaking than teaching in high school or college. There was also some evidence that certification requirements, and what teachers had to do after being initially certificated to continue in good standing, were not attracting the ablest and most promising young people to the profession. The shortage of elementary teachers was realistic and stubborn, and the way out was not clear. Benjamin Fine wrote in the *New York Times,* September 10, 1950, that replacements would be sought "by scraping the barrel," that many teachers would have as little as one year of college work, and that in many communities graduates of high schools would be taken as teachers in the elementary schools. He thought that the shortage of teachers would get worse before it got better. During the decade of 1950, a million elementary teachers would be needed, and only about 200 thousand would be made available, he predicted.

As 1950 approached, public education was becoming more and more secular. Education in the United States during the past half century, and particularly during the past decade or two, had come into closer relationship than ever before with other institutions, agencies, and organizations, industry and business, social service groups, and virtually every other aspect of the community, except the church, where relationships apparently were becoming more and more tenuous. Although when viewed historically education in this country appears as the child of the church and of religion or theology, public education was becoming more and more secular and the issue of Church and State appeared to be getting sharper as the twentieth century advanced. There was complaint from religious groups and the religious press against the growing secularism of public education, and there was some anguish when Mr. Justice Frankfurter of the United States Supreme Court wrote in a decision in 1940, later reversed, that the United States flag was the "symbol of national unity," transcending everything else, and that children could be expelled from school for refusing to salute the flag. And there was further religious anxiety when the court held in the McCollum Case in 1948 that public school buildings could not be used for religious instruction. The apparently increasing tendency toward "statism" in the public schools was disturbing to those who believed that religion had an important place in education.

Attention is now turned to the development of the secondary school during the first half of the twentieth century, to education for all American youth.

Some Suggested Questions and Exercises for Students

1. Compare or contrast a typical American elementary school about the beginning of the twentieth century and in 1950 in (a) physical equipment; (b) curriculum; (c) education of the teachers; (d) financial support and administrative control; (e) extracurricular activities; (f) attention to the health needs of the pupils; (g) other ways.

2. What were the forces or influences (a) economic, (b) political, (c) social and religious, (d) psychological, and (e) others that brought about significant changes in the elementary school between 1900 and 1950?

3. What was the significance of the national committees or commissions on elementary education? What exactly was the result of their work?

4. Energetic advocates of the principles of Pestalozzianism, Herbartianism, Froebelianism, and the philosophy of John Dewey and his disciples tended in some cases to make those principles "go to seed." In what other cases in the history of education have good and promising principles tended to become highly formalized and to "go to seed"?

5. Indicate the significance of the feverish work in the construction and reconstruction of the curriculum in the elementary schools between 1920 and 1950. Did that work reveal: (*a*) Dissatisfaction with the work of the schools? (*b*) General confusion in the aims of American life? (*c*) Advertising or propaganda of pressure groups?

6. State the chief arguments of (*a*) the advocates and (*b*) the opponents of (1) compulsory school attendance laws, (2) child labor laws.

7. Study and report in class on the points made on such laws by (*a*) Giddings, (*b*) Thorndike, (*c*) Forbes.

8. What states had ratified the proposed federal child labor amendment in 1950?

9. What were the most crucial issues facing elementary education in 1950? Show how those issues could be met and solved.

10. Make a study and report in class on the needs of your state (*a*) for buildings for elementary schools, (*b*) for elementary teachers, (*c*) for financial support.

11. Study and make a report in class on the Educational Policies Commission's *Education for All American Children.* On what educational "philosophy" were its recommendations based? How could those proposals be put into effect in your community?

12. Study and report in class on the recommendations made on elementary education by the Regents' Inquiry in New York State.

13. How can more promising and able young people be encouraged to prepare themselves for work in the elementary schools? Be as specific as you can.

14. In early December of 1951 President Colgate W. Darden, Jr., of the University of Virginia made some severe strictures on compulsory education and recommended that it be made to apply only to the elementary schools. His statements were widely published and there was also much editorial comment on them. What were his arguments on the subject? In what way did he invoke the views of Thomas Jefferson, the founder of the University of Virginia?

Some Suggested References and Reading

Bode, Boyd H. *Progressive Education at the Crossroads.* New York: Newsom & Co., 1938.

The purpose of this book is "to contribute to a better understanding of the philosophy in which the progressive movement must find its justification and by which it must be tested."

Brubacker, John S. *The History of the Problems of Education.* New York: McGraw-Hill Book Co., 1947.

Chap. xii ("Elementary Education") throws helpful light on some of the topics discussed in this Chapter.

CASWELL, HOLLIS L., and FOSHAY, A. W. *Education in the Elementary School* (2d ed.). New York: American Book Co., 1950.

A critical review of the development of the elementary school in the United States during the past fifty years. Deals with the characteristics of the program of a good elementary school; the aims of elementary education; children of elementary school age; the organization of the curriculum, and other issues and problems. Contains a brief but useful bibliography.

EDUCATIONAL POLICIES COMMISSION. *Education for All American Children.* Washington, D. C.: National Education Association, 1948.

Attempts to do for elementary education what its *Education for All American Youth* attempted to do for secondary education. Describes "a series of hypothetical schools and school systems such as we hope and believe may be developed in the next ten years." Wears a utopian color.

GULICK, LUTHER H. *Education for American Life.* New York: McGraw-Hill Book Co., 1938.

Statement of the findings and recommendations of the *Regents' Inquiry into the Character and Cost of Public Education in the State of New York.* Pages 49-51 deal with the purposes and functions of elementary education.

KILPATRICK, WILLIAM H. *Education and the Social Crisis.* New York: Liveright Publishing Co., 1932.

"This little book is a call to the teaching profession. . . . Its effort is to summon the profession of education to a study of the stupendous task now looming before us as our civilization faces perhaps its greatest turning point in modern times. . . . New arrangements must be achieved."

KNIGHT, EDGAR W. "The Evolving and Expanding Common School," *The Annals of the American Academy of Political and Social Science.* CLXV (September, 1949), pp. 92-100.

Shows some of the forces that helped to produce the universal elementary and secondary school in the United States.

KNIGHT, EDGAR W., and HALL, CLIFTON L. *Readings in American Educational History.* New York: Appleton-Century-Crofts, Inc., 1951.

Contains many original documents that bear on the subject of this Chapter.

MONROE, WALTER S. (ed.). *Encyclopedia of Educational Research* (rev. ed.). New York: The Macmillan Co., 1950.

Pages 353-83 discuss research on various aspects of elementary education, including development, scope and status, elementary school population, organization and administration, and many other topics. Very useful, especially for students interested in research in elementary education.

NOBLE, STUART G. *A History of American Education.* New York: Farrar & Rinehart, 1938.

An interpretive volume that emphasizes environmental influences on the growth of the curriculum. Chaps. vii-xi and xvii supplement the subjects discussed in this Chapter.

PARKER, S. C. *A Textbook in the History of Modern Elementary Education.* Boston: Ginn & Co., 1912.

Probably the best single account yet available of the growth of elementary education in the Western world. Chaps. xii-xviii bear on some of the topics in this Chapter. The bibliographical notes are very useful.

REISNER, EDWARD H. *The Evolution of the Common School.* New York: The Macmillan Co., 1930.

An excellent account of the origin and growth of the "common" vernacular elementary school in Western Europe and the United States and of the influences that produced it.

ROBBINS, CHARLES L. "Elementary Education," in I. L. Kandel (ed.), *Twenty-Five Years of American Education*. New York: The Macmillan Co., 1924.

Tells the story of the growth of elementary education in the United States during the first quarter of the twentieth century.

SCHORLING, RALEIGH, and MCCLUSKEY, HOWARD Y. *Education and Social Trends*. Yonkers, N. Y.: World Book Co., 1936.

"The schools are faced with making well-informed decisions. Upon what bases shall we fairly and intelligently choose between conflicting ideas?" The world was changing. "There is, however, nothing new about that."

Chapter 3

EDUCATION FOR ALL AMERICAN YOUTH

PREVIEW OF THE CHAPTER

Three types of secondary education have been provided in this country, but the public high school had gained the most commanding position by 1950. . . . The last decade or two before 1900, and many years afterward, had witnessed wide confusion in secondary education. Lack of significant purpose and orderliness was the result of many influences, including the great increase of knowledge and of economic wealth, the findings of the psychological laboratories, the work of G. Stanley Hall, John Dewey, and their students, the impact of industry on education, and increasing interest in industrial efficiency. . . . This confusion in secondary education led to the work of national committees which undertook to bring some order out of the disorder. . . . The report of the Committee of Ten in 1895, the report of the Committee on College Entrance Requirements in 1899, the work of the Carnegie Foundation, the report of the Committee on Economy of Time, 1915-1919, the report of the Committee on the Reorganization of Secondary Education in 1918, and other efforts stimulated wide interest in and discussion of persistent issues in secondary education. . . . The writings of specialists in the subject indicated deep concern about means for improving the work of the high schools. . . . Meantime the rise of regional educational associations and the College Entrance Examination Board had great influence on the improvement of practices in secondary education. . . . Between 1930 and 1950 much experimentation was promoted to further improve the relations between secondary and collegiate education. Among the efforts were the National Survey of Secondary Education in 1933, the Eight-year or Aikin Study of the Progressive Education Association's Commission on the Relation of School and College in the 1930's, the study conducted by the Southern Association of Colleges and Secondary Schools between 1938 and 1945, and other inquiries. . . . Among these inquiries were the publications of the Regents' Inquiry into the Character and Cost of Public Education in the State of New York (1938) and the Educational Policies Commission's *Education for All American Youth* (1944) which undertook to attack some of the issues in secondary education that were widely publicized and discussed. . . . Although some of the confusion that plagued secondary and collegiate education alike in 1900 were removed by these endeavors, nevertheless by mid-twentieth century some of the old issues remained and new ones had arisen.

85

The Types of Secondary Education.—The three main types of secondary education in the United States have been provided by the Latin grammar school, the academy, and the public high school. The first of these was a colonial institution. It began in New England with the establishment in 1635 of the Boston Latin grammar school, which has had a continuous existence, spread to other New England colonies and elsewhere in this country, and reached its greatest development around 1700. Before 1700 at least twenty-seven such schools were reported in Massachusetts, whose act of 1647 required their establishment, and in Connecticut. Before that date students at Harvard came chiefly from such schools in Boston, Braintree, Cambridge, Charlestown, Dorchester, Roxbury, and Salem. The curriculum was mainly the classical languages, and the purpose of this kind of school was the preparation of boys for college where most of them would be fitted for the ministry.

The academy began in the early 1750's with Benjamin Franklin's school in Philadelphia, which grew into the University of Pennsylvania, and extended generally to about the middle of the nineteenth century, except in the southern states where the public high school was late in developing and where the academy continued a principal means of secondary education even after 1900. The academy was open to girls as well as to boys, was sometimes coeducational, and provided a wider curriculum than the Latin grammar school had furnished. It was designed not only as a preparation for college but also for practical life in commercial and business activities. Although its wide educational values were evident and are recognized as important contributions to secondary education in this country, the academy was never considered a public institution as the public high school has come to be.

The public high school had its origin in Massachusetts in 1821 when the English Classical School was established in Boston, and in 1827 that state enacted the first state-wide public high school law in the United States. The full operation of that statute was retarded, however, because the state lacked adequate educational authority to enforce it. But by 1840 there were perhaps a dozen public high schools in Massachusetts and many in other eastern states, and by 1850 they were also to be found in many other states. After the decision in the Kalamazoo Case in Michigan in 1874, the growth of the public high school was greatly promoted. Just as the curriculum of the academy grew out of that of the Latin grammar school, so the curriculum of the public high school developed out of that of the academy. The public high school in the United States represents a repudiation of the aristocratic and selective principle of the European educational tradition. Since 1890, enrollments in secondary schools, mainly public high schools, have practically doubled in this country every ten years.

Confusion in American Education.—But the last decade or two of the nineteenth century witnessed much confusion among educators in the United States. Apparently there was no clear idea of the educational function or of clearly recognized standards of secondary education, and efforts to bring some order out of the confusion led to the establishment of the regional standardizing educational associations, four of which had been formed before 1900. Each of these educational devices grew out of the necessity that was pressing alike in all parts of the country, although perhaps more heavily in some parts than in others. The necessity for better relations between institutions for higher education and the secondary schools had increased rapidly during the latter part of the century.

The conspicuous lack of significant purpose and orderliness in secondary education was the result of several influences. One of these was the great increase in knowledge that had developed during the nineteenth century and had so rapidly and widely expanded that attempts of the secondary schools to keep pace with it led to confusion of subjects and courses. Another influence on secondary education was the great increase in economic wealth which enabled more young people than formerly to go to and remain in school. Still another influence began to come from the laboratories of the experimental psychologists, who seemed to present evidence that tended to deny the validity of the doctrine of formal mental discipline and the transfer of training, with the result that the ancient dogma of disciplinary values in the curricula of secondary education was beginning to fall under suspicion and attack.

Studies by psychologists on individual differences and the social backgrounds of pupils and their choice of careers also began to appear, and soon the theory developed that one purpose of secondary education was to expand its courses so as to do justice both to the individual pupils and to the supporting public. Secondary education was becoming more "democratic" and less aristocratic and selective and was soon to devote itself more and more not to the few, as formerly, but to the many. The duty of the secondary school—specialists on the subject began to say—should be to do its best for each pupil according to his abilities, interests, and needs. Meantime the work of G. Stanley Hall had drawn attention to the significance of the period of adolescence, and that of John Dewey to the general thesis that education is life rather than preparation for life. It was now being said that the purpose of the school was to develop the pupils in their interests rather than to teach them subjects that might be of value to them later; that the principles upon which education should rest should emphasize the present needs of pupils rather than their future needs; that subjects should not be included because of some assumed deferred values; that everything taught should have immediate value. Meantime, also, the force of industry was felt in American education. Interest in industrial efficiency found its way into the school, and the demand for economy and the elimination of waste became almost as insistent in education as it was in industry. One superintendent of schools, for example, justified the elimination of Greek from the curriculum of his community because of its high cost. "The price of instruction in Greek must come down," he said, "or we shall invest in something else."

Still another influence on secondary education in the latter part of the past century and the early part of the present came from the work and reports of national committees which are discussed more fully below. Here it is sufficient to say that the purpose of some of these efforts was to secure desirable uniformity in programs of secondary schools and in the entrance requirements of the colleges. The recommendations of some of these committees were to serve for many years as an important point of departure in the organization of the curricula of secondary schools. The question of the "equivalence" of educational values, which was sharply raised, provoked wide discussion and disagreement. In effect, the significance of some of these studies lay in the implication that one subject in the secondary school was as good as another when taught for the same length of time.

A distinguished educational historian has noted that "it remained for the next generation to show the full import of this implication. . . . On this basis the whole problem of educational value ceased to exist, particularly when fortified later by such questions as mortality and comparative costs of subject matter and by the contributions of psychologists on formal discipline and individual differences." [1] From these reports and wide discussion of their meaning, the principle of election came to be recognized for secondary education. President Charles W. Eliot had established the principle for Harvard, and he and some others had advocated it generally for higher educa-

[1] I. L. Kandel, *History of Secondary Education* (Boston: Houghton Mifflin Co., 1930), p. 475.

tion. This energetic effort of the distinguished president of America's foremost university led Samuel Eliot Morison, the official historian of that institution, later to declare: "It is a hard saying, but Mr. Eliot, more than any other man, is responsible for the greatest educational crime against American youth—depriving him of his classical heritage." [2] But Mr. Morison, in his stricture on President Eliot's contribution to the delinquency of American education, could have noted that probably no characteristic of the schools and colleges of this country is so conspicuous as their tendency to imitate whatever is identified with the fitness and fashion of things educational. What if Mr. Eliot had thrown the prestige of his personality and position in favor of skill in tap dancing or ice skating for a bachelor's degree at Harvard College?

Wide educational discussion throughout the country helped to prepare the way for the establishment of "a national educational currency in terms of norms (or units which came to be more generally used)." This national educational currency came to be known as the "Carnegie Unit," which developed out of investigations made by the Carnegie Foundation for the Advancement of Teaching and came to be employed as a mechanical measure for "evaluating college standards." This instrument of quantitative measurement was designed to help in removing at least some of the anarchy and chaos in secondary and higher education.

Recommendations of national committees, of the Carnegie Foundation, and of inspecting and certificating agencies appear to have had a healthy influence both on the secondary schools and the colleges. The fact that most of the regional standardizing associations placed higher educational institutions before secondary schools in their titles would seem to indicate leadership and perhaps domination of the colleges in the purposes and procedures of these organizations. But there is some evidence to indicate that it was the higher institutions that saved the secondary schools in those years of confusion and during the "unit's golden age." The charge often heard even nowadays that the colleges have dominated the secondary schools in curricula may appear to be correct only in part when viewed historically.

The growth of the secondary school was one of the most striking educational phenomena in the United States during the first half of the twentieth century. In 1900 there were about 15 million Americans in the free public elementary and secondary schools, but only

[2] *Three Centuries of Harvard* (Cambridge: Harvard University Press, 1936), pp. 389, 390.

about 500 thousand were in secondary schools. Out of about 25 million in schools in 1950, there were about 6 million in secondary schools, and it was then predicted that by 1960 there would be 8 million. In the period between 1900 and 1950, the belief greatly strengthened that education above the common elementary school should be provided at public expense for "all American youth." Between 1890 and 1900, private secondary schools had increased in numbers and in enrollments. Prior to 1900, and in some states after that date, the public elementary school and the secondary school had been separate in philosophy and in practice. By 1900 the elementary school had generally come to be considered the common school of the people, to be provided by taxation. But secondary education had not yet come to be widely accepted as a proper function of government, although a very significant court decision in Michigan in 1874 had stated very clearly that secondary schools were comprehended under "common schools," and the Kalamazoo case made it legal in that state for local communities to levy taxes for the support of high schools. A citizen had brought suit to prevent the collection of taxes for a high school and for the salary of a superintendent of schools in Kalamazoo, which had voted for the levy in 1872. The decision, written by Chief Justice Cooley of the Supreme Court of Michigan, reviewed the educational history of the state and then concluded:

If these facts do not demonstrate clearly and conclusively a general state policy, beginning in 1817 and continuing until after the adoption of the present state constitution, in the direction of free schools in which education, and at their option the elements of classical education, might be brought within the reach of all the children of the state, then, as it seems to us, nothing can demonstrate it.

This decision was so forthright and clear that it had great influence on subsequent decisions in similar cases in other states. It ranks as one of the significant judicial decisions involving education in this country. In time the term "common school" was extended to include the high school, if not generally in legislation, then certainly in the way the people came to look upon the public schools. The American people now regard the elementary and the secondary school as comprising their one common school system available to all children and youth at public expense.

The Work of the National Committees.—But before 1900 and long after, there was much confusion in education, and agitation for educational reform in the United States in the latter part of the nineteenth century led to the appointment and reports of three important national committees. The first of these, known as the Committee of Ten on Secondary School Studies, was appointed in 1891 and reported in 1893. The second, the Committee of Fifteen on Elementary Education, was appointed in 1893, and in 1895 made its report, which is discussed in Chapter 2. The third was the Committee on College Entrance Requirements, appointed in 1895 and reporting in 1899. These committees were composed of men who were primarily interested in subject matter in the schools, and who believed in the mental disciplinary theory of education, which the psychologists were soon to bring under a heavy cloud of suspicion and finally to overthrow. The reports of these committees dealt little if at all with questions which numerous educational committees were later called on to deal with, especially the varying abilities, interests, and needs of students and the requirements of the social order. The doctrine of individual differences had not yet been formulated, and serious inquiry had not yet been made as to how the school could build a new social order. That question had to await the onset of the depression that began in 1929. Following that severe economic dislocation, numerous plans were proposed for the schools to build such an order. But achievement of those plans was delayed by the outbreak of the Second World War.

Plans were made by the Committee of Ten [3] for five conferences on the various subjects in the secondary schools : Latin ; Greek ; English ; other modern languages ; mathematics ; physics, astronomy, and chemistry ; natural history, including biology, botany, and physiology ; history, civil government, and political economy ; geography, geology, and meteorology. Of the ninety members selected to work in these conferences, forty-seven were connected with institutions for higher education, forty-two were in the service of public, private, and normal schools, and one was connected with the U. S. Weather Bureau. Among them were many distinguished scholars. The Re-

[3] The members of the Committee of Ten were Charles W. Eliot, president of Harvard, chairman; U. S. Commissioner of Education William T. Harris, James B. Angell, president of the University of Michigan, John Tetlow, headmaster of the Girls' High School and the Girls' Latin School of Boston, James M. Taylor, president of Vassar College, Oscar D. Robinson, principal of the Albany (N. Y.) High School, James H. Baker, president of the University of Colorado, Richard H. Jesse, president of the University of Missouri, James C. Mackensie, headmaster of the Lawrenceville (N. J.) School, Henry C. King of Oberlin College: five presidents of higher educational institutions and one college professor; two headmasters of private secondary schools; one principal of a public high school; and the U. S. Commissioner of Education. *Report of the Committee of Ten on Secondary School Subjects.* New York: Published for the National Educational Association by American Book Co., 1894.

port of the Committee of Ten was based on the reports of these conferences, in which the following questions were used as guides for discussion:

1. In the school course of study extending approximately from the age of six to eighteen years—a course including the periods of both elementary and secondary instruction—at what age should the study which is the subject of the conference be first introduced?

2. After it is introduced, how many hours a week for how many years should be devoted to it?

3. How many hours a week for how many years should be devoted to it during the last four years of the complete course, that is, during the ordinary high school period?

4. What topics, or parts, of the subject may reasonably be covered during the whole course?

5. What topics, or parts, of the subject may best be reserved for the last four years?

6. In what form and to what extent should the subject enter into college requirements for admission? Such questions as the sufficiency of translation at sight as the test of knowledge of a language, or the superiority of a laboratory examination in a scientific subject to a written examination on a textbook, are intended to be suggested under this head by the phrase "in what form."

7. Should the subject be treated differently for pupils who are going to college, for those who are going to a scientific school, and for those who, presumably, are going to neither?

8. At what age should this differentiation begin if any be recommended?

9. Can any description be given of the best method of teaching this subject throughout the school course?

10. Can any description be given of the best mode of testing attainment in this subject at college admission examinations?

11. For those cases in which colleges and universities permit a division of the admission examination into a preliminary and a final examination, separated by at least a year, can the best limit between the preliminary and final examination be approximately defined?

The recommendations of the conferences were not always very specific. Contrary to what might have been expected, the conferences on the old and well-established subjects of Latin and Greek did not urge more time for those subjects, but recognized the just demands of other and newer subjects in the secondary school. The conference on Greek recommended that "the average age at which pupils now enter college should be lowered rather than raised; . . . urges that no addition be made in the advanced requirements in Greek for admission to college." The conference on mathematics recommended that the course in arithmetic in the elementary schools "should be abridged," and that only a moderate allotment of time be given to algebra and geometry; and the conference on geography said that too much time was then being given to that subject "in proportion to the results secured . . . either more should be accomplished or less time taken to attain it." These specialists in the secondary curriculum believed that their subjects should be taught earlier than was then customary, and all the conferences except that on languages believed that the elementary schools should give "perspective views, or broad surveys, of their respective subjects—expecting that in later years these same subjects will be taken up with more amplitude and detail." The answer to question seven above was unanimously negative by the conferences, which made answer to question eight unnecessary, and the Committee of Ten unanimously agreed with the conferences. "Ninety-eight teachers, intimately concerned either with the actual work of American secondary schools or with the results of that work as they appear in students who came to college, unanimously declare that every subject which is taught at all in a secondary school should be taught in the same way and to the same extent to every pupil so long as he pursues it, no matter what the probable destination of the pupil may be or at what point his education is to cease . . ." In only two conferences were minority reports presented.

The reports of the conferences were set out in much detail, some of which was perhaps a bit confusing. But hopefully running through them were frequent statements that reform in the curriculum and of instruction in the secondary schools depended heavily on better teachers in both the elementary and the secondary schools. The need for better teachers was to continue to be a persistent problem which was very acute in 1950 when it was not difficult to demonstrate that good teachers were far more important than the curriculum in the educational process. The report of the Committee of Ten suggested some ways by which better teachers could be had.

That Committee gave attention chiefly to the teaching of subject matter in the secondary schools, to the need for uniformity in content, to the standardization of requirements, to the allotment of time to the subjects, and to admission to college. Confusion in these and other educational issues had led to the movement for standardizing educational associations, beginning with the organization of colleges and preparatory schools in New England in 1885, to be followed by such organizations in other regions. At least two decades were to pass, however, before serious and sustained consideration was to be given to the content of the curriculum in elementary, secondary, and higher education. Interest in the study of the curriculum developed so rapidly after 1920 that by 1950 committees of numerous kinds were "curricking" all over the educational lot. But it was not yet clear whether by the end of the twentieth century the so-called educational profession would have learned that magic in the curriculum alone had not yet been discovered.

In November of 1893, the editor of the *Educational Review* said of the Committee of Ten: "No committee appointed in this country to deal with an educational subject has ever attracted so much attention as this one, and everywhere confidence is felt that the result of its deliberations will be wise and practical. It is not too much to expect that the leading colleges and the best secondary schools will be guided by its recommendations, and that in consequence a long step will have been taken toward providing this country with something like a systematic organization of secondary education. Every branch of the educational system, higher and lower, will feel the good effects of this long-desired reform."

The stubbornness of tradition in education was revealed in the work of the Committee of Ten. In January of 1894, U. S. Commissioner of Education William T. Harris wrote in the *Educational Review* that when the course of study in the secondary schools had been reported on before the National Council of Education in Toronto in 1891, he "did not see that any important results were likely to be secured by the discussion" of the subject. He had found very few teachers in the secondary schools "interested in the question of the relative value of the several branches which tradition has placed in their way." But he believed that with the appointment of the Committee of Ten, it began to appear that "something was to be accomplished that would arrest the attention of all parties engaged in the control of secondary education," and with President Eliot as chairman of the Committee,

...no doubt remained that the work would be thoroughly done and that it would demand and receive the careful consideration of all classes of teachers, whether in secondary, higher, or elementary schools. The report now in press is chiefly the work of the chairman, who has devoted a large amount of his time and strength the past eighteen months to its preparation and to the necessary details of organizing the nine special conferences.

But Harris did not expect the reports of these conferences to be acceptable to all. Some subjects in the secondary school held a strong central position, "made venerable by the long time during which tradition has respected their claims." Chief of these were Latin,

Greek, and mathematics, and the lion's share of the Committee's attention was given to the classics.

Harris expected that the report of the Committee and of the special conferences would result in turning the attention of the "best thinkers among our teachers to the question of the comparative value of the several branches of study. It will thus mark an era in educational progress." In concluding his comments, Harris said: "I feel confident that we shall enter upon a new era of educational study with the publication of this report."

President Eliot wrote in the *Educational Review* of February, 1894, that the primary work of the Committee of Ten was to organize "a conference of school and college teachers of each principal subject which enters into the programs of secondary schools in the United States, and into the requirements for admission to college . . ." The many recommendations for the improvement of teaching, not only in the secondary but also in the elementary schools, would require prolonged study, discussion, and debate if these were to be brought "home to the daily thought of superintendents and teachers," and Eliot hoped that the report of the Committee and the conference reports would be "patiently and candidly discussed in all the various meetings of professional teachers during the coming year . . ." He thought that the conferences and the Committee as a whole had reached a remarkable degree of unanimity in their conclusions. And he suggested that the faculties of law, medicine, and technology could "contribute to the welfare and growth of the secondary schools by conforming their requirements for admission to one or more of the programs recommended for secondary schools by the Committee of Ten." There was also confusion in professional education, on which the searchlight of investigation was to be later turned in the interest of reform. Among the important studies were Abraham Flexner's report on medical education in 1910, Charles R. Mann's study of engineering education in 1918, and Alfred Z. Reed's studies on legal education in 1921 and 1928. The doctrine of free enterprise had been as widely applied in professional education as in academic and collegiate education and had caused confusion.

The Committee set up a clear and definite "quantitative" measure of secondary education, based on the "equivalence of studies," a sort of "national currency" of educational norms which was to receive the blessing of the Committee on College Entrance Requirements in 1899. One subject was soon to be as good as another if studied for the same length of time. When the Carnegie unit was invented some years later, a ready instrument became available for measuring in schooling if not in education. The secondary school was now to be a very different kind of institution, and relations between it and the colleges were to be somewhat harmonized. Freedom was to ring in the elective system, the unit was to have a golden age of at least two decades, as R. L. Duffus has suggested,[4] and the adding machine was to come to be the most indispensable instrument in the offices of registrars. The First World War brought psychological tests to the serious attention of educators as an aid for admission to college. In 1950, however, discussions of the claims of the gifted students and society's obligation to him were becoming the most popular themes for pedagogues.

In March of 1894, Charles De Garmo of Swarthmore College, an energetic Herbartian, had raised in the *Educational Review* a question on the report of the Committee of Ten.

Shall the probable destination of the pupil of the public school make any difference in the matter or method of the studies he pursues? The one hundred men whose opinions are embodied in the report . . . answer, No. So long as he chooses to remain in school, the training given to the son of the artisan or the farmer shall not differ, so far as any given study is concerned, from that of the future scientist, statesman, or professional man. Not only is this principle to hold good for social classes, but it is to be equally valid for the sexes. Evidently the general acceptance of this theory will touch many and widespread interests.

In the first place, private schools owe much of their support to the conviction that public schools do not fit for college. In the next place, many colleges adhere to an antiquated program of studies because private schools consent to honor their requirements, however out of harmony with the times. Furthermore, the people in general have the conviction that higher education is good only for a few professions; that it is confessedly out of touch with the economic world, and that, consequently, it is not for them. Naturally, therefore, they have taken little interest in making the public school a road to the college . . .

It might be assumed that the committee recommends that all students of the public high schools should study the same branches. Nothing could be further from their thought . . . The report will accelerate the reform of the colleges, since it shows that the latter need not inquire so particularly what a student has studied . . . Under this enlarged conception of the scope of higher education, it is now for the first time practicable to coordinate the colleges and the public high schools so that the educational ladder which has been constructed from the kindergarten to the university in Michigan, Minnesota, and other western states is likewise a practicable possibility throughout the Union . . . Of the effect of the report as a whole, there can be but one opinion. It brings to a focus the discussions of a dozen national educational

[4] *Democracy Enters College* (New York: Chas. Scribner's Sons, 1936).

associations and may thus be fairly regarded as the result of the best (unarticulated) American thought upon secondary education. It is in such concrete workable shape that it will prove at once an inspiration and a guide to all who have the direction of secondary education committed to their charge. Though only a beginning, it is a most promising one.

In May of 1894 Francis W. Parker of the Cook County Normal School in Illinois called the report of the Committee "epoch-making," and he proposed some suggestions in regard to its study by the teachers of the country. It should be carefully indexed and a complete syllabus prepared on each conference report, with questions on "the most pregnant subjects," and these materials should be made available to superintendents, boards of education, teachers, and the public generally. The time had come, he said, for something to be done to make teachers' meetings, institutes, and associations more effective, suggestions on these and other matters that were as timely in 1950 as he thought them to be in 1894. The value of the Committee's report would depend in large part, he said, on whether supervisors and teachers of teachers "give those under our charge the best possible opportunites for study and practice" of what he called "the science of education."

The reception received by the report of the Committee of Ten should "give great satisfaction to those concerned in its preparation," said an editorial in the *Educational Review* of March, 1894. "The leading journals and magazines that have a large constituency of intelligent and cultivated readers—such as the *Nation, Harper's Weekly,* the *Outlook,* the *Independent,* the *Dial, Century Magazine,* and the *Atlantic Monthly*—have discussed it at considerable length, and while the criticism is discriminating, the judgments are, on the whole, very flattering. The great importance and significance of the report is recognized by them all."

Then the editor (Nicholas Murray Butler) went on to say that it was as much a compliment to the report that it was sneered at by some people as that it was well received by some others.

The small but noisy class of persons who conspire to produce what have been capitally described as the "fly-by-night educational papers," and those worthies who regard a college as a blot on the face of the earth and a college professor as *ipso facto* an ignoramus, are beating the tom-toms and rallying the faithful against the report, apparently because President Eliot had a hand in framing it. This sort of thing is very puerile and contemptible and vulgar; but the individuals referred to take themselves so seriously, and are taken so seriously by some of those who ought to know better, that a word of warning is often necessary. It is a disgrace to the country, and a severe reflection upon the intelligence of many thousands of our teachers, that these "fly-by-night" papers have the circulation they do.

The editor did not identify these "fly-by-nights." But he published in his magazine in April of 1894 an article from John E. Bradley of Illinois College who looked at the report of the Committee of Ten from the point of view of the small college. He believed that the report illustrated the "progressive spirit in American education . . . That a hundred representative educators should agree with such unanimity upon points so fundamental is in itself a noteworthy fact. That all should concede the need of broader and more comprehensive work is most gratifying." But from the standpoint of the lower schools, he thought some of the recommendations of the Committee were "quite impracticable." He believed that the recommendations about beginning in the grammar schools certain subjects that tradition had placed in the secondary schools—languages, algebra, geometry, and natural science—were not good. The high schools, "now thickly scattered over all the northern states," should be recruiting places for the colleges, and there should be sympathy between the secondary schools and the colleges. The report should serve to increase attendance at colleges

. . . and a large development of true university (postgraduate) work. Two hundred and eight American students were in attendance upon one German university last year. Increasing multitudes of students go abroad each year to find opportunities for study or research which ought to be afforded at home. A much clearer line of division is needed between our collegiate and university work, as well as between the college and the secondary school. Every successful effort to make these three grades of our educational work clear and distinct, and to confine each to its appropriate field and methods, will add symmetry and efficiency to our American educational system.

At that time in all parts of the country there were complaints about the lack of "correct educational ideals," the use of extravagant educational superlatives, and the fact that the catalogues of all higher educational institutions did not always "quadrate with strict moral standards." These were some of the conditions which led to an examination of so-called graduate work and the organization in 1900 of the Association of American Universities. In time Americans were going to Europe in fewer numbers for advanced work. Bradley reported the case of a student who had failed as freshman in a certain college because of low scholarship but was admitted to the second term of the junior class in a neighboring "university." He very much hoped that the Committee's report would make for better standards for admission to and graduation from college and help put a stop to "such occurrences."

At the meeting of the National Educational Association in 1895, W. C. Jones of the University of California gave a paper on action that should be taken by the higher educational institutions and the secondary schools to promote the introduction of the programs recommended by the Committee of Ten. Discussion of the paper led to a resolution:

WHEREAS, The most pressing need for higher education in this country is a better understanding between the secondary schools and the colleges and universities in regard to requirements for admission; therefore

Resolved, That the Department of Secondary Education appoint a committee of five, of which the present president shall be one, and request the appointment of a similar committee by the Department of Higher Education, the two to compose a committee of conference whose duty it shall be to report at the next annual meeting a plan for the accomplishment of this end, so urgently demanded by the interests of higher education.

The two committees were formed and became known as the Committee on College Entrance Requirements; A. F. Nightingale, superintendent of the Chicago high schools, was elected chairman, and William H. Smiley, principal of the Denver high school, was elected secretary. The four regional standardizing associations, then trying to promote the interests of the secondary schools and institutions for higher education, were requested to appoint three representatives to cooperate with the Committee. From the New England Association, Albert Bushnell Hart, John Tetlow, and R. G. Huling were appointed; from the Middle States and Maryland, Melvil Dewey, E. H. Griffin, and Wilson Farrand; from the Southern Association, W. P. Trent, E. A. Alderman, and W. H. Bartholomew; North Central, G. B. Gilbert, J. H. Canfield, and W. H. Butts.

A preliminary report of the Committee made in 1896 and published in the School Review in June of that year was largely a tabular statement of entrance requirements of sixty-seven representative colleges and universities, with résumé and critique of the requirements in the different subjects. This is a very valuable historical document which showed "conflicting, incongruous, and unsatisfactory" practices and the "absolute necessity of radical reforms." The colleges were "much at variance as to what constitutes a liberal education in these closing years of a century which began with scarcely any difference of educational opinion; while the secondary schools, awaiting, on the one hand, the abridgment and enrichment of the common-school curriculum, and on the other, a more uniform expression of opinion of the part of the colleges as to their functions, are suffering from their inability to supply the deficiencies of the former or to satisfy the demands of the latter." Differences in opinion as to what constitutes a liberal education and the functions of secondary, if not in fact elementary, education were perhaps as glaring in 1950 as these had been described in 1896.

At the close of the past century it was generally admitted, in the view of the Committee, that children should have much the same training in the elementary school, but "even in the lowest grades, individual direction should not be lost sight of, as the mind very early gives evidence of a divine implanting which must not be ignored," a point of view that was to receive wider acceptance as the twentieth century moved toward its mid-point. In the secondary school there "must be no Procrustean bed which every pupil by some process of dwarfing or stretching must be made to fit, but natural endowments, as soon as discovered, should have full scope, within certain limitations." The first formal resolution in the final report of the Commission was in favor of "the principle of election" in secondary education. College courses should be so adjusted "that every pupil at the end of a secondary course recognized as excellent, both in the quality and quantity of its work, may find the doors of every college swing wide to receive him into an atmosphere of deeper research and higher culture along the lines of his mental aptitudes." This principle was to have wide application in higher education, under the acceptance of the doctrine of individual differences and the doctrine of the "equivalence" of subjects, during the next fifty years and to make requirements for undergraduate degrees about as heterogeneous as admission requirements had been at the beginning of the twentieth century. Although the Committee meant that programs in secondary schools should not be "purely elective" but should be "eminently elastic, and that elasticity, based on psychological laws, should be recognized by the colleges," the way was now opening for a course for almost everybody and almost everybody for a course in the secondary schools and a degree for everybody and everybody for a degree in the colleges. In 1951 The United States Office of Education showed in one of its studies that 274 "specific subject titles were reported as evidence of efforts to meet needs of increasingly diverse bodies of pupils enrolled in high schools" in the United States.

The Committee on College Entrance Requirements had to deal with the continuing problem of adjusting the requirements of the colleges to conditions in the secondary schools in an effort to harmonize "the relations between the secondary schools and the colleges, to the end that the former may do their legitimate work, as the schools of the people, and at the same time furnish an adequate preparation to their pupils for more advanced study in the academic colleges and technical schools of the country." The proposed investigation created wide interest throughout the country, and the Committee had the cooperation of the American Philological Society, the American Mathematical Association, and the Modern Language Association. The final report of the Committee, published in 1899, which was the result of the work of many specialists in secondary and higher education, proposed the following resolutions:

I. *Resolved,* That the principle of election be recognized in secondary schools.

II. *Resolved,* That the requirements for admission to technical schools should be as extended and thoro as the requirements for admission to college.

III. *Resolved,* That the teachers in the secondary schools should be college graduates, or have the equivalent of a college education.

IV. *Resolved,* That we favor a unified six-year high-school course of study, beginning with the seventh grade.

V. *Resolved,* That in the interpretation of the recommendations of this committee concerning the subjects to be included in the secondary school program and the requirements for admission to college, for which credit shall be given, it is distinctly understood that all secondary schools will not offer opportunities for the pursuit of all these subjects, and that the colleges will select those only which they deem wise and appropriate.

VI. *Resolved,* That, while the committee recognizes as suitable for recommendation by the colleges for admission the several studies enumerated in this report, and while it also recognizes the principle of large liberty to the students in secondary schools, it does not believe in unlimited election, but especially emphasizes the importance of a certain number of constants in all secondary schools and in all requirements for admission to college.

Resolved, That the committee recommends that the number of constants be recognized in the following proportion, namely: four units in foreign language (no language in less than two units), two units in mathematics, two in English, one in history, and one in science.

VII. *Resolved,* That the colleges will aid the secondary schools by allowing credit toward a degree for work done in secondary schools, beyond the amount required for entrance, when equal in amount and thoroness to work done in the same subjects in college.

VIII. *Resolved,* That for students who have met a definite requirement in any science, and who continue the subject in college, it seems to us desirable that there be provided a suitable sequel to the school course in continuation of the study; such students being in no case placed in the same class with beginners.

IX. *Resolved,* That we approve of encouraging gifted students to complete the preparatory course in less time than is required by most students.

X. *Resolved,* That in general we recognize in schools the admissibility of a second year in advanced work in the same subject, instead of a second year in a related subject; for example, two years in biology instead of one year in biology and one year in chemistry, where local conditions favor such an arrangement.

XI. *Resolved,* That it is desirable that colleges should accept, in addition to the year of United States history and civil government already recommended, at least one half-year of intensive study of some period of history, especially of the United States.

XII. *Resolved,* That we recommend that any piece of work comprehended within the studies included in this report that has covered at least one year of four periods a week in a well-equipped secondary school under competent instruction should be considered worthy to count toward admission to college.

XIII. *Resolved,* That it is desirable that our colleges and universities should accept as a unit for admission a year's work in economics, including under this head a course in elementary political economy, supplemented by adequate instruction in commercial geography and industrial history.

XIV. *Resolved,* That we recommend an increase in the school day in secondary schools, to permit a larger amount of study in school under school supervision.[5]

Among other important committees that dealt with the curriculum were the Committee on the Economy of Time and the Commission on the Reorganization of Secondary Education. The first of these was appointed by the National Education Association in 1911, about two decades after the appointment of the Committee of Ten. The work of this Committee, composed of seven members, three of whom were professors of education or of educational psychology, three, superintendents of large city school systems, and one, a college president, illustrated a new method of studying the curriculum. So-called scientific tests were used for the first time to measure the effectiveness of teaching, the materials of instruction, and to examine curricula. The principles of psychology and other tests, not available for use by earlier committees, were employed to discover the most worthy knowledge which Herbert Spencer had tried to find a half century earlier in his remarkable essay, *What Knowledge Is of Most Worth?*

The purposes of the Committee, which worked under the chairmanship of H. B. Wilson, superintendent from Berkeley, California, were to bring about economy of time in the work of schools by the

[5] The report of the Committee appears in *Journal of Proceedings and Addresses, National Educational Association* for 1899, pp. 655 ff.

use of scientific methods, to determine the "socially worth-while in-structional materials," their proper placement in the grades, and their organization to fit what was called the "life-needs" of the pupils, and to eliminate those materials that were no longer considered to be of real worth. Both in personnel and in methods of study, the Com-mittee on the Economy of Time, which made four reports through the National Society for the Study of Education, is believed to have marked a turning point in the study of the curriculum in the United States. The first of the reports of the Committee appeared in 1915 in the fourteenth *Yearbook* of that organization; the second in 1917 in the sixteenth *Yearbook;* the third in 1918 in the seventeenth *Yearbook;* and the fourth in 1919 in the eighteenth *Yearbook.*

One of the most prominent contributions of the Committee's work was perhaps its recommendation of change in the philosophy of American education. In addition to the construction of tests in order to discover the efficiency of instruction, and a study of current materials of instruction in order to determine content, the Committee made a study of human activities in order to discover the most impor-tant information and skills needed by Americans and the institutions and issues of contemporary life in the United States and trends in their development. The Committee brought together the results of numerous scientific studies of the process of learning and tried to apply them to methods of teaching and the selection of materials of instruction. It is not a coincidence that the work of this Com-mittee paralleled or was followed by remarkable activities which swept the country in what is known as the "school-survey" movement, which became a major feature of the so-called scientific study of education. Moreover, so far as a change in the philosophy of edu-cation was to be undertaken, the individual pupil was now to become more than ever before the center of educational interest and attention was now to be given less to his purely intellectual development. By 1950 "the whole child" was a phrase heard on every hand in educa-tional circles. It was doubtless sometimes misinterpreted and over-worked, but the responsibility of the school in developing well-rounded personalities had come to be widely recognized.

The early meetings of this Committee disclosed the influence of the movement for measurement which was rapidly gaining in impor-tance. Careful studies in this field, which had been made by E. L. Thorndike and others, greatly stimulated interest in measuring the results of instruction. As early as 1897, J. M. Rice had published the results of his study of thirty-three thousand school children to find out about their ability to spell. He discovered that children who had spent thirty minutes a day on spelling for eight years did not spell any better than children who had spent only half that time on the subject. Educators and the educational press denounced as "foolish, reprehensible, and from every point of view indefensible the effort to discover anything about the value of the teaching of spelling by finding out whether or not children could spell. They claimed that the object of such work was not to teach children to spell but to train their minds!"

The first report [6] of the Committee on the Economy of Time had largely to do with the investigation of standards of attainment in subjects in the schools, descriptions of experiments then in progress for economizing time in education, and analyses of the allotments of time by grades and subjects in representative cities. Both the first and the second report dealt with descriptions of current practices in the schools, but the second illustrated the fact "that the quantitative study of the school curriculum was slowly but surely concentrating more attention on what *should* be taught and was devoting less energy to the analysis of what *was* taught. By the time the second report was issued, a number of objective curriculum investigations had been completed." The Committee's third report had more largely to do with the effort to discover the skills and factual content which should be taught. "The theory of the quantitative analysis of the curriculum was being rapidly developed . . . It was an orgy of tabulation." Wide discussion of norms and standards continued. The fourth report, in which the Committee exhibited a new phase of the analysis of the curriculum, contained first a bringing together of the numerous scientific investigations of learning, and in it educational workers could find definite recommendations on methods of teaching certain subjects. The era of educational fact-finding, of the questionnaire and of educational surveys, had come, and now learning was to be investigated more and more by the method of the laboratory and tests and testing of wide variety were to sweep the country. [7]

Another important step in the development and improvement of secondary education is believed to have been taken with the report

[6] See Harold Rugg, "Curriculum Making and the Scientific Study of Education since 1910," *Twenty-sixth Yearbook,* National Society for the Study of Education, Part I, pp. 68-71.

[7] Not all school men promptly accepted the theory of the validity of tests in teaching and administration. At the meeting of the Department of Superintendence at Philadelphia in 1913, there was much discussion on measurements and tests, as there had been in the meetings of this organization when Rice was making reports on his studies. Apparently the younger men were more favorable to testing, the older men doubting its value.

in 1918 of the Commission on the Reorganization of Secondary Education which had been set up in 1913 by the National Education Association. Its purposes were as follows:

1. Formulate statements of valid aims, efficient methods, and kinds of materials whereby each subject may best serve the needs of high-school pupils.
2. Enable the inexperienced teacher to secure at the outset a correct point of view.
3. Place the needs of the high school before all agencies that are training teachers for positions in high schools.
4. Secure college entrance recognition for courses that meet the needs of high school pupils.

Fourteen committees worked on the subjects of English, social studies, natural sciences, modern languages, ancient languages, manual arts, music, household arts, business, and agriculture, and on the articulation of the high school and the college, which the Committee of Ten had struggled with and which regional standardizing associations were still struggling with. There was also a committee of review. Each of these committees published reports through the United States Bureau of Education. Subjects in the secondary school on which committees did not report were considered by the National Committee on Mathematical Requirements, of the American Mathematical Association. In 1923 it published a report on the reorganization of mathematics in the secondary school. In 1924 the Advisory Committee of the American Classical League published the well-known *Classical Investigation.* In 1929 and 1930 the American and Canadian Committees on Modern Languages published reports on the teaching of modern languages.

In 1918 the Commission issued its *Cardinal Principles of Secondary Education,* which was widely publicized and in which seven objectives of the curricula of the secondary school were recommended: health; command of fundamental processes; worthy home-membership; vocation; civic education; worthy use of leisure; ethical character. These principles were formulated in an effort to show that what secondary education undertook to do should be determined by the needs of the society it was to serve; by the kind of persons who were to be educated; and in the light of available information on educational philosophy and practice. In this report attention was sharply drawn to the rapidly growing complexity of American life and to the relations of the individual to the state and to national and international matters. The Commission stated the problems of secondary education as follows:

1. The purpose of democracy is so to organize society that each member may develop his personality primarily through activities designed for the well-being of his fellow members and of society as a whole.

2. Education in a democracy, both within and without the school, should develop in each individual the knowledge, interests, ideals, habits, and powers whereby he will find his place and use that place to shape both himself and society toward ever nobler ends.

Herbert Spencer's statement of educational purposes in 1859 had not differed markedly from the cardinal principles set up in 1918, which were to remain fashionable for pedagogical discussions for at least two decades, even if some of the promises of these principles seemed unfulfilled. And in 1938 the Educational Policies Commission of the National Education Association, and the American Association of School Administrators, published *The Purposes of Education in American Democracy* which proposed four instead of seven educational objectives: self-realization, human relationships, economic efficiency, and civic responsibility, which followed a general review of "the objectives of education." These statements were followed by a discussion of the "critical factors in the attainment of educational purposes" which were listed as "the inherent quality of the human stock" to be educated, "the effects of other educative and maleducative agencies outside the schools," and "the efficiency of the schools themselves." In this document the Educational Policies Commission asserted the following:

Education hitches its wagon to a star. It hopes, aspires, and struggles. The democratic theory of social life presupposes that every child and every other member of society should have at least some degree of capacity for improvement and growth. That capacity, however large or small it may be for any given individual, is the fulcrum for the lifting power of democracy. The purposes of education might perhaps be called "directives" more appropriately than "objectives," although the latter word is sanctioned by long usage. These purposes indicate the direction toward which growth should occur. Failure to reach a particular end point with perfection by every child does not constitute failure of the school or of the democratic ideal. Failure comes only when no progress is made.

Following the reports of the Committee on the Economy of Time, the Department of Superintendence of the National Education Association began a series of cooperative studies on a nation-wide scale through a national commission and the research staff of the National Education Association. Six reports, as *Yearbooks,* appeared between 1924 and 1929. The first of these reports appeared in 1924 as the *Second Yearbook,* and dealt with the elementary school curriculum; the second, which appeared in 1925, dealt with research in constructing the elementary school curriculum; the third, which was published in 1926, bore the title, "The Nation at Work on the Public School Curriculum"; the fourth, which appeared in 1927, dealt with the junior high school curriculum; the fifth, which appeared in 1928, dealt with the development of the high school curriculum; and the sixth, under the title, "Articulation of the Units of American Education," appeared in 1929. These publications, each running from 296 to 616 pages, gave careful attention to current practices and provided much material for students of the curriculum. No such collection of scientific materials had ever before been brought together on educational questions. And the study of educational issues was yet a comparatively young "science."

Findings of the Specialists.—Reference to a few of the numerous writings of specialists should indicate the interest in means for improving the work of the schools that was increasing. Charles W. Eliot, who had written effectively on the subject before 1900, published in 1916, two years before the report of the Committee on the Reorganization of Secondary Education, a brief paper under the title "Changes Needed in American Secondary Education," which was followed in 1917 by a paper called "A Modern School" by Abraham Flexner. Both discussions were published in the *Occasional Papers* of the General Education Board. Eliot said that "the best part of all human knowledge has come by exact and studied observation made through the senses . . ." and that the secondary schools should give more attention to the "training of the senses through which the best part of knowledge comes." He recommended more scientific and technical instruction in secondary education, and more attention to the study of music and art, which, for example, were subjects that found their way into the curriculum of American schools very late. He also recommended an increase in the length of the day in school and a decrease in the length of the vacation period in the summer. In 1950 conferences were being held and discussions were being heard in summer sessions and elsewhere on what was called "outdoor education," apparently a kind of education that had to do with the preparation of leaders for the conduct of camps during summer time.

Flexner noted what had been pointed out many times before and has also been pointed out many times since 1917, that tradition was a powerful force in education and that it had largely determined what went on in the schools. He said that much of the time spent on such subjects as the classical languages, mathematics, and even literature had been largely wasted because these had produced few substantial results. The heart of his proposed modern school was to be science, accompanied by a study of industrial society, its occupations and trades; of the organization and the government of society, its history and institutions; and also of a study of what he called aesthetics— languages, literature, art, and music. After the First World War, when the "new college plans" got going with a bang, heavy emphasis came to be placed on teaching collegiate students something about themselves as human organisms (the biological sciences), about the world in which they live (the social sciences), and about the heritages of the past (the humanities). Flexner also said that the curriculum of the secondary school seriously needed revision; useless materials of instruction should be got rid of and the materials which, in his view, were greatly needed should be added.

These papers, by the president of the oldest and most distinguished institution for higher education in the United States and by a man whose influence had already been greatly felt and was to continue to be felt in many aspects of American education, were widely discussed. Partisans of the value of the classical studies were vehement at some of Flexner's suggestions; they sought their day in court in the *Classical Investigation* in 1924. But a concrete result of Flexner's proposals was the establishment of the Lincoln School under the direction of Teachers College of Columbia University. This school, which was to be a new type of educational institution, was endowed by the General Education Board and given wide freedom for experimentation in the curriculum and for instruction in both elementary and secondary educational work. After nearly three decades of operation it encountered litigation in the courts and was finally abandoned by its original sponsors and turned over to New York City as a public school.

Franklin Bobbitt published *How to Make A Curriculum*,[8] one of the earliest books about a subject on which there was to be voluminous writing during the next quarter century. In that work, Bobbitt said that social currents had long been "moving in strange, threatening, and unusual ways," and that education had to "shift its ground in fundamental ways. It must perform functions which it has not hitherto attempted, and discontinue labors no longer serviceable . . . Curriculum-making must find guiding principles which will

[8] (Boston: Houghton Mifflin Co., 1924.)

lead it with all the certainty that is possible in right directions."
In warning against the enthusiasts, however, who were riding off in
many different directions, he noted that many persons delighted
in changes and felt that they were making progress when, as a matter
of fact, they were making only changes. Merely shifting positions
did not necessarily mean progress. "The status quo is usually better
than changes in wrong directions . . ." He advised the simple
assumption,

. . . to be taken literally, that education is to prepare men and women for the
activities of every kind that make up well-rounded, adult life; that it has no
other purpose; that everything should be done with a view to this purpose;
and that nothing should be included which does not serve this purpose. Education is primarily for adult life, not for child life. Its fundamental responsibility is to prepare for the fifty years of adulthood, not for the twenty years
of childhood and youth.

In 1950 it was obvious that some enthusiastic and feverish cur-
riculum-makers had not followed that advice. The fervor of some
of the curriculum-constructionists had often seemed so flaming as to
recall Emerson's suggestion that when the transcendentalists emerged
from their playshops, Nature seemed to say to them: "Why so hot
and hasty, my little Sirs?"

In his Inglis lecture at Harvard in 1930, Thomas H. Briggs of
Columbia, considered one of the most intelligent observers of the
current educational scene, presented severe criticisms of secondary
education in the United States. He said that education should be
considered as "a long-term investment by the state, to make itself
a better place in which to live and in which to make a living, to
perpetuate itself, and to promote its own interests." He concluded
in an accusation that cut three ways: "educational authorities have
made no serious efforts to formulate for secondary schools a curriculum which promises maximum good to the supporting state";
"there has been no respectable achievement, even in the subjects
offered in secondary school curricula"; "no effort has been made,
sufficient to establish in students appreciation of the values of the
subjects in the curriculum such as to insure continued study either
in high schools or independently after compulsion ceases." At about
the same time, Paul Monroe, of Columbia University, was reported
as describing "widespread secondary education of the cultural type
as the cancer of society, the misguided cell which by overmultiplica-
tion destroys the organism that shelters it." On the basis of a very
wide experience in foreign countries as well as in the United States,

he warned against the danger of an unemployed and unhappy "educated proletariat." At mid-twentieth century, Seymour E. Harris, professor of economics at Harvard, warned against the perils of "Millions of B.A.'s, But No Jobs," [9] and presented a dismal picture of the rapidly expanding "proletariat of the A.B. and the Ph.D." and the probable effect on the American economy.

Regional Educational Associations; The College Entrance Examination Board.—Before the rise of regional standardizing associations, some efforts had been made by state universities, sometimes in cooperation with state departments of education, to adjust the differences that had developed between institutions for higher education and the secondary schools, through a form of inspection and accreditation. These efforts seem to have begun in the University of Michigan, which in 1870 recommended that a Commission of Examiners be formed in the faculty to "visit annually such schools as may desire it and give certificates, to those pupils who may be successful in their examinations, to the university." [10] Visitation and certification were begun the following year. High schools were inspected and a list was prepared of those whose graduates the university would admit, upon recommendation by the principal or superintendent, without further examination by the institution. Later this privilege was extended to high schools outside the state. Similar practices were soon developed in Wisconsin, Minnesota, California, and other states, and by 1900 they were rather widely employed throughout the country. It is believed that these efforts tended to bring the secondary schools and higher institutions into a more harmonious relationship.

The regional standardizing associations, which were inventions of educational necessity, began in New England in 1885. Diversity in requirements for entrance to college and in the requirements for the completion of the work of the secondary schools was generally so wide, and the relations between the higher institutions and those schools were so tenuous, that something had to be done to bring some semblance of order out of evident confusion. Attempts to do something about conditions had been made in conferences of New England colleges as early as 1879, 1881, and 1882, and out of these efforts grew the New England Association of Colleges and Preparatory Schools in 1885, to advance "the cause of liberal education by

⁹ *New York Times Magazine,* January 2, 1949. See also his book, *The Market for College Graduates* (Cambridge: Harvard University Press, 1949).
¹⁰ I. L. Kandel, *History of Secondary Education* (Boston: Houghton Mifflin Company, 1930), p. 464.

the promotion of interests common to colleges and preparatory schools." The organization considered uniform entrance requirements and other issues that would improve secondary education in that region; and in 1886 the Commission of Colleges in New England on Entrance Examinations grew out of this organization. In 1902 the New England College Entrance Certificate Board was formed to draw up lists of approved secondary schools whose graduates could enter college on certificate instead of by means of the customary examination. But no secondary school was to be approved "unless it has shown by the record of its students already admitted to college its ability to give thorough preparation for college, or unless it can satisfactorily meet such tests as the Board may establish to determine its efficiency." In 1914 the name of the organization was changed to the New England Association of Colleges and Secondary Schools, which indicated the rapid rise of public high schools.

The New England Association of Colleges and Preparatory Schools was followed in 1892 by the Association of Colleges and Preparatory Schools of the Middle States and Maryland, which stated its primary purpose to be as follows:

The object of this Association shall be to consider the qualifications of candidates for admission to college and the methods of admission; the character of the preparatory schools; the course of study to be pursued in the colleges and schools, including their order, number, etc.; the relative number of required and elective studies in the various courses; the kind and character of the degrees conferred; the methods of organization, government, etc.; the relations of the colleges to the state and to the general educational system of the state and country; and any and all other questions affecting the welfare of the colleges and schools or calculated to secure their proper advancement.

Two years later this association which, like the New England organization and the other regional associations, was to give much attention to the troublesome problems of admission to college, established the College Entrance Board of the Middle States and Maryland. Through the work of Charles W. Eliot and of Nicholas Murray Butler of Columbia University, the College Entrance Examination Board was formed about the end of the century to bring about "as rapidly as possible an agreement upon a uniform statement as to each subject required by two or more colleges in turn. Hold or cause to be held at convenient points, in June of each year, a series of college admission examinations, with uniform tests in each subject, and issue certificates based on the results of such examinations." The several colleges of the Middle States and Maryland were requested by the New England Association "to accept the certificates issued by such joint college admission examination board, so far as they go, in lieu of their own separate admission examinations." This Board became an independent agency, conducted its first examinations in 1901, when 7,889 examinations were given to 973 candidates from 237 schools, and has been very active ever since. The first tests were given in 67 places in the United States and in two places in Europe. Twenty-eight years later more than 22.7 thousand candidates from 813 private and 1,124 public schools were examined in 357 places. In 1948 the number of candidates tested was 78.1 thousand, as against 65.2 thousand in 1947; 46 thousand in 1946; 32.5 thousand in 1945; and 26.1 thousand in 1944. In 1948, 56 per cent of the candidates came from public schools, and 44 per cent from private or independent ones. In 1948 the geographical distribution was as follows:

Region	Percentage	Region	Percentage
New England	22.7	West South Central	1.0
Middle Atlantic	44.3	Mountain	.9
South Atlantic	5.6	Pacific	2.8
East North Central	5.2	Foreign	.8
West North Central	2.0	Unknown	13.9
East South Central	.8		

In that year the examinations were conducted in all the North American states and the District of Columbia, Alaska, the Canal Zone, Guam, Hawaii, and Puerto Rico. Other foreign places in which the Board's examinations were held were Argentina, Australia, Austria, Belgium, Brazil, Canada, China, Colombia, Cuba, Ecuador, Egypt, Ethiopia, France, Germany, Great Britain and its possessions, Greece, Guatemala, Haiti, India, Iraq, Italy, Japan, Korea, Lebanon, Liberia, Mexico, Netherlands and possessions, New Zealand, Norway, Palestine, Peru, the Philippines, Spain, Switzerland, Turkey, Uruguay, Venezuela, and the Virgin Islands.

The examinations used by the College Entrance Examination Board in its early years marked a step forward from the inspection of secondary schools by universities or other agencies and provided for better measuring. Standardized tests of intelligence and achievement, which were later devised, came to be widely used in part for admission to college. Predictions based on them were later examined against the student's collegiate record. In 1922 the Board approved such tests in principle and appointed a committee to prepare them for its use; soon these were being used in its examinations. Tests devised by the American Council of Education, which have been extensively used, were given to 40 thousand students in 121 colleges in 1924, and by 1931 about 150 thousand copies were being distributed for use in 350 institutions for higher education. By mid-century the use of tests of intelligence and achievement had widely spread throughout the United States.

In 1894 the North Central Association of Colleges and Secondary Schools was formed, followed in 1895 by the Southern Association of Colleges and Preparatory Schools, which changed its name in 1912 to the Southern Association of Colleges and Secondary Schools. In 1918 the Northwest Association of Secondary and Higher Schools was formed. In organization and procedure, these associations ran somewhat to a pattern. All of them gave attention to better relations between higher institutions and secondary schools, to the improvement of standards of work in both, and to standards of admission, length of school year and of class periods, preparation and salaries of teachers and their teaching load, buildings and equipment, especially to the equipment of libraries and laboratories, and to many other matters.

These associations have engaged in recent years in many activities not contemplated in their early period. *The National Survey of Secondary Education,*[11] which was published in 1933, was initiated by the North Central Association of Colleges and Secondary Schools. Between 1938 and 1945 the Southern Association of Colleges and Secondary Schools, under its Commission on Curricular Problems and Research, conducted a study of thirty-three public secondary schools in that region, not altogether unlike the Eight-Year Study, often referred to as the Aikin Study, which was conducted in the 1930's by the Commission on the Relation of School and College of the Progressive Education Association. The study by the Southern Association was not as pretentious or as widely publicized as that of the Progressive Education Association, nor was it finished as originally planned because the Second World War made it impossible to follow the graduates of the thirty-three schools through college. In connection with that study, summer conferences were conducted, similar to the workshops of the Progressive Education Association, and there was considerable publication regarding the undertaking, chiefly for the membership of the Southern Association.

The Aikin Study.—The Eight-Year Study was begun in 1932 by the Commission on the Relation of School and College of the Progressive Education Association, under the general direction of

[11] U. S. Office of Education, *Bulletin* No. 17, 1932.

Wilford M. Aikin, with thirty schools in different parts of the country cooperating in the experiment. Its purpose was to determine whether the graduates of "progressive" schools that had not specifically followed college entrance requirements could do as well in college as graduates of so-called traditional schools. The thirty cooperating secondary schools were left free to revise their work as they saw fit, ignoring requirements for college entrance and keeping in mind primarily the interests and needs of the students. Many accredited colleges and universities waived their technical requirements for admission of the graduates of those schools, and instead agreed to admit them "on the basis of their achievements in a broad field and on their scholastic aptitude or intelligence rating." For comparison, a control group of students was selected; for every graduate of the progressive schools, a "matchee" was chosen who had presented the regular credits for entrance to college from a traditional school, and who had about "the same intelligence rating, was of the same race, age, and sex, and represented the same type of family and economic background and the same size of community." Among the findings of the study, which appeared in several volumes, were that "preparation for a fixed set of entrance requirements is not the only satisfactory means of fitting a boy or girl for making the most out of college experience"; that "it looks as if the stimulus and the initiative which the less conventional approach to secondary education affords, send on to college better human material than we have obtained in the past." It appeared that the grades of the progressive school graduates during the first three years of the study were a bit higher than those of the control group and showed a slight lead in every subject except foreign languages, although the differences were not considered statistically significant:

	Progressive	Control group
English	2.54	2.47
Humanities	2.58	2.56
Foreign languages	2.44	2.46
Social science	2.43	2.39
Biological science	2.48	2.47
Physical science	2.46	2.41
Mathematics	2.56	2.44
Other subjects	2.61	2.50

At college, graduates of the thirty schools appeared to take more interest than the control group in all campus activities except athletics. "The guinea pigs wrote more, talked more, took a livelier interest in politics and social problems, went to more dances, had more dates.

Especially concerned with campus affairs were the graduates of the six most experimental schools. There were more dynamos than grinds among them." [12]

Investigations and inquiries such as these seemed healthy in their threats to break what was called the academic lock step and "the ball and chain" of education. These studies were concerned, however, with those graduates of high schools who went to college, and not with the much larger percentage of such graduates who did not go. Equally useful studies, perhaps, could deal with the kind of education young people got in high school who did not get to go to college.

Other Important Studies.—In the 1930's the "Cooperative Study of Secondary School Standards" grew out of conferences and the work of representatives of the regional educational associations which undertook, among other things, to discover (1) the characteristics of an effective secondary school, (2) the means for measuring its effectiveness, and (3) how to make a good school better. The work of this study, in which several hundred secondary schools participated, was placed under the direction of W. C. Eells, as coordinator, and wide publication on this immense effort disclosed interest in phases of secondary educational work that could not have been dreamed of in 1900. The findings of these and other studies on the baffling question of the purposes of secondary education seemed clearly to show the importance of adjusting the work of the secondary school more definitely to the social and economic needs of the people.

The problems of youth had become more and more acute after the First World War, and especially during the economic depression that began in 1929. The years of depression called sharp attention to the problems of American high school youth. These problems had emerged with startling suddenness. About one third of the persons unemployed were between sixteen and twenty-four years of age, and 40 per cent of the employable young people could not find work. The numbers of youth not in school had assumed alarming proportions. Out of these and other conditions came the Civilian Conservation Corps and the National Youth Administration. The principal

---

[12] See Dorothy Dunbar Bromley, "Education for College or for Life," in *Harper's Magazine* (March, 1941); also, *Educational Review* (March, 1941). So-called "essentialists" as well as "progressives" in education will find Dorothy Walworth's *Feast of Reason* (New York: Farrar & Rinehart, 1941) interesting and sprightly reading. One reviewer of this novel, whose theme is "the debunking of the phony factors in 'progressive' methods in education," said that "rabid progressives should tremble in their modern boots."

aims of the NYA were to provide funds for the part-time employment of needy school, college, and graduate students between the ages of sixteen and twenty-four, to enable them to continue their education, and also to provide funds for the part-time employment of youth of families on relief, on work projects designed to give young people valuable experience in work, and also to benefit the communities in which they lived. Howard M. Bell's *Youth Tell Their Story* [13] threw much light on the problems of youth and awakened wide attention to "the lost generation."

As early as 1925 the American Council on Education had drawn attention to the increasing problems of youth and to the need for a national study of the subject. The American Youth Commission, which was organized that year, was composed of sixteen leading American men and women, with Newton D. Baker of Cleveland, Ohio, as chairman, and Owen D. Young, of New York City, as vice-chairman. Homer P. Rainey, formerly president of Bucknell University and later president of the University of Texas, was appointed as director. The Commission undertook to discover the needs of American youth and to appraise the resources and facilities then available for meeting those needs. In 1937 a report of the Commission, under the title *Secondary Education for Youth in Modern America,* [14] discussed the nature of secondary education and the school as a social institution and set up educational objectives and types of activities to meet the needs of youth. The report said that secondary schools must prepare youth for (1) education for citizenship, (2) education for home membership, (3) education for vocational efficiency, (4) education for leisure life, (5) education for physical health, (6) education for mental health, and (7) education for continued learning. To achieve these objectives, it was recommended that the secondary school enlarge the scope of its activities so as to include guidance, extracurricular clubs and organizations, the management of the school, home activities, and contacts between pupils and teachers outside the classroom.

The Commission on Human Relations and the Commission on Secondary School Curriculum, of the Progressive Education Association, which were formed and worked between 1932 and 1942, undertook to grapple with some issues that were being attacked by other commissions and agencies. Meantime the recommendations on

[13] Washington, D. C.: American Council on Education, 1938.

[14] Harl R. Douglass. Washington, D. C.: The American Council on Education, 1937.

secondary education, which were made by the stupendous inquiry into education in the State of New York, were widely discussed.[15] That study recommended that secondary education begin with the seventh grade, with general education the central objective of the program, "by devoting the greater part of the time up to the end of the twelfth grade to the study of general science, human relations, community life, world history, general mathematics, and the arts— subjects which touch many now divided academic topics and which cover matters of direct value and interest to the average American citizen." Broad fields of knowledge were to be presented "in the ways in which they are generally encountered in life and work, and not as semester hours for college entrance." Basic skills, such as reading and writing, particularly for those pupils who were deficient, were to be presented and reviewed. The secondary school was to recognize its "distinct responsibility" for character education; it was to be large enough so that electives could be provided without having classes too small; a guidance service should be established; a pupil would be permitted to leave school after sixteen years of age "if he has a real job." If unemployed, he must continue under the supervision of the school until he reaches eighteen, unless he secures a job meantime. "This program may be in school or not, as the boy and his advisers may determine. Discontinue continuation schools." General vocational education was to be included in the program of "every comprehensive high school," but courses in the subject should place chief emphasis on broad vocational training instead of on the development of specialized skills. New cultural courses were to be added to the program of the secondary school beyond the twelfth grade, and also new subprofessional courses, to prepare youth to enter technical and semiprofessional occupations—wherever such courses were not available.

Graduation from high school was to be based "on readiness to leave school," as judged by the officers of the local school, in accordance with the regulations of the department of education of the state, "and discontinue the Regents' Diploma. The local diploma should specify the work done and the competence achieved." As tests of graduation, the Regents' Examinations were to end and be transformed into examinations designed to test and discover weak spots in the curriculum of secondary education or in teaching. The schools

[15] *Education for American Life* (New York: The McGraw-Hill Book Co., 1938), pp. 46-49. For fuller discussion of the secondary school in this Inquiry, see Francis T. Spaulding, *High School and Life,* same publisher and same date.

themselves should measure the achievement of the pupils through a variety of examinations. Physical and mental health should receive emphasis, and more attention should be given to the gifted and to the handicapped child. Libraries should be improved, and emphasis should be increased on broad reading and expression in English.

Six years after publication of *Purposes of Education in American Democracy,* noted above, the Educational Policies Commission, of the National Education Association, and the American Association of School Administrators published another pronouncement on the subject, this one dealing particularly with the secondary school.[16] This was also widely publicized and discussed, but in some quarters it was considered a bit utopian and somewhat vague and unrealistic. *Education for All American Youth* was the story of education in two imaginary American communities, but the educational principles applied by the study to Farmville and American City were believed by the Commission to be "applicable in any community." The descriptions of the schools for youth in these two communities ("written five years after the cessation of hostilities") and of the "imperative educational needs of youth"[17] differed somewhat in language, at least from aims previously proposed by Herbert Spencer (1859); by the Commission on the Reorganization of Secondary Education (Seven Cardinal Principles, 1918); by the Educational Policies Commission (*Purposes of Education in American Democracy,* 1938); and by other pronouncements on the question of the purposes and function of the secondary school. The ten purposes proposed in *Education for All American Youth* ran like this:

1. All youth need to develop salable skills and those undertakings and attitudes that make the worker an intelligent and productive participant in economic life. To this end, most youth need supervised work experience as well as education in the skills and knowledge of their occupation.

2. All youth need to develop and maintain good health and physical fitness.

3. All youth need to understand the rights and duties of the citizen of a democratic society, and to be diligent and competent in the performance of their obligations as members of the community and citizens of the state and nation.

4. All youth need to understand the significance of the family for the individual and society, and the conditions conducive to successful family life.

5. All youth need to know how to purchase and use goods and services intelligently, understanding both the values received by the consumer and the economic consequences of their acts.

[16] *Education for All American Youth* (Washington, D. C.: National Education Association, 1944).
[17] *Ibid.,* pp. 225-26.

6. All youth need to understand the methods of science, the influence of science on human life, and the main scientific facts concerning the nature of the world and of man.

7. All youth need opportunities to develop their capacities to appreciate beauty in literature, art, music, and nature.

8. All youth need to be able to use their leisure time well and to budget it wisely, balancing activities that yield satisfactions to the individual with those that are socially useful.

9. All youth need to develop respect for other persons, to grow in their insight into ethical values and principles, and to be able to live and work cooperatively with others.

10. All youth need to grow in their ability to think rationally, to express their thoughts clearly, and to read and listen with understanding.

These statements were issued by the hypothetical Commission on Postwar Education of American City, which also issued proposals for action. These included the raising of the period of compulsory education to the age of eighteen or to graduation from high school, "whichever occurs earlier," and to make all three high schools of the community "comprehensive in purposes and programs." A free institution (to be known as the American City Community Institute) above the high school should be established to enable the youth of American City "who wish to do so, to prepare for occupations that require one or two years of training beyond high school and to continue their general education at the same time." This was a sort of "community college" which was widely spreading throughout the United States in the 1940's. The Commission on Postwar Education of American City would have a curriculum for Grades VII through XIV "which will provide for all youth the experiences through which they can best grow in all the ways indicated in the statement of 'imperative educational needs of youth.'" A system of guidance should be begun at once, and plans should be made to get the additional funds needed to enlarge the high school plant so as to take care of more students and to provide for additional educational services such as vocational education and guidance; to help provide the building for the "proposed new community institute"; to find "the annual operating costs of providing education to some 2,000 additional high school students and the students who will enroll in the community institute," and to "provide financial aid to individual students who need to earn money for personal expenses. . . . Begin at once a public relations program for increasing local funds." The funds, the Commission said, would have to come from local, state, and federal sources. Finally, the Commission was to invite the boards of education of the high school districts that surrounded American City to join with the Commission "in planning an educational program to serve the youth of the region as well as the city, and particularly to share in the development of the American City Community Institute which should be a regional institution. Call in the state department of education at once to assist in this cooperative planning." Under the plans of its Commission on Postwar Education, American City was to have a "continuous educational program throughout the period of youth."

The matter of making a curriculum to provide for the ten "imperative educational needs of youth" was disposed of by suggesting "an inclusive course in 'Common Studies' or 'Common Learnings.'" This course would include the fields of "citizenship, economics, family living, appreciation of literature and the arts, and use of the English language. Not less than one third of the student's time should be allowed for this course during Grades X through XII. The teacher of 'Common Learnings' should also serve as general counselor to the students in his or her class."

The second course:

Basic instruction in science would also be one of studies common to all high school youth. Ideally, this instruction should be an integral part of the course in "Common Learnings." At present, however, there is not an adequate supply of teachers qualified to teach science in addition to the other phases of the "Common Learnings" course. For the present, therefore, it seems advisable to include a separate basic course in science in Grade X. This course should be closely related to the course in "Common Learnings." Membership of classes in the two courses should be identical so that teachers of "Common Learnings" and teachers of science can plan their work together, and when desirable pool their class time for work on joint projects. After further experimentation it may be possible to make this basic study of science a part of the work in "Common Learnings."

Either the Educational Policies Commission or its hypothetical Commission on Postwar Education of American City was determined to establish "Common Learnings."

The third course was to consist of instruction in "health and physical education," but this work was also to be considered one of the "Common Studies" or "Common Learnings." But

. . . because physical education activities are quite different in character from those of other classes and require teachers with special qualifications, and because instruction in personal health requires teachers with considerable specialized training in the field, it is recommended that this instruction be given in classes separate from the "Common Learnings" course. Here, also, however, teachers should be alert to opportunities for relating instruction in the different classes.

Either the Educational Policies Commission or the Commission on Postwar Education for American City, through which EPC spoke, was determined to "correlate," "integrate," or "fuse" the curriculum of American City where, it seemed obvious, the ghost of Herbart's "correlation" still stalked.

While some of the problems that had so vexed secondary education in 1900 had been at least partially solved, in 1950 some of them seemed to persist and by that time fresh issues had also appeared. The tremendous inflation of the offerings in the high schools seemed a bit confusing, drew sharp criticisms here and there, and provoked the question whether these schools were promising to do more than they could properly perform. There was evidence that courses, unintelligently proliferated, resulted in economic waste.

In spite of improvements in compulsory attendance and child labor legislation and of continuous attempts to adjust the work of the schools to the varying needs and interests of children, the problems of nonattendance and of truancy were also very acute at mid-century. In the fall of 1949 it was reported by the National League to Promote School Attendance that half of the young people of the United States dropped out of school before finishing their secondary education, and the high rate of dropouts was deplored as "a waste of human resources." Truancy, which was very troublesome, was described by Superintendent William Jansen of the New York City Schools not as a disease but as a system of "a deeply troubled and very often a markedly disturbed personality," the frustration and the unhappiness of youth. Mental hygiene was recommended as one means of curbing truancy and nonattendance. The number of children who quit school could be greatly decreased by the use of a more "flexible, individualized curriculum" that would give prospective dropouts a keener "sense of belonging." And in the spring of 1950 the New York State Vocational and Practical Arts Association, alarmed at the statistics that 50 per cent of the students who entered high school dropped out before finishing its four years of work, also urged a more flexible program of instruction in secondary education and more vocational and practical arts for "those students not suited to academic studies."

Not many months after these discussions of a dismal subject, the National Council of Independent Schools [18] made a statement on

[18] "The Functions of Secondary Education in the United States," *School and Society* (September 23, 1950), pp. 193-95.

what secondary education, whether public or private, should seek to perform at a time when the whole world stood "in the deepening shadows of another possible war." Secondary education had taken on a meaning that was "without precedent in any other time or society" and should be "the great unifying agent in our democracy." These schools must, the statement said, "pass on the national heritage and tradition from which our unity comes." A main reason for the establishment of secondary schools in the early days in this country, and "an impelling force in the development of their descendants, the public and the independent schools, was the determination of successive generations to transmit this tradition by education." That tradition derived from religious faith, from faith in man, and from the "ideal of the widest educational opportunities for all." American children were entitled to the "spiritual heritage" of the past. Central in this American doctrine was also faith in man and in the brotherhood of man and in "the idea of universal education as derived from Thomas Jefferson and spread by Horace Mann and others." The secondary schools of the United States offered "an incomparable instrument" for making "the American way of life" clear and desirable, "cleansed of its dross and materialism." To pass on these articles of faith and this heritage, said the Council, was the primary purpose and function of the secondary school, whether public or private.

To achieve that purpose and to perform that function meant heavy responsibilities for secondary education. It must help young people to perform their intellectual tasks well; must recognize the spiritual quality of man and encourage its growth; must share with the parents the responsibility for the wholesome emotional growth of their children and prepare them to meet their responsibilities "to family, country, and mankind, and to conscience." The secondary schools must also teach their pupils "that freedom must be earned by personal responsibility," and the sense of duty must be built in them "as a permanent habit." They must be taught "to know themselves and to plan for their futures." It was the duty of secondary education to provide for those young people who go beyond the secondary school and also for those who do not.

Specific duties of secondary education, said the Council, was to make its pupils proficient in reading, writing, and mathematics; provide them with some knowledge of "the physical laws of the world in which they live and of the scientific method." All pupils in the secondary schools should be instructed in hygiene, have physical training and opportunity to participate in athletics, "but the last should be clearly subordinate to the more fundamental educational purposes." Secondary schools should develop in their pupils memory and accuracy, powers of observation and of analytical reflective thinking, imagination, the arts of communication, aesthetic appreciation, and "a sense of craftsmanship." The secondary school should also teach its pupils "the rewards of a wise use of leisure." This Aristotle, three centuries before Christ, had highly favored; Herbert Spencer had recommended it in the middle of the nineteenth century; many others between the great Greek philosopher and the eminent English thinker had also done so; and in 1918 the Commission on the Reorganization of Secondary Education had endorsed the idea of the proper use of leisure. The secondary school should also provide "such a stimulating introduction to the lives and works of the great spirits that have moved mankind as to guide pupils to turn to them for pleasure, strength, and inspiration." Guidance should be provided for the pupils, but real guidance, said the Council, "comes from the ways as well as the words of a school or its teachers; it should lead to gains in maturity for individuals and to their increased competence as members of society." The secondary school, the statement continued, while providing for the varied needs of pupils and for their guidance, should be aware that each of them was "entitled to the discipline of hard work and standards commensurate with his ability." The Council also emphasized the high importance of instilling "in all pupils an understanding of the origins and meaning of American democracy." But none of these functions of secondary education, the Council insisted, could the school and its teachers alone accomplish. There must be cooperation between them and the families of the pupils; "they are bounded by the influences of heredity and environment."

New Issues and Old.—During these fifty years of conferences, discussions, and cooperative efforts of many kinds to improve secondary education, much substantial progress in improvement was made. The record of that progress appears in the procedures of those efforts and in the evolution of quantitative standards of secondary educational work. The first half of the twentieth century was marked by continuous quantitative triumphs of secondary education in the United States. The task in the second half of the century was to do qualitatively what had been done so well quantitatively, and that task called for the same kind of faith and courage and persistent effort that the earlier task had required.

While efforts were being made to provide secondary education for all American youth, democracy was entering college. A course for everybody in high school was rapidly becoming a degree for everybody in college. This subject is treated in the next Chapter.

SOME SUGGESTED QUESTIONS AND EXERCISES FOR STUDENTS

1. Compare or contrast (1) the Latin grammar school of the colonial period with a public high school in 1950 in (a) purpose, (b) curriculum, (c) teachers and methods of teaching, and results; and (2) make the same comparison or contrast between an academy and a public high school of 1950.
2. The expansion of the public high school in the United States between 1890 and 1950 was phenomenal. Discuss the principal forces and influences that resulted in that growth: economic, political and social, psychological and scientific.
3. Discuss the conditions in secondary and higher education that made the formation of the regional educational associations the "invention of necessity"? How did the purposes and procedures of these organizations in their formative years differ from their purposes and procedures in 1950?
4. Read the report of the Committee of Ten and the report of the Committee on College Entrance Requirements and compare their recommendations. What "philosophy" or theory of education was reflected in these reports? What were their effects on actual practices in the secondary schools?
5. By 1950, increasing complaint was reported here and there that the schools had "bit off more than they could chew," that they were undertaking to do too much. Discuss the causes of the complaint, indicating whether, in your opinion, the complaint had any foundation in fact.
6. What, in your opinion, were the primary purposes of the American public high school in 1950?
7. In that year the "mortality" of students in high school—their failure to finish its program—was reported as a very disturbing condition. Explain the condition and suggest ways to improve it.
8. Indicate the various governmental and nongovernmental agencies that became concerned about the plight of American youth, especially in the years of depression that followed 1929.
9. Study and report to the class on the activities of the (1) NYA, (2) CCC, (3) any other agencies that operated in the 1930's in behalf of "the lost generation."

10. Read and report in class on the findings and the significance of *The Classical Investigation,* and especially its report on the status of Latin and Greek in the schools in 1924 (pages 249-55 of that study).

11. Briggs, Leonard, and Justman (*Secondary Education,* chap. xix) say that secondary education in this country has never "been guided by a consistent fundamental philosophy." Read that chapter and report in class their reasons for the statement. Is the statement true of the Latin grammar schools? Of the academies? Were not the aims of these two types of schools clearer than the aims of public high schools today?

12. Study and report in class on the Educational Policies Commission's *Education for All American Youth.* On what educational "philosophy" were its recommendations based? How could its proposals be put into effect in your community?

13. Study and report to the class on the recommendations made on secondary education by the Regents' Inquiry in New York State.

Some Suggested References and Reading

Alexander, William M., and Saylor, J. G. *Secondary Education: Basic Principles and Practices.* New York: Rinehart & Co., 1950.
   Deals with modern principles and practices in secondary schools and intended for use in both the preservice and the in-service training of teachers. Provides a description of the modern American high school.

Briggs, Thomas H. *Secondary Education.* New York: The Macmillan Co., 1933.
   Chaps. iv, v, and vi contain historical accounts of secondary education in the United States. Other chapters present issues in and functions of secondary education.

Briggs, Thomas H., Leonard, J. P., and Justman, Joseph. *Secondary Education* (rev. ed.). New York: The Macmillan Co., 1950.
   Chaps. vii ("Functions of Secondary Education"), x ("Remaking the Curriculum"), xviii ("Some Basic Problems in Secondary Education"), and xix ("A Vision of Secondary Education") provide very useful materials for this Chapter. In chap. xix "At no time, from the beginning to the present, has secondary education been guided by a consistent fundamental philosophy." The importance of good teachers is emphasized.

Brubacker, John S. *The History of the Problems of Education.* New York: McGraw-Hill Book Co., 1947.
   Chap. xiv deals with secondary education. Pages 428 ff. bear on topics discussed in this Chapter.

Educational Policies Commission. *Education for All American Youth.* Washington, D. C.: National Education Association, 1944.
   A sort of prophecy of what could happen in secondary education in two imaginary American communities. Undertakes to do for secondary education what *Education for All American Children* attempted to do for elementary education, but it is considered in some quarters as being a trifle unrealistic.

Edwards, Newton, and Richey, Herman G. *The School in the American Social Order.* Boston: Houghton Mifflin Co., 1947.

Chap. xvii ("The Quest for a Content of Education") throws some light on some of the topics discussed in this Chapter. Contains a very useful bibliography.

GULICK, LUTHER H. *Education for American Life.* New York: McGraw-Hill Book Co., 1938.
A statement of the findings and recommendations of the *Regents' Inquiry into the Character and Cost of Public Education in the State of New York.* Pages 46-49 deal with the purposes and functions of secondary education.

INGLIS, ALEXANDER J. *Principles of Secondary Education.* Boston: Houghton Mifflin Co., 1918.
Chap. i gives a good account of the historical development of secondary education; chap. vii discusses its relation to the elementary school; chap. viii treats of its relation to higher education; and chap. x sets out the aims and functions of secondary education.

INGLIS, ALEXANDER J. "Secondary Education," in I. L. KANDEL (ed.), *Twenty-Five Years of American Education.* New York: The Macmillan Co., 1924.
A brief but good account of the influences on and developments in secondary education in the United States during the first quarter of the present century.

KANDEL, I. L. *History of Secondary Education.* Boston: Houghton Mifflin Co., 1930.
Perhaps the best scholarly account of the subject up to 1930. Chaps. ix and xi bear especially on the subjects discussed in this Chapter.

KNIGHT, EDGAR W., and HALL, CLIFTON L. *Readings in American Educational History.* New York: Appleton-Century-Crofts, Inc., 1951.
Chaps. iv and viii contain original materials that bear on some topics discussed in this Chapter.

MONROE, WALTER S. (ed.). *Encyclopedia of Educational Research* (rev. ed.). New York: The Macmillan Co., 1950, pp. 1152-1201.
Articles on research on several aspects of secondary education, prepared by different specialists, are very useful as supplementary materials for this Chapter. Among other subjects the articles deal with research on the general development of secondary education, student population, failures, organization, curriculum, and teachers.

RAINEY, HOMER P. *How Fare American Youth?* New York: Appleton-Century-Crofts, Inc., 1937.
An important report to the American Youth Commission of the American Council on Education which showed the widening gap between youth and American society in finding jobs, in schooling, health, leisure, the family, and the church.

SPEARS, HAROLD. *Secondary Education in American Life.* New York: American Book Co., 1941.
Chaps. iii, iv, and v bear on some of the topics discussed in this Chapter.

——. *The High School for Today.* New York: American Book Co., 1950.
A very readable book which introduces the student to the modern high school to see "What we have" and "How it got that way."

Chapter 4

DEMOCRACY ENTERS COLLEGE

PREVIEW OF THE CHAPTER

So marked were the changes in undergraduate education that its characteristics and functions in 1950 could not have been predicted in 1900 by the most optimistic social and educational prophets. . . . There were new issues in the colleges, but some of those that were persistent at mid-twentieth century had been present at its beginning. Among those issues were the collegiate curriculum, the place of the private and independent institutions, and the increasing belief of Americans in the economic value of academic degrees. . . . The high and increasing costs of higher education caused much anxiety in the 1940's and at mid-century, but John Price Jones pointed out that "the day of the big gift had not gone." The question of federal aid to higher education, the fear of federal control through federal scholarships and fellowships, and the question of exemption from taxes were warmly discussed. . . . Dissatisfaction with the elective system led to much experimentation with the curriculum and to the development of numerous new "college plans." . . . Two unique plans for higher education that attracted national notice were the establishment of a mammoth university in New York, and provision for regional cooperation in higher education in the southern states. . . . The issue of "academic" freedom was very lively during the first half of the century, becoming acute during the two world wars and the intervening economic depression, and at mid-century it was heatedly discussed.

Changes in Undergraduate Education.—The characteristics and functions of the American college in 1900 were very different from those in 1950. As late as 1900, most American colleges were predominantly institutions of liberal arts, with the classical tradition and the disciplinary theory of education very strong. The sciences had not yet arrived as fully as they were to during the first half of the twentieth century, and technology was only slightly in evidence. In 1900 the college generally represented the end of formal education, with very few persons going beyond it; some went to European universities for further study, however, before graduate instruction was provided in this country. Collegiate students were selected, though by a sort of unconscious process—mentally, economically, and socially; only those who showed superior mental aptitude for scholastic interests considered going to college. Poor boys rarely ever worked their way through college as they later came to do. But working one's way through college became in the first half of the twentieth century an important American institution, and self-help students on campuses "were credited by federal tabulations a few years ago with earnings in excess of $32.5 million annually." [1]

Around 1900, the small size of the college usually meant small classes, with personal acquaintance and perhaps personal inspiration and guidance of students by teachers and administrative officers. Many of the so-called problems in higher education in mid-twentieth century had grown out of the fact that this condition had almost entirely changed. In 1900 the college was still predominantly an institution for men, although the issue of coeducation had been heatedly debated for many decades. The report of President F. A. P. Barnard of Columbia, in 1879, had shocked a large part of the educational world of that time by his advocating the admission of women to Columbia College. Ten years earlier, Charles W. Eliot, in his inaugural address as president of Harvard, had said that the attitude of that institution on the education of women was: "The Corporation will not receive women as students in the College proper, nor into any school whose discipline requires residence near the school. The difficulties involved in a common residence of hundreds of young men and women of immature character and marriageable age are very grave. The necessary police regulations are exceedingly burdensome." By 1950, however, with the opening of its law school to women, Harvard had gone coed. [2]

By 1902 the issue of coeducation was hardly as clearly settled as Nicholas Murray Butler of Columbia University believed it was when he wrote: "Coeducation is a dead issue. The American people have settled the matter. Why discuss the matter further?" At about the same time, James R. Angell of the University of Chicago wrote: "To behold the campus dotted with couples, billing and cooing their way to an A.B., is a thing it is said to rejoice Venus or Pan rather than Minerva, and were it the frequent or necessary outcome of coeducation, the future of the system would certainly be in jeopardy." Thomas D. Boyd, president of Louisiana State University, said in

---

[1] Clarence E. Lovejoy, *So You're Going to College* (New York: Simon & Schuster, 1940), p. 150.

[2] See J. Anthony Lewis, "Harvard Goes Coed, But Incognito," *New York Times Magazine,* May 1, 1949.

1910: "The very presence of the opposite sex has a restraining influence, preventing the expression of coarse and unrefined thought. . . . To object to coeducation on the score of morals sounds more like an echo from the past." In 1934 C. A. Richmond, president emeritus of Union College, was reported as saying: "Many believe that the new-found liberty which women have achieved but not fully understood has lowered the tone of our women's colleges both in manners and morals."

In spite of the name "university," Harvard of 1900 was still "a New England college with growing pains," according to the *Harvard Alumni Bulletin* in early 1950. It had only about 1,900 students, 70 per cent of whom came from private schools or private tutors, compared with about 12,000 in 1950; there were only 351 students in the graduate school, as compared with 2,000 in 1950, and the modern schools of law, medicine, and business administration remained in 1900 to be built. The institution had no modern athletic plant, and its endowments were only about $12.5 million as against its nearly $200 million in 1950. Under the caption, "Harvard of Today and Fifty Years Ago," the *Bulletin* said: "The University must somehow continue the growth of the past, and justify its position as a national institution. In our 'classless' society, the vast, complex, modern Harvard must be kept in working equilibrium without sacrificing the precious early liberty of self-direction, and must find at the same time good teaching for the student and for the individual, inward satisfaction."

As 1949 came to a close, increasing concern was being expressed, as it had been expressed for several years by a number of leading educators, over the financial future of higher education in this country whose income from endowments had been steadily declining, with the prospect of philanthropic gifts somewhat clouded, the expenses of maintenance and the costs of construction frightfully high, and estimates of enrollments of students greatly varying. Higher education seemed to be in the midst of many doubts, and these became deeper with the Korean crisis in the summer of 1950. But government and industry were giving two hundred institutions for higher education about $125 million for research, an increase of 500 per cent over prewar years, according to a survey made by the *New York Times,* but a million dollars in 1950 would not buy nearly as much research as in 1939.

The lion's share of the appropriations and grants for research was going into projects in the so-called applied sciences, into fields where the effort was to find the "practical application of principles already discovered in earlier fundamental research," and there was fear that even when funds were made available for basic studies, researches might be steered into directions that would promise immediate practical results. Those educators who were disturbed by these conditions preferred funds for research with no strings tied to them, but apparently the use of much of the money provided for research was being specified rather than being left to the university scholars to use it where it was most needed for basic research. There was also complaint that too little money was being provided for exploration in the social sciences, in economics, sociology, political science, and allied fields. At bit of fine irony in this condition was the fact that the American people were spending untold millions "to develop new inventions for both peace and war. In the case of the atom bomb it was billions. Yet we virtually ignore the crying need for new social techniques to cope with these new creations."

Except for state universities and land-grant colleges, most institutions for higher education in the United States in 1900 were under private and denominational support and control. The trustees were usually zealous and influential representatives of denominational interests, and so also were the presidents and members of the faculty. The practical emancipation of Protestant institutions for higher education from "clerical dominion" was largely a development of the first half of the twentieth century. Apparently, clerical powers in the management of higher education declined, and appeal became louder and louder to business men for endowments. In time, the list of the trustees of institutions for higher education "read like a corporation directory." A study[3] of the governing boards of thirty leading American universities showed that their economic and social composition would have discouraged "those who disapprove of the present secular trend in higher education and who believe that a deep and abiding Christian influence should prevail in the high councils of universities." Only 6.6 per cent of the trustees were clergymen, "and of these, three fifths were Catholic priests." Even an inquiry into such a question would probably have been regarded as improper in 1900.

Commenting somewhat dismally in 1935 on some changes that had taken place in higher education, Stephen Leacock of McGill University wrote in the *McGill News:*

The colleges have got far away from their original mission. They began as places of piety and learning. They did not teach people how to make

[3] H. P. Beck, *Men Who Control Our Universities* (New York: King's Crown Press, 1947).

money. In those days people of gentlemanly birth did not make money—when they wanted it, they took it! The college did not teach men a career—that was done with an axe! But the colleges were supposed to fit men to die; there are no courses in this subject now.

In the place of the older learning, the colleges have embarked on a wilderness of functions. They are gay from noon to night with student activities— they sing, they dance, they act. They run mimic newspapers and mock parliaments and make-believe elections. They put their athletics over with a hoot and a roar that costs more in one season than the old college spent in a decade. In this tumult of activity the "midnight oil" of the pale student of half a century ago is replaced by the two A.M. gasoline of his burly successor.

All this was grand in boom times when life was pitched in that tempo, and when we all grew richer on paper every day. Now the crash has come and the college, like the rest of the world, must get back to facts. Girls and boys of nineteen and twenty have no right to perpetual distraction, to unending "activity," and make-believe autonomy.

Back to the Latin grammar with them. Make them learn the passive subjunctive of a deponent verb. Then they will be ready to die, and thus, since all life moves at back rounds, worthy to live.

Many other glaring differences between higher education in 1900 and in 1950, some on the credit side and some on the debit, could be noted. One difference that must be placed on the credit side was the role of higher education in the national service. By 1950 its actual influence in national affairs had been amply demonstrated in two world wars and in a severe economic depression, and at mid-century the potential influence of higher education in national affairs was generally recognized as of increasing significance in American life.[4]

As indicated in Chapter 1, changes in higher education between 1900 and 1950 were as conspicuous as those that came in elementary and secondary schools. Interest in higher education was increasing around the turn of the century, as shown by the activities of the regional educational associations that had begun in New England in 1885, and in wide discussions of higher education in addresses before educational associations and also in periodicals. As also noted in Chapter 1, the American people by 1900 were becoming very degree conscious, and in that year thirty-nine different kinds of academic degrees were conferred on nearly 16 thousand men and women. Twenty different varieties of honorary degrees were conferred in 1900, the D.D. leading in 273 cases and the LL.D. in 161. Also conferred that year were six honorary A.B.'s, 180 honorary master's

[4] For fuller discussion of this subject see Chapter 8.

degrees, and twenty-three honorary Ph.D.'s. The Ph.D. was awarded as honorary as late as 1912.[5]

In 1950 the different kinds of academic degrees were almost countless, and new degrees were being established annually. In that year degrees were conferred on nearly half a million men and women. More and more were degrees being conferred upon women, a practice that had been frowned upon by "the lords of creation" during most of the nineteenth century and which only in the first half of the twentieth century had become identified with the fitness of things academic. As "frosting for the cake," an almost incredible number of honorary degrees, which had long been fashionable among Americans, were annually conferred about mid-twentieth century. In an effort to find out why people were so eager to acquire academic degrees, the Ohio State University took a poll of its graduate students in the middle of 1950 and discovered, what was doubtless already known, that sheer love of learning was not their highest motive. Sixty per cent of the candidates for the master's degree and more than half of those seeking doctorates were moved toward advanced degrees because, presumably, these meant higher salaries.[6]

The first half of the twentieth century was marked by tremendous increases in higher educational facilities. There were great increases in physical plants, in endowments, in curricula, in faculties, in administrative machinery, in students, and in many academic activities not common in 1900. Among new activities were the growth of summer sessions, the organization of extension divisions and of special schools and colleges, and the establishment of university presses.

The total income of the higher educational institutions of the United States from all sources in 1900 was reported at about $29 million, one fourth of which came from endowments. Benefactions to colleges and universities that year were about $13 million. In 1946 the income was $924 million, with about $90 million coming from endowments, and gifts were about $77 million according to unofficial reports. Official and accurate data on some of these items were difficult to get even in mid-twentieth century.

It is fairly well known, however, that aid for fellowships and scholarships in 1900 was very limited. The total number of fellowships was about 476 and of scholarships about 7.6 thousand. The

[5] For the story of this practice see S. E. Epler, *Honorary Degrees: A Survey of Their Use and Abuse* (Washington, D. C.: American Council of Public Affairs, 1943).

[6] *Time*, July 31, 1950, p. 44.

United States Office of Education reported in 1935 that nearly 67 thousand scholarships and fellowships were available out of nearly $9 million of funds for that purpose, and the number had greatly increased by 1950. C. E. Lovejoy [7] reported in 1940 that 70 thousand students were holding scholarships and fellowships that were valued at more than $10 million annually.

Tuition at Harvard and at Columbia was $150 a year in 1900. Living expenses were estimated at $350 at Harvard and $400 at Columbia. It was reported at the University of California that tuition was free and that living expenses were about $250 a year. At the University of Iowa, tuition was $25 and living expenses were $190. At the University of North Carolina, tuition was $60 and living expenses were $100. It appears that in 1900 publicly supported institutions were in general less expensive than privately supported institutions. By 1950, costs of a college education had so greatly increased all over the United States that further increases in tuition and fees were viewed as unsound public policy. This condition was one of the considerations that led President Truman's commission in 1947 to recommend huge federal funds for scholarships and fellowships.

New Issues in the Colleges.—Two prominent issues in higher education around 1900 were the question of the elective as against the prescribed curriculum and that of the place of the small private or independent college. From Harvard's early days to about 1869, when chemist Charles W. Eliot became president of that institution, the collegiate curriculum had remained about the same everywhere in this country, with a few minor exceptions. The humanities, divinities, mathematics, and logic were the "core." True, the issue between prescription and election had caught the interest of Thomas Jefferson in his plan for the University of Virginia which was chartered in 1819 and opened in 1825, and the Sage of Monticello highly favored election. It had also caught the interest of George Ticknor of Harvard in 1825; of Francis Wayland, president of Brown University, in 1842; later of F. A. P. Barnard of the University of Alabama, later of the University of Mississippi, and later still of Columbia University, and others. In his inaugural address Eliot had pointed out that only a few years before, all students who were graduated from that institution had passed through the same curriculum.

[7] *So You're Going to College* (New York: Simon & Schuster, 1940), pp. 28-45. "You don't have to be a mental giant with consistent A-plus grades to get some scholarships."

Every man studied the same subjects in the same proportions, without regard to his natural bent or preference. The individual student had no choice
of either subjects or teachers. The system is still the prevailing system among
American colleges and finds vigorous defenders. It has the merit of simplicity.
So had the school methods of our grandfathers—one primer, one catechism,
one rod for all children. On the whole, a single common course of studies,
tolerably well selected to meet the average needs, seems to most Americans
a very proper and natural thing, even for grown men.

Then Eliot launched into a justification of the elective system, the
principles of which, he said, had been "gradually developed in this
college during the past forty years." While the liberty of choice at
Harvard was then wide, its limits were still too rigid, Eliot thought.
By 1900 Harvard had made everything elective except English, a
change that led Samuel Eliot Morison, official historian of that institution, to write in 1936: "It is a hard saying, but Mr. Eliot, more
than any other man, is responsible for the greatest educational crime
against American youth—depriving him of his classical heritage." [8]
Cornell's policy was for almost complete election, and great significance was seen in Yale's provision for complete election in the senior
year around 1900. Whether to go to the elective system [9] was being
as widely discussed in 1900 as "general education" or education in
general was fifty years later.

The place of the private or independent institution for higher
education was a lively issue around 1900 as it was at mid-twentieth
century, when it had become increasingly clear that, while the colleges
and universities had fresh problems, most of them were persistently
enduring. At the meeting of the National Educational Association
in 1900, two prominent leaders of higher education had discussed the
subject of the private educational institution; and on the same day,
in early 1950, two distinguished presidents of two eminent independent universities were discussing the same subject. While the
history of higher education in the United States prior to 1870 had
been the history of the small college, after that date, and particularly
after 1900, and more particularly after the First World War, many
institutions developed with huge and by 1950 with phenomenal enrollments. In 1950 there were 2.5 million students in the institu-

[8] *Three Centuries of Harvard* (Cambridge: Harvard University Press, 1936), pp.
389, 390.
[9] See R. Freeman Butts, *The College Charts Its Course* (New York: McGraw-
Hill Book Co., 1939), especially Part III: "The Elective Principle Wins the Day."
Also see R. L. Duffus, *Democracy Enters College* (New York: Chas. Scribner's
Sons, 1936), especially chap. iv: "Let Freedom Ring: The Elective System." Also,
Edgar W. Knight, "Some Early Discussions of the College Curriculum," *The South
Atlantic Quarterly*, XXXIV (1935), pp. 60-78.

tions for higher education of the United States and more than one tenth (280 thousand) were in ten universities. Fifty years earlier, many persons seemed to believe that the small institutions "would soon have no place in the educational economy." At the meeting of the National Educational Association in Charleston, S. C., in 1900, William O. Thompson, president of the Ohio State University, said that there was no disguising the fact that there was "a widespread feeling that the small college has seen its best days" and that there had grown up a sentiment "that the place to educate a boy is in a large crowd. It looks very much as if, in the popular mind, mere bigness was a virtue and littleness a vice."

Thompson pointed out that the criticism of the small college, by inference if not by direct statement, was both unfair and untrue. He thought it not fair to reflect upon the only institutions in the United States which, prior to 1870 or later, had fostered higher education in this country. Moreover, he asserted that the test of greatness of an educational institution was the ability to meet "the emergencies of the hour." He thought the small college had done so in the past as well as the large college or university was doing it in 1900. The larger institutions were young, and "their real value and efficiency are still problematical." The small college had placed important emphasis upon personal contacts between the student and the professors; it had cultivated a respect for scholarship, although no great scholarship was always possible within the limits of a small college, but the honest college had never made pretensions on this point. Scholarship was "the ripe fruit of years of patient toil." Also, the small college had "done great service for its immediate vicinage." Even in 1900 Harvard was still drawing a considerable portion of its students from the immediate vicinity.

At the same meeting in Charleston, William Rainey Harper, president of the University of Chicago, discussed the prospects of the small college and pointed out the basis of belief in its advantages: opportunity of close contact of students and teachers; the higher rank of teachers in the small colleges, while in the larger institutions students were turned over to tutors or instructors; opportunity in small colleges for students to develop responsibility—these beliefs, "in large measure fancied or sentimental, had taken a strong hold upon the public mind." Moreover, the small college was loved and cherished partly because it was small and weak, while the larger institutions were "hated and opposed" because they were powerful. This, said Harper, had been the history of every institution that had become great. He also said that the tradition of this country had been in favor of the small college, in part because of the religious purpose and denominational control with which most of the small colleges stood connected.

Some of the conditions which he thought stood in the way of the development of the small colleges were the modern high school; the decline of sectarianism; the increasing tendency toward specialism; the increase in professional schools; the development of the idea of the university; and the personnel of the faculty—the difficulty of getting the ablest men to work on small salaries in a small college. By 1900 also, the habit of students to move from one institution to another was gaining ground. Migration from the large to the small institutions was comparatively rare, but the migration from small colleges to larger institutions was increasing. In the South and West, the growth of the state university was tending to pinch the small colleges, and there were increasing outcries that state universities were pagan and anti-Christian, and that the students in those institutions were under evil and powerful influences. The facts, however, did not support these charges, Harper said. Lack of financial resources was, after all, one of the greatest difficulties facing the small colleges around the turn of the century. That was also a serious difficulty facing small colleges in 1950. Only 66 per cent of the institutions for higher education in this country, Harper said, had in 1900 more than 150 students, but the number with endowments of less than $100 thousand was reported appallingly large. These were some of the difficulties which confronted the small college in 1900.

Thirty-three years later, President Nicholas Murray Butler pointed to the overvaulting ambition of educational institutions that pretended to be something they were not. He said in his report of 1933: "Nothing is easier than for a college in this country to call itself a university, even though it has not the first characteristic of university organization, method, or ideal. All it need have is ambition to be something which it is not and cannot be." Statistics on higher education, whether official or unofficial, were "wholly meaningless for comparison with statistics in other countries, owing to the lack of any clearly thought out and sound method of classifying institutions of higher education according to their real character rather than according to their self-assumed names." He noted that in that year the *World Almanac* listed 579 universities and colleges in the United States, the United States Bureau of Education listed 567, and the *Statesman's Year Book* listed 1,078.

Harper believed in 1900 that some of the small colleges should be strengthened. The small college was an expression of the American spirit, and unless fundamental change took place in that spirit, there was no reason to suppose the time would ever come when

. . . under proper conditions, there will not be a function and a mission for the smaller institutions. Whatever might be the development of the university spirit, however strong the work of professional education shall come to be, the need of the other kind of institution will continue to exist and to grow; and if only the means may be secured for providing the proper facilities, the work and standing of such colleges will be increased and the advantages of such work will be unchallenged.

In their struggle for existence, however, some of the small colleges might be compelled to become academies or preparatory schools. Many of them at that time were doing work little removed from that of academies, which meant that the term "college" had been misappropriated. The educational and financial resources of many of the small institutions were not sufficient for collegiate work. Harper predicted that 25 per cent of the small colleges in 1900 would survive and would be stronger because of their struggle to survive, but that another 25 per cent would "yield to the inevitable" and would take places in educational work which, "while in one sense lower, is in a true sense higher. It is surely a higher thing to do honest and thorough work in a lower field than to fall short of such work in a higher field."

Harper said that some of the smaller institutions should become junior colleges; there were, he said, at least two hundred

in which this change would be desirable. These institutions have a preparatory school as well as a college course. The number of students in the preparatory school is perhaps a hundred and fifty. In the freshman and sophomore classes they have thirty to forty students, and in the junior and senior classes twenty to thirty. The annual income of these institutions is restricted for the most part to the fees of the students, and will average from all sources, let us say, eight to ten thousand dollars. In order to keep up the name of the college, the income is made to cover the expenses of eight years—that is, the preparatory and the collegiate departments. In order to do the work of the junior and senior years of the college, even superficially, where the classes are so small, as much of the total income is spent upon the instruction during these two years as upon that of the five years below. It is evident that, even with this disproportionate expenditure, the work of the junior and senior college years can be done only in a superficial way because the library and laboratory facilities are meager, the range of instruction is very narrow, and a single instructor is often required to teach in three or four subjects.

But this is not the most significant fact. When the money paid by the students of the first six years has been used for instruction of a few men who are working in the last two years, in order that the college may continue to be known as a college, there does not remain sufficient income to do justice to the work of the lower years. This is an attempt to do higher work at the cost of the lower. Nor are examples of this kind limited to states in the West and South. More than one instance will be found in the state of New York, while in Pennsylvania and Ohio, Indiana, and Michigan such institutions abound.

The reduction of institutions of this class to the rank of colleges which shall do, in addition to the preparatory work, only the work of the freshman and sophomore years, will accomplish several results:

1. The money now wasted in doing the higher work superficially could be used to do the lower work more thoroughly.

2. The pretense of giving a college education would be given up, and the college could become an honest institution.

3. The student who was not really fitted by nature to take the higher work could stop naturally and honorably at the end of the sophomore year.

4. Many students who might not have the courage to enter upon a course of four years' study would be willing to do the two years of work before entering business or the professional school.

5. Students capable of doing the higher work would be forced to go away from the small college to the university. This change would in every case be most advantageous.

6. Students living near the college, whose ambition it was to go away to college, could remain at home until greater maturity had been reached—a point of the highest moment in these days of strong temptation.

The substitution of the six-year institution, including the academic or high-school course, for the present four-year institution, without preparatory work, would, at one stroke, touch the greatest evils of our present situation.

Harper also predicted in 1900 that another change would appear in the development of high schools into junior colleges. This change was already taking place, the establishment of high schools throughout the country being "a new element in our educational machinery which has disarranged the former systems but which has at the same time greatly advanced the interest of education itself. The quickening influence of these institutions is seen not only in the increased number of those who continue their work in the college and the university, nor merely in the fact that a larger number of more intelligent men and women are thus contributed to the various communities, but especially in the fact that the teachers of the schools of a lower grade are vastly stronger and better prepared for their work."

At this time the suggestion was being made that the people would not continue to support public high schools, but Harper noted that they were continuing to support them and that these high schools were constantly increasing their requirements for admission, as well as their facilities for instruction and the length of the curriculum. It was generally recognized that the good high school must have a curriculum of four years, and in some sections of the United States this had been provided.

The next step in the development of this work will be the addition of one or two years to the present courses or, in other words, the carrying of the high school up to the end of the sophomore college year. Already this has practically been accomplished in certain schools in Michigan and in some of our cities. It can be done at the minimum of cost. Today only 10 per cent of those who finished the high school continue the work in college. If the high school were to provide work for two additional years, at least 40 per cent of those finishing the first four years would continue to the end of the sophomore year.

This argument was being made again at the middle of the twentieth century, as it had often been made since 1900. At that time there was wide interest in the "community college," and the rapid growth of this type of institution throughout the United States was very impressive. The United States Office of Education reported in 1950 that 150 colleges had been established since 1948, and the largest number of these were junior or "community colleges" or post-high school institutions. There were then in the United States 500 two-year colleges with enrollments of 500 thousand students. In 1940 enrollments in junior colleges had numbered only 200 thousand. Earl J. McGrath, United States Commissioner of Education, predicted in 1950 that the junior college would take the lead in the movement of an unprecedented growth in higher educational facilities in that decade, and said that by 1960 the number of junior colleges would reach a thousand.

Harper was inclined to criticize the small college because it was everywhere practically the same; every college was a duplicate of its nearest neighbor. "A terrible monotony presents itself to the eye of one who makes any attempt to study the aims and motives of these institutions. All alike try to cover too much ground and, worse than this, all alike practically cover the same ground. A change in this respect is desirable and inevitable. This change will come partly in the way of establishment of colleges for particular purposes; a college, for example, established principally for the study of science; another college established principally for the study of literature; another for the study principally of historical subjects. The principle of individualism, which has already been applied in education to the work of the student and to the work of the instructor, must find application to the work of the institution."

True, the elective system was sweeping the colleges of the country and also finding its way into secondary education; but within a few decades higher education was destined to return somewhat to a measure of prescription, although not as fully as the collegiate curriculum had been prior to 1870. Another prophecy or promise which has remained unfulfilled was Harper's statement that "a further change will be the development of a spirit of cooperation." Apparently, however, not cooperation but competition was to increase among institutions for higher education, although, beginning in the latter part of the nineteenth century, the regional standardizing and accrediting associations had been formed in the interest of cooperation among colleges and between the colleges and secondary schools.

Eight years after Thompson and Harper were talking about higher education in the United States, Robert K. Risk, a graduate of the University of Glasgow, wrote:

No review of American university conditions can be complete unless some attention is given to the small college. There are in the States 622 universities, colleges, and technical schools.... But when full allowance has been made for technical schools, for universities of secondary rank, and for large colleges on the way to become universities, there is a residue of some 400 small colleges scattered all over the country. Of the total, no fewer than 160 have an average of less than 150 students. So it is evident that the small colleges are an important factor in American higher education. Many of them are narrowly sectarian, and others resemble boarding schools both in spirit and in educational standards. But a typical small college of good standing, free from sectarian influences and prejudices, presents many points of interest.[10]

Continuing, Risk wrote:

There are, of course, many colleges which attempt to give a full arts curriculum, including even laboratory courses and advanced classes, upon an income only sufficient to maintain half a dozen competent instructors. There are countless institutions calling themselves colleges, and granting degrees, although their educational capacity is as limited as their spirit is narrow. Probably about a quarter of the colleges of the United States are doing work no higher than that of our secondary schools. You may find a college, whose charter—possibly one of forty years ago—is thoroughly authentic, which has a library of only 1000 volumes, laboratories whose equipment prob-

10 *America at College: As Seen by A Scots Graduate* (Glasgow: John Smith & Son, 1908), pp. 83, 84.

ably did not cost £200, and an income, from all sources and for all purposes, of some £1500 a year. And there is the lower depth of the freak college, which perhaps calls itself a university on its note paper. There are sectarian colleges "where a man may not teach the difference between the subjunctive and the optative mood in the Greek language if he is not sound as to the inspiration of the Book of Job or as to the government of the Church in New Padua." Many of the obscure little colleges are struggling vainly for an existence threatened by the state Universities. Witness the following advertisement from a recent number of the New York *Outlook:*

> College for Sale. Whole or half interest, presidency included. Annual net income $5000. 8218 *Outlook.*

There are colleges where the "Faculty" is drawn entirely from the members of one family, and where one duty of the "President" is to inspect the trunks of students periodically in search of contraband. At some of the Western colleges, there is an academic regulation which forbids freshmen to carry bowie knives and revolvers. And here is an exact copy of the heading on the note paper used by one college president: "Christian University. For Ladies and Gentlemen. College of Arts and Sciences. College of the Bible. Business College. Conservatory of Music. Correspondence Bible School. Faculty Strong. Instruction Thorough. Curriculum Full. Expenses Light." In the case of another college, the applicant for a "Professorship" has to answer these printed questions: "On about how many days in the past year was unable to do full work? On about how many days in the past year, was medicine taken? How long a Christian? Has taught in Sunday School? Has led prayer meetings? Uses wine or liquor? Uses tobacco? Belongs to a secret society? Who can testify as to success in Christian work?" . . . This glance at the freak college may instruct as well as amuse. It serves to illustrate the difficulty of defining "the democratic spirit" which is so often cited in the States as the explanation of what seems incredible, and the apology for what ought to be impossible.[11]

Risk noticed that the American college student was largely engrossed in the social side of collegiate life, and he noted that at Princeton, for example, success or failure in college was bound up for many students with election to the most desirable senior clubs. The other burning interest for the majority of students was athletics; and the passion for spectacular games of football and baseball had reached such a pitch "a few years ago, and the former game had become so honeycombed with veiled professionalism, underhand tactics, and methods of calculated brutality, that a strong reaction set in." The University of Michigan had found it necessary "to limit the number of matches in order to get any work done between them,"

[11] *Ibid.,* pp. 95, 96.

and in many institutions freshmen were barred from the teams to prevent "the importation of disguised professionals." The collegiate athlete, Risk said, had to make some show in his classwork to be kept in college, but this rule was "interpreted with considerable lenience when the reputation of the institution was at stake, and the value of athletic fame as an advertisement was still an important factor in the situation." He was impressed also with the organized applause at games which struck him

... not only as a novelty, but as something grotesque and infantile. When the Princeton team scored or distinguished themselves otherwise, the leader of applause stood up next to the touch-line, faced the stand, and collected the attention of his forces, just as the conductor of an orchestra does. Then with different gesticulations of his arms, each appropriate to a section of the cheer, he led the youths through the devotional rendering of the college yell.

Risk, however, saw in the colleges and universities of the United States some admonition for institutions for higher education in Scotland. He thought that Scotland could learn something from the practices of libraries in American universities which were open "from early morn until late at night" and were freely accessible. The open door and the open shelf and the departmental library for the use of individual classes and seminars he viewed as admirable features of higher education in this country. He said that the Scotch universities were still in bondage to the misconception that the primary duty of a librarian was to protect the books from the students, in contrast to the American conception that his primary duty was to keep books in circulation and see that they were used to the fullest extent, and that every student had the greatest possible facility in using the library. He also commented on "compulsory physical culture" in the American colleges which, however, had been

... badly bitten by the anthropometric craze, and there was a tendency to measure the efficiency of rival institutions according to biceps instead of brains—a tendency illustrated, with regard to athletics, in the remark of a New York parent that if Harvard whopped again at football, he guessed his boy would be sent to Yale. Anthropometricism as a cult has passed, I believe; but the excessive attention has stimulated gymnastics in two ways. Physical culture was found necessary to develop the footballer to his full pitch, and also to keep him in training through the winter; the gymnasium was also all that was left of athletics for the general body of the students, since the training of the teams, and of the squads from which they are drawn, monopolized all attention.

Risk noted that the enormous material resources of higher educational institutions in the United States, which were organized upon most practical lines, "with all the energy and confidence of a new nation," had not yet begun "to produce scholars." Their main interest was in providing "professional and technical education." A professor in Johns Hopkins remarked that American undergraduates were not supposed, upon entering college, to know much "of the world's history prior to the birth of George Washington," and said to Risk: "By the way, you come from Glasgow. Your university is about thirty years old, isn't it?" Risk replied: "My university was founded about half a century before Columbus discovered America." Risk said that in spite of its youth, the American university produced a type of graduate "whose conspicuous characteristics of frankness, hospitality to strangers, readiness to take any amount of trouble on their behalf, and a charm of manner, which the nonacademic American so frequently lacks.... It is a great country, America. In university matters, as in social and political affairs, it does not know where it is going; but it is determined to get there."

Five years after Thompson and Harper, and three years before Risk discussed higher education in the United States, James Bryce commented on the subject. Ambassador from Great Britain to the United States from 1907 to 1913, Bryce had a wide and sympathetic acquaintance with this country and was universally regarded in the United States as the foremost expositor and critic of American institutions, customs, manners, and traits. His distinguished work, *The American Commonwealth,* which had appeared in 1888, proved to be one of the most thorough and penetrating studies ever made of this country. In 1905 Bryce published in the *Outlook* [12] an essay under the title, "America Revisited: The Changes of a Quarter Century," in which he reported some of the changes he had observed. Among those that impressed him most were the prodigious material development of the United States; its swift industrial growth; the remarkable increase in economic wealth and in population; the huge fortunes that had been amassed; the extraordinary absence of pauperism, by comparison with European countries; and the comfort and ease of life for the workingman as well as for others. He noticed that the "easier life" did not mean, however, that life was taken more easily, but in having and spending more money and not doing less work. The stress and rush of life seemed greater than ever before; "everybody, from the workman to the millionaire, had a larger head of steam on than his father had." Time seemed

[12] March 25 and April 1.

more precious, and more pains were taken to save it, and more work was squeezed into the hour and the day. More than ever before, wealth had come to mean power, business was king and had come to overshadow all other activities, and in various new forms had come to make itself felt in politics. Labor unions had strengthened their organization, following the efforts at combination "which the lords of production and distribution" had been making, while the consumer stood by "if not with folded hands, yet so far with no clear view as to the steps which he may take for his own protection." Bryce thought that the consumer's own prosperity at the beginning of the century had helped to make him acquiescent. But long before the first half of the twentieth century had come to a close, relief from the sad plight of the consumer had been sought in American high schools through courses in "consumer education."

Within the years from 1870 to 1905, Bryce observed "a development of the higher education in the United States without a parallel in the world." There were, he said, fifteen or twenty institutions of higher learning "fit to be ranked beside the universities of Germany, France, and England as respects the completeness of the instruction which they provide and the thoroughness at which they aim." He observed ample provision for the study "of those arts in which science is applied to practical ends." In this respect, institutions of higher learning in the United States had gone ahead of Great Britain by reason of larger funds and the increasing "generosity of private benefactors." Along with wide improvement in the range and the quality of higher education had gone great increase in enrollments—greater than the growth of the population—and more and more students were choosing careers in business, in banking, manufacturing, and commerce instead of the professions which were the choices of most students in English universities. Bryce also reported that it was commonly believed in the United States that a "liberal education" was an asset to businessmen, that a young man was "all the more likely to succeed in business if he goes to it with a mind widely and thoroughly trained."

Bryce believed that this feature of American civilization had a very significant bearing on the national life of the country—a sort of antidote to and a balance for the increasingly intense passion "for material progress." The social influence was also important. Graduates, he said, became attached to their colleges and universities, became interested in their fortunes, contributed funds to support them, joined the university clubs which were appearing in many cities as centers of political and social action, and the members were taking active parts in movements for municipal reforms. But the people of the United States, Bryce observed, were not reading serious books as they had in the 1870's when readers were less numerous and less wealthy than they were in 1905. This condition was due in part "to that sense of hurry which makes the ordinary American little disposed to sit down to work his way through a book." It was also due to another recent change, "the passion for looking on at and reading about athletic sports." This new taste in the United States had grown to such vast proportions as to occupy the minds of students, their parents and friends, and the public generally. Baseball and football "matches" excited "an interest greater than any other public events except the Presidential election, and that comes only once in four years."

Twenty-seven years after Bryce and twenty-four years after Risk were writing on the absorbing interest athletics attracted in this country, Henry S. Pritchett, a former president of the Carnegie Foundation for the Advancement of Teaching, whose *Bulletin Number 23* on *American College Athletics* had stirred the colleges of the United States in 1929, playfully proposed in the *Atlantic Monthly* [13] that intercollegiate horse racing be substituted for intercollegiate football so that the players could be released for the pursuit of learning and the bootlegging alumnus could be curbed. "Think what a pot of money a Harvard-Yale horse race would take in!" he exclaimed. Eighteen years later, Marshall Smith and Richard Oulahan, Jr., wrote that intercollegiate football had gone so "big time" that it was "pricing itself out of business," but that for an annual outlay of $275 thousand, not counting the cost of the players and "other hidden expenses," any American college "can have a flashy, bigtime football team." At some institutions the price was a half million a year and, like other academic commodities, was still increasing in cost. [14] In the summer of 1951, when the country was shocked by cheating in examinations at the United States Military Academy, which involved members of its powerful football team, the scandal was attributed in part by some critics to commercialism in the popular intercollegiate sport.

In 1950 questions not altogether unlike those of 1900 were being raised about higher education under private or independent support and control. On the same day in early February of 1950, the presidents of two eminent privately controlled universities dealt some-

[13] Vol. CL (October, 1932), pp. 446-48.
[14] *Life,* October 16, 1950, p. 69. See editorial in the same magazine for September 17, 1951, under the title "Football is a Farce," on the several scandals in basketball, and in football at West Point.

what pessimistically with the future of such institutions. A. Hollis Edens, president of Duke University, said to the Duke Alumni Club of Washington, D. C., that his institution was no longer a rich institution in terms of the cost of operating a great university, and that its present major task "was to provide sufficient funds to do the job. We talked rich a long time. We were a little institution suddenly endowed with great money. Today we are no longer rich. We are talking poor," he said, as he made a strong plea for the support of all private institutions of higher education and declared, as a spokesman in a campaign to raise twelve million dollars for Duke, "It would be a sad day in the United States if private education were squeezed out of business. The United States probably has more privately endowed institutions than it will be able to preserve. Some of them must die. It is our duty to see a sufficient number maintained to do the job ahead." Funds were needed for salaries sufficient to get and retain able professors and to bring into the institution young men of high promise. "We have not kept up in the race of spiraling costs, although we were once ahead in the race for faculty members in the Southeast." Funds were also sadly needed, he said, for buildings and for scholarships, fellowships, and research. "The job of the university today is to train men not so much for vocation but for leadership tomorrow."

At the same time, and a few months before he was to retire from the presidency of Yale University where he had served with great distinction since 1911, for many years as teacher and from 1937 as president, President Charles Seymour warned that privately endowed universities would surely disappear unless they matched the sense of responsibility that state universities had assumed for the welfare of the community. He said that the great state universities and their sensitivity to the needs of the communities of which they were vital parts "provide a challenging example of service for the privately endowed universities. It is important to note that their contributions to the higher learning are of the first order, and their influence in the educational world is steadily increasing." He also said that the state universities "can offer much which lies beyond our competitive efforts, but we have our own peculiar values, the disappearance of which would be the nation's loss. We must be careful to put them at the nation's service.... If we prove our worth, our freedom will not disappear. The price of freedom is service."

At least hinted at here was one of the deadly afflictions that had long characterized higher education in this country, competition. Another characteristic had long been imitation, the apparent effort of colleges and universities to promise to do too many things, and as Charles Dollard, president of the Carnegie Corporation of New York, said in his report for 1949, "to be all things to all men." There appeared all along enough for all the reputable institutions to do, without cutthroat competition and blind imitation or institutional jealousies. When Harry W. Chase was inaugurated as president of the University of North Carolina in 1920, William Louis Poteat, president of Wake Forest College, brought greetings from the other institutions of the state. "Competition?" he asked. "A lady standing on the beach quite ready for the surf explained why she did not go in by saying, 'Another lady is using the ocean.' "

As the second quarter of the twentieth century was closing, many thoughtful persons who saw public support and control of education gradually gaining monopoly were asking the question: "Can private schools survive?" This monopoly had been gained first in elementary education, then in the latter part of the past century and the early part of the present it was substantially gained in secondary education, and there were increasing signs and anxieties that it would eventually extend to higher education. The question was asked in *Harper's Magazine* in its issue of January, 1948, by Russell Lynes who inquired about the future of the independent schools, meaning chiefly the secondary schools, and raised some significant issues about the question. Anyone, he said, who had discussed private schools with public school people found that this question seemed to go beyond matters of the independence of the private schools. If there were no private schools, and if those parents who expend their money and influence on them had to send their children to public schools, would not all public education receive benefit? he asked. Would not those parents become more interested in the quality of education in the public schools and bring pressure to bear to have those schools provide that quality, and would not this reform improve the educational opportunities of all the children of this country?

Lynes believed that this would be the outcome, that the level of education would be raised where appreciable numbers of children were sent away for their education, and that the public schools could do almost anything educationally "if they had the financial support and intelligent backing of the whole community. But few communities (especially the small ones) could afford to have special schools, or even special classes, for the ablest boys and girls. It would be the wealthy suburbs that would benefit first if there were no private schools, and some city school districts in which well-to-do families live." But this raised another question. Would not these special schools or a limited number of better schools in the more favored communities cause a social problem similar to that which the private schools had created, that of special educational privilege of the well to do? Mr. Lynes also thought that there is often confusion between the idea or ideal of equal education for each and everyone and equal educational *opportunity* for each and everyone. He saw peril in any educational system "that tends toward intellectual leveling off, and it is a mistake to think that intellectual leveling off of this sort is democratic. We need a variety of *kinds* of schools as a means of stimulating not merely intellectual growth but also inventiveness and the kind of intellectual independence that is basic to our society. Numerically insignificant as they are, the independent schools can provide an important element in this variety." If the level of education can be raised only from the top, as Frank Aydelotte was quoted as saying,

Then there is a place for schools, free of political and other pressures, that have the resources with which to experiment, teachers who are well paid, and the advantages of a high degree of selectivity among their pupils. The problem is to make the independent schools as good as they claim to be (and this they can do only for themselves); to make them available to those who most deserve them and who will benefit most; and to make them responsible, not only to their closed group, but for the betterment of public education as well.

But he did see that "profound" changes in society, since the prime days of these independent schools

. . . have made them seem as much of an anachronism as the governess in her black frilled cap. The schools are too close to their own problems to see how tradition-bound they appear from the outside, not merely to those who have regarded them with suspicion for years but to many who would like to patronize them but who distrust the imprint which they leave. They are too used to their comforts and luxuries, their often elaborate buildings, or their trappings that emanate decaying refinement, to see that these things have little to do with education and a great deal to do with the spirit that could be their undoing.

There was nothing wrong with their basic aims and ideals and the variety of education these independent schools offered, but if they were to justify themselves, "they had to use their independence not merely as a barricade against the pressures they mistrust but as weapon in the service of the entire community." [15]

15 For further discussion of this question of the private school see "The Function of Secondary Education in the United States" in *School and Society*, September 23, 1950; and in the same magazine for September 8, 1951, on "The Functions of Independent Secondary Education in the United States," statements by the National Council of Independent Schools.

The Economic Value of an Academic Degree.—The almost blind faith of the American people in the economic value of a college education had by 1950 produced a condition that apparently had not been seriously contemplated in 1900: What effect would the mass production of holders of academic degrees have on the American economy? At mid-century, college graduates were finding that their most difficult job of all was the job of finding jobs, and there was much discussion of the subject. A dispatch from Washington in March of 1950 pointed out that for thousands of young people finishing school and looking for jobs that year, the hardest job of all would be to find a job. According to the estimates of the Bureau of Employment Security of the Department of Labor, graduates in 1950 would face the keenest competition for jobs since the early 1940's. The country's economy was not developing new "job opportunities as fast as the schools were preparing young people for their first jobs." To help newcomers to the labor market, a "Job Guide for Young Workers" had been prepared and made available to employment offices. Although many jobs suitable for graduates would be available, newcomers would have to work harder to get them because they would be competing with each other and also with large numbers of unemployed young people already in the labor market. The most numerous jobs available for young graduates were not "in glamour occupations and industries nor in jobs that necessarily require high degrees of skill and training. For the most part they are entry jobs requiring little experience but which offer opportunities for ambitious workers to get started in industry." One of the more important "white-collar" jobs that called for a relatively large number of beginners was that of stenographer, about 200 thousand secretaries, stenographers, and typists being needed annually in business, industry, and the professions. Beauticians would find prospects of employment tougher than in former years "because home beauty aids are reducing the need for beauty operators." Opportunities for young women who had training and wished to be practical nurses and nurse's aids were reported especially good. The total of 41.7 million industrial and commercial jobs was 1.4 million below that of the previous year.

Following the report in 1947 of the President's Commission on Higher Education, which proposed for 1960 an enrollment of 4.6 million students in the institutions for higher education of this country, Seymour E. Harris, professor of economics of Harvard, published "Millions of B.A.'s, But No Jobs," [16] a prospect that had disturbing

[16] *New York Times Magazine,* January 2, 1949.

implications. At the beginning of 1949 collegiate enrollments were about 2.5 millions, but there seemed to have been common agreement among leaders in higher education that the institutions would enroll 3 million by the early 1950's. In 1949 there were more than ten times as many students in colleges as in 1900, and the President's Commission proposed "to double the present output of college graduates within another twenty years," an increase proportionately much greater than the gain in the general population of the country. It was predicted from enrollments in 1949 that at least 10 million would have collegiate diplomas by the 1960's, and two decades later perhaps 15 million, about four times the number of 1949. Harris did not have difficulty in envisioning "a college-bred population of 30 million or even 45 million if one counts all those who have had as much as two years of college. Indeed, if all the recommendations of the President's Commission were carried out, the time would come when we would be confronted with a college-graduate population with as much as 25 to 30 per cent of the nation's labor force." He also pointed out that if it is assumed that in the 1960's collegiate men and women would be seeking the same kinds of employment and in the same proportion as these were sought in 1940, there "would be far more graduates than jobs."

The outlook in the professions was also dark. On the proposed increase in collegiate graduates, seven million people with collegiate diplomas would be looking for jobs in the professions by the 1960's—"a horde of would-be professional workers about four times as great as the number of professional jobs filled by college graduates in 1940." Of course a large proportion of these would be teachers, but he thought it certain "that most of them would not find teaching jobs of any kind. . . . It would require a revolution in finance to increase teaching staffs by a mere 50 per cent within the next twenty years. Even then only three sevenths of the anticipated number of teachers would be able to find jobs in the profession."

In 1940 there were about 338 thousand scientists in this country. If the Commission's proposals should be carried out, the total of scientists would run up to about 942 thousand within the next twenty years. This figure included engineers, and the Commission itself pointed out that engineers faced "a saturated market by 1950."

There were 180 thousand lawyers in the United States in 1940, but under the proposed expanded collegiate program, at least 860 thousand people trained in the law could be expected by the 1960's. These estimates were based on the assumption that collegiate people "would choose the same profession in the same ratio that they did in 1940." Many persons might be discouraged from entering the crowded professions, and economic conditions might keep some students away from college or control their choice of a profession.

Yet, after all allowances are made and exceptions noted, we could still expect an outpouring of college graduates into an economy which probably would not be prepared to receive them. If there are basic changes due in the economy which would eliminate the problem, one cannot imagine what they are.

What would be the result of a rapidly expanding proletariat of the A.B. and the Ph.D.? Obviously any new outpouring of young hopefuls, with their special brand of aspiration and disillusionment, is of vital importance to the American economy as well as to the college graduate himself. If American colleges and universities doubled or tripled their output within the course of a generation, it would be a significant social change. The change has already begun to occur.

For many years the economic value of education had been stressed in the United States. Most people seemed to believe that it paid to go to school, despite the lessons of the depression that began in 1929. Professor Harris warned against putting so much emphasis on the monetary value of a collegiate education, and he urged that more emphasis be put

. . . on the intangible social and cultural values to be derived from learning. The time may be coming when he [the college student] will have to start accepting the idea that education is life, not merely a preparation for it. As John Dewey put it, "Living has its own intrinsic quality and the business of education is with that quality." In any case, the graduates of the next generation will have to find more and more justification for their college education on other than economic grounds.... The boy or girl preparing for college has a right to know what to expect.

In another work [17] Harris elaborated this thesis, and predicted that by 1969 there would be in the United States three college graduates for every job which they were prepared to fill.

Increasing Cost of Higher Education.—The high and increasing costs of higher education in the 1940's and at mid-century were causing many fiscal anxieties and the searching of hearts by trustees, presidents and deans, and their constituencies. The direction of costs had continued upward as the first half of the twentieth century was closing. In 1940 the average cost per student for the entire United States was reported at approximately $375; in 1947

[17] *The Market for College Graduates* (Cambridge: Harvard University Press, 1950).

the figure was reported at approximately $470 and was still rising. Part of the rise was due to the increasing level of prices generally, and part was caused by the growing needs for expanded facilities to carry forward the higher educational program required by the increase in students who as never before were flocking into the colleges and universities. The rising trend in costs was felt by the colleges and universities more severely than by business and industry which could more readily change their prices and more easily increase their income. But the colleges and universities had to do the best they could in order to keep the higher education system of the country from disintegrating or collapsing entirely.[18] If reports could be believed, American higher education at mid-century faced its greatest fiscal crisis and also its heaviest test of merit.

John Price Jones [19] pointed out in 1948 that great pools of wealth may be disappearing, but that the day of the big gift had not yet gone. Gifts by corporations were widening and could be expected to become "an ever-greater factor." There was also an increase in "mass giving," as shown by the great increase in community chests. He thought that the next decade should see philanthropic gifts increase, barring economic dislocation, war, or political disturbances. This prediction or expectation was based on the records of philanthropy in the recent past. Jones estimated that the needs "in a few of the major areas of philanthropy" for the next ten years would be [as shown below], above the annual amounts then being contributed.

Higher education	$100 million a year
Secondary education	$ 44 million a year
Hospitals	$500 million a year
Medical education	$4.5 million a year
Social work	$100 million a year
Religion	$105 million a year

He said that it would require "no great courage to forecast that in the next ten years American philanthropy will be called upon for an increase of at least one billion a year, making the total given away each year over four billions of dollars."

Records of philanthropic giving in the recent past, on which Jones based his prediction or expectation, were impressive. The total of

[18] For the proposals for federal aid to higher education see *Higher Education for American Democracy*. A Report of the President's Commission on Higher Education. Vol. V: "Financing Higher Education." Washington, D. C.: Government Printing Office, 1947.

[19] *The Yearbook of Philanthropy, 1947-48* (New York: The Inter-River Press, 1948), pp. 4, 5.

such giving in the 1940's was more than three billions a year, as against two and one half billions in the 1930's. In the 1940's the money came from the following sources:

From persons who filed income tax returns	$2,575,000,000
From persons not required to pay income tax	26,000,000
From corporations	266,000,000
From foundations	72,000,000
From charitable bequests	202,000,000
From gifts of property by individuals	37,000,000
	$3,178,000,000

Philanthropy, it was pointed out in *The Yearbook of Philanthropy* (page 45) was "the heavy artillery which the body politic is mobilizing in an attempt to maintain, in the face of a world-wide trend toward socialization, the thoroughly American institution of independent higher and professional education." There was a real contest between philanthropy and funds from public taxation for the support of these higher-education institutions, and philanthropy was being forced to assume responsibility, whether it liked it or not. The outcome of the contest would not be quickly decided "unless a war, which always accelerates social evolution, should occur in the next few years." Within two years the crisis in Korea had come.

Between 1945 and 1950, intensive efforts were made by most of the institutions for higher education in the United States to raise money for their varied and increasingly costly activities. In the 1920's they had received an annual average of about $52 million in bequests and gifts. In the 1930's the figure was about $42 million a year; in the first half of the 1940's they had received an annual average of about $43 million; in 1945-46 the figure was about $68 million; and in 1946-47 about $65 million.

In the period from 1920 to 1930 twelve private secondary schools received a total of more than $20 million in gifts and bequests, an annual average of about $2 million. In the decade of the 1930's the total these schools received was about $16 million, or an annual average of about $1.6 million. In the first half of the 1940's they received $4.14 million, or about $830 thousand a year. In 1945-46 the figure was $2.46 million, and the next year it was $2.29 million. The schools that seemed to be most highly favored with gifts and bequests were Phillips Andover and Phillips Exeter, the Hill School, the Lawrenceville School, and the Taft School.

While gifts to higher education had reached in 1950 what has been called "an unprecedented level," so also had expenses, which had greatly outrun income. Out of 630 private colleges from which information was had, one out of five was running deficits, and fiscal conditions in the academic year 1950-1951 were likely to be even more serious. Colleges with small endowments and large dependence on fees from students were facing an uncertain future. Everything academic had gone up in price, "from chalk to footballs," as Charles W. Cole, president of Amherst, was reported as saying. Chalk was up 30 per cent, footballs 59 per cent, steel desks 50 per cent. James Phinney Baxter, president of Williams, noted that even frogs used by teachers of biology had jumped from seventy-two cents to $2.25 a dozen. The costs of running a college campus had increased nearly 70 per cent since 1940.

Fear of Federal Control of Education.—A sharp issue discussed by the Association of American Colleges at its meeting in early 1950 was the need of federal scholarships for needy college students. Apparently, representatives of most of the colleges present favored such federal aid, according to an informal poll taken by a reporter for the *New York Times,* although many supported the proposal "with reservations" and insisted that any such federal funds should be made available directly to the students rather than to the institutions, "and with no strings attached, to avoid even a semblance of federal control." In his budget message in early January, President Truman had asked for a huge appropriation to begin a federal system of scholarships, and the United States Office of Education had outlined the policy of the administration which called for 400 thousand undergraduate scholarships and 37.5 thousand graduate and professional fellowships at a total annual cost of $400 million. In the proposal, provision was also to be made for private loans to students, limited to $1,200 but guaranteed by the government, to "supplement the direct grants."

Basic objection to the proposal for federal scholarships and fellowships came from those who feared increased "statism" and the "welfare state," or the control of education by bureaucracy in Washington. Among those who opposed the proposal was the executive director of the association (Guy E. Snavely) who saw in it an effort at federal control of higher education, and who said that a college education was already available to needy and ambitious students through scholarships under the control of the colleges and universities. He also asserted that large federal subsidies for scholarships would give young people the notion "that we must have a real welfare state where the government will not only guarantee a college education but furnish suitable and good-paying positions thereafter." The retiring president of the organization (Vincent J. Flynn) described the

proposed fellowships as "undemocratic and a form of class legislation," and he saw no reason "why ordinary people should be taxed
to give an education to those whose scholastic aptitude is higher than
the rest. Many of our useful citizens are persons who were far from
leading their class in college." It will be recalled that two members
of the President's Commission on Higher Education, that had reported in 1947 and had recommended federal funds for scholarships
and fellowships, had dissented from its recommendations on the
financing of higher education: Monsignor Frederick G. Hochwalt
and Martin R. P. McGuire.

On the other side of the issue at the meeting in 1950, Bryon S.
Hollinshead, president of Coe College, saw no danger in the program
so long as the scholarships and fellowships were granted to the students and not to the colleges and universities. Edgar C. Cummings,
dean of DePauw University, saw little if any danger of federal control; and Melva Lind, an officer of the American Association of
University Women, said that the program was necessary to equalize
educational opportunities in the United States.

At a meeting of the American College Public Relations Association at the Universtiy of Michigan in early July of 1950, the questions
of the survival of the independent or privately endowed college and
that of federal aid were again discussed in a lively manner. "What
hope is there for the smaller college?" asked the representative of
such an institution. "Where will we get the money to continue to
operate?" At about the same time, Oscar Ewing, federal security
administrator, said that the small colleges, almost without exception,
opposed federal aid. At Ann Arbor the question seemed at least
implicit: Were there too many colleges? "Would it do any harm
to close down many of the colleges, because too many persons are
going to college now?" On this point George Stoddard, president
of the University of Illinois, attacked the philosophy of Seymour
Harris of Harvard who had warned against an oversupply of college
graduates in the American economy. Stoddard thought that American democracy would be strengthened by doubling the number of
college students.

I don't think we need fear that the graduates will become disgruntled or
unhappy if they don't find the jobs they seek. The time is coming when a
general college education will be as common as a high-school education is
today. There is no reason why a bricklayer shouldn't be a college man. His
education would help him use his leisure time better, would help him to
understand some of the problems we face, and would make him a better voter
and citizen.

When Horace A. Hildreth became the ninth president of Bucknell University in 1950, he warned in his inaugural address against government control of all education and against the increasing demand for "giving a college education to everyone who has the ability to go to college." He thought that it "would be tragic if higher education became completely dependent upon government." [20]

Tax-exemption Privileges of Colleges.—A third issue that seemed very acute in higher education at mid-twentieth century had grown out of the tendency of colleges and universities to take advantage of their tax-exemption privileges to operate commercial enterprises in competition with business enterprises that had to pay taxes on their profits. The question was: Should an educational institution, in order to escape taxation, invest its funds in businesses that were generally subject to taxation? As already noted, institutions for higher education in the United States had found themselves financially up against it in the 1940's. Their fixed income had decreased because of lower rates of interest on endowments, enrollments of veterans were declining toward the end of that decade, and the operating expenses of the institutions were reaching levels that were unprecedentedly high. By the end of 1950 it was feared that "half the colleges in the country will be operating in the red—the colleges face their greatest financial crisis in fifty years." They had raised their tuition and fees about as high as possible without crowding out many students, and most of them seemed unwilling to seek a "handout" from the government. The temptation "to go into business" seemed to make a strong appeal in some cases, but there was warning that they should not engage in "unfair competition with private industry."

This issue was before the Association of American Universities in 1950 when recommendations were made on a report by a committee of distinguished educators headed by James R. Killian, Jr., president of the Massachusetts Institute of Technology. Other members were presidents C. W. Darden, Jr. of the University of Virginia, H. W. Dodds of Princeton University, T. S. Painter of the University of Texas, and H. E. Stassen of the University of Pennsylvania. The report of the committee emphasized that the future financial stability of institutions for higher education depended upon exemption from taxation on income or property used for educational purposes, and it asserted that "any impairment of the long-standing principle of tax exemption would be a fatal blow to the educational

[20] *New York Times,* April 30, 1950.

system." The committee saw as a critical need positive measures to conserve and increase the financial resources of the colleges and universities, but advised against the ownership and operation of business enterprises in which exemption from taxes might be claimed by an organization customarily subject to taxation. The committee recommended that the Association of American Universities try to get a change in the federal income tax law which would permit the charitable gifts of an individual in any year to be deducted above the 15 per cent limit. It also recommended that institutions for higher education seek alteration of laws in the various states so as to authorize businesses to make charitable donations.

The tradition and practices of the exemption of colleges and universities from various taxes had already led to some litigation which increasingly caused apprehension among both private and public institutions, and some of the decisions of courts were viewed as "a handwriting on the wall." [21] Under litigation over the issue whether publicly operated institutions should pay the federal tax on admissions to athletic contests, the Supreme Court of the United States, but in a divided opinion, had held in 1938 that the tax must be paid. Two justices dissented spiritedly and asserted that the state's immunity from federal taxation clearly ruled out such a tax. Charters of some of the older privately operated institutions had provided for exemption of their property from taxation, and the dispute became lively whether such exemptions could be removed or altered by statutory legislation subsequently enacted. In some cases the courts had held for exemption; but in the case of Phillips Exeter Academy, in New Hampshire, a state court held a somewhat different view. Chambers believed that if such a case should get to and be affirmed in Washington, it would have "significant consequences for a considerable number of the older privately controlled universities in several states, now enjoying permanent exemption from taxation by virtue of earlier interpretation of their charters by state and federal courts." [22]

Dissatisfaction with the Elective System.—At the beginning of the twentieth century the elective system appeared to be gaining in prestige. It promised to furnish the answers to the growing strength of industrialism, capitalism, and individualism and to provide a solution to problems that had arisen out of the great increase in knowl-

[21] See M. M. Chambers, *The Colleges and the Courts, 1941-45* (New York: The Carnegie Foundation for the Advancement of Teaching, 1946).

[22] Chambers, *op. cit.*, pp. 46, 47. In 1951 it was reported that efforts in California to exempt private schools from taxation were being widely protested.

edge which had been produced by the physical and social sciences. The increasing demands that the advantages of higher education be more widely extended than formerly made election a congenial and comforting theory in higher education. The narrow and pre-scribed curriculum of a few collegiate subjects came gradually to yield to wide election; the view of a liberal education changed and came to include as subjects of study in the colleges the physical and the social sciences, modern foreign languages, and new studies in English. Meantime the great increase in economic wealth, the over-throw of the doctrine of formal mental discipline, and the "discovery" of individual differences had a heavy impact in modifying the col-legiate curriculum, and the old practice of treating all students in the same manner yielded to increasing efforts to provide for their vary-ing interests and abilities. These same forces were operating at the same time in secondary education. Other changes were to appear in the colleges, which were to become more secular and less religious in tone than formerly; rigid regulation of the conduct of students was to be modified in favor of larger freedom and self-reliance; the old aristocratic notion of higher education was to change to a more democratic conception, student bodies became less homogeneous and more heterogeneous, and higher education was gradually to expand in an effort to meet "all kinds of practical needs."

It was only natural under these conditions that considerable con-troversy would develop over the purposes of higher education, even under such changed conditions. Some critics, including Robert M. Hutchins, president of the University of Chicago, who was one of the most vocal of them all, insisted that the way out of the confusion in higher education was through efforts to inculcate "the intellectual virtues, and these are the product of vigorous intellectual effort. Such effort is the indispensable constituent of a university course of study." [23] Hutchins also said: "Education implies teaching. Teach-ing implies knowledge. Knowledge is truth. The truth is every-where the same. Hence education should be everywhere the same. . . . If education is rightly understood, it will be understood as the cultivation of the intellect. The cult of the intellect is the same good for all men for all societies." [24] Educators, he said, should not per-mit students "to dictate the course of study unless they are prepared to confess that they are nothing but chaperons, supervising an aim-less, trial-and-error process which is chiefly valuable because it keeps

[23] *The Higher Learning in America* (New Haven: Yale University Press, 1926), p. 26.
[24] *Ibid.*, pp. 66-67.

young people from doing something worse." He thought that the free elective system which Eliot had introduced at Harvard and which "progressive education" had adapted to lower age groups "amounted to a denial that there was content to education."

The story of higher education in the United States shows that the collegiate curriculum went from prescription to election and then back toward a measure of prescription. From 1636 to about the middle of the nineteenth century, prescription was generally the rule. "Should the time ever come when Latin and Greek should be banished from our universities," prophesied the *Western Review* [25] of Cincinnati in 1820, "and the study of Cicero and Demosthenes, of Homer and Virgil, should be considered as unnecessary for the formation of a scholar, we should regard mankind as fast sinking into absolute barbarism, and the gloom of mental darkness as likely to increase until it should become universal." But some seeds of election were being planted in the early nineteenth century. Among the first proposals for elective courses were those by Jefferson for the College of William and Mary as early as 1779, and later for the University of Virginia which was opened in 1825; by George Ticknor at Harvard in the 1820's; by Francis Wayland of Brown University in 1842, and perhaps by others. Over against these proposals were arguments for the old ideal of mental discipline, as set out in a report by the faculty of Yale in 1828, which defended the prescribed curriculum and the classics as the heart of a liberal arts college. In 1838 F. A. P. Barnard, a graduate of Yale College, became professor of mathematics and natural philosophy in the University of Alabama, and there stood up stoutly for the prescribed curriculum against the elective system and modern studies. Barnard, however, after going from Alabama to the presidency of the University of Mississippi, seems to have shifted his position when he became president of Columbia in 1864. [26] Apparently Barnard, classified with the opponents of election while in the South, later became its energetic advocate. [27] Butts lists fifteen institutions, however, that made efforts toward reform of the curriculum before 1860: the University of North Carolina; Union College in Schenectady, New York; Trinity College in Hartford, Connecticut; the University of Nashville in Tennessee; Hobart College in Geneva, New York; the University

[25] R. Freeman Butts, *The College Charts Its Course* (New York: McGraw-Hill Book Co., Inc., 1939), p. 117.

[26] Butts, *op. cit.,* chap. vii.

[27] See, for Barnard's earlier position, *Report on a Proposition to Modify the Plan of Instruction in the University of Alabama.* New York · D. Appleton & Co., 1855. For his views on election, see Butts, *op. cit.,* 189-94.

of Vermont; Amherst College; Bowdoin College; Columbia College in New York City; New York University; Wesleyan University in Middletown, Connecticut; Lafayette College in Pennsylvania; Oberlin College in Ohio; Norwich University in Vermont; and the University of Rochester in New York.[28]

It will be recalled that Charles W. Eliot devoted to a defense of the elective system a good part of his inaugural address as president of Harvard in 1869 and that he continued to advocate and defend it. His successor, A. Lawrence Lowell, in his inaugural address forty years later, stated that American collegiate students should study "a little of everything," for if they did not, there was no certainty that they would be broadly cultivated, "especially in view of the omnipresent impulse in the community driving them to devote their chief attention to the subjects bearing upon their future career." He thought students in college should devote a considerable part of their time to one subject and take, in addition, several general courses in wholly unrelated fields. Instruction that implied a little knowledge of everything was "more difficult to provide well than any other. To furnish it, there ought to be in every considerable field a general course designed to give men who do not intend to pursue the subject further a comprehension of its underlying principles or methods of thought; and this is by no means the same thing as an introductory course, although the two can often be effectively combined." Three years later, Alexander Meiklejohn, in his inaugural address at Amherst College, deplored the fact that so many of the chairs in the colleges were occupied by professors who had only specialized interest and information, "and it is through them that we attempt to give our boys a liberal education, which the teachers themselves had not achieved."

In these statements and others may be seen the beginning of a definite tendency in the United States toward "general education," which later came to be defined as education in general, especially in the first two years of college. After 1918 this tendency became more and more vigorous, allegedly for the purpose of relating the work of the college to the apparent "life needs" of the students more directly than did the older curriculum. The tendency represented an effort to offset the obvious disadvantages of an inflated collegiate curriculum and the rapid increase in courses which had developed under the unfulfilled promises of election. An examination of the catalogue of almost any representative college nearly anywhere in the United

[28] Butts, *op. cit.*, pp. 131-42.

States showed numerous new courses which covered only a limited section of a field of knowledge and which in most cases proclaimed increasing departmentalization. This great increase in courses may have been a natural result of conditions that appeared after the First World War when multitudes of students crowded into the colleges and universities and when governing higher education authorities became very energetic in expanding their physical plants and educational facilities. When the economic crisis of 1929 brought depression to education, the colleges were forced to re-examine and reappraise their work. Courses in so-called general education began to appear in great numbers, probably, however, not so much from concern of the administration and faculty for the welfare of students as from the interest of the students themselves. There is some significance in the apparent fact that fraternities and sororities and collegiate religious associations manifested concern in assisting entering students to adjust themselves to the life of the campus. A result was that the "orientation" of freshmen, for example, soon became a recognized function of most institutions. Orientation, general, or overview courses also came to be developed in many institutions which began to pay serious attention to general as opposed to specialized undergraduate instruction.

By 1922 at least forty-one colleges were making this kind of provision for their students, as compared with only eleven institutions before the First World War. By 1926 seventy-nine were offering orientation or general courses for standard college credit. And during the next few decades, basic and prescribed courses developed, apparently in the hope of bringing some order out of the chaos which followed the unchecked elective system. New college plans appeared throughout the country and these became very popular almost everywhere. Among the most widely publicized of these were "the Chicago Plan"; the "New Program of Study" at St. John's College at Annapolis, Maryland, based on the "great books" of the intellectual tradition of the Western world and reflecting, it was believed, some of the educational principles of Robert M. Hutchins; the general college of the University of Minnesota, which was widely imitated in many parts of the country; and the Columbia Plan and its survey courses which required an unusual degree of cooperation by the various departments. Among women's colleges that introduced curricular innovations were Sarah Lawrence College of Bronxville, New York, and Bennington College of Vermont. Departmental divisions in organization were avoided at Sarah Lawrence, which had no required courses or grades but attempted to measure the student's achievement in relation to her own ability rather than comparatively or in relation to other students. As originally organized, the work at that institution seems to have been built upon the progressive educational principle of the "activities program," almost complete freedom being allowed the student with reference to her educational program and also to her social life. In theory and practice, Sarah Lawrence differed little if any from Bennington, which had no formal requirements and no traditional rules of residence, class attendance, or final examinations.[29]

These innovations in the collegiate curriculum which were so widely made in the second quarter of the twentieth century, and on which there were voluminous publication and wide discussion, represented many highly creditable efforts to improve the work of the colleges. Among the purposes of these undertakings were the apparent eagerness to break down artificial barriers [30] which had grown up between various fields of learning; to make better provision for the interests and abilities of the individual student; and to improve examinations, in which new practices appeared and on which there was very considerable discussion in committees of faculties and in educational organizations. The United States, through these and other conditions, was rapidly becoming at mid-twentieth century a nation of college men and women. What had long been regarded as the good fortune of youth privileged in economic wealth, or exceptionally aggressive or ambitious, was rapidly becoming, at mid-twentieth century, the reasonable prospect of many more youth than ever before. But the United States was not becoming a nation of college graduates. The high rate of failures continued at alarming proportions among students in college, as it also did among those in secondary school. Reconstruction of the curriculum alone had not been found sufficient to remove fully this academic affliction or to reduce the wailing and the dirging of presidents, deans, and faculties and their personnel clinics. It was growing more and more obvious to thoughtful observers of the American educational scene that better teachers at all levels were needed if the affliction were to be removed and the wailing reduced.

[29] For brief discussions of some of these new college plans see Edgar W. Knight, *Twenty Centuries of Education* (Boston: Ginn & Co., 1940, chapter xv; Butts, *op. cit.*, Part IV; John J. Coss (ed.), *Five College Plans* (New York: Columbia University Press, 1931).

[30] See B. L. Johnson (ed.), *What About Survey Courses?* (New York: Henry Holt & Co., 1937). Contains information on the development of survey courses in the natural and social sciences and the humanities, on composite survey courses, and on the testing of achievement in such courses.

The New York State University; Regional Cooperation.—Two unique plans for higher education in the United States in the 1940's were the establishment of a large and comprehensive university system in New York and the plan for regional cooperation in higher education in the southern states. The State University of New York "came into being as a corporate body in April, 1949," following an act of the legislature the year before on the recommendation of the New York Temporary Commission on the Need for a State University. Owen D. Young was chairman of this commission which had filed its report in February of 1948. The new institution was not intended to compete with any other institution, but its function was "to supply post-high-school education where other adequate facilities either do not exist or for some reason cannot be utilized by qualified students." The new institution was "dedicated to providing facilities in higher education for the qualified youth of the state, regardless of race, color, creed, place of residence, or economic status." A board of trustees was created to have "administrative authority over more than thirty hitherto separate state-supported institutions" which were located in practically every part of the state: eleven teachers' colleges; seven four-year professional colleges; eleven two-year institutes; and two of the four two-year colleges of liberal arts which had been established to provide for veterans. These institutions had faculties of about 3 thousand members, a student population of about 30 thousand, and physical properties valued at more than $85 million.

After many months of consideration and deliberation, and some controversy, the trustees of the University of New York, the youngest of state universities, made public early in 1950 the long-discussed "master plan" for the development of four-year colleges of liberal arts and two-year community or junior colleges in a mammoth $200 million state university system. Those who favored the state university system were convinced that New York had been a bit tardy in providing higher educational facilities for the people of the state. At the hearings on the proposed undertaking, it came out that the constant flow of students from that state to institutions for higher education in the southern states had created such a problem that those institutions had put New York (and other states) "on a quota basis or had to increase their tuition charges to nonresident students." Statistics showed that 45 per cent of collegiate students in upper New York had had to transfer to institutions outside that state for the last two years of their work. The expansion of the private or independent colleges would not solve the problem, in the view of the trustees of the university. High fees would still remain, and the argument that a publicly maintained institution would be in keen competition with the private or independent colleges "did not make sense," these officials also held. They maintained that both types of institutions could live side by side without danger to one another. Alvin C. Eurich, president of the University, pointed out that only one of every eight persons in New York between the ages of eighteen and twenty-one was in full-time attendance at an institution for higher education. Some of the private or independent institutions objected to the state university on the grounds of competition with such institutions, that there were already adequate higher educational facilities in the state, and that it would be less expensive for the state to provide scholarships for needed students instead of creating its own institutions.

The "master plan" of the new university called for one or more two-year colleges in each of the "economic areas" of the state. An increased enrollment of 5.4 thousand students a year in the two-year colleges was planned for each year between 1950 and 1966, and an additional increase of 11 thousand students from 1963 to 1966 which would provide by the latter year a state-wide enrollment "equal to the full student potential of 107 thousand students in two-year programs." In order to accommodate these increased enrollments, new two-year institutions would have to be provided. In 1950 the capacity of the two-year institutions was about 9.3 thousand students. The new facilities would have to be set up by private institutions, by local communities which would receive aid from the state, or by the state itself. An increased enrollment of 4.1 thousand students from the eighteen-year-old through the twenty-one-year-old group was planned for each year between 1950 and 1966 in the four-year programs, and an additional enrollment of 43 thousand was planned for the years 1958 through 1966. These plans called for a statewide enrollment by 1966 "equal to the full student potential of 214 thousand in the four-year programs." No new facilities in four-year colleges were needed immediately, but all the existing facilities in such colleges had to be maintained. The capacity provided in four-year programs in 1950 was estimated at about 160 thousand and could be maintained by the private institutions, by local communities through aid from the state, or by the state itself. But new four-year facilities would be needed between 1960 and 1966, to be maintained by private institutions, by local communities through aid from the state, or by the state itself. This stupendous higher education plan, unlike anything ever before projected in this or any other country, was designed to make provision for those youth in New York who desired to attend "community" or junior colleges at low cost, but it was not designed as a state university in the sense of great institutions such as the Univeristy of Michigan, the University of Minnesota, the University of Indiana, or others in the midwestern or western states. Eurich reported [31] in April, 1950:

Thus, in its first year, the State University of New York has made appreciable and steady progress in providing additional facilities for higher education for qualified youth of the state. This is a formidable assignment. If, within the next ten years, the percentage of youth of college age attending two-year colleges in New York rises to the level already attained in California; and if, at the same time, the number attending four-year colleges rises to the percentage prevailing in the Ithaca region of New York State, almost one third of the youth of college age will be in college. This prediction is based on the reasonable assumption that facilities for higher education in the state as a whole will be about as adequate as they now are in the localities used for comparison. This is a minimum. It is a fact, established by experience, that demand for higher education increases with its availability.

This vast undertaking, Eurich said, would reduce the barriers to higher education for those qualified youth and was worthy of the Empire State. But it deserved and would require the full cooperation of everybody so fortunate as to be connected with it, and informed public support at the community and the state level. "The challenge that it presents comes only once in a generation," he said.

Another unusual plan in higher education and educational administration which attracted wide notice was undertaken in the southern states in the late 1940's. When the Conference of Southern Governors met in 1947, one of its major interests was higher education in the South. These executives and some of their predecessors had seen increasing costs, expanding needs, and increased enrollments calling for more buildings, equipment, and enlarged facilities, as was generally the case throughout the country. Toward the end of 1948, fourteen governors and two hundred educators in the southern states met in Savannah in an effort to "bring to life the nation's first plan for regional education," and they agreed to work together in planning and establishing regional educational facilities. A nonprofit corporation, now known as the Board of Control for Regional Education, was formed, with the governor and three citizens of each signatory

[31] "The Youngest State University," *The Journal of Higher Education*, XXI (April, 1950), 169 ff.

state and a board of consultants to serve with and advise the Board of Control. A charter was provided to become effective upon Congressional consent to the compact, and legislative approval by the signatory states. Under the federal Constitution, no state can enter into any agreement or compact with another state without the consent of Congress. The plan was to establish regional schools in fields of graduate, professional, and technical education where pressing demands were not being met. Plans were also made for a program to promote sound research and investigation into the needs of the region, in collaboration with institutions and groups of institutions, state committees, professional organizations, and public agencies. The participating states made legislative appropriations for work in veterinary medicine ($254 thousand), in medicine ($573 thousand), in dentistry ($517.5 thousand), and $154 thousand for administrative services and operations, a total of $1.4 million. In a short time regional planning in graduate and professional education grew from a proposal to a working program, under which a state not providing medicine, dentistry, or veterinary medicine could send its students to one of the southern institutions which provided such training. The home states of the students paid to the selected colleges $1500 for each medical or dental student and $1000 for each student of veterinary medicine. Actual operation began in the fall of 1949, and in 1950 there were 350 students in the plan. The number was expected to be 600 in 1951. This undertaking was pointed to as one of the fruits of interest in regional planning in the South, which for many years had been examining itself and turning the searchlight on its many pressing problems, in large part through the pioneer work of Howard W. Odum of the University of North Carolina. It is believed that this plan of cooperation in higher education will be successfully achieved. Joint planning and action, it was said, would serve to reduce competition and needless duplication of educational effort. Benjamin Fine, education editor of the *New York Times*, writing on this plan in that newspaper July 24, 1949, said:

It is clear that the project is exceedingly significant. It can help the South build and develop a sound system of graduate and professional schools that will be the equal of any in the country. The implications not only for the South but for the rest of the country are far-reaching. A new pattern has appeared in higher education that will have a profound influence on colleges and universities everywhere.[32]

---

[32] For criticism of the plan see Virgil A. Clift, "Pattern of Discrimination in Public Higher Education," *School and Society*, LXXII (October 7, 1950), pp. 225-28.

The Question of Academic Freedom.—Concern over the old and thorny question of academic freedom, which seems to get sharper in periods of crises, deepened in higher education in the late 1940's and was a very serious issue in 1950. The American Association of University Professors was reported to be "swamped" with complaints of professors who were dismissed or denied promotion because of their alleged political activities, and the organization conducted many investigations in an effort to find out whether or not such professors had just complaints. Ralph E. Himstead, the general secretary of the organization, was reported in May of 1949 as saying that an aftermath of the presidential campaign in 1948 was still being felt in academic circles. At that time members of faculties in several institutions for higher education had complained that they were dismissed because they had given support to Henry Wallace in that election or were active in the Progressive Party, and the organization had been informed of other similar cases. It turned out, however, that most of those professors who had been dismissed did not have academic tenure, and some were on "probationary status" and their contracts were not renewed. Moreover it was often difficult to establish the exact cause for dismissals or failure to renew contracts. It was said that "lack of competence" or some other general reason was sometimes given in explanation. It was also said that the "cold war" was largely responsible for the "unprecedented strain" that was being put on academic freedom at that time. In the spring of 1949 the only outright case of dismissal on grounds of communism was said to have been at the University of Washington. In some other cases the charge of strong sympathy for communism may have been suggested, but it was reported that other grounds for dismissal were probably used.

At that time recent trends in legislation on the subject of academic freedom were noted.[33] Kansas, Massachusetts, and Pennsylvania authorized the dismissal of teachers for disloyalty. Maryland, New Jersey, and New York forbade teachers to hold membership in organizations believed to be subversive, and Maryland and New York authorized the investigation of the loyalty of teachers. Some persons saw in this trend a tendency to the kind of "witch hunting" that followed the First World War. The National Commission for the Defense of Democracy Through Education, which had developed out of the National Education Association, bewailed "the constantly increasing legislation appearing in the various states which impugns

[33] See Benjamin Fine, "Charges of Freedom Curb Rising in Nation's Colleges," *New York Times,* May 29, 1949.

the integrity of the teaching profession by requiring teachers to take oaths other than those required of all officeholders," and viewed "with alarm" the danger in such legislative effort. The Department of Higher Education, at its meeting in the spring of 1949, condemned attempts to limit the activities of teachers and to single them out "for special investigation."

Dr. Fine summarized the major cases at that time. Two professors had been dismissed from the University of Washington for membership in the Communist Party, and another for "neglect of duty." A professor had been dismissed from the University of Washington for supporting the "genetics teachings of Lysenko, Russian Communist, who advocates the theory that acquired characteristics can be inherited." A professor was dismissed from Evansville College in Indiana because, as the institution announced, "his activities both on and off the campus . . . put an end to his usefulness to the institution." The professor had been active in the support of the candidacy of Henry Wallace for the Presidency of the United States. A professor was discharged from Olivet College in Michigan in the summer of 1948 for "ultraliberal views." The following January, five other members of the faculty were discharged, and later ten more resigned voluntarily, making a total of about half the faculty. A professor in the Department of English in the University of New Hampshire, who had served as chairman of the Progressive Party in that state, resigned, and the university announced that he had accepted a position elsewhere, although his contract had another year to run at New Hampshire. Another professor in the same institution was denied promotion, allegedly because of his activities in the local organization of the Progressive Party. A professor at Yale University, who had been an organizer of the Wallace Party in Connecticut and its candidate in 1948 for Congress, was denied reappointment. Yale officials were reported as saying that the professor's "left-wing" activities had nothing to do with his case, but dissatisfaction with his teaching did. In March of 1949, Harold J. Laski of the University of London and a member of the Executive Committee of the British Labor Party was kept from giving lectures at the University of California in Los Angeles. Other colleges took similar action on "Communists or left-wing speakers." In April of 1949 the University of Chicago and Roosevelt College in Chicago were investigated by a legislative committee for "alleged communist activities," but the institutions vigorously denied any taint of communism and defended their faculties and student bodies. The case that seemed to attract wider national notice than the others in 1950 was that of the University of California [34] which was dragged through many meetings of the Board of Regents and finally into court. In April, 1951, a three-man Court of Appeals, by unanimous decision, held that the oath at the University of California was unconstitutional and ordered that those professors who had been dismissed for not signing it be reinstated. It was believed that the effect of that decision, unless reversed by a higher court, would extend beyond the campus of that institution.

Advocates for and opponents of such measures always appeared when loyalty oaths for teachers were under discussion. Much was made of the issue [35] at the inauguration of Gordon Gray of the University of North Carolina in October of 1950. Three of the nation's leading educators were in agreement on the need of unfettered academic freedom in state universities, but two of them, James L. Morrill, president of the University of Minnesota, and Lee A. Dubridge, president of the California Institute of Technology, by implication at least, questioned the value of teacher's oaths. George Stoddard, president of the University of Illinois, did not find such oaths objectionable. He said that they did not serve "to catch Communists, but they may be useful as a means of reducing questionable practices and of establishing perjury in advance of overt subversive acts." The new president appropriately had his say on academic freedom, asserting that it had often been used "as a sort of immunity to Communists and their sidecar passengers," and that these would not be welcome at the University of North Carolina. He could not believe, he said, that firmness prudently exercised toward them would violate the principles of unfettered research and the pursuit of truth. The problem had to be approached "sensibly and with restraint" and without hysteria. Academic freedom had to be preserved at all costs and with no persecution of the innocent.

Not long after the close of the First World War, the American Association of University Professors, in reporting on cases of the dismissal of professors from their posts in colleges and universities, declared:

The liberty of the scholar within the university to set forth his conclusions, be they what they may, is conditioned by their being conclusions gained by a scholar's method and held in a scholar's spirit; that is to say, they must

[34] See George R. Stewart, *The Year of the Oath* (New York: Doubleday & Co., 1950). For a review of this book by Henry Steele Commager and also of Walter Gelhorn's *Security, Loyalty and Science* (Cornell University Press, 1950) see *New York Herald Tribune Book Review*, October 15, 1950.
[35] For further discussion of loyalty oaths for teachers see Chapter 6.

be the fruits of competent and patient and sincere inquiry, and they should be set forth with dignity, courtesy, and temperateness of language.

The statement seemed to represent the position of that organization on the old question of academic freedom which has been in American education since the days of Henry Dunster, who was forced to resign the presidency of Harvard in 1654 because of his views on infant baptism. Samuel Eliot Morison says [36] of this case that when the news got around that Harvard had gone "antipaedobaptist," there was as much dismay and amazement in the neighborhood "as if President Conant should announce his adherence to the Third International." The law of Massachusetts prohibited the questioning of the efficacy of the baptism of infants, and this Dunster had defied by refusing to have one of his own children baptized and in interrupting the baptism of another infant in Cambridge. The saints in the community tried to reason with him, and the Overseers [of the college] begged him to stay on in the presidency, but only on condition that he renounce his views and keep quiet. But he stood by his guns and quit.

Between the case of Henry Dunster and the middle of the twentieth century numerous cases appeared that involved academic freedom. A conspicuous case was that of President Thomas Cooper of the University of South Carolina in the 1830's because he failed or was accused of failing to adjust his scientific views to the theological views held at that time by most South Carolinians. Another case was that of Benjamin Hedrick. He was a native of North Carolina and an honor graduate of its university, but he was dismissed from the faculty of that institution for political heresy. He had expressed, or was reported as having expressed, favor for John C. Frémont for the Presidency of the United States in the newly formed Republican Party. Hedrick had always voted the Democratic ticket, and in August, before his dismissal in October of 1856, had done so in the state elections. No trustee and only one member of the faculty (Frenchman Henry Harrisse) stood up for him and for his right to vote as he pleased. As president of the University of Mississippi, F. A. P. Barnard was charged and tried but exonerated in 1860 by the trustees for not having his theories of slavery on straight. There were many cases in the latter part of the nineteenth century, during the "critical period in American religion," which turned on Darwinism and involved many ministers and teachers.

[36] *Three Centuries of Harvard* (Cambridge: Harvard University Press, 1936), p. 19.

Two very important cases near the end of the nineteenth century should be noted here. Both involved not theological, political, or scientific but economic issues which held the center of the academic stage in 1950 and showed how the center of intellectual or emotional gravity had shifted since the days of Henry Dunster. One of these was that of Benjamin Andrews, president of Brown University, an alumnus of that institution, who had also studied at Newton Theological Seminary and had served his alma mater as professor of political science before becoming its president. His economic views, and especially those on the free coinage of silver, moved the trustees to request him to renounce as unsound economy his views on the question of silver, or if he could not do so, to refrain from advocating them. Andrews resigned, believing that he could not comply with the wishes of the trustees "without surrendering that reasonable liberty of utterance which my predecessors, my faculty colleagues, and myself have hitherto enjoyed, and in the absence of which the most ample endowment for an educational institution would have but little worth." Members of the faculty and of the alumni protested the action of the trustees, to whom a general memorial was made by college presidents and professors and even business men. Among the signers were presidents Eliot of Harvard and Gilman of Hopkins. A special memorial was signed by economists, including professors Taussig of Harvard and Seligman of Columbia. Andrews withdrew his resignation, but soon found educational work in the West more congenial. He served as superintendent of the public schools of Chicago and later as chancellor of the University of Nebraska, from which position he retired in 1909. At about the time that Andrews was suspect at Brown, E. A. Ross was dismissed from his Stanford professorship on charges of favoring free silver, Chinese immigration, and the municipal ownership of franchises. In connection with this case, William Rainey Harper, president of the University of Chicago, gave public guarantee of academic freedom at that institution. Fifty years later his successor, Robert M. Hutchins, stood up for professors at the University of California, and along with others, including members of his faculty and those of the University of Iowa, set out to raise funds to help the ousted professors until they could get employment. In most of the cases of mid-twentieth century the issue was the specter of communism.

The meeting of the National Education Association at Denver in the summer of 1935 claimed to be "a milestone in our democratic civilization," presumably because of its strong stand on academic freedom and tenure. On academic freedom the organization maintained that "administrators, teachers, and schools should have full opportunity to present differing points of view on any and all controversial questions in order to aid students to adjust themselves to their environment and to changing social conditions." And on tenure it reaffirmed "with emphasis its stand in full support of tenure of position of teachers as a means of insuring to the children of the land the best possible instruction." The Division of Research and the editor of the journal of the association were instructed to continue to collect and publish information on tenure, as had been done for several years, and for that purpose the sum of $10 thousand dollars was ordered appropriated.

Since the days of Socrates, the Western world has witnessed many notable contests over what is generally called academic freedom or freedom of teaching. His case, which was one of the earliest instances if not the earliest conspicuous example on record in which the question of the liberty of teaching became the subject of extended inquiry, was in some respects not unlike cases after his time and was in fact similar to some modern ones. Socrates was charged with impiety, criticism of the old gods and of religion, and with corrupting the youth of Athens. He was convicted on the first charge, but the discussion of his case really turned on the second charge. His case was not unlike that of Galileo whose revolutionary theory of the universe many centuries after Socrates and a century before Dunster outraged the popular feeling of the time. In the case of both the Athenian sage and teacher and the Italian astronomer and experimental philosopher, the controversy unfortunately got mixed up with local politics, and freedom of thought became confused with freedom of teaching. This same kind of confusion has many times crept into popular discussions of academic freedom since the days of these eminent men, and was widespread in the United States in the first half of the twentieth century.

Contests over freedom of teaching raged for several centuries around theological questions. Later, the controversies were in the field of politics, later still, in science and its conflicts with theology, and in more recent years such controversies have appeared in the field of economics and the so-called social sciences. Most of the questions of the natural and biological sciences have now passed beyond the boundary of opinion and emotion, but in the social sciences there still remains considerable room for opinion and for emotional outburst, and perhaps less room than in the exact sciences for conclusive and convincing applications of the scientific method. It is at this point that many of those who now venture to explore the fields of the social sciences are likely to be misunderstood if not indeed to do some damage to the cause they seem to try to advance.

During the depression that began in 1929, as during the two world wars, the ancient question of academic freedom was brought forward afresh. Criticisms of the old order were numerous and at times even violent. The fear that freedom of discussion and of teaching would be restricted was rather widespread, especially among certain so-called leaders in pedagogy. There was a new scare about "reds" among faculties and students. But there was nothing novel in this condition. The charge of radicalism in the colleges was made during and just after the American Revolution. In the middle of the next century the charge that college campuses were hotbeds of social and economic radicalism was frequently made, and this charge was used as an excuse for reducing the financial support of higher education. Following the discussions of Darwinism after 1860, controversies again broke out in campus and pulpit in all parts of the country. Professors and ministers were dismissed on charges that their teachings were undermining the faith of the people and should be restricted. And just after the First World War, the fear of Russia drove or seemed to drive many states to enact legislation on what was called "Americanism." Meantime attempts had been made to pass what came to be known as the "pure history" bills and the "monkey" bills. In the depression and again in the Second World War, there was much agitation about "loyalty" oaths. In some of these instances the question of freedom of teaching appeared as a feverish issue, although in the discussions about it there was a bit of unsobered talking and writing.

The verdict of history was not likely to show that the resolution of the National Education Association at Denver was altogether a sobered statement. Reaffirmation with all the emphasis possible in support of tenure of teachers could not in itself insure to children good instruction, which the National Education Association professed to desire. Better teaching could come only through better teachers. And this country, which still has such low standards for teachers, could never have better teachers until its leading educational organization got as aroused about improving their preparation as it did about the question of tenure, which in reality was not very closely connected with freedom of teaching. Moreover, many administrators, teachers, and schools were not competent to present "differing points of view on any and all controversial questions."

Just how, therefore, under the prevailing low standards of preparation of teachers, would such a presentation by them "aid students to adjust themselves to their environment," the resolution of the National Education Association failed to say.

So, also, with the canons which the American Association of University Professors announced. Conclusions gained by the method of scholarship, held in the spirit of scholarship, and the fruits of competent and patient and sincere inquiry, set forth with dignity and courtesy and temperateness of language, were rarely, if ever, actually perilous to a real scholar unless he himself had turned politician and propagandist and a "publicity hound"—which a real scholar rarely allows himself to do. Truth, even when crushed to earth, has a way of arising. Real scholars knew this, and they did not get panicky at any temporary threat to their freedom to seek the truth wherever it may lead and to report it in a gentlemanly manner when they were sure they had found it by scholarly methods.

Not only has freedom of thought been confused with freedom of teaching in these recent discussions, but freedom of teaching has been confused with the idea of tenure. The statement of the American Association of University Professors given above seemed to be sufficient to throw out of court at least some of the cases that had agitated that organization. In some cases, some if not all its criteria of academic liberty had not been observed by the professors who had got into trouble; and whenever these or any other reasonable criteria of academic freedom were disregarded by teachers, then liberty of teaching was likely to be betrayed in the house of its alleged friends, as, for example, when teachers claimed for themselves rights which were generally not accorded to other groups. Academic freedom, like freedom of speech and freedom of the press, was and is a precious thing, but that liberty does not guarantee the teacher in school, college, or university the inalienable right to embarrass the institution in which he is sheltered by making unseasoned and sensational statements on subjects in which he is so often not at home.

Some very pertinent questions arose from the vigorous agitation in the 1940's over loyalty oaths for teachers and freedom of teaching. There was the question whether freedom of teaching was restricted when a teacher was denied the right to use his classroom as a place for partisan propaganda. Was there a denial of academic freedom when a teacher, in reality a public servant, was denied the right to use his position to throw suspicion upon or to condemn institutions which the people had designed and established and maintained and in which most of them seemed to have confidence? Was freedom of teaching denied or abridged when a teacher was restricted from saying anything he pleased to say on any subject he pleased to talk about at any time and place he chose? The teacher, it was said, did not have a vested right to his post, even though he may at times have appeared to believe that he did have such a right. His obligation was to "tell the truth as he sees it and seek to see the truth as it is." But his most binding obligation was to find the truth and reveal it as a scholar and a gentleman. If he spoke or wrote without being competent, did he not weaken or destroy confidence in himself and in his profession and therefore lessen his usefulness to the school, college, or university in which he was serving? But the historically recognized theory of academic freedom was now and then put to an unnecessary strain. Professors who were presumably competent in their fields had been known to fudge on the time set aside for them to teach their subjects and to go outside the scope of the fields in which they were expected to be competent. By 1950 it had become known that the institutions which had been preparing teachers had not been paying too much attention to such subjects as economics, sociology, and government, and that this neglect had made a serious gap in the preparation of instructors. But should not these subjects, it was asked, be presented by persons who were competent in these fields and not by persons outside who were obviously not competent to instruct in them?

There was a point at which it did seem that academic freedom was denied or abridged. Science provides little or no room for emotional evangelism. If what the schools taught was scientifically accurate, apostolic fervor in its presentation was neither necessary nor in good taste. If what was taught was error, it would writhe "with pain" and die "among his worshippers." Moreover, the school, college, or university was coming to be regarded as a partnership of students, teachers, and its supporting constituency. Neither group had a monopoly on rights. Not all the rights in academic freedom were those of the teacher: freedom of teaching was not one thing for the teacher and another for the students or the supporting constituency. The teacher should be protected in his rights, it was argued, but so also should the students and the community and the supporting constituency. Certainly the students should be free from the imposition of mere opinions by the teacher.

In his defense of freedom of teaching, Socrates had failed to point out that the teacher generally deals with persons younger and less experienced than himself, and that a skillful teacher can therefore do harm as well as good. The teacher was not on equal terms with his students because his experience gave him a decided advantage over them. His work as teacher could become a menace to students or community or supporting constituency if he did not exercise restraint and was not also guided by a sense of the fitness of things. Real freedom of teaching was limited by the customs and usages of the community or the supporting constituency of the institution with which the teacher was connected. The best protection a teacher had, or could have, thoughtful observers pointed out in the wide discussions of the subject in the 1930's and 1940's, was not to be found in the lack of restrictions externally and legalistically imposed upon him, by the absence of "pure history" bills, "monkey" laws, or loyalty oaths. His freedom to teach could hardly be separated from his other civil liberties, and it could best be kept secure in the same way that his other liberties were protected. In addition to the limitations of freedom of teaching noted above, there was the limitation set by the rules of good manners, courtesy, honor, by academic *noblesse oblige*. In the restraint that a scholar and gentleman exercised or imposed upon himself resided the community's or the institution's best and surest defense against academic license or abuses of academic freedom. In teaching and in publishing, the teacher was, and still is, expected to teach and to publish as a scholar and as a gentleman. The flaming injunction of the National Education Association in 1935 to "administrators, teachers, and schools to present different points of view on any and all controversial questions" seemed to violate some of the rules of academic freedom. Few of those who were given such marching orders were able honestly and competently to obey them. And it was clear that the rank and file of the teachers would not be able honestly and competently to do so until they were better prepared for the high and serious duties of teaching.

Changes in collegiate education in the United States were accompanied by other developments. Among these were the phenomenal growth in graduate work which became most modish during the first half of the twentieth century; marked changes in medical, legal, dental, and engineering education; the rapid growth of the summer session and of university extension and so-called adult education; the rise of university presses; the expansion of higher education for women and for Negroes; and other developments which are treated in the next Chapter.

SOME SUGGESTED QUESTIONS AND EXERCISES FOR STUDENTS

1. Compare a typical four-year college in 1900 with such an institution in 1950 as to (a) the curriculum, (b) organization and administration, (c) composition of the faculty, (d) extracurricular activities, (e) student welfare.

2. Indicate (a) the economic, (b) the social, (c) the psychological changes that took place in this country after 1900 that increased enrollments in the institutions for higher education.

3. Students will find it very helpful to read and report in class on (a) Lovejoy's So You're Going to College, (b) Beck's Men Who Control Our Universities, (c) Epler's Honorary Degrees: A Survey of Their Use and Abuse, (d) Harris's The Market for College Graduates, (e) Lynes's "Can the Private Schools Survive?" in Harper's Magazine for January, 1948.

4. Two members of the President's Commission on Higher Education dissented from its recommendations on financing higher education. Their dissents appear in pages 65-68 of Volume V of the report. What reasons did the two members give for dissenting?

5. What were the basic objections given at the meeting of The Association of American Colleges in early 1950 to the proposal for federal fellowships and scholarships for college students?

6. In 1950 there was considerable discussion of the question of the tax-exemption privileges of schools and colleges. How did these institutions come to be exempt from taxation? What were the objections to their engaging in commercial enterprises in competition with business enterprises that had to pay taxes on their profits?

7. In his The Colleges and the Courts 1941-45, M. M. Chambers reported on 175 judicial decisions regarding higher education. What were the major issues in these decisions?

8. Read The Higher Learning in America by Robert M. Hutchins and The Higher Learning in a Democracy by Harry D. Gideonse and show how the two statements on higher education differ.

9. Explain the growing dissatisfaction with the elective system, and the tendency after the First World War to establish "new college" plans.

10. What are the arguments for general, orientation, and "survey" courses in the undergraduate college?

11. Look for and report in class on trends in education as revealed by "Education in Review" that appears every Sunday in The New York Times.

12. Look for and report in class on trends in higher education as these are revealed weekly by *Time* and *Newsweek*.

13. Study and report on (*a*) the comprehensive university system established in New York in the 1940's, and (*b*) the plan for regional higher education in the southern states. What were the objections to the Southern Regional Plan?

14. Exactly what do you understand by "academic freedom"? Show why this old and thorny question becomes so acute in economic or military crises. Give the arguments for and against loyalty oaths for college teachers.

SOME SUGGESTED REFERENCES AND READING

ANGELL, JAMES R. *American Education: Addresses and Articles*. New Haven: Yale University Press, 1937.
  A former president of Yale University gives his point of view on several aspects of higher education in the United States.

BABCOCK, F. L. *The U. S. College Graduate*. New York: The Macmillan Co., 1941.
  Asks: Does it pay to go to college? Are the graduates of American colleges richer? happier? better husbands and wives? better citizens? Brings warm interest to cold statistics.

BRUMBAUGH, A. J. (ed). *American Universities and Colleges* (5th ed.). Washington, D. C.: American Council on Education, 1948.
  Concise but comprehensive and useful descriptions of many phases of higher education in the United States. Reveals many significant changes that took place during the 1940's.

BUTTS, R. FREEMAN. *The College Charts Its Course*. New York: McGraw-Hill Book Co., 1939.
  Deals with many of the topics discussed in this Chapter, and especially with the collegiate curriculum. Shows how the prescribed curriculum ruled supreme, then weakened, how the elective system gained the day, and then how new proposals for prescription began to be made.

CHAMBERS, M. M. *The Colleges and the Courts*. New York: The Carnegie Foundation for the Advancement of Teaching, 1946.
  An interesting report on 175 recent judicial decisions regarding higher education in the United States. A very useful volume.

COSS, JOHN J. (ed.). *Five College Plans*. New York: Columbia University Press, 1931.
  Describes new educational developments at Columbia University, the University of Chicago, Harvard University, Swarthmore College, and Wabash College.

DUFFUS, R. L. *Democracy Enters College*. New York: Chas. Scribner's Sons, 1936.
  A vivid account of the ring of freedom in the elective system, education by adding machine, the golden age of the Carnegie unit and why it failed, and educational "new ideals." Good educational history, told in attractive fashion.

FLEXNER, ABRAHAM. *The American College.* New York: D. Appleton-Century Company, 1908.

Presents arguments for strengthening undergraduate work, and makes a vigorous attack on elective studies.

————. *Universities: American, English, German.* New York: Oxford University Press, 1930.

Presents, among other things, sharp criticism of some activities in which some higher educational institutions were engaging and which provoked wide discussion in the circles of the higher learning.

GIDEONSE, HARRY D. *The Higher Learning in a Democracy.* New York: Farrar & Rinehart, 1937.

Considered a reply to Robert M. Hutchins's *The Higher Learning in America.* Gideonse argued that "sheer intellectuality" was not enough, that a sound education introduces the student to the main areas of knowledge. For further attack on Hutchins's philosophy of higher education, see John Dewey, in *Social Frontier,* Vol. III (January, 1937), pp. 137-39.

GRAY, WILLIAM S. (ed.). *Recent Trends in American College Education.* The University of Chicago Press, 1931.

A series of discussions, before the Institute for Administrative Officers of Higher Institutions at the University of Chicago in 1931, on the reorganization of the junior college, of the senior college, and on comprehensive examinations and tests. Also see the following by the same editor and publisher and under the same auspices: *The Junior College Curriculum* (1929); *The Training of College Teachers* (1930); *Needed Readjustments in Higher Education* (1933); *Current Issues in Higher Education* (1937).

HARRIS, SEYMOUR E. *The Market for College Graduates.* Cambridge: Harvard University Press, 1950.

A Harvard professor of economics presents the dismal prospect in the near future of more college graduates than jobs for them, and the probable effect on the American economy.

Higher Education for American Democracy. Vol. V, "Financing Higher Education," of the President's Commission on Higher Education. Washington, D. C.: United States Government Printing Office, 1947.

Presents the arguments for federal aid to higher education which provoked warm discussion throughout the country. Other volumes of the report throw interesting light on many aspects of the subject.

HUTCHINS, ROBERT M. *The Higher Learning in America.* New Haven: Yale University Press, 1936.

A controversial book in which the author holds that "without exception the most important job that can be performed in the United States is first to establish higher learning on a rational basis, and, second, to make our people understand it."

KANDEL, I. L. *The Impact of the War Upon American Education.* Chapel Hill: The University of North Carolina Press, 1948.

Chaps. v and vi bear on some of the topics discussed in this Chapter, especially the curriculum and the idea of a liberal education.

KNIGHT, EDGAR W. *What College Presidents Say.* Chapel Hill: The University of North Carolina Press, 1940.

Selections from the inaugurals and other pronouncements of college presidents on various aspects of higher education from 1864 to 1938, including its purposes and weaknesses, its organization and administration, relations of faculties and students, academic freedom, research, the education of women, and other issues.

KNIGHT, EDGAR W., and HALL, CLIFTON L. *Readings in American Educational History.* New York: Appleton-Century-Crofts, Inc., 1951.

Chaps. iv and viii contain original documents bearing on some of the topics discussed in this Chapter.

LOVEJOY, CLARENCE E. *So You're Going to College.* New York: Simon & Schuster, 1940.

Contains much information on various aspects of higher education in the United States, and interesting facts about such matters as scholarships and how to get them.

SCHMIDT, GEORGE P. *The Old Time College President.* New York: Columbia University Press, 1930.

Shows the high importance of the functions and duties of the chief administrative officer of institutions for higher education in the old days. Excellent for comparison with his functions and duties in the twentieth century. Contains good bibliography on higher education.

The Idea and Practice of General Education. Chicago: The University of Chicago Press, 1950.

An interesting account, by former and present members of the faculty, of the college of the University of Chicago.

TUNIS, JOHN R. *Was College Worth While?* New York: Harcourt, Brace & Co., 1936.

Tells how 541 Harvard graduates of the class of 1911 were getting along after twenty-five years out of Cambridge. Somewhat dismal but arresting: "That lamp of learning, tended by the ancient Greeks, . . . handed down to us in direct line, . . . has at least produced a group of men whose chief ambitions if their record tells the truth are to vote the Republican ticket, to keep out of the bread line, and to break 100 at golf."

Chapter 5

GRADUATE, PROFESSIONAL, SUMMER, AND EXTENSION WORK

PREVIEW OF THE CHAPTER

The first half of the twentieth century witnessed many educational activities not systematically chartered in the nineteenth century. . . . At mid-century the American people had a keener zest than ever before for higher degrees, which had greatly increased in kind and number. . . . Criticisms of the loose manner in which degrees were awarded had long been made, and the story of the master's, the Ph.D., and especially of honorary degrees was not always inspiring. At mid-century, questions of reputable standards were widely discussed. . . . Graduate work in teacher education especially had become big business and was the cause of much confusion. . . . Conditions in medical, engineering, dental, and legal education were also confusing in the latter part of the nineteenth and the early part of the twentieth century, but significant studies in these fields brought great improvements. . . . The wide popularization of higher education through summer sessions and extension services of universities and colleges was a "phenomenon without parallel in the social history of the world." Both of these activities often developed in the face of institutional indifference and sometimes open hostility, but they came to give good accounts of themselves. . . . Interest and activity in adult education was greatly extended, and there was wide publication and discussion of the subject. By mid-century hundreds of thousands of Americans were enrolled in the "invisible university" and were studying where they lived and worked. . . . A very significant educational development, chiefly in the first half of the century, was the university press which seemed "here to stay" and had to be reckoned with by commercial presses.

Unchartered Educational Activities.—The first half of the twentieth century witnessed extraordinary educational activities in directions that had not been systematically chartered in the nineteenth century. Prominent among these new developments were the rapid increase in graduate work, reforms in professional education, especially in medicine, law, engineering, and dentistry, the rapid growth of summer sessions and extension services in higher educational institutions, and the rise of university presses.

The excessive enthusiasm for the possession of advanced academic degrees during the first half of the twentieth century, and the ways by means of which these could be had, often without too much intellectual inconvenience, became manifold and sometimes mysterious. At mid-century the desire to get ahead by degrees burned deeper than ever before in the breasts of Americans, and if their hopes got deferred, their hearts got sick.

An academic degree has been described as the "official recognition bestowed by a university that a certain step or grade has been attained in a branch of learning." But the tendency to increase the number and titles of degrees was pointed out more than seventy years ago when the charge was made that already the "multiplication of degrees" had been carried to an extreme in the United States. It was also said that many of the degrees were worthless because they were given by institutions which by no means came up to university rank in equipment, staff, curriculum, or requirements, and that no distinction was then made between degrees obtained on examination and honorary degrees. In addition to granting degrees on low requirements, criticism was also made of the practice of conferring honorary degrees "either for insufficient reasons or at a price." The result was that the holders of "bona fide degrees from institutions of good standing" were in danger of being classed with those whose degrees were worthless. This danger was still threatening at mid-twentieth century.

Samuel Eliot Morison, the official historian of Harvard, says in his *Three Centuries of Harvard* that "the granting of degrees was the boldest thing President Henry Dunster and the first Board of Overseers ever did; for the conferring of academic titles was a jealously guarded prerogative of sovereignty, to be exercised only by express grant from pope, emperor, or king. It raised Harvard from the status of a collegiate school to a university college, and gave a new incentive to the students, especially after Oxford and Cambridge had recognized Harvard degrees as equivalent to theirs." When President Mather conferred upon himself and on some members of his faculty the degree of doctor of divinity, he is said to have changed Harvard from a college to a university. From that time on the people of this country became increasingly degree-minded.

President A. Lawrence Lowell of Harvard said that "Daniel Coit Gilman did a great work" as the organizer and first president of The Johns Hopkins University, "making in the highest ranges of education the largest single advance in the annals of our country." But he also said that "President Gilman's one mistake, . . . was that of conferring degrees. He would have done better to confer no degrees and let their productions speak for themselves." The third annual report (1878) of this first strictly graduate school to be established in the United States stated that Hopkins had received many inquiries "as to whether candidates not connected with this university might come up at stated times and be examined for the diploma without receiving here systematic instruction."

American Mania for Academic Degrees.—Criticisms of the mania of Americans for academic degrees had been made early. In his report for 1876, the year in which Hopkins was opened, United States Commissioner of Education John Eaton vigorously charged that the sale of diplomas had become a disgrace to institutions of learning in the United States, and he was confident that there should be some way to put "an effectual stop to the occasion of the scandal." Institutions in this country were selling diplomas not only here but also in Europe. Eaton continued to call attention in his annual reports to the fact that some institutions shamelessly advertised degrees for specified sums of money—a scandal and disgrace to the United States—because such institutions were frauds, he asserted.

In 1880, Andrew D. White, the American minister to Berlin, had written to the Secretary of State of the United States of his experiences in Germany with holders of fraudulent American degrees. He said that such cases had "brought disgrace upon the American system of advanced education and upon the American name in general . . ." The practice was ridiculed in a "successful play now running at the Royal Theater in this city" and in a novel by a popular author in Germany. The scoundrel in the book escaped justice in Germany, went to America, and settled down comfortably to practice medicine with a "sham diploma which he has bought for money." At the meeting in 1881 of the American Association for the Advancement of Science, vigorous criticism was made of the "indiscriminate and lavish way in which the Doctor of Philosophy and Doctor of Science were conferred as honorary degrees" instead of as "earned rewards for scientific work and high attainments in philosophic study." [1]

A Question of Reputable Standards.—During the 1880's and 1890's, criticisms of the loose manner in which degrees were conferred continued to be made, and the breezy Edward Lawrence God-

[1] See S. E. Epler, *Honorary Degrees: A Survey of Their Use and Abuse* (Washington, D. C.: American Council of Public Affairs, 1943).

kin of the *Nation* called for a thorough examination of the practice. The country was "swarming with Masters of Arts who had never mastered any arts, and Doctors of Laws who do not know any law, and Doctors of Divinity with whom divinity has very little indeed to do." Such degrees excited the reverence of no human being, but brought higher education "into popular disrepute."

In September, 1892, the *Educational Review* said editorially that protest had reached that publication against those colleges that conferred the degree of doctor of philosophy as an honorary degree. The magazine called this a pernicious and demoralizing practice and stated that at the commencement season in 1892 scores of such degrees were given "without any warrant whatever." No college was justified in giving the Ph.D. at all, and no "university should confer it except for advanced study and research carried on in residence." The journal had been asked to list the institutions that persisted in the abuse and to publish the list from time to time. But it appeared that it might be more "efficacious to print a list of the persons who receive and accept such a degree."

Two months later the same magazine published a communication by Charles W. Super, of Ohio University at Athens, Ohio, who said that a large portion of the college faculties of the United States shared the opinions of the *Educational Review* on this subject. "But what are they to do when boards of trustees take the matter in hand and grant the degree without consulting them?" Cases had occurred in which trustees not only acted without the sanction of the faculties, but against their vigorous protest; there were some men prominent in educational circles "whose influence can be bought with such a low price." There were boards of trustees "shortsighted enough to suppose that the influence of such men will be of more value to an institution authorized to confer degrees than a reputation for care in the bestowal of its honors." He called the degree business in this country a "huge farce." Degree-conferring institutions were usually "liberal in the inverse ratio to their importance."

In 1893 the *Educational Review* said that either because the severe winter and hot spring had killed the crop of locally great men, or for some other reason, the supply of honorary degrees was smaller during the commencement of 1893 than usual. True, it said, hundreds of new D.D.'s and several scores of LL.D's were still at large. The hopelessly discredited M.A. was sparingly used as an honorary degree that commencement season. "But it has already fallen so far that it may as well be allowed to tumble the entire distance."

As late as 1911, the United States Bureau of Education was receiving complaints from abroad of the continued practice of selling degrees or of conferring them indiscriminately or casually. About that time Potomac University of Washington, D. C. was offering the degree of Ph.D. for the completion of four courses, every one of which consisted of only two textbooks, the titles of which were given in the announcement of the university, which offered to supply the books and all necessary expenses for the degree "for $90, payments to suit." Apparently any person to whom this offer was addressed would be accepted without investigation for graduate work *in absentia.*

Odessa University of Odessa, Washington, offered the degree of doctor of divinity in the following letter which was received by the assistant pastor of a large church in the City of Washington:

THE ODESSA UNIVERSITY

(Incorporated under the laws of Congress
of the
United States of America.)

Odessa, Wash.,
September 21, 1911.

Dear Sir: It has been represented to me that you are well entitled to the Degree of Doctor of Divinity, by reason of your work in the Congregational Church. If you care to send ten dollars for our Library and answer a few questions, a Diploma for that Degree will be sent you. A fine diploma hung on the wall of your study will enlarge your reputation.

In a book on the education of Negroes in the United States, published in Paris in 1904, appeared a criticism of diplomas in Negro institutions. Institutions for Negroes, imitating their white brothers, were awarding "diplomas without the least modesty for the university prerogative." It was also charged that degrees were sold. In this book appeared the story of an institution in the South whose administrative and teaching staffs consisted of only two members, and they were of the same family. The father was president and the son was the faculty, both degreeless. They held a faculty meeting and voted to confer the degree of doctor of laws on the president and the degree of doctor of philosophy on the faculty. The book reported another case, that of an eminent Negro preacher who was invited to give the commencement address at a Negro "university" in the South, and he performed the task to the best of his ability.

The institution then proposed to remunerate him by paying his traveling expenses or by conferring on him the degree of doctor of divinity. The minister chose traveling expenses. The book also stated that higher institutions had so overflowed the United States "with learned degrees that these titles have lost the significance which we wish to attach to them. They are not recognized by the universities in Europe." [2]

The master's degree in the United States has had a very capricious and irregular history. For a long time it was awarded as honorary. According to the official historian of Harvard, the class of 1869 was the last of the institution "whose members were allowed to take the M.A. for 'keeping out of jail for five years and paying five dollars,' as the saying was." At mid-twentieth century the master's was now and then conferred as an honorary degree; and the master's in course was causing graduate councils and deans innumerable academic headaches.

By the 1870's candidates for the degrees of master of arts, doctor of philosophy, and doctor of science at Harvard were placed under the direction of "the reorganized academic council," and candidates for the master's there were then required "to pass with high credit four courses of instruction of advanced grade, pursued for one academic year," and also to pass an examination. Under this reorganization, Harvard is said to have conferred "its first earned master of arts degree" in 1874. Yale announced in 1877 that it would confer the master's on bachelors of two or more years' standing who gave "to the academical faculty evidence of having made satisfactory progress in liberal studies . . ." This evidence could be provided by one year's "systematic study (not professional) in New Haven under the direction of the academical faculty, followed by an examination." The earned degree of master of arts seems to have been given at the University of South Carolina in 1812, at the University of Virginia in 1833, at the University of North Carolina in 1856, at the University of Georgia in 1871, at Princeton in 1879, at Brown in 1888, at Pennsylvania in 1891, although it should be said that accurate information on the practice seems not to be available. [3]

The story of the Ph.D. is perhaps a little less confusing than that of the master's, although confusing enough. Fifteen years before

[2] Kate Brousseau, *L'Education des negres aux États-Unis*. Paris: F. Alcan, 1904. Pp. 282-83.

[3] See W. C. John, *Graduate Study in Universities and Colleges in the United States.* Bulletin No. 20, 1934. Washington, D. C.: U. S. Office of Education, 1935. This is good as far as it goes; but at mid-twentieth century there was not available a definitive study of graduate work in the United States.

The Johns Hopkins University was organized in 1876, the first strictly graduate school in the United States, Yale seems to have conferred the first earned Ph.D. in this country. Candidates for this degree were required to pursue studies for at least two years beyond the bachelor's degree, in philosophy and the arts. During that period "universities and even small struggling undergraduate colleges were conferring the Ph.D. on an honorary basis, a very vexing practice that rendered imperative the later development of high Ph.D. standards . . ." [4] At the Universtiy of Pennsylvania the Ph.D. was first conferred as an earned degree in 1870, and three years later Harvard conferred it and the degree of doctor of science. Columbia first conferred the degree in 1875 in the School of Mines. In 1883 the School of Political Science in that institution conferred its first Ph.D. degree, and nine years later the Faculty of Pure Science was established there. Princeton gave the degree in 1879, when the degree of doctor of science was also conferred in that institution; the degree was first given by the University of Michigan in 1876; by the University of North Carolina in 1883; by the University of Virginia in 1885; by Brown University in 1889; and by the University of South Carolina in 1891. In 1870-71 Harvard, Yale, Princeton, Michigan, and Lafayette College reported a total of forty-four students pursuing graduate work, the largest number in any one institution being twenty-four at Yale. In 1872 graduate enrollments numbered about 200. The number in 1880 was about 460; in 1890 about 2.3 thousand; in 1900 about 5.8 thousand; in 1910 about 9.3 thousand; in 1920 about 15.6 thousand; and in 1930 about 47.25 thousand. The number of master's degrees awarded in 1900 was about 1.74 thousand; in 1910 about 2.4 thousand; in 1920 about 3.87 thousand; in 1930 about 14.5 thousand. Doctorates awarded in 1900 were about 340; in 1910 about 400; in 1920 about 530; in 1930 about 2 thousand. Between 1930 and 1950 graduate enrollments increased enormously, and in the latter year more than 60 thousand master's degrees and about 7 thousand doctorates were conferred in course.

By mid-twentieth century questions of standards and of practices in graduate work had been under increasing discussion for a long time. This became very vigorous after the founding of the Association of American Universities in 1900, upon the call of the presidents

[4] Carter V. Good, "History of Graduate Instruction in the United States," in Nelson B. Henry (ed.), *Graduate Study in Education, Part I.* The Fiftieth Yearbook of the National Society for the Study of Education (Chicago: The University of Chicago Press, 1951), p. 3.

of a few of the leading institutions of higher learning. Those institutions invited to participate in discussing the vexatious problems of graduate work included the University of California, Catholic University of America, Chicago, Clark, Columbia, Cornell, Harvard, Johns Hopkins, Michigan, Pennsylvania, Princeton, Stanford, Wisconsin, and Yale. The membership in that organization, whose influence on graduate work has been very marked, gradually increased, and in 1950 it numbered thirty-five institutions. The organization has worked on and formulated standards for and the administration of advanced degrees, with the result that graduate work was greatly improved; efforts were constantly made to safeguard the integrity of higher academic degrees. Before this organization was formed, however, opposition to some practices had been made by the American Philological Association, the American Association for the Advancement of Science, and other learned societies and organizations. There was vigorous opposition to the award of the Ph.D. as an honorary degree, four hundred of which had been awarded between 1872 and 1898. In 1893 the Affiliated Clubs of Graduate Students and the University Senate of the General Conference of the Methodist Episcopal Church had condemned the practice, which continued, however, until as late as 1912. Other organizations which later concerned themselves with issues in graduate instruction included the National Association of State Universities, the Association of Land-Grant Colleges and Universities, the American Association of University Professors, the Department of Colleges and Universities of the National Catholic Educational Association, and perhaps others.

In 1915 the Association of American Universities reaffirmed its belief "that the master's degree should stand for at least one year of bona fide graduate study; that all institutions in the Association should maintain a minimum residence requirement of one year, and that when candidacy for the master's degree is conducted through summer sessions, the required work should be the full equivalent of that otherwise required for the degree sought"—five summer sessions of six weeks each. But as summer sessions and university extension services grew and the demand for the certification of teachers increased, other practices in so-called graduate work developed which did not always equate closely with the resolution of the Association of American Universities. In 1932 that organization expressed belief that there was widespread dissatisfaction with the status of the master's degree, but said that the "immediate standardization of requirements is impracticable in view of the several useful purposes which the degree now serves in different institutions."

By 1950 the ways in which the master's degree could be obtained were more numerous than ever, and most institutions seemed to enjoy freer enterprise in its award than they had had since it was handed out as an honorary degree. Advanced degrees especially appealed to teachers. The relation between degrees and better salaries became closer, and the institutions that provided the easiest ways to degrees generally had the largest enrollments. In 1935, 71 per cent of all successful candidates for the doctorate planned to teach or were engaged in teaching when they received the degree; and 93 per cent of college presidents required either a master's or doctorate for appointment to their staffs. When the certificating bureaus of state departments of education began to increase requirements for teaching in the public schools, better salaries for advanced degrees were guaranteed, and the boom and boon for the teacher-education institutions were on.

Graduate Work in Teacher Education.—It was out of these conditions that graduate work in teacher education had by 1950 become a big part of the big business of graduate work. About one third of all advanced degrees awarded in 1951 were in teacher education, mostly master's, and more than a thousand of the nearly 7 thousand doctorates were in that field, counting the Ph.D. along with the D.Ed., which had been invented as a degree in course. Apparently the fact that advanced degrees in education, especially the master's, gave the holders increased salaries in teaching and managing schools, accounted in part for this rapid growth, but the feverish promotional activities of the managers of teachers' colleges and departments and schools of education in the colleges and universities which were in keen competition for students also helped to account for the phenomenon. Keenly observing critics were saying that some of the teacher-education institutions had resorted to the methods of Chambers of Commerce in bidding for students and those that offered the degrees with the least difficulty were likely to have the largest enrollments. While the possession of the master's degree, which at mid-century could be had in numerous varieties, had generally become a guarantee of better salaries in the public schools, the sources of the degrees were not always the concern of those who gave or got them or of those who engaged the holders for positions. Nor was their content inquired into by those who got or who gave the degrees or by employers. The mere possession of the master's had come to be sufficient to command a larger salary, whether it was conferred by a member of the American Association of Universities or by a feeble department or school of education or by a monohippic normal school. The tendency to fill positions in the schools with degrees rather than with able, cultivated, and broadly educated men and women was coming to be a cause of concern for the quality of the public schools.

It was apparent at mid-century that a careful study of practices in teacher education, especially on the graduate level, was long over-due and increasingly pressed for national attention. It was observed that teacher education had grown up somewhat haphazardly with a bewildering variety of practices of varying and perhaps doubtful standards of excellence, just as had been the case in medical, legal, dental, and engineering education, with the tendency for teacher-education institutions to become trade schools and their products mechanics, instead of centers for ideas and for the generous and broad education of workers in the schools. It was urged that studies such as those made earlier of medical, legal, dental, and engineering edu-cation be provided. Freedom of enterprise and laissez faire were so powerful, and were operating so widely in the education of teachers, and there were so many vested interests in that activity, that pros-pects for such searching and healthy studies were dismal at mid-century. Here and there, however, interest in this issue seemed to be growing, and the Southern Association of Colleges and Secondary Schools was giving some attention to it.

Medical, Engineering, Dental, and Legal Education.—Measured by modern standards, American practices in medical, legal, engi-neering, and dental education were not very reputable until the present century, and that had advanced considerably before some of the sorely needed reforms in these professions were made. On the education for each of these professions, the Carnegie Foundation for the Advancement of Teaching made and published fact-finding studies between 1910 and 1928 which not only provided some important educational history, but more importantly had very healthy effects on these forms of professional education by turning the searchlight on and driving out some spurious practices.

Conditions in medical education were generally very unworthy until after 1910, except in a few places. Bad conditions had reached back to the eighteenth century when only 335 medical degrees of all kinds were conferred and thirty-nine of these were honorary.[5] In the American colonial period, the University of Edinburgh was con-

---

[5] William F. Norwood, *Medical Education in the United States* (Philadelphia: University of Pennsylvania Press, 1944).

sidered the finest medical center in the world and many Americans attended it; but in the colonies there were generally no good arrangements for the study of medicine.   One wishing to do so was generally apprenticed to a practitioner who was looked upon as the young man's preceptor and who had his own ideas about medical standards and rules.   At the termination of the apprenticeship contract, or if no contract existed, if the preceptor decided that the apprentice was qualified to begin the practice of medicine, he issued the young man a certificate to do so.   Abraham Flexner describes the apprenticeship-preceptorial arrangement this way:

It began, and for many years continued to exist, as a supplement to the apprenticeship system still in vogue during the seventeenth and eighteenth centuries. The likely youth of that period, destined to a medical career, was at an early age indentured to some reputable practitioner to whom his service was successively menial, pharmaceutical, and professional: he ran his master's errands, washed the bottles, mixed the drugs, spread the plasters, and finally, as the stipulated term drew towards its close, actually took part in the daily practice of his preceptor—bleeding his patients, pulling their teeth, and obeying a hurried summons in the night. The quality of the training varied within large limits with the capacity and conscientiousness of the master.[6]

Prior to 1800, four medical schools, still in existence, had been founded: Pennsylvania, 1765; Columbia (first known as King's College Medical Faculty), 1767; Harvard, 1782; and Dartmouth, 1797. The early medical colleges enjoyed the benefits of completely free enterprise and regulated their own admission requirements, course of study, length of the period of instruction and the fees, on which each institution depended for its support, a practice that encouraged active competition for students. Effort was not often placed upon a systematic course of study but rather upon the speed and the small cost with which the student could acquire the medical degree. The college that offered the degree on the easiest terms was generally the college that got the most students, as was the case in the middle of the twentieth century in some forms of graduate work in the United States. Because of competition, the course was shortened from six months, as was required in Philadelphia and New York prior to 1800, to sixteen weeks or less. It was this short term that Charles W. Eliot found at Harvard when he became president there in 1869. By 1850, medical colleges in the United States had increased from four to forty, and the annual number of graduates from fifteen to

[6] *Medical Education in the United States and Canada.* The Carnegie Foundation for the Advancement of Teaching (Boston: D. B. Updike, 1910), p. 3.

more than one thousand. But commercialism in medical education, as in legal and dental education, was an affliction which persisted far into the twentieth century. Most of the professional schools were private and proprietary; even those connected with institutions for higher education were generally required to make their own way, the professors, usually practitioners in the community, collecting their own fees.

Eliot "found more bad blood" in Harvard's medical faculty "than in all the rest of the university put together." The students were rowdy and illiterate and many of them had little preliminary education. They were required to attend lectures for sixteen weeks, although they had to wait three years for the degree, to meet the requirement of apprenticeship training with a practicing physician. The examination was given orally on nine different courses, each requiring approximately ten minutes, and passing five out of the nine was necessary for the M.D. degree. Deaths from malpractice by a Harvard medical graduate and anxiety of the Board of Overseers over the bad conditions in medical education at Harvard enabled Eliot to get reforms. These included the requirements of regular tuition fees of students, and salaries for the professors; rigid entrance requirements; a progressive three-year course to be passed regularly by all students at the end of each year; and written examinations. Eliot, in the words of Dr. Oliver Wendell Holmes, a member of the medical faculty, turned the place over "like a flapjack." Some of the reforms went into effect in 1871; entrance examinations were required in 1877. Enrollments dropped in 1872 but were up again in 1879. In 1908, Eliot told the Council on Medical Education of the American Medical Association that with the introduction of the three-year course in 1871 the medical school "began to be endowed. Since we demanded a degree for admission, we have an additional endowment of $4 million. Gentlemen, the way to get endowments for medical education is to improve standards," he was quoted as saying.

Meantime, tendencies toward reform in medical education had been encouraged by the formation of local and state medical societies, and especially of the American Medical Association. Apparently the first efforts to initiate and stimulate reform came from an invitation of the medical societies of Vermont and New Hampshire to similar societies of other New England States and New York to send delegates to a meeting at Northampton, Massachusetts, in 1827, for the purpose of discussing educational reform. Among the proposals made were the forming of a national society; requiring the study of medicine for three years after the A.B. degree before the M.D. could be conferred; requiring full terms of courses; insisting on good moral character in the candidates; making the plan effective July 4, 1829. When the date arrived, however, each school looked to the others to take the lead, and the plan did not develop. In 1835 the Medical College of Georgia suggested concerted action in getting standards for medical education, but no definite step was taken until 1844, at the annual meeting of the New York Medical Society, when a series of resolutions were presented "declaring in favor of the adoption of a fair standard of general education for students before commencing the study of medicine; of lengthening the annual courses of medical college instruction to at least six months . . . ; and of having all examinations for license to practice medicine conducted by state boards, independent of the colleges." After brief discussion, the resolutions were laid on the table until the next meeting when they were freely discussed, but provision for a fair standard of medical education was not made.

After several attempts to get a national meeting, one was finally convened in New York in May, 1846, to establish a national organization for the purpose of elevating standards in medical education. The resolutions offered at that time proposed extending the period of college lectures from four to six months; three years of instruction, including the college lectures; the candidate must be twenty-one years of age and must present the certificate of his preceptor to show when he began his medical studies; the certificate of no preceptor "shall be received who is avowedly and notoriously an irregular practitioner, whether he shall possess the degree or not." It was also recommended that the curricula of the medical colleges be strengthened, and that the number of professors be increased to seven; that preceptors impart clinical instruction to their pupils; that medical colleges show that their candidates for graduation had had hospital experience; that the medical faculties find some efficient means of ascertaining whether their students actually attended the lectures; that preceptors advise their students to attend only those institutions that "rigidly adhere to the recommendations herein contained." It was also recommended that young men should have acquired "a suitable preliminary education" before being received as students of medicine; that the medical profession be guided by the same code of medical ethics; that license to practice be granted by a single Board of Medical Examiners; and that suitable laws should be enacted in each state for the registration of vital statistics and the "adoption of a nomenclature of diseases."

Because of the ease with which medical colleges could get charters from the states to operate, abuses continued. The characteristics of the "proprietary" medical school reflected a "society that worshipped the principles of unchecked free enterprise and unlimited laissez faire." Vested interests were to remain powerful, and for a long time able to prevent the American Medical Association from doing what it should have been able to do—establish national standards for medical education and make the colleges accept them or not be recognized. By 1867 the American Medical Association was able to get agreement on a resolution declaring that "a fair preliminary education equal to a full academic or high-school course ought to be required of all students before entering upon the study of medicine; and that the time of medical study should be four years; including at least three consecutive annual courses of graded medical college instruction of not less than six months each, with hospital clinical instruction during the last college year." As late as 1903 only the Chicago Medical College, later known as Northwestern Medical School, was meeting these standards.[7] A few other institutions followed; and the continued discussion in medical societies and in the medical journals developed a public sentiment that led to the establishment of state boards of health and examination. The American Public Health Association, which had been organized in the 1860's, passed resolutions not unlike those passed by the medical societies. The formation of the Council on Medical Education of the American Medical Association in the early part of the present century, and its energetic activities and the medical survey by the Carnegie Foundation for the Advancement of Teaching in 1910, hastened reforms in medical education in the United States.

The study by N. P. Colwell for the Council on Medical Education and by Abraham Flexner for the Carnegie Foundation for the Advancement of Teaching disclosed wide variations in the practices of medical schools and in the licensing of physicians.[8] This report, which came to have a wide and healthy influence in medical education, set out that the state boards of medical examiners were potentially very useful instruments by which reforms in medical education could be made. These boards could discover the good and the bad schools of medicine by testing the quality of the graduates who had

[7] N. S. Davis, *History of Medicine, with the Code of Medical Ethics* (Chicago: The Cleveland Press, 1903).

[8] *Medical Education in the United States and Canada*, Bulletin No. 4, Carnegie Foundation for the Advancement of Teaching (Boston: D. B. Updike, 1910). This came to be called the "Flexner Report."

been vouched for by the degrees which they held; a large proportion of failures from a school would invite and get serious doubt of its competence and integrity. A state board could also help by refusing its examinations to a graduate from a bad school: "the full weight of its refusal would fall with crushing effect upon the school which had sent him forth," asserted the report.

No institution can long survive the day upon which it is thus publicly branded as feeble, unfit, or disreputable. For the purpose, however, of saving the victims whose cruel disappointment will in time destroy these schools, the arm of the state boards should for the present go beyond the rejection of individuals to the actual closing up of notoriously incompetent institutions. The law that protects the public against the unfit doctor should in fairness protect the student against the unfit school.

The report urged more careful attention by state boards to the amount of general education which a candidate for the examinations by these boards had had prior to his medical education, and said that the "enforcement of even a four-year high school standard will so far clean up the medical field that the state boards will at once be relieved of the duty of dealing with actually disreputable schools. Until that has been accomplished, these boards should be empowered to refuse applicants from the graduates of schools scandalously defective in teaching facilities." Examination for license to practice medicine was undoubtedly "the lever with which the entire field may be lifted." At the time of this report, forty-nine states and territories had eighty-two different boards of medical examiners. "The province of the state in this matter is plain. It cannot allow one set of practitioners to exist on easier and lower terms than another. It cannot indeed be a party to scientific or sectarian controversy. But it can and must safeguard the conditions upon which such controversy may be fought to its finish . . ." The state boards, the report said, had abundantly justified themselves, although they were hardly more than a quarter of a century old; but among the forces that had within that period stimulated improved conditions, the state boards had to be prominently mentioned. As a result of this report and the increasing influence of the American Medical Association, standards of medical education were raised significantly. By 1915 the medical schools had been reduced from 160 [9] to ninety-five

---

[9] For conditions in medical education and comments on the "potential employment" of physicians, see Seymour E. Harris, *The Market for College Graduates* (Cambridge: Harvard University Press, 1949). *Passim.*

and by 1927 to eighty. At mid-twentieth century there were seventy-two four-year and seven two-year medical colleges in the United States with about five thousand men and women being graduated annually.

When the Association of American Colleges met in annual session in 1950, there was much discussion of the role of the professional school in higher education. The profession of medical education was rather severely criticized, and the American Conference of Academic Deans, by resolution, called upon the Association of Medical Colleges to admit more students. In answer to the question why the medical colleges did not themselves decide upon the number of students to be admitted, it was pointed out that the colleges and universities had "lost control over the medical, dental, and veterinary schools." These had their own accrediting agencies which, to a large extent, determined the number of graduates that could be annually "absorbed." One prominent university president was quoted as saying: "I have no voice whatever in our medical school. The dean and the faculty of the school do whatever they wish. If I should interfere in any way, I'd have the Association of Medical Colleges and maybe the American Medical Association itself down on me like a ton of bricks." It was said that one result of this condition was that not many of those who applied for entrance to medical, dental, or veterinary schools could be admitted. The academic deans complained that this was due to an "arbitrary and artificial" formula for admission, and at the same time the deans claimed that the nation needed more doctors.

At that meeting it was reported that of the 25 thousand who applied for admission to medical schools in the fall of 1949, only 6,387 were admitted. About the same ratio was reported for the dental schools, to which 12 thousand candidates applied for the 2,794 places available. The schools of veterinary medicine admitted 858 out of 3,277 applicants. The complaint alleged that many of the rejected applications were good students, but there just was not room for them. It also came out that in 1905 the 160 medical schools in the United States enrolled 26 thousand students and had graduating classes of 5.6 thousand. In 1950 there were seventy-nine medical schools of two or four years with a student body of 23.6 thousand, and in June of 1949 the graduates of these schools numbered about 5 thousand. Meantime, however, the population of the United States had increased from 84 million in 1905 to about 150 million in 1950. In 1905 also there was one medical student to every six undergraduate students in colleges and universities; in 1950 the ratio was one to one hundred.[10]

A slightly different view of the condition which the academic deans saw so dismal was presented by Dr. Howard A. Rusk. He wrote in the *New York Times* of September 10, 1950, that 7 thousand "fortunate young men and women" who were selected from 24.4 thousand applicants to "an average of three or four different medical schools" the spring before, would that month enter upon their first year of medical study. He thought it paradoxical, at first glance, that there were cries for more doctors, that legislation was being prepared to draft physicians into the military service, and that at the same time "thousands of prospective young students are denied the opportunity of studying medicine." And he referred to the views expressed by the American Conference of Academic Deans the previous January. The problem was not so simple as that given by the academic deans, Dr. Rusk thought. The medical schools of the United States, he said, had total enrollments of 25.1 thousand students in 1949. In 1910 the enrollments had been 12.5 thousand; in 1920 there were 12.5 thousand; in 1930 about 21.5 thousand; and in 1940 about 21.27 thousand. With the increase in the number of physicians produced by the medical schools there had been, Dr. Rusk said, "a disproportionate increase in the cost of medical education." Figures showed that the educational cost of operating medical schools had almost doubled between 1941 and 1949, and during those years increased taxation had reduced private funds available for endowments for medical education. One school reported that in 1950 the cost of training a medical student for four years was almost $14 thousand. Tuition fees in 1910 took care of about 70 per cent of the cost of a medical education, but in 1950 these fees accounted for only about 25 per cent of the cost. It seemed obvious that the student could not bear the current high cost of a medical education. The Council on Medical Agencies and Hospitals of the American Medical Association reported in 1950 that the budgets of the medical schools of the country totaled $76 million, an increase of 42 per cent in four years. Dr. Rusk also took notice of the action of a committee in the House of Representatives that voted nine to eight to table a bill that sought to provide federal aid for medical schools, and the proposal of another Congressional bill, also tabled, to provide for a five-year period an annual federal appropriation of

[10] See Benjamin Fine, "Education in Review," *New York Times,* January 15, 1950.

$15 million for construction grants to educational institutions in the fields of health.

Unlimited funds alone for medical education would not make it possible for everybody who wished to do so to attend medical school, Dr. Rusk noted. There were the "interrelated problems of laboratory facilities, clinical training, teaching personnel, and other factors that make medicine the most complicated of professional courses." But in spite of these obstacles, the opportunity to study medicine had practically doubled since 1910 and had "more than kept pace with the growth in population," a statement which clashed somewhat with that of the academic deans. With the closing down of "inferior, second-rate medical schools," due in part no doubt to the Flexner Report, "the number of physicians to every hundred thousand population in the United States declined from 149 in 1909 to 125 in 1929. Since 1929, the ratio has risen steadily, until today it is 133." It was obvious to Dr. Rusk that if the medical schools were to maintain the quality of medical education that was being provided in 1950, "much less expand to meet the present shortage of doctors, they must have financial help. In view of the present national emergency, differences must be resolved and action taken, for some type of Federal aid is an urgent necessity."

In late September of 1950, the Associated Press reported Federal Security Administrator Oscar Ewing, in an address in New York before the American Jewish Congress, as accusing the American Medical Association of blocking federal aid to medical education and of practicing discrimination against Jews. He said that we have been trying, "against the wishes of a single entrenched professional organization," to get federal funds for aid to medical education, at a time when private agencies were not able to make it possible for the medical schools to turn out as many doctors as were needed. And he pointed to the "plain fact" that the cost of producing a doctor was "greater than any medical school can afford." Ewing was also quoted as saying that everybody was for federal medical aid except the American Medical Association, which had been able "to bottle up this plan in a single Committee of the House of Representatives."

An important study on engineering education [11] was made by the Carnegie Foundation and published in 1918. The Society for the

---

[11] Charles R. Mann, *A Study of Engineering Education.* Prepared for the Joint Committee on Engineering Education for the National Engineering Societies (New York: The Carnegie Foundation for the Advancement of Teaching, Bulletin No. 11, 1918).

Promotion of Engineering Education invited the American Society of Civil Engineers, the American Society of Mechanical Engineers, the American Institute of Electrical Engineers, and the American Chemical Society to join them in a joint committee on the subject "to examine into all branches of engineering education, including engineering research, graduate professional courses, undergraduate engineering instruction, and the proper relations of engineering schools to secondary industrial schools, or foremen's schools, and to formulate a report or reports upon the appropriate scope of engineering education and the degree of cooperation and unity that may be advantageously arranged between the various engineering schools." A resolution was later passed which authorized this committee to enlist in the study the cooperation of the Carnegie Foundation for the Advancement of Teaching and the General Education Board. Professor Charles R. Mann of the University of Chicago was chosen to direct the investigation, and representatives of the various societies which sponsored the study expressed the belief that the report possessed high significance "on account of the simple and clear treatment of the complicated problems involved." The report concisely discussed the origin and development of engineering schools and the connection between their curricula "and the changing demands of industrial activities and growth . . ." Another significant characteristic of the report was its discussion of "values and cost," the high importance of "teaching technical subjects so as to develop character," the necessity for laboratory and industrial training throughout the courses, "and the use of good English." Other subjects discussed included the struggle for adequate resources for engineering education, the development of the engineering curriculum, administrative methods in engineering schools, the problem of the progress and the elimination of engineering students, types of instruction in the engineering school, and other problems of engineering education, such as admission, the time schedule, the content of courses, testing and grading, and shopwork. Some of these problems reached back to Rensselaer Institute, which had begun work as early as 1824; the beginning of the scientific school at Yale in 1847; the engineering department of the University of Michigan, which began to confer degrees in 1861; the work of the Massachusetts Institute of Technology, which was chartered in 1861; the influence of the Morrill Act in 1862; the School of Mines at Columbia University in 1864; to the Thayer School at Dartmouth College and to Cornell University in 1867; Worcester Polytechnic Institute in 1868; and to the activities of Illinois, California, Iowa, New Jersey, Maine,

Michigan, New Hampshire, Pennsylvania, Tennessee, Vermont, and Wisconsin before 1870, under the terms of the Morrill Act. Developments in engineering education seem to have been rather rapid between 1870 and 1900.

By 1950 or earlier, interest was growing in the need for giving more attention in engineering and technical schools to the liberal arts and the humanities. A survey of representative schools of engineering, made by the *New York Times* in 1950,[12] indicated that greater emphasis was then being placed "on the humanities (classics and belles-lettres) and social science studies." Many colleges were requiring students in engineering, especially the undergraduates, to take at least 20 per cent of their work in the liberal arts, and some, including Yale University, the California Institute of Technology, and the Carnegie Institute of Technology, were requiring as much as one fourth of the work in the humanities. The educational preparation of the professional engineer in American society, formerly so generally deficient in such fields, needed broadening, it was being said, so that he could participate more effectively in political and economic affairs. Moreover, whereas formerly engineering students often questioned the value of the humanities in their preparation, they were coming more and more to see that a graduate of a technical school was to be more than "just an engineer." By and large, the survey by the *Times* disclosed, "the scientific and engineering students want a broad nontechnical education."

The medical study by Flexner [13] and Colwell in 1910 made a significant national impression, was the subject of numerous comments by the Carnegie Foundation in its annual reports, and had the continuous study and generous support of the General Education Board and the Rockefeller Foundation; and the medical profession itself, through its numerous organizations and especially through the Council on Medical Education of the American Medical Association "maintained a constant scrutiny of medical schools and of standards of medical education. The outcome of all these efforts has been a notable advance in the quality of medical schools, in the facilities for medical education, and in the preliminary training of men for the medical profession," wrote Henry S. Pritchett in 1926.

Following the publication of the medical study, the Carnegie Foundation had many requests for other educational studies, and among these was a request from the Association of Dental Schools

12 See Benjamin Fine, "Education in Review," *New York Times,* April 16, 1950.
13 For further light on the medical study, see Abraham Flexner's autobiography, *I Remember* (New York: Simon & Schuster, 1940), chap. ix.

for a study of dental education. This was undertaken, under the direction of Dr. William J. Gies of Columbia University, and after diligent effort of five years the results were published by the Foundation as Bulletin No. 19 in 1926.[14] Thus the Foundation undertook to do for dental education what it had already done so well for medical and engineering education, to be followed a few years later by a significant study of legal education. In the study of dental education, as in the other studies, brief but excellent historical accounts of the development of this form of professional education were given.

At the time of the study of dental education, there were 44 dental schools in the United States and 5 in Canada, and state boards of dental education had since 1883 maintained a national association. But some of the dental schools were "proprietary" and not parts of institutions for higher education, just as had been the case of medical and law schools. And even some of the dental schools which were integral parts of universities were "conducted as commercial adjuncts and in close accord with the proprietary schools," but most of the independent schools desired to become regular parts of universities. Following the publication of the study of dental education, the number of schools that had been conducted for financial profit began to decrease, as had been the case in medical schools and was to be the case in law schools. Turning the searchlight on educational practices in these professions had very healthy effects.

Dental education in the United States before 1900 had not acquired reputable standing, and dentistry was "practised by an occasional physician or surgeon, many barbers and mechanics, and an increasing number of charlatans." Between the Revolutionary War and 1840 there was "a menacing growth of quackery" against which there were protests by the "conscientious and better educated dentists" who sought through books, pamphlets, papers in medical journals, and broadsides to put a stop to the evil conditions. Meantime attempts to develop dental education under medical auspices had not been successful. Dental education, Dr. Gies said in his report on the subject, had been disdained by medicine.

Between 1840, when the first dental school was chartered by the General Assembly of Maryland as the Baltimore College of Dental Surgery, until 1868, thirteen schools were established, but only one of these, that of Harvard University's dental department, was connected with a university. Sixteen schools were established between 1868 and 1884. By the latter year, nine other universities had fol-

[14] *Dental Education in the United States and Canada* (New York: The Carnegie Foundation for the Advancement of Teaching, 1926).

lowed Harvard's lead and had established dental schools. All but one of the schools founded in connection with universities, unlike the independent or proprietary schools, had survived to 1926. In that year, when the study of dental education was published, there were forty-four dental schools in the United States.

Under the conditions that encouraged commercialism in dental education, primarily for profit for the proprietors, twenty-eight schools had been chartered in Illinois alone between 1883 and 1902. Some of the proprietary schools were

. . . busy diploma mills, which, created under the sanction of indifferent state laws, conducted with the collusion of unworthy dentists, and protected by unfaithful practitioners in posts of public responsibility, freely sold the degree of doctor of dental surgery at home and abroad, to the disgrace of the profession and to the dishonor of dental education. One of these schools, selling its diploma for ten dollars, found a ready market in Germany. Fortunately, when the import of this situation was fully comprehended, organized dentistry promptly brought it to an end. But remembrance of these circumstances clings tenaciously to the reputation of American dentistry in Europe, where the most damaging consequences of these shameful conditions were experienced. [15]

Unworthy commercialism, as Gies called it, fortunately "seems never to have touched the depths reached in medical education; and fortunately also, for dental education, many of the commercial schools were too weak to survive for more than a few years."

In the study by Gies, dentistry was described as not only "a mechanical art for the maintenance of dental functions and facial comeliness, but is one of the most useful means to keep people well and to cure or alleviate disease. It is an important division of health service." In the quality and efficiency of the health service for patients, dentistry "should be made the full equivalent of an oral specialty in the practice of medicine, including the highest attainable efficiency in mechanical reparative measures," but medical knowledge could be practically applied by a dentist "only in proportion to his technical comprehension and ability." This did not mean that a dental student should be required to take all the courses leading to a medical degree, but improvement in dental education in the universities could be made by relating it more closely to medical schools, hospitals, and dispensaries. Improvement could also be made by making the preliminary education and instruction in the basic

[15] See above for complaints about the sale of American academic degrees in this country and abroad in the latter part of the past and the early part of the present century.

sciences practically the same in "general character and adaptability as for medicine; the training peculiar to dentistry should be sufficient to assure both ability to conduct a modern general practice of dentistry and capacity to grow in efficiency; and the most advanced specialties of dental practice should be reserved for optional systematic graduate study." These main objectives could be reached by requiring at least two years of collegiate work, three years of "intensive and well-integrated work in an undergraduate dental curriculum for the training of general practitioners only, the years to be lengthened if necessary; followed by optional supplementary full-year graduate curricula for all types of specialists." Under this arrangement, then known as the "two-three-graduate plan," the general practitioner "could be trained in five years after graduation from high school." In its report for 1925, the Carnegie Foundation said: "The data . . . show that whereas ten years ago graduation from a four-year high school was sufficient for admission to all but two schools, now all require in addition at least one year of approved work in an accredited academic college, and nearly half the number, exactly two years. General adjustment to the latter admission requirements is now clearly in progress."

By 1946 the proprietary dental school, which had so long flourished, had disappeared from the American educational scene. At that time there was no longer any dental school in the United States organized and conducted for its owner's financial profit. Instead, all the 40 schools at that time were legally established "on a nonstock basis," and 36 of these were integral parts of institutions for higher education, 13 of state universities and 23 of privately endowed institutions, four of which received some public support. Of the four other schools, without complete integration with higher institutions, one was affiliated with a privately endowed university but under the control of a separate board of trustees; one was privately supported; and two were integral units in educational institutions, one under public and one under private support, "without university status but organized on a university level in a field of professional education." By 1951 there were two additional schools, one in the University of Alabama and the other in the University of North Carolina.

In 1926-27 the requirement of one year of college work had been established for admission to dental schools. Two to four years of college work became a requirement ten years later; and beginning with 1942, ninety quarter hours of credit, with one year in biology, English, inorganic chemistry, and physics, and one semester in organic chemistry, became the requirements for admission. The most perplexing problem in dental education at mid-century, as it had been for many years, was to secure "adequate support from society to train dentists effectively to do what society insistently asks of them." [16] Gifts for the support of this form of professional education, which the study of dental education in 1926 had anticipated and hoped for, "have not been made in sufficient number and volume," Horner wrote.

Standards in legal education, which had been very low and casual before that time, also began to be raised after 1900. Some of the conditions that had made for slow progress in raising these standards continued, "but their retarding influence has been substantially diminished." [17] Larger organized efforts to improve standards were made after the turn of the century than had been made "by the preceding generation. Previous sporadic attempts of local or state bar associations to accomplish something have been reinforced by the activities of the American Bar Association." In 1893 that organization had strengthened the work of its Committee on Legal Education by forming a section on that subject, which led to the organization of the Association of American Law Schools for the purpose of improving "legal education in America, especially in the Law Schools." Local and state bar associations advocated improvement in the rules governing admission to the practice of law, and slight reforms were made; and the Association of American Law Schools and the bar associations also, independent of action by individual states,

addressed themselves directly to the schools, and promulgated standards backed solely by their own reputation. Thus in one way or another a certain amount of pressure has been exerted upon the law schools. A loosely coordinated system of voluntary associations constitutes the organization upon which the legal profession now [1928] depends for the formulation and advocacy of an improved system of legal education. . . . It has operated primarily as an instrument for selecting, among existing practices, those which are best suited to the development of competency and character in the legal profession, and as an agency for urging their more general adoption. Within these limits it has rendered an important service. However diversified are the educational standards maintained in different jurisdictions, or in different institutions within the same state and even within the same town, the variation would have been still greater if these Associations had not been at work.

[16] H. H. Horner, *Dental Education Today* (Chicago: The University of Chicago Press, 1947).
[17] See Alfred Z. Reed, *Present-day Law Schools in the United States and Canada* (New York: The Carnegie Foundation for the Advancement of Teaching. Bulletin No. 21, 1928).

Our existing system of legal education is a growth that has sprung up within the profession, rather than a structure that the professional organization has deliberately reared. Yet the direction which this growth shall take has already been influenced by professional supervision, to a considerable extent; and in proportion as the organization dedicated to this purpose becomes perfected, it will exercise greater influence over future developments.

In 1890 there had been 61 law schools in this country. Ten years later there were 102 with about 12 thousand students. In 1910 there were 124; in 1920 there were 146; and in 1928 there were 176 schools with about 46 thousand students. Twelve of these were described as "business schools," operated in connection with business or commercial courses; seventeen were operated by the Y.M.C.A. or Knights of Columbus. One correspondence law school was operating in 1900, four such schools in 1910, and one in 1920. Of the 176 law schools in 1928, two required for the degree one or one and a half years of study, eight required two years, and 166 required three years or more. In 1900, eight schools had required only one or one and a half years; forty-seven two years; and forty-seven three years. The "short course" schools were found only in the southern states and Indiana in 1928, when the question was whether or not a period of three years was adequate for legal study. The state requirements that applicants for legal practice must spend a specified time in legal study aroused little controversy among those who favored better standards. In 1860 only nine states or territories out of thirty-nine had had such a requirement; in 1890 nearly half of them had it. Yet in that year only nine states required as much as three years of study, and only five any "proof of even rudimentary general education." [18]

In 1900 requirements for admission to the practice of law were also customarily low, and most members of the legal profession were not easily aroused to a sense of need for reform. Themselves the product of primitive educational methods, they generally owed their own standing in the profession more often to experience gained in the practice of law than to systematic preparation for its practice. "In their own cases the laissez-faire policy pursued by the State had worked out well. It was difficult for them to feel that there was any crying need for change. Furthermore, the element among them which did not appreciate the importance of better preparation for practice were not by any means in entire sympathy with the efforts in this direction that were already being put forth by the law

[18] Reed, *op. cit.*, p. 11.

schools." Those lawyers who had been trained in offices of other lawyers did not favor the proposal that young men should spend their entire preparatory period in law schools.

Continuing, Reed wrote:

Lawyers who had been trained either in offices or in orthodox law schools did not approve of the radical innovations that were being introduced at Harvard. Lawyers who were in actual practice thought that practitioner bar examiners ought to formulate and administer standards of admission, to which law schools should be obliged to conform. Not infrequently, therefore, the particular measures that were recommended by the profession aroused the opposition of the schools. Law school authorities, with their loyal graduates, were not as yet sufficiently numerous or sufficiently united to assume the lead in devising more stringent requirements for admission to the bar. They could and did, however, exert their influence to block reforms that were contrary to the interests of their institutions, and thus contrary to the interests of the community as they understood it.

Insufficient educational machinery, professional apathy, and the conflicting ideals of old-fashioned practitioners and of law-school men all united, therefore, to keep requirements for admission to practice in an unsatisfactory condition. A few states had made provision for central examining boards for admission to the practice of law whose compensation came from the fees of the applicants, and some other means of improving the machinery for admission were used. But so long as widely diverse types of preparation were in vogue, and the state had not declared itself as to which should be preferred, it was impossible to give examinations that would be at once rigorous and yet fair to all applicants.

Since 1918, the Association of American Law Schools has not included in its membership "any law school not connected with a college or university." In the same year, the American Bar Association approved the action taken by many of the law schools of the country that required two years of a college course as a condition of admission to their courses of study, and the Association expressed "the conviction that this should be the minimum requirement recognized by law schools of the first class." In 1922 the Washington Conference on Legal Education resolved: *"Further,* we believe that law schools should not be operated as commercial enterprises, and that the compensation of any officer or member of its teaching staff should not depend on the number of students or on the fees received." Law schools with membership in the Association of American Law Schools, which does many useful educational things besides properly frowning on the crassly commercial type of law school, numbered 107 in 1950.

Summer Sessions and Extension Services.—A very striking fact in the development of education in this country during the first half of the twentieth century, and especially after 1920, was the wide popularization of higher education, said to have been "a phenomenon without parallel in the social history of the world." Two impressive features of that phenomenon were the tremendous growth in summer sessions and the expansion of the extension services of universities and colleges. Although both these activities had their greatest growth in the first half of this century, the roots of each reached back into the latter part of the nineteenth, and in the case of extension, perhaps to the eighteenth century. Both these services developed under difficulties and in the face of institutional indifference if not open hostility.

The summer session, which had not made much headway before 1900, had by the middle of the century become a conspicuous part of the work of the colleges and universities and of the education of teachers. Apparently the first college or university work in the summer had begun at Harvard, but off the campus, under the direction of Louis Agassiz, the famous naturalist, who in 1869 organized "a course of instruction in natural history to be delivered by the seaside in Nantucket during the summer months, chiefly designed for teachers who propose to introduce the study in their schools, and for students preparing to become teachers." Eminent scientists were on the list of instructors announced in the early 1870's after the work had been carried on for a few years chiefly by Agassiz himself. Emphasis was primarily on research for the benefit of university teachers and students and of teachers of science in secondary schools. Similar efforts were later made at Woods Hole, Massachusetts, and at Cold Spring Harbor, Long Island, New York, which stimulated the rise of other schools for biology.

Another influence upon the development of educational work in the summer was that of the Chautauqua Assembly in New York State in 1874, under the leadership of Bishop John H. Vincent of the Methodist Church, an undertaking said to have grown out of a religious camp meeting and a Sunday school institute. Summer meetings with inspirational lectures soon came to be characteristic features of the Chautauqua Assembly, which became popular and was widely imitated throughout the country, an idea that caught on in the universities and later in the colleges. It seems that the first work of this kind on the campus of a university or college was done at the University of North Carolina from 1877 to the middle 1880's. Legislative appropriations were made for the training of young white men for teaching in the public schools of the state, and the Peabody Fund made a grant of $500 to the summer school to help defray the expenses of teachers who were unable to provide them. Provision for the work extended only to men, but the university and the state board of education soon took the position that women should be allowed to attend. Some of the money appropriated by the Peabody Fund was used for that purpose, and the restriction against women was removed when the legislature renewed the appropriation. Legislative appropriations were also made for similar work for Negroes. The work at Chapel Hill was suspended in 1884, to be revived a decade later.

Educational work in the summer was begun at the University of Wisconsin in 1887, initially under the direction of the state teachers' association; at the University of Indiana in 1889; at the University of Chicago in 1892, when, under the organization of the institution on a four-quarter basis, the summer session was made a regular quarter. At Columbia University the summer session was projected after 1900 "in order to accomplish several distinct ends," wrote President Butler in his report for 1913-14. "One of these ends," all of which had been attained by that time, "was to make some provision for the use of the university buildings during what had been the unduly long holiday period of three months." It seems strange now, in the light of the rapid development of the summer session, that the practical-mindedness of the American people would have so long permitted the idleness of their educational plants. But their economic sense finally came to abhor the disuse of their immense educational resources. Another reason given by President Butler for the opening of the summer session at Columbia

. . . was to make it possible for officers of instruction who could not afford to remain without remunerative occupation during so large a part of the year to gain additional compensation while doing work that lay within the University's proper scope and that might well contribute to extend the University's influence. Still another end was to put a stop to the exceptionally bad practice of permitting and even encouraging students to remain idle, when it would be greatly to their advantage, mentally, morally, and physically, to be engaged in systematic study and in preparation for their lifework.

But he added that the main purpose of the summer session in that institution was distinct from any of these:

. . . to demonstrate the essential unity of the University and to provide one place in which that unity might manifest itself without the hampering limitations set by traditions and regulations of the various colleges, schools, and allied corporations included in the University's educational system, in order to prove not only the existence of the University's unity, but its obvious and manifold advantages. For this reason the Summer Session has been maintained from the beginning as a unit.

By 1910 the summer session, usually of a period of six weeks, although in time some institutions began to conduct it for two periods of six weeks each or for other periods, had become a common aspect of higher-education work in the United States. By 1925 at least one fourth of the teachers in this country attended summer sessions. Five years later, attendance in summer sessions in fifteen of the larger institutions was reported as follows:

Institution	Number	Institution	Number
California	7,294	Minnesota	6,210
Chicago	4,957	Nebraska	2,713
Columbia	14.016	Ohio State	4,845
Cornell	2,440	Stanford	1,262
Harvard	2,486	Texas	4,170
Illinois	3,088	Washington	3,686
Iowa	3,493	Wisconsin	5,088
Michigan	4,369		

Except for the years of the depression and the world wars, attendance at these and other institutions for higher education steadily increased between 1930 and 1950. At mid-century, approximately 940 thousand men and women were enrolled in summer sessions in universities, colleges, teachers' colleges, and normal schools, most of them teachers, and in many cities the secondary schools were also providing for work in the summer.

In its early days the summer session was not without its critics, some of whom charged that it was not only sterilizing and discrediting the profession of teaching but also ballyhooing scholarship into backwardness. Some of the critics appeared to believe that this was not a legitimate activity of a reputable college or university, and that the institution maintaining such an educational nuisance would sooner or later lose its prestige. They looked upon the summer school as a jerry-built makeshift, and thought that only professors of superficial, inferior, or doubtful scholarship would teach under such an unorthodox arrangement. They tended to say that the summer session was not a child of honor but rather the issue of the university's misplaced confidence, and that it should be considered unauthorized and spurious and treated as alma mater's illegitimate offspring and not as a son. The critics were not only wrong, but they were not always competent to testify on the subject. More competent were the thousands of men and women, most of them managers and teachers of the schools of this country, who continued to patronize this most popular of all American summer resorts.

If there should be doubt in the minds of those who question the sincerity of students in summer session, it would be rather promptly removed by a visit on almost any warm summer day to hustling and bustling Morningside Heights or Washington Square in New York, to the Midway Plaisance in Chicago, to Jefferson's University at Charlottesville, to sedate Harvard Square, to that great institution just across the Golden Gate at Berkeley, to the comfortably remote village of Chapel Hill, or to any one of a host of other educational centers throughout the United States. Every summer at these educational institutions there were being promoted and maintained some of the most important of all the organized facilities for higher and professional education to be found anywhere in the world. And the high and intelligent purposes and eager vitality of the scores of thousands of students who annually crowded into these places were vigorous rebukes to those who looked upon the summer session and wailed " 'Tis all barren."

Apparently among the warmest supporters of the summer session were those who attended and believed they profited by it. The number itself was impressive; as already noted, more than 900 thousand in 1950. At Columbia University alone, there annually gathered about 15 thousand who were enrolled in more than a thousand courses in charge of about 800 professors and instructors, nearly half of whom were drawn from other institutions. Students went to New York from every American state, from the insular and noncontiguous territories, and from numerous foreign countries. About 70 per cent of the total number were women, and more than half had studied at Columbia previously. Sixty-eight per cent belonged to that group which the critics said was repressed, and when they were not studying in summer session they were teaching in the elementary schools, the secondary schools, normal schools, and teachers' colleges, and on those higher levels of American education where so many weary ones were believed to rest, that is, in the colleges and universities. They were superintendents, supervisors, principals, and teachers from the public schools, fresh bachelors of art from soft southern colleges, staid professors from the ancient institutions in the East, and unlicked cub professors from the colleges of the exuberant West. They came from almost every Middletown in the country.

And they were not educational picnickers, but most of them meant business. On every one of the five teaching days of the six teaching weeks in the largest summer sessions, they could be found in their places in hundreds of different courses that were known in the craft as "education," and through which were exhibited the latest fashions in pedagogy and school management. Principal John Smith and Teacher Mary Jones, of the Middletown public school, were promised by the catalogue descriptions of the courses in which they were enrolled the opportunity to hear about the development, the meaning, the scientific basis, the methods, and the fundamental problems of instruction from the point of view of the various fields of educational thought and practice. And several thousand others from the highways and the byways and the hedges of the American public school system, if at Columbia, for example, joined with Mr. Smith and Miss Jones, even as early as seven-thirty in the morning, Daylight Saving Time, to hear the words of educational salvation fall fresh from the lips of the most distinguished company of scholars and professional educators ever assembled in any institution anywhere since pedagogy first began its triumphal march through this bewildered educational world. And this quest for light and leading these eager students kept up through the lengthened hours of the day and long after the sluggish citizens of Middletown had gone to their virtuous beds.

The roots of university extension and adult education reached back into the past. Benjamin Franklin's *Junto* in 1727, a scientific and literary association which developed into the American Philosophical Society, may be considered somewhat prophetic of developments that were to come in university extension and adult education. The *Junto* included in its membership a copier of deeds, a surveyor, a merchant's clerk, printers, mechanics, shoemakers, carpenters, and a "young gentleman of fortune." It was set up on liberal and democratic principles and provided opportunities for adults without reference to their educational, economic, or social conditions at a time when Harvard and Yale and perhaps other institutions for higher education were classifying their students according to the social prestige of their fathers. Another advocate of what has come to be called adult education was Thomas Jefferson. He would have come to convenient classes in late afternoon or in the evening, when they had finished their daily work, "the mariner, the builder, the metallurgist, druggist, tanner, soapmaker, and others to learn as much as shall be necessary to pursue their art understandingly."

The ideas of university extension and of adult education seem to have been transplanted to this country from England in the latter part of the nineteenth century. And the words "university extension" seem to have had their origin in England where a very striking characteristic of the movement was its close relation to labor, whose representatives and the Workers' Educational Association, founded in 1903, played important parts. But before that time the movement had taken form at some of the English universities. At Oxford, for example, more than 32 thousand extension lectures were arranged between 1885 and 1908 in 577 centers for more than 420 thousand students. Colleges for workingmen had been established before the middle of the nineteenth century. Herbert B. Adams of The Johns Hopkins University, which had organized a workingman's institute as early as 1879, was a strong advocate for the English system for this country; and Melvil Dewey, the librarian of Columbia University, in 1888 urged the Regents of the University of the State of New York to introduce university extension services.

Interest in the idea of university extension and adult education was also stimulated in this country by Bishop John H. Vincent of the Methodist Church, and William Rainey Harper, who was active in the Chautauqua Institution in New York. As pointed out below, that institution clearly had some influence on Harper and his interest in extension when the University of Chicago was opened in 1892, with him as president. Meantime the Philanthropic Society for the Extension of University Teaching, organized in 1890, had sent its secretary, George Henderson, to study university extension in England. He returned, and the name of the Philadelphia Society was changed to the American Society for Extension Teaching, and in the winter of 1890-91 that society organized twenty-three centers for extension teaching.

The purposes of the American Society for the Extension of University Teaching were the extension of higher education "for all classes of the people," of education "through the whole of adult life through methods of study to subjects of everyday interests." In 1900 the Society arranged for the delivery of nearly a hundred courses of lectures at seventy-four centers, and these lectures were attended by nearly 25 thousand people. Attendance at extension classes was about 10 thousand. Subjects were offered in history, literature, music and art, ethics and philosophy, economics, political science and social science, and one course in science. Pennsylvania led in extension centers with forty-three, followed by New York and New Jersey with twenty-one each, by Maryland with seven, and Connecticut with three. The constantly widening use of the society's lectures and university extension work appeared from the list which showed the various auspices under which courses were offered: centers primarily for teachers, 3; under the control of women's clubs, 11;

People's Institute of New York City for working men, 5; educational institutions, 9; New York City Board of Education's "Free Lectures to the People," 14; and regular university extension centers, 53. Within a decade more than a thousand courses, comprising more than six thousand lectures, had been offered, the average attendance of each lecture was about two hundred, and the aggregate attendance about 1.23 million. The movement was extending into many sections of the country through colleges and universities, especially the University of Chicago, The Regents of the University of the State of New York, Rutgers College in New Jersey, the University of Wisconsin, and colleges in California. Reading circles and study clubs on the university extension plan were also being promoted by a Roman Catholic Chautauqua or summer school which had been organized in 1892 at New London, Connecticut, under the auspices of distinguished clergymen and laymen, but was later moved to Cliff Haven, near Plattsburg, New York.

Other undertakings which appear to have had some influence on promoting the idea of university extension and adult education were the American Lyceum, which had begun in Massachusetts in 1826 and which "flourished" for several years; the Brooklyn Institute of Arts and Sciences, 1823; the Boston Society for the Diffusion of Knowledge, which was founded in 1830; and the Chautauqua Institution, which by 1890 had enrolled as many as 60 thousand students for "home study" in systematic reading in ten thousand communities too small to support a lyceum or a library. The Lowell Institute, founded in Boston in 1836 by wealthy John Lowell to bring eminent lecturers there each year for the intellectual benefit of his fellow Bostonians; Cooper Union in New York City, set up in the late 1850's; the Peabody Institute in Baltimore, in 1859; and other similar efforts to diffuse knowledge among people who were unable to go to institutions for higher education may be said to represent the origins of adult education in the modern sense. Josiah Holbrook, founder of the lyceum in this country, had written in 1826 in the *American Journal of Education* on the educational advantages of "associations of adults for the purpose of mutual education." Ten years later, John Lowell left a quarter of a million dollars to support "lectures on natural religion" and on "physics and chemistry with their application to the arts, also on botany, zoology, geology, and mineralogy, connected with their particular utility to man." This benefaction, wrote James Creese [19] in 1941, "has influenced the philosophy and char-

[19] *The Extension of University Teaching* (New York: American Association for Adult Education, 1941), p. 28.

acter of adult education in Massachusetts for more than a hundred years."

An elaborate organization of study at home, as well as on the grounds of the Chautauqua Institution, had appeared in Bishop John H. Vincent's description in 1886 of the purpose and plan of the Chautauqua College of Liberal Arts, directed by Professor William Rainey Harper of Yale, which had as many as six hundred students on the Chautauquan grounds in the summer, "many of them college students, not a few teachers in high schools and academies. Its purpose was to bring advanced students directly under the influence of college teachers, both . . . on the grounds and in home study by correspondence." Bishop Vincent wrote:

> To those who covet educational opportunities of the best kind [but] who cannot leave home to enjoy them. . . . the Chautauqua College of Liberal Arts comes—not with courses of reading, but with prescribed studies, just such as are pursued in the best colleges of the country. . . . In the course of time they read Greek and Latin as well, as intelligently, as do other college students. They read as wide a range of collateral ancient classic literature. They study mathematics. They perform more experiments in chemistry than the average resident college student. In physics, they read, observe, think, and make a report. On every part of the college curriculum they pass written examinations, in the presence of eyewitnesses, and they prepare theses; all of which go on file in the [Chautauqua] University office as proof of patience, fidelity, and ability. . . . Upon the faithful student, honor and reward are put —in diploma and degree.[20]

Apparently it was this experience at Chautauqua that gave Harper his ideas for the plan of organization of the University of Chicago in 1892. One of his tasks was to reconcile, so far as he could, the ideals of graduate work and those "of popular education and community service which Chautauqua represented." His plan called for a five-division organization of the university, one of which was known as the "Division of University Extension, on a par with other divisions, to provide educational opportunities to anyone who was prevented from entering the University Proper—the first division—by 'social or economic reasons.'" This was the first time in the history of American education that "extension" was included in the formal divisions of the plan of a university.

George E. Vincent, president of the University of Minnesota, wrote at about this time that institutions for higher education, faithful to fondness for imitation, "vied with each other in the rapidity

20 *The Chautauqua Movement* (Chautauqua Press, 1886). Quoted in James Creese, *op. cit.*, p. 31.

with which they issue circulars announcing lists of lectures and pro-
posing the organization of centers." Much later he wrote that when
Harper went to Chicago "as its president in 1892, he took with him
all the popular ideas of adult education, and the university became a
most revolutionary place. There was, for instance, the summer
quarter which he instituted. He thought the university plant should
be open all the year round. There were no summer schools then
except at Chautauqua and a few other places; the universities made
it a rule to shut down in June and keep shut until the end of
September. When Dr. Harper broke this rule, one of the large
newspapers published an editorial to prove that, psychologically and
physiologically, it was quite impossible for people to study in the
summertime!" [21]

Vincent was a member of the faculty of the University of Chicago
at the time Harper was working the educational revolution at that
institution, and was torn between his "sympathy with education for
everybody and the feeling of academic exclusiveness that I got from
my friends on the faculty. There was a tendency among them to
stress the social value of the exceptionally able individual; to discover these individuals and to give them opportunity—that was the
important thing. The great masses of mediocre people were relatively
out of the picture." However, when in 1933 he wrote on the subject
again, Vincent said that when he examined "higher education as it
has developed in recent years," he developed "a sneaking sympathy"
with those who said: "How long are we going to center our attention
upon the 'lame ducks' and take care of the mediocre people to the
neglect of those of superior ability? Are there not, after all, only a
few persons of exceptional ability, personality, and character in any
group or community or nation? Why not then devote ourselves to
the really important work in education, the task of finding those
superior persons and giving them a chance to educate themselves?"

This was the philosophy of Thomas Jefferson, who has been presented charmingly as the father of American democracy and who
would give educational preference to the able: "Ten to twenty ge-
niuses should be raked from the rubbish annually." In 1932, Edward
L. Thorndike, the distinguished psychologist, raised serious questions
about the "distribution" of education, and urged more attention to
the able young people. In 1950 the Educational Policies Commission of the National Education Association, and the American
Association of School Administrators, presented a fervid if not too

[21] Mary L. Ely (ed.), *Adult Education in Action* (New York: American Association for Adult Education, 1936), p. 325.

clear a brief for the gifted student in the American schools. The need for giving more attention to the gifted was a subject for discussion before the American Psychological Association in September of that year.

The purposes of university extension services were well stated by Nicholas Murray Butler of Columbia University in his report for 1909-10. There he said that "after ten years' experience, the Summer Session has more than justified itself from every point of view," and he proposed to extend the successful operation of its principles

. . . so as to provide classes and laboratory work in the evening at the University, and both in the evening and during the day in other parts of the city, as well as in the neighboring parts of New Jersey, New York, and Connecticut, for the benefit of those who are not able to avail themselves of the regular courses of instruction. In particular, evening classes will be organized where wage earners, as well as those who are engaged professionally or otherwise during the day, may obtain the best instruction which the University can offer and which they are competent to take, to the end that they may be able to rise in their several callings and professions through greater knowledge of the subject matter with which those callings and professions deal.

In his report five years later, he said that it was "clear that the University may offer through Extension Teaching a new and important service to the city of New York and to the country." And he outlined a program for the thousands of "adult aliens who look forward to becoming naturalized citizens of the United States. . . . It is now recommended that through Extension Teaching there be organized a definite program of study to prepare adult aliens for American citizenship." In his report for 1923-24, Butler said that that part of "University Extension which is known as Home Study is developing in interesting fashion and may yet find ways and means to astonish the University by reason of its value and effectiveness."

Here he pointed out, however, what was noted above, indifference or hostility to these new forms of university work. "The Summer Session, and later University Extension," he wrote, "were both started without any considerable measure of University understanding or University sympathy, but both have proved, whatever their cost, invaluable adjuncts to the University's work and influence and are now universally held in high regard. Home Study, which is at present in the position of a Cinderella, may one day be transformed into a Fairy Godmother. Only the surface of the problem of adult education has been scratched." President Butler believed that closer cooperation by the home, the library, the school, and the university was essential

. . . if the minds of mature men and women are not to be starved through lack of intellectual nourishment and stimulus. . . . The education of youth is suffering from overorganization, from overadministration, and from hysterical overemphasis. The continuing education of the adult, on the other hand, is suffering from lack of organization, from imperfect administration, and from no emphasis at all. If formal education of youth and adolescence amounts to anything, it gives to those who are privileged to receive it a taste and a zeal for knowledge. . . . When the pressure of formal instruction is removed, and when the early stimulus of learning the elements of a trade or a profession has passed, the vast majority of human intelligences plod through life on a dead level. Only now and then is there evidence of real initiative, of mental alertness, and of productive intellectual power. . . . The Home Study Work of University Extension is making ambitious plans to enter upon this field of public service and to cultivate it judiciously and eagerly. No one supposes that the methods of Home Study can displace the personal relationship of teacher and taught, or that it can compete with the closely planned schemes of educational work that have stood the test of generations of use. What Home Study can do, however, is to carry the sparks of scholarship to the dry places of adult life, and light here and there a fire that will give both brightness and warmth to otherwise weary and shut-in lives.

Adult Education in America.—The American Association of Adult Education was organized in 1926 for the following purpose:

Its object shall be to promote the development and improvement of adult education in the United States and to cooperate with similar associations in other countries. It shall undertake to provide for the gathering and dissemination of information concerning adult education aims and methods of work; to keep its members informed concerning the achievements and problems of adult education in other countries; to conduct a continuous study of work being done in this field and to publish from time to time the results of such study; to respond to public interest in adult education, and particularly to cooperate with community group activities in this field, in the formation of study groups whether within or without regular educational institutions; and in other ways to cooperate with organizations and individuals engaged in educational work of this nature, in the task of securing books and instructors; and to serve in such other ways as may be deemed advisable.

In 1929 the Association launched a *Quarterly Journal of Adult Education* which served to keep the membership as well as the general public informed of the organization's activities and also as to what was going on "in the world of adult education, both in America and abroad."

In the year that the American Association for Adult Education was formed, some very important studies on adult education were published, following conferences which had been held under the leadership of Frederick P. Keppel, president of the Carnegie Corporation of New York, and others whose interest he enlisted. Those studies, of significant historical importance, all published by The Macmillan Company in 1926, were: J. S. Noffsinger, *Correspondence Schools, Lyceums, Chautauquas;* O. D. Evans, *Educational Opportunities for Young Workers;* American Library Association, *Libraries and Adult Education;* Nathaniel Pfeffer, *New Schools for Older Students;* and A. L. Hall-Quest, *The University Afield.* From these materials and others that soon became available, Dorothy Canfield Fisher published a book [22] on adult education that was widely read and which "gave the whole field its first general treatment in highly readable form."

In 1935, Morse A. Cartwright, director of the American Association for Adult Education, wrote in *Ten Years of Adult Education,*[23] "Without doubt, the most potent factor in the spread of the adult education idea in the last decade was that contributed by E. L. Thorndike of Teachers College, Columbia University. Discoveries by Thorndike and his associates concerning the ability of adults to learn stirred the imaginations of members of the public and professional leaders of education alike." In *Adult Interests,*[24] a book for "workers in adult education and for students preparing to be teachers of adults," Thorndike noted that for thousands of years there had been "an avowed or tacit assumption of human education that learning belonged primarily to infancy and childhood. . . . It is now seriously challenged for two reasons—that it would be unfortunate under present conditions if it were true, and that it is in fact false." Earlier, in *Adult Learning,*[25] he and his associates had confirmed by experimental evidence the falsity of the assumption, and they had also measured roughly the ability of people to learn up to the age of forty-five years. The experiments showed that the ability of human beings "to learn increased from early childhood" to about the age of twenty-five, and then it declined gradually and slowly at the rate of "about one per cent a year." But the years of childhood were found "to be emphatically *not* the best age for learning, in the sense of the age when the greatest returns per unit of time spent are received."

22 *Why Stop Learning?* (New York: Harcourt, Brace & Co., 1927).
23 (New York: The Macmillan Co., 1935.)
24 (New York: The Macmillan Co., 1935.)
25 (New York: The Macmillan Co., 1928.)

These findings by the eminent psychologist gave a decided stimulus to interest in the movement for adult education.

Before the middle of the twentieth century, the number of men and women who were participating in university extension and adult education, who were "workers by day and students in their free time," ran into millions. Between 1906 and 1913, twenty-eight universities had organized divisions of extension, and twenty-one had reorganized extension departments which had been given up or abandoned during the "lean years" between the success in the early 1890's and 1906 when the University of Wisconsin restored and rehabilitated its extension work. In 1941 it was estimated that almost two million people were enrolled in correspondence courses under the direction of private correspondence schools which were operated for profit; another million were "studying in public evening schools, part-time, and continuation schools; and that there may be 200 thousand more in nonacademic schools, like those meeting in Y.M.C.A.'s." The National University Extension Association had organized in 1915 with twenty-two institutional members. In 1941 its membership consisted of fifty-two extension divisions of universities, which had enrollments of 120 thousand in extension classes, about 50 thousand students in active correspondence courses on the collegiate level, and audiences of 220 thousand for series of lectures directed under the supervision of universities. And these immense figures did not represent all that was then being done in university extension. The figures on the work of urban institutions and of the agricultural extension services of the land-grant colleges were not included. The work of the agricultural colleges was reported by Creese [26] as "being surely the most extensive enterprise of adult education in the world."

By 1948, seventy institutions had membership in the National Extension Association and in that year they reported enrollments of about 484 thousand in extension classes for credit, and more than 193 thousand in noncredit classes. In correspondence or "home study" courses for college credit, more than 150 thousand students were enrolled; and nearly 28 thousand were enrolled in noncredit courses. In high school correspondence or "home study" courses, more than 30 thousand were enrolled; and nearly 250 thousand were enrolled in reading courses, short courses, and institutes.

State universities and land-grant colleges apparently, and quite naturally, have been more active than private and independent institutions in extension activities. Charles R. Van Hise, on becoming

[26] *Op. cit.*, p. 1.

president, had made university extension "a cardinal point" in the program of the University of Wisconsin, generally recognized as the first to organize a state university extension division, and in an address at that institution in 1910, he effectively stated the place of the state university in the educational system of the state. The strength of the institution, Van Hise said, lay in its "close relations to the state," which demanded service of the university, which felt a peculiar obligation to the state; and it was the duty of the university "to instruct young men and women; it is its duty to advance knowledge, and especially those lines of knowledge which concern the development of the state." He also said that it was the duty of the officers and teachers in the institution to serve the state in all directions "in which their expert knowledge will be helpful; it is their duty to assist in carrying knowledge to the people." In this philosophy and tradition, the state universities and the agricultural and mechanical colleges have promoted educational services in many directions.

Although in its formative period educational extension through universities in the United States did not lend itself to easy definition, long before the close of the first half of the twentieth century it had become a real and effective movement, and in some of the larger institutions it had assumed rather elaborate forms of organization, with numerous activities and programs. In addition to extension classes and correspondence study, university extension included exceedingly varied activities, and it had made opportunities for higher education available to scores of thousands of persons. It should be noted, however, that the higher institutions did not themselves originate the idea of extension services, which were begun without any considerable understanding or sympathy by the universities. Both the summer session and extension were looked upon with some suspicion by university faculties, and were considered what Herbert B. Adams is reported to have called parts of the Salvation Army of the educational forces. And while some institutions of mid-century were still reluctant to promote extension activities, earlier indifference had by that time greatly changed. A. L. Hall-Quest reported in 1926 that wherever the university had come in contact "with those who seek and know what they seek, it has evolved a new outlook. . . . The invisible university now enrolls men and women who may study where they live and work." Directors, associate directors, and heads of bureaus of university extension divisions were generally ranked as members of the faculty and were appointed just as were other members. Both the summer session and extension were democratic organizations and, to those who would find the educational rainbow, as American as baseball or apple pie.

The University Presses.—A significant higher educational activity, chiefly a development of the first half of the twentieth century, was the growth of university presses, which Norman Cousins in 1937 described as "probably the most notable development in publishing since the turn of the century." According to Chester Kerr's *A Report on American University Presses,*[27] published by the Association of American University Presses in 1949, Cornell University seems to have been the first institution in the United States to establish a press. This was in 1869. The Johns Hopkins University followed about 1878, the University of Chicago in 1891, Columbia University, the University of California, and Stanford University in 1893, Princeton University in 1905, and Yale University in 1908, according to Kerr. In 1949 the members of the Association of American University Presses had published scholarly books, textbooks for elementary and high schools and colleges, reference works, fiction, verse, drama, and miscellaneous items to a total of 16.5 thousand. During the ten latest fiscal years, these presses had published 5,842 books, and during the year of the study, 727.

For some time a rumor or false story had it that a university press was a device for publishing books that "no one would read," and the purpose, procedure, and the product of university presses were all a bit vague. But all these things were changed during the last few decades of the first half of the twentieth century, when university presses demonstrated that they were "here to stay" in higher educational activities. In 1950, university presses were so active that, according to Kerr, commercial publishers were being kept on their toes. At that time, "1½ per cent of the dollar volume of all books bought and sold in this country came from these lively academic sources," wrote B. B. Perry, Director of the Indiana University Press.[28] The sales of some of the books published by university presses sounded like "best sellers." As a matter of fact, a few of these presses had had some "national best sellers" of surprising variety, and some presses had become rivals of commercial or trade publishers. But in most cases they were allies rather than competitors of com-

[27] A limited supply of this useful study was available in 1951 from the American Council of Learned Societies, Washington, D.C.
[28] "Scholarly Needn't Mean Dull," *New York Times Book Review,* September 24, 1950. See also Bernard Berelson, "Who Reads What and Why," *Saturday Review of Literature,* May 12, 1951.

mercial publishers, and they did "the kinds of publishing that their trade brothers are happy to pass on to them." Moreover, the courageous university presses were reported to undertake the hideous task of teaching scholars and professors, who were inclined to write only for scholars and professors, to write for laymen as well. The Princeton Press was reported to state the purposes and ideals of good university presses some years ago by saying that scholarly books did not have to be insufferably dull; that no books were useful unless people read them; and that there were many people besides those of technically scholarly habits who liked to read books that were really scholarly. Perry said that university presses were not only fixed and permanent parts of higher educational activities but that they "must be reckoned with."

Membership in the Association of American University Presses in 1950 consisted of the University of California, The Catholic University of America, the University of Chicago, Columbia, Cornell, Duke, Florida, Fordham, Georgia, Harvard, Huntington Library, Illinois, Iowa, Johns Hopkins, Kansas, Kentucky, Loyola (Chicago), Louisiana, Metropolitan Museum of Art, Michigan, Michigan State, Minnesota, Nebraska, New Mexico, New York, North Carolina, Oklahoma, Pennsylvania, Pittsburgh, Princeton, Rutgers, South Carolina, Southern Methodist, Stanford, Syracuse, Texas, Toronto, United States Naval Institute, Washington, Wisconsin, and Yale. Cambridge and Oxford in England and a few other presses were affiliated. At mid-century, eleven of the more active presses were in the northeastern part of the United States, eight in the southern states, nine in the midwestern states, three in the southwestern states, and three on the Pacific Coast.

The major purposes of university presses include the extension of the university's "teaching and research beyond the classroom, the laboratory, and the professor's study, by the publication of scholarly research so as to fulfill the function of a higher educational institution in a democracy"; "the widest possible dissemination of tested knowledge," by publishing books that "contribute to an understanding of human affairs whether in the arts or the sciences"; to make known and readily usable the results of scholarship and research by publishing books in all "fields of learning that seem to make a contribution to the sum of knowledge and experience. . . ." and to meet the university's responsibility "for distributing the record of scholarship created as a result of the institution's regular program. . . ." High among the purposes is to see that no "meritorious scholarly work goes unpublished."

Conditions in the preparation of teachers and in teaching are discussed in the following Chapter.

Suggested Questions and Exercises for Students

1. Study and report on the criticisms of the sale of diplomas in the latter part of the past century, as given in the reports of United States Commissioner of Education John Eaton, referred to in this Chapter.

2. Examine the *Nation* and the *Educational Review* for similar criticisms in the 1890's.

3. Read and report on Epler's *Honorary Degrees: A Survey of Their Use and Abuse.*

4. Study and report on the organization and activities of the Association of American Universities, indicating the purposes and the achievements of this organization.

5. Explain how graduate work in teacher education became such a large part of the big business of graduate work, and show why conditions in the certification of teachers and in graduate degrees in education became so confusing.

6. Read and report on the famous Flexner study of medical education in 1910, on Mann's study of engineering education in 1918, on Gies' study of dental education in 1926, and on Reed's study of legal education in 1928. If reforms in these professional fields could be made, why not in graduate work?

7. Study and report on the development of the summer session in American education since 1900. Why was there so often institutional indifference or hostility to this type of educational work?

8. Make a study of and report on the forces and influences which brought about the development of university extension services in this country.

9. What types of extension services are provided in your state?

10. Study and report on the activities of the American Association for Adult Education, indicating the influences that led to the establishment of this organization.

11. Study and report on the activities of the National Extension Association.

12. Compare or contrast university extension services with the services of the American Lyceum in the early part of the nineteenth century, and with those of the Chautauqua in the latter part of that century.

13. Account for the rise and growth of university presses. What are their primary functions?

14. Read and report on Seymour E. Harris's *The Market for College Graduates*. What competent evidence does he offer in support of his gloomy predictions?

SOME SUGGESTED REFERENCES AND READING

ELY, MARY L. (ed.). *Adult Education in Action*. New York: American Association for Adult Education, 1936.
  Very useful for describing the manifold adult educational activities that developed in this country after the First World War.

EPLER, S. E. *Honorary Degrees: A Survey of Their Use and Abuse*. Washington, D. C.: American Council of Public Affairs, 1943.
  Exactly what the title says, this little book is full of lively material on the ancient practice of conferring honorary degrees.

FLEXNER, ABRAHAM, and COLWELL, N. P. *Medical Education in the United States and Canada*. Boston: D. B. Updike, 1910.
  Made and published under the auspices of the Carnegie Foundation for the Advancement of Teaching, and generally known as the Flexner Report, this distinguished study was a very revealing document that brought about far-reaching reforms in medical education practices. Perhaps the most influential educational "survey" ever made in the United States.

FLEXNER, ABRAHAM. *I Remember*. New York: Simon & Schuster, 1940.
  The autobiography of a keen observer and responsible critic of American educational theories and practices over many years. The book pulls no punches. See especially chap. ix for further light on Flexner's medical study.

GIES, WILLIAM J. *Dental Education in the United States and Canada*. New York: The Carnegie Foundation for the Advancement of Teaching, 1926.
  Undertook to do for dental education what the Flexner report did for medical education, with very wholesome results.

GOOD, CARTER V. "History of Graduate Instruction in the United States," in NELSON B. HENRY (ed.), *Graduate Study in Education, Part I*. The Fiftieth Yearbook of the National Society for the Study of Education. Chicago: The University of Chicago Press, 1951.
  A brief but very useful account of the subject of graduate instruction in the United States.

HARRIS, SEYMOUR E. *The Market for College Graduates*. Cambridge: Harvard University Press, 1949.
  A rather gloomy picture of the effects on the American economy of the rapid increase of holders of academic degrees. See also by the same author, "Millions of B.A.'s, but No Jobs," in the *New York Times Magazine*, January 2, 1949.

HOLLIS, E. V. *Toward Improving Ph.D. Programs*. Washington, D. C.: American Council on Education, 1945.
  Contains helpful historical information, deals with "long-range forces that have shaped doctoral work," shows where the degrees were conferred, what agencies employed their holders, and suggests modifications in administrative and instructional procedure.

HORNER, H. H. *Dental Education Today*. Chicago: The University of Chicago Press, 1947.
  Shows how the proprietary dental schools, which had so long flourished, disappeared from the American scene. Very useful.

HURST, JAMES W. *The Growth of American Law.* Boston: Little, Brown, & Co., 1950.
 Pages 265 ff. describe the ways in which lawyers were prepared for practice in the days of the early law schools.

JOHN, W. C. *Graduate Study in Universities and Colleges in the United States.* Washington, D. C.: U. S. Office of Education, 1935.
 A fairly good but brief account of the rise of graduate work in this country. It contains interesting leads to the subject.

KNIGHT, EDGAR W. "The Obligation of Professional Education to the Schools." *School and Society,* LXXIV (October 6, 1951), pp. 209-13.
 Teacher-education institutions "whine that they have been distressed by the tyrannical hand of the graduate school." Urges a thorough and objective study of graduate work in professional education.

MANN, CHARLES R. *A Study of Engineering Education.* New York: The Carnegie Foundation for the Advancement of Teaching, 1918.
 Another important study, under the auspices of the Carnegie Foundation, which had healthy effects in another professional educational field.

MARSHALL, MAX S. "Upward by Degrees." *School and Society,* LXXIII (January 27, 1951), pp. 49-52.
 A ringing warning against the ease with which academic degrees were invented and awarded. "From Boy Scout badge to Ph.D., what is called a badge of merit has become something else."

PIERSON, MARY BYNUM. *Graduate Work in the South.* Chapel Hill: The University of North Carolina Press, 1947.
 Contains a brief discussion of graduate work in the United States before 1900, its beginnings in the South before that date, its organization and administration after 1900, and graduate and professional work for Negroes. Also an excellent bibliography on the subject.

REED, ALFRED Z. *Present-Day Law Schools in the United States and Canada.* New York: The Carnegie Foundation for the Advancement of Teaching, 1928.
 Another important study under the auspices of that foundation which shows how improved standards in legal education came to be established. Valuable educational history.

Chapter 6

TEACHERS AND TEACHING

PREVIEW OF THE CHAPTER

During the first half of the twentieth century, abundant quantitative provisions were made for the training of teachers in the United States. . . . But the responsibility for this work was slowly met by institutions for higher education, although they were urged to undertake the professional education of teachers for the public schools. The University of Michigan seems to have been the first of the major universities to establish a chair for "pedagogics." . . . In 1900, only about 98 thousand prospective teachers were being prepared in six different types of teacher-training institutions, but interest and effort in the preparation of teachers had been somewhat stimulated by national educational committees before that date. . . . Too much of the so-called educational "literature" around 1900 belonged "to the literature of the camp meeting rather than to that of the study," and on its pages "the obviously axiomatic jostled the eternally commonplace," criticisms that could have been made of some educational books at mid-twentieth century. . . . All along there was wide discussion of the need for properly educated teachers. In 1923 G. Stanley Hall wrote that the chief need of education, the "one holy cause" of the world, was a more inspiring teaching personnel. . . . In spite of wide discussion of the subject, the shortage of good teachers, especially in the elementary schools, was a distressing condition at mid-century. So many teachers were teaching subjects and in grades for which they had not been prepared that the question was being raised whether "quotas" should be established in their preparation. . . . Increase in the functions of teachers, inflation of the curricula of the schools, loyalty oaths, and "pure" history and "monkey" bills tended to confuse and irritate teachers in the first half of the twentieth century. . . . Although salaries of teachers were slowly increased, inequalities in them were so glaring as to be offered as a strong argument for federal education-aid to the states. . . . Significant studies were made on teachers and teaching, and these were widely publicized and discussed. But the quality of the young people in preparation for teaching, and that of their teachers in the teacher-education institutions, continued to present a somewhat discouraging condition. How to get and keep in the profession the ablest and most promising people was a perplexing question.

Training of Teachers in the United States.—During the first half of the twentieth century, the American people became increasingly generous in providing for the financial resources of their schools, and by the 1920's public education had reached its loftiest quantitative triumphs. Even allowing for the penchant of the American people for bragging, it can be said safely within the limits of truth that they provided the finest and the most expensive physical equipment for education in the world. In these more visible and tangible ways the educational standards of the United States exceeded those of any other comparable countries.

The American people had also made abundant quantitative provisions for the schooling of their teachers and prospective teachers since New York and Massachusetts had led the way a century or more ago, and particularly since 1900. Five years before Massachusetts established the first public normal school, New York had begun to use academies for the training of teachers, and in 1844 it became the second state to provide a public normal school. Some states followed the pattern set by New York in 1834 for the use of academies as means of teacher-educational work, and some followed the pattern set by Massachusetts in 1839 and New York in 1844 to provide state normal schools. At the outbreak of the Civil War, eight other states had followed Massachusetts and New York and had established normal schools: Connecticut and Michigan in 1849, Rhode Island in 1852, Iowa in 1855, Illinois in 1857, Minnesota in 1858, and Pennsylvania in 1859. By the turn of the century, every state had made some kind of provision for the training of its teachers; but it was not until 1910 that all the American commonwealths had established state normal schools. Apparently the dates of the first establishment of state normal schools are as follows:

State	Year	State	Year
Massachusetts	1839	Vermont	1866
New York	1844	Delaware	1866
Connecticut	1849	Nebraska	1867
Michigan	1849	West Virginia	1867
Rhode Island	1852	Utah	1869
Iowa	1855	Missouri	1870
New Jersey	1855	New Hampshire	1870
Illinois	1857	Arkansas	1872
Minnesota	1858	North Carolina	1876
Pennsylvania	1859	Texas	1879
California	1862	North Dakota	1881
Kansas	1863	South Dakota	1881
Maine	1863	Oregon	1883
Indiana	1865	Virginia	1884
Wisconsin	1865	Louisiana	1884

State	Year	State	Year
Arizona	1885	Montana	1893
Wyoming	1886	New Mexico	1893
Florida	1887	South Carolina	1895
Nevada	1887	Maryland	1896
Colorado	1889	Ohio	1900
Georgia	1889	Kentucky	1906
Washington	1890	Alabama	1907
Oklahoma	1891	Tennessee	1909
Idaho	1893	Mississippi	1910

Facilities for Training Teachers.—Since the modest beginnings for the training of teachers a century ago, made under great difficulties and heavy suspicions, agencies for that purpose so greatly increased meantime that the list itself was very impressive. In addition to normal schools, which were generally transmuted into degree-granting teachers' colleges in the 1920's, there were teachers' institutes; training classes in academies and later in the high schools; summer sessions, and departments and schools of education in the colleges and universities, especially since the early part of the present century; extension classes promoted by institutions for higher education, field courses, and also in recent years that latest and most fashionable device in teacher-education known as the "workshop"; and home-study courses and instruction by mail. Long before 1950, teachers or prospective teachers did not have to depend for pedagogical training upon a restricted campus or a narrow pedagogical course of study. They could then become long-distance students of the science of education and the art of teaching and learn even by correspondence the most fashionable nomenclature in an immense vast pedagogical language.

The battles for the beginnings of institutions for the education of teachers and for making them integral parts of the state's educational system generally had been long and bitter. Even in those states where there was unusual faith in the value of such schools, legislatures were indifferent and often openly hostile, ignorance and prejudice were stubborn, and campaigns against such institutions were waged with much heat. The rise of these institutions was stimulated by the reform movements that had begun in the period of Jacksonian democracy in the second quarter of the nineteenth century and had also promoted the development of the idea of universal schooling. Teacher-training schools, just as universal education, in time developed out of the basic educational needs of young American democracy. The development of institutions for the education of teachers is historically significant because of its basic relation to the continuing task of strengthening the democratic processes in this country. The movement for teacher-training institutions was, therefore, a vital part of the democratic movement for universal education a century ago.

And the outcome of the struggle for normal schools and for other means of training teachers was most fortunate for the idea of universal education. If the advocates of normal schools had failed, the subsequent story of American education would have been very different. Henry Barnard said that a different outcome of the fight in Massachusetts in 1841, when efforts were made to abolish the state board of education and the normal schools after a brief trial, "would have changed the whole condition of public instruction in this country, for a half century if not forever." And a keenly observing foreign visitor to this country, when the initial battle over the establishment of normal schools was raging in the late 1830's, wrote that if the motion to abolish the normal schools of Massachusetts had passed the legislature, "and if no better institutions had been substituted in their stead, the cause of democracy would, by that act, have sustained a severer blow in Europe than it has suffered since the enormities of the French Revolution."

When the movement for teacher-education began a century ago, conditions surrounding teachers and teaching were dismal and dispiriting. The pioneer treatise on teaching published in English in this country (1829), significantly called *Lectures on School-Keeping* by Samuel Hall, quoted a writer in the *Journal of Education* as saying that: "Every person who is conscious of his imbecility in other business, esteems himself fully competent" to teach. And Hall himself wrote: "A portion of those who engage in teaching are such as have received no instruction, except what they derived from common schools. . . . The employment is little more respectable, in their estimation, than manual labor. . . ." More than a century after Hall wrote those words, the *National Survey of the Education of Teachers* reported that about three fourths of the elementary teachers in the United States had no more than two years above high school, and one out of every twenty elementary teachers in 1931 had no schooling beyond the high school.[1]

---

[1] A candidate for admission to the Albany (New York) Normal School in 1841 had only to present himself. A dozen years later, passing an examination in the elementary school subjects was required, along with a knowledge of English grammar and the ability to analyze and parse an ordinary prose sentence. In 1890 no student was desired at a normal school in New York who did "not read readily and intelligibly, spell correctly, and write legibly"—educational qualifications that would have rejoiced the hearts of faculty members in many institutions for higher education at mid-twentieth century.

Teacher-training Institutions in 1900.—Theories and practices in the education of teachers in 1900 were simpler and perhaps less vague and certainly less extensive than in 1950. At the beginning of the century there were only a few ways by means of which teachers could be prepared for the work of the schools, and generally the certification of teachers was still locally administered. There were about 150 public normal schools and about the same number of private ones, but there were only a few departments or schools of education in the colleges and universities. The recommendation of James B. Angell, its president, in 1879 that the University of Michigan establish a chair of the history and art of teaching had attracted considerable notice and some editorial comment and had elicited the applause of Nicholas Murray Butler of Columbia University before the National Educational Association. Only about 98 thousand prospective teachers were in preparation in 1900, and 20 per cent of these had to get their training in public or private secondary schools. Only about 12 thousand were graduated from the normal schools. But the number of graduates of the public and private normal schools that year was at least twice as large as the number that had been reported in 1890.

In at least twenty states in 1918, state normal schools required four years of high school work for admission and the private normal schools were also tending to establish such a requirement, but in some normal schools students were taken from the eighth grade. In 1920 at least four fifths of all the teachers in the United States had preparation of less than two years of study beyond the high school, and one fourth had less than two years in high school. In 1922 the National Association of Teachers Colleges, which had tried to stimulate better standards of admission and graduation, had a membership of ninety-one institutions. In 1950 the list of accredited institutions in that association numbered 248.

The responsibility for the education of teachers was slowly seen and almost as slowly met by the colleges of liberal arts and the universities. Most of them were indifferent, and some of them perhaps openly hostile to such an activity, and this condition accounted in part for the gulf that as late as 1950 separated the work of the professional education of teachers from the other "disciplines" in the same campus.

First Establishment of a Chair of "Pedagogics."—James B. Angell, president of the University of Michigan, was among the first of the university presidents, if indeed not the first, to recommend courses in "pedagogy" as respectable for the university. In his report in 1874 to the Board of Regents of that institution he said: [2]

It cannot be doubted that some instruction in Pedagogics would be very helpful to our Senior Class. Many of them are called directly from the University to the management of large schools, some of them to the super-intendency of the schools of a town. The whole work of organizing schools, the management of primary and grammar schools, the art of teaching and governing a school—of all this it is desirable that they know something before they go to their new duties. Experience alone can thoroughly train them. But some familiar lectures on these topics would be of essential service to them.

Four years later Angell again recommended courses in education, suggesting that for a time perhaps "a nonresident lecturer occupying a part of the year might meet the wants of our students." In 1879 the faculty endorsed the recommendation and the Regents created and filled a chair of "the Science and the Art of Teaching." An official circular sent out in August of 1879 stated the objects of the new chair: To fit students of the University of Michigan "for higher positions in the public school service"; to promote the study of educational science; to teach educational history and theory and comparative education; to "secure to teaching the rights, prerogatives, and advantages of a profession"; and to give "a more perfect unity to our state educational system by bringing the secondary schools into closer relations with the university." The next year Angell said in his report that he was "not aware that there was at that time a chair exclusively for this work in any other American College."

Apparently not unaware of the way the pedagogical wind was about to begin to blow, the National Educational Association at its meeting in 1880 came forward with a resolution on the subject:

RESOLVED: That this Association commends the practice of establishing chairs of Pedagogics in Universities and Colleges, under such arrangements as will put the study of the Science of Education on the same footing as other sciences, in the course of study of these institutions.

Angell's recommendation and the action taken by the University of Michigan led *Harper's Weekly* to applaud that institution in an editorial, "Teaching How to Teach," July 26, 1879: [3]

The University of Michigan is one of the most progressive as well as efficient of our great schools of learning, and adapts itself with singular facility to the situation in a rapidly developing country. It was, we believe, the first

[2] B. A. Hinsdale, *History of the University of Michigan* (Ann Arbor: The University, 1906), p. 83.
[3] P. 583.

of our larger universities to adopt the elective system of study, and its spirit has always been hospitable and generous. The most striking fact in its recent annals is the establishment of a chair of the history, theory, and art of education. The value of such a chair is seen at once from the fact that the public schools of Michigan generally fall under the control of the graduates of the university. The State Normal School is engaged in the same general work, but upon another plane. In a society like ours, whose security depends upon educated intelligence, there is no more important function and service than that of teaching the teachers. The art of the teacher is that of effectively communicating knowledge. But this can be taught, like every art and science, only by those who are especially fitted for the work; and the University of Michigan is fortunate in finding for its new chair apparently the very man to fill it.

The authorities of the university have invited to the new professorship the late Superintendent of the Public Schools of Adrian, Professor Payne.[4] He has been twenty-one years continuously in the public school service of the State, and his admirable influence has been gladly and generally acknowledged. But his efficient administration has only deepened his interest in the philosophic principles of his profession, and his views were fully set forth in a course of lectures delivered last year in the Normal Department of Adrian College, which have commanded the interested attention of "educators" as an admirable exposition of the subject. He is now called to the first chair of the kind established in this country, and the University of Michigan again justifies its position as the head of the educational system of the State.

This action will promote the highest interests of education, not only by tempting future teachers to the training of the university, but by apprising the public that teaching is itself an art, and that the knowledge how to teach may make all the difference between school money well or uselessly spent in the community. Both the educational and charitable systems of Michigan have an enviable reputation, and the good example again set by its university will doubtless be heeded and followed elsewhere.

The Stimulation of Teacher Training.—At the meeting of the National Educational Association in 1891, there was considerable

[4] In addition to his services in public schools, William H. Payne (1836-1907) was for a time president of the Michigan Teachers' Association and editor of its organ, *The Michigan Teacher*. His address on "The Relation Between the University and Our High Schools," given the first year he was at Adrian and published in 1871, strongly advocated a coordinated school system in Michigan and the training of prospective teachers in the science and the art of teaching. This address is said to have attracted the attention of President James B. Angell of the University of Michigan, who invited Payne to the new chair to which the editorial above refers. In 1887 Payne became Chancellor of the University of Nashville and President of Peabody Normal School. Among his many books on education were his edition of David P. Page's *Theory and Practice of Teaching* (1885), *Contributions to the Science of Education* (1886), a translation from the French of Gabriel Compayre's *History of Pedagogy* (1886), *Elements of Psychology* (1890), *Psychology Applied to Education* (1893), and a translation of Rousseau's *Émile* (1893).

discussion of the obligation of the universities "to prepare teachers for the public schools," in which several prominent educational leaders participated. Nicholas Murray Butler, "of Columbia College and the New York College for the Training of Teachers," said that one of "the most interesting chapters in the history of modern education," when it came to be written, would tell the story of the working out of an educational system in the United States that would be suited to the needs and characteristics of the people of this country. The particular issue in educational organization that had to be dealt with at that time, he said, was the coordination of secondary education and the higher educational institutions.   The American college, which had no counterpart in Europe, was an indigenous institution. It had been organized originally as a high school, but had grown "until it has come in some instances dangerously near being a university." The university differed entirely from the college, and owed "a duty to the teaching profession. Originally the university did nothing but train teachers." This duty of the university to the teaching profession had been forgotten; but in recent years attempts had been made to have the university, "wherever it is found, again undertake the inspiration of the teaching profession. In many of our universities chairs of pedagogy are being established. Thought is being devoted to the question. The movement is a great one and is destined to grow." Grow it did. And long before the end of the first half of the twentieth century, most of the colleges and universities had departments and schools or colleges of education.

At the same meeting in 1891, Superintendent George H. Martin, of the Massachusetts public schools, said that the influence of the universities in the education of teachers had not come from those institutions, that it was not "from above downwards," but that the lower schools had had influence on the higher. The creation of departments of pedagogy in the universities had been "the result of demands made upon them by the representatives of the public schools. This influence had come from below."

Also at the same time G. Stanley Hall, president of Clark University, pointed to "the disastrous chasm between the university and the schools. On one side of it we find the Philistinism of the common schoolteacher; on the other the exclusiveness of the university man." Leaders in higher education seemed a bit reluctant to attend the meetings of the National Educational Association, and Hall's practice of attending them had placed him under a bit of suspicion at the hands of his "university brethren." The primary affliction in the educational system, Hall said, was isolation between the lower and the higher schools. But there were hopeful signs on both sides "that the interregnum of divergence is drawing to a close." He had seen three hundred public schoolteachers of New York and vicinity "receiving admirable instruction in a school of pedagogy in New York." But Hall warned on the difficulties that universities had in establishing "schools of pedagogy." The great difficulty he had witnessed at The Johns Hopkins University, where he was "professor of pedagogy," was to find young men who would devote themselves to the study of education. But the field was very inviting and never had there been such an opportunity for young men of promising ability who would burn the bridges behind them and devote themselves "heart and soul to the history and philosophy of education."

Oscar H. Cooper, superintendent of the public schools of Galveston, Texas, told the same meeting of the NEA that the time had come for the colleges and universities of the United States to face their responsibility to public education in this country. These institutions were increasing in their ability to influence public opinion; and the public school was too deeply rooted "in our social organism," and exerted too much influence in national life, to be handled in a flippant way by the institutions for higher education, which should show concern for the improvement of public education. But improvement in the schools below the colleges and universities could not come without earnest and active cooperation between the schools above and those below. Cooper believed that a most important part of the function of the higher institutions was to prepare people to teach in and manage the public schools. Schools of pedagogy or education should be legitimate and essential parts of the curriculum of every higher institution. He noted that the number of young men of collegiate education who had devoted themselves to teaching, even for a brief period, had been gradually diminishing, with the result that the influence of higher education in the public school system had grown steadily less. He urged that the colleges and universities "take hold, in an earnest and vigorous way, of the problem of how best to train teachers," and let them make this an important part of their work. He thought it somewhat alarming that tens of thousands of young men and women would "flock to the short-term, superficial normal schools" which dotted the country. He believed that the teachers of the United States would "greet with proper appreciation and gratitude a movement on the part of our universities toward the recognition of their work as one of the leading learned professions—a recognition which will be secured by the establishment in these universities of properly equipped, well-manned schools of pedagogy."

The study of education in the university was the subject of an address in 1899 before the National Educational Association, by Elmer Ellsworth Brown of the University of California, who observed that every properly so-called profession would ultimately have its own university school for professional training. As a profession, however, education occupied a peculiar position. The university itself was an institution of education, and when the subject of education was pursued as a study in the university, "we have the university looking at itself, as it were—becoming fully conscious of its own processes as well as of the processes of other institutions in which its students may be preparing to teach." This condition helped to explain "the current difficulty in the adjustments of university departments of education to the other university activities. Uncertainties and misunderstandings are unavoidable in making such adjustments. Yet there can be little doubt as to the ultimate outcome. . . ."

The Committee on Normal Schools of the NEA in 1899 commented at length on training or practice schools. These should be places "for illustrating, testing, and at least in part, originating the theory of education," but the first great care of such schools in the teaching process was the children. Originating theory should be subordinated to attention to the children, who should have in practice schools as good training as they could otherwise receive.[5] These schools, which should be under the supervision of the normal schools, should have eight grades and kindergartens, and a student-teacher should not have more than ten or twelve children. There should be "critic" teachers, and practice teaching "was capable of ranking as the most valuable course in the normal school." But its worth depended primarily on the qualities of the critic teachers, one of whom should be assigned to each grade. Provision for "observation work" should be made, but this should "precede actual instruction on the part of the student-teacher." The curriculum of the practice school "should be the correlating center of the normal school" and should directly influence its curriculum.

In its report in 1899, the Committee on Normal Schools of the National Educational Association [6] declared that the faculty was "the

---

[5] It developed in the discussion of the report on practice schools that it was widely thought at that time, as it was later, that these schools could not be as good as those "wholly under regular teachers." There was a presumption against the practice schools as good places for children.

[6] *Journal of Proceedings and Addresses*, 1899, pp. 836-903.

soul" of a normal school, whose function to prepare teachers was unique, and its work meant more than "teaching subjects" and more than "the development of character." It meant "the teaching of subjects that they in turn may be taught," and the development of character that it "in turn may be transfigured into character." The work of the normal school meant "such a preparation for life that it in turn may prepare others to enter fully, readily, and righteously into their environment. Thus, to prepare an individual to lead and direct a little child is a grave responsibility."

The members of the faculty in a normal school should have been trained in "an institution of a higher grade than the one in which he teaches." In the "hierarchy of qualifications" character came first and nothing could take its place; teaching ability came second. This was the ability to "adapt self and subject to pupil," to inspire to thought, feeling, and action, "that kind of work which makes character. Teaching may be defined as causing an individual to think and act physically, mentally, and spiritually." Scholarship came third, and was the "reserve power of every great teacher," commanded respect, and was the fertility of the mind. "Culture" came fourth, to give "tone to the entire being." It was the development "of the finer self," and it came from "wide scholarship—a liberal education baptized by the spirit of the individual." Finally came "a professional spirit and professional ethics," which should characterize every member of the faculty of a normal school.

Those who sought admission to a normal school as students should have *maturity* of mind; *good health and soundness of organs,* a natural fitness to teach, *common sense*—"an intuitive knowledge of common affairs, to know to do the right thing at the right time"; high-mindedness, and native ability. Applicants should have a high school education, including the elementary school course. A dozen years later, L. D. Coffman [7] described the typical female teacher in the United States as

. . . twenty-four years of age, having entered teaching in the early part of her nineteenth year when she had received but four years' training beyond the elementary schools. Her salary at her present age is $485 a year. She is native-born of native-born parents, both of whom speak the English language. When she entered teaching, both of her parents were living and had an annual income of approximately $800, which they were compelled to use to support themselves and their four or five children. The young woman

[7] *The Social Composition of the Teaching Population* (New York: Bureau of Publications, Teachers College, Columbia University, 1911), p. 80.

early found the pressure both real and anticipated to earn her own way very heavy.

It could have been pointed out that the typical female teacher "was more likely to be the daughter of a farmer or a tradesman than of a professional man . . ." An unpublished study made in 1908 showed that those preparing at that time to teach came from "the agricultural and trade classes." Studies made in 1926 by Clyde Hill, and in 1929 by Mary L. Moffett, of "the background of students in teachers' colleges," and summarized by Willard S. Elsbree [8] in 1939, confirmed the findings of Coffman. The typical student in a teacher's college in the late 1920's was "one of a family of four or five children; she was native-born of native-born parents; the father was a farmer, skilled workman, or owner of a small business." The annual parental income of such a typical teacher was between $2,000 and $2,500, and she had been brought up "in a rural community or small town" and differed only in choice of vocation "from her sister who became a stenographer, nurse, or business clerk." Her reading was not very wide.

In 1900, normal training could be obtained in any one of six different types of institutions: public normal schools; public universities and colleges; public high schools; private normal schools; private or independent universities and colleges; and private high schools. In all these types of schools, the number of teachers who were being trained in 1900 was about 98 thousand. About 47 per cent studied in public normal schools, and about 32 per cent in private or independent colleges and universities. Of significance was the fact that in 1900 almost 20 thousand prospective teachers, or about 20 per cent of the total number of normal students, were receiving their training at the secondary level in both private and public high schools. The number of graduates of both public and private normal schools in 1900 was about 11.3 thousand, more than twice as many as had been graduated in 1890.

Interest and effort in the education or training of teachers for the public schools in the United States during the first half of the twentieth century constituted one of the most important chapters in the history of American education during that period. Before 1900, national educational committees, especially the Committee of Ten, the Committee of Fifteen, and the Committee on College Entrance Requirements, had given attention to this persistent issue; some leaders

[8] *The American Teacher* (New York: American Book Co., 1939), pp. 550-51.

of higher education came slowly to recognize the responsibility of the colleges and universities for the training of teachers; and the National Educational Association (later changed to the National Education Association) often pronounced on the subject. But it was not until after the First World War that the need for an adequate supply of properly prepared teachers came to be so widely discussed in the United States. Discussion of this subject continued lively during the heavy economic depression that began in 1929, and during the Second World War, and was an acute issue at the close of the first half of the century.

The Report of the Committee of Ten in 1893 (see Chapter 3) had stated that its recommendations for educational improvements could not be carried out without "more highly trained teachers," and it suggested some means by which these could be had. For the further instruction of teachers in service, summer sessions (Chapter 5), "which many universities now maintain," could be attended by more teachers, especially if help were given them by the communities that they taught in, for the payment of fees for tuition and travel.[9] In the second place, colleges and universities should provide courses for teachers in the towns and cities in which these higher institutions were located—"a reasonable service which the colleges and universities may render to their own communities." And in the third place, the head of the local school system should bestir himself and learn something about "the best mode of teaching any one of the subjects which enter into the school course . . . and help the whole body of teachers under his charge." So also should the principal of the high school help in such a way.

It was noted in Chapter 3 that running through the reports of the conferences in the work of the Committee of Ten was the strong conviction that improvement in the curriculum and instruction in secondary education could best be promoted by better prepared teachers. The report of the Committee emphasized the need for better teachers and suggested some "means of procuring these . . ." It said:[10]

Every reader of this report and of the reports of the nine conferences will be satisfied that to carry out the improvements proposed, more highly trained teachers will be needed than are now ordinarily to be found for the services

[9] In 1950, a Circuit Court of Appeals held in a case that arose in Virginia that expenses incurred by teachers in attendance upon summer sessions were deductible for purposes of federal income taxes.
[10] *Report of the Committee of Ten on Secondary School Studies.* Pp. 53-55.

of the elementary and secondary schools. The Committee of Ten desire to point out some of the means of procuring these better trained teachers. For the further instruction of teachers in actual service, three agencies already in existence may be much better utilized than they now are. The Summer Schools which many universities now maintain might be resorted to by much larger numbers of teachers, particularly if some aid, such as the payment of tuition fees and traveling expenses, should be given to teachers who are willing to devote half of the vacations to study, by the cities and towns which the teachers serve. Secondly, in all the towns and cities in which colleges and universities are planted, these colleges or universities may usefully give stated courses of instruction in the main subjects used in the elementary and secondary schools to teachers employed in those towns and cities. This is a reasonable service which the colleges and universities may render to their own communities. Thirdly, a superintendent who has himself become familiar with the best mode of teaching any one of the subjects which enter into the school course can always be a very useful instructor for the whole body of teachers under his charge. A real master of any one subject will always have many suggestions to make to teachers of other subjects. The same is true of the principal of a high school, or other leading teachers in a town or city. In every considerable city school system, the best teacher in each department of instruction should be enabled to give part of his time to helping the other teachers by inspecting and criticising their work, and showing them, both by precept and example, how to do it better.

In regard to preparing young men and women for the business of teaching, the country has a right to expect much more than it has yet obtained from the colleges and normal schools. The common expectation of attainment for pupils of the normal schools has been altogether too low the country over. The normal schools, as a class, themselves need better apparatus, libraries, programmes, and teachers. As to the colleges, it is quite as much an enlargement of sympathies as an improvement of apparatus or of teaching that they need. They ought to take more interest than they have heretofore done, not only in the secondary, but in the elementary schools; and they ought to take pains to fit men well for the duties of a school superintendent. They already train a considerable number of the best principals of high schools and academies; but this is not sufficient. They should take an active interest, through their presidents, professors, and other teachers, in improving the schools in their respective localities, and in contributing to the thorough discussion of all questions affecting the welfare of both the elementary and the secondary schools.

The Committee of Fifteen, which was appointed in 1893 and which made its report two years later, dealt with the organization of school systems, especially with the coordination or correlation of subjects in the primary and grammar grades (showing the influence of Herbartianism), and with the preparation of teachers. The sub-committee that gave special attention to the training of teachers faced many questions. Among these were those set out below.

The earliest age at which one should be allowed to undertake "a course of professional" work; the requirements of scholarship for entrance on such a course, in the subjects of grammar, historical grammar, rhetoric, literature, arithmetic, algebra, geometry, botany, zoology, drawing, music, history, geography, physics, chemistry, French, German, Latin, Greek, physiology, hygiene, mineralogy; the determination of scholarship by examination or high school diploma; the duration of the professional course; the proportion of time to be given to principles and methods and to the practice of teaching; the extent to which psychology should be studied; the principles of education that could be derived from psychology and allied subjects; the direction which the observation of children should take; the "measurements" that should be made of children, and the apparatus that should be used for the purpose; how much educational history should be studied and in what way, and how it could be made of practical value to teachers; the way in which training in teaching the various subjects of the common school curriculum could be pursued, whether by lectures, writing outlines of lessons, giving lessons to fellow pupil-teachers, the study of books and magazines on methods of teaching; whether a model teacher should be placed over each class in the model school, or every two classes, or should the pupil-teacher be responsible for the teaching of all classes, under the direction of critic-teachers; the best way to observe the work of model teachers; the best way to criticize the practice teaching of pupil-teachers, whether criticism should be made by the teachers of methods, critic teachers appointed especially for the purpose, or by the model teachers; how to test the efficiency of the pupil-teacher in the training school; whether any part of the work of the training school should be the imparting of knowledge, other than in psychology, principles, methods, and educational history; and the basis on which the diploma of the training school should be awarded.

The standards for the education of teachers recommended by this subcommittee were very advanced for the time. The long belief that teachers were born and not made had led to the prevalent belief "that a study of subjects without any study of principles or methods of teaching has been deemed quite sufficient." But modern educational theory and practice, wherever excellent schools were found, confirmed the belief "that there is a profound philosophy on which educational methods are based, and that careful study of this philosophy under expert guidance is essential to make fit the man born to teach," the report of this subcommittee began.

The report also said that "the customs of our best schools conform" to the belief that teachers in elementary schools "should have a secondary or high school education, and that teachers of high schools should have a collegiate education." These were the minimum qualifications that could be accepted, for in "scholarship, culture, and power," teachers in these schools should be four years ahead of the pupils they were to teach. Graduation from high school or proof by examination of the equivalent in scholarship should settle the question of the age of the candidate for a position in elementary school, but that should not be less than eighteen years. Such a candidate "should have studied English, mathematics, and science to the extent usually pursued in high schools," be able to write readily and correctly, and should have studied for two years "at least one language besides English." Skill in music and drawing was desirable, especially the ability "to sketch readily and effectively." The professional training of teachers could be done in normal schools, in normal classes in high schools and academies, and in city training schools.

The extent to which academic or subject matter courses should be taught in teacher-training schools was a question over which wide controversy had waged, and the committee could not be expected to settle it in a paragraph; but so many students entered upon their professional work with such slight acquaintance in academic or subject matter fields as to require instruction in them (a complaint that was to be heard for many decades to come and still is heard); but for a normal school to have to turn aside and teach academic subjects in preparation for professional work impaired the standard and the usefulness of such a school. Proper preparation for admission to teacher-training institutions should settle this question also.

The report also maintained that professional preparation for teaching comprised two parts: *the science of teaching,* which included (1) psychology as a basis for principles and methods; (2) methodology as a guide to instruction; (3) school economy, which adjusts the conditions of work; and (4) history of education, which gives breadth of view." The other part was the *art of teaching.* This was best gained: "(1) by observation of good teaching; (2) by practice-teaching under criticism." Differences of opinion as to the amount of time that should be given to these two parts of professional preparation showed up in the differences in practices in teacher-training institutions, the normal schools giving less and the training schools in cities more time to practice teaching. The committee believed that "not less than half of the time spent under training by the apprentice-teacher should be given to observation and practice, and that this practice in its conditions should be as similar as possible to the work she will later be responsible to do independently."

The committee looked upon psychology as "most important and fundamental of the professional studies which ought to be pursued by one intending to teach." It should be studied at the beginning and at the end of the course, "and its principles should be appealed to daily when not formally studied. The method of study should be both deductive and inductive. . . . The habit of thinking analytically and psychologically should be formed by every teacher. In order to encourage and create a tendency to investigate, a study of "physiological psychology should be made" at the close of the period of professional training. The report also advocated the high importance of prospective teachers' studying and knowing children, as Rousseau had urged thirteen decades earlier. The physical, mental, and moral conditions of the child, his senses of sight and hearing, his likes and dislikes, how to tell the difference between dull and bright children, should be studied. So also should different methods of teaching and of examining, the relative value of individual and group instruction, and the art of questioning.

On the value of the history of education for the teacher the report said:

Breadth of mind consists in the power to view facts and opinions from the standpoint of others. It is this truth which makes the study of history in a full, appreciative way so influential in giving mental breadth. This general advantage the history of education has in still larger degree, because our interest in the views and experiences of those engaged like us in training the young enables us to enter more fully into their thoughts and purposes than we could into those of the warrior or ruler. . . . The history of education is particularly full of examples of noble purposes, advanced thought, and moral heroism. It is inspiring to fill our minds with these human ideals. . . .

But with enthusiasm for ideals history gives us caution, warns us against the moving of the pendulum, and gives us points of departure from which to measure progress. It gives us courage to attack difficult problems. It shows which the abiding problems are—those that can be solved only by waiting, and not tossed aside by a supreme effort. It shows us the progress of the race, the changing ideals of the perfect man, and the means by which men have sought to realize these ideals. We can from its study better answer the question, what is education, what may it accomplish, and how may its ideals be realized? It gives the evolution of the present and explains anomalies in our work. . . .

The proper professional training of teachers called for schools both for observation and for practice, the report said. The pupil-teachers should have opportunity to observe the best methods of teaching, and the best teachers in the regular schoolwork should be chosen for the pupil-teachers to observe. There should be a critic-teacher appointed for the oversight of two pupil-teachers, each of whom should be in charge of a schoolroom; and the critic-teacher might also "supervise one or more teachers for brief periods daily with groups of children." At the close of the school day, the critic-teacher should "meet her pupil-teachers for a report of their experiences through the day." The training course should be two years, one for the theoretical work and one for practice.

Success in practice teaching was measured, the report said, by those tests that apply to all teaching. Do the pupils

. . . grow more honest, industrious, polite? Do they admire their teacher? Does she secure obedience and industry only while demanding it, or has she influence that reaches beyond her presence? Do her pupils think well and talk well? As to the teacher herself, has she sympathy and tact, self-reliance and originality, breadth and intensity? Is she systematic, direct, and businesslike? Is she courteous, neat in person and in work? Has she discernment of character and a just standard of requirement and attainment?

These were some of the questions which had to be answered before a teacher could be described as a failure or a success. Admission to professional training assumed that the prospective teacher had "good health, good scholarship, good sense, and good ability and devotion to teaching." [11]

Although the Committee of Fifteen had been primarily concerned with the elementary school, it had made some important suggestions about the training of secondary-school teachers. These at that time [12] formed one sixth of the 423 thousand public school teachers in the United States, and they were described as "the leading teachers," who gave "educational tone" to the communities and were an inspiration to the great body of teachers. The Committee said that it was of great importance that teachers in the secondary schools "be imbued with the professional spirit" that developed from "sound

[11] Compare these qualifications with those set out by Samuel R. Hall in his *Lectures on School-Keeping* (1829), the first book published in this country in English on the subject of teaching. A reprint of this work was edited by Arthur D. Wright and George E. Gardner and published by the Dartmouth Press in 1929. The pioneer writing in this country on the subject of teaching was Christopher Dock's *Schulordnung*, published in German in 1770.

[12] In 1950, about 36 per cent of the public school teachers in the United States were in secondary schools.

professional culture." The responsible and strategic positions held by teachers in secondary schools called for ripe scholarship, extraordinary ability, "and an intimate knowledge of the period of adolescence which Rousseau so aptly styles the 'second birth.'" The Committee noted that the elementary schools provided for the education of the masses, while the secondary schools provided for the education of social and business leaders, a view that had long separated the education or training of teachers for the elementary schools from that of teachers for the secondary schools and for higher institutions, a view perhaps no less conspicuous in 1950 than it had been in 1895.

The Committee recommended

. . . a place and a plan for the training of teachers for the normal schools. The great body of normal and training schools in the United States are secondary schools. Those who are to teach in these schools need broad scholarship, thorough understanding of educational problems, and trained experience. To put into these schools teachers whose scholarship is that of the secondary school, and whose training is that of the elementary, is to narrow and depress rather than broaden and elevate.

This advice was sound for many teacher-educating institutions at mid-twentieth century.

The plan which the Committee proposed for the training of teachers for the secondary schools called for a degree of scholarship which was "by common consent fixed at a collegiate level." In connection with collegiate preparation, there should be two years of instruction in the science and art of teaching, which would include "psychology in its physiological, apperceptive,[13] and experimental features." There should be training in the principles of education and in methods of teaching subjects in the secondary schools; in "school economy" or management; in comparative education, especially a study of educational systems in European countries and in American states; in the history of education, "the tracing of modern doctrine back to its sources; those streams of influence now flowing and those that have disappeared in the sands of the centuries"; and in philosophy of education "as a division of an all-involving philosophy of life and thought in which unity is found." Provision for observation and practice teaching was also to be made. The Committee on College Entrance Requirements in 1899 recommended "that the teachers in the secondary schools should be college graduates, or have the equivalent of a college education."

13 This shows the influence of Herbart.

Criticism of Early Educational Literature.—So-called educational "literature," especially books on so-called professional education, early invited criticism from scholars, and the criticism continued and became more vocal as the twentieth century advanced. In 1899 Nicholas Murray Butler told the National Educational Association that for two generations Americans had been writing and publishing books on education that "were on too low an intellectual plane to meet the needs of the day." Too many of the books belonged too much "to the literature of the camp meeting rather than to that of the study," and while they were well meant and on the whole did some good, they were not "nutritious as a steady diet. On their pages the obviously axiomatic jostled the eternally commonplace." And he went on to say:

There were exceptions, of course; but out of the fifty best-known books on education which were published here between 1830 and 1890 certainly more than two thirds must be condemned as unscholarly. The reason is not far to seek. Scholarship and care for education as such were divorced. The colleges had rolled the Baconian half-truth, "Knowledge is power," under their tongues so long that it made other condiment unnecessary. Meanwhile the elementary schools and the normal schools were suffering from lack of the scholarship which only the colleges and the yet unborn universities could give. The scholars looked askance at the schools as something beneath them; the schools, unmindful of the fate of perpetual motion, undertook to live on their own scholarship alone. The results were not happy.

Now all this is changed. Dating, perhaps, from President Angell's success in 1879 in securing the foundation at the University of Michigan of the chair which has been successively occupied by Payne and by Hinsdale, and from the elaborate presentation of education as a university subject made by President Barnard of Columbia in 1881 and again in 1882, the movement to bring the upper and the elementary schools together in mutual understanding, and in a spirit of sympathy and cooperation, began to gather headway. It grew rapidly, and in 1894, when the president of the oldest American university, one which had stoutly resisted the inroads of education upon it, made his notable address upon the "Unity of Educational Reform," pointing out clearly the fact that the same principles must govern educational effectiveness at whatever stage of development it is sought, the victory was won. For years before this, President Eliot had himself been a conspicuous example of the new spirit, and now it has come to pass that that university which does not pursue education as energetically as it pursues physics or classical philology is no longer upon a pinnacle. Times have changed, and most intelligent men have changed with them.

The most noteworthy feature of the educational literature of the year is its complete reflection of this new and inspiring point of view. It treats school topics with the seriousness, the care, the scientific method which mark the scholar. Homilies upon education have disappeared before the study of education. As a result, we have the beginnings of an American literature of education which will be permanent.[14]

The same or similar criticism which Butler made in 1899, that too many educational books were not "nutritious as a steady diet," and that in them the "obviously axiomatic jostled the eternally commonplace," could quite properly have been made of some educational books in 1950 and of some in the intervening years. Now and then such criticisms were made. Examples appeared in 1925 in Welland Hendrick's brief treatise on "Pedaguese"; in 1935 in Stephen Leacock's recommendation that collegiate courses in humor be established; in 1938 in Abraham Flexner's comments on the importance of humor in teachers and teaching, and doubtless in comments by other keen observers of the passing educational scene.

Hendrick [15] examined a typical book on education and came up with some amazing exhibits of unclear English composition. For example: "Upon what basis shall the agency of formal education select the experiences that are to function in modifying adjustments?" This sentence illustrated, Hendrick said, the peculiar interchangeability of educational words. There was assurance by the most learned scholars of pedaguese "in the United States, including Guam," that "experiences that are to function in modifying adjustments" may mean the same thing as "the adjustments that are to modify in functioning experiences, or the functions that are to adjust in experiencing modifications, or the modifications that are to experience in adjusting functions." If this explanation should not turn out to be clear to the prospective or in-service teacher for whom these words of pedagogical wisdom were intended, then the following was offered: "The fact that the organization of experience in coherent systems is a fundamental factor in promoting the application of experience to the practical improvement of adjustment is profoundly significant to the process of education." What was really significant, Hendrick thought, was that at first sight the reader may think "this is English; but it isn't."

In 1935, Leacock, a distinguished professor in McGill University, wrote [16] that there was not much common knowledge on humor, and that few people knew anything about it, but he believed that a sense of humor was badly needed in education. Humor had

[14] "Educational Progress of the Year," *Journal of Proceedings and Addresses* (National Educational Association, 1899), pp. 439-43.
[15] *A Joysome History of Education* (New York: A. G. Seiler, 1925), p. 79.
[16] *Humor: Its Theory and Technique* (New York: Dodd, Mead & Co., 1935).

TEACHERS AND TEACHING

been "left clean out of the program of self-improvement." There were collegiate courses in almost everything else: "salesmanship, hotel-keeping, beekeeping, investment and embezzlement"—and in 1950 "supervised necking" was proposed by a professor of sociology in one of the largest state universities—but Leacock could find no course in humor, and of course no academic degrees in the subject, nor was humor required for admission to the profession, of which teaching was reported to be one. So Leacock proposed four collegiate courses in humor: "I. *Elements of Humor,* which would be open, without prerequisites, to "first-year men and fourth-year women"; II. *The Technique of Humor,* which was to be given four hours a week for four years and to lead "to the degree of D.F." (Doctor of Fun). Then followed III, which was a practical course on "How to tell a funny story," and open to men only. The course led "to a government diploma, or license, to tell funny stories in Pullman cars." The cream of the crop in this curriculum, as Leacock set it up, was the graduate or postgraduate course IV, which was to go in the catalogue—description under the title "Tears and Laughter," in which the "highest phase of humor" was to pass from "the ridiculous to the sublime," but was to be open only to the older members of the faculty and first-year women. If Leacock's proposal turned out, as he believed it would, to be educationally epoch-making, a revolution in human thought would develop, and so also would collegiate departments of humor, accompanied by "correspondence courses with circulars and printed testimonials" from satisfied students.

Three years after Leacock was writing on the need for collegiate courses in humor, Abraham Flexner asserted [17] that books on teaching were "proverbially dull" and that "professors of education have frequently taken themselves far too seriously." In 1950 it was professors of education who, generally as before, were writing the books on education which in that year of grace were under as heavy assault as these were when Butler, or Hendrick, or Leacock, or Flexner was so vigorous in criticism of them.

The Need for Professionally Trained Teachers.—Speaking before the National Education Association [18] in 1914, President John W. Cook of the State Normal School, De Kalb, Illinois, vigorously pointed to the need for professionally trained teachers. He noted that 550 thousand teachers the year before had charge of eighteen

[17] Foreword to Henry Simon's *Preface to Teaching* (New York: Oxford University Press, 1938); used by permission.
[18] *Journal of Proceedings and Addresses,* 1914, pp. 113-15.

million children in the public schools of the United States, and that these teachers "were maintained at an annual expense of almost half a billion dollars . . . [and] this vast expenditure does not include interest on an investment of approximately a billion and a half." But the results of this enterprise were far from ideal. One fourth of the children enrolled were absent from school every day, and large as the enrollment seemed, it included only a little more than half the school population. The average child, Cook said, was then receiving only about ninety days of schooling each year. If this should be the record of such a child for the thirteen years between the ages of five and eighteen, it would mean that "the completion of the sixth grade of the elementary school is what we are to rely upon in the way of a common scholarship in perpetuating the institutions of which we are so proud, and which have been established by so immense an expenditure of blood and treasure and toil." Thirty-six years later there were loud complaints about the same kind of condition: too many children were not attending school.

Those conditions had to change and change radically, Cook went on, or some agency other than popular education would have to be relied upon "for the perpetuity of our civilization." But this was not all that lay on the shadow of the picture. If the teachers were properly prepared and skilled in their tasks, the children who did attend school would be better off; "every consideration would seem to demand that the teachers should possess the highest attainable capacity so that no part of this precious fragment of opportunity should run to waste." The watchword of the modern industrial world was "conservation." "Save everything that will yield a profitable atom is the essence of our economic theory. The pride of the manufacturer bears an inverse ratio to the size of the scrap heap. But what of this human scrap heap and what it suggests of all the other scrap heaps if the teaching shall lack in effectiveness because of the poor qualifications of teachers?" Society had dignified the occupation of the teacher by including it in the professional classes. But success had come to teachers through "a wasteful experience; through a violation of this principle of conservation that is the battle cry of the time; through the sacrifice of the richest resource of any people." Cook deplored the fact that the average professional life of a teacher was then liberally estimated at six years, and that eighty thousand new teachers annually found employment in the elementary schools, a turnover that did not suffer much by comparison with conditions in the late 1940's. In 1947 one out of every seven teachers in the United States was employed on a substandard certificate; and as 1950 opened it was reported that 3 million American children were receiving an "impaired" education because of inadequately prepared teachers.

In 1914 Cook declared that the "case is clear. The supreme need of the school is a body of carefully trained teachers. To this end, the professional schools that are designed for their preparation must be multiplied until there shall be a real profession of teaching and no one shall be admitted within its portals who lacks the password." By 1950 more facilities had been provided for the training of teachers in the United States than had been provided in any other country in the world. But too many of the men and women who came out of the institutions for the training of teachers had little more than passwords or catchwords and facile phrases. It was complained that too many of them had the technically required training for some kind of certification but were too often not educated men and women.

Testimony on the importance of education and on the proper education of teachers to carry it on was given by G. Stanley Hall, the eminent psychologist, in 1923 in his autobiography: [19]

Our chief need today is for a great awakening, bringing not one but many radical reforms in its train, such as a widened scope of curricula, a better trained, selected, inspired, and more inspiring teacher personnel, a great increment of resources, etc. But there is no present ground for hope for any such transformation of our system by revolution, and we can only look to the slower processes of evolution in this country, for the following reasons: (1) The great metamorphic advances in the history of education have been due either to a felt need of propaganda, religious or political, or else of a greater industrial or military efficiency. The latter we are too secure and powerful to feel the need of and we lack the enthusiasm and strength of conviction for the former. (2) Another class of reforms has been due to efforts to save a falling state, as in ancient Greece, or to restore one brought low by war, as in Germany after its devastation by Napoleon. We have no sense of decay or debacle, but quite the contrary, so that the salvage motive is lacking, while our country is not humiliated by war but has emerged from the last one more powerful and in some sense less docile than ever before. (3) Another group of reforms have sprung from compassion for the pitiful state of ignorance, and a philanthropic desire to better fit the young for success in a world for which they need an ever more special training. The former has never been a very strong motive here save for promoting the general cause of education by stimulating the war upon illiteracy and by prompting certain private charities and individual efforts for social and economic amelioration. But the latter has inspired many large and small

[19] *Life and Confessions of a Psychologist* (New York: Appleton-Century-Crofts, Inc., 1923), pp. 19-21. Used by permission of the publishers.

donors during the last decade to make bequests which have been beneficient, although some of them have not made for improvement of the system but only for multiplication and too often the duplication of pre-existing institutions.

Industrial education is everywhere more and more needful, and the prostrate economies of Europe need it as never before. But a democracy should give foremost attention to training for citizenship. Thus, because since the [First World] War there has been such a remarkable trend towards democracy, the need of education of the people, who now seem destined to rule themselves as never before, is incalculably increased, for at this critical juncture education has been crippled as never before in modern history since the Thirty Years' War. This form of government, if it is to be safe, is in greater need of popular education than any other form, while the disabilities which the war brought have greatly reduced the efficiency of the educational system of all these newer republics so that in a sense they are stumbling, partially blinded, along the new and more arduous road. Thus, in this reconstruction era, education has suddenly become of far greater importance for the future of the world than it ever was before.

If after reviewing my half century of educational interests and activities, I have a valedictory word to present to the future leaders in this field, it would be the exhortation to believe that education (along with eugenics which, if it comes, will arrive much later) is now becoming the only way of salvation for the world, and to rise to the higher standpoint that sees and measures everything according to its educational value and makes this the supreme criterion of every factor in our complex civilization.

Education has, thus, now become the chief problem of the world, its one holy cause. The nations that see this will survive, and those that fail to do so will slowly perish. Knowledge must henceforth be the light and guide of mankind. More of it must be carried from the original sources, nature and man. This, together with the choicest lessons of our past experience, must be ever more widely diffused, and there must be absolute freedom of both research and teaching. There must be re-education of the will and of the heart as well as of the intellect, and the ideals of service must supplant those of selfishness and greed. Nothing else can save us, and I shall live, and hope to die when my time comes, convinced that this goal is not only not unattainable but that we are, on the whole, with however many and widespread regressions, making progress, surely if slowly and in the right directions.

The Shortage of Good Teachers.—Rarely have schools in the United States had access to an adequate supply of adequately prepared teachers. The shortage of such teachers became very acute during and following the two world wars and in the severe economic depression that came between them, although in 1930 Governor Franklin D. Roosevelt, in an address at Oswego Normal School, warned against an excess supply of teachers and said that there were then 5 thousand qualified women teachers in New York State without jobs. Conditions were disturbing in the 1930's and 1940's. In his very revealing survey of educational conditions, published in the *New York Times* in the early part of 1947, Dr. Benjamin Fine [20] reported that 350 thousand teachers had left the public schools since 1940; that 125 thousand teachers, one in every seven, were serving on emergency or substandard certificates; that 70 thousand teaching positions were vacant because communities could not get the teachers; that 60 thousand teachers had only a high school education or less, and that 175 thousand teachers were new to their jobs each year, twice the turnover that had existed before the Second World War. He also found that the teachers in the United States received an average of $37 a week, but that 200 thousand received less than $25 a week.

Another fact in the discouraging condition was that fewer students were entering the teaching profession than in the past. In 1920, about 22 per cent of all collegiate students were in teachers' colleges; in 1947 only 7 per cent were in such institutions. The shortage of teachers accounted for the closing of 6 thousand schools, and 75 thousand children "will have no schooling during the year" of 1947. Five million children, according to that study, would that year receive an inferior education because of the inadequate supply of teachers. At that time the average teacher had one year less of education than she had had in 1939. One state commissioner of education was quoted as saying: "We no longer ask whether an applicant can read and write. If she looks as though she is able to stand up, we take her." Fifty thousand men had left teaching since 1940 and were not returning to it. [21] Twelve major strikes of teachers had taken place between September of 1946 and February of 1947, when this country was spending only 1.5 per cent of its national income for education. Great Britain was spending an estimated 3 per cent; the Soviet Union was reported as spending much more. There were other appalling educational conditions and inequalities. Some schools spent $6 thousand per classroom unit, while

[20] "Teacher Shortage Imperils Our Public School System," February 10, 1947. The United Press reported Dr. Fine, Education Editor of the *New York Times*, as saying in Florida in August of 1951 that this country would probably have a shortage of 750 thousand teachers by 1960.

[21] See C. W. Bardeen, "The Monopolizing Woman Teacher," *Educational Review*, XLIII (January, 1912), 17 ff. For reply, see an article in the same magazine for that year (pp. 201-2) by Harriet R. Pease. Four years earlier, Bardeen had written in the same magazine "Why Teaching Repels Men." The percentage of men teachers in specific years was reported as follows: 1870 (41); 1880 (43); 1890 (34.5); 1900 (30); 1910 (21); 1920 (14); 1930 (16); 1940 (22); 1944 (15); 1946 (16.6); 1948 (18.8). A foreign observer had earlier noted that the male teacher in the United States would soon be as extinct as the buffalo.

those at the bottom were spending only $100, against the national average of $1600. The survey showed that nearly $5 billion would be needed to bring the educational plants into adequate condition.

Among the causes of the acute shortage of teachers in the 1940's were low salaries, restrictions by the community on teachers, particularly in rural areas, and the demand of the war for skilled and unskilled workers of almost all kinds. Although requirements for certification were generally relaxed, the usual requirements were probably then as at mid-century keeping many able and promising young people out of preparation for teaching. A professor of English at Harvard was quoted as saying that in the ten years of his teaching in that institution, "I have yet to find a first-class person who was preparing to teach in the public school system." General alarm over this educational crisis led to energetic efforts among educational organizations and public-spirited laymen to improve conditions. There were some legislative efforts to encourage young people to go into teaching.

In October of 1949 about 90 thousand teachers, one in ten, were holding emergency or temporary certificates, according to estimates released by the Research Division of the National Education Association, and there were nearly 8 thousand vacant teaching positions. In forty-five of the states, shortages of rural elementary teachers were distressingly large, and thirty-seven states reported similar shortages in the urban elementary schools. The critical shortage in rural sections had been widespread over three or four years, and shortages in urban communities were steadily spreading to more and more states. Thirty-eight states expected that the supply of teachers for elementary schools would continue short for the next few years, whereas the supply of secondary school teachers was expected to be adequate in most of the states. It was estimated in January of 1950 that not fewer than 250 thousand children in city school systems were in part-time sessions, that at least a million children suffered impairment of schooling because of temporary or obsolete buildings, and that another 4 million were suffering because of overcrowded classrooms. In more than half the states, shortages in buildings for urban elementary schools were reported very large, and in about one fourth of the states the shortages in elementary school buildings in rural communities were large, facts ominous for secondary schools when consideration was given to the final effect upon such schools by the increased enrollments in the elementary schools.

Report on a national survey of the subject in early 1950 showed that the schools of the United States were still hampered by a shortage of teachers and the lack of physical facilities.[22] At least 3 million children in the richest country in the world received in the closing year of the first half of the twentieth century "an impaired education," in large part because of the "poorly trained teachers" who had found their way to the payrolls of the schools. All the states in the Union, except Arizona, at that time reported inability to get an adequate supply of adequately prepared teachers for the elementary schools. The schools were then employing 86 thousand teachers on emergency or substandard certificates, an analysis of the data showed, and many "grave problems" faced the schools of the nation. The following May it was reported that the shortage of elementary teachers continued to grow and was one of the most serious issues that faced American education.[23] A spokesman for the National Education Association's Commission on Teacher Education predicted in early 1950 that the addition of 10 million children to the nation's schools in that decade would require a million more teachers, a minimum of 100 thousand a year, but there were only about 20 thousand a year in sight, at the rate of their preparation at that time. This condition would leave a gap of 80 thousand to be filled "in large part by incompetent or poorly prepared teachers."

A few months later *Life*[24] reported that the people of the United States were both complacent and dissatisfied with their schools, which were very good or very bad, getting better or getting worse, were too progressive or not progressive enough, were spending too much or not enough of the blood money of the taxpayers. Nothing, according to the persons interviewed by that magazine, was exactly right with American education. In the main, however, the American people were represented as believing that their educational arrangements were good but not good enough. About 30 per cent of those interviewed on the subject believed that the public schools would get better within five years, but 48 per cent believed they would get worse. About 44 per cent believed that teachers were underpaid, less than 2 per cent believed that they were overpaid, while 34 per cent believed that teachers were getting proper wages. Sixty-seven per cent of those interviewed believed that teachers were better

[22] Benjamin Fine, "U.S. Schools Still Impaired Despite Gains in Teachers," *New York Times*, January 9, 1950.
[23] Benjamin Fine, "Education in Review," *New York Times*, May 7, 1950.
[24] October 16, 1950.

than they were twenty years earlier, 13 per cent believed they were about the same, and 11 per cent believed that teachers in 1950 were not so good as they were in 1930. Nearly 31 per cent believed that more of the public education funds should be spent in their communities for teachers' salaries, while nearly 36 per cent believed that more should be spent on buildings. As late as the fall of 1950, the shortage of teachers was still considered the number one issue in public education in the United States, especially in the elementary schools. Conditions were worse than in 1941, when they were distressingly bad, and there was fear of severe damage to the schools.[25] At a conference in New York in 1950, sponsored by the Educational Records Bureau, the Carnegie Foundation for the Advancement of Teaching, and the American Council on Education, teaching was called the most important profession in a democracy, but the education of teachers was described as "the poorest of all professional departments" and teacher-educating institutions as the "stepchildren" of higher education in the United States.

About a year after this meeting in New York, a writer in a national magazine [26] wrote very caustically about the training of teachers. He signed his name John William Sperry, which was not his name at all. He was a layman and a writer for magazines, who began to worry about the schools that prepared teachers when he visited one, but because he was "engaged in other educational projects" he preferred not to use his real name in the article.

Sperry found some bad conditions in the work of the teachers' colleges and normal schools and other agencies for the education or training of teachers. The "basic facts" were that nobody knew exactly how many teachers' colleges there were in the United States in 1950, because so many of them were trying to become colleges of liberal arts; whatever the number, however, these institutions were providing "a big percentage" of the teachers in the elementary and secondary schools of the country. These schools received less financial support than the colleges of liberal arts, the state universities, the agricultural schools, "or almost any other kind of institution for higher learning." Sperry also reported that teachers in the

---

[25] Benjamin Fine, "Education in Review," *New York Times,* October 1, 1950.
[26] "Who Teaches the Teachers?" *Life,* October 16, 1950, pp. 146-54. Those who may have doubt about the technique of the workshop in the education of teachers may find fun in Sperry's "We're Working in the Workshop," which was sung to the tune of "I've Been Working on the Railroad." For other stinging criticisms of some educational practices at mid-century, see Albert Lynd, "Quackery in the Public Schools, *Atlantic Monthly,* Vol. 185 (March, 1950), pp. 33-38; also, Mortimer Smith, *And Madly Teach* (Chicago: Henry Regnery Company, 1949); Earl Conrad, *The Public School Scandal* (New York: The John Day Co., 1951).

teachers' colleges were not as good as teachers in the colleges of liberal arts and universities; teachers of teachers ranked "close to the bottom" in academic prestige. Teachers' colleges and normal schools he found to have inadequate physical equipment, and they suffered in this respect when compared with colleges of liberal arts and the universities. Moreover, teachers' colleges did not draw as students the cream of the graduates of high schools. Because of these "basic facts," inferior students came to inferior teachers in inferior physical plants and the combination of these conditions did not give promise of getting good teachers in the elementary and secondary schools of the United States. Sperry's picture was very gloomy.

More heartening was the editorial in the same issue of *Life* by Henry Steele Commager, "Our Schools Have Kept Us Free." After noting the tasks that had faced the schools in the past, the eminent American historian pointed out that the American people had placed their public schools "in a cross fire of conflicting demands." Many of the old educational purposes and standards of judgment had disappeared, and new purposes and standards had not been found. The schools, once in educational monopoly in this country, had come to be in keen competition with many other agencies and influences which seemed to reduce the actual educational influence of the schools themselves. But the schools reflected life about them and their failures were those of the society they were designed to serve. "In all this, to reform our schools is first to reform ourselves."

Although arrangements for the training and certification of teachers were very numerous and of numerous variety at mid-twentieth century, many teachers were teaching subjects and in grades for which they had not been prepared and certificated. The State Department of Education of Virginia and the Virginia Education Association reported in the summer of 1951 that 29 per cent of the teachers in the elementary schools and 12 per cent of the teachers in the high schools of that state were teaching subjects and in grades for which they had not had training and appropriate certification. The same or similar conditions were reported in most of the other states at mid-century.[27]

---

[27] The history of the certification of teachers in the United States is very confusing. For many generations localism largely determined the wide variety of practices in the licensing of teachers, and only in the present century have most of the states come to assume certification as a state function. In July of 1951 Massachusetts began a program providing for the state certification of teachers and for the gradual up-grading of certificates so that by 1954 all teachers would be required to hold a bachelor's degree.

Proposals for Teacher Quotas.—By 1950 the question was being raised whether quotas should be established in the preparation of teachers for the public schools. Writing in *School and Society*,[28] John J. Fuller of Winona (Minnesota) State Teachers College said that the movement for establishing such quotas was new, and that it seemed to be "an offshoot of 'selective recruitment.'" Apparently the shortage of teachers, especially for the elementary schools, and efforts to recruit to the teaching profession, had led to this kind of discussion. Several arguments in favor of quotas were reported. The quota system seemed logical. While there was a shortage of teachers for the elementary schools, there was a surplus of teachers in certain subjects in the high school. There was also the question of economy. Why spend taxes to train people for vacancies which did not exist? Also, if people were to have difficulty in getting positions to teach, they should not be encouraged to spend time and money and effort in preparation for those positions. The quota system was needed to protect the positions and the morale of those already in the profession and who had prior interest in the positions that did exist; the quota system was necessary to protect the financial interests of teachers already in service. A surplus of teachers would have a tendency to lower salaries. The quota system would permit early selection; poor prospects for teaching could be weeded out early. And students who desired to go into teaching would "be highly motivated and come to the college with a purpose."

There were arguments against the quota in the preparation of teachers. At best the system of quotas provided "only a stopgap solution. With war babies in effect subsidized by the government, birth rates jumped very markedly. The surge is being felt first in the primary grades. With a falling birth rate, fewer primary teachers will be needed in another few years . . ." The quota system tended to deny to individuals the freedom of "free enterprise" and the right to seek the occupations of their choice. It would tend a bit toward "statism" in education, and would mean that the teacher-educating institutions would have to assume responsibility to get positions for those whom they approved. It was inconsistent "with the democratic principle that schools should recognize and enhance the work of the individual." It would discourage excellent standards in the profession, and would deny the probability that standards for certification would be improved. In the light of existing devices and instruments for predicting success in teaching, the quota system would find itself "on a very questionable foundation." There was

28 LXXII (November 4, 1950), pp. 292-94.

no wide agreement as to what constitutes good teaching.. The quota system would likely increase "mental ill health," would tend to make prospective teachers "conformers" who would be energetic in fitting their thinking to the "officially approved design," and it would thwart "progressive thought and practice in education." It would encourage favoritism, "back scratching" and "apple polishing." It was also believed that the quota system would not be at home in a climate of competition for students, which at mid-twentieth century was a recognized affliction in higher education in the United States.

The increase in the functions of teachers and in what they were expected to do at mid-century as compared with their functions in 1900 was among the very striking educational phenomena in the United States during the first half of the twentieth century. Shortly before 1950 the Association for Supervision and Curriculum Development of the National Education Association asked, "What does better teaching involve?" and undertook to answer its own question.[29] After noting that better teaching was not an accident, and that everything that happened in the school depended on "what teachers and others desire organized education to accomplish and on skills and facilities for achieving what they desire," the association went on to declare its faith in "three fundamental sources to guide teachers in making educational decisions":

1. *Democratic values to which America is committed.*
2. *Realities of the physical and political world, which highlight the needs of individuals and groups in our society.*
3. *Facts of learning and growth, which also highlight human needs and point to effective ways of meeting them. . . .*

Teaching is a complex function having many interrelated aspects. Guided by the foregoing bases for making educational decisions, members of the committee planning this publication selected seven aspects of better teaching which they thought especially significant for emphasis in this book. In the opinion of the committee, better teaching involves the following characteristics:

Fostering security and satisfaction.
Promoting cooperative learning.
Helping pupils develop self-direction.
Fostering creativity.
Helping pupils develop values.
Providing opportunities for social action.
Helping pupils evaluate learnings.

[29] *Toward Better Teaching; A Report of Present Practices.* Yearbook of the organization, 1949, pp. 1-3. Used by permission.

These seven aspects of better teaching state the teacher's responsibility in guiding a learning process dictated by democratic values, realities of the environment, and facts of learning and growth. They also identify desired behavior on the part of pupils, dictated by these same basic factors. The relationships between these three factors and the seven aspects of better teaching formulated by the committee are further developed in the sections which follow.

While some competent critics viewed these "seven aspects of better teaching" as noble sentiments, they also saw them as so vague as easily to cause further inflation of the curricula of the schools and further confuse the teachers whose functions had already confusingly increased. Some years earlier the distinguished historian Charles A. Beard had warned against the tendency to overload the schools:

The teacher is not a physician, a nurse, a soldier, a policeman, a politician, a businessman, a farmer, or an industrial worker. . . . The teacher's principal business is the training of minds and the dissemination of knowledge. . . . If the primary function of the public schools is the training of minds and the dissemination of knowledge that is useful to individuals and society, then the teacher cannot be a firewarden, policeman, soldier, and politician combined. On the contrary, the teacher is another kind of person, with other duties and responsibilities—the duty and responsibility of the scholar.[30]

Throughout the first half of the twentieth century, as had been the case in the latter part of the nineteenth century, the question of recruiting, preparing, and properly rewarding an adequate supply of teachers for the schools was one of the most difficult educational problems that faced the American people. And at mid-century the issue was far from being resolved. In the 1940's the shortage of properly educated teachers again became a serious threat to public education, as had been the case during the First World War and in the great economic depression. The threat in that decade and in other periods of military or economic crisis was extraordinarily serious, with men and women leaving the profession of teaching in large numbers. Some of the causes of the disturbing conditions were not new;[31] some of them were in fact as old as education in this country. But most of the problems in the preparation of teachers and in their work seemed so persistent in 1950 as almost to defy solution. General alarm over the educational crisis at that time led, as often before, to energetic and sometimes feverish if not always

[30] "The Scholar in an Age of Conflict," *School and Society,* XLIII (February 29, 1936), 278-79.
[31] See Willard S. Elsbree, *The American Teacher* (New York: American Book Co., 1939).

effectual efforts among educational organizations and public-spirited laymen to improve the discouraging conditions that faced teachers and teaching and the work of the schools generally. At its annual meeting in the summer of 1950, the National Education Association's Commission on Defense pointed to the enemies of public education in a report that was full of anxieties and fears. In some cases, the report warned, the enemies were within the gates and in ignorance, bigotry, selfishness, and general ill will attacked by day and by night. In February of the following year, when the American Association of School Administrators took over the hotels and the Boardwalk of Atlantic City, the alarms were sounded even more vigorously and disturbingly. The national emergency had added to the troubles of the managers of America's largest social enterprise. Those who heard the Defense Commission's reports of the emboldened enemies of the public schools must have returned to their homes saddened and sobered by the threats to education.

In an address [32] to five hundred prospective teachers in March of 1950, Dean E. O. Melby, of the School of Education of New York University, said that teachers should stop feeling sorry for themselves, that teaching was the greatest profession in the world, and that American teachers held the key to the survival of human freedom not only in this country but in every part of the world as well. He did not believe that low salaries were the principal causes of the difficulties in the profession at that time. In July of 1950, five hundred educators met at the University of Indiana, under the auspices of the National Commission on Teacher Education and Professional Standards, and discussed plans for improving the preparation of teachers in the schools of this country; it was urged that standards should be established that would keep the ill-prepared out of the profession. The American Association of Colleges for Teacher Education had done fairly well as an accrediting agency, it was reported, but many institutions that were not accredited by that organization were sending out graduates who competed for positions in teaching on equal terms with the graduates of properly accredited institutions. This condition was serious, it was said, and it was suggested that what had happened in medicine, law, and other professions might provide a lesson for institutions that sent out teachers. The philosophy of any-one-can-teach would soon disappear, as the philosophy of any-one-can-practice-medicine or any-one-can-practice-law had done, if proper measures were taken. But, as noted in Chapter 5, the prospect for a study of teacher education such as that

[32] *New York Times*, March 19, 1950.

by Flexner in medicine, Reed in law, and Mann in engineering was not bright at mid-century. It was also suggested at the meeting at Indiana University that more was needed than the payment of annual dues for membership in educational associations. Evidence of adequate preparation and of competency was necessary before the general public would come to accept educational associations "as representing a true profession." [33]

In spite of long and wide discussion of the subject, little if any agreement had been reached by 1950 on the "optimum" class size in elementary or secondary schools or in college. Variety in practice appeared in the "teaching load," as in other features of American education. According to a report of the United States Office of Education for 1948, the average daily attendance per teacher for the country as a whole was 24.3, but the range was from 15 to 29.8. States with the lowest and highest average teaching load were as follows:

State with Low Load	Number	State with High Load	Number
South Dakota	15.0	North Carolina	29.8
North Dakota	15.8	Mississippi	29.6
Nebraska	16.8	California	29.2
Montana	18.3	Virginia	28.3
Kansas	18.9	Utah	28.0
Wyoming	19.1	West Virginia	27.7
Iowa	19.2	Arkansas	27.3
		Maryland	27.3

Early and Late Confusion of Teachers.—The first half of the twentieth century saw many efforts to make American teachers loyal and patriotic through legislation and rules on loyalty oaths, although such legislation was not new in this country. Membership in the Established Church of England had been required of teachers in the early Anglican colonies in this country. They had to hold a license from the Bishop of London or his representative in America. In 1776 Massachusetts had enacted a loyalty oath for teachers, New Jersey in 1777 had required schoolmasters to take oaths of allegiance, and Pennsylvania the following year had required that "all trustees, provosts, rectors, professors, masters, and tutors of any college or academy, and all schoolmasters and ushers . . ." take a loyalty oath, which had also been required in Nevada in 1866 and in Rhode Island in 1917, and perhaps elsewhere. In 1921, Colorado, Oklahoma, Oregon, and South Dakota enacted such legislation, and so did

[33] *Ibid.*, July 2, 1950.

Florida, West Virginia, Indiana, California, Montana, North Dakota, Washington, New York, Arizona, Georgia, Massachusetts, Michigan, New Jersey, Texas, Vermont, and the District of Columbia between 1925 and 1935. In the latter year, more than twenty states had such legislation. During and following the First World War, during the great depression that began in 1929, and during and following the Second World War, more or less energetic efforts were made by law to force teachers to be loyal. There was a tendency to a wide epidemic of such legislation in the 1940's. Some teachers and managers of the schools viewed with irritation, and some perhaps with amusement, the legislative efforts intended to thwart tendencies toward alleged subversive activities in the schools.[34] A few of these efforts will serve to illustrate the surge of interest in the matter.

Among the bills here and there was that introduced into the legislature of New York in 1948 to prohibit the use of buildings, maintained in whole or in part by public funds in that state, for any purpose by "any society, association, organization, or group which has heretofore been or may hereafter be determined to be subversive by the attorney general of the United States." The bill, which was to take effect immediately upon passage, was passed, but Governor Thomas Dewey vetoed the measure, as his predecessor, Alfred E. Smith, had done with a similar measure in 1920. Another bill in the legislature of New York was introduced in 1948, to amend the education law of the state "in relation to eliminating from the public schools, superintendents, teachers, and employees who are members of subversive organizations." The first section of the bill stated that the general assembly of New York

. . . hereby finds and declares that there is common report that members of subversive groups, and particularly of the Communist Party and certain of its affiliated organizations, have infiltrated into public employment in the public schools of the state. This has occurred and continues despite the existence of statutes designed to prevent the appointment to or retention in employment in public office and particularly in the public schools of the state of members of any organization which teaches or advocates that the government of the United States or of any state or of any political division thereof shall be overthrown by force or violence or by any unlawful means.

The bill observed that the consequences of such infiltration would be the dissemination of subversive propaganda "among children of

---

[34] For documents on this subject, consult Edgar W. Knight and Clifton L. Hall, *Readings in American Educational History* (New York: Appleton-Century-Crofts, 1951).

tender years, by those who teach them and to whom the children look for guidance, authority, and leadership." The legislature found that members of such unhealthy groups frequently used their offices or positions to advocate the teaching of dangerous doctrines, and were frequently bound by oath to teach and advocate "a prescribed party line or group dogma or doctrine without regard to truth or free inquiry." Moreover, such methods were frequently "sufficiently subtle to escape detection in the classroom." The bill deplored the failure of earlier legislation to prevent this infiltration and consequent menace, "which threatens dangerously to become commonplace in our schools." Then the measure went on to put teeth into the proposed legislation by admonishing the Board of Regents, charged primarily with the responsibility of supervising the educational work of the state, and directing that body "to report thereon regularly to the state legislature." Under the bill, that board was required to "adopt, promulgate, and enforce rules and regulations for the disqualification or removal of superintendents of schools, teachers, or employees" found to be subversive in any city or school district, and to report to the legislature by February 15 of each year the measures taken by the Regents to enforce the law. The General Assembly in North Carolina early in 1949 proposed legislation which would outlaw the Communist Party in that state, but it died in committee.

The Ives Law in New York in 1934 had offered a rather typical case of this kind of legislation. Against the opposition of many civic and teachers' organizations and many influential persons, the measure was enacted, only to be vetoed by Governor Herbert Lehman; but the bill was reintroduced and passed in amended form in special session in July the same year, and Governor Lehman signed it. Under it no one could teach in any school, college, or university whose real property or any part of it was exempt from taxes in the state, until he or she took the oath of loyalty. In the second session of the Seventy-Third Congress (1934), Representative Kenney of New Jersey introduced into the House a joint resolution calling upon the states to require all teachers in public schools and institutions to take the oath to support the Constitution of the United States. It died in the House committee, but at the same session the "Little Red Rider" to the appropriations bill for the District of Columbia required each teacher in the District to sign on each pay day an affidavit that he or she had not taught communism since the last pay day. This legislation was repealed in 1937 when new legislation required teachers in the District to swear that they were not members of any political organization that advocated the overthrow of the government. A similar requirement was made of all teachers and other territorial employees in Hawaii. This issue of loyalty oaths again became heated at the beginning of the Second World War. Some states re-enacted legislation on the subject, and in March of 1949 a total of twenty-one states had some kind of law on the loyalty of teachers, and proposed legislation was pending in others. Other examples of legislation on loyalty oaths that attracted considerable notice included the Ober law in Maryland, the Mehorter-Tumulty law in New Jersey, the Feinberg law in New York, each of which was thrown into litigation, held invalid, and appealed. In higher education, the most widely publicized case that attracted national notice was that of the University of California, which also made its way slowly through the courts; but in the fall of 1951 the Board of Regents of that institution rescinded its oath requirement.

It is to the credit of lawmaking bodies that they were vigilant in trying to safeguard the welfare of the children in the public schools of this country, even if their actions disclosed evidence of heavy pressure groups. Harm does seem to threaten children in times of crisis, whether economic or military, when legislation on teachers' oaths seems energetic and illustrates vigilance.

The pros and the cons of the matter have been set out many times, but advocates of such legislation did not always make clear what they expected to be accomplished by it, and many other good people could see no objection to it. Some advocates of such legislation evidently did not mean to restrict the general civil rights of teachers, but to get at some measure of control over the content and method of the classrooms. In vetoing a bill in New York in 1920, Governor Smith held that the legislation would unjustly discriminate against teachers as a class. Writing in 1935 on the Ives Law in New York, Carl Becker, eminent professor at Cornell University, said that having to sign the statement would irritate many teachers without making them at any time "support the Constitution more loyally or discharge their duties more faithfully than they did before." The agitation over the matter recalled that the test laws passed in this country during the American Revolution produced the following bit of "loyalist poetry" which may have a point nowadays:

> When penal laws were passed by vote,
> I thought the test a grievance,
> Yet sooner than I'd lose a groat,
> I swore the state allegiance.

The attitude of the National Education Association on the employment of Communists as teachers in the schools was given in the following statement in 1949, in substance reaffirmed in 1950 and in 1951:

The National Education Association affirms that the foundations of our American system of government are built in our free public schools. The Association strongly asserts that all schools have an obligation to teach the rights, privileges, and the responsibilities of living in a democracy.

The responsibility of the schools is to teach the superiority of the American way of life, founded as it is on the dignity and worth of the individual; therefore, our youth should know it, believe in it, and live it continuously.

As a measure of defense against our most potent threat, American schools should teach about communism and all forms of totalitarianism, including the principles and practices of the Soviet Union and the Communist Party in the United States. Teaching about communism does not mean advocacy of communism. Such advocacy should not be permitted in American schools.

Members of the Communist Party shall not be employed in the American schools. Such membership involves adherence to doctrines and discipline completely inconsistent with the principles of freedom on which American education depends. Such membership and the accompanying surrender of intellectual integrity render an individual unfit to discharge the duties of a teacher in this country.

At the same time we condemn the careless, incorrect, and unjust use of such words as "Red" and "Communist" to attack teachers and other persons who in point of fact are not Communists, but who merely have views different from those of their accusers. The whole spirit of free American education will be subverted unless teachers are free to think for themselves. It is because members of the Communist Party are required to surrender this right, as a consequence of becoming part of a movement characterized by conspiracy and calculated deceit, that they shall be excluded from employment as teachers and from membership in the National Education Association.

The Association charges the teaching profession with the obligation of providing the best defense of democracy through full participation in making democracy really live and work.[35]

Attempts to restrict teachers and teaching during the first half of the twentieth century appeared in "pure history" bills and in the "monkey bills." As a subject of study required in the schools by law, history had slowly found its way into the curriculum. Massachusetts and Vermont seem to have made it compulsory in 1827, and it appears that by 1860 these states and New Hampshire, Rhode Island, Virginia (1849), and California (1851) had done so. Cali-

[35] *Report of the Committee on Resolutions of the Representative Assembly.* Boston, July 8, 1949.

fornia is reported to be among the first of the states to require the teaching of government, and Virginia seems to have been the first to require the teaching of the history of that state. Between 1860 and 1900, eighteen states had provided for the teaching of history, and after 1900 the number to make such provision rose rather sharply. All the states have at one time or another endorsed the teaching of history as a required subject, but in the main legislation on the matter has been somewhat general.[36]

But textbooks on the subject in time came under close scrutiny. Between 1865 and 1900, some southern states, unhappy about the treatment of the South in textbooks prepared and published in the North, had passed laws prohibiting the use of "partisan" texts in the schools, and some of these laws remained in force for many years. The most active pressure groups for such legislation included veterans' associations in the South. In the North, meantime, efforts had been made to exercise control over texts in history used in the schools, and the Grand Army of the Republic was about as energetic in such efforts as were the veterans in the South. The Catholics were having their problem also, but this was solved by the special preparation of texts for Catholic schools.[37] Opposition in the South after 1865 to "partisan" books recalled opposition before 1860 to northern educational influences in the South, through textbooks, magazines, northern teachers in the South, and the education of Southerners in northern schools. This opposition increased rapidly as the war approached, and after the attack on Harper's Ferry in 1859, many southern students returned home from educational institutions in the North.[38]

After the First World War, patriotic and nationalistic fervor became very vigorous and many laws were enacted on the teaching of history and the social sciences. "Americanism" became the political and educational Shibboleth, and there was a strong tendency toward criticism and censorship of textbooks, to charges of disloyalty of teachers, and even to some "witch hunting." While no section of the country was fully free from this wave of hysteria, it seemed more conspicuous in some places than in others. Six teachers were dismissed from public schools in New York in 1919 for membership in the Communist Party. Some teachers were dismissed on charges

[36] For an excellent account of this subject, see Bessie L. Pierce, *Public Opinion and the Teaching of History in the United States* (New York: Alfred A. Knopf, 1926).

[37] See *The Catholic World*, XXXVI (February, 1883), pp. 658-67.

[38] See Edgar W. Knight, "Southern Opposition to Northern Education," *The Educational Forum*, XIV (November, 1949), pp. 47-58.

of pro-Germanism, radicalism, tactless remarks, alleged unpatriotic activities, and what came to be known as un-Americanism.[39] Many of the "pure history" bills failed to pass, but the wide agitation for such legislation caused much confusion and anxiety.

The subject of academic freedom came to be discussed more widely than at almost any other time. John Dewey was reported as likening the trial and dismissal of some teachers in New York to the Inquisition; and the *New York Evening Post* condemned the Board of Education for its action.[40] In 1926 the Board pronounced on academic freedom in connection with the promotion of a teacher to the headship of a department, by saying that a teacher should not have one set of opinions for the classroom and another for the public. "As a school teacher, he has not the same rights as other citizens to print, publish, or declare his thoughts and opinions. He is no longer at liberty to freely write, speak, or publish. This is not an interference with his rights as a citizen. His rights are as free and untrammeled as they ever were." Superintendent of schools William J. O'Shea was quoted as saying that the educational authorities of New York City did not desire to restrain any teacher's freedom of thought so long as that freedom was kept within reasonable limits, but the teacher must distinguish between license and liberty. He did not see how a teacher could teach children to love American principles and institutions, and then after school hours go out and berate those principles and institutions. Teachers so inconsistent would be called psychopathic and should be sympathized with rather than condemned. The Board of Education had no objection to membership of teachers in organizations, so long as the teachers did not take advantage of their positions to teach un-American doctrines. The editor of the *Nation* [41] questioned the sincerity of O'Shea's declaration of belief in freedom of speech, and said the superintendent resembled those "judges of the inquisition of every period and age of intolerance" who undertook to decide what was reasonable and where liberty

---

[39] See *School and Society*, X (November 22, 1919), pp. 605-6; *New Republic*, XXVI (May 25, 1921); *New York Times*, May 16, 1918 and July 12, 1923.
[40] *School and Society*, VI (December 22, 1917), p. 732. In May, 1950, Superintendent William Jansen of the New York City Schools suspended eight teachers without pay "for insubordination and conduct unbecoming a teacher." The action stemmed from an investigation Dr. Jansen had made, under the education law of New York State, to determine whether there were any Communists in the teaching staff of the city; and he claimed that he had sufficient information about each of the teachers involved to bring them in for questioning regarding their present or past membership in the Communist Party. He did not invoke the Feinberg Law of the state, which barred subversive persons from public school positions, and which had been the center of controversy and was then being contested for its constitutionality.
[41] CXXIII (November 24, 1926), p. 523.

ended. If officials told teachers what to think and say outside school, the free school system would be headed toward destruction.

Laws on Americanism, trials and dismissals of teachers, censorship of textbooks, and similar activities were due in large part to the "Red Scare," and they almost reached the proportions of hysteria in the 1920's. Moreover, there was much unrest in the ranks of labor, and there were some serious strikes; and Attorney General A. Mitchell Palmer, of President Wilson's Cabinet, took the lead in the "Red Hunt" which resulted in the deportation of several hundred alleged radicals, some of whom were arrested without legal warrant and convicted after hasty trials before agents of the Federal Bureau of Investigation.[42] In such a climate of national behavior, it is not unaccountable that teachers also would have fallen under suspicion of governing authority.

Most of the "pure history" bills ran to a pattern. One of these, designed to curb un-American doctrines that were believed to have found their way into history textbooks, was introduced into the legislature of New York in 1923. But it never got out of committee, and the New York Teachers' Union was given credit for its defeat. The bill provided:

Section 680. Use of certain types of books prohibited. No textbook shall be used or designated for use in the schools of any city, union, free school district, or common school district of the state which

(a) ignores, omits, discounts, or in any manner belittles, ridicules, falsifies, distorts, questions, doubts, or denies the events leading up to the Declaration of American Independence, or connected with the American Revolution, or the spirit and determination with which the United States of America has established, defended, and maintained its rights as a free nation against foreign interference, encroachment, and agression, or

(b) ignores, omits, discounts, or in any manner belittles, ridicules, falsifies, distorts, questions, doubts, or denies the deeds and accomplishments of the noted American patriots, or questions the worthiness of their motives, or casts aspersions on their lives.

Section 681. Enforcement of the provisions of the article.

1. The Commissioner of Education shall supervise the enforcement of the provisions of this article, and he shall withhold all public-school monies from any city or district which, in his judgment, willfully omits and refuses to enforce the provisions of this article, after due notice, so often and so long as such willful omission and refusal shall, in his judgment, continue.[43]

---

[42] Harvey Wish, *Contemporary America* (New York: Harper & Bros., 1945), pp. 274-88.
[43] *School and Society*, XVII (March 31, 1923), p. 349.

A bill introduced into the legislature of New Jersey in 1924 read:

No history or textbook or reference book shall be adopted for use or be used in any of the public and private schools located in the State of New Jersey which ignores, omits, discounts, or in any manner belittles, falsifies, misrepresents, distorts, doubts, or denies the events leading up to the Declaration of American Independence or those connected with the War of Independence or any other war in which this country has been engaged, or which ignores, omits, discounts, or in any manner belittles, falsifies, misrepresents, distorts, doubts or denies the deeds and accomplishments of the noted American patriots, or which questions the worthiness of their motives or casts aspersions upon their lives. . . . No such history, textbook, or reference book shall thereafter be placed on the list of histories, textbooks, or reference books which may be adopted, sold, or exchanged in this state for educational purposes, and such history, textbook, or reference book shall be withdrawn from use in all public or private schools.[44]

The bill in New Jersey was opposed by members of the faculty of Princeton University as an interference with freedom of speech, of investigation, and of teaching the truth. If the bill had become law, it would have been impossible to use in the New Jersey schools any history which quoted certain statements of Washington, Jefferson, Lincoln, Theodore Roosevelt, and other great Americans. Opponents of the measure noted that most American heroes had made mistakes and their faults as well as their virtues should be known so that from their experiences Americans could profit. And the *Nation* pointed out, in "Prisons for the Mind," [45] that restrictions on freedom of speech had worked toward the suppression of discussion of new economic and political theories—"the states tumbled over each others' heels in passing antisedition and antisyndicalism laws more drastic than anything during the war itself." And when the pressure became less heavy, morals and education came in for attack.

Urged on by patriotic societies, the American Legion, chambers of commerce, and other organizations, including perhaps the Ku Klux Klan, state legislatures were called on "to stifle by law the quest of truth and guaranty of tolerance in our public schools and state universities." The *Nation* said that "this hysteria is an enslavement of the 'plain people' by themselves—a black hand of ignorance and superstition trying to close the light of future generations."

Searching for, investigating, purging, and banning "un-American" histories were parts of the same crusade for pure Americanism, in which the Sons of the American Revolution and other patriotic so-

44 *The School Review*, XXXII (April, 1924), p. 250.
45 CXVIII (February 27, 1924), pp. 221-22.

cieties played decisive roles, and succeeded in excluding from schools in some places the books of some eminent American historians. Among these were David S. Muzzey, James Harvey Robinson, and George W. Botsford. Aid was lent to investigations in New York by the Lusk Laws. Commissioner of Education William Ettinger of that state named a committee to investigate histories used in the schools, and complaints were made against books by C. H. Van Tyne, Andrew C. McLaughlin, Harry Elmer Barnes, Willis Mason West, and others. Mayor John F. Hylan had a rigorous investigation made of the histories used in the schools of New York City, with David Hirshfield, Commissioner of Accounts, as the chief investigator. Charles Grant Miller, who had led attacks in the Hearst newspapers against un-American textbooks, was named consultant to Hirshfield, and the report of the investigation [46] was ascribed to him. Some of the texts were condemned because they seemed to tend to encourage better relations with Great Britain. Some books were revised in the light of attacks on them, but as the *New York Times* pointed out editorially September 12, 1921, that was hardly the way to rewrite history. Here it was mentioned that the American Federation of Labor might launch a million-dollar campaign to awaken publishers to their responsibilities on these issues.

While these crusades were confined to no one section of the country, apparently they were most vigorous in the northern states. A bill was introduced into the legislature of Massachusetts in 1921 designed to ban from the schools of that state Harriet Tuel's *The Study of Nations*, only to die in committee. Legislation did not, however, always prohibit particular books, but it gave to state boards of education or to chief state educational officers the power to exclude books that were believed to be un-American.

Against these efforts to purge or ban history books used in the schools were many protests. The association of the high school teachers of Washington, D. C., in 1923 adopted resolutions in condemnation of the attacks on histories, and urged the National Education Association "to take such measures as it may deem best to defend the teaching profession against whatever forces now threaten its academic freedom or professional standing," and declared that teachers of history should themselves be the judges of the content of a course in history. And at its annual meeting in 1924, the American Historical Association resolved against the arbitrary methods used

---

[46] For a stinging satire on this investigation, see "The Newest Battle of the Books," in the *Nation*, CXIV (January 25, 1924), p. 88. Perhaps the most nearly complete account of the attacks on histories appears in Pierce, *op. cit.*, pp. 206-94.

by certain newspapers, patriotic societies, fraternal orders, and other groups against textbooks in history and against official censorship. Such propaganda had met "with sufficient success to bring about not only acute controversy in many cities but the passage of censorship laws in several states . . ." The resolution said "that genuine and intelligent patriotism, no less than the requirements of honesty and sound scholarship, demand that textbook writers and teachers should strive to present a truthful picture of past and present, with due regard to the different purposes and possibilities of elementary, secondary, and advanced instruction . . ." Criticism of books should not be based on grounds of patriotism, but only on grounds of fidelity to fact as determined by specialists or tested by evidence. The cultivation in young people of a scientific temper in history, of a spirit of inquiry, and willingness to face harsh facts, were more vital than special interpretation of particular events. Attempts "to foster national arrogance and boastfulness and indiscriminate worship of national 'heroes' " would only encourage "a harmful pseudo-patriotism . . ." The association described as absurd the charges that leading historical scholars were engaged in treasonable activities and propaganda, and that teachers and educational officials were so stupid or disloyal as to put treasonable textbooks into the hands of children. And it further resolved that to continue the feverish agitation would mean "a serious deterioration both of textbooks and of teaching," because reputable scholars would not tolerate the methods that were then being advocated.[47]

Encouraged by many patriotic societies and organizations, the American Legion set out in 1922 to produce a pure American history and three years later came out with a two-volume work under the title of *The Story of Our American People*. In a letter to the *New York Times* July 24, 1925, Professor C. H. Van Tyne, distinguished historian of the University of Michigan, asked what could be expected of a historical work, even though sponsored by the Legion, which had not been written by a historian but rather by a professor of English in the College of the City of New York (Charles H. Horne), and which had to have the approval of the Boy Scouts, the Daughters of the American Revolution, the Daughters of the Confederacy, the Benevolent and Protective Order of Elks, the Knights of Pythias, the Colonial Sons and Daughters, the National Security League, the American Federation of Labor, and other organizations. Presumably, Rotary International had to give its approval. Van Tyne thought that a more appropriate title than *The Story of Our American*

[47] *American Historical Review*, XXIX (April, 1924), p. 428.

People would have been *The Marvelous Story of Us*. And he called attention to the "Holy War Against the Apes" then being so savagely waged in Dayton, Tennessee, and said that such a book as the Legion and Horne had come out with was indeed another war "against scholarship and the quiet laborious efforts of historians to learn the truth and to tell it." He said that in both cases the intellectual history of this country was in the 1920's facing a serious crisis.

Historian John Franklin Jameson severely criticized the Wisconsin law in the *American Historical Review* [48] and pointed out that it merited exhibition in a historical magazine, not only because of the grave considerations that it raised "but also as a curiosity, to be preserved for readers in future years, who may examine it with the same interest with which, in museums of domestic antiquities, we look at old tin lanterns and candle molds, wondering at the quaint, inadequate means of illumination with which our predecessors contented themselves." In his opinion, the law was harmless if justly executed, for of the many textbooks in use at that time none really falsified the facts regarding wars in which the United States had taken part. Under the statute, one could, presumably, say what he pleased about the war with Mexico or with Spain, but with the two wars with England the matter was different. Jameson said that it was "surely disquieting, if not discouraging, to witness these efforts, in Wisconsin and other states, to put back the clock by substituting, for the deliberate judgment of first-rate scholars, the prejudices of the uninformed, of those whose notions of American history have never advanced beyond the point at which they or their fathers were left, in the eighth grade, by the stale textbooks of an earlier time."

Efforts to control the writing and teaching of history were accompanied by efforts to control the teaching of certain aspects of science. While one of the heated issues involved in what is known as "the critical period in religion" in this country in the latter part of the nineteenth century had been Darwin's hypothesis of biological evolution, there were other issues. So-called "higher criticism" and the work of scholars in the textual examination of the Bible had also shocked some of the devout, and threatened to jolt the old-time religion. But after the First World War, and particularly in the 1920's, evolution again reared its head; and legislative resolutions, heated discussions, and in a few cases legislation against teaching as a fact that human beings had "ascended or descended from a lower order of animals" may be considered companions to the agitation, regulations, and legislation about pure histories. Between 1921 and

[48] XXVIII (July, 1923), p. 701.

1929, thirty-seven antievolution bills were introduced into twenty state legislatures.

Kentucky led the procession with a bill in 1921 that lacked only one vote of passage in the lower branch of the legislature. The same year an antievolution "rider" to the general appropriations bill was stricken out in joint committee, after it had passed the upper branch without opposition. In 1923 a similar bill failed in the legislature of Florida, but as a compromise the following resolution was adopted:

WHEREAS, the Constitution of the State of Florida expressly states in section 6 of the Declaration of Rights that, "No preference shall be given by law to any church, sect, or mode of worship, and no money shall ever be taken from the public treasury directly or indirectly in aid of any church, sect, or religious denomination, or in aid of any sectarian institution." And

WHEREAS, The public schools and colleges of this State, supported in whole or in part by public funds, should be kept free from any teachings designed to set up and promulgate sectarian views, and should also be equally free from teachings designed to attack the religious beliefs of the public. Therefore, *Be It Resolved* by the House of Representatives, the Senate concurring: That it is the sense of the Legislature of the State of Florida that it is improper and subversive of the best interests of the people of this State for any professor, teacher, or instructor in the public schools and colleges of this State, supported in whole or in part by public taxation, to teach or permit to be taught atheism, agnosticism, or to teach, as true, Darwinism or any other hypothesis that links man in blood relationship to any other form of life.

In the same year as that of the Florida resolution, the introduction of similar legislation was sponsored by the Fundamentalists in Alabama, Georgia, Oklahoma, Texas, and West Virginia. The bill passed the lower branch in Texas by more than two to one, but died on the calendar of the Senate. The doctrine of evolution was outlawed in Oklahoma by a clause in the bill for free textbooks ". . . that no copyright shall be purchased nor textbook adopted that teaches the 'Materialistic Conception of History,' i.e., the Darwin Theory of Creation *versus* the Bible Account of Creation." Three years later that portion of the statute that related to Darwinism was repealed. In 1925 the legislature of Georgia refused an appropriation to the State Library, ostensibly in fear that it would circulate books on evolution. A Fundamentalist legislator declared that there were only three books worth reading: the Bible, the hymnal, and the almanac. "These are enough for anyone. Read the Bible. It teaches you how to act. Read the hymnbook. It contains the finest poetry ever written. Read the almanac. It shows you how to figure out what the weather will be. There isn't another book that is necessary for anyone to read, and therefore I am opposed to all libraries." [49] A restrictive measure was introduced into the legislature of Louisiana in 1926 and passed one house but was killed by a "parliamentary maneuver" in the other. In the same year a law was passed in Mississippi prohibiting teachers in state-supported schools from teaching "that man ascended or descended from a lower order of animals." Violation of the statute was punishable by a fine of not more than $500 and loss of job.

The Tennessee law on the teaching of evolution, and the Scopes trial that followed it, were widely publicized. Enacted in 1925, this law was the first explicit prohibition against the teaching of evolution:

Section 1

Be it enacted by the general assembly of the state of Tennessee, That it shall be unlawful for any teacher in any of the universities, normals, and all other public schools of the state, which are supported in whole or in part by the public school funds of the state, to teach any theory that denies the story of the divine creation of man, as taught in the Bible, and to teach instead that man has descended from a lower order of animals.

Section 2

Be it further enacted, That any teacher found guilty of the violation of this act, shall be guilty of a misdemeanor and upon conviction shall be fined not less than one hundred dollars and not more than five hundred dollars for each offense.

Section 3

Be it further enacted, That this act take effect from and after its passage, the public welfare requiring it.[50]

Word is said to have reached Tennessee that the American Civil Liberties Union of New York would back any teacher who was willing to stand trial on the violation of the law. John Thomas Scopes and his friend George Rapplegea sat in Robinson's Drug Store in Dayton and made plans to test the constitutionality of the law, which was less than two months old. Scopes was arrested May 5, 1925. On May 16, William Jennings Bryan, antievolutionist, announced that he had been engaged by the World's Christian Fundamental Association to enter the case for the prosecution, and Clarence Darrow and Dudley Field Malone, internationally famous lawyers,

[49] Quoted in Virginius Dabney, *Liberalism in the South* (Chapel Hill: The University of North Carolina Press, 1932), p. 289.
[50] *Session Laws*, 1925, pp. 50, 51. This was passed by a vote of 71 to 5 in the House and by 24 to 6 in the Senate. In 1929 and 1931, the Legislature refused by big majorities to repeal the law. In 1931 the proposal to repeal was defeated in the House by a vote of 58 to 11.

offered their services for the defense, under the auspices of the American Civil Liberties Union. Each of these men—Bryan, Darrow, and Malone—had a genius for publicity, and the Dayton Circus was on. "Right This Way for the Midway" was the caption of an editorial in the Greensboro (North Carolina) *Daily News,* May 18.

Editorially the Charlotte (North Carolina) *Observer* said on May 24:

Each of the three (Bryan, Darrow, Malone) has a penchant for publicity. They would not otherwise be associated with the Tennessee evolution case. . . .

What approaches, therefore, is a great public spectacle, like unto the Kentucky Derby, the Madison Square Garden cat fight of the Democrats, the Loeb and Leopold extravaganza, the Dempsey-Carpentier battle of the century. . . . The case of Scopes, harmless high-school teacher, dissociates itself from education, is divorced from science, has no contact with religion, and is headed for a glorious, knock-down and drag-out, free-for-all scrap with the whole United States for an arena, and with a hundred million cheering fanatics for the audience. Thus is truth sought; thus is religion crucified . . . What matter if behind the ruffles and trumpets there may be a principle involved? Small chance it will stand in the shouting and tumult, in the orgy of lunatic controversy. . . . No matter what decision comes out of the law, no power can stop the relentless search for truth.

. . . never did a small town bask so luxuriously in the limelight of the nation. They are going to have a test of the Tennessee evolution law, and Dayton is rising to its opportunity. Now Dayton is busy with the business side of the situation. Tents are being secured to supplement hotel accommodations. Amplifiers are to be installed to carry to assembled thousands outside the courtroom the argument of the counsel. Railroad companies have been requested to clear all their local sidings for Pullman parking. The big week opens Monday . . . Tennessee will parade the world stage as a Commonwealth determined to regulate affairs in the field of human knowledge; to bring reinforcements through Legislature and the Courts to the Bible, which somehow until now has managed to survive the accidents of time, the assaults of unbelievers, and the sharp attacks of higher critics without Tennessee's assistance. . . . Evolution week at Dayton ought to be harvest time for vendors of hot dogs, bootleggers, pickpockets, pamphleteers, and argufiers of any and all descriptions.

In a commencement speech at Columbia University June 3, Nicholas Murray Butler said:

The Legislature and the Governor of Tennessee have, with every appearance of equanimity, just now joined in violently affronting popular intelligence, and have made it impossible for a scholar to be a teacher in that state without becoming at the same time a lawbreaker.

Courage must now give way to a conformity—to type a sort of spineless corporate opinion, which, operated by prohibitions and compulsions, aims to reduce all individuality, whether of mind or character, to a gelatinous and wobbling mass . . . These new and persecuting barbarians are of a kind with their ancient forbears, who from their seats in the arena gloated with joy as the stricken gladiator or the Christian martyr ended his life in agony.

A quarter century after the Scopes fiasco the anti-evolution law in Tennessee was still on the books. Under a date line from Dayton July 9, 1950, the Associated Press quoted Judge John T. Raulston, who conducted the trial, as saying at the age of 84 that the statute was wholesome and should be enforced. Science and religion clashed in New York State in late 1951 when the Board of Regents announced that examinations in courses in biology in high schools would no longer contain questions relating to the germ theory of disease. This decision, presumably intended to avoid offense to Christian Scientists whose creed was said to discredit such a theory, was made "not through the initiative of the Christian Science Church, which has scrupulously avoided any pressure to impose its own views on public education." The Regents' action followed passage of a statute by the legislature of the state which exempted students from any instruction in hygiene and health that clashed with their religious beliefs. But Norman Cousins, writing in the *Saturday Review of Literature* of December 29, 1951, under the title, "Religion and the Schools," said that the implications of the decision of the Regents were "as startling as they are critical." If the germ theory of disease should be ruled out of examinations in high schools, why not out of biology classes altogether? "What is to stop the same indiscriminate principle from being used in university education, supported in whole or in part by public funds? What about medical schools themselves? If the principle is sound for high-school students why is it less sound for medical school students?" And he asked about the relationship "between the study of knowledge and the use of knowledge."

The Teacher's Salary.—In 1941, the national average of annual salaries for teachers, principals, and other instructional personnel in the public elementary and secondary schools of the United States was $1,507. In 1942 it was $1,599; in 1943 it was $1,728; in 1944 it was $1,846; in 1945 it was $1,995; in 1946 it was $2,254; in 1947 it was $2,639. It was estimated for 1948 at $2,750, and for 1949-50 at $2,985. Comparable figures on salaries are generally out of date before the data can be assembled and verified, but Table 1 shows how the figures appeared for 1947-48. That the highest average salary (in California) was nearly three times that in the lowest state (Mississippi) was given as an argument for federal aid to education. Commenting on these data, the *NEA Journal* said in March of 1950 that the average salary of teachers in the United States "should within a generation reach at least $5,000."

TABLE 1

AVERAGE SALARIES OF EDUCATION PERSONNEL

Rank	State	Average Salary	Rank	State	Average Salary
(1)	California	$3,690	(24)	Colorado	2,540
(2)	New York	3,476	(25)	Minnesota	2,482
(3)	Washington	3,325	(26)	West Virginia	2,364
(4)	Maryland	3,321	(27)	New Hampshire	2,355
(5)	Connecticut	3,249	(28)	Oklahoma	2,277
(6)	Arizona	3,136	(29)	Idaho	2,239
(7)	Rhode Island	3,105	(30)	Louisiana	2,236
(8)	Massachusetts	3,103	(31)	Kansas	2,191
(9)	New Jersey	3,102	(32)	Wyoming	2,187
(10)	Indiana	3,073	(33)	North Carolina	2,114
(11)	Michigan	3,020	(34)	Missouri	2,099
(12)	Illinois	3,016	(35)	Iowa	2,088
(13)	Nevada	2,988	(36)	Vermont	2,066
(14)	Utah	2,968	(37)	Virginia	2,062
(15)	Oregon	2,941	(38)	Alabama	1,957
(16)	Ohio	2,847	(39)	Nebraska	1,919
(17)	New Mexico	2,741	(40)	Tennessee	1,901
(18)	Delaware	2,642	(41)	Kentucky	1,884
(19)	Florida	2,641	(42)	South Dakota	1,883
			(43)	Maine	1,767
National Average		$2,639	(44)	South Carolina	1,742
			(45)	Georgia	1,724
			(46)	North Dakota	1,665
(20)	Pennsylvania	2,597	(47)	Arkansas	1,545
(21)	Texas	2,585	(48)	Mississippi	1,256
(22)	Montana	2,582			
(23)	Wisconsin	2,560			

In the second quarter of the twentieth century, attention was given as perhaps never before to the physical and mental fitness of teachers to teach, when it was reported that scores of thousands of children were on every average school day being taught by substitute teachers because their regular teachers were kept out of school by illness. Besides the serious educational loss, there was also the unfortunate economic loss. Many of the 12 thousand teachers whose places were filled every day by substitutes would either lose their daily wages or that part that was paid to the substitute teachers, besides bills for doctor and hospital. It was reported that in an average school year at least 285 thousand teachers were absent for one or more days because of illness, losing time totaling at least 2 million school days. It was said that, generally speaking, teachers probably had as good health as they would have in some other occupation, for about 15 to 20 per cent lacked the vigorous health necessary "for successful classroom work," although apparently the health of teachers had improved "through the years." Maladjustments of personality, more often than physical disorders, were said to be responsible for failure in teaching, and intense and persistent worries increased the hazards to health. The conditions called for more attention to the health of the teachers, and this matter was getting increasingly worse as the first half of the twentieth century came to a close.[51]

Whatever else may be said about teachers and teaching, and about the difficulty of finding, properly preparing, and adequately rewarding teachers in the schools of the United States, it must be said that the problem has been increasingly recognized and faced in this country in recent decades. In the recognition and the facing of this acute issue, two very comprehensive and significant national studies of the subject should here be noted. One of these was the *National Survey of the Education of Teachers,* provided for by the Congress and included in the survey program of the United States Office of Education, made under the direction of Professor E. S. Evenden of Columbia University, and published in the early 1930's in several volumes. The other was the work of the Commission on Teacher Education, projected by the American Council on Education and published in the 1940's, also in several volumes. The first of these studies, which dealt with the subject quantitatively, showed how inadequate in "amount" and "time" was the education of teachers at the time the data were collected. The sixth volume of the study showed that one out of every twenty elementary teachers in the United States in 1930 had no schooling beyond high school, with the rural schools having the largest percentage in that group.

The other study undertook to view the subject qualitatively and to identify and report better ways than the conventional for the education of teachers. The Commission on Teacher Education was formed in 1938 for a five-year period, and in it many specialists, twenty higher educational institutions, and fourteen school systems and groups of systems cooperated. The final report of the Commission, *The Improvement of Teacher Education,* appeared in 1946,

---

[51] See "Fit to Teach," Ninth Yearbook, Department of Classroom Teachers, National Education Association, Washington, D.C.: 1938. Also Emil Altman, "Our Mentally Unbalanced Teachers," *American Mercury,* April, 1941.

although the leading issues in teacher education had been repeatedly dealt with in its earlier reports. Salaries of teachers, said the final report, were

. . . of basic importance. The worth apparently placed on teaching by the American people (the *average* salary they provided for classroom teachers, supervisors, and principals in 1944-45 was less than $1,800) does small credit to their presumable regard for the welfare of their children and of their society. Salaries must be increased. And since many states are financially unable to raise teachers' salaries to respectable levels through their own efforts alone, federal aid to education is indispensable.

Other conditions which the Commission believed necessary to improve teaching included occupational security, the right of teachers to live a normal life, democratic administrative leadership, and an effective in-service program of teacher education. Out of this comprehensive study came many interesting and useful publications and wide and helpful discussion. Exactly how permanent the influence of that work was and what desirable practices in the education of teachers were or will be promoted by the effort, the future historian will have to report.

It was a bit disturbing, however, to some observers, that the American people seemed slow to learn that adequate salaries and better conditions of preparation, working, tenure, and retirement for teachers were basic to the solution of the most persistent problem in American education. Perhaps no educational emergency was so threatening to the idea of public education as the shortage of teachers, and the strikes and rumors of strikes by those whose loyalty was put to heavy strain and who felt that the public was unconsciously delinquent toward the schools. On Christmas Day of 1946, Dr. Gallup's American Institute of Public Opinion reported "widespread public sympathy with the economic plight of school teachers." [52]

The National Education Association rather consistently continued throughout most of the first half of the twentieth century to resolve on the preparation, certification, salaries, and systems of retirement for teachers. At the meeting of the Representative Assembly of that organization in 1949, resolutions as follows were passed on these subjects:

(*a*) The minimum educational qualifications for all teachers shall be a bachelor's degree with an in-service educational requirement for additional work toward a master's degree or its equivalent.

[52] See the twelve articles by Benjamin Fine in the *New York Times,* beginning February 10, 1947, which dealt with conditions in the nation's schools and colleges.

(b) Minimum salaries with adequate annual increments shall be established which recognize the services and responsibilities of the teacher and compensate for thorough professional education, in-service growth, and years of experience. It is recommended that only evidence of professional education and successful experience shall be used for the determination of salaries.

(c) Teacher-education programs shall be developed that meet high minimum standards that are acceptable in all states.

(d) Certification standards shall be raised, and reciprocal certification between states shall be established. Emergency certificates shall be eliminated.

(e) Existing retirement systems shall be strengthened for all whom they serve by extending benefits on a sound actuarial state-wide basis with reciprocity among states; such systems shall be developed in all areas where they do not already exist. All school-district employees shall continue to be omitted from Federal social security.

Some Studies on Teachers and Teaching.—In 1937, William C. Bagley, of Columbia University, among the most effective and inspiring teachers of teachers this country has ever had, had written that of all "comparable countries, the United States may have the least well-selected and the least well-educated teachers, but beyond peradventure of doubt it has the best-dressed and the best-looking teachers in the world." [53] A decade later, I. L. Kandel of the same institution succinctly summarized the whole matter when he wrote: "It is a paradox in American history that, while faith in education and in the provision of equality of educational opportunity is one of the most deep-rooted of American sentiments, the public esteem of teachers has never paralleled its faith in education. The American public has been trained to spend money on buildings and equipment, but has not yet discovered that its expenditure for teachers is not commensurate with the work expected of them." Going on, he said:

In all discussions of measures to put the idea of equality of educational opportunity into effect, the one, and the chief, factor that would be implemented has, on the whole, not been given the attention that it deserves. Buildings are important; equipment is important; and so are textbooks and materials of instruction. But these only provide the conditions under which the educational process can be carried on. Without well-prepared and well-qualified teachers, none of these conditions has any meaning.

This is as true in the lower grades as it is at the college and university level. In the important series of volumes issued by the President's Commission on Higher Education, Volume IV, "Staffing Higher Education," deserves special attention. Much that appears in this volume can easily be applied to primary or secondary education. Thus, for example, "Stronger personnel and

[53] William C. Bagley and Thomas Alexander, *The Teacher of the Social Studies* (New York: Chas. Scribner's Sons, 1937), p. 5. Used by permission.

better training are required if the objectives of higher education are to be fully realized," could well be generalized by the omission of one word. So could the following concluding paragraph:

"The task ahead of providing faculty personnel adequate for the kind of higher education our Nation requires places a tremendous responsibility upon our democracy. That responsibility is one which must be borne collectively by public and private agencies, by lay and professional citizens, by teachers and administrators. Only pooled efforts can meet the challenge—the challenge to improve democracy by improving higher education."

The key to that improvement, whether in primary, secondary, or higher education, is the teacher. To provide ready access to schools, colleges, and universities does not in itself guarantee equality of educational opportunity. The only guarantee lies in the teacher. This has been recognized in all proposals for the reconstruction of education wherever they have been put forward, not only in the United States but in other countries. The crucial problem everywhere lies in the recruitment, preparation, and remuneration of teachers. The volume, "Staffing Higher Education," is one that should be read by everyone interested in implementing the ideal of equality of educational opportunity and the dedication of education to the realization and enrichment of democracy.[54]

That students in preparation for teaching were generally not as able and as promising as their contemporaries in other departments of the college or university seemed to be noted early, and was clearly observable at mid-twentieth century. In 1927, President Nicholas Murray Butler of Columbia University noted in his annual report that teachers in the United States,

save those exceptions which here as always prove the rule, whether in school, in college, or in university, are and for some time past have been, in large part quite uneducated in any large and justifiable sense of that word. The elaborate training which they have so often received in a sorry substitute for education. . . . What one misses today is that background of good manners, of correct and cultivated speech, of high standards of appreciation in art and in letters, that generous and kindly acquaintance with all that is best in literature, in the fine arts, and in reflective thought, which has always constituted the tie that binds together the men and women of genuinely educational insight and competence.

In their study in 1920 of normal schools in Missouri, William C. Bagley and William S. Learned [55] had found conditions discouraging,

54 "Teachers and Equality of Educational Opportunity," *School and Society,* LXVII (April 24, 1948), pp. 308-9. Used by permission of author and publisher.
55 *The Professional Preparation of Teachers for American Public Schools.* Bulletin No. 14, Carnegie Foundation for the Advancement of Teaching, 1920.

and they commented especially on the evil effects of institutional competition for students, which continued to be a serious affliction in the education of teachers. Eighteen years later William S. Learned and Ben Wood found conditions not greatly improved, if at all, in Pennsylvania.[56] Their study of the relations of secondary and higher education disclosed disquieting conditions on prospective teachers in the higher institutions of that state. Most of the students were "not at home in the lower half of the total college distributions; they exhibit inferiority in contrast with the nonteachers in nearly every department of study; and they show up badly when compared in the same tests with students four years below them who represent the educational problems with which they must be prepared to deal. The ability and attainment of those selected and prepared in special centers for that purpose are consistently and conspicuously below the level of the group as a whole." Learned and Wood saw no good reasons for believing that conditions were less dismal in other states. And they asked whether parents desired to have their children taught in the public schools "by persons of demonstrably less general education than many of those children themselves already possess?" They also significantly said that the "most promising eventual solution for the problem of selecting teachers who both know what to teach and are themselves educated, lies with the schools and colleges that prepare them."

At mid-century, however, most of the teachers' colleges and most of the departments and schools of education in colleges and universities were not making wide and intelligent use of means for selective admission. Most of these institutions seemed to be under such financial or political pressures for enrollment that they could not always reject inferior candidates, when to reject them might mean reduction of income and increase enrollments at competing institutions which might be ignoring or failing to conform to the standards of accrediting set up by the American Association of Teachers Colleges. Competition for students was a grave affliction in the education of teachers at mid-twentieth century, and how to eliminate the unfit candidates from the teacher-education institutions was a persistent problem. But it was generally believed that the quality of the teachers sent out by those institutions would determine more than anything else the prestige, general respectability, and the influence of teaching in the community.

[56] *The Student and His Knowledge.* Bulletin No. 22, Carnegie Foundation for the Advancement of Teaching, 1938, pp. 64-66.

Careful selection of students in the institutions that prepared teachers was believed by most thoughtful observers to be the answer to the serious question of getting able and promising young people, of positive personality, general education and cultivation, to prepare for the profession. One leader in the movement toward this goal said:

> I feel that selective admission is the crucial issue in teacher education. Little can be done until . . . admission . . . is effectively restricted to those who have both the intellectual ability and personal qualities necessary for membership in the most important of all professions in a democracy. . . . If twenty-five institutions have already demonstrated that they can attract and hold students of better than average ability, then why should not all teacher-education institutions do it? [57]

While there was concern about the quality of those young people who were in the teacher-education institutions and preparing for teaching, there was occasional expression of concern about the quality of the teaching personnel in the institutions that undertook to train teachers. Bagley and Learned [58] devoted a whole chapter to this subject. In the normal schools of Missouri in 1920, two thirds of the teachers were of American parentage, nearly one half were born in that state, two thirds of the men came from agricultural, one sixth from professional, and one tenth from commercial families; and one third of the parents of the female teachers in those schools were engaged in trade, less than one third in agriculture, and about one fifth in the professions.

The tentative standards and policies for accrediting members of the American Association of Colleges for Teacher Education defined such a college, but proposed that the quantitative requirements for graduation from such an institution be left to the regional accrediting agencies. So also should the teaching load of the faculty. The "instructional patterns" of the curriculum included general education, teaching fields, professional education, and elective courses in activities. There were also standards on the library, its housing, staff, and budget, and its program of services; on appointment, academic freedom, and tenure; and on financial support, which "should be adequate for and suited to the educational purposes implied in its

[57] Ben Wood and Ruth A. Pedersen, "Results of Selective Admission in Teachers Colleges," *Teacher-Education Journal*, June, 1941, p. 22.

[58] *Op. cit.*, pp. 99-127. For the composition of public school administrators in the United States near mid-twentieth century, see George H. Henry, "Alas, the Poor School Superintendent," *Harper's Magazine*, November, 1946; and for comments on the teaching personnel in teachers' colleges, see "Who Teaches the Teachers?" *Life*, October 16, 1950.

program." On the preparation of the faculty, the standard said that members of faculties of colleges for teacher education should

. . . have special responsibilities beyond the possession of scholarly attainments and a high degree of competency in their special areas of professional service. A person well qualified to teach in such an institution:

a) Is emotionally stable and mature.
b) Reflects high ideals through his behavior.
c) Holds fair-minded attitudes on controversial issues.
d) Shows an active interest in continued professional growth.
e) Regards himself as primarily a college teacher (rather than as a subject matter specialist).
f) Takes a broad (rather than departmental) view of educational problems.
g) Is friendly, democratic, tolerant, and helpful in his relations with students.
h) Has an infectious enthusiasm for teaching that inspires students to want to teach.
i) Has demonstrated skill in methods of instruction appropriate to his field.
j) Leads students to take responsibility for planning and checking their own progress.
k) Inspires students to think for themselves and to express their own ideas sincerely.
l) Organizes materials and prepares carefully for each meeting with a class.
m) Understands the problems most often met by college students.

"The character of a school is fashioned by the character of its teachers," declared the *Regents' Inquiry Into the Character and Cost of Public Education in the State of New York* in 1938, and the educational program proposed by that very extensive and thorough study demanded "far more of the teachers and supervisory officers than is required of them today." [59] Teachers and the "school men," individually and through their educational organizations, and the public and private institutions that were engaged in the preparation of teachers, were called upon "to cooperate for the advancement of the teaching profession in the State." To that purpose the *Inquiry* made some recommendations: [60]

Introduce competition through Regents' rules, into the selection and promotion of teachers throughout the entire State, as is required by the state

[59] *Education for American Life* (New York: The McGraw-Hill Book Co., 1938), p. 55.
[60] *Ibid.*, pp. 56-58. Used by permission of the publisher.

Constitution and as is now attempted in New York City and in Buffalo. The elements to be considered in such competition should include character and cultural influence, teaching ability or promise, broad education, technical training and experience, scholarship, and good health.

Extend tenure to the 20,000 teaching positions not now covered by law as soon as the school systems can be reorganized to provide professional supervision, especially for young and inexperienced teachers. Make the continuing right of all teachers to teach depend on evidence of continued growth and service, determined not solely by courses but also by worth-while scholarship, travel, and community service. Ultimately make retirement compulsory at age sixty-five and provide pensions.

Increase minimum salaries in the rural areas from $800 to $1,200 as soon as central districts are organized throughout the State. This can then be done without any increase in per pupil costs.

Establish twenty annual Regents' Fellowships for teachers, each worth $500 plus the present salary of the teacher winning the award, but not to exceed $3,500 from the State. It should be the purpose of these awards to recognize outstanding teaching wherever it may be found, and to permit a year of travel, further study, or rest.

Strengthen teacher supervision locally, as will be possible with the modernization of the school districts, in recognition of the fact that efficient teaching, particularly by new and inexperienced teachers, requires systematic, professional, and stimulating leadership.

Reduce the number of prospective teachers admitted annually to the state teacher-preparing institutions, and select for training, on a competitive basis, only such candidates as are intellectually and personally promising material for teaching and school administration.

Extend the course for teachers to four years at the present three-year normal schools and authorize them to award the Bachelor's degree. Authorize the state teachers colleges to award the Master's degree to their graduate students. Devote the additional time primarily to general cultural education and individual scholarship, not to instruction in teaching methods.

Bring the teacher-preparing institutions into closer touch with the schools by utilizing one or more of these institutions experimentally for the supervision of teaching in nearby schools.

Organize a permanent Advisory Committee of teachers, school men, and college directors to assist in the revision of the teacher-preparing curriculums, in the development of experimental programs, and in the revision of teacher licensing to include competitive measures of qualification and to eliminate the absurd and rigid, and at times indefensible, aspects of the present system.

Select the staff of teacher-preparing institutions with special reference to scholarship and leadership. Increase top salaries of faculties. Afford these instructors opportunities for study, experimentation, and research. Encourage state teachers' colleges to make use of one another's specialists and particularly inspiring faculty members on an exchange basis. In particular, free the presidents of the teacher-preparing institutions of laborious financial and administrative details so that they may provide more effective leadership.

Reduce the number of teacher-preparing institutions and increase the annual budgets to cover salary increases and improvements in equipment, for those which are continued. Appropriate $8,000,000 for buildings, dormitories, libraries, laboratories, grounds, and equipment.

Trends and issues in educational administration and finance are discussed in the next Chapter.

Some Questions and Exercises for Students

1. Show why the colleges and universities of this country so long delayed providing for the professional education of teachers.
2. Study and give your views on C. W. Bardeen's articles in the *Educational Review* in 1908 and 1912 on men and teaching, and on the reply by Harriet R. Pease in the same magazine in 1912.
3. Study and report on the studies by Bagley, Learned, and Wood, listed in the Suggested References. Show exactly why teaching does not seem to attract the ablest young men and women. How can more of the most promising young people be brought into teaching?
4. Read and criticize Sperry's article, "Who Teaches the Teachers?" in *Life,* October 16, 1950, and Saul's "I'll Stick Up for the Schools," in the *Saturday Evening Post,* April 15, 1950.
5. Causes of confusion among some classroom teachers are said to be the "inflation" of the curricula of the schools and the greatly increased functions of teachers in recent years. Read and comment on some of the criticisms on these conditions.
6. Consult *Readers' Guide to Periodical Literature* and *Education Index* and read and report on some of the more significant articles that have appeared on (*a*) loyalty oaths for teachers, (*b*) the anti-evolution bills, (*c*) the "pure" history bills.
7. Examine the *Book Review Digest* for reviews of some of the more significant books that have appeared in recent years on broad, not technical, subjects in education.
8. Read the article by Emil Altman on "Our Mentally Unbalanced Teachers," in *American Mercury,* April, 1941, and "Fit to Teach" (*Ninth Yearbook* of the Department of Classroom Teachers of the NEA). How would you improve the disturbing conditions which those discussions disclosed?

9. Students in preparation for teaching frequently complain about the overlapping and repetitious nature of both undergraduate and graduate courses they are required to take in professional education for initial certification to teach and to keep their certificates in force. From your experience and observation, comment on this complaint.

10. It is frequently said that teacher-education institutions are rapidly becoming trade schools, and their products chiefly mechanics who have the "know how" but not the "know what," instead of being broadly educated and cultivated men and women. How can this condition be improved?

11. Competent studies of the subject have disclosed that teachers in teacher-education institutions are themselves not as broadly educated and cultivated as teachers in some other departments of the colleges and universities. How can this condition be improved?

12. Lawyers, physicians, engineers, electricians, dentists, pharmacists, nurses, barbers, morticians, beauty-parlor operators, plumbers, real estate dealers, insurance salesmen, and others are required to be examined and certificated by their own peers before they can practice their profession or trade. With teachers, the case is generally quite different. Show exactly how one becomes a teacher in your state.

SOME SUGGESTED REFERENCES AND READING

AMERICAN COUNCIL ON EDUCATION. *The Improvement of Teacher Education.* Washington, D. C.: The Council, 1946.
The final report of the Commission on Teacher Education of the American Council on Education which is very valuable for this Chapter. The student should also consult other publications of the Commission.

BAGLEY, WILLIAM C., and LEARNED, WILLIAM S. *The Professional Preparation of Teachers for American Public Schools.* New York: Carnegie Foundation for the Advancement of Teaching, 1920.
Shows discouraging conditions and the evil effects of institutional competition for students.

BEALE, HOWARD K. *Are American Teachers Free?* New York: Chas. Scribner's Sons, 1936.
Deals with some of the restraints on teachers in the schools of the United States.

CONRAD, EARL. *The Public School Scandal.* New York: The John Day Co., 1951.
A dismal account of conditions. "Teachers are tired and themselves emotionally upset. Confusion reigns at all levels, and only an alerted public can reclaim the public schools from chaos."

ELSBREE, WILLARD S. *The American Teacher.* New York: American Book Co., 1939.
Contains a very good historical treatment of the subject, and excellent discussions of trends in the education of teachers during the first four decades of the twentieth century.

EVENDEN, E. S. *National Survey of the Education of Teachers.* Six volumes. Washington, D. C.: Government Printing Office, 1935.

    Vol. II, "Teacher Personnel in the United States," contains helpful information on the subject of this Chapter, as does also Vol. VI, "Summary and Interpretation," which shows how inadequate was the amount of schooling teachers had when the data were collected.

KNIGHT, EDGAR W. "A Century of Teacher-Education," *Educational Forum,* IX (1945), pp. 149-61.

    Traces the main movements in the schooling of teachers and indicates trends in the present century.

KNIGHT, EDGAR W., and HALL, CLIFTON L. *Readings in American Educational History.* New York: Appleton-Century-Crofts, Inc., 1951.

    Chap. vi contains original documents that throw some light on the subject of this Chapter.

LEARNED, WILLIAM S., and WOOD, BEN. *The Student and His Knowledge.* New York: Carnegie Foundation for the Advancement of Teaching, 1938.

    Shows disquieting conditions, and that students in teacher-education institutions exhibited "inferiority in contrast with nonteachers in nearly every department of study."

LYND, ALBERT. "Quackery in the Public Schools," *Atlantic Monthly,* CLXXXV (March, 1950), pp. 33-38.

    A particularly sharp criticism of practices in the training, certificating, and appointment of teachers. Should be read in connection with Smith's *And Madly Teach* and Saul's "I'll Stick Up for the Schools."

PIERCE, BESSIE L. *Public Opinion and the Teaching of History in the United States.* New York: Alfred A. Knopf, 1926.

    Deals with the questions of the teaching of history and tells of some of the efforts to make history "pure."

SAUL, WALTER BIDDLE. "I'll Stick Up for the Schools," *Saturday Evening Post,* April 15, 1950.

    Attempts to answer some of the critics of the schools, such as Mortimer Smith, below. Strikes back at those "who carp because the schools don't make superhuman citizens out of human clay."

SMITH, MORTIMER. *And Madly Teach.* Chicago: Henry Regnery Co., 1949.

    One of the numerous severe criticisms of the schools and teaching that have appeared in recent years. Charged, with considerable justice, that the schools were trying to do too much.

Chapter 7

TRENDS IN ADMINISTRATION AND SUPPORT

PREVIEW OF THE CHAPTER

Real development in educational administration in the United States came generally in the first half of the twentieth century, but variety in practices was its striking characteristic at mid-century. . . . One of the earliest statements on educational administration in cities appeared in the report of the Committee of Fifteen in 1895. . . . A year later, President Andrew S. Draper of the University of Illinois described education in this country as "a very unsystematic system," but the idealism and determination of the American people worked marked improvements. . . . The American people have all along highly resisted centralized control and bureaucracy in their educational affairs, and localism in organization and administration has continued to be strong. . . . Variety in practices in state educational organization and administration was conspicuous at mid-century, with no uniform pattern developed for state boards of education or for chief state school officers. . . . Variety was also a characteristic in county educational administration in the middle of the century, in spite of long and earnest efforts to improve conditions in rural areas. . . . How to provide funds for the greatly expanded programs of public education was among the most stubborn questions in educational administration at mid-century. . . . By that time public education had become "big business." It was also clear that it was becoming more and more secular, and this condition caused considerable concern throughout the country. . . . Apparently the largest advance had been made by cities, although rural education was receiving increased attention. But issues in educational administration were more numerous and more difficult in 1950 than ever before. Certain trends were clearly observable, and a wide study of the subject was being undertaken under a large grant by the Kellogg Foundation.

Variety in Educational Practices.—In 1938, the Advisory Committee on Education stated that until 1870 "there was no real development in school administration" [1] in the United States, and that it was not until the present century that "school administration

---

[1] Advisory Committee on Education, *Organization and Administration.* Staff Study No. 2.

288

became a professional undertaking." When that Committee made its significant report on the subject in 1938, there were more than 20 thousand state, county, and city school administrators and assistants, and about 35 thousand principals and supervisors employed to direct the public-education activities of the United States, a vast army of persons who presumably required special training and experience for their work in the more than 250 thousand public schools in this country.

The rapid expansion of public education in the United States during the present century has called for such remarkable changes in the organization, administration, and support of educational arrangements as to become among the most conspicuous developments in American education. These changes, which were brought about by the great increase in population and in economic wealth, by the findings of the psychological laboratories, and by the gradual growth of the democratic spirit, were marked not only in the work of the elementary and secondary schools, but they also appeared in higher education, as was noted in Chapter 4. By the middle of the twentieth century, education in the United States had become an immense machine, increasingly standardized and mechanized, the largest public business of the American people.

But whatever else may be said about the matter, education in the United States has all along been marked by variety, which at mid-twentieth century was also a striking characteristic of its legal organization and administration and methods of financial support. The legal organization of public state educational administration reached back to 1784, when New York created its Board of Regents, the first state board of education in this country. The development of state educational administration and organization after that time represented a slow but steady growth from simple and local to complicated organization, with a tendency at mid-century to more or less high centralization.

The administration of education in this country has been entrusted to the various states. The Federal Constitution has been silent on the subject; but by implication, the Tenth Amendment to that document has left to the states the power and the responsibility to organize and direct their arrangements for public education as they please. The constitutions of most of the states place upon their legislatures the obligation to provide for the organization and maintenance of public school systems, and this freedom of action in educational administration helps to explain in part the wide variety of practices in the organization, administration, and support of the public schools throughout the country. While in recent years the Supreme Court of the United States has now and then shown some tendency to become the national school board, by decisions that restricted action by state and local educational authorities, the Court has also noted: "One of the happy incidents of the Federal system" has been the opportunity of the state, "if its citizens choose, . . . to try novel social and economic experiments without risk to the rest of the country." In education, as in other social undertakings, the people of this country have seemed to believe that "in differentiation, not uniformity, lies the path of progress." They have acted, wrote Mr. Justice Louis Brandeis, on this belief and the country "has advanced human happiness, and it has prospered." This strong belief in localism in educational organization and management has always warned against the real or imaginary dangers of interference or coercion from above, and has made for variety instead of uniformity in educational practice. This fear of enforced uniformity had much to do with the long delays in general federal aid to education which had not been provided at the middle of the century.

The power of the legislature of a state over education is now generally recognized throughout this country. As already noted, this power was first exercised, in the sense it is here considered, by the State of New York in 1784 when the law establishing the Board of Regents was enacted, to have some control over the educational institutions that had been authorized there by the English crown. By this legislative act, the first American state board of education was formed and has continued to the present, although it was not given control over the public schools of the state until early in the present century. North Carolina in 1825 established an educational board, under the name of "President and Directors of the Literary Fund," out of which later developed a state board of education. Shortly afterwards Vermont established a form of state educational control, to be followed by similar action in Connecticut, Kentucky, Missouri, Tennessee, and Massachusetts before 1839, and by other states later.

But it was not until 1837 that the first real state board of education was created, by the legislature of Massachusetts. While its main functions were to investigate and make recommendations on educational conditions in the state, its effectiveness developed largely through the vision and energetic work of its distinguished secretary, Horace Mann. His educational services for Massachusetts attracted wide notice throughout this country and in some other parts of the world. By 1860, other states of the Union had established and improved their central boards of education, but years were to pass before effective boards of education were generally provided. The strength of localism, devotion to the doctrine of laissez faire, and the fear of centralized power in the management of local educational arrangements tended to retard the growth of strong state boards of education. Efforts to get state-wide legislation on compulsory school attendance, for example, almost everywhere caused popular resentment to what was believed to be an encroachment of the state into the parental function. Echoes of resentment may even now be heard when a state assumes educational authority and functions with which the people may not be familiar. Some decisions of the Supreme Court of the United States in the second quarter of the twentieth century served to disclose such resentment and attitude, as witness the Oregon decision in 1925, in which the Court held that children could not be compelled to attend public schools, and in the Barnette case (1943), in which it held that children could not be expelled from school for refusing to salute the national flag, although in the Gobitis case in 1940 the Court had held exactly the opposite position.

Pronouncements on Educational Administration.—Among the earliest pronouncements on educational administration by a national committee was that made in 1895 by a subcommittee of the Committee of Fifteen. As noted elsewhere, this committee dealt also with the training of teachers and with the correlation of studies in the elementary schools. The chairman of the subcommittee on the organization of city school systems was Andrew S. Draper, president of the University of Illinois. He and the superintendents of Washington, D. C., W. B. Powell, and of Trenton, New Jersey, A. B. Poland, were in agreement on the report, with superintendents E. P. Seaver of Boston, and A. G. Lane of Chicago, dissenting on a few minor details. The principles which the subcommittee believed "must necessarily be observed in framing a plan of organization and government in a large city school system" were stated as follows: [2]

First: The affairs of the school should not be mixed up with partisan contests or municipal business.

Second: There should be a sharp distinction between legislative functions and executive duties.

Third: Legislative functions should be clearly fixed by statute and be exercised by a comparatively small board, each member of which is representative of the whole city. This board, within statutory limitations, should determine the policy of the system, levy taxes, and control the expenditures. It should make no appointments. Every act should be by a recorded resolu-

[2] The student should read the report in full. This may be found in the *Journal of Proceedings and Addresses*, National Educational Association, 1895, pp. 375-97.

tion. It seems preferable that this board be created by appointment rather than election, and that it be constituted of two branches acting against each other.

Fourth: Administration should be separated into two great independent departments, one of which manages the business interests and the other of which supervises the instruction. Each of these should be wholly directed by a single official who is vested with ample authority and charged with full responsibility for sound administration.

Fifth: The chief executive officer on the business side should be charged with the care of all property and with the duty of keeping it in suitable condition; he should provide all necessary furnishings and appliances; he should make all agreements and see that they are properly performed; he should appoint all assistants, janitors, and workmen. In a word, he should do all that the law contemplates and all that the board authorizes concerning the business affairs of the school system, and when anything goes wrong he should answer for it. He may be appointed by the board, but we think it preferable that he be chosen in the same way the members of the board are chosen, and be given a veto upon the acts of the board.

Sixth: The chief executive officer of the department of instruction should be given a long term and may be appointed by the board. If the board is constituted of two branches, he should be nominated by the business executive and confirmed by the legislative branch. Once appointed, he should be independent. He should appoint all authorized assistants and teachers from an eligible list to be constituted as provided by law. He should assign to duties and discontinue services for cause at his discretion. He should determine all matters relating to instruction. He should be charged with the responsibility of developing a professional and enthusiastic teaching force and of making all the teaching scientific and forceful. He must perfect the organization of his department and make and carry out plans to accomplish this. If he cannot do this in a reasonable time, he should be superseded by one who can.

The government of a vast city school system comes to have an autonomy which is largely its own and almost independent of direction or restraint. The volume of business which this government transacts is represented only by millions of dollars; it calls not only for the highest sagacity and the ripest experience, but also for much special information relating to school property and school affairs. Even more important than this is the fact that this government controls and determines the educational policy of the city and carries on the instruction of tens or hundreds of thousands of children. This instruction is of little value, and perhaps vicious, unless it is professional and scientific. This government is representative. All citizens are compelled to support it, and all have large interests which it is bound to promote. Every parent has rights which it is the duty of this school government to protect and enforce. When government exacts our support of public education, when it comes into our homes and takes our children into its custody and instructs them according to its will, we acquire a right which is as exalted as any right of property, or of person, or of conscience can be; and that is the right to know that the environment is healthful, that the management is kindly and ennobling, and that the instruction is rational and scientific. It is needless to say to what extent these interests are impeded or blocked, or how commonly these rights of citizenship and of parentage are denied or defied, or how helpless the individual is who seeks their enforcement under the system of school government which has heretofore obtained in some of the great cities of the country. This is not surprising. It is only the logical result of the rapid growth of cities, of a marvelous advance in knowledge of what is needed in the schools, of the antagonism of selfish interests by which all public administration, and particularly school administration, is encompassed, and of the lack of plan and system, the confusion of powers, the absence of individual responsibility, in the government of a system of schools. By the census of 1890 there are seven cities in the United States, each with a population greater than any one of sixteen states. The aggregate population of twelve cities exceeds the aggregate population of twenty states. Government for education certainly requires as strong and responsible an organization as government for any other purpose. These great centers of population, with their vast and complex educational problems, have passed the stage when government by the time-honored commission will suffice. No popular government ever determined the policy and administered the affairs of such large bodies of people successfully, ever transacted such a vast volume of business satisfactorily, ever promoted high and beneficent ends, ever afforded protection to the rights of each individual of the great multitude, unless in its plan of organization there was an organic separation of executive, legislative, and judicial functions and powers. All the circumstances of the case, and the uniform experience of the world, forbid our expecting any substantial solution of the problem we are considering until it is well settled in the sentiments of the people that the school systems of the greatest cities are only a part of the school systems of the states of which these cities form a part, and are subject to the legislative authority thereof—until there is a plan of school government in each city which differentiates executive acts from legislative functions, which emancipates the legislative branch of that government from the influence of self-seekers; which fixes upon individuals the responsibility for executive acts, either performed or omitted; which gives to the intelligence of the community the power to influence legislation and exact perfect and complete execution; which affords to every citizen whose interests are ignored, or whose rights are invaded, a place for complaint and redress; and which puts the business interests upon a business footing, the teaching upon an expert basis, and gives to the instruction that protection and encouragement which is vital to the development of all professional and scientific work.

We have undertaken to indicate the general principles which we think should be observed in setting up the framework of government of a large city school system. While we have no thought that any precise form of organization which could be suggested would, in all details, be imperative, we are confident that the form or plan of organization is of supreme consequence, and that any which disregards the principles we have pointed out will work to disadvantage or lead to disaster.

Superintendent Seaver's dissent was as follows:

I find myself in general accord with the doctrines of the report. There is only one feature of it from which I feel obliged to dissent, and that is an important though not necessarily a vital one. I refer to the office of school director. I see no need of such an officer elected by the people, and I do see the danger of his becoming a part of the political organization for the dispensation of patronage.

All power and authority in school affairs should reside ultimately in the board of education, consisting of not more than eight persons appointed by the mayor of the city, to hold office four years, two members retiring annually and eligible for reappointment once and no more. This board should appoint as its chief officer a superintendent of instruction, whose tenure should be during good behavior and efficiency, and whose powers and duties should be to a large extent defined by statute law, and not wholly or chiefly by the regulations of the board of education. The superintendent of instruction should have a seat and voice but not a vote in the board of education. The board of education should also appoint a business agent, and define his powers and duties in relation to all mattters of buildings, repairs, and supplies, substantially as set forth in the report in relation to the school director.

All teachers should be appointed and annually reappointed or recommended by the superintendent of instruction, until after a sufficient probation they are appointed on a tenure during good behavior and efficiency.

All matters relating to courses of study, textbooks, and examinations should be left to the superintendent and his assistants, constituting a body of professional experts who should be regarded as alone competent to deal with such matters, and should be held accountable therefor to the board of education only in a general way, and not in particular details.

Superintendent Lane's dissent was as follows:

I concur in the recommendations of the subcommittee on the organization of city school systems as summarized in the concluding portion of the report, omitting in item 3 the words "And that it be constituted of two branches acting against each other." Omit in item 5, "but we think it preferable that he be chosen in the same way that members of the board are chosen and be given veto power upon the acts of the board." I recommend that the veto power be given to the president of the board.

When these statements on educational administration were made in 1895, the professional study of the subject had scarcely begun.

Pedagogy, or education (as it was later to be called), was a most minor subject of professional study and few colleges or universities had chairs or departments in the field, which was to expand with lightning speed during the next fifty years. Little had been written on educational administration or educational finance in 1900, and instruction in these subjects was likely to be largely the recollections of practical experience. Before the close of the first half of the twentieth century, however, the literature in these fields had become voluminous, and courses in educational administration and educational finance were covering the campuses of the country like an Atlanta (Georgia) newspaper is reported to cover the "Empire State of the South"—like the dew. Examination of the "offerings" in these subjects in schools of education in the large universities or even in teachers' colleges revealed that multitudes of proliferated courses were then being provided in major and minor aspects of administration and finance.

American Idealism in Education.—In 1896 Andrew S. Draper, president of the University of Illinois said, in an address before the National Educational Association,[3] that the United States had a very great system for extending popular education in this country, but "a very unsystematic system" which he believed to be "characteristic of a youthful but great people." The public school, he said, was the product of pioneers whose numerical growth had been phenomenal, whose energy had been intense, whose ambition for self-improvement had been extraordinary, and whose swift development of general quick-wittedness and cooperative institutional life had excited the admiration of the world. During the fifty years that passed since that appraisal of this country's educational effort, the American public school reached some of its lofty triumphs, and at mid-twentieth century it ranked so high among the noble achievements of democracy that the American people looked upon this immense social enterprise with a greater admiration and a more pardonable pride than the public school had enjoyed a half century before.

[3] *Journal of Proceedings and Addresses*, 1896, p. 201. This organization had begun in 1857 as the National Teachers' Association, to become the National Educational Association in 1870, and to be chartered by the Congress in 1906 as the National Education Association. An important part of the story of the growth of public education in the United States can be traced through the addresses, proceedings, and resolutions of this organization. See Chapter 9. The membership in this organization grew from 43 in 1857 to 170 in 1870, to 2,700 in 1884, to 7,000 in 1894; dropped to 4,500 in 1904; rose to 7,000 in 1914, to 138,000 in 1924, to 154,000 in 1934, to 271,000 in 1944, to 437,855 in 1950, and in 1951 to 465,266, when 46 per cent of the teachers in the United States had membership in that association, according to the *NEA Journal* for September of that year.

That admiration and pride arose in large part from the fact that no instrumentality of democracy had brought more comfort or held out more hope to the people of this country than that of public education. This most fascinating part of the entire American democratic epic had long stood as a sign and symbol of opportunity for their advancement in this world. It appeared to have raised the level of the lives of the American people and to have given them hope which they could have had by no other earthly means. For this and other reasons the American people continue to cherish their schools. Their faith in the power of education has been so strong as to appear at times almost pathetic. Moreover, most of the American people seem to know that their schools represent one of their most deep-seated human interests and activities because they have witnessed the struggles of public education to develop in the face of many stubborn and discouraging obstacles.

These obstacles had been numerous. The American common school had its origin in part in conflicts that flourished in contending economic interests. It was born in poverty and obscurity and in its early years was fed sparingly by the crumbs of charity and philanthropy. Often its way was obstructed by pedagogic politicians or political pedagogues and indifferent if not hostile ecclesiastics. The principle of educational equality, now generally accepted in most of the American states, was slow to gain strength because schooling was generally regarded as the privilege of the well to do and favored and not as a right of the masses. Almost everywhere in this country the principles of public support and control of education, and free, nonsectarian, and compulsory education, now commonly accepted, were bitterly contested before winning acceptance in the public mind and passing into established practice. But over many stubborn and discouraging obstacles the common school won its way through a stalwart idealism and vigorous determination.

Resistance to Centralized Control.—This idealism and this determination were characteristic of the faith of the American people in their dream of universal education. And these qualities had almost always stood in solemn protest against autocratic and bureaucratic control in education, as in other public interests and activities of the American people. But some observers of the educational scene in 1950 seemed to see in the rapid tendency to such control in the administration of the schools the most insidious threat ever made to the integrity of public education in this country and to a healthy local interest in its work.

Many such observers saw a definite tendency in recent years to remove the schools further and further away from the people and to entice or coerce them to look more and more to their state capitals or to Washington for their Santa Claus. This tendency, the observers said, was bound to stifle local interest and local initiative and effort and to discourage the sense of local educational responsibility among the people. Some searching questions were being asked: Does high centralization in educational administration increase the morale of teachers? Does it give definite assurance of the wise use of educational funds and protection against their waste? Does it guarantee security against mediocrity and partisan political control in educational management? Does it always guarantee equality of educational opportunity, which had become a sort of watchword or slogan or Shibboleth of the American people? These observers seemed to see the tendency to high centralization and bureaucratic educational control as a significant warning to public education, which in mid-twentieth century faced its greatest test of merit. They said that educational bureaucracy easily promoted partisan political purposes but could never freely serve legitimate educational purposes; that centralized officialism was not hospitable to the long-established tradition and principles of public education in this country and could become hostile to its best interests and those of American democracy in general.

Highly centralized control or bureaucracy in educational administration tended, keen observers said, to increase educational paper work and bookkeeping and clerks, to exalt the function of the "administrator," however mediocre he may be, and to develop the "administrative attitude" which can so easily overshadow the primary function of the school—which was to teach. Intelligent critics warned in the middle of the twentieth century that if the American people did not become more vigilant about the rapid trend toward high centralization in the administration of their schools, the important business of education could easily reach the point that the important business of salvation is believed to have reached in the sixteenth century when one of the greatest revolutions in history took place. The Protestant Revolt was brought on, it was said, in part by ecclesiastical bureaucracy and theological bookkeeping, because the theologians had made religion a very complicated matter. Highly complicated administration could easily develop an education priesthood in this country, observers pointed out.

A reasonable minimum of state supervision or oversight to safeguard state educational funds was considered desirable. But this should not mean bureaucratic interference with the administration of the local schools or with the content of educational programs. Such interference could easily lead to the regimentation of education and through it to the regimentation of the minds of the people. The danger of such regimentation was already appearing in some states by 1950, and was becoming all the more menacing because public education in this country had grown in stature and in the confidence of the people through local interest, local initiative, and effort of responsible local agencies. Any theory or practice that was likely to retard or destroy that interest, initiative, and effort was bound to be harmful to public education and eventually to bring it into disrepute. In American education there was no place for the political methods of statism or of the police state, the critics said. Eternal vigilance was as much the price of educational as of any other kind of liberty.

The danger of partisan political interference was explicitly or implicitly warned against by the American Association of School Administrators in its resolutions in March of 1950, when it strongly opposed state laws requiring loyalty oaths for teachers, the use of public funds for private or parochial schools, and urged the strengthening of the United States Office of Education:

> We reaffirm the position of the Association in urging Congress to establish the United States Office of Education as a nonpartisan, independent agency, governed by a national board of education. This board should be composed of representative laymen, appointed for long, overlapping terms by the President with the consent of the Senate. It is also recommended that this board shall appoint a professionally qualified commissioner of education to serve as its executive officer.

Some observers of the current scene, however, did not exactly see how such action would remove the danger of politics in education on a national scale.

Two years after the report of the Committee of Fifteen, and its discussion of the organization and administration of city school systems, and one year after Andrew S. Draper, president of the University of Illinois, had discussed before the National Educational Association the "very unsystematic system" of educational arrangements in this country, the president of the Board of Education of Louisville, Kentucky, T. H. Watkins, read a paper before that national organization [4] on variety of methods of selecting boards of education in American cities. He found that of fifty cities with a population of 22 to 50 thousand, the average size of the board of

[4] *Journal and Proceedings,* 1897, pp. 988-93.

education was twelve members, the average term was three years; that forty-one elected their boards by popular vote and nine appointed them; that in seventeen cities the members of boards served from wards, in thirty-one they served "at large," and in two cities there was a combination of both methods. At that time the largest boards were reported in Allegheny (Pa.), with eighty-four members; Reading (Pa.), with sixty-four; Brooklyn, with forty-five; Philadelphia and Pittsburgh, with thirty-eight each; Providence (R. I.), with thirty-three; Cincinnati with thirty-one; Newark (N. J.), with thirty; Lynn (Mass.), Milwaukee (Wis.), New York City, and Chicago, with twenty-one each; New Orleans and Rochester (N. Y.), with twenty each; and Syracuse (N. Y.), with nineteen members. The smallest boards were in Evansville (Ind.), with three members; Memphis, with five; St. Joseph (Mo.), Des Moines (Ia.), and Kansas City with six each. Dividing the country roughly into North, South, and West (including Indiana but not Ohio in the West), the average size of city school boards was: North, twenty-four; South, thirteen; and West eleven members, "showing that in territorial development the tendency is toward smaller boards." This tendency appeared to be continuing fifty years later.

The high average in the North in 1897 was believed to be due, "to no small extent," to Pennsylvania, in which "the conservatism of Teutonic blood is not prone to innovation and experiment." Pittsburgh at that time, for example, was divided into thirty-eight districts, each with a board of six directors who were elected in the districts by popular vote, each for a term of three years. These district boards had powers to levy taxes, borrow money, purchase grounds, construct buildings, and appoint teachers. The central board of education of the city was composed of thirty-eight members, one elected from each district for a period of three years, and had charge of all high schools, paid the salaries of all teachers, adopted the course of study for the entire city, and purchased books and supplies which were provided free to all pupils. The central board received funds by appropriation from the city council, the amount being included in the general levy. Funds required by the district boards were raised by direct taxation in the districts.

Statistics and answers to inquiries led Watkins to conclude that the tendency near the turn of the century was toward smaller boards and longer terms than those of that time. He believed that "nine will ultimately prevail as the model number of members," and that a term of three years for each member would become popular. Sentiment seemed to be growing in favor of members, whether appointed or elected by popular vote, to serve from the city at large rather than from wards or districts.

On questions of the composition and powers of city school boards, Watkins did not care to give "ventilation" of his personal views, which would not be as valuable "as opinions already at hand of well-known and experienced educators." One of these, the president of Packer Collegiate Institute, recommended at the Boston Woman's Educational Association, about 1897, that the educational and the business administration of public schools "should be kept as separate as possible," and that there should be "centralized authority and responsibility in each of the administrations," a development that was to come rather generally in larger places throughout the country before 1950. The board of education should have "a committee on instruction." In a city of as heterogeneous a population as Boston had, the board of education "should be appointed (probably by the mayor), not elected by the people." Boston at that time had a board of twenty-four members, elected by popular vote for a term of three years.

D. C. Gilman, president of The Johns Hopkins University, was quoted as saying that in a large city

. . . there should be a small board of education, made up of the best men that can be enlisted, without regard to the wards in which they reside. This board should serve without pay, but it should be relieved of details by properly paid clerical assistants. It should include men who are as capable as the water commissioners, the park commissioners, the police commissioners, the harbor commissioners are capable of directing a very important branch of the public service.

Gilman also said that the proper administration of the educational system of a city required competent persons in charge of financial matters, buildings and equipment, and "education," and that these persons should be paid adequately and should be "held to strict accountability by the general board." The need, he said, was not only for accountants of fidelity and accuracy, and properly qualified inspectors of buildings who understood "the arts of construction, heating, and plumbing," but especially "educational guides and leaders, men and women, worthy of appointment in any institution because of their knowledge, character, and administrative powers, as well as their devotion to the service of the public through the agency of the public school system. They should be supervisors and inspectors of the work of instruction."

An article in the *School Board Journal* for April of 1897, by Frank A. Fitzgerald, discussed the subject of the best type of board of education, and said:

It is a question of communities, of development, and of evolution. Each community has its own problems to solve, its own peculiar environments, and the needs of this community vary at different periods of its growth. In communities where the board of education is large, there is usually a developing public sentiment in favor of a change from a large board to a small board. In communities where the board of education has been for a number of years a small one, there is a tendency in favor of a larger or more representative body. Nor can one general law be laid down upon the question whether members of boards of education shall be appointed by the mayor or by judges of the district court, elected by the people at large, or by wards. It is, of course, important that the quality of the members of the board of education shall be high. But there is room for a great deal of discussion as to what we mean by quality. It is not at all certain that the most cultivated and best educated people in the community will make the best members of a board of education. There are many instances where representatives from this class of people have been distinctly the worst members on the board, so far as the interests of the schools are concerned. Reform boards that are elected during times of excitement, with the idea of correcting some great alleged evil, and composed of the best citizens, are often much worse, so far as the interests of the schools are concerned, than their predecessors.

The really vital interests of the schools, so far as they are affected by the efficiency or nonefficiency of a board of education, are the treatment by the board of questions involved in the election of a superintendent and teachers, the dismissal of teachers, and questions concerning the course of study and the adoption of textbooks.

The best schools are to be found where the people in charge are not clamoring for more power, and where they are not changing the course of study every other year. Primarily, the character of the work done in schools depends upon the quality of teaching. All the other accessories are incidental and immaterial.

A few simple changes in the bylaws of a board of education will greatly simplify the problem. The object of any rational reform is threefold: (1) To segregate the purely professional sides of the schools, as far as the initiative is concerned, into the hands of the superintendent. (2) The maintenance of a certain freedom among the teachers and principals, within certain board limits. (3) The segregation of the interests represented by the business side into such simple forms as will enable the members of the board of education to do more than their duty without devoting an undue amount of time to the public service.

The board of education ought to run the schools, through its executive officers. It ought not to be forced to spend hours of its time debating details.

If reformers would confer with the right spirit with their local school boards, instead of rushing off to the legislature to secure new legislation, wise changes could easily be made.

State Administration of Education.—Variety of practice in state educational administration appeared at the middle of the century in the prescriptions of qualifications or restrictions for membership on state boards of education. Most of the forty states that had such boards prescribed some qualifications or restrictions. Among these were the requirements that each Congressional district must be represented; that one or more members must or must not be engaged in educational work; that not more than a specified number may have membership in the same political party; that no member may be connected with a business that published textbooks; that no member may hold another elective or appointive office, and perhaps other restrictions, which have often called for interpretation by the attorney general or the courts. Educational qualifications were generally not prescribed for membership on state educational boards, but most boards for which data were available in 1950 were composed of members who had attended college. The term of office of members also varied widely in 1950, from three years in two states (Delaware and Kansas) to thirteen years in one state (New York). Compensation for service on state school boards also varied. Members generally were not paid salaries, but all, except perhaps *ex officiis* members, received expenses, a *per diem*, or both.

According to W. W. Keesecker,[5] specialist in school legislation in the United States Office of Education, provision for state boards of education was made before 1950 in the following States:

New York (1784); North Carolina and Vermont (1820-29); Connecticut, Kentucky, Massachusetts, Missouri, Tennessee (between 1830 and 1839); Arkansas and Michigan (1840-49); California, Indiana, Kansas, New Hampshire, Oregon, and Utah (1850-59); Alabama, Florida, Louisiana, Maryland, Mississippi, Nevada, New Jersey, New Mexico, Texas, Virginia (1860-69); Colorado, Delaware, South Carolina (1870-79); Arizona (1880-89); Idaho, Montana, Oklahoma, Wyoming (1890-99); Georgia, Washington, West Virginia (1900-9); Pennsylvania, Minnesota (1910-19); Maine (1949). This table accounted for forty states, Maine being the

---

[5] *State Boards of Education and Chief State School Officers.* Bulletin 1950, No. 12. Washington, D. C.: Government Printing Office, 1950, p. 8. Illinois, Iowa, Nebraska, North Dakota, Ohio, Rhode Island, South Dakota, and Wisconsin in 1950 had no state boards of education in the usual sense, but some of these states had boards that dealt primarily with higher education.

latest to join those "that have established general state boards of education." [6]

The decade of the 1940's was full of changes that had to do with the selection, the composition, the organization, and the duties and powers of state boards of education. At least sixteen states enacted legislation on these subjects: Arkansas and Oregon in 1941; Georgia and North Carolina in 1943; Missouri, with constitutional changes in 1944 and legislative changes in 1945; Indiana, Kansas, and New Jersey in 1945; Massachusetts, Vermont, Washington, and West Virginia in 1947; Colorado with constitutional changes in 1948 and legislative changes in 1949 which reconstituted its board, and in the latter year Texas also reconstituted its state board; Maine in 1949 for the first time created a board, and New Hampshire in 1950 removed the governor from its board.

Around 1940 governors were *ex officiis* members of boards of education in fifteen states, but apparently around mid-century there was a trend to remove them from such boards. In the decade of the 1940's they were removed from membership in Arkansas, Georgia, Indiana, Missouri, New Hampshire, and North Carolina. Keesecker reported two other "trends" in state educational organization. One of these was to remove the power to appoint the chief state school officer from the governor, and to give it to the state board of education (Maine and Massachusetts), and the other was to remove the power of appointment of state boards by the governor (Maine, Texas, and Washington), although action by so few states could hardly be called a "trend." The removal of *ex officiis* members from state boards of education, or deprivation of their privilege of voting, was also reported in several states, including Colorado, Indiana, Kansas, Missouri, North Carolina, Washington, and West Virginia. Delaware, however, added two *ex officiis* members to its board.

It was obvious at mid-century that no uniform pattern for the composition of state boards of education had yet developed. Variety in practice continued, despite recommendations of countless "surveys" and wide discussion of the subject. State boards of education in the United States at mid-century still had Topsy-like characteristics. Eighteen states in 1950 provided in their constitutions for state boards of education, and twenty-two made such provision by statute. Provision for larger board was made in the 1940's in Arkansas, Colorado, Indiana, Massachusetts, Missouri, New Jersey, North Carolina, Texas, Vermont, Washington, and West Virginia,

---

[6] For specific legal requirements by states for membership on state educational boards in 1950, see Keesecker, *op. cit.*, pp. 17-18.

but in 1950 the size of state boards ranged from three members in Mississippi to twenty-one members in Texas. A few states in the 1940's abolished their constitutionally created boards and established new ones; and Colorado and Texas adopted the system of the popular election of members from congressional districts. Notwithstanding variety in practice in their composition and organization, for many years legislation increased the responsibility of state boards of education "for policy making in educational affairs, and also toward enhancing its administrative facilities by enlarging the staff of the state departments of education." In some cases the staffs are numerous. One chief state school officer, who had several hundred persons in his organization, was asked how many persons worked in it. He is reported to have replied, "About half of 'em."

As noted above, some states provided by constitution and others by statute for their state boards of education. According to Keesecker,[7] the form of provision in forty states in 1950 was as shown in Table 2.

TABLE 2

PROVISION FOR STATE BOARDS OF EDUCATION

State	Constitutional Provision	Statutory Provision	State	Constitutional Provision	Statutory Provision
Alabama	—	X	Missouri	X	—
Arizona	X	—	Montana	X	—
Arkansas	—	X	Nevada	—	X
California	X	—	New Hampshire	—	X
Colorado	X	—	New Jersey	—	X
Connecticut	—	X	New Mexico	X	—
Delaware	—	—	New York	X	—
Florida	X	X	North Carolina	X	—
Georgia	—	X	Oklahoma	X	—
Idaho	X	—	Oregon	—	X
Indiana	—	X	Pennsylvania	—	X
Kansas	—	X	South Carolina	X	—
Kentucky	—	X	Tennessee	—	X
Louisiana	X	—	Texas	X	—
Maine	—	X	Utah	X	—
Maryland	—	X	Vermont	—	X
Massachusetts	—	X	Virginia	X	—
Michigan	X	—	Washington	—	X
Minnesota	—	X	West Virginia	—	X
Mississippi	X	—	Wyoming	—	X

[7] *Op. cit.*, p. 11.

As in some other phases of state educational organization and administration, localism was strong. There was long opposition to full-fledged "regular" chief state school officers, by whatever name they were called. Gideon Hawley, the first officer of the kind provided for in New York in 1812, was kicked out and his office abolished a decade later. Apparently Hawley had offended the sensitive politicians of the commonwealth. The secretary of state was designated *ex officio* superintendent of the common schools, and this continued to be the status of the office until 1854 when it was recreated as a separate office under the title of superintendent of public instruction. In 1904 the name was changed to commissioner of education and this had continued as late as 1950.

Chief state school officers *ex officiis* were common practices for a long time. Among the states that provided for such arrangements at one time or another were Alabama, state comptroller; Arizona, governor; Arkansas, secretary of state; Colorado, territorial treasurer; Connecticut, commissioner of the school fund, principal of the normal school; Delaware, state auditor; Florida, secretary of state, registrar of public lands; Idaho, territorial comptroller; Illinois, secretary of state; Indiana, state treasurer; Louisiana, secretary of state; Maryland, principal of the normal school; Minnesota, chancellor of the state university, secretary of state; Mississippi, secretary of state; Missouri, secretary of state; Nebraska, state librarian, territorial auditor; New York, secretary of state; Ohio, secretary of state; Oregon, governor; Pennsylvania, secretary of state; Rhode Island, secretary of state; Tennessee, secretary of state, state treasurer; Texas, state treasurer; Virginia, second auditor; Wyoming, territorial auditor, state librarian.[8] Today, however, every American state has a full-time chief state school officer.

The titles of chief state school officers vary, as do also their duties and salaries. In 1940 the titles ran to nine, and in 1950 to six, different designations. In twenty-seven states the title was superintendent of public instruction; in thirteen, it was commissioner of education; in four, superintendent of education; in two, superintendent of schools; in one, director of education (Rhode Island); and in one, superintendent of free schools (West Virginia). The title of superintendent of public instruction seemed to have been most commonly used at mid-twentieth century.

As may be noted above, the office of state superintendent of schools was appointive in the early days. The first of these, in New

8 Keesecker, *op. cit.,* p. 26.

York in 1812, was filled by the Council of Appointment which was composed of four senators who were to be chosen by the legislature. The provision in 1836 for a state superintendent of public instruction in Tennessee called for his appointment by the legislature. Massachusetts in 1837 made provision for the first real state board of education in this country, and the board was to name its secretary, whose duties were those of the chief state school officer of that state. Horace Mann was appointed to the post, which he filled with great distinction from 1837 to 1848. Henry Barnard was similarly appointed the first chief state school officer of Connecticut in 1838, and later of Rhode Island. Calvin Wiley became the first state superintendent of common schools of North Carolina in 1852 by legislative appointment, as did Caleb Mills in Indiana, Cyrus Pierce in Michigan, John Swett in California, and others. Appointment was the practice in the *ante bellum* period rather than popular election, which was later to become the most widely used method by which the chief state school office was to be filled. Thirty-one states by 1896 had come to choose this officer by a vote of the people, thirty-four states were doing so in 1920, thirty-two in 1940, and twenty-nine in 1950, when the tendency seemed to be away from that method of choice to appointment by the state board (thirteen states) or by the governor (six states). Missouri in 1944, and Colorado in 1948, made constitutional change to appointment by the state board of education; and the legislature of Massachusetts in 1947, and of Maine in 1949, changed the method from appointment by the governor to appointment by the state board. Texas in 1949, by statutory legislation, changed from popular election to appointment by the state board of education.

Educational qualifications of the chief state school officer are usually not specified in the states that elect him by popular vote. In some of these states, and in some of those that select by other methods, something, often a bit vague, is said about the matter: "recognized ability as school administrator," "such professional qualifications as shall be deemed appropriate," "high educational standing," "hold highest type of state teachers' certificate," "experienced educator," "educational attainment and breadth of experience in the administration of public education and of the finances pertaining thereto," "experienced educator," "shall be selected solely on ability and professional qualifications," and the like. But there have been cases in which the power of "politics," partisan and even ecclesiastical, has been the determining influence in the selection of chief state school officers.

The law of Texas, which in 1949 changed the method of choice from vote of the people to appointment by the state board of education, says:

The State Commissioner of Education shall be a person of broad and professional educational experience, with special and recognized abilities of the highest order in organization, direction, and coordination of education systems and programs, with particular abilities in administration and management of public schools and public education generally. The Commissioner of Education shall be a citizen of the United States and of the State of Texas for a period of not less than five (5) years immediately preceding his appointment; of good moral character; shall be eligible for the highest school administrator's certificate currently issued by the State Department of Education; and shall have a minimum of a Master's Degree from a recognized institution of higher learning. He shall subscribe to the oath of office required of other State officials.

Variety in practice appeared also in regard to chief state school officers, their official titles, qualifications, duties, and compensation. The first state to provide for this officer was New York in 1812, with the title of "Superintendent of Common Schools," at a salary of $300 a year. His chief duty was "to digest and prepare plans for the improvement and management of the common school fund," which had been formed in 1805,

. . . and for the better organization of common schools; to prepare and report estimates and expenditures of school monies, to superintend the collection thereof, to execute such services relative to the sale of lands, which now are or hereafter may be appropriated, as a permanent fund for the support of the common schools . . . ; to give information to the legislature respecting all matters referred to him by either branch thereof . . . ; and generally to perform all such services relative to the welfare of the schools as he shall be directed to perform, and shall, prior to his entering upon the duties of his office, take an oath or affirmation for the diligent and faithful execution of his trust. His office was to be kept "at the seat of government."

Tennessee in 1836 created a Board of Commissioners of Common Schools, to be composed of the treasurer of the state, the comptroller of the treasury, "and an executive officer, to be called the Superintendent of Public Instruction," who was to be appointed for a period of two years by joint vote of the two branches of the legislature, and to serve as chairman of the board. His salary was to be $1,500 a year, and he was to enter into bond in the sum of $100 thousand, "conditioned for the faithful discharge of the duties of his office; and shall take an oath to support the constitution of the United

States, the Constitution of the State, and an oath of office." He was required "to prepare and submit an annual report to the legislature, containing a full and comprehensive statement of the amount and condition, together with plans for the improvement and management of the common school fund, and such a plan for the organization of a system of common schools as he may think advisable, and such other matters relating to his office and to common schools as he shall deem expedient to communicate." Robert H. McEwen was appointed to the post, and was reappointed for a second term that began in February, 1838; but there was considerable discontent with his administration of the school funds, and hints that he had been guilty of fraud led to inquiry. A legislative committee was appointed to investigate the case, which resulted in a majority report that McEwen had defrauded the funds of the schools of about $120 thousand. When his term of office expired in February of 1840, legal action was instituted against him and his securities, but the litigation dragged out for a decade and wore some color of politics. Final settlement was made in the sum of about $10 thousand. Meantime the school funds were taken from the hands of the state superintenden' and placed in control of the state bank.

Following recommendation of Governor Edward Everett, in 1836, Massachusetts created a state board of education consisting

. . . of the governor and lieutenant governor, and eight persons appointed by the governor with the advice and consent of the council, each to hold office eight years from the time of his appointment, one retiring each year in the order of appointment; and the governor, with the advice and consent of the council, shall fill all vacancies in the board which may occur from death, resignation, or otherwise.

The board of education was authorized to

. . . appoint its own secretary, who, under its direction, shall make the abstract of school returns . . . ; collect information respecting the condition and efficiency of the public schools and other means of popular education; and diffuse as widely as possible throughout the commonwealth information of the best system of studies and method of instruction for the young, that the best education which public schools can be made to impart may be secured to all children who depend upon them for instruction.

The secretary was required to

. . . suggest to the board and to the legislature, improvements in the present system of public schools; visit, as often as his duties will permit, different parts of the commonwealth for the purpose of arousing and guiding public sentiment in relation to the practical interests of education; collect in his office such schoolbooks, apparatus, maps, and charts as can be obtained without expense to the commonwealth; receive and arrange in his office the reports and returns of the school committees; and receive, preserve, and distribute the state documents in relation to the public-school system.

In addition, the secretary was required, under the direction of the state board of education, to

. . . give sufficient notice of, and attend such meetings of teachers of public schools, members of the school committees of the various towns, and friends of education generally in any county, as may voluntarily assemble at the time and place designated by the board, and shall at such meetings devote himself to the object of collecting information of the condition of the public schools of such county, of the fulfillment of the duties of their office by members of the school committees of all the towns and cities, and of the circumstances of the several school districts in regard to teachers, pupils, books, apparatus, and methods of education, to enable him to furnish all information desired for the report of the board. . . .

For these and other services the secretary was to have an annual salary of $2,000 "and his necessary traveling expenses incurred in the performance of his official duties after they have been audited and approved by the board; and all postages and other necessary expenses arising in his office, shall be paid out of the treasury in the same manner as those of the different departments of the government." The incidental expenses of the board of education "and the expenses of the members thereof incurred in the discharge of their official duties, shall be paid out of the treasury, their accounts first being audited and allowed."

After some discussion there as in other states that provided for a chief state school officer before 1860, North Carolina in 1852 created the office to be filled by the legislature for a term of two years and at an annual salary of $2,000 to be paid out of the Literary Fund which had been set up in 1825. Strong recommendations for the creation of the office, by Governor William A. Graham, especially in 1848, led to this action. Calvin Wiley, a leading Whig, was appointed every two years from 1852 to 1866 by a Democratic legislature at a time when partisan or ecclesiastical politics had not yet come to be such a consideration as it was later to become in local, county, and state educational administration there and elsewhere throughout the country. It was very doubtful at mid-twentieth century whether a member of a minority political party could have been comfortably elevated to the chief state school office in any American state, whether by popular election or appointment by governor or state board. The theory that to the victors belong the spoils came to apply widely in educational administration.

Wiley's legal duties in North Carolina differed little from those of chief state school officers in other states before 1860. In North Carolina and in many other states, the schools were administered locally by county educational authorities who examined and certificated persons as teachers. The state superintendent was required

> . . . to collect accurate and full information of the condition and operations of the system of free or common schools in each county in the state; of the size of the school districts; to inform himself as well as possible of the causes, whether local or general, which have affected the success or impede the operations of the system in different sections; to consult with experienced teachers, when possible, and to collect statistics and information of matters materially affecting the cause of education in the state;

He made annual report to the governor and the legislature. Although his authority was largely hortatory and advisory, he was expected to superintend the work of the common schools "and to see that the laws in relation thereto are enforced; to call on the chairmen of the different boards of county superintendents who fail to make returns to him" according to law. He was to see, especially, that funds distributed to the counties from the Literary Fund were properly applied to the schools, and the state superintendent, under direction of the Literary Board, from which after 1868 developed a state board of education, was required to have an eye out for all funds that should properly come to the Literary Fund. In his annual report, the state superintendent of common schools was to deal with many matters and to make "such suggestions and recommendations as he may deem proper." It was illegal for him to "use his official position for the purpose of propagating sectarian or political party doctrines." He was subject to removal by the Literary Board.

The annual salaries of the chief state school officers in 1948 were reported as follows: [9]

State	Salary	State	Salary
Alabama	$5,700	Colorado	$4,000
Arizona	5,000	Connecticut	10,000
Arkansas	5,000	Delaware	10,000
California	12,000	Florida	9,000

[9] The Council of State Governments, *The Forty-eight State School Systems,* p. 186. Up-to-date facts on this subject, as on many other public education subjects, are most difficult to get. In the case of the salaries of chief state school officers, the figures may change from time to time by legislative action.

State	Salary	State	Salary
Georgia	7,500	New Mexico	$6,000
Idaho	4,000	New York	20,000
Illinois	9,000	North Carolina	6,600
Indiana	7,200	North Dakota	3,300
Iowa	6,000	Ohio	6,500
Kansas	5,000	Oklahoma	4,800
Kentucky	5,000	Oregon	6,600
Louisiana	7,500	Pennsylvania	12,000
Maine	7,000	Rhode Island	6,000
Maryland	15,000	South Carolina	7,500
Massachusetts	11,000	South Dakota	4,800
Michigan	7,500	Tennessee	6,600
Minnesota	8,000	Texas	6,000
Mississippi	7,500	Utah	6,000
Missouri	7,500	Vermont	6,000
Montana	4,200	Virginia	9,960
Nebraska	5,000	Washington	4,000
Nevada	4,800	West Virginia	6,000
New Hampshire	8,000	Wisconsin	6,500
New Jersey	15,000	Wyoming	4,800

Educational Administration in Counties.—The educational administration of the counties and rural areas of the United States, like that of the states and of urban communities, underwent some marked changes during the past four or five decades, but also like state and city organization and administration, rural school administration showed wide variety in practice at the middle of the century. About two decades earlier, N. W. Newsom had written: [10]

The educational literature dealing with school administration reveals much criticism of the office of county superintendent and its personnel in many states. It is said that the office is too much mixed with politics; that the personnel lacks academic training and experience, and is below the standards of district and city superintendents; that the powers, duties, and responsibilities of the county superintendent are not sufficiently definite; that the superintendent lacks clerical assistance and traveling expenses; that the salary attached to the office is insufficient to secure high-grade professional service; and that the position is uncertain, due to the political nature of the office.

It was reported that in 1950 some of these criticisms were "still valid in certain states. It is likewise true today that in some states the county superintendency has not attained the full stature which conditions warrant. Nevertheless the position has grown and is continuing to grow in importance in many states where grave shortcomings were prevalent twenty years ago." [11]

[10] *The Legal Status of the County Superintendent.* Bulletin 1932, No. 7. Washington, D. C.: Government Printing Office, 1932. P. 1.

[11] *The County Superintendent of Schools in the United States.* Yearbook, February, 1950, Department of Rural Education, National Education Association, p. 28.

The office of county superintendent, just like that of the state superintendent, developed through various stages, but it was not until after 1900 that closer attention than formerly was given to its strategic importance in public educational work. As was the case with the state superintendency, the duties of the office of county superintendent of schools were often performed by or entrusted to other officers—the county clerk, county judge, county land commissioner, or chairman of the board of county school visitors.

Beginning with Delaware in 1829, the county superintendency of schools had been rather rapidly established, and by 1879 only four of the thirty-eight states had not yet established the office; but of those thirty-four states, seven had already abolished it. Some states created the office, then abolished it, and then re-established it. Apparently, Connecticut, Massachusetts, and Rhode Island have "never had a school official representing the county as a whole." County and rural area superintendents "functioned" in 1950 in all the states except Delaware and Nevada; in these states all educational duties that were not performed by the local educational districts were performed by the state departments of education. The other forty-six states in 1950 reported nearly 3,400 county superintendents of schools. In the six New England States, two or more towns could form a supervisory education district under one superintendent, and a similar practice was followed in some towns in New York. In these seven states there were about 450 supervisory union or district superintendents of education. But the most common form of organization for county schools in 1950 was known as the "intermediate district superintendency." This has been defined as an area that comprises the territory of two or more basic administrative education units, with a board or a supervisory officer or both responsible for supervising the financial, administrative, or educational functions of the area. Three fifths of all county superintendents in the United States at that time were engaged in the "county intermediate district plan of organization." There were twenty-seven states which used this plan, and of these, only sixteen had a county board of education for each county.

In 1950 there were twelve states in which the county-unit plan was used. In these states there were no intermediate school districts, administrative functions below the state level being performed by the local district which was either a county or an independent unit, usually in a city. All education districts in Florida and West Virginia were county units, and the county superintendent of schools administered all the schools of the county, both urban and rural. The only educational system in Maryland that was not under the administration of a county superintendent was that of Baltimore. In Virginia the unit of educational administration was known as a division, and seventy-five of the divisions were counties. Ten divisions consisted of two counties each, one division was made up of three counties, two comprised a city and a county, and twenty-two were county districts. Utah in 1950 had twenty-four education districts, each of which comprised an entire county. In spite of education "surveys" and pronouncements of theorists in educational administration, at mid-century variety rather than uniformity was the practice in county or rural educational administration, as it was in state and to a less degree, perhaps, also in urban educational administration. But with increased financial aid by the state to the local school, the duties of the county superintendent had greatly enlarged. Their paper work had increased immensely, and in many cases adequate clerical assistance had not been provided.

Variety appeared in the educational requirements, the methods of selection, the duties, and the compensation of county superintendents of schools. As late as 1880 no state specifically required that these officers be graduates of colleges or normal schools, nor did any state specify any definite amount of education experience. Then, as now in many places, "politics" had much to do with the selection of the chief county school officer. As late as 1930 "only four states had enacted laws requiring normal school or college graduation of county superintendents, and fourteen prescribed teacher's certificates as the only educational requirement." [12] In 1950, twelve states required five or more years in college (Connecticut required six years), and in all the following states this officer was appointed: Connecticut, New Hampshire, Vermont, Indiana, Iowa, Michigan, Ohio, Pennsylvania, Louisiana, Maryland, Utah, and Virginia. Four years of college work were required by eighteen states: Maine, Massachusetts, New York, Arizona, Arkansas, California, Illinois, Michigan (in counties below 30 thousand population), New Jersey, Oklahoma, Oregon, Washington, Wisconsin, Alabama, Florida, Kentucky, North Carolina, and West Virginia. In nine of these states, county superintendents were appointed; in seven they were elected by popular vote (Arizona, California, Illinois, Oklahoma, Washington, Wis-

---

[12] *The County Superintendent of Schools in the United States.* Yearbook, February, 1950, Department of Rural Education, National Education Association, p. 42.

consin, and Florida) ; and in Oregon and Alabama they were elected or appointed.[13] The states that required less than four years of collegiate work were Colorado, Idaho, Kansas, Minnesota (no requirements stated), Mississippi, Missouri, Montana, Nebraska, North Dakota, South Carolina (no requirements stated), South Dakota, Texas, Wyoming, Georgia, New Mexico (no requirements stated), and Tennessee. In all these states except Tennessee, the county superintendent of schools was elected by popular vote. In more than a third of the counties in that state, provision was made for appointment by the county court. In a few counties in South Carolina and Texas, county superintendents of schools were appointed.

Variation was also marked in the length of the term of county superintendents of schools, from one year to an indefinite period, but in 1950, twenty-four states prescribed four years as the term. There was also a wide difference in salaries. In 1930 the median annual salary of county superintendents was reported at $2,312. In 1950 it was reported at $4,010. Five states had county superintendents who were paid $900 or less a year, and twelve states had a total of 191 superintendents who received less than $2,000 a year. At the other extreme there were a few county superintendents who received $10,000 a year or more. Twenty-four states reported 252 county superintendents who in 1950 received salaries of $6,000 or more. The states in which they were paid the largest annual median salaries in 1950 were Maryland, New Jersey, California, Pennsylvania, Connecticut, North Carolina, New Hampshire, Virginia, Louisiana, New York, Illinois, and Utah. In all these states except Illinois, the county superintendents were appointed. The states in which the lowest salaries were paid were Minnesota, Arizona, North Dakota, Wyoming, South Dakota, Idaho, Montana, Washington, Oklahoma, Nebraska, Kansas, and Colorado. In all these states the county superintendents were elected.

Interest in education in rural places had long attracted the attention of the educators of this country. In 1951 about half the nation's public school children were attending rural schools, and a little more than half the teachers of the United States were in rural communities. A nation-wide survey conducted by the *New York Times* [14] indicated that the rural schools were giving "many children an inferior education." Visits to representative rural schools by Dr. Benjamin Fine, education editor of that paper, disclosed "almost shocking conditions. Nearly 3.5 million children are being deprived of an adequate education this spring because of inadequate buildings, poorly trained teachers, double sessions, and part-time instruction. More than one out of four children in rural schools is getting a Grade B education." Because of the better salaries generally paid in urban communities, teachers were leaving rural schools whenever they could. Moreover, some of the rural teachers complained that they did not have the same protection of tenure that most teachers in cities had. "The local school boards frequently insisted on retaining the right to determine whether a teacher is to be rehired. As a result, the rural teacher is never certain whether she is to be re-employed for the coming year, even though she is doing satisfactory work." The survey also showed that working conditions were less satisfactory in rural than in urban places. What was reported as one bright spot, however, was the increase in the number of school districts that were being consolidated, and the passing of the "one- and two-room little red schoolhouses. . . ." Incomplete figures showed that in 1950 more than 104 thousand buses were being used daily to transport more than 6 million children to nearly 44 thousand schools, at an annual cost of more than $180 million. The miles of routes traveled one way were more than 2.28 million.

In 1925 there had been about 200 thousand one-teacher schools in the United States. In 1950, according to The Council of State Governments,[15] there were 75 thousand one-teacher schools, with Illinois leading the list with 6,778. Iowa followed with 5,637; Missouri with 5,272; Wisconsin with 4,475; Minnesota with 4,421; Kentucky with 3,462; Kansas with 3,090; Michigan with 2,942. The smallest numbers of one-teacher schools were in Rhode Island with 26, Utah 28, Delaware 48, Nevada 93, Connecticut 115, Massachusetts 128, New Hampshire 133, New Jersey 136, Maryland 165, Washington 167. At mid-century the gravest needs in rural education were for well-trained teachers and better school buildings. It was estimated that at least $5 billion would be required for the construction of buildings before adequate facilities could be provided.

National interest in rural education reached back many years. The Smith-Lever Act of 1914 was a result of the report of the Country Life Commission which President Theodore Roosevelt had appointed in 1908 to examine into the needs of the people in rural areas and to recommend remedies for the conditions that needed improvement. That study stimulated increased interest in rural life. The Department of Rural and Agricultural Education of the National Education Association had been formed in 1907, reor-

[15] *The Forty-eight State School Systems* (Chicago: 1949, p. 194).

ganized as the Department of Rural Education in 1919, and since 1936 had been the Division of Rural Service of that Association. The Country Life Commission, the Department of Rural Education of the NEA, and numerous other agencies and activities stimulated interest in improving conditions of rural education. At mid-century there was some evidence to indicate that education in rural areas would receive more attention than formerly from educational leaders.

The Provision of Funds for Education.—How to pay for public education was a question that increasingly pressed for solution between 1930 and 1950, and it was very evident that the great increases in elementary and secondary schools in the fall of 1950 did not make the question less persistent. With the prediction that increases in enrollments for several years following 1950 would be about one million a year, the question was how to find the money to pay the bill. The size of the financial problems for public education in 1950 was huge. At that time some states were spending for public school support a percentage of their total income twice as great as were other states. The percentage of total personal income that went into public education in the states in 1937-38, in 1947-48, and in 1949-50 appears in Table 3.[16]

Public Education as "Big Business."—By mid-twentieth century, public elementary and secondary education had become "big business" which required huge funds. Receipts for public elementary and secondary schools were about $4.85 billion, including funds raised by the sale of bonds. The value of school property in 1948, the latest year for which data on the subject were available, was reported at $9.2 billion, about $385 per pupil enrolled, and a billion more than was reported in 1946. In addition to physical plants, the school systems of the country owned permanent funds and income-producing lands valued at $700 million, income from which was used for school purposes. The indebtedness of the schools, which had been $3.1 billion in 1932, was $2 billion in 1946, about $2.6 billion in 1948, and much larger in 1950 when the need for new buildings and for repairs on old ones was heavier than ever before in the history of the country. Payments in interest on indebtedness were about $76 million in 1948, and school bonds outstanding in that year were about $2.4 billion. Expenditures for the construction of school buildings in 1900 had been $35 million. In 1910 they were

16 *Public School Finance Programs of the Forty-eight States.* Washington, D. C.: U. S. Office of Education, Circular No. 274, 1950. P. 87.

TABLE 3.

PERCENTAGE OF TOTAL PERSONAL INCOME EXPENDED FOR PUBLIC EDUCATION

State	1937-38		1947-48		1949-50	
	Per Cent	Rank	Per Cent	Rank	Per Cent	Rank
Alabama	2.71	39	2.90	17	2.77	16
Arizona	5.48	2	3.91	2	3.87	3
Arkansas	2.81	33	2.39	32	2.48	25
California	3.69	16	2.58	28	2.28	32
Colorado	3.76	12	3.05	11	2.74	18
Connecticut	2.24	47	1.91	46	1.79	48
Delaware	2.25	46	1.93	45	2.20	37
Florida	3.18	26	2.95	16	3.36	10
Georgia	2.71	38	2.25	37	2.41	26
Idaho	4.54	6	3.05	11	2.75	17
Illinois	3.47	18	1.98	44	2.04	44
Indiana	3.75	13	2.84	19	2.62	20
Iowa	4.25	8	2.62	26	2.58	23
Kansas	3.76	11	3.14	8	3.00	8
Kentucky	2.80	34	2.45	31	2.33	30
Louisiana	3.40	20	2.77	21	3.46	7
Maine	2.49	43	2.07	42	2.34	29
Maryland	2.33	44	1.99	43	2.14	38
Massachusetts	2.59	42	2.77	48	2.06	42
Michigan	3.32	22	2.64	23	2.61	21
Minnesota	3.54	17	2.67	22	2.60	22
Mississippi	2.74	37	2.63	25	2.24	33
Missouri	2.75	36	2.20	38	1.95	46
Montana	4.28	7	3.42	5	2.65	19
Nebraska	3.20	25	2.29	35	2.05	43
Nevada	2.59	41	2.49	29	2.37	27
New Hampshire	2.65	40	2.25	36	2.21	35
New Jersey	3.45	19	2.30	34	2.31	31
New Mexico	4.16	9	4.04	1	4.11	1
New York	3.22	24	2.09	40	1.95	45
North Carolina	3.71	14	3.03	13	3.50	5
North Dakota	5.27	3	2.83	20	2.80	15
Ohio	3.09	28	2.36	33	2.12	40
Oklahoma	5.03	4	2.96	15	3.04	11
Oregon	3.24	23	2.89	18	3.50	5
Pennsylvania	2.84	31	2.16	39	2.12	40
Rhode Island	2.19	48	1.87	47	1.80	47
South Carolina	3.10	27	3.10	9	2.90	13
South Dakota	5.99	1	2.96	14	2.21	36
Tennessee	2.82	32	2.64	24	2.57	24
Texas	3.70	15	3.18	7	3.50	5
Utah	4.87	5	3.82	3	3.98	2
Vermont	2.80	35	2.48	30	2.36	28
Virginia	2.32	45	2.08	41	2.24	34
Washington	3.05	29	3.24	6	2.85	14
West Virginia	3.38	21	3.43	4	2.90	12
Wisconsin	3.04	30	2.59	27	2.12	40
Wyoming	3.86	10	3.05	11	3.38	9
Averages	3.24	—	2.45	—	2.39	—

$70 million; in 1920, about $154 million; in 1930, about $371 million; in 1940, about $258 million; and in 1950 about half a billion dollars. At mid-century it was reported that, at current costs of construction, at least ten billion dollars would be needed for school buildings by 1960 in order to provide for the rapidly increasing school population, who would also call for more teachers as well as for more buildings and equipment. Competition for the school dollar, by salaries for teachers and by the demands for enlarged physical facilities, became keener than ever before as the second half of the twentieth century opened.

By 1948 all the states had made some provision for pensions or retirement for their professional educational staffs, and in many cases for all educational employees, and many states and cities had also made some kind of provision for all their employees, both educational and noneducational. In 1950, retirement funds for the staffs of public elementary and secondary schools were reported at more than $1.7 billion.

It may be seen in the preceding pages that variety still marked practices in state organization and administration of public education in the United States in 1950, a condition which generally had historical explanation. The same may be said of public education support in which variations were as glaring as those in organization and administration in the forty-eight states at mid-twentieth century. Just as state legislatures could establish any form of educational organization and administration they chose, so also they could make for public education support any arrangements they cared to make. The educational "principles" in both cases may have appeared to be "American," but in the development of their practical application, localism or regionalism had generally operated.

The decline of the importance of permanent public school endowments in the support of education has been marked in the United States during the present century, although these means of educational support had been considered rather important in the nineteenth century. So-called "literary funds" had been created rather widely in the various states, beginning in Connecticut and Delaware before 1800, in New York in 1805, Tennessee in 1806, Virginia in 1810, Maryland in 1812, New Jersey in 1816, Georgia in 1817, Maine, New Hampshire, Kentucky, and Louisiana by 1821, and in Vermont, North Carolina, Pennsylvania, and Massachusetts by 1834. South Carolina seems to have been the only state that had not established a permanent public school endowment before 1860. The oldest purpose or incentive for such funds seems to have been to provide free schools with as little tendency as possible to resort to the pain of direct taxation, but the results of these endowments were not always wholesome. Now and then they were exploited or mismanaged, and their promises were often unfulfilled. The importance of permanent endowments as a means of public school support declined, and by 1900 less than 6 per cent of the total revenue for such support was derived from that source. By 1920 less than 3 per cent came from such endowments.[17]

After 1900, and particularly after the First World War, taxation and legislative appropriations for educational purposes gained in importance, and taxes for schools gradually increased. The evils that had resulted from dependence for school support upon such uncertain sources as permanent endowments served to increase legislative concern for the support of the schools, and state legislatures gradually came to follow more definite fiscal policies. For example, California in 1919 increased the grant of the state from $15 to $17.50 per year for each pupil in average daily attendance in its elementary schools, and by constitutional amendment the next year, and by legislative enactment on the subject, that figure was raised to $30 per pupil. At the same time, California increased its appropriation from $15 to $30 for each pupil in high school. Massachusetts, which led "the Union in the antiquity of her practice of supporting schools overwhelmingly by local taxation," made some extraordinary changes in school support. In 1915 that state derived from local taxation about 97 per cent of its total revenues for schools. Soon it frankly recognized the necessity of changing this policy, and it provided the use of a part of the proceeds of its income tax as an annual current fund to be known as the general school fund. A result was that whereas that state in 1915 had provided only 1.82 per cent, five years later it furnished more than 12 per cent for educational purposes.

Meantime old types of taxation for schools began to give way to new types generally throughout the country. The old types included general property taxes and poll taxes for educational purposes. During the first quarter of the twentieth century, the poll tax for school support was abandoned in many states, although these taxes continued to be used for that purpose in counties and towns. Meantime,

---

[17] See Fletcher H. Swift, *History of Permanent Common School Funds in the United States* (New York, Henry Holt & Co., 1910). Also by the same author, "Public School Finance," in I. L. Kandel (ed.), *Twenty-Five Years of American Education* (New York, The Macmillan Co., 1924), pp. 199-224.

also, a rather strong tendency developed to depend less than formerly upon general property taxes for educational purposes, although in 1925 these still remained rather widely used. At that time twenty states levied a tax on real and personal property for public school support. The change in the national life in the United States from almost exclusively agricultural occupations to a large measure of manufacturing and commercial activities brought about a change in this condition.

Whereas wealth was formerly represented almost entirely by real and personal property, during the first quarter of the twentieth century wealth and property more and more tended to become corporate, and this change led to a form of income tax for educational and other purposes. By 1925 more than thirty states levied taxes on stocks in corporations, some levied them on savings banks, and a large number on inheritances. Louisiana in 1920 provided for a severance tax on natural products taken from the soil, except on agricultural products. A few states levied taxes on ores for support of education, as well as upon timber, sand, gravel, gas, oil, and other natural products.

During the first few decades of the twentieth century, the importance of local educational support increased. About 68 per cent of the total receipts for public support for education came from local sources around 1900. In 1920 the figure was more than 83 per cent, according to Swift, apparently the largest increase in local support for education being in the South Central and the South Atlantic States. In spite of a certain tendency toward centralization and of some court decisions, and also in spite of the pronouncements of educational theorists that the public schools were state institutions rather than local ones, nevertheless in actual practice the public schools in this country seemed to become more and more local institutions during the first quarter of the present century. A result of this condition was the report from all parts of the United States that funds for public school support were inadequate. Most of the states in 1925 seemed to be trying to support their schools under a local system.

In time, however, in an effort to equalize educational revenues, educational burdens, and educational opportunities, the states became more and more conscious of the need for trying to find adequate educational revenue from units stronger than local school districts. It was out of this change that interest in larger educational units, such as the state and the nation, began to develop. The county also came to loom larger than formerly in importance in matters of organization, administration, and support of education. The county system as a means of better educational arrangements came to attract wide attention throughout the country. Meantime, also, the subject of federal education aid attracted more and more attention. The Smith-Lever Act of 1914 provided federal aid in extension work in agriculture and home economics, to be followed three years later by the Smith-Hughes Act which marked the entry of the federal government in aiding vocational education and the training of teachers and supervisors for that work. In 1918 the Smith-Sears Act provided for the vocational rehabilitation of disabled soldiers and sailors, and the Smith-Bankhead Act of 1920 provided for the vocational rehabilitation of civilians who had been disabled in industry or otherwise. From these modest beginnings, made without much experience to go on, the federal government by 1950 had widely extended its aid for educational services in the states, territories, the District of Columbia, and to institutions. The cost of these services amounted to nearly $3 billion by the middle of the century, but at that time general federal aid for education had not been achieved.

Federal appropriations for various services to education for the year ending June 30, 1948, which did not change very much during the next few years, were reported as follows:

For the support of land-grant colleges	$ 5,030,000
Agricultural experiment stations	8,030,807
Cooperative agricultural extension service	27,455,370
Vocational education below college level	25,035,122
Vocational rehabilitation	18,000,000
School lunches	54,000,000
Schools in war-congested areas	6,646,340
Education and training of veterans	2,122,292,440
Value of surplus property for schools—Army and Navy donable property	201,406,636
Value of surplus property for schools—real property	284,473,734
Construction cost of property to schools enrolling veterans	79,446,379
Equipment value of property to schools enrolling veterans	87,013,725
Funds for Federal government services to education, including U. S. Office of Education, Office of Vocational Rehabilitation, Bureau of Indian Affairs, U. S. Military and Naval Academies, Howard University, Public Schools of Panama and the District of Columbia	34,034,986
Total	$2,953,785,539

A federal program of considerable magnitude and significance was that of lunches for children in elementary and secondary schools, for the support of which federal funds increased from $12.6 million in 1940 to $92.2 million nine years later. This program was begun in a small way during the depression in the 1930's, in part to justify the use of surplus agricultural products and to give work to persons who were unemployed. Its promotion was stimulated by persons interested in agriculture, in education, and in the physical and mental health of American children. There were criticisms, however, that the program was encouraged in part to support prices of agricultural commodities, and that it was not primarily educational in principle or practice. Under the program, assistance to nonpublic schools was regarded with some apprehension by the critics. And there was also criticism that local education officials were required to deal with numerous federal agencies in the administration of the program. This requirement greatly added to their administrative chores and "paper work." But the enterprise was vigorously defended by the Task Force of Herbert Hoover's Commission on Public Welfare which published its study in 1950.[18]

Most of the total budgetary identifiable and available sums of money being obligated for education by the federal government at mid-century were for items connected with war or defense, such as educational facilities for veterans, schools in defense areas, preservice or in-service education for those in the armed forces, military research through universities, or for raising the educational level of the armed forces. If such items as training in military service schools, the various educational activities of the Atomic Energy Commission, and the surplus war property given or sold at heavy discount to educational institutions should be included, the sums would be much larger. As many as nine departments or independent agencies of the government, working through numerous subagencies, were making large grants or entering into contracts with colleges and universities for research.[19] Between 1947 and 1949 federal funds for research in higher institutions practically doubled. The sum in 1949 was more than $160 million; and in his message on the budget to the Congress in the early part of 1950, President Truman emphasized the role of education and research in American democracy.

[18] Hollis P. Allen, *The Federal Government and Education* (New York: McGraw-Hill Book Co., 1950). This is the complete study by that important commission on public welfare in the United States and is very useful for students and teachers of educational history, particularly on the subject of federal relations to education.

[19] For the extent of these appropriations see Allen, *op. cit.,* p. 143.

As already noted, general federal educational aid had not been provided by 1951. Prior to the 1920's, when the subject came to be widely discussed and vigorously advocated and opposed, such aid had been a matter of much concern, especially in the years from 1870 to 1890, when the Hoar Bill and the Blair Bills were before the Congress. In 1870, George F. Hoar had introduced into the House of Representatives a bill to establish a national system of education which, although it was voted down, was nevertheless the beginning of an intense struggle which was to be waged for many years over the relations of the national government to education in the states. This bill was a significant attempt to impose by law a nationally controlled system of education. Between the failure of the Hoar Bill and the revival of interest in federal aid to education after the First World War, there had been wide interest in the Blair Bills of the 1880's. Eleven bills for federal aid were introduced into the Congress between 1872 and 1880, but only four came to the floor and only two received consideration, one by the House and one by the Senate. Each of these passed in the chamber in which it had originated, but failed in the other chamber.[20] From 1884 to 1890 the Blair Bills were before the Congress, and discussions of these legislative efforts resembled the debates and discussions that went on in the 1940's. Fear of mixed schools in the South, fear of complete federal domination of education, and the complexity of the religious implications in public education were sharply revealed in the earlier debates as in the later ones.

Proposals for federal aid were numerous in the 1940's and widely discussed. In the middle of March of 1950, however, the Committee on Education and Labor of the House of Representatives rejected, by a vote of thirteen to twelve, after it had been discussed behind closed doors for more than a month, a bill for federal aid to education in the sum of $300 million annually which had already been approved by the Senate. The proposal was finally caught up in a national religious controversy which had become very heated the previous summer. The issue of Church and State was sharper than ever before, with the exchange of opinions between Francis Cardinal Spellman and Mrs. Eleanor Roosevelt in the summer of 1949 assuming proportions that made it an important educational event of the decade. Some court decisions did not make the issue less sharp.

[20] See Gordon C. Lee, *The Struggle for Federal Aid. First Phase: A History of the Attempts to Attain Federal Aid for the Common Schools 1870-1890* (New York: Bureau of Publications, Teachers College, Columbia University, 1949).

The House Committee turned down amendments to prohibit the use of federal funds for parochial and private schools, and also amendments to require such use. The decisive test found advocates of both extremes voting against the bill, along with strong opponents of federal aid to education and those who believed that the issue had become "too hot to handle" in an election year.[21]

In March of 1951 the campaign for federal aid was renewed as a means of "furthering the mobilization effort." In Washington, Senator Lister Hill of Alabama, long a vigorous advocate of such aid, warned the United States Senate that efforts at defense were being impeded by the poor schools in the United States. He said that inadequate schooling since 1948 had cost the armed forces the equivalent of fourteen divisions because of rejections, and that the loss of these men could well mean the difference between military victory and defeat; and he said that conditions in education in the United States would not greatly improve without federal aid. At about the same time, Earl J. McGrath, United States Commissioner of Education, was saying in an address in New York that the conditions of the schools had reached the danger zone, and that federal aid could not safely be "put on the shelf" during the national emergency. Education was one of the first lines of defense and the stake of the nation in it was greater than ever before because of the nature of the conflict with communism. He said that inequities in education in this country were glaring and tragic.

The percentages of receipts for the support of public elementary and secondary schools in the United States for 1939-40 and for 1949-50, from federal, state, county, and local sources, are given in Table 4; [22] the percentages of estimated state, county, and local revenues for public elementary and secondary schools, from taxation on property and from other sources in 1949-50, appear in Table 5.[23] Educational facilities for which public funds were provided in 1949-50 appear in Table 6,[24] and additional educational services for which public funds were provided in 1949-50 are shown in Table 7.[25]

---

[21] In December of 1948, the Chamber of Commerce of the United States published *Which Way Education?* in which the arguments for and those against federal aid to education were given. See Edgar W. Knight and Clifton L. Hall, *Readings in American Educational History* (New York: Appleton-Century-Crofts, Inc., 1951), pp. 386-99.

[22] *Public School Finance Programs of the Forty-eight States.* Washington, D. C.: U. S. Office of Education, Circular No. 274, 1950, p. 71.

[23] *Ibid.*, p. 72.

[24] *Ibid.*, p. 79.

[25] *Ibid.*, p. 81.

TABLE 4

RECEIPTS FOR SUPPORT OF PUBLIC ELEMENTARY AND SECONDARY SCHOOLS

State	Federal		State		County		Local	
	1939-40	1949-50	1939-40	1949-50	1939-40	1949-50	1939-40	1949-50
Alabama	4.0	1.5	54.2	75.8	23.4	19.7	18.4	3.0
Arizona	4.7	1.5	20.8	36.0	33.8	7.3	40.7	55.2
Arkansas	3.2	5.1	44.2	62.7	3.5	1.3	49.1	30.9
California	3.6	1.5	46.3	53.3	1.9	0.7	48.2	44.5
Colorado	0.7	1.3	9.1	21.9	19.7	11.6	70.5	65.2
Connecticut	0.5	1.4	9.1	22.8	0.0	0.0	90.4	75.8
Delaware	7.0	2.3	85.9	89.2	0.0	0.0	7.1	8.5
Florida	1.0	1.2	51.2	53.4	16.8	21.9	31.0	23.5
Georgia	1.6	5.4	56.8	67.7	16.4	16.6	25.2	10.3
Idaho	1.1	2.1	15.9	25.7	22.8	19.2	60.2	53.0
Illinois	0.9	1.1	10.0	18.9	0.1	0.0	89.0	80.0
Indiana	0.7	1.4	33.9	39.4	0.6	0.0	64.8	59.2
Iowa	0.9	1.6	1.4	17.6	2.5	0.8	95.2	80.0
Kansas	1.1	1.4	12.4	18.5	13.5	20.2	73.0	59.9
Kentucky	2.1	4.5	40.4	38.5	26.4	0.0	31.1	57.0
Louisiana	1.6	5.9	52.7	67.4	29.0	24.1	16.7	2.6
Maine	1.2	2.3	15.8	27.6	0.0	0.0	83.0	70.1
Maryland	1.1	1.3	21.6	40.0	31.0	31.3	46.3	27.4
Massachusetts	0.6	1.1	10.3	18.2	0.0	0.0	89.1	80.7
Michigan	2.1	1.2	42.1	57.6	0.4	0.2	55.4	41.0
Minnesota	1.1	1.9	36.0	46.6	1.4	5.2	61.5	46.3
Mississippi	2.9	6.3	37.4	51.7	19.2	12.2	40.5	29.8
Missouri	1.1	0.7	32.1	38.8	1.2	6.8	65.6	53.7
Montana	1.3	4.2	13.9	28.9	17.5	35.2	67.3	31.7
Nebraska	1.3	2.1	6.6	5.9	0.9	1.2	91.2	90.8
Nevada	3.9	6.4	22.0	36.9	48.8	31.5	25.3	25.2
New Hampshire	6.1	2.4	5.2	6.5	0.0	0.0	88.7	91.1
New Jersey	2.7	0.9	6.0	19.1	14.4	0.9	76.9	79.1
New Mexico	1.1	1.9	78.8	84.7	8.6	10.1	11.5	3.3
New York	0.4	1.0	33.1	46.7	0.0	1.2	66.5	51.1
North Carolina	2.8	3.1	65.7	78.1	23.3	12.9	8.2	5.9
North Dakota	1.2	1.4	19.9	26.9	7.7	20.5	71.2	51.2
Ohio	4.9	1.2	35.5	36.4	1.4	0.2	58.2	62.2
Oklahoma	1.7	2.7	39.2	42.9	7.1	17.8	52.0	36.6
Oregon	0.8	1.3	1.9	28.6	23.9	0.5	73.4	69.6
Pennsylvania	0.7	1.0	21.0	37.6	0.0	0.0	78.3	61.4
Rhode Island	1.0	1.9	10.5	18.7	0.0	0.0	88.5	79.4
South Carolina	2.0	4.4	48.6	64.0	5.2	5.6	44.2	26.0
South Dakota	1.7	1.9	16.0	13.0	3.3	11.0	79.0	74.1
Tennessee	1.8	3.5	34.0	63.3	48.5	25.1	15.7	8.1
Texas	1.0	2.2	42.2	49.9	0.8	0.2	56.0	47.7
Utah	7.1	1.9	39.1	53.1	32.6	13.2	21.2	31.8
Vermont	7.6	1.6	15.6	31.7	0.0	0.0	76.8	66.7
Virginia	4.5	2.6	32.4	40.7	37.1	30.7	26.0	26.0
Washington	1.0	2.9	62.5	68.5	5.2	0.0	31.3	28.6
West Virginia	1.1	4.1	51.2	62.4	47.7	33.5	0.0	0.0
Wisconsin	3.5	1.5	21.5	22.6	8.8	3.1	66.2	72.8
Wyoming	8.5	1.8	18.8	44.6	20.2	9.6	52.5	44.0
Averages	1.7	1.9	30.3	42.7	6.7	5.6	61.3	49.8

TABLE 5

PERCENTAGES OF ESTIMATED SCHOOL REVENUES FROM VARIOUS SOURCES

State	Percentages from Property Taxes				Percentages from Other Sources			
	State	County	Local	Total	State	County	Local	Total
Alabama	5.1	20.0	0.0	25.1	71.8	0.0	3.1	74.9
Arizona	0.0	7.4	56.0	63.4	36.6	0.0	0.0	36.6
Arkansas	0.0	0.0	32.5	32.5	66.1	1.4	0.0	67.5
California	0.0	0.8	43.6	44.4	54.1	0.0	1.5	55.6
Colorado	0.0	11.7	66.1	77.8	22.2	0.0	0.0	22.2
Connecticut	0.0	0.0	74.4	74.4	23.1	0.0	2.5	25.6
Delaware	0.0	0.0	8.7	8.7	91.3	0.0	0.0	91.3
Florida	0.0	19.2	23.7	42.9	54.1	2.9	0.1	57.1
Georgia	0.0	17.5	10.9	28.4	71.6	0.0	0.0	71.6
Idaho	0.0	17.0	48.2	65.2	26.3	2.6	5.9	34.8
Illinois	0.0	0.0	80.9	80.9	19.1	0.0	0.0	19.1
Indiana	0.0	0.0	58.9	58.9	39.9	0.1	1.1	41.1
Iowa	0.0	0.8	80.0	80.8	17.9	0.0	1.3	19.2
Kansas	0.0	20.5	60.8	81.3	18.7	0.0	0.0	18.7
Kentucky	0.0	0.0	58.5	58.5	40.3	0.0	1.2	41.5
Louisiana	8.0	15.6	2.8	26.4	63.6	10.0	0.0	73.6
Maine	0.0	0.0	65.6	65.6	28.3	0.0	6.1	34.4
Maryland	0.0	31.4	27.5	58.9	40.5	0.3	0.3	41.1
Massachusetts	0.0	0.0	79.9	79.9	18.4	0.0	1.7	20.1
Michigan	0.0	0.0	38.6	38.6	58.3	0.2	2.9	61.4
Minnesota	0.0	4.8	43.4	48.1	47.5	0.5	3.9	51.9
Mississippi	0.0	11.6	31.3	42.9	55.2	1.4	0.5	57.1
Missouri	0.0	0.0	48.6	48.6	38.9	4.9	7.6	51.4
Montana	0.0	36.8	32.2	69.0	30.2	0.0	0.8	31.0
Nebraska	0.0	1.2	92.3	93.5	6.0	0.0	0.5	6.5
Nevada	0.0	33.6	23.5	57.1	39.4	0.0	3.5	42.9
New Hampshire	0.0	0.0	92.6	92.6	6.6	0.0	0.8	7.4
New Jersey	0.0	0.0	78.7	78.7	19.3	0.9	1.1	21.3
New Mexico	1.0	10.0	3.4	14.4	85.3	0.3	0.0	85.6
New York	0.0	0.0	48.7	48.7	47.1	1.2	3.0	51.3
North Carolina	0.0	8.9	4.7	13.6	80.6	4.4	1.4	86.4
North Dakota	0.0	19.8	43.2	63.0	27.3	1.0	8.7	37.0
Ohio	0.0	0.0	61.5	61.5	36.8	0.2	1.5	38.5
Oklahoma	0.0	3.9	28.7	32.6	44.0	14.4	9.0	67.4
Oregon	0.0	0.4	70.6	71.0	29.0	0.0	0.0	29.0
Pennsylvania	0.0	0.0	56.4	56.4	38.0	0.0	5.6	43.6
Rhode Island	0.0	0.0	80.0	80.0	19.0	0.0	1.0	20.0
South Carolina	0.0	4.6	24.0	28.6	67.0	1.2	3.2	71.4
South Dakota	0.0	10.2	70.5	80.7	13.2	1.1	5.0	19.3
Tennessee	1.7	20.6	5.9	28.2	63.9	5.4	2.5	71.8
Texas	5.0	0.0	46.8	51.8	46.0	0.2	2.0	48.2
Utah	19.2	11.5	29.6	60.3	34.9	2.0	2.8	39.7
Vermont	0.0	0.0	66.7	66.7	32.3	0.0	1.0	33.3
Virginia	0.0	31.5	21.7	53.2	41.8	0.0	5.0	46.8
Washington	0.0	0.0	29.5	29.5	70.5	0.0	0.0	70.5
West Virginia	0.0	35.0	0.0	35.0	65.0	0.0	0.0	65.0
Wisconsin	0.0	3.2	72.6	75.8	22.9	0.0	1.3	24.2
Wyoming	13.5	8.9	41.6	64.0	31.9	0.9	3.2	36.0
Medians	0.0	3.6	45.2	58.7	39.2	0.0	1.3	41.3

TABLE 6

EDUCATIONAL FACILITIES SUPPORTED BY PUBLIC FUNDS

State	Nursery Schools	Kindergarten	Grades 1-12	Grades 13-14	Adult or Evening Schools	Summer Schools	Recreation Program
Alabama	—	—	X	—	X	—	—
Arizona	—	—	X	—	—	—	—
Arkansas	—	—	X	—	—	—	—
California	—	X	X	X	X	—	—
Colorado	—	—	X	X	—	—	—
Connecticut	X	X	X	—	X	—	—
Delaware	—	—	X	—	—	—	—
Florida	—	X	X	X	X	X	X
Georgia	—	—	X	—	—	—	—
Idaho	—	—	X	—	—	—	—
Illinois	—	X	X	—	—	—	—
Indiana	—	—	X	—	—	—	—
Iowa	—	—	X	X	—	—	—
Kansas	—	—	X *	—	—	—	—
Kentucky	—	—	X	—	—	—	—
Louisiana	—	X	X	—	—	—	—
Maine	—	X	X	—	X	—	—
Maryland	—	—	X	X	X	—	—
Massachusetts	—	—	X	—	—	—	—
Michigan	—	X	X	X	X	—	X
Minnesota	—	X	X	—	—	—	—
Mississippi	—	—	X	—	—	—	—
Missouri	—	—	X	X	X	—	—
Montana	—	—	X	—	—	—	—
Nebraska	—	X	X	—	—	—	—
Nevada	—	—	X	—	—	—	—
New Hampshire	—	X	X	—	—	—	—
New Jersey	—	X	X	—	X	—	—
New Mexico	—	—	X	—	—	—	—
New York	—	X	X	—	X	X	—
North Carolina	—	—	X	—	—	—	—
North Dakota	—	—	X	—	—	—	—
Ohio	—	X	X	—	X	—	—
Oklahoma	—	—	X	X	—	—	—
Oregon	—	X	X	—	X	X	—
Pennsylvania	—	X	X	—	X	—	X
Rhode Island	—	X	X	—	—	—	—
South Carolina	—	—	X	—	X	—	—
South Dakota	—	—	X	—	—	—	—
Tennessee	—	—	X	—	—	—	—
Texas	—	—	X	—	—	—	—
Utah	—	X	X	X	X	—	—
Vermont	—	—	X	—	—	X †	—
Virginia	—	—	X	—	X	—	—
Washington	X	X	X	X	X	—	X
West Virginia	—	—	X	—	—	—	—
Wisconsin	—	X	X	—	—	—	—
Wyoming	—	—	X	—	—	—	—
Number of States	2	19	48	10	17	4	4

* Grades 1 to 8.
† Includes only vocational classes and summer kindergartens.

TABLE 7

Additional Services for Which Public Funds Were Provided, 1949-50

State	Administration and Supervision	Education of Exceptional Children	Vocational Education	Audio-visual Education	Free Textbooks	Special Teachers	Pupil Transportation	Health Services	School Lunches	School Library
Alabama		X	X		X					
Arizona	X		X		X				X	
Arkansas		X	X	X	X		X			
California		X	X				X			
Colorado		X	X				X			
Connecticut							X	X		
Delaware	X	X	X		X		X			
Florida	X		X	X	X	X	X			X
Georgia	X		X				X			
Idaho		X	X				X		X	
Illinois	X	X	X				X		X	
Indiana	X	X					X			
Iowa			X		X		X			
Kansas		X	X		X					
Kentucky		X	X	X	X	X	X	X	X	
Louisiana	X	X	X		X	X	X	X		X
Maine	X	X	X	X		X	X		X	
Maryland	X	X	X	X	X		X			X
Massachusetts	X	X	X				X			
Michigan	X	X	X		X		X			
Minnesota	X		X		X		X		X	
Mississippi		X	X				X			
Missouri					X		X			
Montana		X	X				X			
Nebraska			X							

328

Nevada			X				X			
New Hampshire	X		X				X			
New Jersey	X	X	X			X	X			
New Mexico					X		X			
New York		X	X			X	X		X	
North Carolina	X		X		X					
North Dakota			X				X			
Ohio		X	X	X			X			
Oklahoma		X	X		X		X			
Oregon		X	X				X	X		
Pennsylvania	X	X	X				X	X		
Rhode Island	X								X	
South Carolina	X		X			X	X			
South Dakota			X				X	X		
Tennessee	X	X	X	X	X		X		X	
Texas	X		X							
Utah	X		X				X			
Vermont		X	X	X	X		X		X	X
Virginia	X	X				X		X		
Washington		X			X		X			
West Virginia	X	X					X			
Wisconsin		X					X			
Wyoming							X			
Number of States	23	30	41	6	16	8	40	6	9	4

329

Trends in Education in 1950.—It is noted in Chapter 6 that the certification of teachers, the history of which is very confusing, was long looked upon as a local administrative function, and that only in the twentieth century did certification come to be assumed as a function of the state. Localism in this activity long resisted the intrusion by the state and made for a wide variety of confusing practices. There was little uniformity of practice in a given state, and often certificates in one county would not be considered good in another in the same state. "Reciprocity" in certification was not a common practice. In 1898 only three states issued all teaching certificates. The number of states that did so was five in 1903; fifteen in 1911; twenty-six in 1921; thirty-six in 1926; thirty-nine in 1933; and in 1950 all states except Massachusetts seemed to do so. In that state, certificates were generally issued by local educational authorities. That state in 1951 began a program which provided for the state certification of teachers and for the gradual upgrading of certificates, so that by 1954 all teachers in Massachusetts would be required to hold a bachelor's degree. But even at mid-century the many ways of getting and keeping in force certificates to teach school were generally manifold if not mysterious.

During the first half of the twentieth century some trends in this administrative activity were observable. In addition to the tendency of the state to issue certificates, with centralization in a bureau of the state department of education, reports on approved training in educational institutions, and increasingly in summer session, came to be substituted for examinations; the abolition of "life" certificates; the giving up of "blanket" certificates, and making provision for certificates on the basis of educational preparation and the kind of work teachers were prepared to do; increasing the training for certificates, with a tendency toward four years of collegiate training or more; and apparently increasing requirements in professional education. At mid-century this was bringing much complaint on the ground that so many of the required courses in education, on both undergraduate and graduate levels, were overlapping and repetitious. Although progress was made in the quantitative requirements for the education of teachers, there was some sober questioning about the qualitative requirements, especially in professional education.

The resistance of local educational authorities to certification, as to some other educational functions by the state, was prolonged and bitter in some states, and sometimes the issue was fought through several sessions of legislatures. But as the state came more and more to pay the piper, it came more and more to call the tune.

It was noted above that near the end of the past century, T. H. Watkins reported on the trends in educational administration in the cities of the United States, observed the large size of the boards of education at that time, and predicted that these would soon be reduced in the interest of educational effectiveness. Two decades later a widely recognized authority on educational administration wrote that urban districts had up to that time offered "the largest opportunities for constructive educational leadership," and that much of the advance that had been made in educational administration had been due in large part to the cities. In forms of organization and administration, in supervision and equipment, and in the extension of educational services and advantages, the city school district had been the pioneer.[26] Instead of many school boards or committees, such as counties had, there was only one school board in those cities that had come to develop a unified plan of educational organization and administration. In the generation that has passed since Cubberley wrote, further advances have been made in the best organized and administered urban places, where at mid-century some of the best principles of educational administration could be found. With the growth of the number and size of cities and the increase in their educational functions and services, schools in urban localities came to differ markedly from schools in villages and rural communities. Urban educational matters received more consideration and discussion, although during the first half of the present century, education in rural communities came to receive increasing attention. In 1950, half of all the children in the public elementary and secondary schools of the United States were enrolled in separately organized city school systems.

Questions on educational administration at mid-century were more numerous and more difficult, and otherwise differed markedly from those of 1900. The management of schools was no longer the simple and local requirement that it had been earlier, when its details were fewer and less exacting. "School management," as it was first called as a subject of professional study, was only in its infancy in 1900, as already noted. But before 1950, American colleges and universities had come to offer countless courses in so many minute phases of educational management as to invite the criticism that some of the institutions were failing to send out broadly educated leaders and were rapidly becoming trade schools and turning out mere mechanics. The condition provoked some searching questions, and here and there

[26] E. P. Cubberley, *Public School Administration* (Boston: Houghton Mifflin Company, 1916), p. 433.

some tonic satire which tended to annoy some professors of the subject.

Around the middle of the century, some of these were asking themselves: Was educational administration, especially in the cities, "in a critical period of transition, both as practiced and as taught? If so, what are the critical factors, and what are promising ways of seeing us through?" They also asked about the "constructive steps" that could be taken at once "to dramatize the need for improving the working conditions of the typical school administrator with a view to improving educational leadership," which some of them seemed to think some were losing.

Another question which was being asked at the middle of the century was whether the environment of the modern American city could be so "influenced that a climate favorable to progressive and dynamic school administration can actually emerge?" The word "dynamic" had come to be widely and often loosely used in professional educational circles, although no clear definition of it seems to have been offered by members of the craft. It was also noted that the administrators were acquainted with the rising tide of dismissals, terminations, and resignations that were affecting the superintendencies of large city school systems of the United States, manifestations reported as symptoms only, however, of much deeper difficulties. Apparently, it was pointed out, the entire administration of large city school systems was on trial and under test, "and usually within a climate that is anything but favorable toward progressive school leadership." The interest of the citizens had to be aroused if cohesiveness in the school system itself was to be maintained. Conditions required new and bold thinking, it was said, and inquiry was made as to what "some of that thinking would be like."

Moreover, in those times "of conflicting ideologies," it was said that there was special need for renewed consideration of the proper place of "official authority" for the control of educational policy. A practicing superintendent of a big city system, who wore the doctoral ermine of a flourishing school of education, irreverently asked whether the institutions that were training the educational administrators of the country had failed to meet their responsibilities. Other questions which were being asked about educational administration at mid-century concerned means of reducing the energetic activities of heavy pressure groups. And finally, the head of a great university got up and embarrassingly asked exactly what was meant by democratizing education, and what should be the attitude of the administrators toward the teachers' union. The words democracy, leadership, challenge, and service were so frequently on the lips of the administrators as now and then to seem a bit empty.

A study of developments in recent decades seems to exhibit certain trends in state educational administration which were not in evidence in the latter part of the past and the early part of the twentieth century. According to Keesecker [27] some of these trends were the following:

1. An increase in legislative activity affecting the composition and organization of state boards of education.
2. The restriction of state control over education by the governor (1) by his removal from state boards of education and (2) by a trend away from the appointment of state boards by the governor.
3. The abolition of constitutionally created *ex officiis* state boards.
4. The removal of all *ex officiis* members from state boards of education.
5. The removal of professional educators from membership on state boards.
6. An increase in the number of members on state boards.
7. The selection of state boards by popular vote.
8. The selection of state boards by school-board conventions.
9. Increased legislative and policy-making responsibility of state boards.
10. Broadening the scope and functions of general state boards of education.

Promising efforts in studying issues of public educational administration appeared in conferences on the subject which were held at Endicott, New York; Madison, Wisconsin; Clear Lake, Michigan; and at Cornell University in the late 1940's and in 1950, under the auspices of the National Conference of Professors of Educational Administration and other organizations. Reports of these conferences were issued on "Developing Leaders for Education," "Educational Leaders: Their Function and Preparation," "Emerging Programs for Improving Educational Leadership," and "Programs for Preparing Educational Administrators in 1950," all of which threw helpful light on various phases of this important subject.

What may be considered the first organized study of the issues and difficulties of educational administration in the United States was announced in the fall of 1950, to be undertaken under a large grant from the W. K. Kellogg Foundation to the graduate schools of education of Columbia University (Teachers College), the University of Chicago, Harvard University, the University of Texas, and the

[27] *Op. cit.,* pp. 109-10.

George Peabody College for Teachers. Proposal for the study, which was to extend over five years, had been made a few years earlier by the American Association of School Administrators. While much progress had been made during the first half of the twentieth century in advanced work in educational administration, educators were reported as generally believing that however encouraging progress in that direction had been, conditions in 1950 were far from satisfactory, and that there was room for much improvement. At that time many superintendents and principals in public school systems had been awarded the master's degree, and an increasing number had received the doctorate in educational administration, the Ph.D. or the doctorate of education (Ed.D.), which was rapidly becoming almost as common among the school people as the master's degree had been two decades earlier.

There were several major purposes of the significant Kellogg study: to improve the methods of recruiting, selecting, and the preservice of those preparing for work in educational administration; to improve the professional in-service of those who enter upon such work; and to improve what had come to be called the "internship" in educational administration, which was a system of cooperative arrangements between graduate schools of professional education and public school systems under which beginners in the work could gain some preliminary practical administrative experience. This was one of the most comprehensive studies ever attempted for educational improvement in the United States. Its key word was "cooperation," and the outcome of the immense undertaking was hopefully awaited, but only the future could disclose the extent of its practical success.

Statements of national income, expenditures for public elementary and secondary schools, and the percentage of the national income "in current dollars" for elementary and secondary education, by decades, from 1900 to 1950 were approximately as shown in Table 8.

TABLE 8

NATIONAL INCOME AND EXPENDITURES FOR EDUCATION

	National Income	Educational Expenditures	Percentage
1900	$ 17,965,000,000	$ 214,964,618	1.20
1910	31,430,000,000	426,250,434	1.36
1920	73,999,000,000	1,036,151,209	1.40
1930	75,003,000,000	2,316,790,384	3.09
1940	81,347,000,000	2,344,048,927	2.88
1950	250,000,000,000	4,600,000,000	1.84

The figures for expenditures included the total outlay for buildings and current costs in school districts, the states, and the federal government. The National Education Association stated in 1950 that every prediction of the trend of national income for the next half century was for steady increase. "It is likely that the present national income will be doubled by the year 2000. It is clear that we are able to support our public schools adequately, if we wish to do so, without strain upon the financial condition of the country." [28]

The next Chapter deals with education in the United States during military and economic crises.

SOME QUESTIONS AND EXERCISES FOR STUDENTS

1. Account for, and report to the class, the fact that variety rather than uniformity was the striking characteristic of educational organization, administration, and support in the United States in 1950.
2. Show why the district system of public educational administration persisted so long in some states.
3. Look for and report on any survivals of objections to highly centralized educational control in your state.
4. Explain why chief state school officers were generally appointed before 1860, but at the middle of the twentieth century most of the states elected them by popular vote.
5. Indicate (a) any advantages and (b) any disadvantages you see in the popular election of county superintendent of schools.
6. Examine and report on the recommendations of the President's Advisory Committee on Education on the reorganization of local school districts. On consolidation and transportation.
7. Account for the fact that permanent public school endowments ("literary funds") were often mismanaged in the early days.
8. Study and report on the arguments on federal aid to education presented by (a) the President's Advisory Committee on Education in 1938, (b) the Chamber of Commerce of the United States in 1948.
9. Indicate any evidence you can find which seems to show that public education in the United States was becoming more and more secular around the middle of the twentieth century.
10. Show why questions on public educational administration were more numerous and more difficult at mid-twentieth century than in 1900.
11. Study the story of the certification of teachers in your state. What are the arguments for and against the administration of this educational function by the state?

[28] *Our School Population: Annual Report of the Profession to the Public.* Washington, D. C., 1949-50, p. 15.

12. Indicate and explain the "trends" in public educational administration in 1950.

SOME SUGGESTED REFERENCES AND READING

ALLEN, HOLLIS P. *The Federal Government and Education.* New York: McGraw-Hill Book Co., Inc., 1950.
  Very useful on federal activities in education.

AMERICAN ASSOCIATION OF SCHOOL ADMINISTRATORS. *Standards for Superintendent of Schools.* Washington, D. C.: The Association, 1939.
  A preliminary report of the Committee on the Certification of Superintendents of Schools, which contains tentative recommendations on the subject.

——— *The Superintendent of Schools and His Work.* Washington, D. C.: The Association, 1940.
  Final report of the Committee on the Certification of Superintendents of Schools, with recommendations.

BRICKMAN, W. W. "The School and the Church-State Questions." *School and Society,* LXXI (May 6, 1950), pp. 273-82.
  Reviews extensive literature on an issue that had become very acute at mid-twentieth century.

DUKE UNIVERSITY LAW SCHOOL. *Law and Contemporary Problems.* Durham, N. C.: 1950.
  A very significant symposium on the relation between religion and the State, on decisions of the Supreme Court on religious issues, the separation of Church and State, and on allied subjects.

KEESECKER, W. W. *State Boards of Education and Chief State School Officers.* Bulletin 1950, No. 12. Washington, D. C.: Government Printing Office, 1950.
  Shows the historical development of the legal organization of state educational administration and its practices at mid-century. Very useful for some topics discussed in this Chapter.

KNIGHT, EDGAR W., and HALL, CLIFTON L. *Readings in American Educational History.* New York: Appleton-Century-Crofts, Inc., 1951.
  Contains many original documents that bear on topics discussed in this Chapter.

MORT, PAUL R. *State Support for Public Schools.* New York: Teachers College, Columbia University, 1926.
  Discusses the equalization of educational opportunity, cost of a minimum educational program, and the division of financial support between the state and local administrative divisions.

NATIONAL EDUCATION ASSOCIATION. *Your School District.* Washington, D. C.: The Association, 1948.
  Provides a useful analysis of the structure of local educational administration, and furnishes the history of local district organization in several states.

——— *The County Superintendent of Schools in the United States.* Washington, D. C.: The Association, 1950.
  Throws much light on some topics discussed in this Chapter. Contains useful bibliographies.

STRAYER, GEORGE D., JR. *Centralizing Tendencies in the Administration of Public Education.* New York: Teachers College, Columbia University, 1934.
  A very good treatment of those tendencies in Maryland, New York, and North Carolina.

THE COUNCIL OF STATE GOVERNMENTS. *The Forty-Eight State School Systems.* Chicago: The Council, 1949.

   Contains much useful and significant, as well as some disturbing, information on the organization, administration, and support of public education in the United States at about the middle of the twentieth century.

U. S. OFFICE OF EDUCATION. *Public School Finance Programs of the Forty-Eight States.* Washington, D. C.: U. S. Government Printing Office, 1950.

   A very useful treatment of practices in public support of education in the United States around 1950.

Chapter 8

DURING MILITARY AND ECONOMIC CRISES

PREVIEW OF THE CHAPTER

Education in the United States suffered heavy jolts during the first half of the twentieth century. Two of these came during military crises, and one during the worst economic dislocation the country had ever had. . . . The impact of the First World War was felt chiefly in higher education. Cooperation of the colleges and universities with the national government through the Students' Army Training Corps brought the emergency home to those institutions. . . . The Committee on Education and Special Training of the War Department, in working with the colleges and universities, greatly strengthened the machinery and process of mobilization. . . . That experiment demonstrated the capacity of higher education to perform a highly patriotic and effective service in the national welfare. But the SATC was also the fiscal and budgetary salvation of many colleges and universities. . . . The record of the patriotic services of higher education was more extended during the Second World War, when the National Conference of College and University Presidents on Higher Education pledged united effort to decisive military victory. . . . Through the Army Specialized Training Program and the Navy College Training Program, more than 200 thousand trainees were participating in many significant programs in more than 600 colleges and universities by the summer of 1943. . . . The impact of the Second World War was also felt in secondary education. . . . The Second World War led to wide publication and discussion of the place of liberal and humanistic studies in higher education, in contrast to heavy vocational emphasis, and there were sharp criticisms of current educational practices. . . . The impact of the severe economic depression that began in 1929 was strikingly conspicuous. The behavior of the American people toward their educational arrangements was very different from that in any other economic dislocation. Educational budgets were sharply slashed, school terms were reduced, teachers went without their pay, and confusion in education was nationwide. . . . The critics of the schools were more numerous than ever before: professional educators, editors, ministers, commencement pulpiteers and baccalaureateers, and many other persons tore into education and had little that was good to say about the schools. . . . A study of 9 thousand editorials on education in twenty-five leading newspapers in the early 1930's, by Charles R. Foster, Jr., was very revealing. . . . An earlier study by Royce S. Pitkin showed that education had generally prospered in other periods of depression.

Twentieth-century Crises in Education.—During the first half of the twentieth century, education in the United States suffered heavier jolts than it had ever before had, two of these coming from the impacts of military crises and one from the severe economic dislocation that began in 1929. I. L. Kandel has noted that the connection between education and military victory had been recognized since the early part of the nineteenth century.

Thus the Battle of Waterloo was won on the playing fields of Eton, and the Battle of Sedan by the Prussian schoolmaster. As wars have become global and all the resources of the nations engaged in them must be drawn upon, it is inevitable that the normal life of all, whether in the combat services or far from the fighting fronts, should be completely disrupted. Under such conditions, the normal progress of education is seriously affected.[1]

The impact of the First World War was felt chiefly in higher education and was not so widespread as that of the Second World War, which touched not only the colleges and universities but the elementary and secondary schools and also the institutions that trained teachers. Moreover, many parents were drawn into industries of war, home life was disrupted, juvenile delinquency and the proper care of children presented new and baffling difficulties, and the entry of teachers into the military and other services connected with the war caused a serious crisis in this country.

In the Second World War, the national government had the benefit of its experience of cooperation with institutions for higher education in the First World War, through what was known as the Students' Army Training Corps, when that military emergency brought home to the colleges and universities their heavy responsibilities for aiding national defense. How those responsibilities were met by the institutions during the first of these military emergencies is a brief but important chapter in the history of education in this country. The record of the higher institutions and their students, in the experiment of the SATC, though of short duration, was one of high courage and patriotic devotion.

When the United States entered the First World War in April of 1917, the regular army of this country numbered about 120 thousand enlisted men. When the Armistice was signed fourteen months

---

[1] *The Impact of the War Upon American Education* (Chapel Hill: The University of North Carolina Press, 1948), p. 3.

later, the total number of American men recruited for the army exceeded 4 million, and this expansion of that arm of the military service had been promoted in no small way by the Committee on Education and Special Training of the War Department, which helped greatly to strengthen the machinery and process of mobilization. Under that committee, vocational training detachments were operated at more than 150 institutions for higher education for the training of technicians, and units of the SATC (collegiate section) were later established in 525 colleges and universities. Contracts between the War Department and the institutions called for the training of 220 thousand soldiers in the vocational section and 200 thousand in the collegiate section, before June 30, 1919.

Cooperation in Wartime.—The immediate need which led to the creation of the Committee on Education and Special Training was the shortage of technicians. Early in this unique experiment, it was found that 200 thousand more technicians were needed than were available, and that the army required more than 500 different forms of technical skills. By April of 1918 there were 6 thousand men in technical and vocational training in 15 institutions, and by July of that year, 50 thousand were in training in 147 institutions. This work continued throughout the summer, and each month 25 thousand men, technically trained in these schools, were delivered to the army. One of the most significant facts about this program was that 130 thousand physically fit men were accepted for service in the technical and vocational detachments, and 130 thousand men were delivered to the army, "each with added technical skill which rendered him a more useful member of the military establishment."

The collegiate section was established for the purpose of developing "as a great military asset, a large body of young men in the colleges," by providing efficient military instruction, and by requiring that students in the SATC maintain an academic standard higher than the usual "pass mark" in the institutions. Another purpose, as stated by Secretary of War Newton D. Baker, was the prevention of "unnecessary and wasteful depletion of the colleges through indiscriminate volunteering, by offering to the students a definite and immediate military status." In this way collegiate training became identified with national service. That part of the program was just getting organized in the fall of 1918 when an epidemic of influenza swept the country, which affected nearly every one of the SATC units and made it almost impossible for either the military or the academic work to be done as it had been planned. For nearly a month, little was done at any of the schools. Then came the Armistice on November 11, demobilization was ordered, and by December 20 of 1918 about 165 thousand student-soldiers were returned to civilian status. But the experiment demonstrated the capacity of higher education for a highly patriotic and effective service and devotion to the national welfare. This patriotism and devotion, if now and then colored a bit perhaps by immature sentimentality, were in no way decreased by the fact that the SATC was the fiscal and budgetary salvation of some of the institutions for higher education. The official report of the experiment, conducted without any experience or precedent and under great difficulties, testified that in general there was no thought of fiscal gain in the institutions, and the undertaking was pronounced a success. Out of the official report came recommendations for the Reserve Officers' Training Corps which was later formed in many educational institutions throughout the country.

The more extended record of service by the higher institutions in the national emergency that broke upon the American people on December 7, 1941, was also one of intelligent patriotism and high courage. Shortly after that "day of infamy," the National Conference of College and University Presidents on Higher Education met in Baltimore and pledged President Roosevelt "the total strength of our colleges and universities—our faculties, our students, our administrative organizations, our physical facilities. The institutions of the United States are organized for action, and they offer their united power for decisive military victory and for the ultimate and even more difficult task of establishing a just and lasting peace."

Work of the Leaders of Higher Education.—These leaders knew, however, that all that was needed to win the war could not then be accurately defined, nor could the total present or future resources of trained manpower be accurately appraised or predicted. New needs would doubtless arise as the months passed. But one thing seemed clear: the presidents of the colleges and universities were not only willing, but eager, to offer all their resources in the effort to win the war; and they believed that the surest and quickest way to victory was "the full, energetic, and planned use of all our resources and materials." They pledged full cooperation with the National Resources Planning Board and other agencies of the national government, warned against the danger of "competitive bidding for faculty and students by government agencies and by industry," and emphasized the necessity for the conservation of adequate personnel at all levels of education so that effective instruction in the schools could be maintained and an adequate supply of trained men and women could be continuously provided. The leaders of higher education urged appropriate plans to meet the shortages of teachers in the schools, of workers in community programs, of county agents, leaders in the 4-H Clubs, home demonstration agents, and other leaders in rural life. They also urged the importance of retaining, "as far as practicable, a degree of uniformity" among the institutions for higher education with regard to wartime changes in the academic calendar and credit systems, "while making adjustments in the interest of acceleration."

These college and university presidents frankly recognized the increasing requirements of the government and industry for men and women trained in the technological and professional skills necessary in the war, and the necessity for preparing such workers as speedily as possible. But they urged that adjustments in the curricula should be made intelligently, and that changes should be consistent with national needs and educational standards. While the acceleration of higher education programs seemed necessary, this should be undertaken "without lowering of established standards of admission to college." In spite of this advice, however, there were here and there apparent tendencies toward "bargain basement" educational practices.

One of the most significant resolutions at Baltimore had to do with the obligation of the colleges and universities to give more attention to health education: individual health was "essential to national efficiency and to national war effort." At that time about a million men had already been rejected for military service because of their inability to meet the minimum standards of physical fitness which it required. All institutions were urged to take the steps "necessary to bring each individual student to his highest possible level of physical fitness"—sound advice for education in a country at war, but equally sound for education in times of peace. The applications of science to military purposes had been heavily required in the First World War, but the demand was even more exacting in the Second World War, which was largely a conflict of technology. That struggle the college and universities were called upon to help win.

With the lowering of the draft age to eighteen in November of 1942, the anxieties and difficulties of the institutions for higher education, already very nervous, greatly increased. By that action only a small number of young men subject to the regulations of selective service could plan on going to college, and only a few of those that entered could claim deferment from active military service as "potentially necessary." Attempts to remove some of the uncertainties of the colleges and the young men were made later that year by the Army and the Navy in consultation with the War Manpower Commission, the Navy Advisory Council on Education, and responsible national committees that had been set up earlier. Out of this consultation and planning, arrangements were made to make as full use as possible of the higher institutions to prepare men for military service and for war industries and essential civilian activities. The main results were the ASTP (Army Specialized Training Program) and the NCTP (Navy College Training Program), plans for which were published in early December of 1942. A little later, the first list of the institutions selected to participate in these undertakings was published: for the ASTP, 249 colleges and universities, and 51 for the NCTP. Nineteen institutions were selected for both programs, the curricula of which were prepared by national authorities recommended by the United States Office of Education and the American Council on Education, by the Navy's Advisory Committee on Education, and by special consultants from the higher institutions. The institutions were selected, as had been the case of the SATC in the First World War, on their facilities for providing the instruction required, adequacy of provisions for housing and subsistence, and charges for overhead.

As carefully as these programs seemed to have been planned, there was in them evidence of confusion and uncertainty, the blame for which, however, cannot be placed at the door of any one interested group. The Army-Navy testing program by which students were selected was so bewilderingly mammoth, and the assignment of selected students to the selected colleges and universities was so annoyingly delayed, that the Committee on Relationships of Higher Education to the Federal Government, in April of 1943, expressed "deep concern with the present status and apparent prospects of the major section of the Army Specialized Training Program." But the program did get under way in the summer of 1943, and by October of that year, 628 institutions and 212.5 thousand trainees were participating in the work as shown in Table 9.[2]

By December of 1943, when the peak was reached, there were 380 thousand men in specialized training in 489 colleges and universities. After that time this work was gradually reduced, and "the basic phase of the ASTP was terminated in April, 1944, and the other

[2] I. L. Kandel, *The Impact of the War Upon American Education* (Chapel Hill: The University of North Carolina Press, 1948), p. 156.

programs a few months later. The place of the ASTP was taken by the Army Specialized Training Reserve Program (ASTRP), which had been begun on August 9, 1943."

TABLE 9

SPECIAL PROGRAMS OF INSTITUTIONS FOR HIGHER EDUCATION, OCTOBER, 1943

Program	Institutions *	Trainees
Army Specialized Training	216	129,080
Army Air Forces	151	66,512
Navy College Training	244	9,193
Navy Air Force	17	7,743
	628	212,528

* Total number of institutions, eliminating duplications, 440.

In 1944 the critical conditions in higher education were brought to the attention of the Congress by resolution in the House of Representatives on June 21 of that year. Its purpose was to study the effects on higher institutions of reduced enrollments, and recent and prospective reduction in the Army and Navy training programs, "with a view to determining means by which such effects may be alleviated." These issues affected the national interest and welfare because the effect of the war had fallen heavily upon enrollments, finances, and instructional staffs. These unhappy conditions were to be greatly improved under the G. I. Bill of Rights. Enrollments of civilian students in 1944 and 1945 were only 54 per cent of what these had been in 1940, there was a sharp decline in instructional staffs, and institutional income in 1944 and 1945 was 67 per cent of what this had been in 1940. Army and Navy contracts had taken care of about 50 per cent of the income in men's colleges and in some coeducational institutions. Colleges for women were not so seriously affected, but the teachers' colleges were generally hit hard. Through the Women's Army Auxiliary Corps (WAACS), Women's Reserve of the Navy Reserve (WAVES), Women's Reserve of the Coast Guard and Marines (SPARS), women increasingly entered these branches of the military service. But these opportunities were not provided exclusively for women in, or who had been to, college, and it did not seem necessary to alter the programs for the higher education of women.

War's Impact on Secondary Education.—The impact of the war on secondary education was also heavy. High school students were not returning to school, but were going to work; go-to-school and back-to-school drives were launched; educational organizations passed resolutions on the alarming conditions; the High School Victory Corps was organized; and other efforts were made to get and keep children in the high schools, enrollments in which dropped from 6.7 million in 1941 to 5.5 million in 1944, a decline which could not be accounted for entirely by the decline in birth rate or by the adoption of a policy of acceleration. Discussion of needed changes in the curricula of the secondary schools greatly increased as a result of these conditions.

If the institutions for higher education were going to help win the war, some persons believed it necessary to revise their curricula and programs. Others questioned the wisdom of doing so. But collegiate degrees came to be offered in three, two and a half, and even in two years; many academic traditions were abandoned, and increased emphasis came to be placed on "speeding up," with much stress upon technological and immediately practical courses. This emphasis tended to disturb advocates of the humanities and of "liberal" learning. Questions were raised as to whether the trend toward acceleration and vocationalism would furnish the real solution to some of the acute issues in higher education, even in the emergency of war, and on the possible effect of the trend on the further impairment of higher educational standards that needed instead to be strengthened. Some persons asked whether education in the humanities and liberal arts was not as important in times of war as in times of peace. In its extensive programs in the colleges and universities, the Navy had insisted that a broad and well-grounded education was of great importance in the emergency, and by implication asked whether higher education could afford to scrap those subjects that had been considered so important for so many centuries.

The Place of Liberal and Humanistic Studies.—This issue led to wide publication on and discussion of liberal and humanistic studies in the institutions for higher education. Significant had been the publication in 1938 by the Carnegie Foundation for the Advancement of Teaching of *The Student and His Knowledge,* based on a study, made by W. S. Learned and Ben Wood, of secondary and higher education in Pennsylvania, and in the Graduate Record Examination, developed by that Foundation in cooperation with colleges and universities. The tests used in this examination were built on the general principles that had been used in the Pennsylvania study. The rapid expansion of courses, due not only to the expansion of knowledge but also to efforts of the colleges to fit their curricula to the "temper of the multitude," had caused some concern after the First World War. This concern had led, as noted in Chapter 4, to much experimentation with survey courses, orientation courses, general courses, and "general education," which I. L. Kandel says "resulted in courses offering a little of everything in relation to fields of knowledge and nothing in particular." [3] Higher education between the two wars had been characterized by "mechanical and external devices," in some cases indulged in to enlist public interest and support. Walter A. Jessup, president of the Carnegie Foundation, pointed to competition as one of the causes.

Just now we are in a mood to follow the new. Not only do we like to buy a new model of motor car or radio; we are attracted by the "new education." In bidding for favor, we are streamlining the job—our current models glitter with gadgets that smack of the factory and the salesman. Perhaps a college can gain by adopting sixteen cylinders, hydraulic brakes, and air-flow design. Perhaps so. Or it may be that a college should be organized with multiple tubes and high-fidelity loud-speaker. But certainly the college that rests its case on doing something new or adopting some gadget of the moment would do well to consider the long road it must travel. It might well recognize that the institution must be administered with a view to its whole task—not a temporary task of exploitation or publicity of news releases or reorganization of the current pattern, whatever it may be, but a task to be measured ultimately by the effect of the college upon the student himself. The president of a small college recently said, "We know that we are accepting students who cannot do our work. We know that we are carrying these students forward to graduation. In our present situation we are under such pressure that we feel that we have no other choice. Our campus morale is affected by numbers, and a reduction in attendance is looked upon as a slump—as though the institution were losing ground." The general result is constant college competition for students. [4]

There were sharp criticisms of current educational practices by many persons, including Robert M. Hutchins and Mortimer Adler of the University of Chicago; Mark Van Doren of Columbia University, whose *Liberal Education* in 1943 provoked considerable discussion; Stringfellow Barr and Scott Buchanan of St. John's College; and by the weekly broadcasts of "Education for Freedom, Incorporated," between December of 1943 and March of 1944, on the purposes and the meaning of liberal education. At about the same time the American Council of Learned Societies undertook to

[3] *Op. cit.*, p. 182.
[4] "The American College," in *Twentieth Educational Yearbook*, I. L. Kandel (ed.), the International Institute of Teachers College, Columbia University, 1943, pp. 180, 181.

stimulate interest in the humanities through local and regional conferences on the subject. The report of a Harvard Committee on the Objectives of a General Education in a Free Society, which President Conant appointed in the spring of 1943, was published in 1945, and under the title, *General Education in a Free Society,* was widely read and discussed. In his annual report to the Board of Overseers of Harvard in 1943, President Conant wrote: "The primary concern of American education today is not the development of the appreciation of the 'good life' in young gentlemen born to the purple. It is the infusion of the liberal and humane tradition into our entire educational system. Our purpose is to cultivate in the largest possible number of our future citizens an appreciation of both the responsibilities and the benefits which come to them because they are Americans and because they are free." It was reported in the *New York Times* of April 16, 1950, that the leading scientific schools of the United States were then giving more attention than formerly to liberal arts, and that responsible educators throughout the country were "convinced that general education and the social sciences have a vital part to play in the total educational program of the technical man. It is not enough, they say, to train a good engineer; he must also know how to be a responsible citizen. As one college president recently remarked, the scientist must not only know how to make an H-bomb, but he must also know how to prevent it from destroying the world."

The statistics of the census also came up for fresh discussion. The census of 1920 had disclosed that a little more than 7 per cent of the total population of the United States over twenty-one years of age could not write in any language, "regardless of their ability to read." By 1930 this figure had changed to 5.3 per cent. In 1940 the question of literacy did not figure in the census, but instead "the highest grade of school completed" was used. In that census it was shown that of 73.7 million persons over twenty-five years of age, 3.8 per cent had not completed one year of schooling, while nearly 10 per cent had completed from one to four years—a total of almost 14 per cent of those over twenty-five years of age with less than five years of schooling. The reports of selective service disclosed that 676 thousand men had been rejected for mental or educational weaknesses, "which meant that they had less than the four years of schooling which was set up as the standard of functional literacy." About 350 thousand men who registered for the draft had signed their names with a mark. It was reported in 1946 that "as many men were lost to the United States military services in World War II on account of physical unfitness as our country had under arms in all theaters of World War I." These deficiencies were viewed as great "a handicap to war production as they were to military efficiency. They are as great a liability in peace as in war."

The facts of illiteracy and of the physical defects of young men, which the draft in the First World War had revealed, were shocking, and the lessons for the schools which those facts set out were clear. It was also clear in the Second World War that those lessons had not meantime been learned by the teachers and managers of the schools and by the supporting public; and it was charged that the alarming conditions revealed by the draft in the Second World War had to be chalked up against the failure of the schools. It appeared that the resolutions made during and immediately after the First World War, to do something about the educational and physical weaknesses which that emergency had disclosed, had lasted only during the period of compulsion.

Effects of the Economic Depression.—A third heavy jolt that American education felt came from the onslaught of the economic depression that began in 1929; and if the impacts of the two world wars were observable, those of the economic dislocation were strikingly conspicuous. Education in the United States had seemed to hold the confidence of the American people during the decades that followed the awakening in the second quarter of the nineteenth century, and more especially during the prosperous years that preceded the fateful autumn of 1929. Those who doubted the effectiveness of public education and its guiding philosophy, and those who cynically opposed its expansion and support, seemed to be growing smaller in number during the first three decades of the present century, and an increasing number of Americans were almost lyric in their praise of public education. But conditions changed with startling suddenness after 1929, and by 1931, heavy and violent hands were laid upon the schools and other educative and cultural agencies, including libraries, throughout the country. And when the teachers and managers of the schools returned to their work in September of 1931, most of them were less certain than they had ever been before of their way or their pay in a confused and confusing educational world.

Not only were the salaries of the educational workers cut, but almost everything that they had been engaged by the public to do was denounced as aimless and ineffective if not indeed actually vain and empty. The teachers and managers of schools, and their work, were assailed as never before, and there was the cry from one end of the country to the other that much of so-called education and many of the educators were altogether barren. It was not amazing, therefore, that the educational workers were distraught, because they and the schools were being tried as by fire.

Educational budgets were suddenly slashed, and many of the teachers were cut off with a shilling. Such a means of economy in the schools had never before been resorted to by governing authorities, even in the many well-defined economic depressions that the country had witnessed in the past century. The record, on the other hand, seemed to show that in other dark economic crises, plans for extending educational facilities had been made. Sessions of more than forty state legislatures in 1931 disclosed that advanced educational legislation and increased means of educational support would not be possible, and that the schools would find it difficult to retain the financial support they had gained prior to the depression. Appropriations to schools, colleges, and universities were greatly reduced, salaries of teachers were drastically cut, annual increments in salaries were denied, the teaching load and size of classes were increased, in some cases school terms were shortened, programs for buildings were held up or abandoned altogether, and many teachers were in their schoolrooms without contracts. Cities that formerly maintained annual terms of nine and ten months now found it impossible to provide more than six or seven. Debts, deficits, and the depression were pointed to as the causes of the crisis in education.

Some Critics of the Schools.—Also, never before had the work of the schools come in for such heavy criticism from so many different directions. The severest of the criticisms came from the educational experts themselves, the pedagogical high priests, professors of education, who for a long time had had their way in setting the styles for the teachers and managers of the schools. These critics condemned almost every feature of the democratic theory and practice of public education which had so long been the proud boast of the American people. The elementary school was attacked for low standards of discipline and for chaos in its curriculum, as well as for the inadequate preparation of the teachers and the fact (apparently only then discovered) that most of them were women. The secondary school was assailed as an educational fetish and an arid and purposeless luxury; higher education was pointed to as positively degenerate; colleges were headed straight for the demnition bowwows; coeducation was pronounced unsafe. An easy curriculum, automobiles and liquor as partners in the "charming combination," which along with the leisureliness of students, fraternities, and sororities, "those splendid centers of hypocrisy," and the autocracy of professional athletic coaches made for deterioration of higher education and cultural death.

To the criticisms of the professional educators were added those of the press and the pulpit, and this only increased the frustration of those who had charge of the nation's largest public business. Never had so much been written and spoken about the schools. It was charged in the public prints that teachers were content with nothing less than attempts to cover the earth in the curriculum; that they acquiesced in, when they did not instigate, all sorts of devices to make the schools take over the functions of the home, the church, and the policeman, while the main problem that faced the teachers was that of teaching boys and girls reading, writing, and arithmetic. One editor of a daily paper of national circulation expressed fear that "any and every sort of quack, pretentious mountebank, and pious fraud can invade the field of education," and he pointed to the difficulty of dislodging the pedagogical charlatans. "The average layman knows that he is quite unequal to such a task; so he becomes an easy victim for educational 'experts' with fifty-seven varieties of expensive idiocy."

The pulpit pointed to the shortcomings and sins of education, and indirectly charged to educational failures the broken fortunes, broken homes, and the epidemic of suicides that accompanied the depression. The Federal Council of Churches of Christ in America, in a pronouncement made in 1932, blamed greed for the economic crisis and declared that economic exploitation, through which the acquisitive instinct has submerged the sense of social responsibility, "was bearing and eating its own bitter fruit." By implication at least, education should have done something about the sad condition. And Warden Lewis E. Lawes, of Sing Sing Prison, told the National Education Association that the schools had done little or nothing to mold character, and that there was a missing link between character and education. The aspirations of education, as proclaimed in resolutions of educational associations, were noble, he said, but the records of police departments, children's courts, juvenile homes and reformatories told a very different story.

During these dismal years for the schools, commencement seasons provided superior platforms for their critics. Crops of sermons by pulpiteers and addresses by baccalaureateers offered more advice for the salvation of the educational world than the old orb had ever before had. Many causes of the bad state of things were revealed in these commencement efforts. A Secretary of the Treasury in President Franklin D. Roosevelt's cabinet disclosed to the graduating class of one large university that the lack of music in the schools had caused the feverish runs on the banks and was largely responsible for the depression. Astrology in business, buncombe in politics, superstition in daily life, and exaggerated and perverted emotions were described as the deadliest afflictions of the American people, which the schools should have removed. President Nicholas Murray Butler told 5 thousand men and women whom he decorated with academic degrees in 1933 that the social order rested upon a moral rather than an economic foundation, and unless the gain-seeking motive of the American people were subordinated to the ideal of human service, grief and disaster would continue to becloud and distress the world. If the graduates in the depression years heeded the cheerless words spoken at their commencements, they must have been aware that they were taking their diplomas into a very forbidding world. Competent observers of those exhibitions must have remarked the extraordinary procedure of the baccalaureateers and pulpiteers in the higher seats of learning who presumed to tell young men and women in brief addresses what those temples of light and leading should have been teaching them for four years. But it was likely that the advice in these commencements was to go the way of that of their predecessors and successors, and be forgotten soon after it was heard.

Advocates of public education in those dark days were apparently less vocal than its carping critics. In order to find out about public opinion on American education, a study [5] of a representative segment of the American press for the years 1930-35 showed about 9 thousand editorials on education in twenty-five leading newspapers throughout the United States. These editorials, constituting 3.67 per cent of all editorials in the papers for that period, disclosed 44.5 per cent favorable to, 32.4 per cent neutral on, and 23.2 per cent adversely critical of American education. Next to "the general value of education," in terms of high frequency of mention, Foster reported that "King Football" was still king; but editorial references to the value of education were not discussions of the purposes and aims of education and how these were to be achieved, but were "essentially declarations of belief in the value of education or in praise of some educational institution. Inspection of them shows that in most cases they are simply

[5] Charles R. Foster, Jr., *Editorial Treatment of Education in the American Press* (Cambridge: Harvard University Press, 1938). Materials drawn from this study are here used by permission. For a later analysis of opinion on the public schools, see *Life* for October 16, 1950.

that and nothing more. . . ." Foster also got the "overwhelming"
impression from the editorials that a major concern of the American
public, when it thought about its schools, was "money. . . . The
public doesn't care much about what educators do, as long as it
doesn't cost too much." Nearly 15 per cent of the editorials on
educational matters dealt with finance, "the dominant center of
attack":

> The evidence that money matters have greatly concerned the critical public,
> while scarcely needing elaboration, rests on the fact that of all the editorial
> references to education covered in this study, 1,878, or 14.8 per cent, have
> to do with educational finance in its various phases. This figure does not in-
> clude 420 additional references to teachers' salaries, included under another
> heading in the tabulation. Nor does it include numerous editorial allusions
> to educational finance made in a passing fashion not seeming to justify their
> inclusion in this group.
>
> Some newspapers devote one third or more of their editorial comment on
> education to costs. For example, the *Denver Post* treats of this subject in 33
> per cent of its topical references to education. Under this head, in the
> *Charleston News and Courier,* come 35 per cent of the educational comments.
> This assumes more significance when one pauses to consider the vast possible
> range of discussion on educational topics. . . . [6]

Next to the general value of education, to athletics, and to finance,
topics in terms of frequency of mention were set out as follows:
administration; public responsibility for the support of education;
teachers' salaries; methods and procedures; ability and character of
teachers; centralization, unification, and consolidation; health and
safety of pupils; political influence of the schools; civic education
and social studies; morale and behavior of pupils; freedom of teaching; miscellaneous matters concerning pupils; grants and gifts to
higher education; general efficiency of the schools, the skill and ability
of graduates; military training and militarism; pupils' opinions and
their expression; teachers' organizations; progressive education, activity programs and the child-centered school; professional schools
and courses; academic freedom of pupils; research; influence of education on the character, attitudes, ideals, and citizenship of young
people; achievement of pupils; attendance at school; propaganda and
indoctrination; equalization of educational support; federal aid to
education; illiteracy; adult education; "fads and frills"; vocational
and educational guidance; federal department of education; extracurricular activities; the education of teachers; expansion of educa-

[6] *Ibid.,* pp. 43-44.

tional facilities; discipline; public interest in education; compulsory education; play and physical education; state control of education; art and music; character education; intelligence testing; methods of mass education; student publications; summer schools; civic activities of pupils; modern languages; transportation of pupils; education of defective and handicapped children; use of school buildings for community activities; married teachers; failures of pupils; tenure of teachers; courses, conventions, and institutes for teachers; controversial issues in the schools; formal mental discipline and the transfer of training; safety patrol work; examinations; sex education; debating in the schools; home-study courses; adjustment of pupils, problem children; necessity for improving school buildings; homogeneous grouping; annuities, retirements, and pensions for teachers; continuation schools; aptitude testing; nursery schools; elective courses in the schools; and the promotion of teachers (mentioned only once as against 1,168 times that the general value of education was mentioned).

"Fads and frills" ranked thirty-seventh in a list of ninety-eight topics in terms of frequency of mention, but what was meant by the term was not always clearly stated. The *Chicago Tribune* for October 26, 1931, said, ". . . the frills must go," whereas the *Des Moines Register* for April 10, 1933, was high in its praise of music in the schools of that city, and the *New York Times* of February 28, 1934, declared that music belonged to "the fundamentals of education," and in another editorial for February 3 of that year had said that the finer things in the schools were not frills. The *Dallas News* of March 18, 1932, warned against contracting the curriculum unduly "in a spirit of false economy," and the *Boston Post* of March 12, 1934, pointed out that three centuries before the arts of reading and writing were considered frills, that two centuries before arithmetic was considered a fad, and that a century ago civics, geography, and history were looked upon as frills. While some editorials criticized the expenditure of public money on "fads and frills," few of them identified "fads and frills" specifically. The *Atlanta Constitution* said on March 12, 1933, that ". . . the faddists . . . have foisted upon school committees and superintendents a multitude of unnecessary and costly new notions of pseudo education . . . ," but did not say what those costly notions were. The *Los Angeles Times* said that the curfew had rung for furbelows of "special education," and urged trimming of the frills, but did not identify them. During these depression years the most frequently named "fads and frills" included music, art, sewing, commercial classes, cooking, home economics,

vocational training, visiting teachers, physical education, health services, swimming pools, fine buildings, supervision and other overhead
costs, visual education, and research.

The *New York Daily News* admitted that only one twenty-eighth
of the money spent on public education in New York City was spent
on what that newspaper called frills, but asked on April 18, 1932:

> Don't some of those items seem a little frivolous in times which call for
> making every public dollar count? And oughtn't parents who want their
> children taught drawing, music, sewing, or speech improvement be willing to
> pay for such instruction instead of charging it to the taxpayers? Is a public
> kindergarten better than a home for a child?

On May 18, 1933, the same paper asked:

> What is education, and how much education should society furnish free to
> the children who will take over when they grow up? . . . Well, we believe
> everybody should know how to read, write, and figure, and should know the
> history of his own country pretty well and something about the history of
> the rest of the world. That doesn't seem open to any argument at all.

> We think, too, that every child should be taught how to care for and use
> and develop his or her body. In other words, we favor athletics and physical
> training and sensible health education for all children.

> We wouldn't say, however, that this necessary education included esthetic
> dancing or eurythmic didoes, or other kinds of faddist instruction.

> It seems particularly useless to us to teach drawing, sewing, cooking, and
> music to all comers at the taxpayers' expense. We don't believe, for instance,
> that a girl who can't learn from her mother how to cook and sew is going
> to learn much more about these things in school. There is more than a
> suspicion that artists and musicians are born, not made; and whether that is
> true or not, it certainly is true that both of these professions are crowded
> already.

Newspaper Opinion of the Schools.—Public opinion on the issues
of the establishment of a federal department of education with representation in the cabinet, and on federal aid to education, was reflected, if not too significantly so, in newspaper editorials in the period
from 1930 to 1935. The subject of a strong federal department of
education was mentioned or discussed ninety times in the twenty-five
newspapers referred to, and about half the editorials were favorable
and thirty-four were opposed to such a department. A few editorials
were classified as neutral. But forty-four of the favorable editorials
appeared in two newspapers, the *New York Evening Journal* and the
Chicago Herald and Examiner. The thirty-four unfavorable editorials appeared in thirteen papers. "It must be concluded, then, that

in the newspapers dealing with the issue, the establishment of a strong federal department of education is distinctly opposed, except in three newspapers. And forty-four of the forty-five favorable comments, as already noted, appear in two of the three." The question of a strong department of education in Washington, however, must be separated from the question of federal aid to education, Foster pointed out. Federal aid to education was favored by three fourths of the editorials on the issue, while about 14 per cent adversely criticized the granting of such aid. Apparently the favorable attitude on this subject "was based largely on local needs and only infrequently because of any recognition of the principle which calls for equalization of educational opportunity in all parts of the country."

Typical of the moderate arguments against federal aid in the period between 1930 and 1935 was an editorial in the *Des Moines Register* on November 6, 1932:

> This is simply the old problem that arises over and over again, of how far it is advisable to go in obtaining efficiency through centralization of control, at cost of close contact between the supervising body and the locality under control. . . . Proposals to centralize certain phases of educational control in the federal government have already gained prominent support. But it is doubtful whether many friends of education would advocate placing entire control of the schools with a bureau in Washington.

The *New Orleans Times Picayune* believed that the question needed much study, but that the alarm over centralizing education in Washington was out of proportion to the "immediate danger." The *Denver Post* thought that the federal government had enough to do without taking on the schools, and added that when advocates argue that a federal system of education will give equality of educational opportunities, "the thing they have in mind is a federal dole for school districts." The *Philadelphia Inquirer* applauded local self-government as basic in the American system and tradition, argued for "home rule" in education, and favored limiting the functions of the United States Bureau (now Office) of Education to those of a "clearing house." The *Milwaukee Leader* hoped that if the Bureau should be elevated to a department in the national government, "it will be hedged about with restrictions which will leave education in the hands of the states and local communities where it belongs, and that the department will serve only as a clearing house and fact finding agency." The *Birmingham News* declared that public opinion in this country was overwhelmingly opposed to the creation of a federal department of education with representation in the cabinet, and that the best educational interests of the country required that that opinion remain that way. The *New York Times* expressed opposition to a federal department of education and to grants of money to the states for educational purposes if such grants depended upon conditions imposed by the federal government. The *Atlanta Constitution* said July 24, 1930, that opposition to President Herbert Hoover and Secretary of the Interior Ray Lyman Wilbur ". . . puts a perfect snuffer on the hopes of those misguided educators and teachers who yearn to be cogs in a vast federal educational centripetal machine with a suction pipe into the national treasury."

In the conditions revealed by Foster appeared two major implications: (1) "the introduction of new subjects in the schools and provision of new educational services must be 'right' in principle and provably so; (2) the guidance of public opinion must be accepted as a corollary of educational administration, in order to assure a reasonable public readiness to experiment in new fields." In general, it appeared from this study that if editorial comments reflected the public attitude toward education, "the general feeling toward teachers and administrators is good." It was apparent that the schools and the teachers were in high "position to serve society well if they but guard the prestige which they have and build from it."

Nowhere was the plight of education in the depression years more seriously recognized than in the annual meetings of local and national educational organizations. The meetings of state associations were concerned with local troubles, but those of national groups reflected the educational misery of the entire country. The spirit of these men and women was fervid and militant, and most of their deliberations and addresses voiced protest against the past decade of greed, debauchery, and irrational individualism in American life, and made pleas for a more healthy attitude toward public service in general. True, there was some evidence that not all those who managed and taught the schools had fully emerged from their bewilderment and dismay at the harsh realities of retrenchment in education. They knew that the flush years of prosperity were in the past, that the boom era of educational development was halted, that large budgets which formerly went unchallenged were now closely trimmed, and that the appropriations actually allowed were more closely watched. This strange condition tended to subdue and disquiet these leaders, some of whom revealed a fear of insecurity, while a few seemed to find it difficult to attain perspective sufficient to estimate the full meaning of the educational crisis. They were alarmed not only by attenuated financial resources but also by criticisms of their work.

Some of them appeared to be blinded by the afterglow of the rapid conquest of this country by public education before 1929. Those idealists who in fair-weather days had come to look upon dubious realists as educational unbelievers and heretics were now shocked and terrorized by cuts in their budgets. Some of them were deceived by what critics called the superficial quickness of the development of public education, which had been phenomenal, while they continued to place a sort of blind faith in gigantic administrative and supervisory organization and counted the strength of their work in terms of size and numbers. A few, perhaps, had failed to distinguish clearly between education and schooling. It was only natural, therefore, that public school managers found themselves in the wilderness of educational confusion. While they knew that they and their work were confronted with insecurity, it was cheering to observe that even if their morale tended to weaken, most of them whistled their way through the educational graveyard.

It was also not improbable that some leaders felt a bit responsible for the mess that education was in; certainly they knew that, whether justly or not, critics had charged to education a part of the general economic and social collapse. Although there were signs in support of the view that some leaders had been weakened spiritually by the disaster which had overtaken their work materially, a careful observer could also discern symptoms of recovery. It appeared that, notwithstanding the attacks upon it, education had a strong constitution and that its leaders were ready and eager to do their full part to maintain the high quality of it; that in spite of the suffering which education had undergone during the past few years, it still showed elasticity and capacity for adaptation. Though "bruised with adversity," the fight for mere existence seemed to call out its latent forces and the loyalty of its leaders, and the crisis through which education was passing promised to serve to purify their work and to renew their vitality.

There was no effort to disguise the fact that education of almost all kinds and degrees was not only on the defensive but heavily under fire. The school administrators knew that their salaries and the salaries of their teachers, as well as of other public servants, were open and easy targets for economy sharpshooters. The foes of public education then, as at midcentury,[7] had easy access to vehicles of publicity, and the average citizen was likely to be misinformed or kept in ignorance about the hard-earned gains of education in the past. It also seemed clear that the public, then as always, needed

[7] See Arthur D. Morse, "Who's Trying to Ruin Our Schools?" *McCall's*, September, 1951.

intelligible information about the schools; that the school people feared that they themselves had been a bit smug, perhaps remiss in their obligation to keep the public accurately and adequately informed about the schools, and not alert enough to prevent the distortion of information by critics and ill-wishers on the cost and the work of the schools. Many superintendents were frankly confessing these sins, most of them admitting the necessity for checking waste in the schools. Not only were they aware of this need, but they also seemed to know that they must maintain and increase their educational solvency if the basis of public confidence and good will was to be restored and preserved.

It was impressive to observe that these managers of the biggest public business in the United States were also becoming aware that taxation in this country had reached a stage of considerable seriousness, and that its burden was one of the most stubborn obstacles in the path of educational as well as general business recovery. They also seemed to know, or appeared to be learning, that probably the American people had not yet developed a solid and accepted philosophy of taxation. While those who spoke on the subject held that economy in education was desirable at all times, they urged as of utmost importance that essential school services should be maintained; and they pointed out that the demands upon the schools were heavier than in times of prosperity. But some of these leaders in educational administration seemed to believe that economies could be made by better organization and administration. Better budgetary practices, the elimination of useless and costly mechanical equipment, and a better revenue system were urged.

The conviction also seemed strong that the training of teachers demanded reorganization and redirection. There was a sort of common agreement that there had been an unintelligent multiplication and duplication of courses in normal schools, teachers' colleges, and departments of education—conditions which had developed during the period of rapid educational growth. In the opinion of many leaders, the time seemed ripe for a thorough and systematic revision of this work. Specifically, it appeared that most of those who had the responsibility for training teachers believed that teacher-training agencies, especially university departments of education, should relate themselves more closely to subject matter, even though specialists in subject matter in the past may have discharged their obligations reluctantly and perhaps ineffectively. More fundamental courses were recommended: courses in education should be related more closely to the other social sciences so that students in education might learn that the school is an important part of the American social order. This subject received considerable attention at meetings of the American Association of Teachers' Colleges and of the National Society of College Teachers of Education.

Among those who were managing and directing the schools of this country was discernible the belief that American education of all kinds and conditions might be able to get along with less administrative organization. Some of these leaders unfortunately had been taught, or had taught themselves, to look upon organization as the sacrament of ritualistic educational administration. While the moratorium in education was being discussed, mild and often even severe criticisms were being made against the huge educational machinery which grew up in this country during the days of prosperity and from which some afflictions were believed to have come.

It was charged during these depression years, as it was to be charged at mid-century, that the fountainhead of the attack upon the schools everywhere resided in "large taxpayers and the institutions which represent the wealthier and privileged elements in the community." It was also charged that those who made the least use of the public schools, who were the least dependent upon them because of superior economic status, who gave their children by means of private teachers the same things which they denounced as extravagances when supplied in less measure to the children of the masses, were the most active critics of the schools. Under cover of the depression and the cry of economy, the efficiency and attractiveness of the schools were being threatened. The critics said that the cause of the economic catastrophe was identical with the cause of the educational crisis.

The National Survey of School Finance, authorized by Congress in 1931, reported early in 1933 that a third of the school children of the country were receiving inadequate instruction, and that the depression was endangering the standards for millions of others. The depression was one of the causes of the unhappy condition, but not the sole cause. Most of the states, the survey report stated, would find it difficult to support adequate educational systems, even in times of economic prosperity, because the old methods of school support had broken down. Half the states obtained 90 per cent, or even more, and most of them 80 per cent of the support of the schools from general property levies. Instead of continuing the prevalent practice of depending upon property taxation for school maintenance, that burden should be widened by the imposition of other taxes, the report urged. Five years later the need for a wider distribution of public support of education was emphasized in the report of the President's Advisory Committee on Education.

While the report of this finance survey was being distributed to the legislatures and governors of the various states, the lawmaking bodies and chief executives in most of these states were holding or preparing to hold legislative sessions in 1933, and many of them were already saying, by messages, bills, and acts, that the need was for more than a redistribution of the burden of school support. The burden itself must be lightened, they cried; the cost of education must come down, they demanded. Reduced cost of government was a definite mandate from the people themselves, including that mythical "man in the street." Long before their election, hundreds of legislators were pledged to bring down public expenditures. Expert advice from the economists, political scientists, educators, and humanitarians had been sought, and sometimes respectfully heard and occasionally taken, in more prosperous times. In fact, millions had been spent on the services of "experts" during such times, but some of it casually and perhaps even unintelligently. But not so now. *Dies irae* had come. The year that saw an expert vacate the White House to an advocate of justice to the "forgotten man" set out to record itself on taxation in many a state capitol in 1933. Long before the statesmen reached the statehouses they had prepared drastic economy measures, and some of the Solons had offered bills to slash almost before their chaplain had offered his initial petition for blessings upon their deliberations. In 1932 the National Education Association had made a very stirring presentation that undertook to show that expenditures for education were very inadequate.

Comparing the expenditures for education and for other purposes of government, it was noted that the total of all federal, state, and local expenditures showed that the cost of highways and waterways had been far out of proportion to that of schools. President Hoover's Research Committee on Social Trends had revealed that between 1915 and 1929 the cost of highways and waterways increased 160 per cent, while that of education had increased only 120 per cent, both expenditures being given in terms of the dollar in 1915. Meantime the federal cost of highways had increased 1,100 per cent, while the federal cost of education had increased only 90 per cent. On needed retrenchment in public services, the survey of social trends concluded:

The immediate effects produced by depression can scarcely be taken as adequate guides to long-time tendencies. Reductions in governmental costs do not necessarily imply widespread abandonment of established activities.

The roads to economy are many. Governmental organization, whether in national, state, or local jurisdiction, still falls short of the standards of efficiency which in principle are generally accepted. Reorganization of conflicting and overlapping agencies and governments, improved techniques of overhead management, adjustment of salary scales to changes in living costs—these offer opportunities for saving which cannot be overlooked. If, however, activities have been undertaken which under changed conditions meet no active public demand, their disappearance will not be long delayed.

But the critics continued to point to the menace of the cost of schools. Some of them, of course, admitted the necessity of education, but they also continued to charge extravagance for so-called fads in education. The editor of the *Saturday Evening Post,* writing in that publication on January 14, 1933, said:

It is to our credit that our realization of the benefits of learning is practically universal, and that we do not willingly deny our children anything we believe to be for their good. So strong is this tradition that "education" has become a vertable abracadabra, a magic word, a word with which to conjure incredible sums out of the pockets of the people. Woe unto the politicians or legislatures that would not unlock their treasuries to the word "education."...

Too long have we been at the mercy of the supereducators and their craze for novelties. If they were idle or dishonest or incompetent, we should know how to cope with them; but they are none of these. They may swamp their employers with added taxes, but they are as honest as the day is long, and they fight for their convictions with the dauntless spirit of Christian martyrs who would face the lions of Nero in the arena rather than buy their lives by dropping a pinch of incense upon the altar of Diana.

As 1933-34 advanced, official reports continued to reveal the deepening crisis in education. More than at any time during the depression were the quality and the existence of the schools at stake in many communities in the United States, according to a statement by Commissioner George F. Zook of the United States Office of Education: "We find ourselves in the grip of a social difficulty from which we shall extricate ourselves only with the greatest effort and pain." The closing of schools because of the lack of funds had deprived 100 thousand additional children of educational opportunity in the autumn of 1933. Altogether about 2.28 million children of school age were not in school. About 2 thousand rural schools in twenty-four states had failed to open, although few if any city public schools had been closed. Many private and parochial schools were closing, and at least sixteen institutions of higher education had been discontinued since 1932. In some communities so-called free public schools had been forced to charge tuition and to admit only those children whose parents could pay the fees. One fourth of the cities had shortened their school terms; more than seven hundred rural schools were expected to run not more than three months during the year. The terms in practically every great American city were one to two months shorter than they had been seventy-five years before. These conditions were reported to be in sharp contrast to conditions in European countries, and the problem in the United States was becoming more serious every day. One out of every four teachers was receiving less than $750 a year, and it appeared that soon one out of every three would receive less than that amount; about 40 thousand rural teachers received less than $450 each in 1933-34. One out of every thirteen Negro teachers was receiving $25 per month or less.

Reports from 700 typical cities of the country showed that many if not most of them had reduced or eliminated art instruction, music instruction, physical education, home economics, industrial art, and health services. About 200 thousand certificated public school teachers were unemployed; thousands of teachers had been dismissed from private schools and colleges. Few of the graduates of teacher-training schools were able to find positions. About 26 thousand teachers would have been needed to operate the city schools on the 1930 basis, and 76 thousand teachers would have been needed in the country as a whole, on the 1930 basis, for the multitudes of children who were not in school. About 7.28 thousand more children were enrolled in the high schools of the country in 1932 than in 1930, although about 115 thousand fewer children were in the elementary schools, the first decrease in the history of the country. The abolition of child labor in industry under the National Recovery Act had placed about 100 thousand children in the high schools. The schools of the United States in the year 1933-34 were trying to give instruction to pupils who had increased by more than a million since 1930, and on funds decreased by about $368 million. The depression had crushed real estate values and in turn crushed education. Tax delinquencies, lower assessments, mortgage problems, tax limitations, school funds in closed banks, differences in wealth—these were some of the conditions facing education four years after the depression began.

Under these conditions, a renewed interest in the federal financing of education was evident. Conferences on the emergency were held in many parts of the country, and the educators urged a national plan. President Hoover had called a meeting of leaders in Washington toward the end of 1932. Early in 1933 an important conference was held at Columbia University, and later that year the National Conference on the Financing of Education met at that institution under the auspices of the Joint Commission on the Emergency in Education of the Department of Superintendence and the National Education Association. At that conference William F. Russell, dean of Teachers College, presented a significant paper on the federal financing of education, in which he made a plea for substantial federal support as a part of the recovery program, asserting that "the federal government should make grants at once for this purpose in almost any form; and that looking forward to more normal times, studies should be undertaken to determine the irregularities that exist from state to state and the methods necessary to surmount them." This view was shared by numerous other leaders throughout the country, and as the new year of 1934 opened, the way toward federal aid of education seemed brighter than at any other time in the history of the country; but by mid-twentieth century it had not yet been achieved.

Impressive during these lean years was the loyalty of the teachers and other educational workers. Reports from all over the country showed that they were ready and willing to do their full part. While the minds of the American people were in a ferment under conditions which thoughtful men and women had said, a few years before, could never be, when confidence had weakened in the political, economic, financial, and even educational leadership of the country, the teachers patiently carried on. Thousands of them went unpaid, were unable to meet payments on life insurance or on their homes, and were forced to borrow to the limit on insurance policies and in some cases from loan sharks. Occasionally, militant action appeared among them, such as that of the Chicago teachers who were patient no longer and who refused to be distracted or entertained by the picturesque profanity of a leading citizen of Chicago, where finances had been notoriously muddled. Hunger and destitution menaced the homes of thousands of its teachers and other school employees, some of whom were not paid for many months by America's second largest city that boasted a $20 million opera house, a $100 million lake-front park, and a modernistic "Century of Progress," but could not pay the men and women who instructed their children. The plight of the teachers in Chicago received much publicity, but conditions there must have differed only in extent from those in many other places in the country. Equally desperate and perhaps more hopeless conditions appeared in the rural schools throughout the southern states and in many sections of the Middle West.

But while public education was threatened with something little short of a complete breakdown in vast areas of the United States, with demands for further retrenchment from taxpayers' committees, citizens' commissions, bankers, power interests, merchants' associations, and real estate groups, the teachers generally preferred "to make personal sacrifices rather than have the children denied their educational birthright." They shared manfully in such sacrifices, and in doing so again earned their right to demand that the public be mindful of those whose well-being should be its first concern—the children. The teachers knew that the agonizing human calamity that faced American life brought them fresh responsibilities which could not be evaded; that the way out of the hysteria was through not less but more real education, the most important of all public services; that there was the need for economy—and economy they approved so long as it did not vitally affect the welfare of the children. But they also knew that the feverish agitation and demand for economy could easily be turned into campaigns whose catchwords would cripple the schools, and that an emergency, whether due to war, pestilence, flood, famine, or economic disturbances, was an additional reason for maintaining the educational work in unimpaired vitality. American teachers again demonstrated during the depression that they were among the least self-seeking groups of American citizens—that seldom was money-mindedness dominant among them. The teachers set good examples for many other citizens whose resources and opportunities were larger, and proclaimed sympathy and fellowship with the ideal of American education, probably more clearly than any other group of people. During the distress that followed 1929 they retained their belief that the most substantial possessions are not land and goods, which are always within the reach of depressions and bankruptcies and moths and rust. Faith in childhood, on the other hand, was to them an imperishable and indestructible possession that remains with human beings after they have been robbed or stripped of those possessions that are unable to defy adversities or to outlive calamities.

The crisis which education confronted in the early 1930's led to the question of the behavior of the American people toward education during other economic depressions. Studies disclosed that during the past century the United States had faced a dozen or more well-marked economic crises, each accompanied by conditions of lowered production, shrinkage in capital, bankruptcies, falling prices, reduced earnings, wage cuts, unemployment, unrest, and distress. But during these depressions education was pointed to as the foundation of public well-being and public well-doing, and it was cherished as the source of American life. Faith in the regenerative powers of education seemed to have remained robust during those distressing times.

School Gains Despite Depressions.—In *Public-School Support in the United States during Periods of Economic Depression*,[8] Royce S. Pitkin showed that very large gains were made in the maintenance of public educational facilities during and following other economic crises in the United States, that the American people made substantial increases in public support, and that those increases more than kept pace with the increase in school attendance. Information examined for several states revealed that schools, rather than other functions of government, were usually favored during economic crises, that wherever reductions were widely made in public expenditures, reductions for education were less than for general governmental purposes, and that in some states public school support actually increased, while the costs of other public services decreased. The study also showed that considerable progress was made in educational legislation during years of depression.

Not a single serious depression was studied that did not have its accompaniment of better laws relating to the schools. Normal schools have been established in many states under such conditions; requirements for certification have been raised; better compulsory-education laws have been enacted; provision has been made for the education of the physically and mentally handicapped; entire state systems of schools have been reorganized; and better schemes of supervision have been put into operation.

Among the various phases of legislative activity relating to education during the lean years, perhaps the most noteworthy is that relating to financial support. As one reads of the attempts, made during successive periods of diminished income, to provide the funds necessary to carry on the type of school system that the American people seemed to desire, one sees a tendency to constantly enlarge the unit of support as a means of insuring a more equitable distribution of the burden. The activity of the educational leaders of the early years of the last century in the field of finance reminds us that the movement to equalize the tax burden and to provide equal educational opportunity is not a recent one. Different methods of distributing the state's funds for education have been tried under the stimulus of hard times. New sources of revenue have been found at times when the burdens of the owners of real estate have made them more vocal than usual. In fact, the whole range of educational finance has been the subject of increased attention during the

[8] Brattleboro, Vermont, 1933.

recurring periods of depression with which the people of America have been afflicted.

Other developments during these periods have been those relating to the upward extension of the public school, such as the growth of the high school and the state university. The curriculum has been widened, school libraries have been provided, and textbooks made free during depression years. Plans for the retirement and pensioning of teachers have been establishd.

Why the American people behaved toward their schools in the depression that came after 1929 in a manner so different from that in which they had behaved in other economic crises is not easily ascertained. The excuses, as already noted, were depression, debts, and deficits. But it may not have been unlikely that their strange behavior was due in part to their disillusionment with the unfulfilled promises of American education. Throughout many decades before the gigantic economic dislocation of 1929, many claims, some of them perhaps extravagant, had been made for the wonder-working powers of public education, and probably most Americans had come to depend too much on schooling as the sovereign solvent of all their ills and inadequacies, and all their economic, social, moral, and spiritual problems. When the heavy economic blow fell, it was not unnatural for those who had placed so much faith in schooling to turn savagely on their own handiwork.

What the schoolmen had to say about educational and other issues during the first half of the twentieth century is discussed in the next Chapter.

SOME QUESTIONS AND EXERCISES FOR STUDENTS

1. In your study of the effects of war upon education, what effects do you find in the American Revolutionary War? In the Civil War? In the Spanish-American War?

2. Indicate why, in more recent times, war has come to have such heavy impact on education, especially in those countries involved in military struggles.

3. Examine and report on the conclusions Kandel drew from his study of the impact of the Second World War on education in the United States.

4. Compare or contrast the demonstrable educational effects of the First World War with those of the Second World War.

5. What new emphases in education in the United States came to be made as a result of the two world wars? (I.e., literary, health and physical education, vocational training, humanities.)

6. Exactly what effects did the economic depression in the 1930's have on education in your state? On finances for schools, educational legislation, school terms, education of teachers?

7. What is the evidence that the public schools of the United States may have been wasteful during the years of prosperity prior to 1929?

8. What is the evidence that the depression years stimulated interest in federal aid to education? Why had not such aid been provided by mid-twentieth century?

9. Study the education page of the *New York Times* (Sunday) during the 1930's for information on conditions and trends in education during that decade. Make a similar study of the education section in *Time*.

10. What is the evidence, if any, that the communities which had provided good schools before the depression suffered least educationally during the depression?

11. Compare or contrast the commencement speeches and sermons in the depression years with those in the fair-weather days in the 1920's. With those at mid-twentieth century.

12. How, if at all, did the huge expenditures for national defense around mid-century affect public educational expenditures in your state?

13. In what way or ways did the federal government assist education in your state during the depression years?

14. Examine Pitkin's study of education in other depressions and make a similar study for your state during the economic crises that he studied.

15. What is the basis of the criticisms of religious leaders, that lack of religious instruction was a major deficiency of American education in recent decades?

16. Examine the study by Foster, and make a similar study of the leading newspapers in your state for the period which he studied or for some other suitable period. Examine the religious press of your state to see what educational issues it discussed for the same or other period or periods.

SOME SUGGESTED REFERENCES AND READING

ALLEN, HOLLIS P. *The Federal Government and Education.* New York: McGraw-Hill Book Co., 1950.

    The original and complete study of education for the Hoover Commission Task Force on Public Welfare, and very useful on federal educational activities.

AMERICAN COUNCIL ON EDUCATION. *Organizing Higher Education for National Defense.* Washington, D. C.: The Council, 1941.

Shows that the higher educational institutions desired and sought in every way to render the greatest possible service to the immediate needs of the defense program.

AMERICAN COUNCIL ON EDUCATION. *Higher Education and the War.* Washington, D. C.: The Council, 1942.
Contains much useful information that throws light on some subjects discussed in this Chapter.

BARCK, OSCAR T., JR., and BLAKE, NELSON M. *Since 1900: A History of the United States in Our Times.* New York: The Macmillan Co., 1947.
Chaps. viii, "From Peace to War," xxvi, "Preparing for Total War," xxix, "Problems of Peace and World Organization," and xxx, "Social Trends During Peace and War," greatly supplement the materials in this Chapter.

BROWN, FRANCIS J. *Educational Opportunities for Veterans.* Washington, D. C.: Public Affairs Press, 1946.
Tells the story of the legislation on the G. I. Bill of Rights and the educational opportunities which that act provided for veterans.

EVENDEN, EDWARD S. *Teacher Education in a Democracy at War.* Washington, D. C.: American Council on Education, 1942.
Prepared for the Commission on Teacher Education, this little volume discusses the implications of war for the education of teachers, points out lessons from the First World War, and shows "our tragic failures during the war of 1917-18 to profit from either our own experiences or those of our allies."

FAULKNER, H. U. *American Political and Social History.* New York: Appleton-Century-Crofts, Inc., 1943.
Chaps. xxxvi, "The World War," xxxviii, "Life in the Postwar Decade," and xlii, "America Goes to War," throw light on some of the topics discussed in this Chapter.

FOSTER, CHARLES R., JR. *Editorial Treatment of Education in the American Press.* Cambridge: Harvard University Press, 1938.
Shows that of the 9,000 editorials in twenty-five leading newspapers between 1930 and 1935, about 44 per cent were favorable to, 32 per cent neutral on, and 23 per cent adversely critical of American education.

KANDEL, I. L. *The Impact of the War Upon American Education.* Chapel Hill: The University of North Carolina Press, 1948.
An excellent study by a careful scholar who examines the educational deficiencies disclosed by the Second World War and shows that higher education seemed to lack "a sense of direction."

KNIGHT, EDGAR W. "The Scourge of the Schools." *Outlook and Independent,* CLIX (December 2, 1931), pp. 430-31, 448.
Shows that legislative action in some states set the schools back many years and lowered the morale of their teachers and managers.

KNIGHT, EDGAR W., and HALL, CLIFTON L. *Readings in American Educational History.* New York: Appleton-Century-Crofts, Inc., 1951.
Chaps. ix, x, and xi contain original materials that bear on some of the topics discussed in this Chapter.

LANGDON, EUNICE. "The Teacher and the Depression." *Nation,* CXXXVII (August 16, 1933), pp. 182-85.
Discusses the tragic effects of the economic depression that began in 1929 on the teachers in the schools of the United States.

METZENBAUM, JAMES. "The School Crisis and What Can Be Done About It." *Forum,* LXXXIX (June, 1933), pp. 365-69.

Reports that debts and extravagance were eating the heart out of public school funds.

PARRISH, WAYNE W. "The Plight of Our School System." *Literary Digest,* CXVI (September, 1933), p. 32.

Shows that many states lost gains made slowly over a period of ten or more years, and summarizes data on closed schools, shortened terms, reductions in salaries, and other dismal educational conditions.

PITKIN, ROYCE S. *Public School Support in the United States During Periods of Economic Depression.* Brattleboro, Vermont, 1933.

Compares public behavior toward education during depressions in 1837, 1857, the 1870's, 1893, 1907, and 1921, and shows that the American people passed through those economic dislocations without crippling the schools, but by aiding them.

TODD, L. P. *Wartime Relations of the Federal Government and the Public Schools, 1917-1918.* New York: Teachers College, Columbia University, 1945.

Shows, among other things, that the wartime experiences revealed a lack of agreement on the proper function of education in American democracy; that war-inspired educational campaigns were of doubtful value; and that some of those efforts were marked by emotionalism.

WICKER, R. W. "Racketeering on Parnassus." *North American Review,* CCXXXV (June, 1933), pp. 529-36.

Shows that education in the United States during the great depression was "on the spot," and that the intelligent financing of the public schools had broken down.

Chapter 9

WHAT THE SCHOOL MEN SAID

PREVIEW OF THE CHAPTER

The apparently unfailing principle in social history that education of whatever period or place reflects the conditions in which it exists finds illustration in the addresses and resolutions of the National Education Association. . . . Official pronouncements of the NEA during the first half of the twentieth century reflected the changing moods in education in this country during that period. . . . Throughout those years, this immense educational organization seemed generally to favor the things they would be expected to favor and to oppose those they would be expected to oppose. But the motto suggested in 1900 for these educational workers, "In essentials, unity; in nonessentials, liberty," enabled them to disagree on the issue of "technical tests" in the early part of the century and on that of "progressive" as opposed to "essentialist" education in the 1930's, and mildly now and then on other issues. . . . Throughout these fifty years, the NEA consistently resolved, however, on the high purpose of the common school in the United States, on the great importance of improving the qualifications of teachers and the conditions of their teaching, on federal aid to education, on the strengthening of the Office of Education in Washington, for the representation of education in the President's cabinet, the improvement of the physical surroundings of the schools, on suitable ethical instruction, recreational facilities, and on other issues. Now and then the association applauded the efforts of those institutions for higher education that mildly and perhaps piously undertook "to remove the taint of professionalism that has crept into student sports," and it severely condemned the use of alcohol and narcotics. . . . The association took note of the changing conditions that demanded training for commerce and the industries as well as for the professions, endorsed democracy in educational administration, favored the exclusion of secret societies from the schools, and urged more attention to physical and health education. . . . Always the NEA reaffirmed its faith in public schools, "owned and controlled by the people," and now and then it looked askance at any efforts to get public aid for private and parochial elementary and secondary schools, an issue that was becoming more and more acute at mid-century. . . . As the First World War approached, the NEA recognized that "the first duty of the hour is wholehearted national loyalty," and it expressed its supreme wish to give the fullest service "for the sacred cause of our country and our allies, in defense of democracy and righteousness," urged the teaching of patriotism in the schools, endorsed the Student Army Training Corps, the Americanization of un-American elements in the population, and the removal of illiteracy. . . . The NEA found itself in hearty accord with the decision of the Supreme Court of the United States, affirming the validity of the Eighteenth Amendment to the Constitution; it urged English as the language of instruction in the schools; it advocated cooperation in safeguarding American youth "from cigarette smoking and kindred vices"; and it sought an effective method for ridding the schools of inefficient teachers; it agreed with the American Legion that thoroughgoing instruction in American history and civics should be provided; it urged more attention to individual differences among children; it favored a national child labor amendment; recommended the widest observance of American Education Week; applauded the Parent-Teachers' Association as one of the greatest educational movements of the time; and urged the continuous study of the curriculum and more attention to rural education. . . . The NEA endorsed the work of philanthropic foundations as a means for developing and promoting the educational interests of the country; suffrage for women; vocational guidance; it viewed the war in Europe in 1915 "as a tragedy without parallel in history," and approved the American School Peace League and the observance of Peace Day; approved the League of Nations; recognized the distinction between the professional administration of schools and lay boards of education elected by the people; warned against federal interference in and control of education; endorsed the implanting of a feeling of brotherhood with all mankind so as "to obliterate the misunderstandings that breed war"; urged the teaching of respect for law and order "as a chief purpose of education"; endorsed the proposed nation-wide observance of the 200th anniversary of the birth of George Washington to be held in 1932, and preparation for the celebration of the Horace Mann Centennial in 1937; recommended that the Pact of Paris be taught in the school, and that international Goodwill Day be appropriately observed; vigorously opposed retrenchment in education; commended President Franklin D. Roosevelt for creating the National Youth Administration and establishing the Civilian Conservation Corps; commended and asked support for the Future Teachers of America; urged the promotion of intercultural relations and the teaching of the work of the United Nations as a part of civics; deplored strikes among teachers; called for support of the World Organization of the Teaching Profession; urged UNESCO to expand its educational activities, and declared that a program of education and re-education should be given high priority in the occupied areas of Germany, Austria, and Japan; it vigorously opposed Communists as teachers in the public schools of the United States.

Education Reflects Social and Economic Conditions.—An apparently unfailing principle in educational and social history is that education of whatever time or place is a reflection of the life in which it exists, of the conditions about it. Educational theories and practices, like other human activities, seem to be subject to the pressures and demands of public opinion, more often, perhaps, than such theories and practices are molders of public opinion; more often than not education seems to follow rather than to lead. This principle of reflection is abundantly illustrated in the resolutions of the National Education Association,[1] which during the first half of the present century, as in other years, apparently reflected the changing moods of the times.

At its meeting in Charleston, South Carolina, in 1900, the Association applauded the common school as "the highest hope of the nation" in the development of character, in the training of intelligence, and in the diffusion of information, and suggested as a safe motto: "In essentials, unity; in nonessentials, liberty; in all things, charity." But this benign pedagogical principle, if accepted, was not to remain fully in practical application throughout all the next fifty years. After the organization of the Progressive Education Association in 1918, and its energetic and vocal activities for two decades or more, full agreement on controversial issues was not always had, especially after the Progressives and the Essentialists declared a cold pedagogical war. The issue between the two groups was always sprightly and often amusing, if never clearly defined, and it provoked wide discussion and now and then pious recriminations. The Essentialists called the Progressives "softies," and the Progressives called the Essentialists "fogies." Each side illustrated the truth of George Bernard Shaw's pithy remark that most people are down on what they are not up on, or perhaps Cicero's penetrating observation that "it seems an unaccountable thing how one soothsayer can meet an-

---

[1] This organization had been formed in Philadelphia in 1857 as the National Teachers' Association, and from that date to 1870 it bore that name. During those years the organization never had more than two hundred members, and until 1866 women were not given the privilege of active membership. At the meeting in Cleveland in 1870, the name was changed to The National Educational Association by the union of the American Normal School Association, which had been organized in 1858, and the National Association of School Superintendents, which had been organized in 1865. In 1906 The National Education Association of the United States was chartered by Congress, and in 1917 it took up headquarters in Washington, D. C. Membership grew from 43 in 1857 to 170 in 1870, to 2.7 thousand in 1884, to about 7 thousand in 1894, dropped to 4.5 thousand in 1904, rose to 7 thousand in 1914, to 138 thousand in 1924, to 154 thousand in 1934, and to 271 thousand in 1944. In 1950 the organization had a membership of 437.8 thousand, and in May of 1951 the membership was 465.2 thousand, about 46 per cent of the teachers in the United States.

other without smiling." The battle raged; and while the conflicting advice of those who sat in the seats of the pedagogical mighty may have brought some confusion to many of the teachers and managers of the schools in the Middletowns of the United States, it must have brought a bit of relief also. It served to recall the report by an attaché in the Department of State in Washington of a conference between Secretary John Hay and the Chinese Minister Wu Ting Fang over the imbroglio caused by the Boxers in China. Reporters for the press were eager to learn the outcome of the conference, and the clever attaché finally informed them that "Mr. Hay was a little hazy and Mr. Wu a trifle woozy."

The controversy between the Essentialists and the Progressives so gained in heat, if not light, that in 1938 it seemed worthy of the attention of the public opinion statistician, Dr. George Gallup, and his American Institute of Public Opinion. That organization asked a spokesman of each side to define the real point or points at issue. The spokesmen obliged, but their replies, instead of being declaratory, were cautiously couched in the form of questions that were hardly any better answered in 1950 than these had been in 1938. William C. Bagley of Teachers College, Columbia University, speaking for the Essentialists, asked: "Should our public schools prepare boys and girls for adult responsibilities through systematic training in such subjects as reading, writing, arithmetic, history, and English, requiring mastery of such subjects, and, when necessary, stressing discipline and obedience, with informal learning recognized but regarded as supplementary rather than central?"

William H. Kilpatrick of the same institution, speaking for the Progressives, asked: "Should our schools make central the informal learning of experience and activity work, placing much less stress on formal, systematic assignments, discipline, and obedience, and instead seeking to develop pupil initiative, discipline, and responsibility as well as mastery of basic subjects, by encouraging pupils to show initiative and develop responsibility, with teachers, while in control, serving primarily as guides?"

At the meeting of the American Association of School Administrators in 1938, there were some arguments over the issues of the Progressives and the Essentialists. The quarrel also broke out in New York City where the officials of the school system felt called upon to defend the activity programs that had begun there a few years before as a six-year experiment with about 50 thousand children. Also, the alumni of Lincoln School of Teachers College, Columbia University, which had been on a progressive basis since its establishment about two decades earlier, were given a chance to say what they thought of its method. As in most disputes over educational matters, opinion on the controversy was divided. Some of the alumni said "Yes" and some said "No" to the question: "Did the progressive methods of the school help you then or later?" Opponents of the progressive experiment in the schools of New York City charged "atheism" and "communism." Advocates of the experiment replied "Nonsense."

Changing Moods in Education.—At its meeting in 1900, the National Education Association resolved that the purpose of the common school in this country was to attract and to instruct the rich as well as to educate the poor. Within the walls of the common school "American citizens are made, and no person can safely be excluded from its benefits." It also resolved that the extension of the American common school system to Cuba, Puerto Rico, and the Philippines was an imperative necessity, so that knowledge could be generally spread in those outlying territories, and that the "foundations of social order and effective local self-government may be laid in popular intelligence and morality." It urged the Congress to provide for the reorganization of the United States Bureau of Education "upon broader lines"; viewed with satisfaction the rapid extension of provision for more nearly adequate secondary and higher education as well as for technical, industrial, and commercial education; and resolved that every safeguard should be thrown around the profession of teaching and its proper compensation. It also noted that the effectiveness of a public school system was to be judged by the character and the intellectual power of the pupils and "not by their ability to meet a series of technical tests. The place of the formal examination in education is distinctly subordinate to that of teaching." The Association also renewed its pledge to carry on the work of education in a spirit "which shall be not only nonsectarian and nonpolitical" but in the ideals of national life and character.

The resolution on "technical tests" recalls another fight among the educators. Three years earlier Dr. Joseph M. Rice had published in the *Forum* his findings on the spelling ability of 33 thousand school children which revealed, among other things, that children who had spent thirty minutes a day for eight years on spelling did not spell any better than children who had spent only half that time on the subject. These findings did not meet with the hearty approval of the educators of this country. They and the education press denounced as "foolish, reprehensible, and from every point of view indefensible" the effort to discover anything about the value of the teaching of spelling by finding out whether or not children who had studied the subject could spell. The critics of the findings of Dr. Rice argued that the object of spelling was not to teach children how to spell but to develop their minds. His findings in spelling and other investigations were received with derision by the Department of Superintendence of the National Education Association. At its meeting in 1912, that body of educational leaders voted, after a heated discussion and by a small majority, against the measurement movement. But two years later a Committee on Tests and Standards made a favorable report to the organization which was adopted by a majority vote.

Consistency of the NEA's Position.—In 1901, at the meeting in Detroit, the Association declared that the progress and the happiness of a people existed in direct ratio to the universality of education. "A free people must be developed by free schools." Provision for the universal education of American youth was pronounced "the duty of every state in the union, and residents of territories under the direct control of the national government, including the Indian territory, Alaska, and the new possessions," must receive the benefits of free education at the hands of the government. The work of William T. Harris and of the United States Bureau of Education was applauded for "invaluable service to the cause of education throughout the United States." The Association reiterated its statement that the public school should be the center of the educational life of the community in which it was located, and especially in rural districts. Public libraries for the use of everybody in such communities were needed to promote educational extension courses which would draw both the young and the old. It was the view of the Association that if the public school could be freed from the ravenous influence of partisan politics and left untouched "by the narrowness of rigid sectarianism," it could become the real center of a broader intellectual life in the community. Emphasis was also placed by resolution on the teaching in the elementary schools of subjects that would have a bearing upon the ethical, physical, and aesthetic nature of the child, as well as upon his purely intellectual nature. "Sober, industrious, intelligent, honest, cultured citizenship should be the result of public school training in the United States." But it was declared that the public school system would not be wholly free until every grade from the kindergarten up to and including the university should be opened "to every boy and girl of our country." The public school system of the state should be a unit from bottom to top, and private institutions were admonished to work in harmony with the ideals of public education, so far as their special purposes would permit them to do so. Educational legislation, said the educators, should not wait for public sentiment, but should lead public sentiment when necessary. They applauded the liberality of men of wealth in making donations to educational institutions; affirmed the principle that children had the same right to protection by law from ignorance as well as from abuse, neglect, and hunger, cordially approved those states that had enacted compulsory education laws, and heartily recommended supervision, which was lacking in most rural communities. It also strongly recommended the consolidation of rural schools and the transportation of pupils at public expense, and urged larger support and control of teacher-education institutions. "Normal schools free to persons preparing to teach are an absolute necessity in a perfected system of education." No one should have charge of a school who had not been previously prepared for teaching, and there should be a limit to the time one could serve "as an apprentice in the vocation of teaching," a perspective that had not been fully gained in every school when the half century came to a close. It was also the belief of the Association that the standards of school architecture should be improved for proper seating, heating, lighting, ventilation, and the ornamentation of school buildings. These standards should be as definite as those for teaching, the educators said.

In 1902, at Minneapolis, the Association emphasized the high importance of increasing and improving the qualifications of teachers and expressed the hope that soon there would be a standard for them as definite "as is now fixed by the best schools in the country for the training of physicians and lawyers," whose standards were to be markedly raised during the next half century. The Association also made a plea for unity of effort in the complete education of the child, "constantly keeping in mind that the present division of instruction into elementary, secondary, and higher is for administrative purposes only"; it again urged the consolidation of rural schools and public and free transportation of pupils; more attention of all local educational authorities to make proper adaptation of courses of study to the needs and abilities of the pupils; the employment of teachers on merit only and without political considerations; improvement in the construction of schoolhouses and in lighting, heating, seating, and ventilation, hygiene, and sanitation; approved the organization of summer schools for teachers; applauded men and women of wealth who were aiding education, and especially Andrew Carnegie's gift of $10 million for the Carnegie Institution in Washington, which by 1949 had expended $40 million and had assets of $59 million. The Association praised "the heroic work" for public education in the southern states where the Conference for Education in the South had been organized in 1897 and which had for many years conducted energetic campaigns to arouse the people to the need for better educational facilities and to a willingness to provide them. The Association also noted "that familiarity with the English Bible is rapidly decreasing among the pupils in our schools," and hoped for a change in public sentiment that would permit and encourage its reading, but "not in the interest of sectarian instruction."

The Association again urged the Congress to organize and strengthen the United States Office of Education on broader lines because of the increased responsibilities placed on it by the necessity for the reorganization and administration of public school systems in the recently added territory of the United States; and it reiterated its pronouncements that the common schools of the country were for the education of all the people and were the only barrier against "class distinctions which have no place on American soil." At that time, and for some years later, private secondary schools were flourishing in many parts of the country, and in some communities public high schools had not yet come into their own.

Forty-six years later, Russell Lynes asked in *Harper's Magazine* [2] "Can the Private Schools Survive?" and answered that there was nothing wrong with their basic aims and ideals but that "profound changes in society" made it necessary for the private schools "to use their independence not merely as a barricade against the pressures they mistrust but as a weapon in the service of the entire community." In the early part of 1950, Charles Seymour, president of Yale University, said that the state universities and their sensitivity to the needs of the communities of which they were vital parts provided "a challenging example of service for the privately endowed universities" which had their "own peculiar values, the disappearance of which would be the nation's loss. We must be careful to put them to the nation's service. . . . If we prove our worth, our freedom will not disappear. The price of freedom is service." At the same time, A. Hollis Edens, president of Duke University, was saying: "It would be a sad day in the United States if private education were squeezed out of business. The United States probably has more

[2] January, 1948.

privately endowed universities than it will be able to preserve. Some of them will die. It is our duty to see a sufficient number maintained to do the job ahead." [3]

In Boston, in 1903, the Association pointed out that teaching would not be a suitably attractive and permanent career until teachers were properly paid and assured of undisturbed tenure during efficiency and good behavior; said that the strength of public education in this country lay in the regard of the people whom it served and in their willingness to sacrifice for it; that the highest ethical standards of conduct and of speech of teachers should be insisted upon, and a code of professional conduct clearly understood and rigorously enforced by public opinion; that school boards and school grounds should be arranged so as to serve as effective agencies for educating not only the children but the people as a whole "in the matters of taste"; and declared that it was the duty of the school to lay the foundations of character in the young so that they would have "reverence for the majesty of the law."

At the meeting in St. Louis in 1904, the Association again urged the preservation of the United States Bureau of Education in integrity and dignity; said that inadequate compensation for educational work was driving many people from the schools and preventing many promising young people from entering the profession; urged educational supervision in every school; emphasized the necessity for the development of public high schools and for improving the rural schools, the merit system in determining the employment and retention of teachers, and said that women of equal character and efficiency and successful experience were equally entitled with men "to the honors and emoluments of the profession," and also advocated the enactment and rigid enforcement of proper laws relating to child labor.

At Asbury Park in 1905, the Association pointed to the establishment of rural high schools as one of the most gratifying evidences of educational progress in this country, urged that industrial education include agricultural as well as manual training, and recommended the use of urban school buildings for free vocational and evening schools. It asserted that the ultimate purpose of public education was to teach children how to live righteously, healthily, and

[3] For a discussion of the small private college at about the turn of the century, see: "The Small College: Its Work in the Past," by William O. Thompson, president of Ohio State University, and "The Small College: Its Prospects," by William Rainey Harper, president of the University of Chicago, in the *Journal of Proceedings and Addresses of the National Educational Association*, July, 1900, pp. 61-87, and referred to in Chapter 4.

happily. Every school should inculcate "the love of truth, justice, purity, and beauty through the study of biography, history, ethics, natural history, music, drawing, and manual arts." It also recorded its approval "of the increased appreciation among educators of the fact that the building of character is the real aim of the school."

At the same time, the Association congratulated those schools and colleges that were making efforts "to remove the taint of professionalism that has crept into student sports," but professionalism in athletics in the schools and colleges was to increase greatly during the years ahead. A study of inaugural addresses and other speeches and papers by college presidents disclosed that these educators had about as much (or even more) to say about intercollegiate football as about any other subject in education during the first four decades of the twentieth century.[4] Charles W. Eliot had not discussed the subject in his inaugural address as president of Harvard in 1869, but in 1908 he wrote: "The exaggeration of athletic sports in schools and colleges remains a crying evil, and there are no clear signs that any effectual remedy is taking effect. . . ." The issue was to become more and more critical; and in 1932 Henry S. Pritchett, a former president of the Carnegie Foundation for the Advancement of Teaching, proposed the substitution of intercollegiate horse racing for intercollegiate football. The game had become so popular and was so widely discussed that it was later described as "dementia Americana."

In 1905 the Association observed with great satisfaction the tendency of cities and towns to replace large with small school boards to determine general educational policies, but to entrust all executive functions "to salaried experts." It also stated that local taxation supplemented by state taxation was the best means for public school support; and observed that a free democracy could not long continue without state-supported schools administered by representatives chosen by and responsible to the people, an observation Thomas Jefferson had made a century and a quarter earlier.

In 1907 at Los Angeles (there was no meeting in 1906), the Association noted with approval that the qualifications of teachers were increasing annually, and that higher standards would logically lead to higher salaries. It heartily approved of efforts then being made to determine the proper place of industrial education in the schools, and of the use of urban school buildings for vocational and evening schools and lecture courses for those adults and children who had been obliged to leave the day schools prematurely. Many

[4] Edgar W. Knight, *What College Presidents Say* (Chapel Hill: University of North Carolina Press, 1940).

of the resolutions of earlier years were repeated, and in addition, the Association recognized that "a present demand for separate higher instruction for women is greater than existing colleges for women can supply," although the Association was not seeking to determine the merits of coeducation as against the separation of the sexes in institutions for higher education. It also deplored secret societies, fraternities, and sororities in the schools, and urged educational authorities to abolish them. It regretted "the purely theoretical work which still characterizes much of our so-called training of teachers." Significant also was the resolution of the Association that year "that the forces of this world should be organized and operated in the interest of peace and not of war."

At the meeting in Cleveland in 1908, the Association commended the establishment of trade schools, industrial schools, and evening continuation schools in urban communities, in the interest of the commercial and industrial welfare of the country, and recommended the subordination of highly diversified and overburdened courses of study in the grades "to a thorough drill in essential subjects." The next four decades were to witness, however, more and more subjects added to the courses of study not only in the elementary schools but also in the secondary schools and colleges and universities, and energetic and sometimes feverish activities in the construction and reconstruction of the curriculum at all levels.

Indefiniteness of and confusion in aims was to become a conspicuous characteristic of American education before the first half of the twentieth century had passed into history. Although educational aims had been few and rather specific in 1900, by 1935 more than 1500 social aims of English, more than 300 aims of arithmetic in the first six grades, and more than 800 generalized aims of the social studies had been stated in courses of study and in special studies. The Association also pointed to the importance of giving consideration to the individuality of pupils so that they could be instructed in the light of their limitations and capacities, reflecting the influence of scientific studies on individual differences and other products from the laboratories of the psychologists. It urged closer attention to the training of children in morals and in business and professional ethics so that the coming generation of men of affairs would have "a well-developed abhorrence of unfair dealing and discrimination." The state should provide all children with the rudiments of an education.

At the meeting in Denver in 1909, the Association pointed to the changed conditions of the twentieth century that demanded schools for the training of youth for commerce and the industries as well as for the professions, but said that the purpose of free common schools must continue to be chiefly culture for the individual "and the transmission to posterity of the results of the investigations and deliberations of the past." It came out strongly for democracy in the administration of education, the importance of expert supervision, of better and more numerous high schools, of more schools for the education of teachers and a merit system for their appointment and promotion. All secret organizations of whatever sort should be excluded from the social life of the schools, and more attention should be given to the promotion of physical and health education through the diffusion of scientific information. School buildings and all school equipment should be more widely used for community interests and social betterment, and rural school districts should be consolidated. The work of the philanthropic foundations was heartily endorsed as means for developing and promoting the educational interests of the country.

In Boston in 1910 the Association reaffirmed its faith in the public schools "owned and controlled by the people." The time had arrived, it said, for the establishment of an international council of education; it complained of the abuses of the labor of children in industry, and reattested its declaration in connection with the Hague Conference that teachers of this country and of all nations must cooperate in "this commanding movement of our time for the world's peace." It also asserted its unalterable opposition to any division of public school funds among private or sectarian schools, and declared "that any appropriation from the federal or state treasuries in support of private educational institutions is in direct contravention of the fundamental principles upon which our system of American public school education has been founded." This issue was to continue and to grow more and more sharp as the decades passed. In the closing years of the half-century, it was vigorously injected into the proposal before the Congress for federal aid to schools. Wrangling members of the House Labor Committee in the spring of 1950 found themselves at odds over religious and administrative differences that had blocked direct federal aid to schools for many months. The burning issue was whether such aid should be provided only for public schools or also made available to private and parochial schools. In 1947 the Supreme Court of the United States had held constitutional the use of public school transportation for nonpublic-school children (New Jersey Bus Case), but in 1948 had held unconstitutional the use of public school buildings for religious instruction (McCollum Case).

At the meeting in San Francisco in 1911, the Association repeated some of its earlier resolutions and urged suitable ethical instruction in the elementary schools to supplement the moral training given in the home, and expressed favor of all measures tending to secure the health of children. The hygienic and other requirements of school buildings and grounds were regarded as important steps in improving educational conditions: size of rooms, window space, corridors, stairways, exits, ventilation, indoor and outdoor equipment of school buildings, playgrounds, "thus rendering possible the standardizing of schoolhouses, rooms, and appliances." The physical equipment of the schools should be open to the pupils and their parents and families as opportunities for recreation outside the regular school hours. Compulsory school laws should be strengthened; instruction in occupations should be given; and the children were "recognized as the most precious natural resource of the nation." Progressive principles should be applied to the education of girls in the schools and women in the colleges, "as are already provided for boys and men." Advances in the cause of world peace during the past year encouraged the Association to urge a wider dissemination of knowledge upon that vital subject.

The next year in Chicago, the Association reaffirmed its belief in the use of the schools as recreational centers, urged wider effort for the increase in the salaries of teachers, applauded interest in the cause of world peace, and protested against the movement to establish compulsory military training in the schools, not designed primarily for military purposes, "as reactionary and inconsistent with American ideals and standards." Normal schools and teachers' colleges should give courses in sex hygiene with a view to introducing this subject into the public schools. The Association also went on record in favor of suffrage for women, and in changes in the courses of study in the public schools and in methods of teaching, so as to assist pupils in the ready application of the knowledge they may acquire "to actual life conditions." Vocational guidance for youth was recommended, and the federal government was urged to enact a law that would improve the home, the shop, and the farm through vocational training. School districts should provide grounds in proportion to the size of the school buildings, "not less than a square rod for each child." The Association also approved the movement for a national university.

At Oakland in 1915, the Association looked upon the war in Europe "as a tragedy without parallel in history," approved the American School Peace League, the organization of peace leagues among pupils, the observance of Peace Day, and the dissemination of information on international relations. It again declared opposition to compulsory military training, urged the promotion of international relationships in education, science, art, and social service as of fundamental importance, by coordination "of the organized forces of the civilized world." It recognized the importance of the movement to promote child welfare, of improved conditions in rural education, of provision for school supervision as distinct from teaching, and expressed itself unequivocally in favor of better salaries, security of tenure, retirement annuities, and better working conditions of teachers. It also said that every child of school age must be provided with that kind of education "which will be best adapted to meet his peculiar educational needs," and called for increased financial resources for the schools. In New York City in 1916 the Association endorsed the movement for the promotion of citizenship education inaugurated by the Bureau of Nationalization of the Department of Labor, again declared its belief in suffrage for women, urged higher professional standards and tenure of teachers, and seemed to weaken a bit on the subject of military training in the schools. It recognized that communities or the states could introduce such training "as may seem wise and prudent," but said that it should be strictly educational and that military ends should not pervert educational purposes and practices.

The NEA and the First World War.—The next year, in Portland, Oregon, the Association recognized "that the first duty of the hour is wholehearted national loyalty," and expressed as its supreme wish the giving of fullest service "for the sacred cause of our country and our allies, in defense of democracy and righteousness"; rejoiced that the young people of the country had manifested such a splendid spirit of patriotic devotion to the national cause; said that physical education and medical inspection of school children should be emphasized as never before; recommended "that the government give every encouragement to genuine military training" in technical institutions, colleges, and universities; urged thrift and the conservation of resources, suffrage for women, a national university, a national Department of Education under a secretary in the President's cabinet; "the protection of teachers and institutions from designing partisanship," and improved salaries for teachers "commensurate with conditions of living." Every teacher should teach patriotism, whether by heroic story, song, biography and history, social ethics, or "revised and vitalized civics." The final resolution was "as President Wilson has given us the vision, we ask the blessing of God upon the cause of the nations in alliance to save the world from militarism and autocracy."

In Pittsburgh in 1918, the Association recommended that the national government share with the states the responsibility of providing funds and the organization, administration, and supervision for Americanizing and making literate the adult population of the entire country; urged that the government encourage the states to establish uniform minimum standards of health services, training for citizenship, "and preparation and compensation of teachers, through financial aid distributed to the states enforcing these standards, the amount to which any state is entitled to be determined on a simple basis." In this year a bill was introduced in the Congress to create a Department of Education in the national government and to appropriate money for federal cooperation with the states in the encouragement and support of public education. The Association said that it was the patriotic duty of taxpayers and lawmakers to provide sufficient funds "to ensure a living and a saving wage to the teachers of the country"—and urged the immediate enactment of a federal child labor law that would meet the objections found by the Supreme Court of the United States in the law declared unconstitutional by that tribunal, so that a greater number of children would have adequate protection. Efforts were being made to give increased protection to children and women in industry. In 1916 Congress had enacted a law [5] excluding from interstate commerce any goods from factories or mines that employed children under fourteen years of age, but the Supreme Court in 1918 held the act unconstitutional. Attempts to achieve the same purpose were later made by an act that imposed a tax of 10 per cent on the net profits of factories that employed such children, and this was also held unconstitutional in 1922 by the same Court.

The Association also approved the plan of the government by which young men above eighteen years of age could enlist in the army and continue their collegiate work, the reference being to the Student Army Training Corps. It called for the teaching of patriotism by every teacher from the kindergarten to the university; urged careful consideration of the training of girls for efficient and intelligent participation in the civic and social life of their communities, states, and the nation; urged the states to adopt the prohibition amendment; favored a national university and a national department of education, the protection of teachers from "unwar-

[5] Keating-Owen Child Labor Act.

ranted dismissal by employing bodies," and the ballot for women; said that boards of education should make health and physical education a major subject, "with equal rating with all other school subjects"; instructed the Commission on the Emergency in Education to investigate what was being done and the most acceptable methods used in sex education; and favored amendment of the Smith-Hughes Act to prevent the possibility of establishing "a dual system of schools in any state."

At Milwaukee in 1919, the Association voted that, as a result of the "Great War" a high level of patriotic, intelligent, and competent citizenship should be emphasized, that the un-Americanized elements be Americanized; that illiteracy be removed, that English as the universal language of instruction be used in the schools, that a high degree of physical and moral fitness be insisted upon "for both the responsibilities of peace and the duties of war on the part of all our people." It urged the passage by the Congress of the Smith-Towner Bill and the creation of a Department of Education in the national government, with a secretary in the President's cabinet; that a year of compulsory civic, physical, and vocational training be provided; that a campaign be waged to enlist all teachers as active members of the Association; that more adequate financial support for public education be provided; that legal means be provided by which factional politics could not get control of the schools; called for better rural schools, more flexible and adaptable courses of study, methods of instruction, and systems of promotion to meet the needs of all classes of children; recommended compulsory education to the age of sixteen and compulsory continuation schools to the age of eighteen; the compulsory registration of minors and more effective enforcement of compulsory school laws; compulsory classes in Americanization for all illiterates and all who could not read and write the English language with a proficiency equal to a sixth grade standard as a condition necessary for admission to citizenship; again called for legal provision for the use of English as the language of the school, and for compulsory physical education; stood up boldly for an annual minimum of $1,000 for teachers; heartily approved the League of Nations and urged the Congress to recognize it in the interest of "peace and happiness of all people and the propagation and preservation of true democracy"; and urged the governors of all the states to work for the ratification of the woman suffrage amendment.

In 1920 at Salt Lake City, the Association stated that those who entered upon public school services should have a minimum of four years of carefully planned preparation "following up graduation from a four-year high school"; reaffirmed its faith in the Smith-Towner Bill; urged salaries attractive enough to retain good teachers then in the service and to induce promising young men and women to prepare for teaching, and urged provision for the retirement of superannuated teachers. It said that provision should be made for schoolrooms sufficient in number "to give each child a seat for a full-day session"; that facilities for the education of teachers should be extended and improved; that vocational training should be provided, but should not be allowed to overshadow general or cultural education; emphasized the importance of kindergartens; and urged Connecticut, New Hampshire, Vermont, Tennessee, North Carolina, and Florida speedily to ratify the woman suffrage amendment; called for such changes in the Smith-Hughes Act as would avoid interference with the autonomy of the states in vocational education; recommended definite plans for physical training in every school, better rural schools, state supervision of both private and public schools, and the use of the English language as the vehicle of instruction in private and public schools; the selection of the highest types of citizens as members of school boards without regard to sex or politics; cooperation in safeguarding youth "from cigarette smoking and kindred vices"; found itself in hearty accord with the decision of the Supreme Court of the United States in affirming the validity of the eighteenth amendment; urged permanent tenure for efficient teachers and some effective methods of ridding the profession of inefficient personnel.

The following year, at Des Moines, the Association recognized the importance of a well-educated and professionally trained teacher in every schoolroom, and again urged tenure for teachers, a single salary schedule in the elementary and the high schools, based upon education, professional training, and successful experience; pointed to the inadequate program of rural education; recognized the distinction between the professional administration of the schools and lay boards of education elected by the people; commended the demand of the American Legion that thoroughgoing instruction in American history and civics be required of all students for graduation from elementary and high schools; and again endorsed a Department of Education in the federal government and federal aid to education, the removal of illiteracy, the Americanization of the foreign-born, a program of physical and health service, the better training of teachers, and the equalization of educational opportunity as embodied in the Towner-Sterling Bill then pending in the Congress.

In Boston, in 1922, the Association reaffirmed its unqualified support of federal aid and federal recognition of public education "without federal interference in any way with state or local control"; urged the Congress and state legislatures to recognize the supreme importance of public education and to provide adequate funds for its support; again gave its unqualified approval to permanent tenure for efficient teachers during good behavior, and better salaries and retirement funds for teachers; objected to a bill in the Congress which would place the education of the foreign-born in charge of the Naturalization Bureau, and expressed its belief that international peace and good will could be brought about by mutual understanding and confidence which could be more speedily realized by education than by any other means.

At Oakland-San Francisco in 1923, the Association again urged federal aid to education without federal interference; said that more attention should be paid to individual differences among children; warned against narrow economies in the support of education; recognized the principle that education is a function of the state; urged fuller support for teacher-training schools and colleges, and better salaries for teachers and their promotion on merit alone, and the removal of fear of destitution of teachers through adequate retirement allowances; deplored the educational evils brought on by politics "in the case of the highest educational office in the Commonwealth of Pennsylvania"; favored a child labor amendment to the Constitution of the United States, urged courses in physical education and recreation in all the schools and colleges in the country, and said that the primary purpose of the teaching of American history was to inculcate in the people "a lasting devotion to America and her institutions."

In Washington, D. C., in 1924, the Association again urged a Department of Education with a secretary in the President's cabinet; acknowledged the contribution to education by private institutions and enterprises; urged a professional code of ethics for teachers and administrators and called for better-trained teachers, asked that state educational associations exert every effort to improve standards in the teacher-training institutions, and called for improved retirement systems and for equal pay to men and women teachers of equal qualifications; said that the Constitution should be taught in all the upper grades of the elementary schools; emphasized the need of moral and social guidance for young people, and endorsed the National Conference on Outdoor Recreation. It also urged upon the Congress and the President of the United States the wisdom of requiring the reading and writing of English understandingly as a qualification for citizenship; expressed opposition "to war except as a means of national defense"; advocated the prompt ratification by the states of the child labor amendment recently passed by the Congress; and deplored the narcotic addiction and the "spread of the use of heroin among youth." It said that teachers should inspire respect for law, recommended the widest observance of American Education Week in the schools, churches, and civic centers of all communities, and asked that teachers in Alaska and Hawaii should not be required to pay federal income taxes.

In Indianapolis in 1925, the Association went on record as favoring the implanting of a feeling of brotherhood with all mankind so as "to obliterate the misunderstandings that bred war"; called attention to the need for adequate financial support of schools, adequate programs of health and physical education, the importance of training teachers, again expressed the importance of wholesome respect for law, and reaffirmed its position on the subject of child labor. It urged adequate provisions for tenure and retirement and a minimum salary schedule for teachers, and a Department of Education with a secretary in the President's cabinet. At its meeting in Philadelphia the next year, the Association again urged a Department of Education in the federal government; repeated its position on child labor and on the teaching of respect for law "as a chief purpose of education"; urged the reading and writing of English understandingly as a qualification for the admission of the foreign-born to citizenship and to the privilege of voting; noted with pleasure the increase in professional requirements for teachers, and improvements in tenure, pension, and retirement laws; and affirmed its faith in the value of competitive athletic sports, but said that public recognition should be given to distinguished achievement in scholarship "so as to avoid the appearance of giving athletics first place in school life." It believed that international peace rested upon international good will, which in turn rested on international understanding.

In 1927 at Seattle, the Association expressed the belief that the minimum of preparation for teaching should be not less than four years beyond graduation from high school; that better salaries should be paid to teachers; that educational and vocational guidance was a primary obligation of organized education; that special classes should be provided for the subnormal, the physically handicapped, and delinquent children; emphasized the importance of adult education; and said that all administrative officers of states, counties, and cities should be selected on the basis of their professional qualifications by lay boards of education, and that such boards should be elected on a nonpartisan ballot, chosen at large for relatively long terms "so arranged as to make it impossible to select a majority of the members of the board at any one election." It also urged that schools be financed on a state-wide basis, and that state departments of education should be strengthened. Again it called for a Department of Education in the federal government, and recommended physical and health education and the teaching of the evil effects of narcotics and alcohol. The tendency of state legislatures in the 1920's to enact laws compelling or forbidding the teaching of particular subjects or topics in the schools was viewed by the Association as "an unwise and dangerous practice," and if continued would change the educational institutions "now consecrated to the teaching of the truth, into prejudiced schools devoted to the interest of special propaganda." It praised "every legitimate means for promoting world peace and understanding among the peoples of the earth."

At Minneapolis in 1928, the Association called the Parent-Teachers' Association one of the greatest educational movements fostered during the past quarter of a century, again urged a fair and just retirement of teachers and improvement of conditions of tenure, and said that the study and investigation of the curriculum was one of the most important educational projects of the time; urged the removal of adult illiteracy; approved all means for creating international understanding and peace; and called for proper protection of academic freedom, which meant "not the propagation of unsound or revolutionary theories, but rather the exercise of initiative and independence in the preparation of individuals for freedom in a democracy." It emphasized the importance of physical education and mental health; pointed to the necessity for adequate business procedures in the administration of education; and commended the work of the United States Bureau of Education, which was being done too often "with meager funds and inadequate equipment." It reaffirmed its belief that a Department of Education should be established in the national government.

In Atlanta in 1929, the Association recommended the continuous study of the curriculum to determine the subjects children should be taught in school; commended "the studies of early childhood for their contribution to an understanding of child growth and development"; called for counselors in junior and senior high schools, a Congressional appropriation for the study of rural education throughout the nation, said there should be more emphasis upon teaching respect for law as the foundation of democratic liberty, commended teachers for increasing their training through extension classes and summer sessions, called for the just retirement of teachers, emphasized the importance of adult education and the work of free public libraries, the continued observance of American Education Week, and rejoiced that "by solemn agreement among the nations of the world, war has been renounced as an instrument of policy in the settlement of international disputes. . . ." It also extended greetings to the National Congress of Parents and Teachers and again urged a Department of Education with a secretary in the President's cabinet.

At the meeting in Columbus, Ohio, in 1930, the Association declared its belief in equal educational opportunity for every child "regardless of residence, capacity, or handicap, and that free education through elementary and high school should be within the reach of every boy and girl"; urged Congressional relief of the emergency in rural education; recommended that adequate financing of the schools was the first duty of the localities, states, and nation; said that free public library service should be as general as free educational service; urged the continued observance of American Education Week, and praised the kindergarten for its good influence in the development of the child. It also went on record as favoring more attention to children who are hard of hearing, and recommended medical treatment and instruction in lip reading; deplored the commercialization of athletics in schools and colleges, but emphasized the need for physical education; and reaffirmed its position in favor of the Eighteenth Amendment and on the teaching of the evil effects of alcohol, tobacco, and narcotics upon the human system. Again it resolved against commercialized child labor as economically unsound, unjust to children, and injurious to the state, and favored a constitutional amendment which would permit the enactment of a national child labor law. It also said that legislation should be enacted to safeguard for uses of education "a reasonable share of the radio broadcasting channels of the United States"; endorsed the proposed nation-wide observance of the 200th anniversary of the birth of George Washington to be held in 1932, and preparations for the celebration of the Horace Mann Centennial in 1937; recommended for teachers four years of training beyond the four-year high school; urged the Congress to appropriate funds for a national survey of teacher training; commended the National Congress of Parents and Teachers; recommended that the Pact of Paris be taught in the schools, and that international Goodwill Day be appropriately observed. It again recommended a Department of Education with a secretary in the President's cabinet, and expressed appreciation to President Herbert Hoover and Secretary Ray Lyman Wilbur for the appointment of the Advisory Committee on the Relation of the Federal Government to Education and plans for the White House Conference on Child Health and Protection.

At the meeting in Los Angeles in 1931, the Association called for a system of taxation for education "which is equitable, wide in its application, and which establishes a fair balance between direct and indirect taxes"; condemned ill-considered cuts in budgets for schools, reductions in salaries of teachers, and other shortsighted policies then being followed because of the economic depression; pointed again to the evil effects on the human organism of alcohol, tobacco, and narcotics; favored the Eighteenth Amendment and laws enacted under it, and declared that "character should be a major objective in education." Handicapped children should receive special care; opportunities for the education of the teacher should be "adequate, rich in content, and practical in application"; favored tenure laws that would protect teachers from losing their jobs "because of political, personal, religious, or any unjust reasons," but did not prevent the dismissal of incompetent, immoral, or unprofessional teachers. The continued observance of American Education Week and of International Goodwill Day was urged, along with the participation of the schools in the observance of the 200th anniversary of the birth of George Washington.

In 1932 in Atlantic City, the Association favored economy in the administration of the public schools, but vigorously opposed any retrenchment which would injure the children either by lowering educational standards, impairing the morale of teachers, or eliminating those subjects and activities which contributed to the health, culture, or vocational training of the people. It condemned the tendency to increase the size of classes beyond the point of efficiency, the shortening of school terms, reduction of salaries of teachers, and the elimination of services and activities designed to promote health, recreation, vocational, and cultural opportunities. Again it recommended federal aid to education, and said that funds should be made available by the national government "for the resumption of public projects, federal, state, and local, which had been planned and approved but which have been discontinued solely for lack of funds," with such aid from the national government coming through the Reconstruction Finance Corporation. At the meeting in Chicago in 1933, the Association resolved that the solvency of schools was dependent upon the application of scientific principles of taxation;

objected to any retrenchment in education as measures of economy unless it preserved the educational rights of childhood and was based on scientific professional principles; asserted that the management of educational affairs must be nonpolitical and professionally directed, and that public education must be free; condemned the practice of tuition charges in high schools, and said that the greater part of the local costs of education should be borne by the state. Teachers should be assured of adequate compensation and protection from unjust discharge, and there should be a reasonable limitation on the size of classes and the freedom of teachers from unnecessary worry and hampering restrictions. Teachers should not be discriminated against because of marital status, and they should receive equal pay for equal work regardless of sex; kindergarten training should be provided for all children of kindergarten age; instruction should be given in the schools on the evil effects of alcohol and narcotics; educational workers should keep the public informed of the purposes and work of the schools; and the Research Division of the Association was requested to collect and widely disseminate facts on movements against public education. Lay organizations, Parent-Teachers Associations, the American Association of University Women, the National League of Women Voters, the Business and Professional Women's Clubs, and service clubs, the American Legion, the American Federation of Labor ("and many newspapers and magazines") working to protect the schools from injury should have the cooperation and appreciation of all teachers and educational authorities. A vigorous protest was made against those communities that had failed to pay or had otherwise discriminated against their teachers "in meeting public financial obligations."

In 1934, in Washington, D. C., the National Education Association endorsed the growing practice of stressing in the classroom through subject matter and projects "the cultural heritages of various national, ethnic, and racial groups"; endorsed the child labor amendment to the Constitution; recognized the important educational place of the moving picture, and joined with other educational, patriotic, and religious organizations "in demanding a high type of moving pictures for the boys and girls of America"; pointed to the importance of teaching the evil effects of alcohol and narcotics on the human body, and expressed disapproval "of any false advertising or propaganda on this subject"; recommended the expansion of the Civilian Conservation Corps for the purpose of "equipping the boys for regular occupations after discharge"; endorsed the plan of the United States Office of Education for the creation of a commis sion on the problems of youth; said that the need for tenure for teachers was never so imperative, and instructed the use of $10 thousand for the work of a committee to study the subject; opposed further retrenchment in the services of the schools; and endorsed the social policies of slum clearance and provisions for sanitary and attractive homes for the underprivileged classes, unemployment insurance for all workers, including teachers, and state pensions for widows who needed such aid. Noting that the annual income of the schools of the United States "has been reduced more than five hundred million dollars," the Association pledged itself to make every effort to have introduced into the Congress and to secure the passage of a bill for a direct grant of not less than $500 million to be distributed to the school districts "according to average daily attendance and lack of adequate tax resources." It also said that the major part of the local cost of education should be borne by the state, that scientific tax laws should be enacted in all the states "to the end that all forms of wealth shall bear their just shares of the cost of government and education," and said that the making of educational budgets and the appointment of teachers should be free from political or other special groups.

In Denver, in 1935, the Association reaffirmed its position on federal educational aid, commended President Franklin D. Roosevelt for creating the National Youth Administration and for the appropriation of $50 million to assist needy youth, and the establishment and continuance of the Civilian Conservation Corps; said that teachers and educational administrators should have full opportunity to present differing views on controversial issues to help students "adjust themselves to their environment and to changing social conditions," but promptly asserted that the "fundamental principles of American democracy are the best so far devised by the mind of man to govern a free people," and pledged itself "so to teach the youth of this land." It again called for adequate laws on tenure, for provision for kindergartens, extensive constructive recreational programs, and for the passage of the child labor amendment to the Constitution. It opposed compulsory military training in the schools, and it paid tribute to the memory and influence of William T. Harris, "great educational philosopher, superintendent of schools in St. Louis, President in 1875 of the National Educational Association, and United States Commissioner of Education for seventeen years," the centennial of whose birth was that year being observed.

In 1936, in Portland, Oregon, the Association again stated its stand on tenure for teachers "as a means of insuring to the children of the land the best possible education," reaffirmed its position on "freedom of teaching and full opportunity to present differing points of view on any and all controversial questions," deplored the rider to the appropriations bill of the District of Columbia, passed the year before, which limited freedom of teaching there; reaffirmed its opposition to compulsory military training in the public schools, colleges, and universities; approved the Inter-American Conference for peace in the Western Hemisphere to be held that year in Buenos Aires, called for a Division of Youth Education and Guidance in the United States Office of Education, urged prompt and complete restoration of full educational programs in those states that had suffered serious curtailment; reaffirmed with emphasis the principle of federal educational aid, and urged the passage of Senate Bill 4,793 which had been introduced in the second session of the Seventy-Fourth Congress, reaffirmed its position on the necessity for independence of education in the administration of local, state, and federal governments, and opposed the administrative merging of education "with functions generally classified as welfare services."

The next year, in Detroit, the Association repeated its position on a Division of Youth Education and Guidance in the United States Office of Education, urged provision for adult education, directed its officers to continue efforts for federal aid to education, and endorsed the principles as given in the Harrison-Black-Fletcher Bill; urged better means for promoting education in rural communities; and recommended a committee to study the matter of adjusting "the supply of adequately trained teachers to the demand for teachers" in the interest of establishing a balance "between the number of qualified candidates for teaching and the prospective demand for teachers." (Seven years before, Governor Franklin D. Roosevelt had warned in the State of New York against the danger of a surplus of teachers.) The Association also repeated its adopted policy of opposition to war as a method of settling international disputes, and declared that the best way to maintain peace in the world was through "education for peace, including the truth about the causes of war and the means of alleviating such causes; the teaching of war aims and the extent to which these have been attained through warfare; nationalization of the war munitions industry to take the profits out of war and preparation for war; an amendment to the Constitution to provide that, except in case of actual invasion, war may be declared only by vote of the people; an amendment to the Constitution to legalize automatically the draft of the material and industrial resources of the country for the successful prosecution of war." It repeated its position on tenure for teachers; commended President Franklin D. Roosevelt for the appointment of the Advisory Committee on Education; urged the independence of education from local, state, and federal governments; objected to the administrative merging of education with public welfare agencies; protested against loyalty oaths for teachers; advocated further development of educational programs by radio; urged that American Education Week be observed in the schools; endorsed the work and reports of the Educational Policies Commission and the work of the Horace Mann Centennial Committee; expressed appreciation for the work that had been done by members of the Congress, by newspapers, and by other means to get repeal of the "Red Rider" restriction upon teachers in the District of Columbia; praised the kindergarten; commended the steps that were being taken to restore the educational programs in those states that had suffered serious curtailment, and urged that "this forward movement" be continued. It endorsed the proposal of the American Council on Education that studies be made of the status of the education of teachers and the work of the American Foundation for the Blind.

At the meeting in New York City in 1938, the Association again recommended federal aid to education without federal control; condemned any campaigns of propaganda for the indiscriminate reduction of taxation without regard to social needs; opposed any measures designed to place a constitutional limitation within the various states; said that teachers should not be called upon to teach without pay in any so-called emergency, when the public had the ability to provide additional funds and failed to do so; urged the continued study of the certification of teachers and of adjusting the supply of properly trained teachers to the demand for teachers; reaffirmed its position on permanent tenure for teachers "as a means of insuring the children of the land the best possible instruction"; opposed discriminatory oaths for teachers; recognized the "serious problems confronting youth through unemployment, social maladjustment, unequal educational opportunities, and financial stress," and recommended the cooperation of all agencies and organizations concerned with the problems of youth; urged all teachers to continue to promote international good will; favored "the largest possible budget for the Association's public relations activities in order that it may (1) expand its present service through the radio, press, lay organizations, and other agencies, and (2) make available to state and local associations and school officials expert advice on publicity." It also recommended that American Education Week be observed in all the schools, and that the President of the United States and the Congress "work intelligently, cooperatively, and unselfishly for world peace."

At its meeting in 1939, the Association commended and asked support for the "Future Teachers of America," an organization which had grown out of the Horace Mann Centennial in 1937. It also urged promotional activities to recruit promising young people for teaching, and asked that institutions engaged in the education of teachers permit only well-qualified candidates to enter. The Association said that all systems of tenure should be operated by established educational authority, and offered the experience, advice, and facilities of the National Education Association in efforts to secure adequate systems of tenure. Teachers were urged to participate in the civic and political life of their communities, states, and the nation in every way not inconsistent with their positions. It also endorsed "institutes of professional relations" to train teachers in teacher-student, student-professional, and teacher-public relations. It called for democracy in school administration, and said that teachers should use the principles set out by the Educational Policies Commission. Also, the school should cooperate with advisory committees in planning trade education.

In 1940 the Association urged that teachers be selected according to merit and not residence, and urged Departments of Public Relations to interpret the needs and accomplishments of the schools and to oppose reactionary forces. It also called for a survey of the legal status of women as a guide to the association in outlining activities in the area of equal rights. The next year the Association asked for educational standards in federal educational positions equal to the standards required by existing agencies, condemned the certification of inadequately prepared teachers, recommended that, when there is a shortage of teachers, small units be combined instead of issuing temporary certificates, or that teachers be brought from other places to fill the vacancies. It also called upon the teachers to work for retirement systems, and asked for an amendment to the Hatch Act that would allow all teachers to exercise their civic rights. It opposed the employment in any educational institution of any person who was a member of any organization that advocated changing the form of government of the United States by any means not provided by the Constitution. It also recommended that teachers assume greater responsibility in cooperation with parents and citizens, and that conferences with labor, industry, and agricultural and civic groups be held to promote plans for defense. The Association believed that no textbooks for public schools should be adopted unless recommended by committees of teachers, who were urged to do all in their power to promote national unity.

In 1942 the Association opposed the lowering of standards for certification, asked that the United States Employment Service co-operate in bringing in teachers from other areas, commended increases in salaries that had been made and asked for more increases in order to keep the teachers in and maintain the efficiency of the schools, and repeated its recommendation of 1941 that teachers work for the promotion of systems of retirement. It called for equal rights for men and women in the schools.

In 1943 the Association recommended adequate salaries both for the sake of the teachers and for the schools, called for supplementary aid from larger governmental units, and asked that teachers consider the services of patriotism before leaving their positions. It urged that teachers continue to uphold the traditions and ideals "which are the priceless heritage of Americans," and recommended adequate salary schedules and the financial support of education. A constructive program should be developed to counteract the forces which were contributing to juvenile delinquency, through the enforcement of all laws designed to protect the interests of youth, and proper guidance to enable youth to serve their country in ways for which they were best qualified. Because many "war activities" were claiming so much of the time of children, the schools were urged to maintain the required days of actual school attendance. The United States should participate in an international effort to establish peace and order under law. In 1944 the Association urged schools and colleges to recruit promising young people for preparation for teaching, expressed appreciation for increases in teachers' salaries and called for more increases, urged the maximum exemption of retirement pay from income taxes, and recommended sick leave as necessary for efficiency in the schools. In 1945 the Armed Services Institute was commended for developing standards of evaluation for military courses.

In 1946 the Association urged that standards be maintained, that emergency certificates for teachers be discontinued, and that certificates be reciprocal among the states; urged the federal government, schools and colleges, and lay groups to set up scholarships to attract able young people to the profession; asked for higher salary scales, again urged the exemption of retirement pay from income taxes, recommended sick leave, called for an accreditation agency for new schools that were being established under the G.I. Bill of Rights, and accepted the need for some phases of military education in the school. In 1940 the Association had urged no interruption of the usual educational program by the "regimentation of youth, characteristic of totalitarian systems," and in 1941 had said that there should be the least possible interference with necessary educational services as a result of military training. In 1947 the Association accepted provisions for national defense, the next year it urged adequate national defense as defined by Congress, and in 1949 it proclaimed that the federal government had the right to provide for national defense when necessary. In 1946 the Association urged that education be represented in UNESCO, and asked that an educator be director of that organization. It also urged the promotion of intercultural relations and the teaching of the work of the United Nations as a part of civics. In the same year the organization urged that the moral and spiritual aspects of life, and the conservation of natural resources, be taught in the schools, and expressed its appreciation for the veterans of the war.

In 1947 the Association called for programs of housing and school lunches, for the direction of the United States Office of Education by a board of laymen with a professionally qualified executive, urged no duplication of existing agencies, called for the support of the United Nations and UNESCO as preparation for world citizenship, urged support of UNESCO, that languages and culture be increased in the schools, commended the "Future Teachers of America," urged that emergency certificates be discontinued, and that a minimum of four years of collegiate work be required at that time for teaching, and that five years be required in the future, and condemned strikes by teachers. Recommendations on salaries, tenure, and sick leave were frequently repeated.

In 1948 the association went on record as favoring a bachelor's degree, and in-service training for those who held the master's degree, called for public and private scholarships, urged compromise to improve salaries and to prevent strikes among teachers, called for adequate retirement pay and a change in the tax structure, requested that "teacher rating scales" be discarded, called upon teachers to oppose all groups that undertook to undermine the Constitution of the United States, and said that teachers should participate in civic life; it called for support of the World Organization of the Teaching Profession, for the adequate financing of the United States Office of Education with an independent professional commissioner, and that the work of the office be directed by a national board appointed by the President, with long overlapping terms, urged UNESCO to expand its educational activities, recommended the reorganization of small schools for greater economy, said that the United Nations should be taught as a part of civics, that the rights, privileges, and responsibilities of living in a democracy should be taught, and that American youth should be indoctrinated in the American way of life so that they could know it, believe in it, and live in it continuously. The organization also recommended the teaching of recreational and creative activities in the schools, which should be expanded to fourteen years and include summer camps.

In 1949 the Association urged the requirement of a bachelor's degree and later a master's degree for teaching, called for the recruiting of teachers, especially in the elementary field, urged democratic procedures in the adjustment of salaries for teachers who should have higher salaries, called for a uniform-pay salary scale, and asked for extra pay for extra work. It called for using democratic procedures in sick leave, and said that members of the Communist Party should not teach or be members of the National Education Association. Teachers should participate in public affairs for the purpose of increasing their prestige. It also called for an exchange of teachers and for support of the World Organization of the Teaching Profession. As it had done many times before and was likely to do many times later, the Association urged federal aid to education, that the United States Office of Education be nonpolitical and have no parallel agencies, repeated its request for the support of the United Nations and UNESCO, urged that adult education become a part of the work of the schools, that there should be teaching about Communism, the conservation of natural resources, moral and spiritual aspects of life; recreational and creative activities should be provided, and the school system should be expanded to include the nursery school, kindergarten, junior colleges, and summer camps.

In 1950 the Legislative Commission of the National Education Association of the United States adopted a statement reaffirming the policy of that association on the matter of national aid to public elementary and secondary schools, as follows:

For approximately thirty years the Representative Assembly of the NEA has in annual meeting adopted by overwhelming vote a policy urging federal aid, under state and local control, to assist the states in paying the current costs of operating their public elementary and public secondary schools, with a view more nearly to equalizing educational opportunity in the United States.

The National Education Association of the United States supported S246, which passed the Senate by a vote of 58 to 15, May 5, 1949. The most significant issue in this legislation is the preservation of state and local control of educational policy. The Association urges strict adherence to the provision of Section Six of this act which, in careful observance of the principle of state and local control of educational policies, authorizes the state to expend the federal funds appropriated to them under the act "for any current expenditure for elementary or secondary school purposes for which educational revenues derived from the state or local sources may legally and constitutionally be expended in such state."

The Association is without reservation opposed to any provision in any federal-aid-to-education measure which, in the administration of funds thus made available, is directed at bypassing the provisions of the federal constitution, state constitutions, state laws, and the educational agencies established by the respective states for the administration of their public elementary and public secondary schools.

Two months after this action, the American Association of School Administrators reaffirmed its devotion to the ideals and principles of the American system of government and its support of an adequate defense plan, urged the continued use of the United Nations as an instrument of peace, and declared itself in favor of "charter amendments to enable the United Nations to enact, interpret, and enforce world law to prevent war." It called upon the school systems of the country to become familiar with the principles of UNESCO; said that the program of education and re-education should be given high priority in the occupied areas of Germany, Austria, and Japan; recommended renewed emphasis in the curriculum on the wise use of human and natural resources; urged a minimum standard of four years of professional preparation for the certification of teachers in all public schools, and that prospective teachers be carefully screened and given more guidance and advice concerning the qualifications and requirements for successful teaching; opposed loyalty oaths for teachers and opposed Communists as teachers; called for an extension of the program of public education from kindergarten through the fourteenth grade, more funds for schools, federal aid without federal control, federal aid for school buildings, the establishment of the United States Office of Education as a nonpartisan, independent agency under a national board of education with a professionally qualified commissioner, praised the appointment of Earl J. McGrath as commissioner, urged that state departments of education be strengthened, that school administration be made professional, noted with satisfaction the increasing participation of lay organizations in cooperative educational planning, and expressed its appreciation to the National Congress of Parents and Teachers. It strongly expressed its belief in the principle of the separation of Church and State, and opposed the use of public funds for private and parochial schools. To this resolution one member of the Committee on Resolutions, Superintendent James L. Hanley of Providence, Rhode Island, dissented, because it injected the sectarian issue into the report. That issue was decisive shortly afterwards in shelving in the House the federal aid bill that had already been passed by the Senate.

At the meeting of the American Association of Colleges for Teacher Education in Atlantic City in the early part of 1950, that organization warned against the union of education and politics and resolved that the American schools must be kept independent and free from the afflictions that come from a union. In the discussion on the resolution it was pointed out that in many communities and states, politics played a large part in the operation of public schools. Under the title, "Freedom from Partisan Politics," the resolution said: "Colleges for teacher education can serve best when they can be operated in terms of educational policies rather than the dictates of political interests. We recommend that schools be divorced from partisan politics at the local, state, and national levels," a recommendation that had been made many times by the National Education Association during the preceding half century. A companion resolution called for a federal board of education as a means of eliminating political influence on the national level, although it was not clearly indicated how partisan politics could be prevented on the national level if not on local and state levels. That resolution called for making the United States Office of Education an independent agency under a federal board of education, to consist of nine to thirteen lay citizens, to be appointed by the President of the United States for overlapping nine- to thirteen-year terms, and empowered to appoint the United States Commissioner of Education as its executive officer and, upon his nomination, the staff members of the Office of Education. The same organization voted for federal aid to education without federal control, and urged the teaching of "world understanding" so that school children could be given "wholesome attitudes of neighborliness, mutual respect, and understanding of foreign people"; recommended a minimum of five years of collegiate work for teachers in all school systems, the reduction of the size of classes whenever it was excessive, and stated that in elementary and secondary schools the size should not be above twenty-five. It also made a plea that collegiate teaching be improved and strengthened, and declared that the universities and graduate schools were not affording adequate preparation for teaching in colleges.

The resolutions of the Representative Assembly of the National Education Association in San Francisco, in July of 1951, included some that had been passed earlier: that "education is the inalienable

TABLE 10

MEMBERSHIP IN NEA AND AFFILIATED STATE ASSOCIATIONS

States and other areas	Estimated number of teachers 1950-51	Membership in National Education Association			Rank of Col. 5	Membership in Affiliated State Associations		Percent NEA membership is of state membership 1951	Rank of Col. 9
		May 31, 1950	May 31, 1951	Percent of teachers members 1951		May 31, 1950	May 31, 1951		
1	2	3	4	5	6	7	8	9	10
Total	1,002,672	453,797	465,266	46	.....	856,502	880,156	53	.....
★★★★Alabama	22,000	14,863	15,701	71	15	15,575	15,856	99	5
★★★★Arizona	5,200	4,365	4,278	82	7	4,394	4,337	99	7
★★★★Arkansas	13,954	10,413	10,666	76	11	11,532	11,884f	90	12
★★★★California	68,518	34,588	33,564	49	24	57,617	58,450	57	28
★★★Colorado	10,040a	4,667	4,382	44	30	7,500b	9,105	48	30
★★★Connecticut	11,700	3,252	3,537	30	41	9,902	10,315	34	42
★★★★Delaware	2,175	1,140	1,319	61	21	1,685b	2,003	66	20
★★★Florida	18,844a	4,980	4,822	26	46	14,005	14,968	32	44
★★★★Georgia	24,900a	10,933	11,371	46	26	16,747	17,062	67	19
★★★★Idaho	4,950	4,571	4,582	93	3	4,539	4,561	100	3
★★★★★Illinois	46,568	24,676	25,911	56	23	41,500b	42,079	62	21
★★★★Indiana	25,867	15,931	16,344	63	18	26,015	26,824	61	24
★★★Iowa	23,400	8,340	8,657	37	34	22,377	22,780	38	36
★★★Kansas	17,500	12,028	12,637	72	13	17,118	17,563	72	17
★★★Kentucky	19,371	9,636	8,524	44	29	17,852	17,439	49	29
★★★Louisiana	20,000	4,475	4,618	23	48	11,579	12,235	38	37
★★★Maine	7,040	2,454	2,476	35	35	6,571	7,040	35	41
★★★★Maryland	10,051	6,569	6,846	68	16	7,384	8,050	85	13
★Massachusetts	24,910	5,739	5,046	20	50	20,000b	19,500b	26	48
★★Michigan	38,000	11,700	12,302	32	38	32,667	33,200	37	39
★★Minnesota	21,121	5,697	5,586	26	43	17,289	17,094	33	43
★★★Mississippi	16,000	3,841	3,654	23	49	8,974	9,103	40	34
★★★Missouri	24,200	11,296	11,623	48	25	25,834	26,580	44	32
★★★★Montana	5,100	3,872	4,201	82	6	4,175	4,615g	91	11
★Nebraska	12,627	3,629	3,861	31	40	11,818	12,490	31	45
★★★★Nevada	1,300	1,103	1,035	80	10	1,064	1,040	100	4
★★★New Hampshire	3,162	1,537	1,416	45	28	3,210	3,136	45	31
★★New Jersey	30,500	11,872	11,462	38	32	27,135	27,621	41	33
★★★★★New Mexico	5,662	3,850	4,183	74	12	5,782	6,828	61	22
★New York (Except NYC)	47,800	12,894	12,234	26	45	47,120b	49,000	25	50
New York City (5 Boroughs)	34,000	664	570	2	53	26,400d	27,200d	2	53
★★★★North Carolina	29,700	11,928	13,550	46	27	20,916	22,152	61	23
★★★★North Dakota	6,375a	2,723	2,479	39	31	5,897	6,240	40	35
★★★★Ohio	45,684	25,921	27,070	59	22	43,520	44,586	61	26
★★★★Oklahoma	19,014a	6,767	7,052	37	33	17,586	19,143	37	40
★★★★Oregon	11,500	8,812	9,261	81	9	8,600	9,125	101	1
★★★★Pennsylvania	61,242	37,702	38,824	63	17	53,760	53,209	73	16
Rhode Island	3,950a	301	264	7	52	3,911	4,044	7	52
★★★★South Carolina	17,450	5,348	5,357	31	39	8,779	8,999	60	27
★South Dakota	7,500	1,539	1,873	25	47	7,479	7,235	26	47
★★★★Tennessee	22,640	19,810	20,314	90	4	20,553	20,923	97	8
★★★Texas	55,800	15,995	18,573	33	37	46,823	49,236	38	38
★★★★Utah	5,684	5,415	5,729	101	1	5,920	6,157	93	10
Vermont	2,650a	724	686	26	44	2,581	2,666	26	49
★★★★Virginia	22,240a	13,156	13,573	61	20	17,340	17,750b	76	15
★★★★Washington	16,700	12,950	13,559	81	8	13,331b	14,457i	94	9
★★★★West Virginia	16,222	14,285	14,439	89	5	14,396	14,611	99	6
★Wisconsin	21,500	6,869	6,341	29	42	22,589	22,538	28	46
★★★★Wyoming	2,695	1,526	1,645	61	19	2,566	2,701	61	25
OUTLYING POSSESSIONS									
★★★★★Alaska	653	393	472	72	14	275c	576	82	14
★★★★District of Columbia	3,596	1,573	1,217	34	36	2,000	1,717	71	18
★★★★Hawaii	3,470	3,234	3,398	98	2	3,220b	3,360	101	2
★★Puerto Rico	9,947	144	1,650	17	51	9,100c	8,773	19	51
Other Possessions		14	3	....		....	....	....	....
Foreign		1,093	529	....		....	....	....	....

a Estimated by state department of education.
b Estimated by officials of state education associations.
c Membership for May 31, 1948.
d Estimated on the basis of 80% of teachers.
e Membership for May 31, 1949.
f Membership for May 2, 1951.
g Membership for April 16, 1951.
h Membership for March 31, 1951.
i Membership for April 20, 1951.

right of every American; that it is essential to our society for the promotion and preservation of democratic ideals. Therefore, the Association declares its convictions and challenges its members to leadership in attaining the objectives of this covenant." It also declared its belief that every child of whatever race, "belief, economic status, residence, or physical handicap should have the fullest development in mental, moral, social, and physical health, and in the attitudes, knowledges, habits, and skills that are essential for individual happiness and effective citizenship in a democratic nation and cooperative world," a creed with which few if any men of good will could argue. It endorsed "enriched curriculums," socially desirable environment that would "give a background of more fertile experience," expanded health services and physical fitness programs in the schools, the prohibition of child labor, better school-attendance laws, vocational and educational guidance, unified community recreational programs, and "the right to unfettered teaching." Teachers had certain responsibilities and rights and should be protected by sound retirement arrangements, by credit unions in cases of financial emergencies, and from discharge "for nonsubversive political, religious, personal, or other unjust reasons by effective tenure laws." Teachers had a right to organize and to participate in "determining" educational policies and school management. "Members of the Communist Party should not be employed in our schools." The association commended efforts toward international good will, toward national defense and the preservation of democracy, and called again for federal aid to education, as it had done many times before, but warned against the dangers of federal control. It urged the expansion of "school services," and provision for a national board of education which would select "a professionally qualified commissioner of education. . . ."

Table 10 exhibits membership in the NEA and in affiliated state education associations as of May 31, 1951 as given in the *NEA Journal* for September of that year.

In the next and final chapter, attention is given to some educational trends and developments not specifically treated in preceding chapters.

Some Questions and Exercises for Students

1. Study the resolutions of the NEA for the position of that organization on (*a*) the effects of alcohol and narcotics on the human system; (*b*) physical and health education; (*c*) illiteracy; (*d*) federal aid to education; (*e*) national university; (*f*) the education of women; (*g*) the education of the Negro; (*h*) partisan politics in educational ad-

ministration; (*i*) military training in the schools; (*j*) international cultural relations; (*k*) academic freedom; (*l*) Communists as teachers.

2. Probably the most influential organization affiliated with the National Education Association was the American Association of School Administrators, formerly the Department of Superintendence. Make a study of the forty-eight chief state school officers to find out about their formal schooling, degrees (earned or honorary), membership in scholarly groups such as Phi Beta Kappa and Sigma Xi, age, sex, native state, method of appointment or election, and length of time in the superintendency.

3. Make a similar study for (*a*) city and (*b*) county superintendents in your state.

4. American Education Week was established in 1921 by the NEA in cooperation with the American Legion and the United States Office of Education, and in 1938 the National Congress of Parents and Teachers joined these organizations in promoting this special week. The purpose was to secure for the United States an educational program "adequate to meet the needs of the twentieth century . . ." Each year a week was designated as American Education Week, usually in the fall, with a general theme or slogan and a special slogan for each day. From the *Journal of the NEA,* which annually publishes the program, compile a list of the slogans from year to year, and note how these reflected the mood of the times. For example, in 1922 the slogan was "No illiteracy by 1927—it can be done," but in 1924 it was "No illiteracy by 1930."

5. Make a study of and report on the activities of the Research Division of the NEA, which began in 1922.

6. Study the addresses of the presidents of the NEA by decades since 1900 for educational trends which those addresses revealed.

7. Study the resolutions of the NEA and of the AASA for the same purpose.

8. On what educational issues did these groups appear consistent in their pronouncements over the half century?

Some Suggested References and Reading

Fenner, Mildred Sandison. *NEA History: Its Development and Program.* Washington, D. C.: The Association, 1945.
    A brief but well-written account of the origin and growth of the National Teachers' Association (1857-1869), the National Educational Association (1870-1906), and the National Education Association since 1906, which gives the high lights of the activities of this energetic organization.

KNIGHT, EDGAR W. *What College Presidents Say.* Chapel Hill: The University of North Carolina Press, 1940.

A study of the inaugurals and other addresses of American college and university presidents from 1864 to 1938, which seemed to show, as did the addresses and resolutions of the National Education Association, that these leaders of higher education generally said and wrote what they were expected by their constituencies to say and write, and that when they undertook to say or write what they were not expected to say or write, they were soon not allowed to say or write anything.

NATIONAL EDUCATION ASSOCIATION. *Journal of Addresses and Proceedings.* Washington, D. C.: The Association, 1900-1951.

This Chapter is based largely on the official reports and resolutions of the annual meetings of that organization, which should be available to students in most of the colleges and universities.

NEA Journal. Washington, D. C.: Published by the Association.

This house organ of the largest education association in the United States was begun in 1921, having been preceded by the *Bulletin.* The editorials reflected changed and changing educational conditions, as did also the contributed articles and papers by leading educators.

Chapter 10

OTHER TRENDS AND DEVELOPMENTS

PREVIEW OF THE CHAPTER

In 1951 the national government was bringing to a close one of the most extensive and significant educational experiments in which it had ever engaged, but many measures were then before the Congress to extend the benefits of the G.I. Bill of Rights to future veterans. . . . Efforts toward better international understanding through educational activities increased during the closing years of the first half of the twentieth century. . . . Although precedents for it were very old, the philanthropic foundation was a significant development of the first half of the century and represented fiscal assets of about $2 billion of private wealth, with the immense Ford Foundation being the youngest and the largest of this form of trust to channel "private wealth to public or general welfare purposes." . . . Remarkable scientific progress had been encouraged in no small part by the philanthropic foundation. At mid-century, President Harry S. Truman recommended the establishment of the National Science Foundation to encourage and develop a national policy for the advancement of "basic research and education in the sciences." . . . At mid-century there was much evidence of confusion in science, and disillusionment with the laboratory. However, at the diamond jubilee meeting of the American Chemical Society in 1951 James B. Conant, president of Harvard University, made some comforting predictions about developments in science during the next half century. . . . Negroes in the United States made greater progress in education during the first half of the twentieth century than ever before. . . . The higher education of women, which had been slow to develop, rapidly advanced, and when Harvard opened its law school to "God's second mistake," the old issue of coeducation seemed to be finally settled. . . . As the first half of the century was coming to a close, interest in federal aid to education to the states increased, but the significant recommendations of the President's Advisory Committee on Education in 1938 had not yet been passed into application as the second half-century began. . . . The health-consciousness of the American people was keener at mid-century than ever before, with the general death rate the lowest on record, but accidents were affecting the American economy more than disease. . . . Educational organizations and journalism had phenomenal growth. . . . Athletics in educational institutions continued increasingly to absorb the interest of the American people, who were shocked, however, in 1951 at scandals in intercollegiate sports. West Point's experience highlighted the unfortunate conditions, but the president of one ancient seat of learning resigned on account of alleged academic irregularities in favor of athletes. . . . The last three or four decades of the first half of the century saw an apparently increasing tendency of the Supreme Court of the United States to become the national school board, a condition that caused considerable anxiety. . . . The first half of the century witnessed the growth of the so-called scientific study of education, of the educational survey, and of the construction and wide use of objective tests in educational work. . . . But at no time in its long history had American education been subjected to such severe attacks and criticisms as it suffered in the 1940's. . . . In the midst of much confusion, the National Citizens Commission was formed in the spring of 1949 to stimulate cooperative educational action in local communities.

The National Government in Education.—In the summer of 1951, the United States was bringing to a close one of the most extensive and significant educational experiments in which it had ever engaged, in which during the preceding seven years it had expended $14 billion on the education and training of the veterans of the Second World War. Tuition alone had cost $3.5 billion, and at the peak of the undertaking in 1947 more than a million veterans had crowded the college campuses of the country. In the summer of 1951 about a half million were still in college under the G.I. Bill of Rights. In a survey made by the *New York Times* [1] it was reported that "educators everywhere believe that the G.I. program was successful." The administration of funds for this vast undertaking had cost $2 billion, and although in some respects it was inefficient, "in the main the money was wisely spent and properly used."

Legislation on the G.I. educational program, designed to provide federal assistance for those service men and women who desired further educational opportunities, had been approved in 1944, and by amendments the original statute was altered so as to permit veterans to get as much as four years of education—depending upon the length of their service—to be paid for by the national government. Under the program, veterans received, in addition to tuition, monthly allotments for subsistence that ranged from $75 to $120, according to the number of their dependents, and also free textbooks and other necessary educational supplies. Subsistence allotments for the seven years cost about $9.9 billion; tuition, about $3.5 billion; equipment, about $376 million; supplies, about $86 million; and

[1] July 22, 1951.

counseling about $26 million. Under the program, veterans were permitted to go to secondary and technical schools or colleges, or receive training on jobs or at farming. About 3.4 million attended schools below college level; about 2.35 million attended college; about 1.63 million received on-the-job training, and about 760 thousand had training on farms. The program was conducted by more than seventy regional offices under the Veterans Administration, and by the end of 1946 about 30 thousand persons were employed to conduct its affairs. Government checks had been sent to 46 thousand educational institutions, and subsistence checks to 1.6 million veterans. By 1951 the number of employees had been reduced to about 9 thousand.

Carl R. Gray, Jr., Administrator of Veterans Affairs, was quoted as saying that the program, which was a new departure in benefits for veterans, had been very effective and had "achieved much that had been hoped for it." It had been "a program of hope for the veterans—hope for new careers, for promising futures, and for successful readjustment to civilian life." It was believed that the G.I. Bill of Rights had set a precedent for benefits to future veterans, and many G.I. measures were before the Congress in the summer of 1951. It was said that most of the known abuses in the G.I. program had arisen "from administrative difficulties inherent in the law and from the sudden impact of large numbers of veterans upon the educational system."

Education and Better International Understanding.—Efforts toward better international understanding through educational activities increased as the close of the first half of the twentieth century approached. Some educational undertakings of more than national scope followed the Second World War and were watched with much interest: the interchange of American and British teachers; a program of traveling fellowships abroad, proposed and set up under Public Law 584 of the 79th Congress, approved in August, 1946; the establishment of Japan's International University; the activities of the International Institute of Education; and the organization and activities of UNESCO.

The British-American Exchange of Teachers was inaugurated with the school year of 1946-47 in a program that followed an official request from Great Britain to the State Department in Washington. The program provided for 74 teachers from each country in 1946-47. The American teachers represented 29 states. This number was later increased, and the program was accounted a great success. The exchange teachers, who were carefully selected, exhibited great interest and enthusiasm for the undertaking.

The program, however, began under many difficulties. As the exchange got under way, there were severe shortages of teachers in both countries, difficulties of travel, and shortages of living quarters; but the success of the program was due in large part to the cooperation which it had from local educational authorities in both countries. In addition "to the intangible results," it was and still is believed that constructive and definite educational benefits would develop for both countries from the undertaking, and that useful studies in which guest and host teachers would collaborate would come to publication. One of the major purposes of this interesting cooperative educational effort was the promotion of understanding and good will between Britain and the United States.

The Fulbright Act, under Public Law 584, was initiated by James W. Fulbright, senator from Arkansas, a former Rhodes scholar and former president of the university of that state. Under this legislation, provision was made for sending American students abroad for study, with their expenses paid from the sale of surplus war equipment, and for receiving foreign exchange students in this country. The law also provided for "financing studies, research, instruction, and other educational activities of or for American citizens in schools and institutions of higher learning" in foreign countries, or of the citizens of such countries in American schools and institutions of higher learning. The act further provided for the appointment of a Board of Foreign Fellowships by the President of the United States. This board represented cultural and educational student and war veterans' groups, the United States Office of Education, the Veterans Administration, and both state-supported and privately endowed educational institutions.

These efforts showed a remarkable change in the attitude of this country. Opposition to the European education of Americans had been vigorously voiced here as early as the seventeenth century, and energetic opposition continued through the Revolutionary War and even afterward.[2]   Noah Webster had been very sharp in his criticism of the practice, George Washington had viewed it with "indescribable regret," and Thomas Jefferson and others had warned against it. The General Assembly of Georgia had declared that sending youth abroad for education was a humiliating "acknowledgment of

[2] See Edgar W. Knight, *A Documentary History of Education in the South Before 1860* (Chapel Hill: The University of North Carolina Press, 1950), Vol. II.

the ignorance or inferiority of our own." The assembly expressed its displeasure over the issue by enacting a law which made aliens of those Georgians under sixteen years of age who resided three or more years abroad for their education, and excluded them from holding office for such a term upon their return. These expressions in the early days of this country disclosed a fear that foreign education would warp the minds of young Americans and make for disloyalty to their nation and to the institutions at home. The recent efforts in the exchange of teachers and students were viewed as heartening signs that the American people were growing much more world-minded. The exchange of students and teachers was not without precedent, although in these two programs new principles seemed to appear. There had been an annual exchange of graduate students between the signatory nations of the treaty of Buenos Aires in 1936, a major purpose of which was the promotion of Pan-American understanding. And for several years South American countries had been sending picked students to the United States for work in certain fields, including public health and education.

Of much interest was the announcement in the early part of 1950 that Japan's International University would be opened in 1952, that American professors would be engaged for it, and that one or more international houses would be provided for American and other foreign students and research workers. These undertakings were part of the report of the Educational Exchange Survey Group which investigated educational conditions in Japan at the invitation of General Douglas MacArthur. The International University was to be nonsectarian, and its purpose was to develop a program of graduate education based on democratic philosophy and Christianity. Secretary of State Dean Acheson in endorsing the plan said: "The faculty, both Japanese and international, is to be Christian, but there is to be no attempt to proselytize, for freedom of religion is one of the most important of freedoms." There were to be graduate schools of education, social work, citizenship, public administration, and a college of liberal arts, all designed to prepare leaders in education for the schools and colleges of Japan, for public service, and for social-welfare work.

Another significant activity was that of the Institute of International Education which had been founded in New York City in 1919. Its overseas activities greatly widened, and by 1950 more than 2 thousand foreign and American students were aided through fellowships and scholarships—a large increase over the preceding year. Fifty-nine countries were represented in this program. It was also pointed out in the report of the Institute that 277 fraternities, sororities, and students' groups, as well as private organizations and individuals, had assisted the program of bringing foreign students to the United States. In addition to this activity, the Institute answered 100 thousand inquiries from persons interested in foreign studies, and gave advice to 10 thousand persons in its New York offices. The Institute's *News Bulletin* has wide circulation. The program of the Institute in 1951 included bringing students and specialists to the United States from Germany, Austria, and Japan, in cooperation with the Department of State and the United States Army. A program of the Korean government called for sending students to study in this country.

The organization and activities of United Nations Educational, Scientific, and Cultural Organization (UNESCO) were also considered very significant. During the years of the Second World War, the public and the educational profession showed a growing interest in the promotion of educational and cultural relations on an international basis, and the creation and development "of an international agency for education to promote understanding and cooperation among the peoples of the world as a guarantee of peace." An important part of this immense task "was the reconstruction of education in the Axis countries and the re-education of their peoples." This program was undertaken by the army military governments (to be assisted later by civilian educators), as each of the Axis countries went down to military defeat. "Education Missions" were sent to Japan and Germany in 1946 to advise the military governments in the over-all educational reorganization and reconstruction of those countries. Official reports of these activities followed the same year: "United States Education Mission to Japan" and "United States Education Mission to Germany."

Another part of this effort was to provide aid, especially material aid, to the liberated countries in the rehabilitation of their school systems. This was provided first through the United Nations Relief and Rehabilitation Administration and then through UNESCO, which at its first meeting in Paris in 1946 undertook to raise funds for the purpose. The same year the International Commission for International Educational Reconstruction was formed, also to raise funds to aid educational rehabilitation abroad. Another important phase of the work was the plan to create an international educational agency. Interest in this proposal had been stimulated by the Council of Allied Ministers of Education in London in 1942, and by "Education and the United States," reprinted in Washington the next year, and written by the American Council on Public Affairs—a report which grew out of discussions of a Joint Commission of the Council for World Citizenship and the London International Assembly. Attention was gradually turned to still other aspects of educational reconstruction by many organizations, and wide publication and discussion on the subject continued.

After some delays and uncertainties, the decision was made to include in the United Nations Charter the subject of education as one of the important instruments for the maintenance of peace in the world. The constitution of UNESCO was adopted at a conference of official representatives of forty-four countries in London in November, 1945, and had to be ratified by at least twenty of the forty-four signatory nations before the organization could come into being. In 1946 the Congress authorized the President to accept membership of the United States in UNESCO and to establish a National Commission on Educational, Scientific, and Cultural Cooperation. Both these actions, taken without opposition in either branch of the Congress, were unique in the history of this country.[3]

The broad purposes of UNESCO included the stimulation of educational relief and the reconstruction and equipping of schools, universities, libraries, churches, and museums. In the Philippines, 362 libraries had been destroyed; in Belgium, four museums were in ruins; in Poland 6.3 thousand teachers had been killed; the University of Vienna had been wrecked; more than 1.3 thousand churches in Yugoslavia had been destroyed; 1.5 thousand grade schools had been leveled in France; and this was just the beginning of the damage which needed speedy alleviation. Cooperation in all efforts to obtain a "free flow of information and free travel" was another broad purpose of the organization, along with the promotion of production and the distribution of publications, films, and radio broadcasts, and the stimulation of an interchange of scientists, educators, and students. Other aims were to spread knowledge throughout the world, to teach the illiterate half of the world to read and write, to educate people to live in peace, to promote education in health through personal and community hygiene, to stimulate adult education, and to encourage academic, vocational, and domestic skills. And there were even further aims in view: to sponsor international institutes for the theater, music, and literature; to aid in the translation of great books and to collect information on the arts and sciences; to help identify and remove social, religious, and racial tensions unfavorable to peace;

---

[3] See I. L. Kandel, *The Impact of the War Upon American Education* (Chapel Hill: The University of North Carolina Press, 1948).

to encourage inquiries on the principles of human rights, democracy, and liberty; to analyze the basis of the ideological conflicts that lead to wars; to encourage the conservation of the world's natural resources; to promote research centers throughout the world; to open up hitherto uninhabitable areas; and to stimulate scientific developments to the benefit of mankind.

The first meeting of UNESCO was held in Paris in 1946, the second in Mexico City the following year, the third in Beirut in 1948, and the fourth in Paris, the organization's headquarters, in Florence in 1950, and in Paris in 1951. The reports of these meetings indicated the magnitude of UNESCO's plans and activities in the interest of understanding and peace. High confidence in the success of this enterprise was widely expressed, but any appraisal of its ultimate and permanent success, as of the "Education Missions" to Japan and Germany, must await the future historian.[4]

Philanthropy and Education.—A most significant development of the first half of the twentieth century, although precedents for it were very old, was the philanthropic foundation, which has been described "as a legal instrument for channeling private wealth to public or general welfare purposes." This kind of trust, which in the United States at mid-century represented assets of more than $2 billion of private wealth, was "the product of a relatively mature capitalist society." Motives for creating the more than 700 philanthropic foundations in the United States between 1900 and 1950 (more than 500 of them active in mid-century) have been difficult to ascertain. While surplus private "wealth, social sensitivity, and the prevailing tax structure have been contributory factors" in their creation, the services which these foundations have performed have been determined, indirectly at least, by public opinion, which has sometimes suspected the motives of some of the foundations.

Before some of the large foundations were created in the early part of the twentieth century, a few smaller trust funds had been set up for educational purposes. Apparently the first of these in English-speaking North America was the Benjamin Syms bequest in 1634, to which was added the bequest of Thomas Eaton in 1659, for the endowment of a free school in Virginia. This fund was small, but

---

[4] In addition to other reports, the student should examine *Fundamental Education,* a report of a special committee to the preparatory commission of UNESCO, New York, 1947. This book "lays the groundwork for one of UNESCO's major undertakings—the attempt to provide education for the immense numbers of people who lack the most elementary means of participating in the life of the modern world." The idea of "fundamental education" was more than an effort "to make the entire population of the world literate."

it was still active in Elizabeth City County in that state at mid-twentieth century. Larger and more prosperous bequests were those of Benjamin Franklin to Boston and to Philadelphia toward the end of the eighteenth century, a thousand pounds sterling to each, to provide loans to "young artificers of good character." In each case the principal was to be held for a century, at the end of which time the Boston fund amounted to $391 thousand, and that of Philadelphia to $90 thousand. The major part of each was then used for public works, under the terms of the bequest and in the discretion of the managers, and the remainders were reinvested for another century. According to E. V. Hollis,[5] in 1904 Boston used $408 thousand of its fund to build Franklin Union in that city, and four years later Philadelphia used $133 thousand to endow Franklin Institute there. The remainders of the funds were then "reinvested for another hundred years, or until 1991."

Stephen Girard's bequest in 1830 for building and endowing a school in Philadelphia for "poor male white orphans" has been of vast service,[6] and at mid-twentieth century had increased to nearly $90 million. In 1846 Smithsonian Institution was established in Washington, D. C. under the bequest of James Smithson, an Englishman, "for the increase and diffusion of knowledge among men." This was followed in 1867 by the George Peabody Fund of $2 million to give educational aid to the stricken southern states—"this I give to the suffering South for the good of the whole country." In 1882 John F. Slater created a fund of $1 million "for the uplift of the lately emancipated people of the southern states, and their posterity, by conferring on them the blessings of Christian education." In 1908 Anna T. Jeanes of Philadelphia left the sum of $1 million to nearby Swarthmore College if that institution would give up intercollegiate football forever. The college declined the gift tied with such strings, and through that circumstance still another fund was provided for the education of Negroes in the southern states. The following year Caroline Phelps Stokes left $1 million to promote, among other worthy objects, "the education of Negroes, both in Africa and the United States." In 1915 Julius Rosenwald created a fund, which bore his name, to aid in the construction of modern schoolhouses for Negroes in the rural sections of the South. But as

---

[5] *Philanthropic Foundations and Higher Education* (New York: Columbia University Press, 1938), pp. 20, 21. See also, by the same author, the article on foundations in Walter S. Monroe (ed.), *Encyclopedia of Educational Research* (rev. ed.) (New York: The Macmillan Co., 1950), pp. 485-89.

[6] See B. G. Wittels, "Lucky Sons of Stephen Girard," *Saturday Evening Post,* December 13, 1947.

important and as useful as these foundations were, they did not compare in the extent of their influence with the large educational endowments established by John D. Rockefeller, Andrew Carnegie, Mrs. Russell Sage, Mrs. Stephen Harkness, and others after 1900.

Some of these philanthropic foundations were mammoth undertakings. Thirty of the largest in 1950 owned 87 per cent of the combined assets of the 505 that were active at that time, the capital assets of the major trusts having been increased between 1930 and 1950. Eight of these thirty were the Carnegie and the Rockefeller trusts; these controlled 64 per cent of the capital assets of all the active foundations. At that time 73 per cent of these philanthropic assets was held by foundations with headquarters in New York City.

These large trusts were under the direction of self-perpetuating boards of trustees who were reported to be generally of the same economic and cultural status as that of the trustees of the larger and richer universities and colleges, persons who had "a high degree of economic and social security and who belong to the better clubs and fashionable churches." The officials of the foundations were often drawn from officials of institutions for higher education and their advisors were usually members of college and university faculties. Most of the big foundations established before 1915 held their capital assets in perpetuity, but only about one fourth of those established in the 1940's so held them.

The fields of activities of these large trusts were many and varied, but education claimed their major interests. Education was followed by social welfare, health, recreation, religion, racial relations, international relations, public administration, economics, and other miscellaneous activities. Institutions for higher education received most of the grants for educational purposes. The concentration of grants was so heavy that twenty universities received 73 "per cent of the total granted to colleges and universities during the twentieth century by a selected group of foundations." About three hundred and ten institutions for higher education shared in the other 27 per cent. By 1920, the foundations had provided $220 million toward the general endowments of colleges and universities, on such conditions that an additional $660 million were provided by other persons for those endowments.

In addition to these activities, the foundations had been very generous in providing funds for pensions of college teachers, for fellowships and scholarships, for research activities in independent "institutes" and societies, legal, medical, dental, engineering, and teacher education, music, art, library science, forestry, agriculture, and many other fields of effort. Much philanthropic aid found its way to research and work in the noncontroversial physical and natural sciences, especially in the early years of the activities of the foundations; but in more recent years funds have gone increasingly to such work in "the controversial areas of the social sciences . . ." which were marked by remarkable changes in the latter part of the first half of the twentieth century.

The youngest of the major philanthropic trusts at mid-twentieth century was the huge Ford Foundation which in assets topped all the others, and in March of 1951 was reported to be the world's richest foundation. Its fiscal assets were reported to be about a half billion dollars. This trust, which had had its inception in 1936 with Edsel Ford's initial gift of $25 thousand, was fully set up in 1950 when the gigantic estates of Henry Ford and his son Edsel were settled, and the immense funds were earmarked to be spent for "human welfare" through a tax-exempt agency known as The Ford Foundation. One commentator on this great fund observed: "If the tax collector doesn't remember Ford kindly, a lot of other people will." [7]

In a financial statement issued in March of 1951, Henry Ford II, chairman of the trustees of the trust, said: "Until such time as the trustees may consider it practical and desirable to dispose of all or part of its principal fund, the only source of funds available for the work of the foundation will be the liquid assets and future dividends from its investments." At the end of 1950 the liquid assets were reported at nearly $79 million. The bulk of the net assets consisted of 3,089,908 shares of Class A nonvoting stock of the Ford Motor Company, which represented gifts received between 1937 and 1950 from the late Henry Ford and the late Edsel Ford and their estates. Assets other than the Ford stock were listed as more than $3 million in cash, nearly $84 million in United States Treasury bills and certificates of indebtedness, $5 million in real estate, and a half million in other assets. The trustees determined that the funds could most wisely be spent in promoting progress and understanding in five large areas: peace, freedom and democracy, economic well-being, education, and human behavior. In late 1950, when it initiated its active program, The Ford Foundation was "already on its way toward becoming a major factor in the American school and college

[7] James R. Miller, "He's Got to Give Away $25,000,000 a Year," *This Week Magazine, New York Herald Tribune,* September 2, 1951; also Robert L. Heilbroner, "The Fabulous Ford Foundation," *Harper's Magazine,* CCIII (December, 1951), pp. 23-32.

picture." On its "five areas for action" was this statement: "The Ford Foundation will support activities to strengthen, expand, and improve educational facilities and methods to enable individuals more fully to realize their intellectual, civic, and spiritual potentialities; to promote greater equality of educational opportunity; and to conserve and increase knowledge and enrich our culture." The foundation at once took steps to implement two major parts of the educational work of the United States by providing a Fund for the Advancement of Education, with an initial grant of $7 million, and a Fund for Adult Education with an interim grant of $3 million, which were expected to play a large part in educational research and investigation during the next decade.

Instead of appointing a university or college president or some other official collegian to direct the spending of the funds, the trustees selected Paul C. Hoffman for that responsible position. He had been president of the Studebaker Corporation and later was head of the Committee for Economic Development. He had just finished spending, in two and a half years, $10 billion as administrator of the ECA. He took office with The Ford Foundation at the beginning of 1951 under instructions: "Collect the best brains you can find and start spending." Among these best brains were Robert M. Hutchins, formerly head of the University of Chicago; Chester C. Davis, formerly president of the Federal Reserve Bank of St. Louis; H. Rowan Gaither, Jr., an attorney of San Francisco and chairman of the Rand Company; and other persons who had reputations to speak of.

According to report, the general public did not always understand the purposes of the philanthropic foundations, and curious requests for grants marked and marred the experience of the older trusts all along. One critic of philanthropic trusts pointed to "the tactics of grant-seekers as constituting the seamy side of philanthropy." The late F. P. Keppel, president of the Carnegie Corporation, said that some of the questionable methods applicants for grants would use ranged from "mild wheedling to anything short of murder." He told of one college president, a chronic applicant, who called one day at Dr. Keppel's office and calmly announced: "I am not here today to ask for money." Dr. Keppel answered by asking, "How much is it you don't want?"

The trustees of the new Ford Foundation soon learned that because the announced and widely publicized aims of the immense trust covered considerable ground, many persons mistakenly came "to think of it as a grab bag, available for the financing of almost anything." Applications for grants came in at the rate of $100 million a month and included "some bizarre requests": for the support of a plan to improve the human race by financing matrimony among college students, the assumption being that they would produce bright children; the request of an elderly lady for a grant to enable her seventy-year-old and unhappy brother to get banjo lessons; of an inventor who asked aid to manufacture hot-air balloons to use in weather research; of another grant-seeker who urged funds to convert the Mediterranean Sea into a fresh-water lake. But the trustees proceeded on the theory "that people should not come to the Foundation, but that we should go to them—with our program." That program promptly assumed large proportions and tackled big projects, among which were overseas activities, aid to the Free University of Berlin, the National Committee for a Free Europe, an International Press Institute, the Free Russia Fund, a Resettlement Campaign for Exiled Professionals, a Fund for the Advancement of Education, scholarships for younger college and university professors, and a Fund for Adult Education. Toward the support of these activities The Ford Foundation had by the end of 1951 laid out about $25 million.[8]

A Half Century of Scientific Progress.—In the stimulation of investigation and research in the natural and social sciences, in a half century that was marked by a "social restlessness" and remarkable scientific progress unlike anything that any other similar period in the history of the race had seen, the philanthropic foundations played no small part. By 1950, science had so come into its own that when people spoke or thought of progress they usually meant progress in science and technology. As was indicated in Chapter 1, science had been in its infancy in 1900 as compared with science in 1950, for between the two dates new and startling scientific theories and applications opened up widely before the eyes of men: aircraft, automobiles, radio-telephonic communications, broadcasting and television, radar, synthetic rubber, electron tubes, and marvelous discoveries in medical science: antibiotics, vitamins, hormones, penicillin, sulfa drugs, and

[8] The W. H. Kellogg Foundation, incorporated in Michigan in 1930 "to advance the health, education, and well-being of children without regard to race, creed, or geographical boundary" directed its activities mainly toward the advancement of child health and welfare. In 1947 its fiscal assets were reported at about $47 million. At mid-century, however, this trust was sponsoring, through a grant of $3 million, a five-year study designed to improve the profession of school administration. The grant was made to the graduate schools of education in Columbia University (Teachers College), the University of Chicago, Harvard University, the University of Texas, and George Peabody College for Teachers. This was said to be the first time that concerted attention on such a large scale had been given to the preparation of the managers of the public schools of the United States.

a host of other discoveries on which the scientists had been diligently at work. The half century had witnessed two devastating world wars, but it also witnessed new scientific benefits, wide social reforms, the conquering of diseases, more human comfort and less human drudgery, and all these changes had wide educational significance.

The role of research in American democracy and life was emphasized by President Harry S. Truman in his budget message to the Congress in 1950 when he recommended the establishment of the National Science Foundation. After again recommending federal aid to education in the states, he said:

The Government is investing hundred of millions of dollars in research—primarily in applied research in the military, atomic energy, and health fields.

We must consider, however, not only the ways in which the great reservoir of scientific knowledge already at our disposal can best be utilized, but also the best paths to follow for the discovery of further basic knowledge.

To this end we urgently need a National Science Foundation to stimulate basic research and to assure an effective balance among the Federal research programs. By developing a national research policy and by formulating a truly national research budget, it should be possible to relate the activities of public and private institutions in a concerted effort to advance all frontiers of knowledge.

The budget provides $500 thousand for the administrative expenses of the proposed National Science Foundation, in the expectation that the Congress will enact legislation, already passed by the Senate, to establish it.

This recommendation followed several years of study of proposed legislation, hundreds of pages of testimony by experts on science, medicine, and education, and the National Foundation was established in May of 1950. But the Congress approved only $225 thousand for its organizational and administrative expenses for the year, although the sum of $14 million had been set as the first year's request. The legislation proposed for the foundation provided for dealing with "fundamental research, which was to be neither military nor secret," but as finally enacted, the bill authorized the Secretary of Defense to call upon the foundation to engage in military research whenever he deemed it necessary. Even with its restricted appropriation, it was believed possible for this newcomer among federal agencies to get off to a good start. Commenting on the undertaking, the *New York Times* [9] said that since it "would have to husband its resources, it is to be hoped that the foundation will avoid unnecessary duplication of work done by other scientific agencies. There are

[9] May 14, 1950.

fashions in research as there are in automobiles and clothes, with the result that some fields are more highly developed than others." Any "lopsidedness" in research could be corrected, that paper thought, "if the foundation maps out the whole field of science for the purpose of discovering where research is already being conducted on an adequate scale, and where it has hardly begun."

The primary function of the National Science Foundation was to encourage and develop a national policy for the advancement of "basic research and education in the sciences." Most scientists looked upon basic research as almost in the nature of "critical material," as Dr. Alan T. Waterman, director of the foundation, was reported as saying when he appeared before a subcommittee of the House in 1951 to urge adequate support for its work. Unless steps were taken to encourage basic research "at its source, so that the 'stock pile' is being constantly replenished, we may some day find ourselves with greatly reduced stores of the new ideas and basic concepts on which our technology depends." Few scientists disagreed with this point of view, although some of them thought that an appropriation of $14 million would not be sufficient for the foundation. At mid-century the United States was spending $2 billion a year "on research of all types in the natural sciences." But the foundation's board of twenty-four distinguished persons, headed by James B. Conant, president of Harvard, believed "that they could put the money where it would do the most good—into replenishing the stock pile of scientific ideas." The atomic bomb had been built "on the basis of fifty years of intensified study of subatomic forces, beginning when Wilhelm Konrad Roentgen discovered X rays." The fear among those scientists who took this long view was that basic studies might be "stamped out in the rush to make something useful of what we already know." It was pointed out that when funds were made available chiefly for "applied" scientific research rather than for basic investigations, competent scientists had to shift their efforts.

Moreover, endowments of universities could no longer carry the full load of basic research, and taxes were tending to dry up support from philanthropic sources; hence the need for more generous support of basic research by the federal government. Industrial leaders acknowledged their debt to the scientific work of the universities, but stockholders were "understandably" not willing to use funds of their companies "in a research project unless it looks as if it would pay a return." [10]

[10] See Robert K. Plumb, "Science in Review," *New York Times*, August 19, 1951; also an editorial on the foundation in that paper, September 2, 1951.

The foundation's board decided that the best place to begin its program was with fellowships to young people who had demonstrated promising scientific ability. Another place where its funds would be used was in the support of "exploratory research by competent scientists whose work is now handicapped because of inadequate financial resources." A third major function of the foundation would be "to support projects whose importance to the military defense of the nation is presently recognized." In August of 1951, however, it seemed clear that science had not yet had an impressive influence on the Congress. The House Appropriations Committee recommended that the National Science Foundation receive for the fiscal year $300 thousand instead of the $14 million requested by President Truman on the advice of the foundation's executive board —a drastic cut which, it was hoped, would be restored by the Senate. The American Association for the Advancement of Science, among the senior scientific societies that had stood up for the foundation, took "the unprecedented step of advising its members to write to their senators."

"Disillusion with the Laboratory."—Notwithstanding the great advances in scientific work, there was evidence at mid-century that science was probably as confused as the world for which it had been working. The theoretical or "pure" scientist was still looked upon as a dreamer and visionary, even while tearing the atom apart and showing how its energy could be coaxed to work for the welfare as well as for the destruction of human beings and the confusion of their affairs in the world. Even before the middle of the century dissatisfaction with the "Great God Science" had developed. Two decades earlier Joseph Wood Krutch had written under the title, "Disillusion with the Laboratory," [11] that science had "seemed to promise to increase the power to control nature and the accidents of human lives. We do not, we cannot, actually doubt even the most fantastic of the verities which the scientist announces, since his boasted power to foretell and control, upon the basis of his hypothesis, has been too often vindicated to permit of skepticism, and when he tells us that soon we shall be doing this or that, we know from experience that we had best believe him. Yet our belief is without enthusiasm—even, perhaps, a little perfunctory or impatient—because all his successes seem to achieve and to promise less than they once did. . . . Science has always promised two things not necessarily related—an increase, first, in our powers, second, in our happiness and wisdom, and we

[11] *Atlantic Monthly,* March, 1928.

have come to realize that it is the first and less important of the two promises which it has kept most abundantly."

Since the 1920's, and particularly after the onset of the great economic depression that began in 1929, many criticisms were heard of the social and political institutions of this country. During the fair-weather days, it was fashionable in some quarters to use scientific arguments to prove the insignificance of man and his small importance in the universe, and at the same time to romanticize his self-efficiency and to teach that his salvation depended upon the extent of his scientific knowledge. But in the confusion and unsettled conditions of modern science, some of the greatest scientists stepped forward and declared that if there was taint of materialism in this powerful age, it should not be charged against science but against man's spiritual unpreparedness for the gifts of science. Michael Pupin, eminent for his researches in electrical communications, said that political science, sociology and education, psychology, and theology may have failed to teach men and women that there are spiritual powers in the human heart which could be employed for the good of mankind. As 1950 approached, confusion apparently increased. Walter Lippmann noted that no mariner "ever enters upon a more uncharted sea than does the average human being born in the twentieth century. Our ancestors thought they knew their way from birth through eternity, but we are puzzled about day after tomorrow."

Near the middle of the twentieth century, Anthony Standen, who took a "first" in chemistry at Oxford and then studied chemical engineering at the Massachusetts Institute of Technology, published "a sweeping and savage little book called *Science Is the Sacred Cow*," [12] in which he declared that the world was divided into two groups: "scientists, who practice the art of infallibility, and non-scientists, sometimes contemptuously called laymen." He saw the scientists as "pleasant and even modest fellows," but their collective "ego" was neither pleasant nor modest. They showed infatuation with their own scientific minds, and seemed to think "they are entitled to pour scorn on other subjects from a very great height," although he admired their practical results: "Better things for better living." Unfortunately, however, scientists seemed "overbearing, overpraised, and overindulged," and it was not the results of science but the "scientific method" or "scientific attitude" or a variety of other "hidden, mystical virtues" that they advertised most. It was a delusion for laymen to believe that science was a "cure-all

[12] (New York: E. P. Dutton & Co., 1950.)

for mankind," infallible and above criticism. "What with scientists who are so deep in science that they cannot see it, and nonscientists who are too overawed to express an opinion, hardly anyone is able to recognize science for what it is, the Sacred Cow of our time." Even physics, "science at its best," and chemistry, presented serious contradictions, by making claims to "the discovery of immutable truths, and yet scoff at all philosophical absolutes." The truths of physics and chemistry were not truths at all, but "a body of well-supported probable opinion only, and its ideas may be exploded at any time." And Standen asked: "Is the universe to be thought of in terms of electrons and protons? Or . . . in terms of Good and Evil? Merely to ask the question is to realize at least one very important limitation of physics." The other scientists, the biologists included, were guilty of the same limitation and spent much time trying to define their mystic terms, with "ludicrous" results. The psychologists, among the worst, were torn among the gestaltists, the behaviorists, the functionalists, and the reflexionists, and expended their energies in "formulating the obvious" and in "guesswork in gobbledygook" without having "anything really important to say about man." It was possible, Standen said, "to go clear through a course in psychology without ever hearing what the various virtues are." He also thought that the layman should steer clear of the advice of the social scientists. Mathematics was the only exact science, he said, but even it had become the tool of all the other sciences which had "substituted the *is* for the ought." And he added: "That is why we must never allow ourselves to be ruled by scientists. They must be our servants, not our masters."

It was an old complaint that increase in man's scientific knowledge and technological "know how" had not been "accompanied by a corresponding sense of moral obligation, meaning that we have not yet succeeded in curbing abuses of scientific discoveries and inventions either in peace or war," wrote Waldemar Kaempffert, science editor of the *New York Times*.[13] He pointed out that Sir Oliver Lodge, forty years before, had doubted whether man was "spiritually and morally fit to make rational use of such a technical triumph." Kaempffert went on to say that science had so far "been applied chiefly in fathoming the secrets of matter and motion, technology chiefly in winning wars and improving man's material condition. If the proper study of mankind is man, science is still in a primitive state" because it knew less about man than about the atom. If and

[13] "The Past Century—and the Next—in Science," *New York Times Magazine,* September 9, 1951.

when a renaissance should come in science, where it was sorely needed, it would "devote at least as much research to man's abilities and shortcomings as it has devoted to the synthesis of drugs and plastics. In the past, science has taught man how to conquer his environment. It has still to tell him why he behaves as he does, and teach him how to conquer himself."

About the time Kaempffert was writing this, James B. Conant, President of Harvard, one of the distinguished scientists who had made the first atomic bomb, was looking into the crystal ball— plastic of course—and telling the diamond jubilee meeting of the American Chemical Society that he had no fear of atomic war, and he predicted that solar energy for industrial purposes would prove more valuable than atomic energy. He predicted "neither an atomic holocaust nor the golden abundance of the atomic age." On the contrary, he saw "a worried humanity endeavoring by one political device after another to find a way out of the atomic age. And by the end of the century this appears to have been accomplished, but neither through totalitarianism nor by the advent of world government." In his view, neither the forces of evil nor those of good would prevail to the extent that had been foreshadowed in recent years by some dismal prophets of gloom. Mankind, the distinguished chemist predicted, would manage by the narrowest margin to avoid World War III, would learn to harness the inexhaustible source of solar energy, to produce fresh water from sea water in order to make garden spots of deserts, and there would be an era of peace and prosperity. "To my mind the prospects today are more hopeful than they were two years ago," he comfortingly declared. The people of the free world had been "awakened from their dreams of an easy peace; they have faced up to the realities of the mid-twentieth century. Before long they will be armed and ready. When that day comes, the fear of Communist aggression will cease to haunt Western Europe. When that day comes, one can begin to talk about a real settlement of the international situation," President Conant was quoted in the press as saying. The place of schooling in this strange scientific age may not have been clear to everybody. But to the educators it had seemed clear enough. Following the blasting of Hiroshima in early August of 1945, and following their fondness for slogans, the educators hastened to make "Education for the Atomic Age" the catchword of their conventions.

The Negro's Progress in American Education.—Despite their manifold handicaps, the American Negroes made greater progress in education during the first half of the twentieth century than in any of their other activities. The increase of their attendance at public schools had been especially highly marked, and there had also been a marked increase in their attendance at higher educational institutions. But Harvard had been established nearly two centuries, the College of William and Mary more than 130 years, and Yale more than 125 years before the first Negro received a collegiate degree. John Russwurm had been graduated from Bowdoin College in 1826. Charles S. Johnson [14] says that Russwurm "added to this accidental distinction that of being the founder of *Freedom's Journal,* the first Negro newspaper." For twenty years following his graduation, only seven other Negroes were graduated from recognized colleges, and by 1860 there had been only twenty-eight. In 1900 there were ninety-nine colleges for Negroes in the United States, with 2.6 thousand students, and that year 156 baccalaureate degrees were conferred. Although the number of institutions for Negro higher education had increased to only 108 in 1950, enrollments in them had increased to 74.5 thousand, and baccalaureate degrees to more than 13 thousand, and there was increasing attendance of Negroes in higher institutions in those states that did not provide separate schools for the two races. While the number of bachelor's degrees had increased eighty-four times in a half century in the Negro colleges, the corresponding figures for all institutions for higher education in the United States was sixteen. Negro college faculties had increased from 1.5 thousand in 1900 to 5.8 thousand fifty years later. At the beginning of the century, Negroes composed only 57 per cent of the faculties in these institutions. In 1950, the figure was above 90 per cent. The educational and general income of the Negro colleges meantime had grown from about $1 million to approximately $40 million, but even this was a somewhat slower increase than appeared in the income of higher education as a whole. In 1900 the total value of all Negro collegiate property was reported at close to $8 million. In 1948, the latest date for which comparable statistics were available in 1950, this figure was about $120 million. Prior to 1951, no Negro college offered work above the master's degree, but in that year North Carolina College, at Durham, a publicly supported and controlled liberal arts college for Negroes, was enabled by an ap-

[14] *The Negro College Graduate* (Chapel Hill: The University of North Carolina Press, 1938), p. 7. The great leader, Booker T. Washington, was the first Negro to receive an honorary degree from a New England institution, a master's from Harvard in 1896. For a moving account of this event see his *Up From Slavery* (New York: Doubleday, Doran & Co., 1938), pp. 295-302.

propriation by the state of North Carolina to enter upon work for the Ph.D., especially in the field of professional education. Prior to 1936, some 132 Negroes had received this degree and 155 Negroes had been admitted to Phi Beta Kappa. By 1950 many more had received that degree and had membership in that scholarship society.

Negroes have been a part of the national citizenship since the adoption of the Fourteenth Amendment to the Constitution of the United States in 1868. At that time illiteracy among them was close to 90 per cent. By 1930 this had declined to about 16 per cent, but the problem of Negro illiteracy constituted at mid-century a large part of the entire problem of illiteracy in the United States. In 1940 about 75 per cent of all Negro workers were classified as unskilled or semi-skilled, and less than 3 per cent as professional. In conditions of health, crime, and delinquency, the Negroes suffered disproportionately when compared with the whites. Death rates among them were higher, with tuberculosis, cardiac diseases, and diseases of infancy the major causes of death; and as a group they furnished an excess proportion of the inmates of state and Federal prisons and reformatories. The improvement of the health of this minority group to the point where it would compare favorably with the white people would wipe out many disabilities from which Negroes suffered, improve their economic condition, and stimulate their native abilities. Statisticians and other experts for insurance companies said that health was "basic to the general welfare of the Negro as it is to no other race," a condition that placed heavy responsibilities on the schools.

The Higher Education of Women.—As pointed out in Chapter 4, the higher education of women was long an acute issue in the United States, where such provision was slowly made and coeducation was stubbornly resisted. Nevertheless, the higher education of women rapidly advanced during the first half of the twentieth century. And when, at mid-century, Harvard University opened its law school to what pessimistic Friederich Wilhelm Nietzsche had called "God's second mistake," the issue seemed finally resolved. For, as went Harvard, always identified with the fitness and fashion of things educational, so always would most of the other institutions for higher education sooner or later be likely to go.

There had been misgivings about the higher education of women throughout most of the nineteenth century, by the end of which, however, sentiment on the subject was beginning to change. When in 1879 F. A. P. Barnard, president of Columbia University, advocated the admission of women to the undergraduate college of that institution, he is said to "have convulsed the educational world of that day." A decade earlier, Charles W. Eliot of Harvard had said in his inaugural address that that ancient institution would not admit women as students in Harvard College nor in any of its other schools whose discipline required residence near it. The difficulties involved in a common residence "of hundreds of young men and women of marriageable age are very grave. The necessary police regulations are exceedingly burdensome. The Corporation are not influenced to this decision, however, by any notions about the innate capacities of women. The world knows next to nothing about the natural mental capacities of the female sex." Six years later Eliot wrote in the *New England Journal of Education* that if

. . . women had not been cheaper than men, they would not have replaced nine tenths of the men in the American public schools . . . The superiority of men to women, or of women to men, has nothing to do with the matter . . . That frequent changes of teachers should result from having nine tenths of the teachers women is a necessary consequence of two stubborn facts: first, that women have not the physical endurance of men, and secondly, that the great majority of female teachers stop teaching at marriage, an event that does not stop a man's teaching . . . It is quite unnecessary to this argument to undervalue the work of women in schools . . . This protest is directed against the excessive employment of women, into which towns have been let from motives of false economy."

A few years later James B. Angell, president of the University of Michigan, said that women graduates were doing their full share of winning a reputation for that institution and were "justifying the wisdom of the Regents who opened to them the opportunities for a thorough classical training." J. L. Pickard, president of the State University of Iowa, wrote in 1893 that women's physical nature demanded a different treatment "as to hours of study, as to times of physical exercise and the character of such exercises, as to regularity and uniformity of tasks assigned." But he believed that young men and women could be educated together as well as in separate schools, and "a strong plea may be made for coeducational colleges on the score of economy." In 1894 John C. Kilgo, president of Trinity College in North Carolina, pointed out that boys and girls grew up in the same homes, played together in the yards, went to school, Sunday school, and to picnics together, and were expected to be social companions and to marry when they reached adulthood. He saw no reason why their collegiate education should be separate. Three years later, when Trinity College was opened to women, he wrote that the innovation was "cheered most enthusiastically by the women," and marked "a new era in our state and its future will vindicate the wisdom of Mr. Duke." [15]

In the same year that Kilgo was writing about Trinity's being opened to women, E. A. Alderman, president of the University of North Carolina, a near neighbor of Trinity College, wrote that that institution "should open its postgraduate courses to women of the state. Then perhaps it might enter into the purpose of some good man or woman with a heart for good deeds to build such a foundation for women here as would give them equal facilities with their brothers and also make for the softening of our manners and the humanizing of our life." In 1902, James R. Angell, of the University of Chicago, wrote in *Popular Science Monthly:* "To behold the campus dotted with couples, billing and cooing their way to an A.B. is a thing, it is said, to rejoice Venus or Pan rather than Minerva, and were it the frequent or necessary outcome of coeducation, the future of the system would certainly be in jeopardy." The same year, Nicholas Murray Butler of Columbia University wrote in the *Journal of Education:* "Coeducation is a dead issue. The American people have settled the matter. Why discuss the matter further?" G. Stanley Hall, president of Clark University, told the National Education Association in 1904:

> It is now well established that higher education in this country reduces the rate of both marriage and offspring . . . I think it established that mental strain in early womanhood is a cause of imperfect mammary function, which is the first stage of the slow evaluation of sterility . . . A boy forced to see too much of girls is sure to lose something, either by excess or defect, from the raw material of his manhood. The higher education of women involves all the difficulties of that of men, with many new problems of its own. The girls' colleges think it wisest to train for self-support, and hold that if marriage comes, it can best take care of itself. I urge the precise reverse.

The same year, James B. Angell of the University of Michigan told the same association: "As it seems to be by divine ordination that the sexes are compelled to grow up together, I think that in the West, at least, we shall continue to believe that they may be properly educated together, under such reasonable regulations as good sense will suggest." [16]

---

[15] Washington Duke made a large gift to the college on condition that it be opened to women. In 1924 his son, James B. Duke, richly endowed the institution, which became Duke University.

[16] For other views of college presidents on the subject of coeducation and the higher education of women, see Edgar W. Knight, *What College Presidents Say*

During the First World War, girls of Radcliffe College, tenuously coordinated with Harvard College, were admitted for the first time to the famous Widener Library of Harvard, but to avoid amorous trouble they were required to sit together behind pillars at the end of the room; and when the Lamont Undergraduate Library was opened, it was announced that girls would not be admitted to its facilities: there were too many "corridors and alcoves," the librarian was quoted as saying, and "if we should let girls in we should have to hire a force of patrolmen to watch the dark corners, at enormous expense"—an argument similar to one which President Eliot had used in 1869 against having women at Harvard.

But conditions were rapidly changed in regard to the higher education of women. In the 1940's, after more than three centuries of high masculine tradition and prestige, Harvard enlisted on the side of coeducation and as a wartime measure permitted juniors, seniors, and graduate students of nearby Radcliffe to attend its courses. Paul Buck, dean of the Faculty of Arts and Sciences, said that it was a "recognition which I do not think we can properly escape in the future, that Harvard assumes an interest in the education of women." One Boston newspaper rushed its sheets to the streets, screaming on the first page "Harvard Goes Coeducational," which is said to have chilled some of the officials of the ancient institution. One dean was reported as fearing that further extension of coeducation might some day furnish Harvard with coeducational cheer leaders in the football stadium, a prospect which some Harvard men would probably view as dark and forbidding. Another official imagined boys and girls whispering together in library corners, or walking arm in arm under the trees on the banks of the Charles River. How could boys and girls study together and "still avoid each other's oppressive continuous presence?" it was asked.[17]

In October, 1949, Harvard took another step towards coeducation when it was announced that beginning in the fall of 1950 qualified women would be admitted to its famous law school. Lewis quoted Dean E. N. Griswold as saying that women had "made a place for themselves in the law . . . have come a long way since they were first admitted to membership in the American Bar Association in 1918. Opportunities for women in the law are still limited. . . . It

(Chapel Hill: The University of North Carolina Press, 1940), pp. 299-311. For other original documents on the subject, see Edgar W. Knight and Clifton L. Hall, *Readings in American Educational History* (New York: Appleton-Century-Crofts, Inc., 1951).

[17] See J. Anthony Lewis, "Harvard Goes Coed, But Incognito," *New York Times Magazine,* May 1, 1949.

is our expectation that we will admit only a small number of unusually qualified women students, for the present, at least." With that action, however, which was approved by the governing board of Harvard at the request of the faculty of the law school, all branches of higher scholarship at that institution were opened to women. The Divinity School did not accept women for degrees, but they were admitted to courses in the history and philosophy of religion. Graduate training was available to women in administrative and personnel work in business, although in 1949 the Graduate School of Business Administration did not accept women. The School of Public Health had awarded its first degree to a woman in 1938, the School of Dental Medicine was open to women, as was also the School of Design, and in 1949 Harvard's Medical School conferred the M.D. on women for the first time.

Viewed in retrospect, resistance to the higher education of women and to coeducation seems irrational and cruel, and it may be a bit difficult for American people of the mid-twentieth century to understand. Brave were those who in the earlier years had dared raise their voices in behalf of the educational rights of women. In his *Essay on Projects,* published near the end of the seventeenth century, Daniel Defoe had said that one "of the most barbarous customs in the world, considering us a civilized and Christian country, is that we deny the advantages of learning to women," to whom he would deny "no sort of learning." His essay did not arouse much enthusiasm in England. Mary Wollstonecraft's *A Vindication of the Rights of Women* was published in 1792 in England, and republished in Philadelphia two years later, and this startling challenge to the supremacy of "the lords of creation" is said to have been an ominously indicative in that sphere as Rousseau's *Émile* was said to have been in another sphere.

But less than a century ago, American women were under not only heavy educational disabilities but also heavy civil, social, political, and economic disadvantages. The English common law which prohibited a married woman's ownership of property, for example, remained the rule in most American states until far in the last decades of the nineteenth century, when many states had modified their legislation on the subject in the direction of greater justice for women. Moreover, theology seems to have been an obstacle to women's rights, even though human personality and respect for it were considered essentials of both Christianity and democracy. St. Paul advised young Timothy: "Let a woman learn in quietness, with all subjection, but I permit not a woman to teach, nor to have dominion over man." Wives should submit themselves unto their husbands as "unto the Lord"; and St. Peter called woman "the weaker vessel." Generally, the professions were closed to women. When the first medical degree was conferred on a woman in 1849 by Geneva Medical College in Western New York, many people said that Elizabeth Blackwell was either a mad or a bad woman. It should also be recalled that physical health and robustness in women were under heavy suspicion, a delicate state of health being considered an additional feminine attraction. Women were to be ethereal and delicate clinging vines, and not overzealous in finding a trellis on which to climb. In such a climate of opinion it was not strange that vigorous advocacy of educational and other rights of women could not have been very fashionable. Advocates of such rights were often subjected to the criticisms of the conservative and of some of the clergy who prophesied that educational rights equal to those of men would dissolve the family bonds and cause the home to disintegrate.

But conditions greatly changed and by mid-twentieth century the battle had just about been won. In 1950 women received 121 thousand of the 498 thousand academic degrees awarded in the United States, about 103 thousand of the 433 thousand bachelor's, about 17 thousand of the 58 thousand master's, and 643 of the 6.6 thousand doctorates, most of them in coeducational institutions. The field in which women had the largest number of majors for all three degrees was education. For the bachelor's degree, this was followed by English, home economics, business and commerce, sociology, music, psychology, history, art, languages, and chemistry. For the master's degree, education was followed by social work, English, home economics, history, languages, and chemistry. For the doctorate, English, which followed education, was followed by psychology, chemistry, languages, and history. New York led all the states in the number of each degree awarded, followed for the bachelor's by Texas, California, Pennsylvania, Illinois, Ohio, Massachusetts, Michigan, Indiana, Minnesota, Wisconsin, Oklahoma, and Tennessee. For the master's, New York was followed by Texas, Illinois, Massachusetts, Pennsylvania, Michigan, California, Ohio, Wisconsin, and Colorado. For the doctorate, Illinois followed New York and was in turn followed by California, Pennsylvania, Massachusetts, and Iowa.

Progress in Federal Aid to Education.—Advocates of proposals for federal aid to education after the First World War looked upon the failure of the national government to provide assistance for general education as "a failure of the American system to follow through for the most basic of all our American institutions. It is a failure to carry forward the democratic idea of more equal educational opportunity for all American children." Emphasis was given to this interest in the report of the President's Advisory Committee on Education in early 1938, when Federal grants to the states for educational purposes were recommended to begin in 1939-40 ($70 million) and to be increased through 1944-45 to $190 million. The Committee recommended the continuation of the usual grants for vocational education in the public schools, for vocational rehabilitation of the physically disabled, instruction in the land-grant colleges, agricultural experimentation, extension work in agriculture and home economics, and such other federal aid as had become customary.

New grants recommended by the Committee in 1938 were to be divided into several major funds, to be distributed to the states according to their educational needs and abilities. The largest of these funds was intended for elementary and secondary schools; the second was for the preparation of teachers and other educational personnel; the third, for the construction of schoolhouses; and the fourth for the improvement of state educational administration, which in most states was greatly needed. Other purposes for which funds were recommended were "civic, general, and vocational part-time adult educational activities," to be used through schools and colleges and allocated on the basis of the adult population; for rural library services; and for scholarship aid, reading materials, and the transportation of pupils in both public and nonpublic schools. There was some doubt about the legal use of public funds for the transportation of private school pupils, but in 1947 the Supreme Court of the United States settled that issue in the New Jersey (Everson) Bus Case, when that tribunal held constitutional a statute in that state which provided for the transportation of nonpublic school pupils in publicly owned busses.

Throughout the report of the President's Advisory Committee on Education, there was emphasis on educational inequalities in the United States, notwithstanding the tremendous educational progress that had been made during the past three or four decades. The report showed that there were 127 thousand local school jurisdictions in the nation, most of which raised their school funds separately; and that, for example, in Iowa the most prosperous school district had 275 times more wealth per child than the poorest district. In some states the ablest school districts could provide $100 or more per child for every dollar provided by the poorest districts. Under the recommendations of the Committee, the rural sections of the United States would have been especially benefited. Bills to carry the recommendations into effect were introduced in both houses of the Congress in 1939 and were awaiting hearings in 1941, when war drums began to beat again and war clouds to hang heavily over the heads of millions of children throughout most of the world.

After the onset of the great depression in 1929, the problems of American youth became more acute than ever before in the history of the United States. The years of the depression called sharp attention to the problems of high school youth. One third of all persons unemployed in this country were between the ages of sixteen and twenty-four years, but 40 per cent of the employable young people were unable to find work. Out of these conditions grew new federal educational activities, especially the Civilian Conservation Corps (CCC), the Federal Emergency Relief Administration (FERA), the National Youth Administration (NYA), as an independent division of the Works Progress Administration, under an order which "prescribed rules and regulations relating to student-aid projects and to employment of youth on other projects under the Emergency Relief Appropriation Act of 1935." The number of young people between the ages of sixteen and twenty-four years who participated and received aid in the programs of the NYA rose from about 470 thousand a month during the first half of 1936 to more than 580 thousand during the first half of 1937, after which time the appropriations were reduced, although this form of relief work was continued.

In 1910, William James of Harvard had written an essay under the title, "The Moral Equivalent of War," [18] in which he advocated an organization of youths to combat the ravages of nature. He believed that such an organization could do much to preserve for a peace economy the moral equivalents of the martial ideas and virtues of unity, surrender of private interests, and the development of loyalty, discipline, and hardihood. "To various and sundry hardy tasks in forests and fields, on roads and in mines, on ships, would our gilded youths be drafted off according to their choice, to get the childishness knocked out of them, and to come back into society with healthier sympathies and sobered ideas." Whether consciously or not, it seems to have been on some such ideas as these that the CCC was established, although relief was avowedly one prominent purpose of the organization.

[18] See F. A. Silcox, "Our Adventure in Conservation," *Atlantic Monthly*, December, 1937. For a fuller account of some of the activities of the CCC, FERA, and NYA, see Edgar W. Knight, *Education in the United States* (3d rev. ed., Boston: Ginn & Co., 1951), pp. 627-34.

When Adolph Hitler went into Paris in 1940, apparently American educational leaders began for the first time since the First World War to think seriously about the relation of education to crises in democratic societies, and especially about its relation to threats to American democracy. Following the summer of 1940 there were more pronouncements on education and democracy, and education and national defense, than ever before. National and local educational organizations, college and university presidents, prominent political figures, publicists, and leaders in other fields of endeavor in American life began to emphasize that "a changed world situation calls for educational policies in support of national defense." Military and diplomatic events in Europe seemed to have aroused in many people in the United States "grave concern regarding the future of their way of life and even of their existence as an independent nation." Early in September of 1940, a committee representing forty organizations met in Washington for the purpose of mobilizing the educational forces of the country in the interest of national defense; and the Executive Secretary of the National Education Association and the President of the American Council on Education became co-chairmen of a nation-wide Committee on Education and National Defense. One of the objects of this organization was to disseminate information regarding developments of defense in the United States, while other purposes were to encourage the maintenance and improvement of educational opportunities essential in a long-range national program, and the immediate and continuous representation of organized education for effective cooperation with the National Defense Council, the Federal Security Agency, and other governmental divisions. All these efforts were answers to Hitler and those who were under the delusion from which he and others like him suffered.

The Congress had meantime provided for summer training programs in schools and colleges for workers essential to national-defense industries. By July 15, about 30 thousand workers were enrolled in these programs, and a month later there were nearly 93 thousand. By October, the number was about 242 thousand, with six hundred cities, representing practically all the states, cooperating in the effort. Later, the Congress made additional appropriations, for training in vocational schools, high schools, colleges, universities, and rural schools, youth and adults as workers to speed up defense industries and governmental services. Short courses in institutions for higher education and in schools of engineering, designed to meet the shortage of engineers in fields essential to national defense, and vocational or related or necessary instruction for young people employed on work projects of the National Youth Administration. Never before had a military or other emergency led so vigorously to the harnessing of the educational resources of this country.

Educational and other conditions during and following the First World War had led the National Education Association and its Department of Superintendence, which later came to be called the American Association of School Administrators, to create the Joint Commission on the Emergency in Education in 1932, with a board of more than four hundred regional consultants to cooperate in its activities. These included a program of action for the purpose of trying to meet the acute educational difficulties that had grown out of the depression. The work of the Commission was very effective through regional conferences, radio broadcasts, news letters, the dissemination of useful information about the schools, and surveys of those organizations that were antagonistic to and those that favored public education. Particularly important were the Division of Administrative Service, the Research Division, and the Division of Publications.

In 1936 the Educational Policies Commission was established upon recommendation of the Joint Commission on the Emergency in Education which had discontinued its activities in 1935. The purpose of this Commission was to take a comprehensive view of life in the United States in an effort "to stimulate thoughtful, realistic, long-term planning with the teaching profession; to encourage desirable changes in educational purposes, procedures, and organization; to review recommendations for the improvement of education; to make the best practices in education known and used throughout the country; and to develop a more effective cooperation among various groups interested in educational improvement." Composed of more than a score of distinguished educators, this Commission engaged in extensive research and published many useful books, including *The Unique Function of Education in American Democracy, The Structure and Administration of Education in American Democracy, The Purposes of Education in American Democracy, Education and Economic Well-being in American Democracy, The Education of Free Men in American Democracy, Learning the Ways of Democracy,* and many others. At mid-century the Educational Policies Commission was still very energetic and was engaged in many useful enterprises.

The important relation between public library services and public education came to be increasingly recognized as the twentieth century advanced. Although books and the services of libraries were highly important educational allies, the development of public libraries had not been as rapid as lovers of books and leaders in library work had hoped and expected. Even in wealthy centers, getting adequate support for libraries continued to be difficult, and in the smaller and rural communities there was a sad lack of free public library facilities. A report of the American Library Association in 1938 showed that about 45 million people in the United States at that time did not have access to the services of free public libraries, and of the 3.1 thousand counties in the United States, fewer than three hundred had provided county-wide library service. The American people were then spending about thirty-seven cents per capita annually for such service, with two states at the bottom of the list spending only two cents. Massachusetts led the list with $1.08. New York was spending sixty-two cents. In twenty-two states, half the population did not have access to free public library services. According to the American Library Association, one dollar a year was considered a reasonable per capita expenditure for free public library services, an estimate that was increased in the 1940's to $1.50 for good and to $2.00 for superior services in communities of 25 thousand population or more. The President's Advisory Committee on Education in 1938 considered this activity so important that it recommended grants-in-aid for the encouragement of such services.

The principle of state aid for public libraries had been slow to pass widely into practical application, although small grants had been made for the purpose in New England and some other eastern states before 1900. By 1896 the American Library Association was able to report such aid in Connecticut, Maine, Massachusetts, New Hampshire, New York, New Jersey, Rhode Island, and Vermont, with Delaware and Maryland following later. By 1941, grants had been provided in about eighteen states, and by mid-century in several others, with the movement gradually gaining interest and strength.

Instruction in Health and Accident Prevention.—The health consciousness of the American people was keener at mid-twentieth century than ever before, and was well reflected in the work of the schools. The year 1948 marked the centennial of the public health movement which had been set in motion in England in 1848 with the passage of the first public health legislation and the organization of the first general board of health in London. The first half of the twentieth century had been marked by advances in medical science and public health unequaled in all previous human history. From courageous beginnings, extraordinary changes developed in sanitary and hygienic services which made human life safer, more comfortable, and happier.

Within the first half of the century, the medical inspection of school children and the supervision of their health greatly advanced and came to play an important part in the work of the schools. By 1911 more than four hundred cities in the United States had provided for some form of medical inspection and the work of nurses in their schools, and nearly half the states had medical inspection laws, following the lead of Massachusetts which in 1906 had enacted the first legislation on the subject. By the middle of the century, the medical inspection of school children was rapidly becoming a regular part of the work of the schools in practically all the states, although there was variety rather than uniformity in practices. Attention was also being increasingly given to supervised health, recreational, and safety activities, and to mental hygiene in the schools. Work in these new directions had been stimulated by the White House Conferences on Child Health and Protection which had begun in 1930 under the influence of President Herbert Hoover, who was long actively interested in child welfare work. Among the recommendations of the first conference was one on the rights of children: ". . . of every child, regardless of race, or color, or situation, wherever he may live under the protection of the American flag," a statement which was given wide circulation and had an effect in the work of the schools. The American people came to recognize the importance of good school buildings and surroundings, of the mental hygiene programs in the schools, and of the health both of the children and the teachers. Attention was being given more and more to handicapped children, to those hard of hearing, to the blind, the crippled, and to those of low-grade intelligence. These new responsibilities markedly differed from those of the schools at the beginning of the century.

The general death rate at mid-century was the lowest on record, and the American people were enjoying better health than ever before, according to a report of Surgeon General Leonard A. Scheele of the United States Public Health Service. Improved conditions were due to a decline in deaths by communicable diseases, notably influenza and pneumonia, which were listed together, and tuberculosis, which at the beginning of the century had been the chief causes of death. In 1950, these diseases ranked sixth and seventh, respectively; influenza and pneumonia at 38.2, and tuberculosis at 30.2, per 100 thousand people. In that year, more than 16 million patients had received bed care in hospitals, about 14 million had had chest X rays, and more than 2 million had visited their departments of public health to be examined for venereal diseases. The darker side of the picture showed that cancer and cardiac diseases were increasingly enormously as killers. The death rate from cancer in 1948 showed an increase of 12 per cent over 1940, and that from cardiac diseases an increase of 11 per cent. Mental diseases were reported as the primary causes of ill health and disability. The increase in cardiac and mental diseases, alcoholism, and accidents was a "symptom of cultural conflicts" which had their origin in the physical environment, Dr. Scheele reported, but he saw enormous gains ahead for American health and the health of the world in the next half-century.

But accidents were affecting the American economy more than any disease, and insurance companies and the National Safety Council were trying to drive that fact home. The Travelers Insurance Companies of Hartford made some impressive observations about this gruesome blot on the American scene in *The Human Race,* the fifteenth annual booklet of data on accidents on streets and highways, in "the hope that a bit of satire may succeed in personalizing the lessons of safety where sterner warnings have failed . . ." It was disclosed that more than 32 thousand people had been killed and 1.4 million injured by motor vehicles in 1948. Fatalities on highways had declined a bit since the end of the Second World War—a tribute "to the safety job that has been done. But the injured millions should be constant reminders that the job is far from completed." Many schools were putting in courses on safety for drivers of automobiles and for pedestrians, a step that led some critics to point to the "inflation" of the curriculum in the high schools, and advocates to urge that the colleges and universities do something about the problem of safety. It was pointed out that accidents caused more loss of working years than any disease. The estimated annual cost in loss of wages, including the value of anticipated earnings, for deaths and permanent disabilities, medical expenses, overhead costs of insurance, property damage, and indirect costs associated with occupational accidents was $7.4 billion.

Growth of Educational Organizations and Journalism.—In Chapter 1 brief notice was taken of the great increase in educational organizations and the rapid growth of educational journalism in the first half of the twentieth century. These natural developments in education were not unlike those in other interests and activities of the American people, who have a genius for organization and a fondness for imitation in education as in other matters.

In *The Great American Band Wagon*,[19] a sprightly discussion of American exaggerations, Charles Merz called attention to the mania of the people of the United States for membership in organizations and especially in secret societies, and pointed out that of the sixty million adults in this country in 1928, at least half of them belonged to about eight hundred active secret orders, "each member with a watch charm or a countersign or password." Americans, he said, were the world's greatest joiners. "Who really knows his country without at least one password?" he asked. He said that Americans imitatively joined the Ancient Free and Accepted Masons, the Odd Fellows, the Knights of Pythias, the Daughters of Rebekah, the Maccabees, the Red Men, the Elks, the Modern Order of the White Mahatmas, the Rotarians, Kiwanians, Civitans, Epworth Leaguers, Friends of Self-Determination of Rhodesia, and hosts of other organizations, not to mention the countless country, motor, luncheon, and discussion clubs and societies for the prevention of this or that thing or for the achievement of some other.

In imitation, or for more worthy purposes, or from economic, social, political, or professional motives, people engaged in educational work have exhibited the same or similar tendencies to organize and have membership in educational associations, organizations, and societies, which by 1950 were myriad and increasing as conspicuous features of the American educational scene. The growth of educational organizations was accompanied by the rapid expansion of educational journalism, for most of the associations had their own "house organs." At mid-century there were more than seven hundred and fifty educational periodicals in the United States, listed under nearly fifty different classifications, each representing some organization, and educational journalism had become big business. In addition to the journals of national educational associations, there were journals of state educational associations, state or regional journals issued by professional organizations, by state departments of education, by city boards of education, and many other agencies. There were journals dealing with adult education, psychology, mental hygiene, secondary education, elementary education, higher education, home economics, guidance, religious education, consumer education, visual education, parents-teachers, administration, supervision, history of education, vocational education, Negro education, libraries, industrial arts, language, science, rural education, speech, teacher education, and many other subjects. There were thirty-six separate

[19] (New York: The John Day Co., 1928.)

titles under the topic of health, physical education, and safety. Between 1940 and 1945, at least ninety new educational journals were projected in this country, and almost every year saw one or more new periodicals go to press, at least for a time, for the mortality rate of educational journals has been high.

Educational journalism, which seems to have begun before the organization of educational associations as these are nowadays known, had its modest beginnings in the early part of the nineteenth century with the work of Albert and John Pickett in the publication of the *Academician* in New York, which did not have a long life. The organization in the 1820's of the American Lyceum in Massachusetts and of the Western Academic Institute and Board of Education in Cincinnati, and a few other organizations, including some state educational associations, were followed in 1857 by the National Teachers' Association which developed into the National Education Association, and which by mid-twentieth century had a mammoth membership, and affiliated with it were many scores of organized groups interested in some phase of education.

American ventures in educational journalism seem to have been influenced by educational journals in France and Germany, but attempts of general magazines in this country to include comments on educational subjects may have had some effect on the early efforts to establish strictly educational periodicals. But there were other reasons. Horace Mann wrote, in the educational journal which he began in Massachusetts in 1839 and edited for several years, that the primary purpose of the publication was the improvement of the schools and the promotion of other means of education in that state. Henry Barnard, who made a journal for Connecticut a personal venture and expended much of his own money to keep it going, said that its purpose was the advancement of education in that state. In 1852 the *Ohio Journal of Education* said that its purpose was "to awaken the whole community to a lively sense of the importance of education to a free people, and of the common school as a means by which all the youth of the state are to be educated."

By 1860 fifteen educational journals had been begun by state educational associations, apparently the first in Illinois. This was followed by journals in Rhode Island, New York, Massachusetts, Ohio, Michigan, Indiana, Wisconsin, Missouri, North Carolina, Alabama, Vermont, Kentucky, Connecticut, and Iowa. State departments or boards of education undertook the publication of educational journals before 1860, apparently in the following order: the *Ohio Common*

School Journal, edited by Samuel Lewis, and the *Michigan Journal of Education,* edited by J. D. Pierce, both in March of 1838. Similar journals followed in a few other states.

The dismal part of the story of educational journalism in this country has been its high mortality rate. Inadequate financial support and inadequate editorial direction were the major causes of death. Paid subscriptions seem to have been few in the early days, and the exchange with other journals increased expenses without producing revenue. Even Henry Barnard's eminent effort, the *American Journal of Education,* seems not to have exceeded five hundred paid subscriptions for any issue before 1860, and it is said that it cost Barnard personally as much as $1,300 an issue to keep it solvent. The average yearly circulation of all educational journals in the United States in the 1840's was reported at about 13 thousand, and in the 1850's about 32 thousand, figures which have clearer meaning when compared with the 40 or 50 thousand subscribers to a few of the state educational magazines in 1950. Many expedients were resorted to in the early days to get subscriptions. One state allowed 5 per cent to be added to the examination grades of teachers who subscribed, and another is said to have permitted applicants for certificate to teach to subscribe to the educational journal in lieu of taking an examination.

Horace Mann and other early educational leaders fully believed in educational organizations and journals as important educational auxiliaries. But Mann had a hard time making his journal go. In a letter to a Virginian who was interested in trying to start a journal in his own state, Mann wrote:

> Unless your prospects are better than mine have been, I can give you no encouragement. My common school journal makes an octavo volume of about 400 very large pages. I have edited it now for seven years as a labor of love—that is, for nothing; and it has hardly defrayed the printer's bills. I wish I could offer to send you a complete copy of it, but should have to buy it for that purpose, and therefore you will have to excuse me.

Critics who look askance at educational organizations and journals should again be reminded that education reflects life about it and is more imitative than original. If alcoholics and atheists, the American Friends of Lafayette, bottlers of carbonated beverages, horseshoe pitchers and homeopaths, petroleum geologists and pipe-organ pumpers, advocates of the abatement of noises or of the perpetuation

and encouragement of barber shop quartet singing could organize
(and they did) and start a magazine, in the strict American tradition,
why should not teachers of English, Latin, French, Spanish, and
Portuguese, the social sciences, home economics, typewriting, swimming, vaulting, tap dancing, educational superintendents, principals,
supervisors, or other defensive groups be allowed to do so? They
were and they did, with president, vice president, secretary, executive
committee, and, of course, treasurer.[20]

Athletics and Education.—It was pointed out in Chapter 3 that
athletics in educational institutions in the early years of the twentieth
century had already come to absorb the wide attention of the American people. Ambassador James Bryce of England, in 1905, commented on the passion of the people of the United States "for looking
on at and reading about athletic sports," and three years later Robert
K. Risk of Scotland observed, rather critically, the very large place
intercollegiate sports held in American life. As the century advanced,
interest in these activities greatly increased, difficult problems continued to arise in them, questionable and downright bad practices developed, and at mid-century athletics perhaps absorbed more attention than any other activity in educational institutions, not only in
the colleges and universities but in secondary schools as well. In
1951, the people of the United States were shocked by proved charges
of "throwing" basketball games; and in August of that year, when a
cheating scandal at the United States Military Academy, alleged to
have been closely connected with commercialism in football, was aired
and widely publicized, the American people were horrified and
saddened. American youth seemed to be in a bad plight if practices
in their popular intercollegiate sports could fall so heavily under
suspicion.

In the middle 1920's the Carnegie Foundation for the Advancement of Teaching had undertaken inquiries into school and college
athletics at the request of some influential organizations, including
the Association of American Colleges, the Association of Colleges
and Secondary Schools of the Southern States, and the National Collegiate Athletic Association. The results of the studies were published by the foundation in 1929 as Bulletin Number Twenty-Three,
American College Athletics, and Bulletin Number Twenty-Four, *The
Literature of American School and College Athletics.* While the

---

[20] The largest of the educational associations was the National Education
Association, which had been formed in 1857. In May of 1951, this organization had
a membership of 465 thousand, about 46 per cent of the teachers in the United
States. See Chapter 7.

studies were being made and after their completion, the foundation significantly commented in its annual reports on conditions in athletic sports in the educational institutions of the United States.

Such sports could be made beneficial in education, but not until commercialization had been stopped and they were no longer allowed "to retain their pre-eminence in our distorted scale of academic values." The taint of commercialism removed, intramural sports could be made educationally serviceable if these had institutional support

. . . sufficient to make resort to the methods of the showman and the professional sport promoter unnecessary. Hitherto athletics has absorbed the college; it is time for the college to absorb athletics. . . . . Any institution whose alumni, undergraduates, and faculty desire wholesome and rational athletics can have it both within its own walls and in modified competition with rivals. A college that sets about securing such athletics to itself may suffer defeat on the playing field, its registration may diminish, and its constituency may clamor; but its faculty will in time discover a change in the scholastic temper of its student body, and its undergraduates will learn the distinction between true athletic sport and noisy and scruple-diminishing competition."

The chief causes of defects in college athletics, said the foundation's reports, were commercialism and the negligent attitude toward the educational service for which higher education in the United States existed. The educational opportunities that athletics could afford were neglected by the methods of management, coaching, and play, and by the rapid growth of athletics, which had made it impossible for institutions to consider fully "the problems involved in local situations." Institutions had depended principally "upon catchwords, like 'faculty control' or 'athletics for all,' and the imitation of practices at sister colleges, without due regard to their effect upon the imitating institutions." Another source of neglect appeared "in the field of morals and conduct," where energetic and "vociferous proponents of college athletics have claimed for [them] far greater benefits than athletics can possibly ever yield . . . and have hailed the shadow as the substance. Commercialism has always obliterated the nonmaterial aspects of athletics." These studies of athletics for the foundation were fact-finding rather than fault-finding efforts, and while some improvements in the situation seemed promising, clearly radical changes were needed. In 1933 former President Henry S. Pritchett, of the foundation, said that the removal of commercialism from collegiate athletics would come only when the institutions provided an intellectual life that appealed more strongly to their students "than the glamour of commercial shows financed in the name of the college and fostered by a demoralizing publicity." It was in connection with the studies made by the Carnegie Foundation that Dr. Pritchett was led to write his playful suggestion that intercollegiate horse racing be substituted for football, as noted in Chapter 4.

In 1951, when charges of "throwing" basketball games were made and sustained and ninety cadets were dismissed from West Point in a cheating scandal in examinations, the nation was shocked and intercollegiate athletics were probably discussed more widely than at any time since the disclosures by the Carnegie Foundation in the 1920's. De-emphasis of intercollegiate athletics, especially of the major sports, was demanded, with here and there admissions by some institutions of irregularities in the conduct of sports. It was charged, perhaps with some justice, that departments of physical education, favored and flourishing at mid-century, had been invented to accommodate strong physical, but not so strong intellectual, athletic talent; and that athletes were receiving grades in courses in physical education which they did not attend. There were even reports of tampering with the transcripts of high-school athletes to enable them to attend college and get on varsity teams; and in some cases trustees behind closed doors probed charges of questionable athletic conduct in their institutions, and there was shuffling of coaching staffs.

The scandal at West Point badly hurt the powerful football squad of the famous academy where there were more anxious weeks than the institution had had in all its century and a half of existence. Most of the cadets stood up for the honor code and upheld the action of the officials of the academy; support also came from many quarters throughout the country, "and it was apparent that there would be no backing down. . . . It was evident, as well, that the great majority of the cadets, untouched by the scandal, felt that their errant colleagues should pay the penalty of dismissal." The academy, however, was submitted to heavy pressures "to stay its hand," to give the cribbers another chance or less severe punishment; parents appealed to President Harry S. Truman and to members of the Congress, and some parents personally represented the cases of their sons to Major General Frederick A. Irving, the academy's superintendent.

There was wide publicity in the press and on the radio, and much editorial comment on this distressing matter. In its lead editorial of August 12, 1951, the *New York Times* said that there was reason "for much sober and painful reflection" over the scandal, that obviously the honor code of the academy must be repaired, and that in the investigation the whole question of undue emphasis on "competitive athletics in the educational structure" called for serious attention. Conditions in intercollegiate sports demanded "very straight thinking and forthright action." The fact that at least one dismissed member of the academy's football squad had "already received offers to play at five different universities" seemed to show the need for a broad inquiry into athletic conditions.[21] But it was reported that Columbia University would "not even consider" admitting any of the transferees from the Point; that neither the University of Virginia nor Washington and Lee University wanted anyone who had been dropped or suspended from another institution; that Pennsylvania State College, before making up its mind, would wait to see whether the academy indicated "discredit or dishonor" on the transcript. But the powerful voice of Francis Cardinal Spellman, Archbishop of New York, was reported as offering the educational institutions under his jurisdiction as asylum to the unhappy cadets, and in doing so he quoted Alexander Pope: "To err is human; to forgive divine." The University of Notre Dame announced through the Associated Press that there was room in that institution for any of or all the ninety expelled cadets, "free if they can't pay," but there was no place for them on the football fields of the fighting Irish. An unidentified "very wealthy man" offered to foot the bills if the cadets needed financial help and would stay off varsity athletics.

While the storm raged, Democratic Congressman John F. Kennedy of Massachusetts wrote [22] that the West Point scandal called attention to the graver issue of the "outmoded system" for making appointments to the service academies, into which young men were finding their way

. . . by political favoritism, inadequate screening, and misplaced emphasis on qualities that are of little importance in military leaders. . . . Our present system, developed to insure the supremacy of the civilian over the military, makes the majority of appointments to West Point and Annapolis a personal prerogative of Senators and Representatives. That system is far from a success, especially when our safety may hinge on our ability to draw into the service academies young men who are best fitted to meet the vast responsibilities that will later be placed upon them in our armed forces."

These academies, he said, were not attracting the best men, and he asserted that "an undesirably high number of graduates, upon whom the government has spent large sums of money, fail to stay with

---

[21] The *New York Times* on the same date carried revealing articles on the same subject by Murray Illson ("Education in Review") and by Richard H. Parke ("West Point Is Recovering from Its Serious Shock").

[22] *New York Times Magazine*, August 19, 1951.

the armed services." Congressmen frequently made their appointments on grounds of "first come, first served," or on grounds of political obligation or friendship. From 1945 to 1947 there were 380 resignations from undergraduates at West Point and 306 from Annapolis; and 30 per cent of the graduates of the naval academy, of the classes of 1943 to 1946, resigned their commissions. Resignations from the military academy were fewer, "but too great a percentage of young men consider the academies as a place of refuge rather than as the foundation of a life's career in the service of their country." The ways to improvement lay in more rigid physical and mental tests and more careful screening all along the line. Between 12 and 30 per cent of Congressional appointees failed to pass the physical examinations given at the academies. "We dare not continue to pick men who may direct another war with new weapons and new techniques by methods developed almost a century ago and shown to be wanting."

A survey had been conducted by the *New York Times* and published in a series of six articles in that paper by Charles Grutzner in March of 1951, on the impact of athletics on education. The survey disclosed that most educators, in the forty colleges and universities queried, agreed that "intercollegiate sports, particularly football and basketball as played in huge stadiums and arenas as a multimillion-dollar business" were ridden by several evils. But there were differences of opinion as to how the evils could be eliminated. Some representatives of higher education believed that more nearly uniform rules and stricter enforcement of them might improve the conditions "without losing any of the 'big time' aspects of college games." Others were of the opinion that football and basketball had grown too big "and must be cut down in size before they do further injury to academic standards and democracy in education." Some educators seemed to favor, others oppose, "scholarships" and other subsidies to athletes. The way out of the bad conditions and the evil days on which intercollegiate sports had fallen was not clear at mid-century.

There was the comment that the general "reactions" to the press reports of the West Point scandal were more disturbing than the occasion that led up to these reports. "More has been said in extenuation than in condemnation of the offense," said I. L. Kandel in an editorial in *School and Society*.[23] Examinations, he said, intensified competition; strained students so intensely that they cannot resist temptation; involved parents whose children try not to disappoint them; "or, from another approach, home conditions have been and

23 August 18, 1951, p. 107.

are so unfortunate as to predispose to cheating . . . Back of the whole unfortunate episode is the general atmosphere which has in recent years called insistently for more direct emphasis in education on moral and spiritual values." And he quoted John Dewey as saying, on the eminent philosopher's seventieth birthday: "Our present American ideal seems to be 'Put it over—and make it snappy while you do it.' I do not imagine this state of things will endure forever." Severe criticisms of alleged academic irregularities in favor of athletes at the ancient seat of learning of the College of William and Mary in Virginia led in September of 1951 to the resignation of the president, John E. Pomfret. A few weeks later the faculty of that institution issued a statement through the Associated Press that charged the sports scandal there to an ambitious athletic program that was "obscuring and corrupting" the real purposes of the institution, was steadily sapping "the academic standards of the college," "vitiated the most elementary standards of honest and right conduct," and "tarnished the bright tradition of the honor system which William and Mary has cherished for generations."

One of the sharpest criticisms of athletic badness appeared in an editorial, "Football Is A Farce," in *Life* on September 17, 1951, in which it was asserted that the entertainment value of the game was doubtful because the coaches "in their greed to win games and keep earning better money than the philosophy professors" had so tampered with and changed the rules of football as to make it impossible for spectators to follow the players, yet many of the institutions for higher education seemed to consider the game their greatest contribution to the United States. It would have been thought, said the editorial, that after the basketball scandals of the winter before and the cribbing scandal at the Military Academy, the colleges would have learned their lesson, and that intercollegiate athletics would come in "for a little healthy de-emphasis," but right then the big argument in academic circles was over television rights, and "if anything, football is going to be bigger and more expensive than ever this fall." The coaches appeared to be more callous and less competent than their salaries and their speeches would indicate, but final blame for the bad conditions had to be placed on the presidents. The real question was "Why do we have colleges, why do we spend close to $3 billion a year on them and why are we trusting 2.2 million of our brightest young people to their tender mercies this year? . . . What we really want is that old American goal of a genuine education for everyone who is capable of absorbing it." The American people looked to the college teachers and especially to the college presidents, "for firm and impartial guidance along the road to culture and morality . . . We put a lot of faith in our colleges, and we deserve to have it justified." The college presidents could not shirk their responsibilities in the athletic crisis. These would say that they did not sell the tickets, and in fact had nothing to do with football. "Maybe not, Mr. President, but someone is certainly committing the crime in your name . . . Whether you are an active conniver in this fraud or just the victim of a camel under the tent, you appear equally guilty to the casual bystander. Better forget about those stadium bonds and start worrying about your real franchise in American life."

The U. S. Supreme Court and Education.—The last three or four decades of the first half of the twentieth century saw an apparently increasing tendency of the Supreme Court of the United States to become the national school board, as Mr. Justice Jackson put it in the significant McCollum Case in 1948.[24] Prior to 1900 that tribunal had handed down only four decisions affecting education, and during the next two decades it handed down only three. But between 1920 and 1950 its decisions on educational issues became increasingly numerous.

The great increase in educational cases that made their way to Washington reflected extraordinary changes and conditions in American education during the first half of the twentieth century, when it became the largest public and social enterprise in the United States. Among the changes and conditions that increased litigation, perhaps the most significant included the phenomenal growth of the public school itself and its rapid tendency toward secularization, which called for judicial interpretations, especially of the First and the Fourteenth Amendments to the Constitution of the United States. The extension of the activities of education and also of the government, and its regulations that affected the economic and social life of the American people, had direct bearing on issues that required judicial decision.[25]

In addition to the decision in the famous Dartmouth College Case in 1819, the other educational decisions before 1900 were the Girard

[24] Edward S. Corwin, "The Supreme Court As National School Board," *Law and Contemporary Problems*. Durham, N. C.: Duke University School of Law, Winter, 1949, pp. 3-22. In the same publication, see Milton R. Konvitz, "Separation of Church and State: The First Freedom," pp. 44-60; Charles Fahy, "Religion, Education, and the Supreme Court," pp. 73-91; Russell N. Sullivan, "Religious Education in the Schools," pp. 92-112; William A. Mitchell, "Religion and Federal Aid to Education," pp. 113-43.

[25] See Ward W. Keesecker, "Supreme Court Decisions Affecting Education," *School Life*, XXXI (February, 1949), pp. 4-7; and "Recent Federal Court Decisions Affecting Education," in the same magazine, XXXIII (October, 1950), pp. 6-7.

College Case in 1844, the Springfield Township Case in 1859, and the Cummings Case in 1899. The Dartmouth College Case is too well known to call for comment here. In the Girard College Case, the court held that the will of Stephen Girard, under which the college was established and which excluded ministers and missionaries of the Gospel from entrance to the institution, was not so disparaging to the Christian religion as to make void, under the constitution and laws of Pennsylvania, the will of Girard under which the college was endowed. In the Springfield Township (Indiana) Case, the court held that a state could refuse to apportion its funds to schools which received aid from a township (derived from federal land grants) until schools not receiving such aid were equal to those that did receive it. In the Cummings Case (Georgia), the court held valid the maintenance of a high school for white children without providing a similar school for Negro children.

The number of educational cases before the court began to increase in the first decade of the present century. In a South Dakota case in 1908, the court upheld the policy of the United States Office of Indian Affairs in using public treaty and trust funds of Indians to obtain, by contract, the education of Indian children in private Catholic schools. The same year, in the fairly well known Berea College Case, the court upheld a statute of Kentucky which prohibited an educational institution from giving instruction to both whites and Negroes, a statute which was repealed in 1950. In 1910, the court, in a Kansas case known as the International Textbook Case, held that instruction by correspondence was commerce among the states, under the commerce clause of the Federal Constitution, and that such commerce could not be obstructed or encumbered by state legislation. In 1915 the court held, in a University of Mississippi case, that legislation prohibiting secret societies in an institution did not violate any rights guaranteed by the Constitution of the United States. In 1923 the court held, in a Nebraska case, that a statute that prohibited the teaching of foreign languages in private schools clashed with the Fourteenth Amendment by depriving persons of liberty and property without due process of law, and was also an arbitrary interference with the liberty of parents to control and educate their children and with the liberty of teachers to pursue their lawful calling. The principle of law invoked in this decision, which invalidated legislation in several other states, was not unlike that invoked in the well-known Oregon Case in 1925.

In that case the court held that children of compulsory school age could not be compelled to go to public schools. The statute which would make such a requirement had the approval of the people of Oregon, but it was held invalid on the ground that it violated liberties guaranteed by the Federal Constitution, in that the statute denied parents the right to educate their children wherever they saw fit, and also that it deprived private schools of their property without due process of law.

In a Mississippi case in 1927, known as the Gong Lum Case, the court held that a "child of Chinese blood, born in, and a citizen of, the United States, is not denied the equal protection of the laws by being classed by the state among the colored races who are assigned to public schools separate from those provided for the whites, when equal facilities for education are afforded to both classes," a fine point that was to come in for further judicial refinement in decisions that were later handed down in other racial cases.

In a case from Louisiana, the court in 1930 held valid a statute providing for free textbooks for children in private schools, and seventeen years later the court gave a somewhat related decision in the New Jersey Bus Case, in which it was held valid to transport, by public means, nonpublic school children to parochial schools. But in 1948 the court held in the widely publicized McCollum Case (Illinois) that public school property could not be used for religious instruction. When that decision was given, many communities, which were providing for religious instruction under what was known as the "released-time" arrangement, were thrown into considerable anxiety and confusion by this word from Washington.

Following the decision in the McCollum Case, 3 thousand communities in forty-six states that had "released-time" programs in religious instruction, in which 2 million "pupils of all faiths had been enrolled in weekday religious classes," faced the aggravating question whether or not such instruction of children in the public schools could be legal. But in the summer of 1951, the Court of Appeals of New York State answered yes. Parents in Brooklyn had brought suit charging that the "released-time" program, which had been in operation in New York City since 1941, was a clear violation of the principle of the separation of Church and State, but in a six-to-one decision the highest court of New York State held that it did not violate that principle. That court said that the program in New York differed markedly from that in Champaign where instruction in religion had been given in public school property, whereas in New York City the children were dismissed from school to get religious instruction elsewhere if their parents so desired. In the opinion of the New York court, the decision in the McCollum Case did not hold

. . . that all released-time programs are per se unconstitutional . . . The Constitution does not demand that every friendly gesture between Church and State shall be discountenanced. The so-called "wall of separation" may be built so high and so broad as to impair both State and Church . . . It must also be remembered that the First Amendment not only forbids laws "respecting an establishment of religion," but also laws "prohibiting the free exercise thereof." We must not destroy one in an effort to preserve the other.

During and following these and other decisions involving religious issues, there were complaints that education in the United States which, historically, was a child of the church and religion, was becoming more and more secular. The issue of "Church and State" was becoming increasingly sharper, and the apparent tendency to "statism" in education was disturbing to those Protestants and Catholics alike who believed that religion had an important place in education. There was the charge from a prominent Catholic that the court had "officially exiled God from our schools," and that the decision in the McCollum Case violated "constitutional requirements for separation of Church and State."

Some other significant educational decisions of the Supreme Court in the 1930's and 1940's involved religious and racial issues.[26] Among those that turned on religious issues were the flag-saluting cases, especially the Gobitis Case in 1940 and the Barnette Case in 1943. In the Gobitis Case from Pennsylvania, the court sustained a ruling of a local school board that required children to salute the national flag as a condition for attendance at school. In that decision Mr. Justice Frankfurter wrote that the flag was the "symbol of national unity" and transcended everything else; and that children of Jehovah's Witnesses (who were the center of the controversy) could be expelled from school for refusing to salute the flag. In the similar Barnette Case, the court in 1943 reversed its earlier decision and held that children could not be dismissed from school for refusing to salute the flag. The religious beliefs of Jehovah's Witnesses, said the court in this decision, from which Mr. Justice Frankfurter dissented, included a literal version of the command: "Thou shalt not make unto thee any graven image . . ." In the view of the court, Jehovah's Witnesses looked upon "the flag as

[26] For original documents on court decisions on religious and racial issues, consult Edgar W. Knight and Clifton L. Hall, *Readings in American Educational History* (New York: Appleton-Century-Crofts, Inc., 1951), chaps. ix and xi.

an 'image' within this command. For this reason they refuse to salute it."

There were several cases on racial issues. One of the most significant was the Missouri or Gaines Case in 1938, in which the court held that when a state provided legal education within its borders for whites, it must make the same provision for Negroes with the same qualifications as those of whites, else equality of legal rights would be denied; and that the payment by the state of out-of-state tuition for Negroes did not remove this discrimination. The obligation of the state to provide equal protection to all its citizens could be met only by legislation operating within its own jurisdiction. The constitutional principles set out in this decision were invoked in many other cases by mid-century.

Differences in salaries of white and Negro teachers had long been the practices in states which maintained separate schools for the two races. In 1940, the Fourth United States Court of Appeals held that such differences were discriminatory and unconstitutional. Many suits at law followed this decision, and at mid-century states with separate schools for the whites and the Negroes were moving toward removing the differences in salaries.

By 1950 other cases had reached Washington, and in June of that year some noteworthy decisions were handed down by the Supreme Court on racial issues in education. In one of these the court held that Herman M. Sweatt must be admitted to the law school of the University of Texas, even though the state had established a separate law school for Negroes, because the two schools did not offer substantial equality in the opportunities for white and Negro law students. In another case, the court on the same day held that the University of Oklahoma must stop the classroom segregation of G. W. McLaurin in its graduate school. McLaurin had been required to sit apart from the other students in an anteroom adjoining the classroom, to sit in a designated place in the library, and to sit at a designated table in the cafeteria, and have his meals at a time different from that of other students. The court held that "state-imposed restrictions which produce such inequalities cannot be sustained."

The issue of "separate but equal facilities" was lively and widely discussed at mid-century. In a Louisiana case known as Plessy vs. Ferguson, the court in 1896 had held constitutional the state regulation of interstate trains that called for "separate but equal" facilities. But in 1950 the court held a different view and said, in a transportation case and in the cases of the University of Texas and the University of Oklahoma, that "separate but equal facilities" were not sufficient in either education or transportation. In doing so the court struck another blow at segregation. Under these decisions changes came in the dining-car practices of railroads, and state universities that had never before done so were beginning to admit Negroes. While these educational cases were concerned with higher education, there was growing anxiety that the lower schools also would be involved.[27]

Education in the United States in 1950 was still a function of the state, but at that time it was clearer than ever before that state educational legislation and administrative policies and practices must not clash with the Constitution of the United States. Every state was expected at that time to maintain and administer its educational arrangements within the limits of the Constitution of the United States, as interpreted by the Supreme Court. On this relation of the educational systems of the states and the Constitution, the court itself had significantly spoken. In the Gobitis Case, Mr. Justice Frankfurter, speaking for the court, said:

. . . the courtroom is not the arena for debating issues of educational policy. It is not our province to choose among competing considerations in the subtle process of securing effective loyalty to the traditional ideals of democracy, while respecting at the same time individual idiosyncrasies among a people so diversified in racial origins and religious allegiances. So to hold would in effect make us the school board for the country. That authority has not been given to this Court, nor should we assume it.

In a similar case from West Virginia, in which the court in 1943 reversed its decision in the Gobitis Case, that tribunal said:

The Fourteenth Amendment, as now applied to the States, protects the citizen against the State itself and all of its creatures—Boards of Education are not excepted. These have, of course, important, delicate, and highly discretionary functions, but none that they may not perform within the limits of the Bill of Rights. That they are educating the young for citizenship is reason for scrupulous protection of Constitutional freedoms of the individual, if we are not to strangle the free mind at its source and teach youth to discount important principles of our Government as mere platitudes.[28]

In the case from West Virginia the court also said that

. . . we apply the limitations of the Constitution with no fear that freedom to be intellectually and spiritually diverse or even contrary will disintegrate

[27] For the historical development and legal status of separate schools, see *Journal of Negro Education,* XVI (Winter, 1947).
[28] See Keesecker, *op. cit.*

the social organization . . . Freedom to differ is not limited to things that do not matter much. That would be a mere shadow of freedom. The test of its substance is the right to differ as to things that touch the heart of the existing order.

Commenting on this assertion, Keesecker said: "However much one may cherish the rightness of any decision, it is difficult to fathom the influence which the court's vigorous views may have on future education, especially if the accelerating frequency of decisions continues." In his view, there could be no question of the principle of judicial review of educational as of other issues, but it was the frequency of decisions by the court and the force of its views that presented a "new and important factor for consideration in the field of education." In the light of the rapid extensions of state legislative activities in education, "and also the prevailing judicial emphasis upon defending the rights and freedoms of individuals under the extended meaning of the First and Fourteenth Amendments as against state legislative policies, it is reasonable to expect an increasing number of other decisions from the high tribunal which will in time significantly affect public education in the United States."

How to slow down the disturbing educational changes by the process of litigation in court had been suggested, by implication at least, in the Gobitis Case, in which the court said:

> Judicial review, itself a limitation on popular government, is a fundamental part of our constitutional scheme. But to the legislature no less than to courts is committed the guardianship of deeply cherished liberties. . . . To fight out the wise use of legislative authority in the forum of public opinion and before legislative assemblies rather than to transfer such a contest to the judicial arena serves to vindicate the self-confidence of a free people.

In the McCollum Case, decided in December, 1948, Mr. Justice Jackson qualified his opinion of concurrence with the majority opinion by the following significant reservations:

> I think it is doubtful whether the facts in the case establish jurisdiction in this Court, but in any event that we should place some bounds on the demands for interference with local schools that we are empowered or willing to entertain. I make these reservations a matter of record in view of the number of litigations likely to be started as a result of this decision.
>
> A Federal Court may interfere with local school authorities only when they invade either a personal liberty or a property right protected by the Federal Constitution. . . . We must leave some flexibility to meet local conditions, some chance to progress by trial and error.[29]

[29] Quoted in Keesecker, *op. cit.*, pp. 4-6.

The Scientific Study of Education.—Other developments in education during the first half of the twentieth century appeared in educational surveys,[30] which became fashionable and were widely used in almost all parts of the United States, and the extensive use of objective tests, both practices an outcome of the so-called scientific study of education. While the earlier surveys were of the personal estimate type, those that were later made were on a more nearly scientific basis through the use of objective standards of educational measurement. Critics of the mechanical and external devices used in the educational survey charged that these techniques were often indulged in for publicity purposes; but while the recommendations of the surveyors were not always fully accepted or promptly acted upon by governing educational authorities, the method of the educational survey did seem useful to public school systems and to educational institutions as guides for the diagnosis and treatment of educational shortcomings.

Among the earliest of the educational surveys in the first half of the twentieth century were those made by Paul H. Hanus, of Harvard University, of the schools in Montclair, New Jersey, in 1911; of Baltimore, the same year, by E. E. Brown, United States Commissioner of Education, and others and said to be the first "descriptive and comparative type of school survey" in this country; of Boise, Idaho, in 1912, by Edward C. Elliott of the University of Wisconsin, George D. Strayer of Columbia University, Charles H. Judd of the University of Chicago, and others; of New York City in 1912 by Hanus and other educational experts; of Cleveland in 1915-16, by Leonard P. Ayres of the Russell Sage Foundation, and others. Other surveys were made under the direction of Abraham Flexner of the General Education Board, of the school system of Gary, Indiana; of Bridgeport, Connecticut, under the direction of James H. Van Sickle, superintendent, of Springfield, Massachusetts; of Portland, Oregon, by Cubberley and others; and of Springfield, Illinois, by Ayres and others. These and other subsequent and perhaps less extensive edu-

[30] Perhaps the earliest educational survey in this country was made in South Carolina in 1825, by request of the legislature of that state to the faculty of South Carolina College, now the University of South Carolina. This survey, signed by Thomas Cooper, the president, for himself and colleagues, was followed by a study of education in that state by Stephen Elliott and James H. Thornwell, of that institution, in the 1830's; and by another, in 1846, by R. E. W. Allston, at the request of the State Agricultural Society of South Carolina. Another study was made the following year by a committee, of which Henry Sumner was chairman. Sumner said that the results of the earlier studies were "splendid nothings," a fate that was to overtake some educational surveys in the United States in the first half of the twentieth century. See Edgar W. Knight and Clifton L. Hall, *Readings in American Educational History* (New York: Appleton-Century-Crofts, Inc., 1951), pp. 331-40.

cational surveys were designed to find the weak and the strong points in the educational work of the system studied and to indicate ways for improvement.

Techniques for the school survey had become rather well developed before 1920, and between that date and 1950 few if any features of educational administration were so modish. The survey method was widely applied to state school systems and to institutions for higher education, often through aid from the philanthropic foundations and under advice from the United States Office of Education. Many of the studies were made under the direction of the Institute of Educational Research, Division of Field Studies, of Teachers College, Columbia University. A result of this work was the establishment of bureaus or departments of research in city and state school systems, in departments and schools of education in colleges and universities, and in teachers' colleges. This development led to the organization of the National Association of Directors of Educational Research, later known as the Educational Research Association, to promote research in educational administration, supervision, and teaching.

One of the most extensive and comprehensive of all the surveys was the Regents' Inquiry into the Character and Cost of Public Education in the State of New York in the 1930's, under the direction of Luther H. Gulick, with Owen D. Young as chairman of the commission of the inquiry, and Samuel P. Capen as associate director. This immense study was undertaken in recognition of the tremendous changes that "have come into the life of the boys and girls and men and women of this State, especially since the First World War . . ." The findings and recommendations of the inquiry appeared in a general report entitled *Education for American Life: A New Program for the State of New York*.[31] Other volumes dealt with various phases of education in the state.

The survey movement was accompanied by the increasing construction and use of objective tests of mental ability and measurements of achievement, which also became so popular throughout the United States as to be almost regarded with awe and blind reverence and devotion. Testing and the use of statistical techniques tended to became faddish. The movement reached back at least to the work of Francis Galton in England, who applied the statistical method to studies of heredity, and to that of Alfred Binet and Thomas Simon in France, who in the early part of the twentieth century

[31] (New York: McGraw-Hill Book Co., 1938.)

published a series of standardized mental tests and a scale for the measurement of intelligence. In this country the movement attracted the attention of James McKeen Cattell, Franz Boas, and Edward L. Thorndike of Columbia University, of Lewis M. Terman of Stanford University, and of many other distinguished educational scientists throughout the United States. The testing movement was greatly stimulated during the First World War when tests of intelligence were constructed and widely used in the army, and during the Second World War when even more extensive use was made of them. Long before 1950 the literature on this subject had become very voluminous and was still growing. Until the use of objective tests and measurements caught on, however, the movement was resisted and there was a storm of protest against it. The reports of findings in tests of the abilities of school children to spell, made by J. M. Rice in the latter part of the nineteenth century, and of other studies, did not receive the approval and blessing of the National Education Association until the second decade of the twentieth century.

By the aid of the so-called scientific method in education, of which the survey and testing were important parts, educational administration and supervision underwent extraordinary changes. Through these techniques attempts were made to apply the mathematical attitude to the study of education, to measure with irritating exactness and certitude differences in native abilities, character, conduct, and achievement of individuals, and to substitute objective and presumably precise methods of measurement for subjective and presumably inexact methods. So fascinating were these new educational techniques that superintendents of schools and teachers who questioned their validity or neglected to make use of them were considered outmoded, and their usefulness was often questioned. The vocabulary of the educational workers had to include such terms and words as "mean," "median," "mode," "coefficient of correlation," "probable error," "mean deviation," "standard deviation," and "I.Q.," or they were looked upon as relics of an unscientific age and attitude.

A significant feature of higher education at mid-century was the growing interest in and widespread use of objective tests for admission to college. In 1948 the testing activities of the American Council on Education, the Graduate Record Examination, and the College Entrance Examination Board were merged to form the Educational Testing Service. In the first report in 1950, by Henry Chauncey, president of the new organization, it was noted that during the first eighteen months of the activities of ETS more than 5 million of its tests were administered, and that more than three quarters of a million students took tests for admission to colleges, medical, law, and graduate schools and service academies. The research staff of the organization was then developing "new measures of aptitude and personality to aid in counseling and guidance. Tests and other devices to measure relative attainment of fundamental objectives of education, particularly at the high-school level," were also in the research stage, but it would be several years before these would be ready for general use, it was reported.

Attacks on Education in 1950.—Public education in the United States at mid-twentieth century was under heavier attacks than it had been subjected to in all its long history. "It happened in Pasadena, California, it almost happened in Englewood, New Jersey, it may be happening in your own child's school today," wrote the editor of *McCall's* in introducing Arthur D. Morse's "Who's Trying to Ruin Our Schools?" in the September, 1951, issue of that magazine. Morse's article dealt with "the shame of Pasadena" which had been disclosed by David Hulburd's book, *This Happened in Pasadena,* with the attacks made in "an attractive, prosperous community" in New Jersey, and especially with the activities of Allen Zoll and his National Council for American Education, with Lucile Cardin Crain's publication, *Educational Reviewer,* and with Major General Amos Fries' (Retired) publication, "ironically titled," *Friends of the Public Schools.* Zoll and his work had been attacked and his name called by the National Education Association earlier in the year, and there were many suspicions about the work of Crain and of Fries. But Morse could have mentioned, as less vulgar and more subtle and satirical criticisms of the schools, Mortimer Smith's *And Madly Teach,* which had appeared in 1949, Bernard Iddings Bell's *Crisis in Education,* the same year, Albert Lynd's "Quackery in the Public Schools," which appeared in the *Atlantic Monthly* in March of 1950, and perhaps other criticisms of the schools which were less billingsgate than those of the triumvirate of critics he did point to. It was quite fashionable at mid-century, as it had been during the great economic depression that began in 1929, to tear into the schools and their work.

Criticisms, which were very numerous throughout the roaring 1940's, took many forms. In the early part of that decade, the results of an inquiry conducted by the *New York Times* [32] into the knowledge which college students had of history startled many people, but

[32] April 4, 1943.

the report was said to have had the effect of making the study of the subject compulsory in secondary schools and in colleges. One alarming result of the study was the discovery that 25 per cent of the 7 thousand students in thirty-six universities did not know that Abraham Lincoln was President of the United States during the Civil War; 30 per cent did not know that Woodrow Wilson was President during the First World War; and 84 per cent of them, in the bicentennial anniversary of Thomas Jefferson's birth, could not name two of the contributions made by that great American. But there were differences of opinion about the reliability and the validity of the test. A progressive dean of a progressive school of education said the questions in the test were not important; and a versatile professor of education disclosed that information was not worth anything unless it was worth something. A professor in a technological school did not see what the questions had to do with winning the war. Nearly a decade later the same newspaper conducted a similar study of students' knowledge of geography, with similar gloomy findings.

Early in that decade the National Association of Manufacturers undertook to discover, in a large and widely publicized investigation, what the young people of the United States were studying in the secondary school, which served to indicate some fear or misgivings of that organization that the schools were contributing to the delinquency and corruption of youth and leading them straightaway to economic and social sin. The results of the association's examination of several hundred textbooks in history, civics, sociology, and economics were awaited with interest. Those who looked upon the effort as subversive, and an obstruction to freedom of teaching, heard from the association itself the expression of hope that the undertaking would "encourage manufacturers in every community to cooperate wholeheartedly with their local educational authorities in analyzing sound means by which the concept of free enterprise and the details of its operation may be taught in the schools." The free enterprise which the NAM enjoyed in this study should have encouraged distillers, morticians, realtors, football coaches, opponents of intolerance, and other defensive groups to scrutinize the materials of instruction in the schools. It is highly probable that if it had not been for public education, the NAM could not have enjoyed free enterprise in its businesses or in making an examination of schoolbooks. But while the task was reported to be undertaken in the strict scientific temper, with a staff consisting of an able director, two typists, a Marxist, a liberal, and an independent of conservative leanings, who came up with more than twelve hundred pages of single-spaced typescript of more than half a million words, the results turned out not to be earth-shaking.

Formation of the National Citizens Commission.—In the midst of much confusion and numerous severe criticisms of public education, the National Citizens Commission for the Public Schools was formed in the spring of 1949, after some years of exploratory meetings, on "the problems and opportunities of public school education in the United States," by a group of citizens "not professionally identified with education, religion, or politics." This organization was unique in that it was the first independent national association dedicated to efforts to improve public education "through cooperative action by citizens in the local communities." Roy E. Larsen, president of *Time,* who became chairman of the group, said: "First, we must find out what some of the present notions are as to the purposes and practices of education. Then we must come through with our own thoughts."

The first annual dinner meeting of the new organization in early 1950 was significant. A letter was read from President Truman, who said that the schools of the United States "must be strengthened and improved if they are to equip today's children and youth to meet the need for intelligent, patient, and constructive leadership as the future unfolds." James B. Conant, president of Harvard, an energetic leader in the organization, described it as "one of the outstanding events in the history of education in this half-century." In a stirring address, General Omar B. Bradley, Chairman of the Chiefs of Staff, said that "if some dramatic incident could shock the American people to an awareness of public education, they would react as unitedly as they did at Pearl Harbor," but he pointed to "a parade of embarrassing statistics" that showed failure to accomplish this purpose. "The growing inadequacy of our public school system is creeping up in every community," he told a thousand interested people at the dinner, that "year by year community by community, we are watching one of the great strongholds of democracy being weakened." Preoccupation of the American people for the past ten years "with saving this nation, and its way of life, from aggression has frequently left the grade schools and high schools of our communities behind." He believed that the American people could "recapture this democratic power if citizens in every community will hold meetings like this one tonight." Notwithstanding the obvious achievements of public education, appraisal of the schools by local citizens was of paramount importance, President Conant told the gathering. The public school was "the symbol of the special contribution which this republic has made to the concept of democracy," and the future of public education had significance which far transcended "the immediate issues." Chairman Larsen saw some of the contemporary problems of education in the United States directly related "to its phenomenal growth and success as an American institution. Many of our schools are in serious trouble because the demands made upon the schools have outrun their capacity to meet those demands." [33] Improvement in public education, he said, depended upon backing "with the *total citizen resources* of the community." Commented the editor of *The Nation's Schools* in its issue of September, 1949: "The National Citizens Commission for the Public Schools may be the greatest boon to public education since the American Lyceum."

The Commission, which had received initial financial support from the Carnegie Corporation and the General Education Board, and whose members did not represent any organization or groups, set out to encourage the formation of groups in communities for the purpose of improving their local schools. The organization would also act as a clearinghouse to enable such groups to have the benefit of the experience of others, "in the hope that community efforts now being carried on in isolation can benefit from the continuing encouragement and pooling of information which the Commission will provide." In order to encourage a wider and more active public interest in public education, the Commission cooperated with the Advertising Council "in a campaign designed to dramatize the problems and opportunities of public school education in newspapers, in magazines, on outdoor posters, and on the radio." The injunctions to the public were: "Find what problems your local public schools are facing. Take an active part in helping to solve them."

. . . . . .

This book appears at the end of an extraordinary half-century in which education in the United States reached its most lofty quantitative triumphs in the face, nevertheless, of heavy jolts from wars and economic depression and also from severe criticisms of its theories and practices. The First World War jarred respect for mankind,

[33] Inflation of the curricula of the schools, and methods of certification of teachers, came in for much criticism. One critic said that the schools were undertaking to teach everything "except how to come in out of the rain," and that the training and certification of teachers had become so complicated and intricate that "Socrates himself would find it very difficult to be certified."

brought on fatigue of the human spirit, encouraged cynicism, and led many people to believe that in the primitive passions and ruthlessness of warfare men saw themselves revealed as they really were. During the economic crisis that began in 1929, and in both world wars, discussed in Chapter 8, the mood of the times reflected itself in the schools and in other educational and cultural activities, and more hard things were then said about education than had ever before been heard.

If the First World War and the economic depression dealt heavy body blows to education and to the hope of peace and prosperity in the world, the Second World War did not greatly restore or increase that hope. Instead, the last two decades of the first half of the twentieth century witnessed the world as giving itself over almost completely to hatred and violence, and there developed the gravest threat that had ever been made to the democratic way of life and education. The people of the world saw war become stronger and stronger as the destroyer of human values; they saw the physical sciences come to owe much of their progress to the production of weapons of war, and science cultivated in large part to prostitute the humane gifts of science. There was also evidence that in the United States the people were taking democracy and some of its precious freedoms for granted—freedom of speech, the press, of religion, and of assembly, which reached back into the distant past and had been won through bloody centuries. All these unhealthy conditions were reflected in education.

It was pointed out above that as the first half of the twentieth century came to a close, criticisms of American education were perhaps more numerous and sharper than ever before, and that there was much confusion in the immense educational arrangements that the American people had established for themselves. The phenomenal growth of education and its apparent success during those fifty years may have helped to explain some of the many issues, as well as much of the confusion, in it at the close of the period. Besides, it was very obvious that the heavy demands upon the schools, and their difficulty in meeting them, added to their confusion.

Notwithstanding the crises and the attacks which American education had faced, it had given a fairly good account of itself, and it remained at mid-century the key to American democracy, just as American democracy remained the key to education in the United States. Intelligent criticisms of education had always been healthy; perhaps few thoughtful people would have denied in 1950 that some educational follies had been committed. Intelligent educational criticisms tended to dispose educational workers to serious reflection.

These workers, as well as those who sat in judgment on their work, and the parents and public generally, perhaps needed to learn, however, that "ruin and recovery are alike from within," as Epictetus said in his golden manner many centuries ago. It also seemed clear that the American people had to keep constantly in mind that chastened thinking under compulsion usually continues only during the period of duress, and that resolutions, however noble, can never sustain themselves without an active display of will.

In his heartening editorial in *Life,* October 16, 1950—in an issue which was devoted in large part to criticisms of American education —the eminent American historian, Henry Steele Commager, emphasized the immense tasks that faced education in this country, in large part because the American people had come to place their schools "in a crossfire of conflicting demands." Many of the old purposes and standards of judgment had gone, and new purposes and standards had not yet been found for American education. The schools once had an educational monopoly; but in recent decades these had come so rapidly in keen competition with other agencies that the educational influences of the schools had themselves markedly reduced. But the schools reflected life about them and their failures were those of the society of which they were integral parts. If the schools were to be reformed, Commager said, there had to be reform of the American people themselves.

SOME QUESTIONS AND EXERCISES FOR STUDENTS

1. Study and report on the primary purposes of the G.I. Bill of Rights for the benefit of veterans of the Second World War. In what way or ways did that program set a precedent for benefits to future veterans? What Congressional plans were made to extend such benefits to veterans of the Korean War?
2. Make a study and report on the purposes and activities of UNESCO. What do you understand by that organization's program of "fundamental education"?
3. What was the purpose of the British-American exchange of teachers? What was the evidence of the success of the program?
4. Discuss the purposes of the Fulbright Act and report on the success of its program.
5. What were the purposes of the Japanese International University, in the development of which the United States was to participate?
6. Discuss the purposes and activities of the Institute of International Education which was founded in 1919.

7. Study and report on the "Education Missions" to Japan and Germany at the close of the Second World War.

8. Discuss the purposes and the advantages and disadvantages or dangers, if any, of the large and powerful private philanthropic foundations or trusts. In what way or ways did the Kellogg Foundation and the Ford Foundation differ in purposes and activities from those set up in the early part of the twentieth century?

9. What were the purposes of the National Science Foundation that was recommended by President Truman and established in 1950? What have been its achievements?

10. In what way or ways had the great advances in scientific progress brought "disillusion with the laboratory" by the middle of the twentieth century? In what way or ways were people spiritually unprepared for the gifts of science, as one great scientist put it?

11. Discuss the comforting predictions of scientific development during the next half century, which James B. Conant made at the diamond jubilee meeting of the American Chemical Society in 1951.

12. Make a study and report on the educational progress of the Negroes during the first half of the twentieth century, noting especially decisions of the Supreme Court of the United States on the subject of educational facilities for Negroes equal to those for white people.

13. Study and report on Kandel's *The Impact of the War on American Education,* noting the educational deficiencies which he saw disclosed by that military crisis.

14. Show the primary reasons why provisions for the higher education of women, and especially coeducation, were so long delayed in the United States.

15. Trace the movement for federal aid to education since 1900, and show why it had not been achieved by 1951.

16. Study and report on the work of the Educational Policies Commission of the National Education Association.

17. At mid-century, accidents were reported to be affecting the national economy more than disease. What do you consider the obligation of the school in such a condition?

18. Account for the rapid growth of educational organizations and journals in the first half of the twentieth century.

19. What was the real significance of the athletics scandals that were so widely publicized and discussed at mid-century? What can be done to improve conditions in athletic sports? Read the editorial on college football in *Life,* September 17, 1951, and show how you would answer it.

20. Make a study of the major educational cases that came up for decision before the Supreme Court of the United States in the second
quarter of the twentieth century, and discuss the alleged tendency
of that tribunal to become the national school board. On what
issues did most of those decisions turn?

21. What was the significance of the wide use of "surveys" and of
objective tests in educational work in the second quarter of the
twentieth century?

22. Account for the many heavy attacks that were being made on education in the United States at mid-century, and undertake to answer
them. What was the basis for the charge that the curricula of the
schools had become highly inflated, and that the demands on the
schools were too many and too heavy for them to meet?

SOME SUGGESTED REFERENCES AND READING

"Critical Issues and Trends in American Education." *The Annals,* The American
Academy of Political and Social Science, CCLXV (September, 1949).
Devoted entirely to the many aspects of education in the United States at mid-
twentieth century, the student may find in this publication very useful material
prepared by specialists on the various topics treated.

HEILBRONER, ROBERT L. "The Fabulous Ford Foundation," *Harper's Magazine,*
CCIII (December, 1951), pp. 25-32.
A very thoughtful article on the youngest and richest of the great philanthropic
foundations, but asks some pointed questions about the great trust. "In Hoffman's own words: 'The Ford Foundation has the biggest blank check in history.'"

HOLLIS, E. V. *Philanthropic Foundations and Higher Education.* New York:
Columbia University Press, 1938.
A comprehensive historical study of the rise, development, and activities of the
private educational trusts. Contains a very useful bibliography on the subject.

JOHNSON, CHARLES S. *The Negro College Graduate.* Chapel Hill: The University
of North Carolina Press, 1938.
An excellent account of the story of the higher education of Negroes since
the graduation of John Russwurm from Bowdoin College in 1826.

KANDEL, I. L. *The Impact of the War Upon American Education.* Chapel Hill:
The University of North Carolina Press, 1948.
Contains useful material that bears on some of the topics discussed in this
Chapter, especially the G.I. Bill of Rights, the Fulbright Act, federal aid to edu-
cation, and international cultural relations.

KNIGHT, EDGAR W., and HALL, CLIFTON L. *Readings in American Educational
History.* New York: Appleton-Century-Crofts, Inc., 1951.
Contains original documents on some of the subjects discussed in this Chapter.

KNIGHT, EDGAR W. *Education in the United States* (3d rev. ed.). Boston: Ginn &
Co., 1951.
Chap. xx contains considerable material on some of the topics treated in this
Chapter.

"UNESCO'S Work in Education." *Harvard Educational Review,* XX (Summer, 1950).

Devoted entirely to the educational work of UNESCO, the various chapters are written by specialists and throw considerable light on the activities of this unique educational organization.

Wittels, B. G. "Lucky Sons of Stephen Girard." *Saturday Evening Post,* December 13, 1947.

A sprightly story of the unique foundation on which Girard College in Philadelphia has had such a long and useful development.

INDEX

Academic degrees, in 1900 and in 1950, 131, 132; conferred on women, 431; excessive enthusiasm for possession of, 182; Samuel Eliot Morison on, 182; A. Lawrence Lowell, on President Daniel Coit Gilman's "one mistake" as president of The Johns Hopkins University, 182, 183; American mania for, 183; Andrew D. White, on fraudulent, 183; Edward Lawrence Godkin on, 183, 184; *Educational Review* on the Ph.D. as an honorary degree, 184; Charles W. Super on, 184; United States Bureau of Education has complaints about the spurious granting of, 185; Potomac University in Washington, D.C., offers easy, 185; Odessa University sells, 185; a Negro "university" in the South offers a commencement speaker either traveling expenses or an honorary degree for his services, 185, 186; Affiliated Clubs of Graduate Students opposes easy, 188.

Academic freedom, 25, 26, 167-76; American Association of University Professors concerned with, 167; trends in legislation on, 167; University of Washington involved in, 167, 168; National Commission for the Defense of Democracy Through Education deplores legislation on, 167; Department of Higher Education of the NEA condemns restrictions of, 168; Benjamin Fine reports major cases on, 168; Harold J. Laski prevented from lecturing at the University of California at Los Angeles, 168; heated issue at the University of California, 168, 169; American Association of University Professors pronounces on, 169, 170; early cases involving, 170-71; NEA pronounces on, 171, 172; Socrates early victim of, 172.

Academician, The, early educational journal, 10; (Albert and John Pickett), 440.

Academy movement begins, 86.

Accidents, effects on the national economy, 438; heavy costs of, 13, 14; instruction in prevention of, 436.

Acheson, Dean, on Japan's International University, 410.

Adams, Herbert B., interest in adult education, 212.

Adler, Mortimer, 346.

Administration, educational, Nicholas Murray Butler makes rather savage attacks on, 23; trends in, 288-337; pronouncements on by Committee of Fifteen, 291-95; numerous courses in, 295, 331, 332; resistance to centralized control in, 296, 297; state, 302-11; county, 311-14; developments in, 333-35; Kellogg Foundation aids study of, 333, 334.

Adolescence, G. Stanley Hall on the significance of, 87, 88.

Adult education, Thomas Jefferson's interest in, 211; Herbert B. Adams' interest in, 212.

Advisory Committee on the Relation of the Federal Government to Education, 391.

Affiliated Clubs of Graduate Students, oppose easy academic degrees, 188.

Agassiz, Louis, 207.

Aikin (Eight-Year) Study, sponsored by the Commission on the Relation of School and College of the Progressive Education Association, 113-15.

Airplane flight, first successful, 4, 14.

Alderman, Edwin A., on the higher education of women, 428.

Allen, Hollis P. (*The Federal Government and Education*), 322 *n.*

American Association of Adult Education, purposes of, 217, 218; publications of, 218.

American Association for the Advancement of Science, opposes easy advanced degrees, 188.

American Association of Colleges for Teacher Education, 259, 282, 283, 401.

American Association of School Administrators, opposes loyalty oaths, 298, 334, 400, 435.

American Association of Teachers Colleges, 281, 282.

American Association of University Professors, 188.

American Association of University Women, 392.

American Bar Association, committee on legal education of, 204.

American Chemical Society, 199, 424.

Date Due

Demco 293-5